ENVOINFORMATICS

ENVOINFORMATICS

Editor
Professor (Dr.) Arvind Kumar
FLS (London), FASc (Swiss), FISEC, FSESc, FAZ, FZA (Gold Medalist)
Pro-vice Chancellor
S.K.M. University, Dumka – 814 101 (Jharkhand)

2008
DAYA PUBLISHING HOUSE
Delhi - 110 035

ISBN10 81-7035-478-1
ISBN13 978-81-7035-478-9

Published by : **Daya Publishing House**
1123/74, Deva Ram Park
Tri Nagar, Delhi - 110 035
Phone: 27383999
Fax: (011) 23260116
e-mail : dayabooks@vsnl.com
website : www.dayabooks.com

Showroom : 4760-61/23, Ansari Road, Darya Ganj,
New Delhi - 110 002
Phone: 23245578, 23244987

Laser Typesetting : **Classic Computer Services**
Delhi - 110 035

Printed at : **Chawla Offset Printers**
Delhi - 110 052

PRINTED IN INDIA

Preface

Enviroinformatics is the new movement of environmental management. It plays a key role in safeguarding our planet's future. The last one decade has witnessed the emergence of Enviroinformatics as a major thrust area in the global scientific scenario. As the interface between the two most rapidly advancing fields of biological and computational sciences, enviroinformatics is immense in scope and vast in applications. The analysis of environmental information using database and statistical techniques in order to accelerate and enhance environmental research is the target of enviroinformatics.

The environment looms large on the global political agenda. The increased attention is the result of several factors: increased awareness of the environmental damage caused by economic activity; rapid population growth; the perception of the earth as a single biosphere; and more recently, the end of the Cold War. During the past few decades, the scientific community has uncovered new information on the environmental consequences of human kind's interaction with the earth. Much of this has found its way into the popular media. As a consequence, the public has some familiarity with issues such as global warming, ozone depletion, nuclear pollution, and hazardous waste disposal. This period has also seen accelerating population growth, growth that has thrown into stark relief the problems caused by the inadequate supply of food and resources in certain localities and by the mal-distribution of food on a global level.

As environmental scientists work to unravel the complexities of our global environment, a challenging new field is emerging in the engineering community. Enviroinformatics will help scientists make sense of large, complex data sets gleaned from environmental monitoring. Now-a-days, tremendous amounts of data pour in from satellite systems, GPS networks, ground-based remote sensing, every aircraft, every ship, and every weather station. All of these are collecting information about the environment, and that data set is growing every day. There has to be a way of assimilating all that data and making it accessible to scientists.

After pollution is created, you have to try to remediate it. But remediation can take many years and can cost a lot of resources because the environment has a very slow response time. Preserving the environment is one of the great morale duties of enviroinformatic scientists. Much of the work by environmental engineers should be centered on trying to lessen man's impact on environment. Keeping this fact in view, the present book "*Enviroinformatics*" has been undertaken. This book is the unique compilation of the most recent and informative research articles of internationally acknowledged experts in the field of Environmental informatics with the intention of providing a sufficient depth of the subject to satisfy the needs at a level which will be comprehensive and interesting. This book will be useful to the students, research scholars, scientists in the field of environmental management and ecoplanners, environmental engineers, politicians and other people with similar interest.

I consider myself extremely fortunate in having got the invaluable support and erudite suggestions of eminent persons like Prof. (Dr.) Christian Ulrichs of Germany, Dr. M. A. Kabir Chowdhury of Malaysia, Prof. Dr. Ahmed H. Al-Harbi of Saudi Arabia, Prof. Tej Kumar Shrestha of Nepal, Prof. P. V. Dehadrai, Former Director, CIFRI, Dr. Dilip Kumar, Director, CIFE, Mumbai, Prof. K. C. Pandey, Former V. C. (Lucknow), Prof. A. R. Yousuf of University of Kashmir, Srinagar (J & K), Professor N. C. Datta of Calcutta University, Professor S. K. Konar of Kalyani University, Professor D. K. Belsare of Bhopal University, Professor Professor U. C. Goswami of Gauhati University, Professor P. C. Mishra of Sambalpur University, Professor P. Natarajan of Kerala University, Professor P. S. Murthy of Bangalore University, Professor Ajit Varma of JNU, Professor A. L. Bhatia of Jaipur University, Professor A. K. Mittal of BHU, Professor S. P. Hosmani of Mysore University, Professor K. Kapoor of Udaipur University, Professor K. B. Reddy of Nagarjuna University, Professor M. Vikram Reddy of Pondicherry University, Professor B. K. Tiwari of NEHU, Professor G. Tripathi of Jodhpur University, Professor R. Ramalingam of Annamalai University, Professor Sharif U. Ahmad of Nagaland University, Professor G. K. Kulkarni of Aurangabad University, Professor S. U. Mehram of Nagpur University, Professor S. K. Battish of PAU, Professor B. M. Sharma of Manipur University, Professor B. D. Joshi of Hardwar University, Professor G. C. Pandey of Faizabad University, Professor K. C. Sharma of Ajmer University, Professor M. Raziuddin of Hazaribag University, Professor U. S. Bagde of Mumbai University, Professor Gurdeep Singh of I. S. M., Dhanbad, Dr. P. K. Goel of Karad, Professor S. P. Roy and Shri Tribhuwan Poddar of Bhagalpur University, Bhagalpur for encouragements.

I also express my deep sense of gratitude to my parents whose blessings have always prompted me to pursue academic activities deeply. I am also thankful to my wife, *Kumari Bimla* and my two lovely sons, *Kumar Pallav Shivshankaran* and *Kumar Prasun Ramakrishnan* whose natural smiles extended to me relief all through this tiresome endeavour.

Last but not the least, I am also thankful to Mr. Anil Mittal, Proprietor, Daya Publishing House, New Delhi for taking keen interest in bringing out of this book. Finally, I will always remain a debtor to all my well wishers for their blessings, without which this book would not have come into existence.

Professor A. Kumar

Contents

	Preface	*v*
1.	**Informatics on *Aeromonas hydrophila* and Motile *Aeromonad septicemias* of Fish** *Arvind Kumar and Partha Bandyopadhyay*	1
2.	**Removal of Cadmium from Water and Wastewater by Economic Method** *Y.C. Sharma, M. Mahto and S.N. Kaul*	22
3.	**Influence of Chromium and Cadmium on Germination, Seedling Growth and Photosynthetic Pigments of Soybean [*Glycine max* (L.) Merr.]** *K. Sankar Ganesh, Al. A. Chidambaram, P. Sundaramoorthy, L. Baskaran and M. Selvaraju*	29
4.	**Ultrasonic Investigation on Aqueous Ternary Electrolytes of Some Mineral Salts** *T. Sumathi and A.N. Kannappan*	35
5.	**Environmental Audit: Sign Post for Sustainable Industrial Economy** *N.S. Raman*	40
6.	**Evaluation of Groundwater Resource of Faridabad District, Haryana, India** *Madhuri S. Rishi*	47
7.	**Studies on the Effect of Bavistin (Carbendazim) on Seed Germination and Growth of Some Vegetable Crops** *P. Sundaramoorthy, K. Sankar Ganesh, L. Baskaran, Al.A. Chidambaram and S. Natarajan*	57
8.	**Seasonal Variations in Ambient Air Quality of Jalgaon Urban Centre** *Nilesh D. Wagh and S.T. Ingle*	62

9. **Drought Tolerance of Coriander (*Coriandrum sativum* Linn.) Genotypes in Rainfed Vertisols** 73

Lakshmi Narasmimha Rao Kamineni, Giridhar Kalidasu, C. Sarada

10. **Comparison of Rate of Copper Ion Induced Oxidation of Lipoprotein in End Stage Renal Diseased and Renal Transplant Patients: An *in vitro* Study** 78

C.S. Parameswari, B. Vijaya Geetha, R. Vijaya Kumar

11. **Activation of Green Gram Amylase by Calcium Chloride** 84

T. Devasena, S.K. Chithreswari and J. Christinal

12 **Mite Pest Scenario and their Status Associated with Common Vegetables** 88

Rabindra Prasad, Uday Kumar Prasad, Sanjay Kumar Sathi and Devendra Prasad

13. **Screening of Antimutagenic Effects of Green and Black Tea (*Camellia sinensis*) in Reverse Mutation Assay** 94

K.S. Santhy, S. Namitha, Sherly P. George and P. Arulraj

14. **Effect of Larval Size and Weight on Pupation Site Preference in Different Species of Drosophila** 101

N.B. Vandal and N. Shivanna

15. **Protective Effect of *Mucuna pruriens* Seed on Ethanol Treated Rat Brain ATPases** 107

G. Krishnamoorthy and A. Sivamady

16. **Efficacy of Rapid H_2S Test for Detection of Fecal Contamination in Drinking Water** 111

D.H. Tambekar, N.B. Hirulkar, S.R. Gulhane, Y.S. Banginwar and N.S. Bhajipale

17. **In vitro Sensitivity Study of Phytopathogenic Fungi Against Indian Piper** 118

J. Das, S. Goswami, R. Gupta and M. Begam

18. **Integrated Management of Brinjal Fruit Borer (*Leucinodes orbonalis* Guen.) through Varietal Resistance and Judicious Insecticidal Application** 123

Rabindra Prasad, Rajesh Kumar, Udaya Kumar Prasad, Muneshwar Prasad and Devendra Prasad

19. **Insect Pests Scenario in Rice Agroecosystem in Ranchi, Jharkhand** 129

Rabindra Prasad, Sanjay Kumar Sathi, Udaya Kumar Prasad, and Devendra Prasad

20. ***In vitro* Antimicrobial Activity of Citric Acid Against Multiple Drug Resistant Uropathogens** 137

A.V. Gomashe and P.M. Tumane

21. **Enhanced Salinity Tolerance of Tomato [*Lycopersicon esculentum* (L.) Mill.] Plants as Affected by Paclobutrazol Treatment** 141

B. Sankar, R. Somasundaram, P. Manivannan, A. Kishorekumar, C. Abdul Jaleel and R. Panneerselvam

22. **Seed Invigoration in Indian Bean (*Lablab purpureus* L.)** 145

R.L. Moharana, D.P. Khuntia, S.J. Pramanik and A.K. Basu

23. **Integrated Control of *Rhizoctonia solani* by Leaf Extract of *Argemone mexicana* and *Trichoderma viride*** 151
H.S. Shukla and P.V. Ramaiah

24. **Disease Related Laser Use Survey at Indore** 157
Varsha Jain, K.N. Chaturvedi and M.M. Prakash

25. **Spontaneous Positive Geotropic Shoot Development in Onion** 161
M. Babu Rao

26. **Ethnoveterinary Practices by Santhal Tribe in Jamtara District of Jharkhand** 163
A.K. Mandal and B.B. Dutta

27. **Hydrophytic Plants Used as Vegetable in Dharawad District of Karnataka** 167
N.M. Rolli, M.G. Nadagouda, R.H. Ratageri, H.C. Lakshman

28. **Preparation of Value Added Products by Utilizing Low Value Deep Sea Fish Bull's Eye (*Priacanthus hamurur*)** 171
L. Suragihali Siddappa, C.V. Raju, Jayanaik, M.H. Bhandari and Basavakumar

29. **Study of Algal Flora in Rice Fields of University Campus, Bhagalpur, and Bounsi, Banka (Bihar)** 176
Braj Nandan Kumar

30. **Marine Actinomycetes: A Potential Source for L-asparaginase** 180
P. Dhevagi and E. Poorani

31. **Biological Treatment of Azodyes** 199
P. Dhevagi and K. Sujatha

32. **Groundwater Quality of Bhadravathi Town, Karnataka State** 216
Vijaya Kumara, J. Narayana, K. Harish Babu, Devidas Kamath and E.T. Puttaiah

33. **Phycological Aspects and Water Quality Assessment in the Rivers of Andhra Pradesh, India** 234
P. Manikya Reddy and V. Venkateswarlu

34. **Determining the Genetic Variability in *Dioscorea alata* L. in Tirunelveli Hills in Tamil Nadu** 243
A. John De Britto, N. Nirmal Kumar and R. Mahesh

35. **Effect of Colchicine on Various Morphological Characters in *Cucumis pubscens* Willd.** 247
M. Babu Rao

36. **Diversity of Phytoplankton in Mani Reservoir, Hosanagar, Karnataka** 251
D.N. Veerendra S. Manjappa and E.T. Puttaiah

37. **Water Pollution and its Effect: An Overview** 255
Rajendra Prasad Singh, M.T. Dan and Umapati Sahay

38. **Control of Cabbage Butterfly, *Pieris brassicae* Linn. with Some Recently Developed Neem Extracts** 263
M. Bhubaneshwari Devi

39. **Studies on the Pollen Foraging Behaviour of Rock Bee, *Apis dorsata*, at Mannampandal, Nagai District, Tamil Nadu** 268
S. Thiripurasundari, M. Varadharajan and V. Mathivanan

40. **Mosquitocidal Effect of the Plant Extract Against the Yellow Fever Mosquito, *Aedes aetypti* L.** 275
Renugadevi Arasappan and T. Thangaraj

41. **Effect of Ethanol and *Mucuna pruriens* Seed on Rat Liver** 281
G. Krishnamoorthy and A. Sivamady

42. **Diurnal Variation in Ayyanakere Lake, Western Ghat Region of Chikmagalore, Karnataka** 288
S. Thirumala, B.R. Kiran, E.T. Puttaiah, Vijayakumara, K. Harish Babu & D. Basavaraja

43. **A New Species of Retractocephalus Haldar and Chakraborty, 1976 (Apicomplexa : Conoidasida) from a Coleopteran Insect in West Bengal, India** 293
Monali Chatterjee and T.K. Kundu

44. **Evaluation of Ginger Varieties for High Altitude and Tribal Area of Andhra Pradesh** 299
M. Mutyala Naidu, M. Padma, K.M. Yuva Raj and P.S.S. Murty

45. **Performance of Different Cluster Bean Varieties** 302
M.M. Naidu, K.P. Pathy, V. Ganesh Babu and R. Sreenivsulu

46. **Performance of Different Turmeric Varieties in High Altitude Area of Andhra Pradesh, India** 305
M. Mutyala Naidu, M. Padma, K.M. Yuva Raj and P.S.S. Murty

47. **Rapid Composting of Irrigated Pearl Millet Straw** 309
J. Kannan and P. Singaram

48. **Plankton Diversity at Gopnath, Gulf of Khambhat, Gujarat** 315
Kauresh D. Vachhrajani and Pradeep C. Mankodi

49. **Studies on the Status of Drinking Water Quality of Bharatpur Area in Rajasthan** 325
Deepshikha Garg, R.V. Singh and Sunita Goyal

50. **Alterations in Kidney Transaminases After Combined Exposure to Sulphur Dioxide and Nitrogen Dioxide in Albino Rat** 333
Asha Agarwal and Shaista Parveen

51. **Plant Diversity Status of Constructed and Sewage Polluted Pond, Dharwad, Karnataka** 337
R.H. Ratageri and T.C. Taranath

52. Alterations in the Carbohydrate Metabolism of *Vigna mungo* (L.) Hepper as Affected by Cobalt Stress 344

K. Jayakumar and P. Vijayarengan

53. Effect of Chronic Exposure of Cadmium on Histology of *Sarotherodon mossambicus* 348

D.V. Muley, R.B. Patil, R.S. Dabhole and D.S. Redekar

54. Population Dynamics and Bioefficacy of *Raphidopalpa* (Aulacophora) *foveicollis* (Lucas) (Coleoptera : Chrysomelidae) on *Lagenaria vulgaris* Ser. in Barak Valley of Assam 355

Dilip Nath and D.C. Ray

55. Crop Density, Growth and Yield Attributes of Lowland Rice as Influenced by Different Level of Fertilizer Nitrogen Substitution through Poultry and Livestock Wastes 364

S. Ramesh, S. Ravi and B. Chandrasekaran

56. Growth, Yield, Nutrient Uptake and Soil Fertility Status of the Succeeding Rice Crop as Influenced by the Residual Effect of Nitrogen Substitution through Livestock Wastes in the Preceding Rice Crop 370

S. Ramesh, S. Ravi and B. Chandrasekaran

57. Agrometeorological Assessment and Amelioration of Rural Food Security 377

S. Venkataraman

58. Natural Enemies of *Helicoverpa armigera* (Hubn.) on Pigeon Pea from Western Maharashtra 381

T.V. Sathe and T.M. Chougale

59. Effect of BGA and Sea Weed Extract (Plant Growth Stimulant) and Fertilizer on Yield of Mungbean (*Vigna radiata*) Variety Vaibhav 384

D.D. Dudhade and B.M. Jamadagni

60. Effect of Phosphorus and Seed Rate on the Yield of Bold Seeded Kabuli Chickpea 387

D.D. Dudhade and B.M. Jamadgni

61. Plankton Diversity in Riverine Ecosystem of South Assam and Tripura 390

Dilip Nath and D.C. Ray

62. The Occurrences of the Heavy Metals from Three Reservoirs of Satara District (Maharashtra), India 394

Sandhya M. Pawar and Sanjay S. Sathe

63. Growth and Yield Response of Rice to Solid Waste of a Paper Mill of Orissa 399

B. Padhy, P.K. Gantaye, K.C. Lenka and Sabita K. Padhy

64. Fluctuation of AM Fungi Infection and its Importance on Certain Forest Tree Species 407

M.G. Nadagouda, R.H. Ratageri, N.M. Rolli and H.C. Lakshman

65. Arbuscular Mycorrhizae (AM) Fungal Association in Some Rare, Medicinal Plants **415**

R.H. Ratageri, M.G. Nadagouda, N.M. Rolli and H.C. Lakshman

66. Foundry Industry and Latest Pollution Control Technologies **423**

Y.C. Sharma

Index **429**

Chapter 1

Informatics on *Aeromonas hydrophila* and Motile *Aeromonad septicemias* of Fish

Arvind Kumar[1] and Partha Bandyopadhyay[2]

[1]Environment Science Research Unit, Post Graduate Department of Zoology, S.K.M. University, Dumka – 814 101, Jharkhand, India

[2]Research & Development Division, Latika Sea Food Pvt. Ltd., Jalalkhanbard, Contai – 721 401, Purba Medinipur, West Bengal, India

ABSTRACT

Aeromonas hydrophila is the most common bacteria in freshwater habitats. The presence of these bacteria, by itself, is not indicative of disease and, consequently, stress is often considered to be a contributing factor in outbreaks of disease caused by these bacteria. *A. hydrophila* infected internal organs through the digestive tract or through uninjured skin under conditions of crowding. Biochemistry, genetics, and serology of the motile *Aeromonas* taxon are heterogeneous, the taxonomic position of this genus has been unstable. Upon microscopic examination, the bacteria appear as short (0.5 × 1.0 μm), gram-negative bacilli. Phenotypically, motile aeromonads are cytochrome oxidase positive, ferment glucose with or without the production of gas. Motile aeromonads that have been taken from lesions on diseased fish have been shown to have a greater chemotactic response to skin mucus than isolates that were obtained as free-living organisms from pond water. However, the composite nature of virulence observed both inter- and intra-specifically among the motile aeromonads may be best defined by looking at synergistic relationships between virulence factors. Oxytetracycline (Terramycin) has been the drug of choice for treating motile aeromonad septicemias in fishes. Chloromycetin, like oxytetracycline, was effective in treating fish when it was administered orally. However, its use is prohibited in food fishes and discouraged in other fishes.

Keywords: *Aeromonas hydrophila, Fish, Septicemia.*

Introduction

Aeromonas hydrophila and other motile aeromonads are among the most common bacteria in freshwater habitats throughout the world, and these bacteria frequently cause disease among cultured and feral fishes. From descriptions of fish diseases in the early scientific literature, Otte (1963) speculated that septicemic infections in fish caused by motile aeromonads were common throughout Europe during the Middle Ages. Although the bacterial etiology of these early reports was inconclusive, the pathology was similar to that observed with red leg disease in frogs, in which *A. hydrophila* was identified as the causal organism. Because many bacteria isolated from fish with hemorrhagic septicemias in fish were often misidentified, it is now recognized that certain isolations of bacteria ascribed to the genera *Pseudomonas, Proteus, Bacillus, Aerobacter,* and *Achromobacter* actually belonged to the genus *Aeromonas.* The exact etiology of disease involving aeromonads is complicated by the diverse genetic, biochemical, and antigenic heterogeneity that exists among members of this group. Consequently, motile aeromonads are often referred to as a complex of disease organisms that are associated with bacterial hemorrhagic septicemias and other ulcerative conditions in fishes. Although motile aeromonads appropriately receive much notoriety as pathogens of fish, it is important to note that these bacteria also compose part of the normal intestinal microflora of healthy fish (Trust *et al.*, 1974).

Therefore, the presence of these bacteria, by itself, is not indicative of disease and, consequently, stress is often considered to be a contributing factor in outbreaks of disease caused by these bacteria. Such stressors are most commonly associated with environmental and physiological parameters that adversely fish under intensive culture. As one such example, Eisa *et al.* (1994) have shown that the prevalence of motile aeromonad septicemia in cultured and wild Nile tilapia (*Oreochromis niloticus*) was 10.0 per cent and 2.5 per cent respectively; it was 18.75 per cent and 6.25 per cent in cultured and wild Karmout catfish, respectively. Ventura and Grizzle (1987) produced systemic infections more readily among channel catfish (*Ictalurus punctatus*) by abrading their skin prior to exposing the fish to the bacterium. These researchers further showed that *A. hydrophila* infected internal organs through the digestive tract or through uninjured skin under conditions of crowding (13.1 g of fish/L) and high temperature (24°C). Such infections did not occurred when catfish were held at a lower density (5.2 g of fish/L) and temperature (18°C). In another interesting study, Peters *et al.* (1988) subjected subordinate rainbow trout (*Oncorhynchus mykiss*) to social stresses of cohabitation with dominant cohorts and then exposed these fish to infection by *A. hydrophila*. By comparison to their dominant counterparts, the subordinate trout showed physical evidence of stress based on elevated plasma glucose concentrations and increased leukocyte volumes. Following exposure to the pathogen, the bacterium was also recovered from more organs and with greater prevalence among the subordinate fish than from their dominant cohorts. In feral fish, other factors may be important stressors that trigger motile aeromonad septicemias. Toranzo *et al.* (1989), for example, described the occurrence of such an epizootic associated with spawning stress among gizzard shad (*Dorosoma cepedianum*) in the Potomac River (Maryland, U.S.A.).

Motile aeromonads primarily cause disease in cultured warm water fishes: minnows, bait fishes, carp (*Cyprinus carpio*), channel catfish (*Ictalurus punctatus*), striped bass (*Morone saxatilis*), largemouth bass (*Micropterus* salmoides) and tilapia. The pathogen may also affect a variety of cool and cold-water species, but is not necessarily restricted to fresh water environments. Rahim *et al.* (1985) have isolated *A. hydrophila* from wounds of five species of brackish water fish including species; *Platosus anguillaris, Lates calcarifer, Epinephelus megachir, Labeo ruhita* and *Serotherodon nilotica*. Thampuran *et al.* (1995) have not only isolated motile aeromonads from raw and processed products of marine fish, but also from marine fishing grounds, as well.

Taxonomy and Classification

Biochemistry, genetics, and serology of the motile *Aeromonas* taxon are heterogeneous, the taxonomic position of this genus has been unstable. Kluyver and van Niel (1936) transferred many organisms that were associated with hemorrhagic septicemias in fish within the genera *Bacillus, Pseudomonas, Proteus,* and *Aerobacter* into the new genus *Aeromonas.* These aeromonads were short, gram-negative, motile bacilli with a single flagellum that fermented glucose with or without the production of gas. Snieszko (1957) later divided the genus into three species: *A. hydrophila, A. punctata,* and *A. liquefaciens.* In Snieszko's scheme, *Aeromonas liquefaciens* contained most of the fish pathogens. Schubert (1967) confirmed that there was enough biochemical similarity to establish the genus *Aeromonas,* but invalidated species-specific distinctions. Later, Popoff and Vernon (1976) demonstrated that the motile aeromonads could be classified into two distinct species: *A. hydrophila* (composed of the organisms previously described as *A. punctata* and *A. liquefaciens),* and a new species that they named *A. sobria.* Biochemically, *A. hydrophila* hydrolyzes esculin and ferments both salicin and arabinose, whereas *A. sobria* does not utilize these compounds (Lallier *et al.,* 1981). Motile aeromonads may be pleomorphic but generally produce circular, smooth, raised colonies on agar.

Upon microscopic examination, the bacteria appear as short (0.5 × 1.0 µm), gram-negative bacilli. Phenotypically, motile aeromonads are cytochrome oxidase positive, ferment glucose with or without the production of gas, and are insensitive to the vibriostatic agent 0/129 (2,4-diamino,6,7-di-isopropyl pteridine). In addition, the bacteria produce 2,3 butanediol and reduce nitrate to nitrite. Hsu *et al.* (1984) noted that all (n = 164) of the isolates of motile aeromonads that they studied produced acid from fructose, galactose, maltose, mannitol, trehalose, dextrin, and glycogen; 99.4 per cent of the strains produced acid from glucose, 98.8 per cent from mannose, and 98.2 per cent from glycerol. Acid production from other carbohydrates (arabinose, salicin, cellobiose, sucrose, and lactose) varied. Shotts *et al.* (1985) also found that all *A. hydrophila* complex strains hydrolysed albumin, casein, and fibrinogen; most strains also digested gelatin (99.9 per cent), hemoglobin (94.3 per cent), and elastin (73.2 per cent), but none of the strains hydrolyzed collagen. Further phenotypic differentiation of the seven most commonly isolated motile aeromonads obtained from clinical isolates may be accomplished using the criteria of Carnahan *et al.* (1991) and modified by Joseph and Carnahan (1994) as described in Table 1.1. However, Austin and Austin (1989) have shown that *A. hydrophila, A. sobria,* and *A caviae* comprise the most predominant clinical isolates that are typically associated with fish.

Pathology

Motile aeromonads cause diverse pathologic conditions that include acute, chronic, and covert infections. Severity of disease is influenced by a number of interrelated factors, including bacterial virulence, the kind and degree of stress exerted on a population of fish, the physiologic condition of the host, and the degree of genetic resistance inherent within specific populations of fishes. Motile aeromonads differ interspecifically and intraspecifically in their relative pathogenicity or their ability to cause disease. Under controlled laboratory conditions, De Figueredo and Plumb (1977) found that strains of motile aeromonads isolated from diseased fish were more virulent to channel catfish than were those isolated from pond water. Lallier *et al.* (1981) performed studies on rainbow trout (*Oncorhyncus mykiss,* formerly *Salmo gairdneri)* to compare the relative virulence of *A. hydrophila* and *A. sobria,* as taxonomically described by Popoff and Vernon (1976). Their results indicated that strains of

A. *hydrophila* isolated from either healthy or diseased fish were more virulent than strains of *A. sobria*. Additionally, *A. sobria* was not isolated from fish with clinical signs of motile aeromonad septicemia (Boulanger *et al.*, 1977). Paniagua *et al.* (1990), for example, collected aeromonad isolates along the River Porma, Leon Province (Spain) and found that their isolates grouped within three species; *A. hydrophila* (n=74 strains), *A. sobria* (n =11 strains), and *A. caviae* (n = 12 strains). The authors additionally observed that 72.02 per cent of *A. hydrophila* isolates and 63 per cent of *A. sobria* isolates were virulent for fish by intramuscular challenge, but all of the strains of *A. caviae* were avirulent. Pathologic conditions attributed to members of the motile aeromonad complex may include dermal ulceration, tail or fin rot, ocular ulcerations, erythrodermatitis, hemorrhagic septicemia, red sore disease, red rot disease, and scale protrusion disease.

Table 1.1: Differentiation of Common Motile Aeromonads Isolated from Clinical Specimens as Described by Carnahan *et al.* (1991) as modified by Joseph and Carnahan (1994). All bacterial isolates to this point would be short gran negative, oxidase-positive bacilli that ferment glucose and are resistant to the Vibrostatic agent.

Characteristic[a]	*A. hydrophila*	*A. veronii bv. sobria*	*A. veronii bv. veronii*	*A. caviae*	*A. scubertii*	*A. janddaei*	*A. trota*
Esculin hydrolysis	+	–	+	+	–	–	–
Voges-Proskauer reaction	+	+	+	–	V	+	–
Pyrazinamidase activity	+	–	–	+	–	–	–
CAMP-like factor (aerobic only)	+	+	+	–	–	V	–
Arabinose fermentation	V	–	–	V	–	–	–
Mannitol fermentation	+	+	+	+	–	+	+
Sucrose fermentation	+	+	+	+	–	–	–
Ampicillin susceptibility	R	R	R	R	R	R	S
Carbenicillin susceptibility	R	R	R	R	R	R	S
Cephalothin susceptibility	R	S	S	R	S	R	R
Colistin susceptibility[b]	V	S	S	S	S	R	S
Lysine decarboxylase	+	+	+	–	+	+	+
Ornithine decarboxylase	–	–	+	–	–	–	–
Arbutin hydrolysis	+	–	+	+	–	–	V
Indole production	+	+	+	–	+	+	+
H2S production[c]	+	+	+	–	–	+	+
Gas from glucose	+	+	+	–	–	+	+
Hemolysis (TSA with 5 per cent sheep erythrocytes)	+	+	+	V	+	+	V

[a] +: positive for >70 per cent of isolates; –, negative, *i.e.* positive for <30 per cent of isolates; V, variable; R, resistant; S, susceptible.

[b]MIC (single dilution), 4 µg/mL.

In the acute form of disease, a fatal septicemia may occur so rapidly that fish die before they have time to develop anything but a few gross signs of disease. When clinical signs of infection are present, affected fish may show exophthalmia, reddening of the skin, and an accumulation of fluid in the scale pockets (Faktorovich 1969). The abdomen may become distended as a result of an edema and the scales may bristle out from the skin to give a "washboard" appearance (Figures 1.1 and 1.2). The gills may hemorrhage and ulcers may develop on the dermis. Ogara *et al.* (1998) noted severe eye pathology and heavy mortality among yearling and older rainbow trout accompanying a severe outbreak of motile aeromonad septicemia. The condition at first affected one eye progressed into the other eye, after which the orbits ruptured causing blindness and death. Similarly, Yambot and Inglis (1994) described an acute mortality among Nile tilapia in which the most apparent clinical signs included opaqueness in one or both eyes, accompanied by exophthalmia and eventual bursting of the orbit. Motile aeromonads were isolated from the eyes, liver and kidneys of affected fish. Histopathologically, fish may exhibit epithelial hyperplasia in the foregut; leptomeningeal congestion in the brain, as well as a thrombosis and inflammation in the perisclerotic region and corneal epithelium of the eye (Fuentes and Perez 1998). There my also be a severe branchitis, as indicated by leukocytic infiltration and dilation of the central venous sinus Grizzle and Kiryu 1993). These authors also noted that catfish with septecemic or latent infections had enlarged nuclei in the branchial epithelium and that there was a significant correlation between the presence of these gill lesions and the severity of hepatic and pancreatic lesions. Rodriguez *et al.* (1993) further noted that there was an increase in bacterial acetylcholinesterase activity in the brain tissue of moribund fish.

Systemic infections were characterized by diffuse necrosis in several internal organs and the presence of melanin-containing macrophages in the blood Ventura and Grizzle 1988). Internally, the liver and kidneys are target organs of an acute septicemia. The liver may become pale or have a greenish coloration while the kidney may become swollen and friable. These organs are apparently attacked by bacterial toxins and lose their structural integrity (Huizinga *et al.*, 1979). Even when tissue

Figure 1.1: Scale Protrusion on a Carp (*Cyprinus carpio*) Caused by *Aeromonas hydrophila*

Figure 1.2: Severe Distention and Accumulation of Ascites in the Abdomen of a Goldfish (*Carassius auratus*) Caused by *Aeromonas hydrophila.* Also note the "washboard" effect of the dermis caused by the protrusion of scales from the body surface.

damage in the liver and kidneys is extensive, the heart and spleen are not necessarily damaged. However, splenic ellipsoids are often centers of intense phagocytic activity by macrophages. Bach *et al.*, 1978 observed pathological changes in the spleens of fish injected with virulent *A. hydrophila,* whereas fish infected orally showed little or no splenic involvement. Bacteria were present within the reticular sheaths of the ellipsoids, where intense phagocytic activity by macrophages occurred. Phagocytized bacteria divided intracellularly and extracellularly and destroyed the endothelial and reticular cells of the ellipsoids. The lower intestine and vent, which sometimes protrude from the body, are often swollen, inflamed, and hemorrhagic. Additionally, the intestine is devoid of food and may be filled with a yellow mucus-like material. Chronic motile aeromonad infections manifest themselves primarily as ulcerous forms of disease, in which dermal lesions with focal hemorrhage and inflammation are apparent (Figures 1.3 and 1.4). Both the dermis and epidermis are eroded and the underlying musculature becomes severely necrotic (Huizinga *et al.,* 1979). Inflammatory cells are usually lacking in the necrotic musculature, whereas the adjacent epidermis undergoes a hyperplasia that results in a raised margin. At this stage, the infection has usually become systemic and pinpoint hemorrhages (petechiae) may occur throughout the peritoneum and musculature. Fish with only cutaneous infections may have several types of concealed lesions including increased amounts of lipofuscin and haemosiderin in the liver and spleen; however, most visceral organs were not necrotic (Ventura and Grizzle 1988).

Aeromonas hydrophila was generally considered to be a secondary invader in red sore disease, in which the primary etiological agent was believed to be the protozoan ciliate *Epistylis* (Rogers 1971). Recently Hazen *et al.* (1978b) reexamined the etiology of red sore disease and found that *A. hydrophila* was present in 96 per cent of the initial lesions on fish, whereas *Epistylis* was present in only 35 per cent of such lesions. Furthermore, electron microscopy showed that *Epistylis* lacked structures that produced lytic enzymes and, therefore, could not initiate the development of lesions. This study strongly suggested that *A. hydrophila* is indeed the primary etiological agent of red sore disease and that *Epistylis* is a secondary pathogen that rapidly colonizes the dermal lesions initiated by bacterial

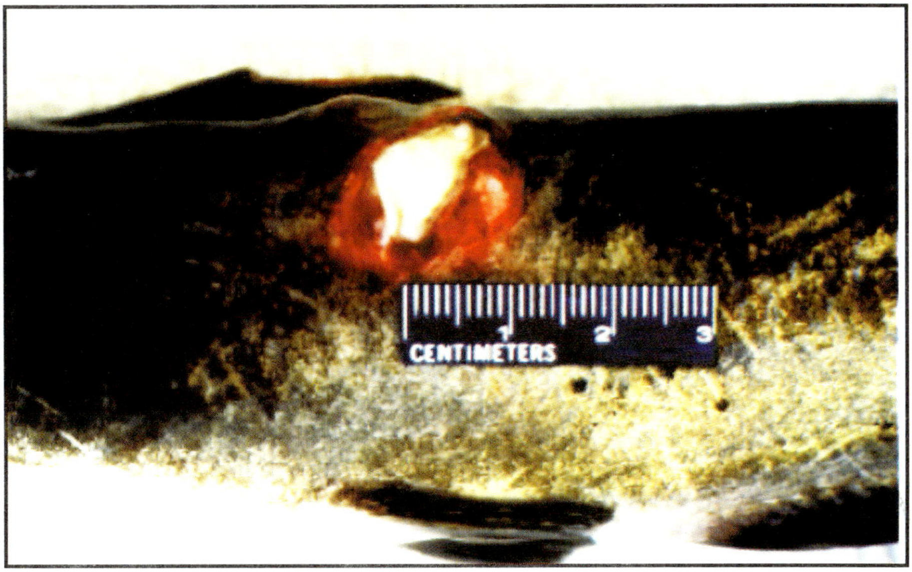

Figure 1.3: Lesion Produced by *Aeromonas hydrophila* in the Dermis of a Channel Catfish (*Ictalurus punctatus*)

Figure 1.4: Hemorrhage and Ulcerations Caused on the Dermis of American Shad (*Alosa sapidissima*) by *Aeromonas hydrophila*

proteolytic enzymes. In frogs and other amphibians, *A. hydrophila* infections cause distention of capillaries on the ventral surface of the legs and abdomen, giving them the red coloration that is the source of the name of the disease;–red leg. Outbreaks of aeromonad septicemias in frogs and warm water fishes usually occur in the spring and coincide with an increase in water temperature. Resistance to disease is lowered at this time because aquatic organisms are often anemic and have a substantial decrease in serum proteins resulting from periods of dormancy and starvation that occurred during the winter. Huizinga *et al.* (1979) also indicated that rising water temperatures increased metabolism, decreased overall condition, and stressed the fish. Stressed fish increased production of corticosteroids, which in turn increased their susceptibility to infection. Motile aeromonads can also cause disease in warm-blooded vertebrates. In immunocompromised human hosts, for example, *A. hydrophila* may cause septic arthritis, diarrhoea, corneal ulcers, skin and wound infections, meningitis, and fulminating septi cemias (Von Gravenitz and Mensch 1968; Davis 1978). Clinical isolates of *A. hydrophila* have been obtained from retail foods (fish, seafood, raw milk, poultry and red meats) and all isolates had biotypes identical to those of enterotoxin-positive strains (Palumbo *et al.*, 1989). The ability of these bacteria to grow competitively at 5°C may be indicative of their potential as a public health hazard. However, most *A. hydrophila* were reduced to non-detectable levels on catfish filets cooked to 70°C (Huang *et al.*, 1993).

Virulence Factors

The ability of a pathogen to locate, attach to, and subsequently infect a susceptible host is a primary step in the development of disease. Consequently, factors produced by motile aeromonads, which can facilitate contagion, are important elements of bacterial virulence. In fact, motile aeromonads that have been taken from lesions on diseased fish have been shown to have a greater chemotactic response to skin mucus than isolates that were obtained as free-living organisms from pond water (Razen *et al.*, 1982). Ascencio *et al.* (1998) have shown that *A. hydrophila, A. caviae*, and *A. sobria* can actually adhere to animal cell lines that have mucous receptors. These workers also determined that the proportion of *A. hydrophila* strains which bound various mucins was significantly greater than the proportions of *A. caviae* and *A. sobria* that acted similarly. Trust *et al.* (1980) also indicated that *A. hydrophila* had adhesive agglutination characteristics which facilitated attachment to eukaryotic cells. Electron microscopy further demonstrated that motile aeromonads produce fimbriae (pili) that facilitate adhesion but these structures were common to cells regardless of their virulence (delCorral 1990). The results of the latter study, therefore, suggest that attachment may facilitate contagion but prevented correlation between haemagglutination, yeast cell co-agglutination and virulence. In addition to adhesins, Dooley and Trust (1988) characterized a tetragonal surface protein array consisting of a 52 KD protein from virulent isolates of *A. hydrophila*. This S-layer was also reported by Ford and Thune (1991) among motile aeromonads that they isolated from clinically diseased catfish. The existence of such layers structurally permeates bacterial cell membranes which generally increases cellular hydrophobicity. The increased surface tension enhances resistance of the bacterium to complement-mediated serum lysis and phagocytosis by leukocytes. Indeed, Gado (1998) noted that virulent aeromonad isolates from Nile tilapia share a common resistance to the killing effect of tilapia serum. Byers *et al.* (1986) have also shown that *A. hydrophila* can produce siderophores that confer resistance against the ability of serum transferring to inhibit bacterial growth.

Many studies have attempted to further delineate the virulence mechanisms of motile aeromonads. Kou (1973) found that many of the virulent, avirulent, and attenuated aeromonads that he studied possessed hemorhagic factors and lethal toxins. The virulent bacteria had quantitatively more toxic potential than did their avirulent or attenuated counterparts. Olivier *et al.* (1981) indicated that both *A. hydrophila* and *A. sobria* produced enterotoxins, dermonecrotic factors, and hemolysis. Although both species produced hemolysis on blood agar plates at 30°C, only *A. hydrophila* did so at 10°C. Because these researchers were working with salmonid fish, they suggested that the hemolysis of red blood cells by *A. hydrophila* at temperatures comparable to those of the water in which fish live may at least partially account for the difference in virulence between A. *hydrophila* and *A. sobria.* Enterotoxins, haemolysins, proteases, haemagglutinins, and endotoxins produced by this complex of bacterial organisms have been the subject of much research (Cahill 1990). However, the composite nature of virulence observed both inter- and intra-specifically among the motile aeromonads may be best defined by looking at synergistic relationships between virulence factors. For example, Rigney *et al.* (1978) found that individual injections of either endotoxin or hemolysin alone did not produce clinical pathology in frogs. However, when both the endotoxin and hemolysin were injected in the same inoculum, frogs exhibited pathology that mimicked clinical signs of red leg disease. Thune *et al.* (1982a) also found that channel catfish were tolerant to injections of endotoxin alone at concentrations up to 400 ìg endotoxin per 7.2 g of fish. However, an extracellular cell-free extract of a spent culture medium had an LD_{50} value of 15.7 µg protein within 48 h after its injection into 7.2 g fish. Thune *et al.* (1982b) later showed that this extract contain was proteolytic but not hemolytic. Two proteases were further refined from this extract; one was heat labile and had an LC_{50} concentration of 18 µg of protein per gram of fish, and the other was heat stable and had an LC_{50} concentration of 3 µg of protein per gram of fish. Allan and Stevenson (1981) also found hemolytic and proteolytic activities in crude extracellular preparations from *A. hydrophila.* These researchers indicated that aeration increased growth rates, cell yield, and the amount of proteolytic activity. Proteolytic activity was reduced, however, when cultures were incubated at 37°C. Furthermore, extracts from a protease deficient mutant were more toxic to fish than were similar extracts from isogenic wild strains. Because the extract from the protease deficient mutant had a fivefold increase in hemolytic activity, Allan and Stevenson concluded that hemolysin, not protease, was the principal virulence factor of *A. hydrophila.* The results of other studies, however, might caution against such conclusions.

Although Rogulska *et al.* (1994) found that haemolytic activity was high in 93 per cent of very pathogenic strains of *A. hydrophila* and the activity was also also high in 87.5 per cent of pathogenic *A. sobria.* Measurement of hemolytic activity alone was not the decisive characteristic in terms of isolate virulence because even some (15 per cent) avirulent *A. hydrophila* isolates were hemolytic. Additional measurements showed that a combination of high hemolytic and high proteolytic activity, which was detected in 90 per cent of virulent *A. hydrophila* strains and 87.5 per cent of the *A. sobria* strains, may be a better measure of total virulence. Only one non-pathogenic strain of *A. hydrophila* had high levels of both activities. Rodriguez *et al.* (1992) have purified a metalloprotease, a serine protease and a haemolysin from culture supernatants of *A. hydrophila.* Each of these factors has lethal activity for rainbow trout. The metalloprotease had a molecular weight of 38 kD, was stable at 56°C for 10 min, had no cytotoxic activity but produced an LC_{50} value of 150 ng/g of trout. The serine protease had a molecular weight of 22 kD, was also stable at 56ºC for 10 min, possessed cytotoxic activity and also had an LC_{50} value of 150 ng/g of trout. The haemolysin was alpha -hemolytic and had a molecular weight of 68 kD and produced an LC_{50} value of 2 µg/g of trout. The haemolysin was stable at 56ºC deg for 20 min and at 60ºC for 10 min. Because the haemolysin possessed esterase activity on beta - naphthyl acetate, Rodriguez *et al.*, suggested that the compound may be distinct from either alpha–or beta–haemolysin. Casc'on *et al.* (2000) have cloned a gene encoding elastolytic activity, ahyB, from *Aeromonas hydrophila.*

A hydrophila B is synthesized as a pre-proprotein which is further processed into a mature protease and a C-terminal propeptide. The protease hydrolyzed casein and elastin and showed a high sequence similarity to other metalloproteases. Results of a recent molecular analysis, which was conducted by Zhang *et al.* (2000) to underscore genetic differences between virulent and avirulent isolates, confirms that virulence among the motile aeromonads depends upon a multiplicity of factors. Their results showed that 22 DNA fragments were present in most of the virulent strains and that these genes encoded for five known virulence factors of *A. hydrophila* including haemolysin (hlyA), protease (oligopeptidase A), outer-membrane protein (Omp), multidrug-resistance protein and histone-like protein (HU-2). These same fragments were mostly absent in the avirulent isolates that were examined.

Identification and Diagnosis

Presumptive diagnosis of *A. hydrophila* may be based on the species of fish affected, the past disease status of those fish, and the presence of clinical signs of disease. However, bacteria must be isolated and identified biochemically to provide a definitive diagnosis. Either Tryptic Soy Agar (TSA) or Brain-Heart Infusion Agar (BRIA) is a suitable medium for the primary isolation of motile aeromonads from diseased fish. Because mixed bacterial infections are common in fish affected with hemorrhagic septicemias, it is often difficult to isolate pure cultures of a single species of motile aeromonads from clinically diseased tissues. In order to facilitate the recovery of motile aeromonads upon primary isolation, Shotts and Rimler (1973) designed a differential medium for selective isolation of motile aeromonads. This medium, termed R-S agar, is prepared by dissolving the following ingredients (grams) in distilled water to a volume of 1 liter: L-lysine hydrochloride (5.0), L-orninthine hydrochloride (6.5), L-cystine hydrochloride (0.3), maltose (3.5), sodium thiosulfate (6.8), bromothymol blue (0.03), ferric ammonium citrate (0.8), sodium deoxycholate (1.0), novobiocin (0.005), yeast extract (3.0), sodium chloride (5.0), and agar (13.5). The mixture is constantly stirred, heated to boiling for 1 min, and brought to pH 7.0. The medium is cooled to 45°C, dispensed into sterile petri dishes, and can be refrigerated in plastic sleeves until used.

After inoculation, R-S agar should be incubated at 37°C for 24 to 48 h, to ensure optimal differentiation of bacteria. Colonies of motile aeromonads are yellow; those of *Pseudomonas, Escherichia*, and *Enterobacter* are green; and those of *Edwardsiella* are green with black centers. Although *Proteus*

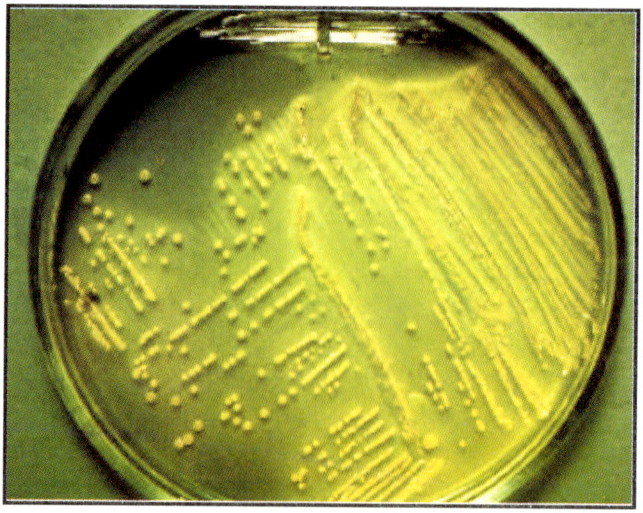

Figure 1.5: Growth of Yellow Colonies that are Characteristic of *Aeromonas hydrophila* after incubation on Rimler-Shotts Agar

vulgaris and some *Citrobacter* are also yellow on R-S agar, these colonies have black centers that indicate the bacteria are producing hydrogen sulfide gas. Although R-S agar has facilitated primary isolation of motile aeromonads, yellow colonies should not be accepted as a basis for definitive diagnosis. *Aeromonas salmonicida* will also produce yellow colonies on R-S agar, but unlike the motile aeromonads growth of this bacterium is inhibited at 37°C. Davis and Sizemore (1981) also indicated that R-S agar supported the growth of a limited number of yellow colonies whose DNA homology ratios were inconsistent for the genus *Aeromonas.* Many of these isolates, especially those obtained from low-salinity sites, were also identified by the API 20E system as *A. hydrophila.* Therefore, additional biochemical tests should be performed on isolated colonies that have been cloned from purified colonies on either TSA or BHIA. It is important to note that reactions inconsistent for the species can occur if one uses colonies picked directly from from the differential R-S agar medium. For example, Overman *et al.* (1979) found that 8 per cent of the isolates they examined were cytochrome oxidase negative when taken from differential media. Glucose fermentation is a critical reaction that differentiates the motile aeromonads from species of *Pseudomonas* (Bullock 1961). Bacteria are inoculated into two tubes of Oxidation Fermentation (OF) basal medium supplemented with 1 per cent glucose. The medium in one tube is overlaid with a plug of sterile petrolatum and both tubes are incubated at 25°C for 24 to 48 h. Results are interpreted as follows: yellow coloration in both tubes indicates acidic fermentation of glucose typical of *Aeromonas,* whereas yellow coloration only in the tube without petrolatum indicates oxidation of glucose characteristic of *Pseudomonas.* A single tube modification of this test was described by Walters and Plumb (1978), in which a tube is prepared with twice the amount of glucose medium contained in the two-tube test. After incubation, a yellow coloration throughout the tube indicates fermentation, whereas a yellowish coloration only at the top of the medium indicates oxidation. Motility can also be determined by examination for diffused bacterial growth away from the origin of inoculation. Production of gas is evidenced in either test by the formation of bubbles in the medium. Although most strains of *A. hydrophila* produce gas during the fermentation of glucose, some motile aeromonads isolated from diseased fish are anaerogenic–that is, they do not generate gas (Ross 1962). Because motile aeromonads are ubiquitous and have considerable antigenic diversity, serodiagnostic identification is not reliable. Agglutination procedures, fluorescent antibody tests (Eurell *et al.*, 1978, Soltani and Rabani Khorasgani 1999), and immunoenzyme procedures (Lewis 1981, Mishra 1998) have been adapted for use within homologous antigen/antibody systems. These assays may accurately detect strains of motile aeromonads against which homologous detection antibodies were developed, but detection of heterologous strains makes serodiagnostic identification impractical. Fliermans and Hazen (1980) found that a total of three different antisera to *A. hydrophila* gave a positive fluorescent antibody reaction with only 27.5 per cent of the *A. hydrophila* isolates tested. Therefore, the lack of an effective polyvalent antiserum specific for *A. hydrophila* still limits reliable serodiagnostic detection of this pathogen. Calabrez and Lintermans (1993) have also developed a Polymerase Chain Reaction (PCR) technique which has been used to detect strains of *A. sobria* in water, sediments, and fish. Genetic analysis suggests that there are presently 14 genomospecies recognized within the aeromonads (Joseph and Carnahan 1994) and, consequently a number of species-specific PCR tests would need to be developed and run on individual clinical samples in order to achieve accurate diagnosis.

Serology and Vaccination

Motile aeromonads are one of the most taxonomically and antigenically diverse groups of bacteria pathogenic to fish. The amount of antigenic diversity inherent within this group is especially expressed within H and O somatic antigens. Ewing *et al.* (1961) described 12 Oantigen groups and 9 H-antigen groups. Each group was further divided into a number of additional serotypes. Chodyniecki (1965) also found a high degree of antigenic diversity among strains of motile aeromonads obtained from the same population of fish and even from different organs of the same fish. Monovalent bacterins were initially prepared against *A. hydrophila*, but these vaccines only provided acceptable levels of protection against challenge with a homologous bacterium. Fish were not immune to infection by heterologous strains of *A. hydrophila* (Post 1966; Schaperclaus 1967). Although some strains of motile aeromonads have common somatic antigens (Rao and Foster 1977; Lallier *et al.*, 1981), it has been consistently demonstrated that a monovalent antiserum could agglutinate only a small percentage of the total isolates examined. Kingma (1978) produced seven rabbit antisera to heat stable antigens of seven isolates. Collectively, these antisera agglutinated only 19.5 per cent of the total number of motile aeromonad isolates studied. Despite the tremendous degree of serological diversity that exists within this taxon, Mittal *et al.* (1980) found that strains of *A. hydrophila*, which were highly virulent for rainbow trout, shared a common O-antigen. Furthermore, these bacteria did not agglutinate in acriflavine, settled after boiling, and resisted the bactericidal activity of normal mammalian sera. In contrast, low-virulence strains of *A. sobria* did not share the common Oantigen; these bacteria settled after boiling and were lysed by normal mammalian sera. Schachte (1978) also found that the delivery of vaccine by injection or immersion or *per os* stimulated differential kinetics of antibody production. However, no significant protection against natural exposure to heterologous *A. hydrophila* was afforded to channel catfish vaccinated by any of the methods. Anbarasu *et al.* (1998) found that formalin inactivated vaccines were superior to heat killed preparations, especially when the bacterins were injected with adjuvants. Thune and Plumb (1982) found that both sac fry and swim-up fry vaccinated by immersion in sonicated polyvalent bacterin were protected against challenge with homologous bacteria, indicating an early onset of immunocompetence in channel catfish. This study was important because *A. hydrophila* causes a severe problem in channel catfish in spring and early summer, when fry are abundant. The early onset of immunocompetence among channel catfish fry indicates that immunization, if effective, could be used to reduce outbreaks of *A. hydrophila* infection. Regardless of whether whole cells, freeze-thawed cells, or cell sonicates were used, Thune and Plumb (1982) further indicated that injection was superior to either immersion or spray vaccination for developing humoral antibodies. However, cell sonicates evoked the best antibody response. Sonication may disrupt the cell and allow better processing of certain somatic antigens (*e.g.*–bacterial lipopolysaccharide). Consequently, Baba *et al.* (1988) were able to evoke better protection against *A. hydrophila* among carp that were vaccinated with crude lipopolysaccharide (LPS) rather than whole-cell, formalin killed vaccine. Immersion of fish in the LPS vaccine for 2 h at 25°C was more efficacious and less stressful than injection, but vaccination with crude LPS did not invoke an observed humoral immune response as measured by bacterial agglutination, passive haemagglutination and agar gel diffusion tests. Because of the antigenic diversity that exists among this complex group of organisms, additional vaccination strategies included research on development of polyvalent vaccines, immunization against inactivated extracellular toxins (toxoids), and the development of vaccines consisting of cellular antigens plus toxoid. Liu (1961) noted that the biological activity of extracellular toxins from motile aeromonads was neutralized by a single antiserum prepared against an isolate of *A. liquefaciens* (synonym for *A. hydrophila*). He therefore concluded that the motile aeromonads shared extracellular antigens. Bullock *et al.* (1972) also indicated that aerogenic and anaerogenicstrains of *A. hydrophila* possessed common extracellular antigens. Schaperclaus (1970) recognized that common carp (*Cyprinus carpio*) vaccinated against *A. hydrophila* developed both agglutinating serum antibodies against cellular antigens and antitoxic activity against extracellular antigens. In a later study, he found that common carp vaccinated by intraperitoneal injection of bacteria produced more circulating antibodies than did carp vaccinated by the oral route (Schaperclaus 1972). Furthermore, vaccination with soluble extracellular antigens was more efficacious and provided a wider base of protection against heterologous serotypes than did vaccination with whole-cell antigen. Shieh (1987) found that Atlantic salmon immunized by intramuscular injections of extracellular protease from *A. hydrophila* were protected from challenge with the homologous and some heterologous isolates of *A. hydrophila*. Shieh (1990) repeated these studies and produced similar results when *A. sobria* extracellular protease was used as the immunogen and challenges were conducted with homologous and heterologous strains of the same bacterium. However, no report was made on the ability of extracellular protease derived from one of these species to cross protect against the other motile aeromonad species. Despite the great amount of research that has been expended to develop a safe and efficacious vaccine, there is still no product that has been licensed for use against the motile aeromonads within the United States.

Occurrence and Range

Motile aeromonads cause diseases wherever bait fishes or warm water or ornamental fishes are propagated. To a lesser extent, these bacteria also initiate disease in coldwater species. Although diseases associated with motile aeromonads are most severe among fish that are propagated under conditions of intensive culture, these bacteria may also affect feral fish and are common in the intestinal flora of apparently healthy fish (Trust *et al.*, 1974). The bacterium is ubiquitous and occurs in most fresh water environments. It can be found both in the water column and in the top centimeter of sediment (Hazen 1979). Motile aeromonads are adapted to environments that have a wide range of conductivity, turbidity, pH, salinity, and temperature (Hazen *et al.*, 1978a). Temperature optimums may depend upon the particular strain under investigation, but generally range from 25°C to 35°C. Consequently, most epizootics among warm water fishes in the southeastern.

These are generally reported in spring and early summer (Meyer 1970). Pond water, diseased fish, and diseased frogs, as well as convalescent frogs and fishes, may become reservoirs of infection. Certain algae (Kawakami and Hashimoto 1978) and other protozoa (Chang and Huang 1981) that are grazed upon by fish can harbor motile aeromonads. In the latter study, *Tetrahymena pyriformis* was experimentally shown to graze on populations of *Aeromonas hydrophila*. The bacterium, at concentrations of 1×10^6 cells/mL co-existed with the protozoan. If a second bacterial species was introduced, predation by the protozoan increased. In reservoir studies, Hazen (1979) found high densities of *Aeromonas hydrophila* in mats of decomposing *Mypiophyllum spiaatum* and, enterically, within largemouth bass, several other species of fish, turtles, alligators, and snails. The densities of *A. hydrophila* were highest in the water from March to June, although a second peak occurred in October. Mean monthly densities of *A. hydrophila* were positively correlated with incidence of incubation in largemouth bass. Largemouth bass from thermally altered parts of the reservoir had a significantly higher incidence of infection. Kawakami and Hashimoto (1978) found greater quantities of *A. hydrophila* (as many as 103 cells) in algae fed upon by ayu (*Plecoglossus altivelis*) than were present in the water itself where the density of *A. hydrophila* was generally less than 10 cells/mL. Osborne *et al.* (1989) found high densities of motile aeromonads within the environment during midsummer when sedimentary chlorophyll sub(a) and water temperature were highest. This also correlated temporally with the highest prevalence of dermally ulcerated striped mullet (Mugil cephalus) that also contain large concentrations of the bacteria within their stomachs and on their skin. The authors suggest that mullet graze on bacteria-laden sediment for algae and consequently bioaccumulate the pathogen within their guts and on their skin which, in turn, enhances disease. Thus, the intestinal tract or epidermal abrasions are likely portals of bacterial entry. Under conditions of stress, it is even likely that some strains of motile aeromonads that are ordinarily part of the normal gut flora become pathogenic. It is believed that infection occurs in winter, when fish are relatively inactive, and that the disease breaks out in spring. Aquarium fish, which are usually maintained at constant water temperature, can develop this disease at any time. Rainbow trout appear to be among the most susceptible of the salmonids that develop motile aeromonad septicemias.

Methods of Control

Prevention

Effective hatchery management is the best approach to avoid infections and subsequent epizootics caused by these bacteria. In water reuse hatcheries, both ozonation (Colberg and Lingg 1978) and filtration combined with ultraviolet irradiation (Bullock and Stuckey 1977) effectively eliminate the threat of *A. hydrophila*. Colberg and Lingg (1978) showed that a specific microbial oxygen demand was exerted during batch ozonation that caused greater than a 99 per cent mortality of bacteria within a 60-second contact during continuous flow exposure at 0.1-1.0 mg ozone per liter. Calesante *et al.* (1981) eliminated recurrent motile aeromonad mortality among muskellunge (*Esox masquinongy*) fry by ultraviolet irradiation of lake and well water supplies during egg incubation and yolk absorption. Motile aeromonad septicemias are generally mediated by stress. Elevated water temperature (Esch and Hazen 1980), a decrease in dissolved oxygen concentration, or increases in ammonia and carbon dioxide concentrations have been shown to promote stress in fish and trigger motile aeromonad infections (Walters and Plumb 1980). The monitoring of environmental variables can therefore enable one to forecast stressful situations and possibly avoid problems before they arise. Wherever this disease occurs frequently, pond fish should not be handled but transferred only after water temperature is high enough for fish to be active and feeding normally (Rychlicki and Zarnecki 1957). Mortalities were reduced dramatically (80-90 per cent) when fish, at the time of spring transfer, were injected intraperitoneally with 10-20 mg of chloromycetin or by dissolving 10-20 mg chloromycetin in water per kilogram of fish (5-10 mg/lb). However, this drug is not registered for use on food fish nor is it legal to treat fish prophylactically (in the absence of disease). It is prudent that managers should avoid introducing fish into their hatcheries that have recently undergone infection. Shipments of new eggs should be surface disinfected to prevent contamination of facilities and stocks. Wright and Snow (1975) found that either acriflavine (500-700 mg/L for 15 min) or iodine as Betadine (100-150 mg/L iodine for 15 min) successfully disinfected eggs of largemouth bass (*Micropterus salmoides*), but neither Roccal nor formalin was effective. When warm water fishes are held in tanks or hauled in trucks or plastic bags, the value of adding disinfectants or antibiotics should be examined. The most promising compounds include chloramphenicol, oxytetracycline, chlortetracycline, and a mixture of penicillin and streptomycin added to water at a rate of 10-15 mg/L. Again, it is important to note that the use and administration of such prophylaxis must be in compliance with local regulations.

Treatment

Oxytetracycline (Terramycin) has been the drug of choice for treating motile aeromonad septicemias in fishes. The drug is approved for use with pond fishes, channel catfish, and salmonids. It is administered in feed at a daily rate of 50 to 75 mg/kg of fish for 10 days. Fish must be withdrawn from treatment for 21 days before they are stocked or eaten. This treatment sometimes produces dramatic results when it is administered for even 2 or 3 days, and is particularly effective when fish become infected after they have been handled, crowded, or held under stress for short periods of time (Meyer 1964; Meyer and Collar 1964). Furanace, though not registered for use in the United States, is extremely effective against motile aeromonads if the affected fish are immersed for 5 to 10 minutes in water containing 1-2 mg/L furanace, or by maintaining fish for 1 week in water containing 0.1 mg/L drug.

However, furanace can be toxic to fishes if used improperly (Mitchell and Plumb 1980). Chloramphenicol (chloromycetin) was successfully used to treat frogs with red leg disease by gastric intubation of 3 to 5 mg per 100g of frog for 5 days, twice daily. Chloromycetin, like oxytetracycline, was effective in treating fish when it was administered orally. However, its use is prohibited in food fishes and discouraged in other fishes because it is the drug of last resort in certain human diseases–*e.g.*, typhoid fever. Indiscriminant use of chloramphenicol can result in drug resistance and thus reduce the value of the antibiotic in human medicine. Against strains of motile aeromonads that show multiple drug resistance, piromidic acid administered orally has been experimentally shown to be more effective than either chloromycetin or oxytetracycline (Katae *et al.*, 1979). However, this drug is not registered for use on food fishes in the United States and European Union.

References

Allan, B.J., and R.M.W. Stevenson, 1981. Extracellular virulence factors of *Aeromonashydrophila* in fish infections. *Canadian Journal of Microbiology*, 27: 1114–1122.

Anbarasu, K., Thangakrishnan, K., Arun, B.V., and Chandran, M.R., 1998. Assessment of immune response in freshwater catfish (*Mystus vittatus* Bloch) to different bacterins of *Aeromonas hydrophila. Indian Journal of Experimental Biology*, 36: 990–995.

Ascencio, F., Martinez-Arias, W., Romero, M. J., and Wadstrom, T., 1998. Analysis of the interaction of *Aeromonas caviae, A. hydrophila* and *A. sobria* with mucins. FEMS *Immunology and Medical Microbiology*, 20: 219–229.

Austin, D.A., McIntosh, D. and Austin, B., 1989. Taxonomy of fish associated *Aeromonas* spp., with the description of *Aeromonas salmonicida* subsp. *smithia* subsp. nov. *Systematic and Applied Microbiology*, 11: 277–290.

Baba, T., Imamura, J., Izawa, K., and Ikeda, K., 1988. Immune protection in carp, *Cyprinus carpio* L., after immunization with *Aeromonas hydrophila* crude lipopolysaccharide. *Journal of Fish Diseases*, 11: 237–244

Bach, R., P.K. Chen and G.B. Chapman, 1978. Changes in the spleen of channel catfish *Ictalurus punctatus* Rafinesque induced by infection with *Aeromonas hydrophila. Journal of Fish Diseases*, 1: 205–217.

Boulanger, Y., R. Lallier and G. Cousineau, 1977. Isolation of enterotoxigenic *Aeromonas* from fish. *Canadian Journal of Microbiology*, 23: 1161–1164.

Bullock, G.L., 1961. The identification and separation of *Aeromonas liquefaciens* from *Pseudomonas fluorescens* and related organisms occurring in diseased fish. *Journal of Applied Microbiology*, 9: 587–590.

Bullock, G.L. and H.M. Stuckey, 1977. Ultraviolet treatment of water for destruction of five gram-negative bacteria pathogenic to fishes. *Journal of the Fisheries Research Board of Canada*, 34: 1244–1249.

Bullock, G.L., P.K. Chen and H.M. Stuckey, 1972. Studies of motile aeromonads isolated from diseased warmwater and coldwater fishes. Page 21 In: *Abstracts of the Annual Meeting of the American Society for Microbiology*, Philadelphia, Pennsylvania, 23–28 April 1972.

Byers, B.R., D. Liles, D., P.E. Byers and J.E.L. Arceneaux, 1986. A new siderophore in *Aeromonas hydrophila*: Possible relationship to virulence. *NATO Advanced Research Workshop on Iron, Siderophores and Plant Diseases*, Wye, Kent (UK), 1–5 July 1986, 117: 227–232.

Cahill, M.M., 1990. Virulence factors in motile *Aeromonas* species. *Journal of Applied Bacteriology*, 69: 1–16.

Calabrez, M.C.T., P. Lintermans and J.H. Vosjan, 1993. The polymerase chain reaction (PCR) technique as a specific and sensitive detection method for *Aeromonas salmonicida* and *Aeromonas sobria* in natural ecosystems (water, sediment, and fish). In: *International Council for the Exploration of the Seas. Marine Science Symposia*, 21–23 June 1993, Copenhagen, 201: 189–190.

Calesante, R.T., R. Engstrom-Heg, N. Ehlinger and N. Youmans, 1981. Cause and control of muskellunge fry mortality at Chautauqua Hatchery, New York. *Progressive Fish-Culturist*, 43: 17–20.

Carnahan, A.M., S. Behram and S.W. Joseph, 1991. Aerokey II: a flexible key for identifying clinical *Aeromonas* species. *Journal of Clinical Microbiology*, 29: 2843–2849.

Casc'on, A., J. Yugueros, A. Temprano, M. S'anchez, C. Hernanz, J.M. Luengo, and G. Naharro, 2000. A major secreted elastase is essential for pathogenicity of *Aeromonas hydrophila*. *Infection and Immunity*, 68: 3233–3241.

Chang, M.C. and T.C. Huang, 1981. Effects of the predation of *Tetrahymena pyriformis* on the population of *Aeromonas hydrophila*. National. *Science Council Mon.*, 9: 552–556.

Chodyniecki, A., 1965. Comparative serological studies on somatic antigens of *Aeromonas punctata* Zimmerman strains isolated in the course of septicemia in trout. *Acta Hydrobiologica*, 7: 269–278.

Colberg, P.J. and A.J. Lingg, 1978. Effect of ozonation on microbial fish pathogens, ammonia, nitrate, nitrite and biological oxygen demand in simulated reuse hatchery water. *Journal of the Fisheries Research Board of Canada*, 35: 1290–1296.

Davis, J.W. and R.K. Sizemore, 1981. Nonselectivity of Rimler-Shotts medium for *Aeromonas hydrophila* in estuarine environments. *Journal of Applied and Environmental Microbiology*, 43: 544–545.

Davis, W.A., J.G. Kane and V.F. Garagusi, 1978. Human *Aeromonas* infections: a review of the literature and a case report of endocarditis. *Journal of Medicine*, 57: 267–277.

De Figueredo, J. and J.A. Plumb, 1977. Virulence of different isolates of *Aeromonas hydrophila* in channel catfish. *Aquaculture* 11: 349–354.

Del Corral, F., E.B. Shotts, Jr. and J. Brown, 1990. Adherence, haemagglutination and cell surface characteristics of motile aeromonads virulent for fish. *Journal of Fish Diseases;* 13: 255–268.

Dooley, J.S. and T.J. Trust, 1988. Surface protein composition of *Aeromonas hydrophila* strains virulent for fish: identification of a surface array protein. *Journal of Bacteriology*, 17: 499-506.

Esch, G.W. and T.C. Hazen, 1980. Stress and body condition in a population of largemouth bass: implications for red-sore disease. *Transactions of the American Fisheries Society*, 109: 532–536.

Eissa, I.A.M., A.F. Badran, M. Moustafa and H. Fetaih, 1994. Contribution to motile *Aeromonas* septicaemia in some cultured and wild freshwater fish. *Veterinary Medical Journal Giza*, 42: 63–69.

Eurell, T.E., D.H. Lewis and L.C. Grumbles, 1978. Comparison of selected diagnostic tests for the detection of motile *Aeromonas* septicemia in fish. *American Journal of Veterinary Research*, 39: 1384–1386.

Ewing, W.H., R. Hugh and J.G. Johnson, 1961. Studies on the *Aeromonas* group. United States Department of Health, Education and Welfare. Public Health Service, Communicable Disease Center, Atlanta, Georgia. 37 pp.

Faktorovich, K.A., 1969. Histological changes in the liver, kidneys, skin and brain of fish sick with red rot. In: *Infectious Diseases of Fish and their Control.* Division of Fisheries Research, Bureau of Sport Fisheries and Wildlife. Washington, D. C. Translated from the Russian by R.M. Howland, pp. 83–101.

Ford, L.A. and R.L. Thune, 1991. S-layer positive motile aeromonads isolated from channel catfish. *Journal of Wildlife Diseases*, 27: 557–561.

Fliermans, C.B. and T.C. Hazen, 1980. Immunofluorescence of *Aeromonas hydrophila* as measured by fluorescence photometric microscopy. *Canadian Journal of Microbiology*, 26: 161–168.

Fuentes, R.J.M. and H.J.A. Perez, 1998. Isolation of *Aeromonas hydrophila* in the rainbow trout (*Oncorhynchus* mykiss). *Veterinaria, Mexico*, 29: 117–119.

Gado, M.S.M., 1998. Studies on the virulence of *Aeromonas hydrophila* in Nile Tilapia (*Oreochromis niloticus*). *Assiut Veterinary Medical Journal*, 40: 190–200.

Grizzle, J.M. and Y. Kiryu, 1993. Histopathology of gill, liver and pancreas and serum enzyme levels of channel catfish infected with *Aeromonas hydrophila* complex. *Journal of Aquatic Animal Health*, 5: 36–50.

Hazen, T.C., 1979. Ecology of *Aeromonas hydrophila* in a South Carolina cooling reservoir. *Microbial Ecology*, 5: 179–195.

Hazen, T.C., G.W. Esch, R.V. Dimock and A. Mansfield, 1982. Chemotaxis of *Aeromanas hydrophila* to the surface mucus of fish. *Current Microbiology*, 7: 371–375.

Hazen, T.C., C.B. Fliermans, R.P. Hirsch and G.W. Esch, 1978a. Prevalence and distribution of *Aeromonas hydrophila* in the USA. *Journal of Applied and Environmental Microbiology*, 36: 731–738.

Hazen, T.C., M.L. Raker, G.W. Esch and C.B. Fliermans, 1978b. Ultrastructure of red sore lesions on largemouth bass (*Micropterus salmoides*): association of the ciliate *Epistylis* sp. and the bacterium *Aeromonas hydrophila*. *Journal of Protozoology*, 25: 351–355.

Hsu, T.C., E.B. Shotts and W.D. Waltman, 1985. Action of *Aeromonas hydrophila* complex on carbohydrate substrates. *Fish Pathology*, 20: 23–35.

Huang, Y.W., C.K. Leung, M.A. Harrison and K.W. Gates, 1993. Fate of *Listeria monocytogenes* and *Aeromonas hydrophila* on catfish fillets cooked in a microwave oven. *Journal of Food Science (USA)*, 58: 519–521.

Huizinga, H.W., G.W. Esch and T.C. Hazen, 1979. Histopathology of red-sore disease (*Aeromonas hydrophila)* in naturally and experimentally infected largemouth bass *Micropterus salmoides* (Lacépède). *Journal of Fish Diseases*, 2: 263–277.

Joseph, S.W. and Carnahan, A., 1994. The isolation, identification and systematics of the motile *Aeromonas* species. *Annual Review of Fish Diseases*, 4: 315–343.

Katae, H., K. Kuono, Y. Takase, H. Miyazaki, M. Hashimoto and M. Shimizu, 1979. The evaluation of piromidic acid as an antibiotic in fish: An *in vitro* and *in vivo* study. *Journal of Fish Diseases*, 2: 321–335.

Kawakani, H. and H. Hoshimoto, 1978. Occurrence and distribution of *Aeromonas* in surface water and algae in river water. *Journal of the Faculty of Fisheries and Animal Husbandry*, Hiroshima University, 17: 155–164.

Kingma, D.A., 1978. Studies on some selected isolates of the fish pathogen *Aeromonas hydrophila. M.Sc. Thesis.* University of Georgia, Athens, Georgia. Kluyver, A. J. and C. B. van Niel, 1936. Prospects for a natural system of classification of bacteria. Zentralbl. Bakteriol. 94: 369–403.

Kou, G.H., 1973. Studies on the fish pathogen *Aeromonas liquefaaiens*–II. The connections between pathogenic properties and the activities of toxic substances. *Journal of the Fisheries Society of Taiwan*, 2: 42–46.

Lallier, R., D. Leblanc, K.R. Mittal and G. Olivier, 1981. Serogrouping of motile *Aeromonas* species isolated from healthy and moribund fish. *Journal of Applied and Environmental Microbiology*, 42: 56–60.

Lewis, D. H, 1981. Immunoenzyme microscopy for differentiating among systemic bacterial pathogens of fish. *Canadian Journal of Fisheries and Aquatic Sciences*, 38: 463–466.

Liu, P.V., 1961. Observations on the specificities of extracellular antigens of the genera *Aeromonas* and *Serratia. Journal of General Microbiology*, 24: 145–153.

Meyer, F.P., 1964. Field treatments of *Aeromonas liquefaciens* infections in golden shiners. *Progressive Fish-Culturist*, 26: 33–35.

Meyer, F.P., 1970. Seasonal fluctuations in the incidence of disease on fish farms. In: *A Symposium on Diseases of Fishes and Shellfishes*, (Ed.) S.F. Snieszko. American Fisheries Society Special Publication 5, Bethesda, pp. 21–29.

Meyer, F.P. and J.D. Collar, 1964. Description and treatment of a *Pseudomonas* infection in white catfish. *Applied Microbiology*, 12: 201–203.

Mishra, S.S., 1998. Use of dot immunoassay for rapid detection of pathogenic bacteria *Vibrio alginolyticus* and *Aeromonas hydrophila* from shrimps and fishes. *Indian Journal of Marine Sciences*, 27: 222–226.

Mitchell, A.J. and J.A. Plumb, 1980. Toxicity and efficacy of furanace on channel catfish *Ictalurus punctatus* (Rafinesque) infected experimentally with *Aeromonas hydrophila. Journal of Fish Diseases*, 3: 93–99.

Mittal, K.R., G. Lalonde, D. Leblanc, G. Olivier and R. Lallier, 1980. *Aeromonas hydrophila* in rainbow trout: relation between virulence and surface characteristics. *Canadian Journal of Microbiology*, 26: 1501–1503.

Ogara, W.O., P.G. Mbuthia, H.F.A. Kaburia, H. Sorum, D.K. Kagunya, D.I. Nduthu and D. Colquhoun, 1998. Motile aeromonads associated with rainbow trout (*Onchorhynchus mykiss*) mortality in Kenya. *Bulletin of the European Association of Fish Pathologists*, 18: 7–9.

Olivier, G., R. Lallier and S. Lariviere, 1981. A toxigenic profile of *Aeromonas hydrophila* and *Aeromonas sobria* isolated from fish. *Canadian Journal of Microbiology*, 27: 230–232.

Osborne, J.A., Fensch, G.E. and Charba, J.F., 1989. The abundance of *Aeromonas hydrophila* L. at Lake Harney on the St. Johns River with respect to red sore disease in striped mullet (*Mugil cephalus* L.). *Florida Scientist*, 52: 171–176.

Otte, E., 1963. Die heutigen Ansichten Uber die Atiologie der Infektiosen Bauchwassersucht der Karpfen. Wien. *Tieraertzl. Monatsschr*, 50: 996–1005.

Overman, T.L., R.F. D'Amato and K M. Tomfohrde, 1979. Incidence of oxidase variable strains of *Aeromonas hydrophila*. *Journal of Clinical Microbiology*, 9: 244–247.

Palumbo, S.A., Bencivengo, M.M., Corral, F. del; Williams, A.C., Buchanan, R.L., and Del Corral, F., 1989. Characterization of the *Aeromonas hydrophila* group isolated from retail foods of animal origin. *Journal of Clinical Microbiology*, 27: 854–859.

Paniagua, C., Rivero, O., Anguita, J. and Naharro, G., 1990. Pathogenicity factors and virulence for rainbow trout (*Salmo gairdneri*) or motile *Aeromonas* spp. isolated from a river. *Journal of Clinical Microbiology*, 28: 350–355.

Peters, G., M. Faisal, T. Lang and I. Ahmed, 1988. Stress caused by social interaction and its effect on susceptibility to *Aeromonas hydrophila* infection in rainbow trout *Salmo gairdneri*. *Diseases of Aquatic Organisms*, 4: 83–89.

Popoff, M. and M. Vernon, 1976. A taxonomic study of the *Aeromonas hydrophila-Aeromonas punctata* group. *Journal of General Microbiology*, 94: 11–22.

Post, G., 1966. Response of rainbow trout (*Salmo gairdneri)* to antigens of *Aeromonas hydrophila*. *Journal of the Fisheries Research Board of Canada*, 23: 1487–1494.

Rahim, Z., K.M.S. Aziz, M.I. Huq and H. Saeed, 1985. Isolation of *Aeromonas hydrophila* from the wounds of five species of brackish water fish of Bangladesh. *Bangladesh Journal of Zoology (Bangladesh)*, 13: 37–42.

Rao, V.B. and B.G. Foster, 1977. Antigenic analysis of the genus *Aeromonas*. *Texas Journal of Science*, 29: 85–92.

Rigney, M.M., J.W. Zilinsky and M.A. Roug, 1978. Pathogenicity of *Aeromonas hydrophila* in red leg disease of frogs. *Current Microbiology*, 1: 175–179.

Rodriguez, L.A., A.E. Ellis and T.P. Nieto, 1992. Purification and characterisation of an extracellular metalloprotease, serine protease and haemolysin of *Aeromonas hydrophila* strain B32: all are lethal for fish. *Microbial Pathogenesis*, 13: 17–24.

Rodriguez, L.A., A.E. Ellis and T.P. Nieto, 1993. Effects of the acetylcholinesterase toxin of *Aeromonas hydrophila* on the central nervous system of fish. *Microbial Pathogenesis*, 14: 411- 415.

Rogers, W.A., 1971. Disease in fish due to the protozoan *Epistylis* (Ciliata: *Peritrichia*) in the southeastern U.S. Proceedings of the Southeastern Association of Game and Fish Commissions, 25: 493–496.

Rogulska, A., J. Antychowicz and J. Zelazny, 1994. Haemolytic and proteolytic activity of *Aeromonas hydrophila* and *A. sobria* as markers of pathogenicity for carp (*Cyprinus carpio* L.). *Medycyna Weterynaryjna*, 50: 55–58.

Ross, A.J., 1962. Isolation of a pigment-producing strain of *Aeromonas liquefaciens* from silver salmon (*Oncorhynchus kisutch)*. *Journal of Bacteriology*, 84: 590–591.

Rychlicki, Z. and S. Zarnecki, 1957. Die Zator Karpfenaufzuchtmethode und deren Einflus auf die Beseitigung der Bauchwassersucht. *Z. Fisch*, 5: 423–442.

Schachte, J.H., 1978. Immunization of channel catfish, *Ictalurus punctatus*, against two bacterial diseases. *Marine Fisheries Review*, 40: 18–19.

Schaperclaus, W., 1967. Probleme der Karpfenimmunitat gegenuber *Aeromonas punctata* und Fragen der antigenen struktur des bak- teriums. *Z. Fisch. Hilfswiss.* 15: 129–138.

Schaperclaus, W., 1970. Experimentelle Untersuchungen zur Ermittlung der wirksamsten Impfantigene fur eine aktive Immunisierung von Karpfen gegen *Aeromonas punctata. Z. Fisch. ND* 18(3-4):227-257.

Schaperclaus, W., 1972. Orale and parenterale aktive Immunisierung von Karpfen gegen *Aeromonas punctata. Arch. Exp. Veterinarmed*, 26: 863–874.

Schubert, R.H.W., 1967. The taxonomy and nomenclature of the genus *Aeromonas* Kluyver and van Niel 1936. Part I. Suggestions on the taxonomy and nomenclature of the aerogenic *Aeromonas* species. *International Journal of Systematic Bacteriology*, 17: 23–37.

Shieh, H.S., 1987. Protection of Atlantic salmon against motile aeromonad septicaemia with *Aeromonas hydrophila* protease. *Microbios Letters*, 36: 133–138.

Shieh, H.S., 1990. Protection of Atlantic salmon against *Aeromonas sobria* infection. *Microbios Letters*, 43: 171–172.

Shotts, E.B. and R. Rimler, 1973. Medium for the isolation of *Aeromonas hydrophila. Journal of Applied Microbiology*, 26: 550–553.

Shotts, E.B., T.C. Hsu and W.D. Waltman, 1985. Extracellular proteolytic activity of *Aeromonas hydrophila* complex. *Fish Pathology*, 20: 37–44.

Snieszko, S.F., 1957. Genus IV. *Aeromonas* Kluyver and van Niel 1936. In: *Bergey's Manual of Determinative Bacteriology*, 7th ed., (Eds.) R.S. Breed, E.G.D. Murray and N.R. Smith. The Williams and Wilkins Co., Baltimore, Maryland, pp. 189–193.

Snieszko, S.F., 1978. Control of fish diseases. *Marine Fisheries Review*, 40: 65–68.

Soltani, M. and M. Rabani Khorasgani, 1999. Evaluation of indirect immunofluorescent antibody technique for detection of *Vibrio anguillarum* and *Aeromonas hydrophila* infections in cultured fish and prawn. *Journal of the Faculty of Veterinary Medicine*, University of Tehran. 4: 73–78.

Thampuran, N. and P.K. Surendran, 1995. Incidence of motile aeromonads in marine environment, fishes and processed fishery products. pp. 352–358, 1998, (Technological advancements in fisheries. Proceedings of the National Symposium on Technological Advancements in Fisheries and its Impact on Rural Development held at Cochin by School of Industrial Fisheries, Cochin University of Science and Technology during December 5 to 7, 1995.

Thune, R.L., T. E. Graham, L.M. Riddle and R.L. Amborski, 1982a. Extracellular products and endotoxin from *Aeromonas hydrophila:* Effects on age-O channel catfish. *Transactions of the American Fisheries Society*. 111: 404–408.

Thune, R.L., T.E. Graham, L.M. Riddle and R.L. Amborski, 1982b. Extracellular protease from *Aeromonas hydrophila:* Partial purification and effects on age-O channel catfish. *Transactions of the American Fisheries Society*. 111: 749–754.

Thune, R.L. and J.A. Plumb, 1982. Effect of delivery method and antigen preparation on the production of antibodies against *Aeromonas hydrophila* in channel catfish. *Progressive Fish-Culturist*, 44: 53–54.

Trust, T.J., L.M. Bull, B.R. Currie and J.T. Buckley, 1974. Obligate anaerobic bacteria in the gastrointestinal microflora of the grass carp (*Ctenopharyngodon idella)*, goldfish (*Carassius auratus) and* rainbow trout (*Salmo gairdneri). Journal of the Fisheries Research Board of Canada*, 36: 1174–1179.

Trust, T.J., I.D. Courtice and H.M. Atkinson, 1980. Hemagglutination properties of *Aeromonas.* In: *Fish Diseases*, (Ed.) W. Ahne. Third COPRAQ, Springer Verlag, Berlin, pp. 128-223.

Ventura, M.T. and J.M. Grizzle, 1987. Evaluation of portals of entry of *Aeromonas hydrophila* in channel catfish. *Aquaculture*, 65: 205–214.

Ventura, M.T. and J.M. Grizzle, 1988. Lesions associated with natural and experimental infections of *Aeromonas hydrophila* in channel catfish, *Ictalurus punctatus* (Rafinesque). *Journal of Fish Diseases*, 11: 397–407

Von Gravenitz, A. and A.H. Mensch, 1968. The genus *Aeromonas* in human bacteriology. *N. English Journal of Medicine*, 278: 245–249.

Walters, G.R. and J.A. Plumb, 1978. Modified oxidation fermentation medium for use in identification of bacterial fish pathogens. *Journal of the Fisheries Research Board of Canada*, 35: 1629–1630.

Walters, G.R. and J.A. Plumb, 1980. Environmental stress and bacterial infection in channel catfish, *Ictalurus punctatus* Rafinesque. *Journal of Fish Biology*, 17: 177–185.

Waltman, W.D., E.B. Shotts and T.C. Hsu, 1982. Enzymatic characterization of *Aeromonas hydrophila* complex by the API-ZYM system. *Journal of Clinical Microbiology*, 16: 692–696.

Wright, L.D. and J.R. Snow, 1975. The effect of six chemicals for disinfection of largemouth bass eggs. *Progressive Fish-Culturist*, 37: 213–217.

Yambot, A.V. and V. Inglis, 1994. *Aeromonas hydrophila* isolated from Nile tilapia (*Oreochromis niloticus* L.) with "Eye Disease". International Symposium on Aquatic Animal Health, Seattle, WA (USA), 4–8 September 1994. University of California, School of Veterinary Medicine, Davis, CA. p.103.

Zhang, Y.L., C.T. Ong and K.Y. Leung, 2000. Molecular analysis of genetic differences between virulent and avirulent strains of *Aeromonas hydrophila* isolated from diseased fish. *Microbiology*, 146: 999–1009.

Chapter 2

Removal of Cadmium from Water and Wastewater by Economic Method

Y.C. Sharma[1]*, M. Mahto[2] and S.N. Kaul[1]

[1]Environmental Laboratories, Department of Applied Chemistry IT-BHU, Varanasi – 221 005

[2]Environmental Engineer, JSPCB and Ph.D. Scholar, Ranchi – 834 003

[3]Director Grade Scientist, WWT Division, NEERI, Nagpur – 440 020

ABSTRACT

Economically viable removal of cadmium has been investigated. For the purpose a locally available non-toxic mineral has been tried. On lower initial concentrations of Cd, the removal (per cent) was found to be greater and removal decreased at higher initial concentrations. The removal (per cent) increased from 41.0 to 80.3 per cent by decreasing the concentration of cadmium in solution from 2.0×10^{-4} M to 0.5×10^{-4} M at 6.5 pH, 100 rpm, 0.01 M $NaClO_4$ ionic strength. pH plays an important role in the removal of cadmium. Rate of the removal was calculated by Lagergren's model and was found to be 5.10×10^{-2} min^{-1} in optimum conditions. The process of removal proceeds with intraparticle diffusion and the value of the coefficient of intraparticle diffusion was found to be 3.25×10^{-10} cm^2 S^{-1}. The parameters can be used for designing a treatment plant for treatment of Cd(II) rich waters and wastewaters economically. The effect of temperature revealed an exothermic nature of the process of removal.

Keywords: Cd(II), Economic removal, Adsorption, China clay.

[#] Corresponding Author.

Introduction

Metallic species are indispensable for economic and industrial development of all nations. Most metals have applications in various industries and this application is growing day by day (Nriagu, 1988). Sources of these metallic species into water environment are both natural and anthropogenic (Moore and Ramamoorthy, 1984; Adriano, 1986). Like most other metals cadmium also has multifarious uses. Cadmium is widely used in alloys, electroplating, Ni-Cd batteries and paint pigments (Kannan, 1995).

Main source of cadmium pollution to water systems is through the discharge of untreated wastewater from the above applications. From toxicological view point, this metal comes in the category of non-essential both for human beings and plants. As the human body does, not have a homeostatic control for Cd, this becomes highly toxic for them, as cadmium is a potent enzyme inhibitor and causes several health problems. This metal has been reported to be teratogenic for many animals. Precipitation, ion-exchange, extraction, etc. have been the popular methods for removal of cadmium from water and wastewater but these methods pose some problems in different ways. Villaescusa *et al.* (2004) have reported significant removal of metal cations by grape stalk waste. Laderia and Ciminelli (2004) used an oxisol for adsorption of Arsenic. Min *et al.* (2004) reported improved removal of cadmium from water by innovative application of juniper fiber and nutshell carbon which was found to produce superior results for removal of trace cations from drinking water (Ahmedna *et al.*, 2004). Carbonaceous materials (Hanzlik *et al.*, 2004) have also been reported for cadmium removal and the process is cost effective. Adsorption on activated carbon and activated charcoal has been recognized as a popular choice for treatment of cadmium rich wastewater and also for other metallic species (Teker *et al.*, 2004; Matsui *et al.*, 2004) but all of these processes are cost intensive inhibiting their large scale application to the developing nations. Because of the high treatment cost of water and wastewater by activated carbon etc scientists world over are engaged in the search of economically viable alternatives (Sharma, 1995; Sen and De, 1987; Villaescusa *et al.*, 2004 and Viraraghavan, 1997). Emphasizing on the economic aspect of treatment of Cd(II) rich wastewaters the present communication aims at use of China Clay, a clay mineral as an alternate to the otherwise costly activated carbon.

Materials and Methods

The adsorbent, China Clay was procured from *Patharghat* (*Bihar*). In order to keep the process of cadmium removal low, it was used as such without any pretreatment in the experiments after crushing and passing through a sieve of 100 μm. The average particle size was measured by particle size analyzer model HIAC-320 (ROYCO Instrument Division USA) and the surface charge by Lazer Zee Model 1-500 (Penkem Inc., New York, USA). The surface area of the adsorbent was determined by a 'Three Point' N_2 gas adsorption method using Quantasorb Surface area analyzer, Model 1-QS/7 (Quanta chrome Corp., USA) and porosity by Mercury Porosimeter. The chemical analysis of the adsorbent was done according to IS 1527 Bureau of Indian Standards (1960).

Batch adsorption experiments were carried out by agitating 1.0 gm of adsorbent with cadmium solutions of desired strength, temperature and pH in different glass bottles in a shaking thermostat at 100 rpm. Equilibrium time was determined by shaking the cadmium solution with adsorbent for different time intervals. At the end of equilibrium time the adsorbent was separated from solutions of cadmium by filtration and the progress of removal was determined by determining the amount of cadmium in the supernatant spectrophotometrically (Standard Methods, 1998) using a spectrophotometer (UV 2100 model, Shimadzu, Japan). 1M NaOH/HCl maintained the pH of the solutions.

Results and Discussion

Chemical Characterization of China Clay

The chemical characterization of China Clay was carried out by Bureau of Indian Standard Methods (1960) and the results of analysis are given in Table 2.1. The analysis shows that SiO_2 and Al_2O_3 are its main constituents, oxides of other metals are present in traces. Other parameters are also presented in Table 2.1.

Table 2.1: Characterization of China Clay

Constituents	SiO_2	Al_2O_3	*CaO*	Fe_2O_3	*MgO*	*Loss on Ignition*	*Mean Diameter*	*Surface Area*	*Density*	*Porosity*
% by Weight	46.22	38.40	0.86	0.68	0.37	13.47	100 μm	13.52 m^2g^{-1}	2.69 gcm^{-3}	0.33

Determination of Time of Equilibrium and Optimum Cadmium Concentration

Study of the effect of contact time and concentration on adsorption of Cd(II) on China Clay shows that removal increased from 41.0 to 80.3 per cent (Figure 2.1) by decreasing the concentration of cadmium in solution from 2.0×10^{-4} M to 0.5×10^{-4} M at 6.5 pH, 30°C temperature and 0.01 M $NaClO_4$ ionic strength. The removal is rapid in initial stages and then gradually decreases and acquires equilibrium in 80 min time. This finding reveals two important features: the process is highly dependent on initial concentration of cadmium and the time of equilibrium is independent of the initial solute concentration.

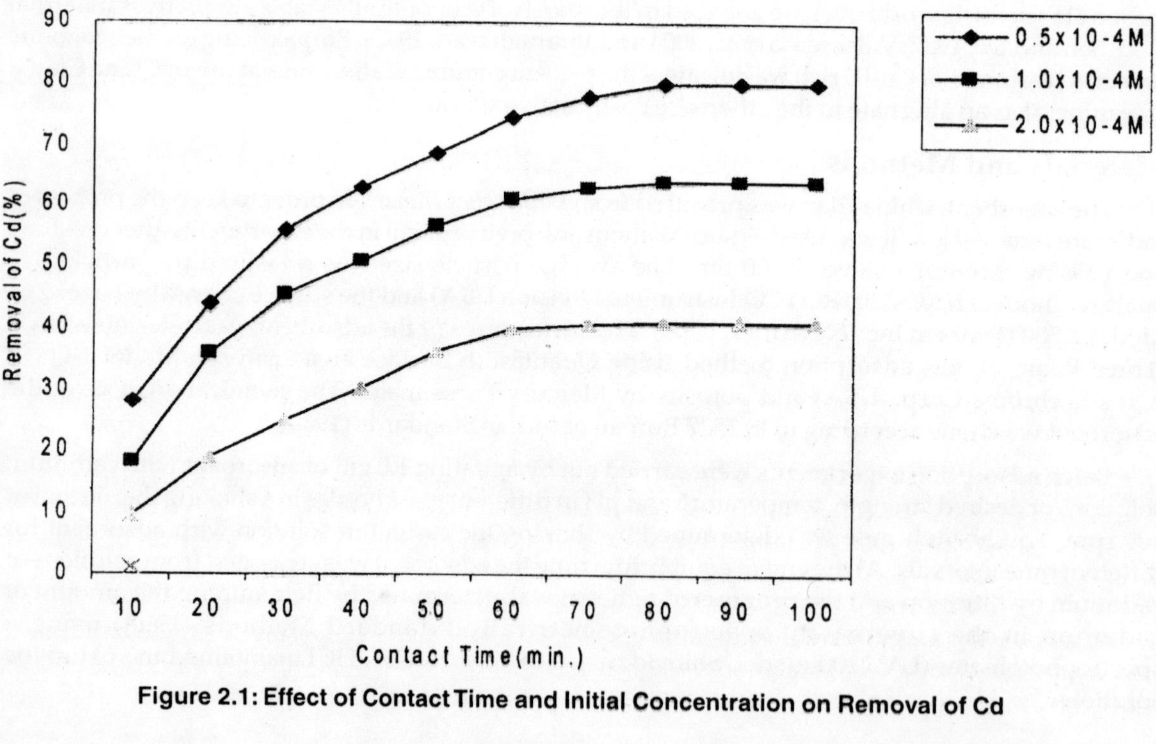

Figure 2.1: Effect of Contact Time and Initial Concentration on Removal of Cd

The contact of the solute and the adsorbent must be eliminated after the equilibrium time and this finding has lot of practical importance.

Effect of pH on the Removal of Cadmium

pH plays an important role in most adsorption processes and in the present system also the effect of this parameter was studied on the process of removal. The adsorption of cadmium was found to be maximum (86.6 per cent) at pH 9.5 (Table 2.2) out of the different values of pH 2.5, 4.5, 6.5 and 9.5. It

Table 2.2: Maximum Removal (per cent) of Cadmium by Adsorption on China Clay

Concentration of Cd in solution: 0.5×10^{-4} M

Ionic Strength: 0.01 M $NaClO_4$, Temperature 30±0.5°C

pH	2.5	4.5	6.5	9.5
Removal	9.3	41.4	80.3	86.6

was, however, found to be minimum (9.3 per cent) at 2.5 pH. It is expected that the deprotonated surface in the alkaline range would favor the uptake of Cd(II) and the same has been found to be applicable in the present studies. In aqueous environments, oxides and oxide minerals are covered with hydroxyl groups, S–OH, which are amphoteric in nature. Adsorption at H^+ and OH^- is thus based on the protonation and deprotonation of surface hydroxyls (Stumm, 1987).

$$\underset{\text{protonation}}{SOH_2^+} \rightarrow \underset{\text{neutral surface}}{SOH + H^+} \rightarrow \underset{\text{deprotonation}}{SO^- + H^+} \quad (1)$$

The variation of adsorption with change in pH shows two distinct regions of interest:

1. Between pH 2.0–4.0, the variation in adsorption is quite small, and
2. Beyond pH 4.0, there is a significant increase in the removal and an adsorption edge can be noticed with a maximum at around pH 9.5.

In the first region, ion-exchange mechanism may be operative due to interactions at constant charge sites (planer sites):

$$Cd^{2+} + 2(Al, SiO)^- Na^+ \leftrightarrow (Al,SiO)_2 Cd + 2 Na^+ \quad (2)$$

This type of mechanism has also been suggested Huang and Rhoads (1989). The second region which is greater than pH_{zpc} is very much influenced by pH. This region involves the interaction of solute with constant potential sites (edge sites) of the adsorbent.

Dynamics of Removal

The study of the dynamics of the process of removal of cadmium on China Clay and the rate of the process of removal was determined by using the well known Lagergren' s model (1898):

$$\log (q_e - q) = \log q_e - K_{ad}/2.303 . t \quad (3)$$

where,

q_e and q (both mgg^{-1}) are the amounts of cadmium adsorbed at equilibrium and at any time 't' respectively, K_{ad} (min^{-1}) is the rate constant of adsorption. The plots of 'log $(q_e - q)$ vs t' (Figure 2.2) are linear and indicate the fitness of the model for the present system. The values of K_{ad} were calculated

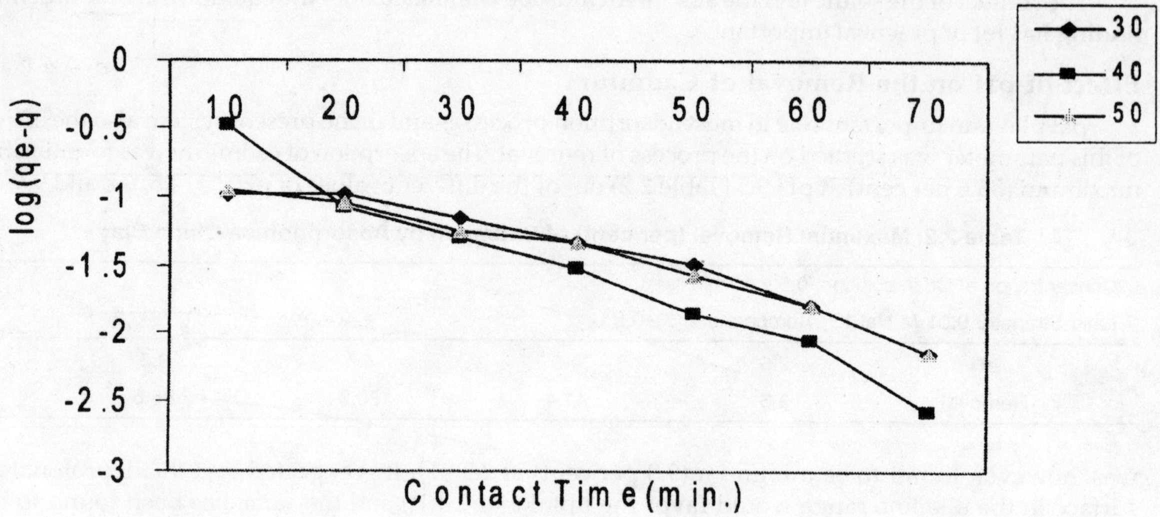

Figure 2.2: Dynamic Modelling for the Removal of Cd by Economic Method

graphically and were found to be 5.10×10^{-2} min^{-1}, 4.82×10^{-2} mini, and 4.12×10^{-2} min^{-1} at 30, 40 and 50°C respectively.

Intraparticle Diffusion Studies

Almost in all rapidly stirred batch reactors there always exists a possibility of intraparticle diffusion (McKay, 1998; Westell *et al.*, 2003; Laderia and Ciminelli, 2004). This process of intraparticle diffusion is rate limiting in many adsorption processes. For the present system this possibility was studied and the values of the constant of intraparticle diffusion were determined as follows:

$$D = 0.03\ r_o^{\ 2}/t_{1/2} \qquad (4)$$

where,

'D' is a coefficient of intraparticle diffusion, r_o(cm) is the radius of adsorbent particles, and $t_{1/2}$ (min) is the time for half adsorption of cadmium by China Clay. The value of 'D' as calculated from the above expression was found to be 3.25×10^{-10} cm^2s^{-1} and this value of 'D' indicates intraparticle diffusion to be the rate controlling step (McKay and Porter, 1997; McKay and Sweeny, 1997).

Effect of Temperature

The removal of cadmium decreased from 80.3 to 51.3 per cent (Figure 2.3) by increasing the temperature of the process from 30 to 50 °C at 0.5×10^{-4} M initial concentration of cadmium, 6.5 pH, 100 µm particle diameter and 0.01 M $NaClO_4$ ionic strength. Decreasing pattern of adsorption with increasing values of temperature reveals the exothermic nature of cadmium adsorption on China Clay. As the process of cadmium removal followed first order rate equation, the values of rate constants of adsorption at different temperature were determined by the graph of 'log ($q_e - q$) vs t' (Figure 2.2). The values of K_{ad} obtained are given in Table 2.3. It is clear from this Table that value of K_{ad} are in decreasing pattern with increasing temperature, indicating the exothermic nature of the present process. The increased escaping tendency of the cadmium at elevated temperature may be another explanation to this finding.

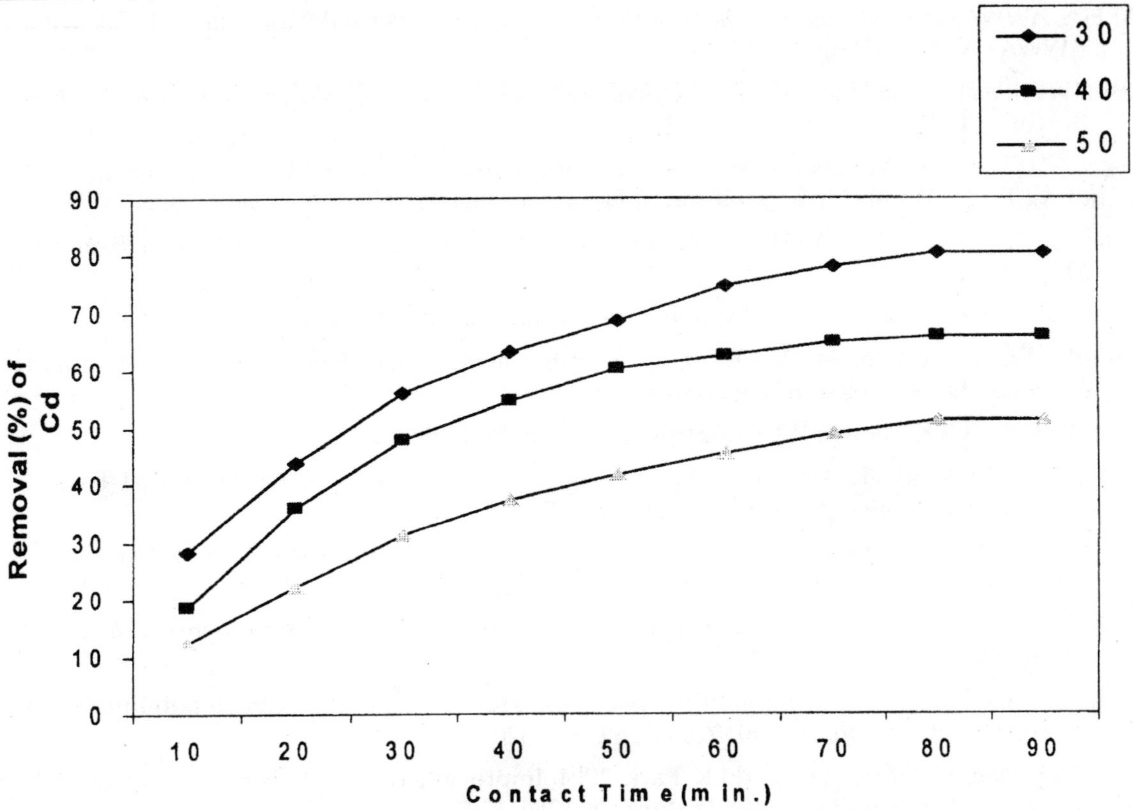

Figure 2.3: Removal (%) of Cadmium by Adsorption on China Clay

Conclusions

From the above studies the following conclusions may be drawn:

1. The removal (per cent) of Cd was found to be higher in low concentration ranges and pH is another important parameter controlling removal of cadmium by adsorption on selected adsorbent.
2. Values of the rate constant of removal process are determined by Lagergren' s model. The values of K_{ad} indicate the exothermic nature of the process.

Intraparticle diffusion plays important role during the removal of cadmium in the present system.

Table 2.3: Values of Rate Constant of Adsorption at Different Temperatures

Temperature (°C)	*K_{ad} (min^{-1}) (x 10^{-2})*
30	5.2
40	4.5
50	3.4

References

Adriano, D.C., 1986. *Trace Elements in the Terrestrial Environment*. Springer-Verlag, N.Y.

Ahmedna M.L., W.E. Marshall, A.A. Husseiny, R.M. Rao and I. Goktepe, 2004. The use of nutshell carbons in drinking water filters for removal of trace metals. *Water Research*, 38: 1062–1068.

APHA, AWWA, 1998. *Standard Methods for the Examination of Water and Wastewater*, 20th Ed., APHA/AWWA/WEF, Washington, DC.

BSI (1960). *Indian Standard Methods of Chemical Analysis of Fire Clay and Silica Reftactory Materials.* Bureau of Indian Standards, IS: 1527.

Hanzlik, J., J. Jehlicka, O. Sebek, Z. Weishauptova and V. Machovic, 2004. Multicomponent adsorption of Ag(I), Cd(II) and Cu(II) by natural carbonaceous materials. *Water Research*, 38: 2178–2184.

Huang, C.P. and Rhoads, E.A., 1989. Adsorption of metallic species on clays. *J. Colloid and Interface Sci.*, 31: 230–236.

Kannan, K., 1995. *Fundamentals of Environmental Pollution*. I. S. Chand and Co. Ltd., India.

Laderia, A.C.Q. and Ciminelli, V.S.T., 2004. Adsorption and desorption of arsenic on an oxisol and it's constituents. *Water Research*, 38: 2087–2094.

Lagergren, S., Bill K. *Svenska Vatens Kapersed Handle*, p. 24, 1898.

Matsui Y., A. Yuasa and K. Arica, 2001. Removal of a synthetic organic chemical by PAC-UF systems-I: Theory and modeling. *Water Res.*, 35: 471–477.

McKay, G., 1998. Adsorption of dyestuffs from aqueous solutions with activated carbon. *Water, Air, Soil Pollut.*, 12: 307–317.

McKay G. and Sweeny, A.G., 1997. Principles of dye removal from textile effluents. *Water, Air Soil Pollut.*, 14: 3–11.

McKay, G. and Porter, J., 1997. Equilibrium parameters for the sorption of copper, cadmium and zinc ions onto peat. *J. Chem. Tech. Biotechnol.*, 69: 309–320.

Min, S.H., Han, J.S., Shin, E.W. and J.K. Park, 2004. Improvement of cadmium ion removal by base treatment of juniper fiber. *Water Research*, 38: 1289–1295.

Moore, J.W. and Ramamoorthy, S., 1984. *Heavy Metals in Natural Waters*. Springer-Verlag, N.Y.

Nriagu, J.O., 1988. A silent epidemic of Environmental metal poisoning. *Environmental Pollution*, 50: 139–161.

Sen, A.K. and De, A.K., 1987. Adsorption of mercury (II) by coal fly ash. *Water Res.*, 21: 885–888.

Sharma, Y.C., 1995. Economic treatment of Cd(II) rich hazardous waste. *J. Colloid and Interface Sci.*, 173: 66–71.

Stumm W., 1987. *Aquatic Surface Chemistry*. Wiley Interscience, NY.

Teker M., O. Saltabas and Imamoglu, M., 1997. Adsorption of cobalt by activated carbon from the rice hulls. *J. Environ. Sci. Health*, A32: 2077–2086.

Villaescusa, I., Fiol, N., Martinez, M., Miralles, N., Poch, J. and Serarols, J., 2004. Removal of copper nickel ions from aqueous solutions by grape stalkwastes. *Water Res.*, 38: 992–1002.

Viraraghavan T. and G.A.K. Rao, 1991. Removal of Cd and Cr from wastewater using fly-ash. In: 45th *Purdue Industrial Waste Conf. Proc.* Lewis Pub., Michigan, pp. 517–527.

Westell, J.C., Chen, H., Zhang, W. and Brownawell, K., 2003. Sorption of linear alkylbenzene sulfonates on sediment materials. *Environ. Sci. Technol.*, 33: 3310–3318.

Chapter 3

Influence of Chromium and Cadmium on Germination, Seedling Growth and Photosynthetic Pigments of Soybean [*Glycine max* (L.) Merr.]

K. Sankar Ganesh, Al. A. Chidambaram, P. Sundaramoorthy, L. Baskaran and M. Selvaraju

Environmental Biology Laboratory, Department of Botany, Annamalai University, Annamalainagar, Tamil Nadu, India

ABSTRACT

In the present investigation, the influence of chromium and cadmium on germination, growth and photosynthetic pigment response of soybean was studied. The different concentrations (0, 5, 10, 25, 50, 100, 200 and 500 mg/l) of chromium and cadmium were used for germination studies of soybean. The seeds treated with distilled water is maintained as control. There was a gradual retardation of germination and growth parameters like root length, shoot length, fresh and dry weight and photosynthetic pigments like chlorophyll and carotenoid content with gradual increase of heavy metal concentration. No germination was observed at 500 mg/l concentration. The heavy metal chromium was found to be more toxic to soybean when compared to cadmium.

Introduction

Heavy metal pollution is a worldwide problem. Among the heavy metals, chromium is one of the major metal pollutants like cobalt, copper, zinc, lead and cadmium. (Vander Veen and Huczengal, 1980; Barcelo *et al.*, 1985; Bishnoi *et al.*, 1993; Mehta *et al.*, 1996). The chromium is released during chemical processes such as electroplating, leather tanning, textile printing, textile preservation, metal finishing. The industrial effluents with heavy metal adversely affect plant growth and development when it is used for irrigation (Sheoran and Singh, 1993; Prasad, 1995). It depresses growth of plants even at relatively low concentrations. The negative effect of chromium on growth, photosynthesis and respiration and mineral nutrition of plants were reported.

Cadmium is present as a contaminant in automobile tyres, motor oils, soldering electrical parts, plating at steel, fungicides, plastics and coal (Chauhan *et al.*, 2004). Water is mainly contaminated by disposal of industrial wastes containing cadmium. There are few reports of cadmium affecting germination, growth and chlorophyll biosynthesis in different crops (Muthuchelian *et al.*, 1988, Sheoran *et al.*, 1990; Saravanan *et al.*, 1997; Hindu and Hera, 2001). The objectives of the present study is to investigate the effect of chromium and cadmium on germination, growth and photosynthetic pigments response of soybean [*Glycine max* (L.) Merr.].

Materials and Methods

The present investigations were carried out with soybean [*Glycine max* (L.) Merr.] seeds. Soybean seeds were obtained from Shakthi Soya's (P) Ltd., Coimbatore. The healthy seeds were surface sterilized with 0.2 per cent mercuric chloride solution for two minutes and then they were thoroughly washed with tap water to avoid surface contamination if any. The seeds were treated with different concentrations of chromium and cadmium solution (0, 5, 10, 25, 50, 100, 200 and 500 mg/l). The 10th day old seedlings were analysed for various morphological parameters such as germination percentage, root length, shoot length, fresh weight and dry weight. The photosynthetic pigments like chlorophyll (Amon, 1949) and carotenoid (Kirk and Allen, 1965) were estimated in both the control and heavy metal treated soybean seedlings.

Results and Discussion

In the present study, the increased concentrations of chromium and cadmium resulted in significant reduction in germination percentage, root length, shoot length, fresh weight and dry weight of soybean seedlings (Tables 3.1 and 3.2). Similar results were reported earlier due to chromium and cadmium toxicity (Bindhu and Bera, 2001; Shalini Purohit *et al.*, 2003; Lakshmi and Sundaramoorthy, 2003; Dahiya *et al.*, 2003; Hsu and Kao, 2003; Aery and Rana, 2003). The reduction in germination, growth, fresh and dry weight of seedlings at higher chromium and cadmium concentrations may be due to the deleterious effect of heavy metal on the hydrolytic enzymes present in the storage organs as observed in other crops (Sawhney *et al.*, 1990; Sheoran *et al.*, 1990; Dua and Sawhney, 1991). Growth inhibition at higher cadmium levels may be linked either to a lower mitotic activity in the root meristematic zone and/or to an inhibition of cell enlargement in the elongation zone as consequence of decreased cellular turgor (Gabbrielli *et al.*, 1990). The decrease in fresh and dry mass of plant was mainly due to the inhibition of water uptake and enlargement of root cells (Mukherjee and Mukherjee, 1979). Cadmium has been reported to inhibit seed germination and seedling growth of *Triticum aestivum* (Kalita *et al.*, 1993) Phytotoxicity of cadmium is manifested by stunting, chlorosis, reduction in photosynthesis, wilting and necrosis.

The effect of chromium and cadmium on biochemical changes are furnished in Tables 3.3 and 3.4. Total chlorophyll and carotenoid content of seedlings were significantly affected by heavy metals. They showed a gradual decline with increase of chromium and cadmium concentrations. The reduction in chlorophyll content may be due to interference of heavy metals with pigment metabolism (Muthuchelian *et al.*, 1988). Similar findings were noted earlier due to the increase in the concentration of cadmium chlorophyll 'a' chlorophyll 'b' total chlorophyll and the ratio of chlorophyll a/b decreased. It was observed that chlorophyll 'a' was more than chlorophyll 'b" in both treated and untreated plants (Bindu and Bera, 2001).

Table 3.1: Effect of Different Concentrations of Chromium on Germination Studies of Soybean [*Glycine max* (L.) Merr.]

Chromium Concentrations (mg/l)	*Germination Percentage*	*Root Length (cm/seedlings)*	*Shoot Length (cm/seedlings)*	*Fresh Weight (g/seedling)*	*Dry Weight (g/seedling)*
Control	95 (±8.55)	5.86 (±0.5274)	11.68 (±1.0512)	3.267 (±0.2940)	0.453 (±0.0407)
5	90 (±8.10)	5.16 (±0.4644)	10.06 (±0.9054)	2.492 (±0.2242)	0.345 (±0.0310)
10	85 (±7.65)	4.58 (±0.4122)	8.28 (±0.7452)	1.963 (±0.1766)	0.336 (±0.0302)
25	75 (±6.75)	3.68 (±0.3312)	7.02 (±0.6318)	1.778 (±0.1600)	0.299 (±0.0269)
50	70 (±6.30)	2.54 (±0.2286)	5.38 (±0.4342)	1.527 (±0.1374)	0.256 (±0.0225)
100	50 (±4.50)	2.08 (±0.1872)	3.05 (±0.2745)	1.212 (±0.1090)	0.220 (±0.0198)
200	25 (±2.25)	1.48 (±0.1332)	1.86 (±0.1674)	0.978 (±0.0880)	0.162 (±0.0145)

±: Standard deviation.

No germination was observed beyond 500 and 1000 mg/l.

Table 3.2: Effect of Different Concentrations of Cadmium on Germination Studies of Soybean [*Glycine max* (L.) Merr.]

Cadmium Concentrations (mg/l)	*Germination Percentage*	*Root Length (cm/seedlings)*	*Shoot Length (cm/seedlings)*	*Fresh Weight (g/seedling)*	*Dry Weight (g/seedling)*
Control	98 (±8.82)	11.5 (±1.035)	21.66 (±1.9494)	3.478 (±0.31302)	0.690 (±0.0621)
5	95 (±8.55)	11.0 (±0.99)	21.20 (±1.908)	2.708 (±0.24372)	0.630 (±0.0567)
10	90 (±8.1)	10 (±0.9)	20.5 (±1.845)	2.098 (±0.18882)	0.568 (±0.05112)
25	80 (±7.2)	9.1 (±0.819)	18.6 (±1.665)	1.795 (±0.16155)	0.485 (±0.04365)
50	70 (±6.3)	8.5 (±0.765)	18.0 (±1.62)	1.723 (±0.15507)	0.398 (±0.03582)
100	60 (±5.4)	6.2 (±0.558)	17.0 (±1.53)	1.400 (±0.126)	0.228 (±0.02052)
200	30 (±2.7)	5.2 (±0.468)	12.0 (±1.08)	1.000 (±0.09)	0.182 (±0.01638)

±: Standard deviation.

No germination was observed beyond 500 and 1000 mg/l.

Table 3.3: Effect of Different Concentrations of Chromium on Biochemical Studies of Soybean [*Glycine max* (L.) Merr.]

Chromium Concentrations (mg/l)	*Chlorophyll 'a'*	*Chlorophyll 'b'*	*Total Chlorophyll*	*Carotenoid*
Control	0.0267±0.0024	0.0256±0.0023	0.0523±0.0047	0.9129±0.0821
5	0.0259±0.0023	0.0247±0.0022	0.0506±0.0045	0.8478±0.0762
10	0.0230±0.0020	0.0206±0.0018	0.0436±0.0439	0.2681±0.0691
25	0.0201±0.0018	0.0164±0.0014	0.0365±0.0032	0.3728±0.0281
50	0.0171±0.0015	0.0114±0.0010	0.0285±0.0025	0.1706±0.0153
100	0.0102±0.0009	0.0053±0.0004	0.0157±0.0014	0.1497±0.0134
200	0.0047±0.0004	0.0027±0.0002	0.0074±0.0006	0.0313±0.0028

±: Standard deviation.

No germination was observed beyond 500 and 1000 mg/l.

Table 3.4: Effect of Different Concentrations of Cadmium on Biochemical Studies of Soybean [*Glycine max* (L.) Merr.]

Cadmium Concentrations (mg/l)	*Chlorophyll 'a'*	*Chlorophyll 'b'*	*Total Chlorophyll*	*Carotenoid*
Control	0.0307±0.0027	0.0296±0.0026	0.0603±0.0054	1.8152±0.1633
5	0.0285±0.0025	0.0272±0.0024	0.0557±0.0050	1.5200±0.1368
10	0.0262±0.0023	0.0235±0.0021	0.0497±0.0044	0.9216±0.0829
25	0.0240±0.0021	0.0195±0.0017	0.0435±0.0039	0.7806±0.0702
50	0.0200±0.0018	0.0178±0.0016	0.0328±0.0034	0.5208±0.0468
100	0.0151±0.0013	0.0118±0.0010	0.0269±0.0024	0.4308±0.0387
200	0.0105±0.0009	0.0078±0.0007	0.0203±0.0018	0.4000±0.0360

±: Standard deviation.

No germination was observed beyond 500 and 1000 mg/l.

Decrease in chlorophyll content due to heavy metal treatment may be either because of reduced synthesis or accelerated degradation of the pigment (Wickliff *et al.*, 1980). From this present study, the various concentrations of chromium and cadmium solutions have different effects on the initial growth of soybean. The cadmium showed less toxicity when compared with chromium in soybean seedlings. Since the higher concentrations of heavy metals is toxic growth of seedlings. It is necessary to reduce the heavy metals present in the wastewater. So, it can be concluded that the industrial wastewaters should be properly treated before they get discharged into the nearby water bodies. It was also reported that there was no germination observed beyond 500 mg/l.

Acknowledgement

The authors are thankful to Dr. R. Panneerselvam, Professor and Head, Department of Botany, Annamalai University for providing laboratory facilities.

References

Aery, N.C. and D.K. Rana, 2003. Growth and cadmium uptake in barley under cadmium stress. *J. Environ. Biol.*, 24(2): 117–123.

Arnon, D.I., 1949. Copper enzymes in isolated chloroplasts polyphenol oxidase in *Beta vulgaris. Plant Physiol.*, 24: 1–15.

Barcelo, J., C.A. Poschenrieder, A. Ruano and B. Gunse, 1985. Effect of chromium (Cr-VI) on mineral element composition of bush beans. *J. Plant Nutr.*, 8: 211–217.

Bindhu, S.J. and A.K. Bera, 2001. Impact of cadmium toxicity on leaf area, stomatal frequency stomatal index and pigment content in mungbean seedlings. *J. Environ. Biol.*, 22(4): 307–309.

Bishnoi, N.R., L.K. Chugh and S.K. Sawhney, 1993. Effect of chromium on photosynthesis, respiration and nitrogen fixation in pea (*Pisum sativum* L.). *J. Plant Physiol.*, 142: 25–30.

Chauhan, S.S., S.K. Khatik and P.R. Dikshit, 2004. Cadmium a pollutant element. *J. Industrial Pollution Control*, 20(2): 235–246.

Dahiya, D.S., N. Kumar, J. Bhardwaj, P. Kumar, A.S. Nandwal and M.K. Sharma, 2003. Interactive effect of chromium and phosphorus on growth, dry matter yield and their distribution in wheat shoot. *Indian J. Plant Physiol.*, 8(2): 129–132.

Dua and S.K. Sawhney, 1991. Effect of chromium on hydrolytic enzymes in germinating pea seeds. *J. Environ. Exp. Bot.*, 31: 133–139.

Gabbrielli, R., T. Pandolfini, O. Vergano and M.R. Palandri, 1990. Comparison of two serpentine species with different nickel tolerance strategies. *Plant and Soil*, 122: 271–277.

Hsu, Y.T. and C.H. Kao, 2003. Changes in protein and amino acid contents in two cultivars of rice seedlings with different apparent tolerance to cadmium. *Plant Growth Regulation*, 40: 147–152.

Kirk, J.T.O. and R.L. Allen, 1965. Dependence of chloroplast pigments synthesis on protein synthetic effects of actilione. *Biochem. Biophys. Res. Cann.*, 27: 523–530.

Lakshmi, S. and P. Sundaramoorthy, 2003. Effect of chromium on germination and biochemical changes in blackgram. *J. Ecobiol.*, 15(1): 1–11.

Mehta, R., K. Gupta, D.S. Dahiya and N. Kumar, 1996. Effect of chromium(VI) on growth, yield and biochemical constituents of sunflower (*Helianthus annuus* L.). In: *Resource Management of Frazil Environment*, (Eds.) R.K. Bhel, A.P. Gupta, A.L. Khurana and A. Singh. pp. 159–162, CCS AAU, Hisar and MMB, New Delhi.

Mukherjee, S. and C. Mukherjee, 1979. Characterisation of cadmium effect in different plant materials. *Indian J. Expt. Biol.*, 17: 265–269.

Muthuchelian, K.S., Maria, Victoria Rani and K. Paliwal, 1988. Differential action of Cu^{2+} and Cd^{2+} on chlorophyll biosynthesis and nitrate reductase activity in *Vigna sinensis* L. *Indian J. Plant Physiol.*, 31(2): 169–173.

Prasad, M.N.V., 1995. Inhibition of maize leaf chlorophylls, carotenoids and gas exchange functions by cadmium. *Photosynthetica*, 31: 635–640.

Rai, V.N., R.D. Tripathi and Kumar, 1992. Bioaccumulation of chromium toxicity on growth, photosynthetic pigments, photosynthesis, *in vitro* nitrate reductase activity and protein content in a chlorocoaeleam green algae *Glancolystis aostochinearum. Chemosphere*, 25: 1722–1732.

Saravanan, S., A. Subramani, P. Sundaramoorthy and A.S. Lakshrnanachary, 1997. Influence of cadmium on germination and growth behaviour of *Arachis hypogaea* (Linn.) var. VRI.2. *Geobios*, 24: 167–170.

Sawhney, V., I.S. Sheoran and R. Singh, 1990. Nitrogen fixation, photosynthesis and enzymes of ammonia assimilation nodules of mungbean (*Vigna radiata*) grown in presence of cadmium. *Indian J. Exp. Biol.*, 28: 883–886.

Shalini Purohit, T.M. Varghese and M. Kumari, 2003. Effect of chromium on morphological features of tomato and brinjal. *Indian J. Plant Physiol.*, 8(1): 17–22.

Sheoran, I.S. and R. Singh, 1993. Effect of heavy metals on photosynthesis in higher plants. In: *Photosynthesis-photoreactions to Plant Productivity*, (Eds.) Y.P. Abrol, P. Mohanty and Govindjee. Oxford and IBH Publishing Co. Pvt. Ltd., New Delhi, pp. 451–468.

Sheoran, I.S., H.R Singal and R. Singh, 1990. Effect of cadmium and nickel on photosynthesis and the enzymes of the photosynthetic carbon reduction cycle in pigeon pea [*Cajanus cajan* (L.) Hepper]. *Poll. Res.*, 16: 29–31.

Vander Veen, C. and Huczengal, 1980. Combating river pollution taking the Rhine as an example. *Progress in Water Technology*, 12: 1035–1059.

Wickliff, C., H.J. Evans, K.R. Center and S.A. Roussel, 1980. Effect of cadmium chlorophyll biosynthesis. *J. Environ. Qual.*, 9: 180–184.

Chapter 4

Ultrasonic Investigation on Aqueous Ternary Electrolytes of Some Mineral Salts

T. Sumathi[1] and A.N. Kannappan[2]

[1]Department of Physics, DDE, Annamalai University, Annamalainagar - 608 002

[2]Department of Physics, Annamalai University, Annamalainagar - 608 002

ABSTRACT

Ultrasonic velocities and densities of sodium sulphate and magnesium sulphate have been measured in urea-water mixture with composition 30 : 70 mixture at 303, 308 and 313 K. Various parameters such as adiabatic compressibility (β_{ad}), apparent molal compressibility (ϕ_k), apparent molal volume (ϕ_v), limiting apparent molal compressibility (ϕ^o_k) and limiting apparent molal volume (ϕ^o_v) have been calculated. These parameters have been utilized to throw light on solute solvent interactions. The effect of temperature on these parameters has also been discussed.

Keywords: Electrolytes, Alkali cations, Solute-solvent interaction.

Introduction

The study of ultrasonic velocity leads to a better understanding of the nature of interactions between solute and solvent. That is why, of late an increasing interest has been shown in the study of physico-chemical, behaviour and molecular interaction in a variety of liquid mixtures of electrolyte. Such studies have been carried out by several workers (Ramanathan and Ravichandran, 2004; Pandey and Akhtar, 1996; Nikam *et al.*, 2004). The main objective of the present investigation is to explore molecular interactions in ternary electrolytic mixture as not much data is available in such systems in literature. The mineral salts like sodium sulphate and magnesium sulphate are important constituents of biofluids and soil fluids. The main ionic solutes in biofluids are the alkali cations *viz.*, Na^+ and Mg^{2+} in small amount, the common anions are the small amounts of So_4^{2-}. The ionic solutes have two important functions:

1. They are normally responsible for the osmotic pressure of biofluids.
2. The ion Na^+ is mainly responsible of extra cellular and intracellular fluids of soils.

In the present investigation, density and velocities of sodium sulphate and magnesium sulphate in urea-water mixture at different temperatures have been measured and other acoustical parameters are calculated in order to interpret the nature of interactions in the systems.

Materials and Methods

Since the electrolytes used are Analar-R grade (99.9 per cent pure), they have been taken as such without any purification. Required amount of water and urea are taken to prepare the binary mixtures in a clean dry conical flask with ground stopper.

The required quantity of the electrolyte for a given molality has been dissolved and similar procedure adopted for different molalities of, electrolyte. Ultrasonic velocity has been measured using ultrasonic interferometer with an accuracy of ±0.1 per cent at a frequency of 3MHz. The temperature of the liquid was maintained constant to an accuracy of ±0.1 k. The density of the mixture was measured using 5 ml specific gravity bottle.

Different thermodynamic parameters such as adiabatic compressibility (β_{ad}), apparent molal compressibility (ϕ_k), and apparent molal volume (ϕ_v) have been calculated for sodium sulphate and magnesium sulphate in urea water mixture at 303, 308 and 313K.

The adiabatic compressibility is deduced from the equation:

$$\beta_{ad} = \frac{1}{U^2 p} \qquad \text{....(1)}$$

The apparent molal compressibility (ϕ_k) is calculated as,

$$\phi_k = \frac{1000}{mp_0}(\rho_0\beta - \beta_0\rho) + \frac{\beta_0 M}{\rho_0} \qquad \text{....(2)}$$

where,

$\beta\rho$ and $\beta_0\rho_0$ are the adiabatic compressibility and density of solution and solvent respectively, m is the molal concentration and M is the molecular weight of the solute. ϕ_k is a function of *m* as obtained by Gucker from Debye Hukel theory and is given as:

$$\phi_k = \phi^0{}_k + S_k m^{1/2} \qquad \text{....(3)}$$

where,

$\phi^0{}_k$ is the limiting apparent molal compressibility at infinite dilution and S_k is a constant.

The apparent molal volume can be deduced from the equation:

$$\phi_v = \frac{1000}{mp_0}(\rho_0 - \rho) + \frac{M}{\rho_0} \qquad \text{....(4)}$$

The apparent molal volume has been found to differ with concentration according to Mason's empirical relation as

$$\phi_v = \phi^o_v + S_v m^{1/2} \quad ....(5)$$

where,

ϕ^o_v is the limiting apparent molal volume at infinite dilution and S_v is a constant.

Results and Discussion

The measured ultrasonic velocity and density are listed in Table 4.1. The computed adiabatic compressibility (β_{ad}), apparent molal compressibility (ϕ_k) and apparent molal volume for the two salts are listed in Table 4.2. The limiting apparent molal compressibility and limiting apparent molal volume along with the constants. S_k and S_v at differed temperatures are listed in Table 4.3. From the Table 4.1, it is noticed that ultrasonic velocity increases with increase in molalities and temperature. The values of density increase with increase in molalities and decreases with rise in temperature.

Table 4.1: Values of Density (ρ) and Velocity (U) of Sodium Sulphate and Magnesium Sulphate in Urea-water Mixtures

Molality of Salt (m)	*ρ kg m⁻³*			*U ms⁻¹*		
	Temperature (K)			*Temperature (K)*		
	303	*308*	*313*	*303*	*308*	*313*
			Sodium Sulphate			
0.0000	1075.7	1072.8	1071.7	1627.4	1633.7	1637.9
0.2001	1100.7	1096.9	1094.8	1661.6	1663.1	1665.5
0.4000	1123.5	1120.2	1118.2	1689.0	1691.4	1695.2
0.6000	1146.5	1142.1	1140.3	1711.5	1715.3	1718.6
0.8000	1167.2	1164.1	1161.7	1736.2	1741.1	1745.0
1.0000	1189.7	1184.7	1183.8	1772.1	1773.6	1777.8
			Magnesium Sulphate			
0.2000	1097.5	1093.6	1092.6	1658.4	1660.2	1663.1
0.4000	1118.7	1114.9	1112.9	1673.9	1678.4	1680.8
0.6000	1136.8	1132.5	1129.5	1692.9	1695.9	1699.8
0.7999	1153.5	1150.2	1149.8	1711.8	1716.5	1718.0
1.0001	1171.4	1166.6	1163.9	1733.4	1735.3	1737.4

From the Table 4.2 it is clear that β_{ad} decreases with increase in concentration at all temperatures in both the salts indicating the solvation of ions or increased ion-solvent interaction (Ishwara and Shivakumar, 1998).

It is observed from the Table 4.2, the ϕ_k and ϕ_v values are negative for both the electrolytic solution over the entire range of molrality and temperature. Both ϕ_k and ϕ_v values decrease with increase of temperature. The above observation suggests that the ϕ_k values for the electrolytic solution are comparatively higher than that of the solvent, thereby indicating a strong ion-solvent interaction.

Table 4.2: Values of Adiabatic Compressibility (β), Apparent Molal Compressibility (ϕ_k) and Apparent Molal Volume (ϕ_v) of Sodium Sulphate and Magnesium Sulphate in Urea-water Mixtures

Molality of Salt (m)	$\beta \times 10^{10}$ pa^{-1}			$-\phi_k \times 10^{10}$ m^2N^{-1}			$-\phi_v$ m^3 mol^{-1}		
	Temperature (K)			Temperature (K)			Temperature (K)		
	303	308	313	303	308	313	303	308	313
				Sodium Sulphate					
0.0000	3.5101	3.4925	3.4782	–	–	–	–	–	–
0.2001	3.2906	3.2961	3.2929	1504.55	1373.77	1300.70	116.15	112.27	107.72
0.4000	3.1201	3.1204	3.1120	1364.97	1316.00	1292.75	111.09	110.46	108.47
0.6000	2.9776	2.9759	2.9691	1272.49	1237.04	1219.46	109.70	107.66	106.68
0.8000	2.8422	2.8338	2.8269	1208.09	1194.97	1179.18	106.33	106.38	104.97
1.0000	2.6766	2.6834	2.6727	1205.48	1173.42	1169.26	105.98	104.31	104.60
				Magnesium Sulphate					
0.2000	3.3130	3.3176	3.3090	1341.38	1213.21	1184.85	101.33	96.94	97.51
0.4000	3.1903	3.1840	3.1806	1150.37	1113.89	1078.18	99.93	98.11	96.11
0.6000	3.0694	3.0702	3.0642	1066.80	1027.82	1002.60	94.67	92.75	89.89
0.7999	2.9585	2.9508	2.9467	1006.93	992.23	981.35	90.42	90.20	91.10
1.0001	2.8412	2.8466	2.8463	981.11	951.16	930.99	88.96	87.43	86.02

Table 4.3: Values of Limiting Apparent Molal Compressibiliy ($\phi_k°$), Limiting Apparent Molal Volume ($\phi_v°$), the Constants S_K and S_v of the Salts in Urea-water Mixtures

Temperature	$-\phi_k° \times 10^8$ m^2N^{-1}	$S_k \times 10^8$ N^{-1} m^{-1} mol^{-1}	$-\phi_v°$ m^3 mol^{-1}	S_v m^3 $kg^{½}$ $mol^{-3/2}$
		Sodium Sulphate		
303	17.35	5.66	123.83	18.65
308	15.47	3.83	119.08	14.50
313	14.36	2.72	111.60	6.82
		Magnesium Sulphate		
303	15.96	6.49	113.57	24.69
308	14.18	4.78	107.32	18.99
313	13.72	4.49	107.27	20.20

The similar trend is observed in ϕ_v also. The decrease in ϕ_v is due to strong ion-ion interaction. The negative values of ϕ_v indicate eletrostrictive solvation of ions (Aswar *et al.*, 2000).

In Table 4.3 the limiting apparent molal compressibility φ°k values are negative and decrease with increase in temperature. The negative $\phi°_k$ values may be due to loss of compressibility of solvent because of strong electrostrictive forces of ions (Upadhyaya, 2000).

The positive S_k values which measure solute-solvent interaction (Muhuri *et al.*, 1996) decrease with rise in temperature. The values of limiting apparent molal volume $\phi°_v$ are negative for both the electrolytic solution at all the temperature indicating the presence of interaction between the ions and solvent (Parmer *et al.*, 1989). The values of S_v is a measure of ion-ion interaction (Jha and Jha, 1990) decrease with increase in temperature.

From this investigation it is noticed that existence of ion-solvent interactions resulting in attractive forces, promote the structure making tendency in sodium sulphate solutions while ion-ion interactions resulting in dipole-dipole, dipole-induced dipole and electrostrictive forces enhances the structure breaking properties in the case of magnesium sulphate solutions.

References

Aswar, A.S., Kulkarni, S.G. and Rohankar, P.O., 2000. Ultrasonic, volumetric and viscometric studies of some substituted acetophenones in THF-water, DMF-water and dioxane-water co-solvents at 303.15k. *Indian J. Chem.* 39A: 1214–1217.

Ishwara Bhat, J. and Shivakumar, H.R., 1998. Study on acoustic behaviour of potassium thiocyanate in aqueous and various, non-aqueous, solvents at 298-313k. *Indian J. Chem.*, 37A: 252–256.

Jha, D.K. and Jha, B.L., 1990. Partial molar volumes and partial molar compressibilities of Zn SO_4 Cd SO_4 $Zn(No_3)_2$ $Cd(NO_3)_2$ and $Cdcl_2$, *Ind. J. Pure and Appl. Phys.*, 28: 346–349.

Muhri, Prakash, K., Das Bijan and Hazra K. Dilip, 1996. Apparent molar volumes and apparent molar compressibilities of some symmetrical tetra alkylammonium bromides in 1,2-dimethoxyethane. *Indian J. Chem.*, 35A: 288–293.

Nikam, P.S., Mehati Hason, Pawar, T.B. and Sawant, A.B., 2004. Ultrasonic velocity and allied parameters of symmetrical tetra alkylammonium bromides in aqueous ethanol at 298.15k. *Indian Journal of Pure and Applied Physics*, 42: 172–178.

Pandey, J.D. and Akhtar, Y., 1996. Ultrasonic studies of aqueous concentrated electrolytic solutions at 298.15k. *J. Pure Appl. Ultrason.*, 18: 108–113.

Parmer, M.L., Khanna, A. and Gupta, V.K., 1989. Partial molar volumes and viscosities of some transition metal sulphates in aqueous urea solutions. *Ind. J. Chem.*, 28A: 565–569.

Ramanathan, K. and Ravichandran, S., 2004. Ultrasonic study of mixed salt solutions of ammonium sulphate and ammonium chloride. *J. Pure Appl. Ultrason*, 26: 12–17.

Upadhyaya, S.K., 2000. Ultrasonic study of molecular interactions and compressibility behaviour of lithium soaps in 50 : 50 per cent (v/v) benzene methanol mixture. *Ind. J. Chem.*, 39A: 537–540.

Chapter 5

Environmental Audit: Sign Post for Sustainable Industrial Economy

N.S. Raman

Senior Scientist, NEERI, Nehru Marg, Nagpur – 440 020

ABSTRACT

Indian industries are diversifying into progressively more capital intensive and energy intensive areas which are degrading the environmental quality. Considering the future environmental and energy scenarios, the impact the industry has on environmental quality and occupational health/safety of industrial workers, Environmental Audit (EA) deserves to be adopted as a pre-requisite for sustainable development and sound environmental management of industries.

EA is a structured and comprehensive mechanism for ensuring that the industrial activities do no adversely affect the environmental quality and the economy of the industrial sector improves as a consequence of improved process and energy effectivity as also the occupational health and safety. This article emphasises that the successful EA programme investigates all possibilities of energy saving, material saving and water budgeting through conservation of resources, to protection of environment. The article presents the various options for environmental management in Indian industry, including reactive control measures on one hand and anticipative preventive strategies on the other hand.

The article stresses that EA would entail a "cradle to grave" approach while reviewing EA skills and audit protocols alongwilh discussion of key environmental audit techniques.

Introduction

There is a great human urge for better living standards with all the comforts and luxuries. This tendency has resulted in rapid industrialization, which is bound to continue in future.

Industrialization is considered to be a yardstick of a nation's development and all developing economics are grappling with this issue how to manage the increased demands on environment and energy without adversely affecting the economy and environment.

Indian industries are diversifying into progressively more capital intensive and energy intensive areas which are degrading the environmental quality. Indian industry cannot afford to ignore current growing environmental concerns. Environmental issues are not just esoteric, but involve assessment of critical business issues such as cost.

Environmental protection is nowadays no longer a task that can be addressed in isolation. It must be integrated into development and production in order to prevent new environmental problems from arising, in the first place. Only close collaboration between technological facilities and industry can help environmental technology to keep one step ahead in long term to achieve sustainable development through industrial economy.

In reality, the objective of considering environmental aspects as apart and parcel of developmental projects is to achieve:

1. Sustained development with minimal environmental degradation.
2. Prevention of long-term environmental side effects incorporating mitigative measures so that the remedies do not become unmanageable and prohibitive.

In India, "Environmental Audit" should be considered as a sign post to achieve sustainable development. Implementation of Environmental Audit warrants increasingly interventionist policies which influence technological considerations preceding investment decision making, in-such a way that resource utilization is also the cost of environmental protection, and damages are minimised while economic productivity and innovative capacity is maximised.

Sustainable development may be achieved through implementation of Environmental Audit (EA) which aims at large scale technological substitution towards environmentally benign technologies such as clean technologies of production that conserves resources, generate less pollution, provide direct economic benefits and stimulate the growth of industries as well as national economy, recycle and reuse technologies for end of the pipe treatment that render the otherwise demand non-productive activity of waste treatment as profitable proposition.

Environmental Audit in Indian Context

Environmental audit in Indian context should take cognizance of the following:

1. Environmental audit undertaken in developed countries comprises two components, *viz.*, assessment and verification of environmental systems
2. Endeavour on environmental protection thus far in India has relied on strict regulatory measures with little regard to economic productivity
3. Preventive and reactive approaches do not complement each other In the current practices of environmental management in India as reflected in legislative, administrative and policy formulations.

Thus the Environmental Audit in the context of free market economy in India, is to be defined as a pragmatic management tool comprising systematic, documented, periodic and objective evaluation of production and environment management systems to ensure resource conserving modes of manufacturing, and cost-effective environmental protection as a consequence of Improved material, water and energy effectivity, for enhanced economic productivity and acceptable environmental quality and health of employees and general public.

The above definition recognizes the potential for resource conservation in manufacturing processes with concomitant reduction in the cost of production, pollution control, and comprises comparative analysis of the process technology in use vis-à-vis the state-of-the-art technology available in that sector with concomitant implication on raw materials and energy use effectivity, as also the quantity and characteristics of residues.

The definition inter alia considers shifts towards cleaner production technologies through comparative analysis of various competing alternatives in industrial sectors based on technological, economic, societal and environmental considerations as a part of Environmental Audit.

Evolution of Environmental Audit in India

Industrial activities in India have lead to environmental problems by excessive consumption of resources and release of deleterious effluents, emissions, and residues. Efforts to prevent, abate, and control pollution have relied on classical methods for influencing human behavior namely, motivating commitment and introducing competition. Examples of these methods are seen in various laws, regulations, and standards; financial incentives and labeling of environment friendly products. In India, there are some 250 enactments that have a bearing on the environment. As a matter of practice in India, polluting industrial units are persuaded by Pollution Control Boards to take steps to comply with the prescribed emission standards, under threat of prosecution in case of default.

With the experience of environmental damage caused by industrial activities, introspection and analysis become increasingly elaborate, and various names were given to this process. Some of the names given earlier on the basis of scope are quality control survey; environmental review; environmental diagnostic study; and health, safety and environmental audits. In the global context, the United Nations has issued a set of recommendations for Industry Information disclosure, but these are yet to be implemented even in the developed world. This may be an a real in which India could take a lead.

Recognizing the importance of the environmental audit, procedures were first enacted under the 1986 Environment (Protection) Act by the Ministry of Environment and Forests [Notification No. GSR 329 (E), dated March 13, 1992]. This notification required that the industrial units furnish environmental audit reports. By an amendment [Notification No. GSR 386 (E), dated April 22, 1993], the term for the document has been revised from *Environmental Audit* Report to *Environmental Statement*.

An environmental statement must be submitted by every industry, operation, or process requiring consent under Section 25 of the water (Prevention and Control of Pollution) Act of 1974 or under Section 21 of the Air (Prevention and Control of Pollution) Act of 1981 or both, or authorization under the Hazardous Wastes (Management and Handling) Rules of 1989 issued under the Environment (Protection) Act of 1986. The statement must be submitted to the concerned state pollution control board for the period ending March 31 in the prescribed format by September 30 every year.

The aim of an environmental statement of an environmental audit is to facilitate supervision and, at the same time, gain information on the measures to be taken by an industrial unit in regard to compliance with the company's internal policies and with the Indian regulations in force. The environmental statement enables industrial units to take a comprehensive look at their industrial operations and facilities, and to understand material flows in order to focus on areas in which waste reduction, and consequently saving in input costs might be possible.

Design and Implementation

Environmental Audit is relevant equally to the Developed and Developing countries, through it is not to be applied in an identical manner.

Environmental Audit should typically be a combination of Process Audit Material Audit, Compliance Audit, Energy Audit, Environmental Quality and Health and Safety audit. In fact, energy and environment are now well recognized as intricately related issues; the two sides of the same coin. Both energy and environmental issues demand immediate attention–energy because of its impact on the economic well being of a nation, and environment because, it is a prominent indicator of a nations physical health.

Environmental Audit should be used as asystematic and powerful tool to study the existing facilities in each industry and lead to assessment and identification of areas where improvements could be made to conserve material, water and energy. Consequently, optimum material, water and energy consumption targets/norms are to be established with a high degree of objectivity for monitoring, controlling and modifying the system/operations.

Environmental Audit aims "To Produce Better While Polluting Less" which is a real challenge and a necessary step for an industry.

The inputs to be considered in an environmental audit to conserve resource is depicted Figure 5.1. EA aims at evaluating whether an industry uses raw materials and energy at a reasonable and economic cost. A better understanding of the basic principles and general pattern of an industry is an important step in EA to undertake and encourage efficiently the implementation of waste elimination (raw materials and energy).

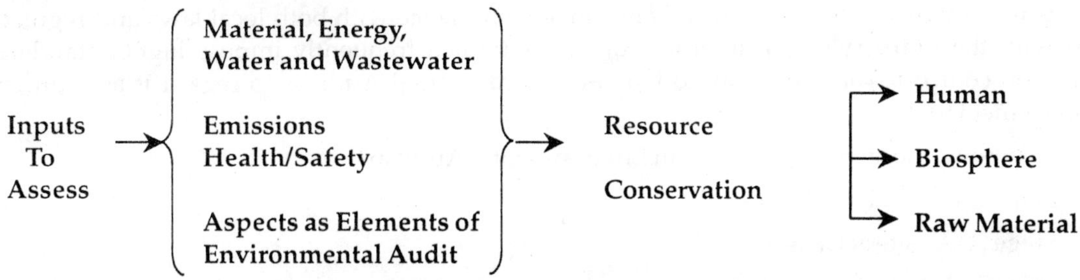

Figure 5.1: Environmental Audit: A Step Towards Resource Conservation

Pollution generally represent a loss: Loss of raw materials, energy, by-products or final products. EA tries to spare the environment by limiting the residues and wastes while implementing the conditions of production.

Procedures which define a formal EA programme should be readily standardized, which allows a particular facility, group of facilities, or programme to be contemplated in a logical and comprehensive manner.

EA process can be a powerful means of achieving the objectives. Regardless of the specific industry to be audited, there are usually 3 elements in an EA process:

Environmental Audit Guidelines

Since EA is long ranged and complex activity, written guidelines are required to ensure consistency of approach. The EA guidelines ensure that interviews, site inspections, filing and reporting are standardised.

Pro Audit Questionnaire/Audit Protocols

A document is required to be prepared to initiate the EA process in an industry to help collect the necessary audit information, coordinate facility or programme staff to be interviewed, arrange for the logistics of an EA visit.

Environmental Audit Workbook

EA workbook should include all that is necessary to support an environment auditor including the pertinent synoptic reviews of pertinent regulations with which an industry deals with.

"Environmental Audit" typically involves five distinct, yet interrelated, basic steps:

1. Understanding Internal Management System
2. Assessing the soundness of an industry's Internal control
3. Gathering Environmental Audit evidence
4. Evaluation of Environmental Audit findings
5. Reporting Environmental Audit findings

Environmental Audit Approach

One phenomena of increased environmental concern is the environmental audit. Environmental audits usually meant to systematically examine compliance with both local laws and regulations, and with the industry's own internal guidelines (which frequently impose higher standards of pollution control). The ideal way to look at Environmental Audit is to regard it as a pragmatic management tool.

Generally, the steps involved in an Environmental Audit are:

Stage 1: Pre-audit activities

Stage 2: On-site activities

Stage 3: Post-audit activities

The following steps are generally adopted while conducting Environmental Audit in an industry:

1. The preparatory study of salient design and operating data.
2. Site visit by a joint team (Including operating personnel and Environmental Audit Consultants) for plant familiarisation and for interview sessions with operating personnel to appreciate constraints, bottlenecks and margins in operation and to obtain salient design and operating data on process, water, material and energy aspects.
3. Based on above, base-case (s) of operation, material, water and energy profiles are developed.
4. Development of Environmental Conservation Schemes supported with techno-economic analysis.
5. The recommendations of the Environmental Audit may be classified as process oriented or equipment oriented. Process oriented recommendations may Include changes in operating

parameters, modifications to the processing schemes and improved utilisation of operating margins.

Energy Effectivity

Energy is an essential input for economic development. The development of energy sources is highly capital intensive and large investments are required to meet demands of energy for the different sectors of economy. The demand for electricity, coal and petroleum products is estimated as 798 billion KWH, 460 million tonnes and 125 million tonnes respectively in the year 2006–07. The estimated gap between demand and production of commercial sources of energy in the terminal year (1996–97) of the eighth Five Year Plan is given in Table 5.1.

Table 5.1

Sources	*Coal (Million Tonnes)*	*Petroleum Products (Million Tonnes)*	*Electricity (Billion KWH)*
Demand	311	81	450*
Production	308	44**	448*
Gap	3	37	2

*: Gross generation requirements.

**: Indicates petroleum products availability from 47.08 million tonnes of indigenous crude oil production.

The formulation and implementation of national energy policies have been dominated by economic and technological concerns. As on date, the inter-relationships between energy use and environmental quality have received increasing attention, and the energy supply systems is now often strongly influenced by various environmental issues. Although this tendency has been most marked in industrialized countries, it is now quite evident in the recently industrializing nations including India. Hence the authors strongly feel that energy effectivity has to be seen in any industry as a part of Environmental Audit.

India's energy mix is dominated by coal, an energy source with severe environmental repercussions. The environmental consequences of the energy development cause for reaching damage at both the national and regional levels through hazardous gas emissions and contamination of water and land.

Table 5.2 highlights the potential for energy conservation in various sectors, and specially large energy intensive industries. This potential should be realised through measures whose capital and life cycle costs are less than that needed to generate equivalent amounts of energy supply. Our experience while conducting Environmental Audits indicates that 10–15 per cent of the potential savings can be realized by adopting no-cost house keeping measures. A substantial portion of balance potential can be realized with minor process/technology improvement measures. The pay back period for such measures range from a few months to less than 2–3 years.

Material Audit

Material Audit as a part of environmental audit aims at better management of the sequence of the material flow in the process of fabrication. For material savings on the basis of material audit, a material balance scenario is developed which highlights the possibilities of raw material savings leading to decrease in the costs of production.

Table 5.2: Energy Conservation Potential

Sector	*Potential (per cent)*
Economy wide potential	Upto 23
Agricultural	Upto 30
Industrial	Upto 25
Transport	Upto 20
Domestic and commercial	Upto 20
Industries	
Textiles	20–25
Pulp and paper	20–25
Foundries	15–20
Glass	15–20
Fertilizers	10–15
Cement	10–15
Chlor-Alkali	10–15
Aluminium	08–10
Iron and steel	08–10

Source: 1) IMWG Report 1999.

2) World Bank Industrial Energy Efficiency Project Proposal 1989.

Note: The potential is with respect to house keeping, retrofitting and minor process modification measures and does not include potential as a result of technology changes.

Material Audit benefits the environment, and will yield better production, thereby, "producing better while polluting less".

In one of our environmental audit studies, it is shown that an excess amount of about 0.04 t of sulphur per tonne of calcium bisulphite can be saved if proper stoichiometric quantities of chemicals are used for calcium bisulphite preparation.

In an environmental audit study conducted in an industry, it was revealed that savings to the tune of Rs. 125 lakhs per annum can be achieved if the recommendations are implemented in the areas of material/process, energy, water and wastewater and house keeping measures.

Epilogue

Environmental stability is going to be the mega issue of the twenty first century and a point on which global politics of economics would revolve. Our endeavour and thrust should be on the macro-management of the economy. We must therefore emphasise on Environmental Audit wherein the opportunities for Environmental Conservation in Indian Industries can be exploited depending on factors like vintage of the plant and the environmental awareness of the operating personnel. Environmental Audits carried out generally identified opportunities which could lead to a saving of 20–25 per cent on the existing energy bill, 40–45 per cent on existing water usage and 25–30 per cent on existing material use. Even if a small fraction of these benefits is realized, the profit can adequately compensate for Environmental Audit studies.

Whether such an audit should be carried out with in-house resources only or whether outside consultants also need to be called-in, will very much depend on the nature of an industry, the relevant expertise available within an industry, the past experience with environmental audits and the magnitude of the task. Based on our Environmental Audit experience of Indian Industries, the authors have no hesitation in recommending that Environmental Audits should be carried out earnestly and in a detailed manner on a regular basis. It is heartening to note that Environmental Audit studies conducted so far has revealed enormous potential to achieve increased productivity and improved environmental conditions. EA may be viewed as a sign post for sustainable Industrial development.

Chapter 6

Evaluation of Groundwater Resource of Faridabad District, Haryana, India

Madhuri S. Rishi[#]

Centre for Environment and Vocational Studies, Panjab University, Chandigarh - 160 014, India

ABSTRACT

In this article, an attempt has been made to quantify groundwater resources of Faridabad district (Haryana) at block levels *viz.*, Faridabad, Ballabhgarh, Hathin, Hodal and Palwal, based on the modified norms by NABARD (National Bank for Agricultural and Rural Development, India) and in the light of various groundwater investigations carried out during 1992–1993. The estimations reveal that out of the five blocks only one (Hathin) falls in the white (safe) category, whereas three *viz.*, Ballabhgarh, Hodal, and Palwal fall in grey (semi-critical) category. In contrast, Faridabad block falls in dark (most critical) category. The results assume great significance in the light of utilization of groundwater for various domestic and agricultural purposes.

Keywords: *Groundwater resources, Faridabad district, Monsoon water recharge, Non-monsoon recharge, Potential recharge, Groundwater draft, Unrecoverable losses, Groundwater balance.*

Introduction

The study area forms a part of Faridabad district that lies between 27°52′N to 28°23′N latitudes and 77°06′E to 77°32′E longitudes. Administratively, Faridabad district has been divided into five

[#] E-mail: madhuririshi@gmail.com.

community development blocks namely, Faridabad, Ballabhgarh, Hathin, Hodal and Palwal. The elevation of the water table to the mean sea level varies between 180m to 198m. The groundwater flow in the northern parts of the district is towards east and southeast *i.e.*, towards river Yamuna and downstream. The master slope of the water table is towards southeast and south. The hydraulic gradient varies from 0.35m per km. in the northeastern and eastern parts to 2.1 m per km. in the south and southwestern parts of the district. In the central region, its average value is about 1.45 m per km. The area forms a part of flat alluvial plain without any conspicuous topographic feature and in general, the climate of the area is of continental character (Basu, 1989). Around 85 per cent of the total annual rainfall is received during June to September (Southwestern monsoonal period). Most part of the study area is irrigated by Western Yamuna canal and its distributaries and has high irrigation density. Groundwater balance of Faridabad district has been worked out on the modified norms of National Bank for Agriculture and Rural Development (NABARD, 1986). The raw data regarding rainfall, flood prone areas, irrigation inputs, types of crop cover, nature of soil cover, shallow water level areas and groundwater draft were obtained from various Government and semi-government agencies engaged in the related works. The data in the respect of areas suitable for groundwater development based on the chemical quality of shallow water zones, were modified in the light of results of various groundwater investigations carried out during 1990–1993 (Sharma, 1996).

Methodology

It involves the estimation of groundwater balance for a normal rainfall year and the other information needed in these calculations was taken for the years 1990–1993 (GWEC, 1986). The total annual recharge is estimated as a sum of normalized monsoon, non-monsoon and potential recharge. The monsoon recharge is computed as a sum of net change in the groundwater storage during pre- and post-monsoon periods and the gross groundwater draft during the monsoon period from which, sum of recharge during monsoon period from canal seepage, recycled water from surface and groundwater irrigation are subtracted. For calculating non-monsoon recharge, area considered suitable for development coupled with IMD normal rainfall during non-monsoon and rainfall infiltration index are considered. While calculating potential recharge, recharge from shallow water table and recharge from flood prone areas are taken into consideration.

The total annual draft includes the groundwater draft for different groundwater structures and the unrecoverable losses due to evapo-transpiration coupled with effluent losses. Data related to shallow water table areas, net geographical area suitable for development, water level fluctuations, normal rainfall for both monsoon and non-monsoon period and the canal seepage is taken into consideration. In order to calculate groundwater worthy areas, under lain by saline water (EC > 6000 micro-siemens/cm at 25°C) along with areas occupied by the hard rocks were subtracted from the total geographical area.

The total groundwater resources thus calculated would be those available for domestic, agricultural and industrial purposes. In the state of Haryana, requirements for domestic and industrial purposes do not exceed 6 per cent; but 15 per cent of the total are kept for these requirements (Dogra, 1996). Under the present concept of usable resources, the draft component deducted is only from the groundwater structures used for irrigation as the other components are negligible. The domestic and industrial draft has already been accounted for and 15 per cent of the total groundwater resources left for these purposes. The computation of the water balance has been carried out only for the fresh and marginally saline areas. Saline zones were excluded as these occupy very small portions of the total geographic area. The basic equation employed for computation of groundwater balance is as under:

Groundwater Balance = Total annual recharge – Net annual draft

= (Monsoon recharge + Non monsoon recharge + Potential recharge) – Net annual draft

Results and Discussion

In the study area, the major sources of groundwater recharge include recharge from canal network, precipitation, irrigation return flow, recharge from flood prone areas, recharge from surface water bodies and sub surface groundwater inflow. Chatervedi's formula (given below) was used to calculate recharge from rainfall as the study area falls under alluvial cover.

$$R\rho = 2.0\,(R - 15)2/5$$

where,

$R\rho$: Recharge in inches and

R: Rainfall in inches.

As per the adopted norms, recharge for the study area should vary between 20–25 per cent of normal rainfall but percentage of rainfall infiltration appears to be less than these figures. Only a small portion of the annual precipitation gets into groundwater storage as the major portion comprises surface run off to the streams while a part goes into the atmosphere by the process of evapo transpiration (Walton, 1970).

Groundwater Worthy Areas

The whole area under investigation is groundwater worthy as it is neither underlain by saline water on large scale nor occupied by hard rocks (Bhumla and Abrol, 1972). Small areas even though underlain by saline water were neglected.

Recharge Due to Monsoonal Rainfall

While calculating the monsoonal recharge, area suitable for development, average water table fluctuation and the specific yield values were taken into consideration and the recommended water table fluctuation approach was followed. The average seasonal water table fluctuation has been evaluated from water level data of observation wells and the fluctuations in water table were taken as the difference between the lowest pre-monsoon and the highest post-monsoon levels. The computations are based on the data of average seasonal fluctuations measured at observation wells from 1990 to 1993.

The change in the water table fluctuation in an aquifer corresponds to the rainfall of the observation year. As the rainfall may deviate for a particular year from the normal rainfall, hence the estimated rainfall recharge should be corrected for the long-term normal rainfall recorded by Indian Meteorological Department (IMD). While calculating the groundwater recharge during the monsoon period, the following formula has been used:

$$S = A \times U \times (\text{WTF from June to October})$$

where,

S: Recharge due to monsoon rainfall in m^3

A: Groundwater worthy areas in km^2

U: Specific yield

WTF: Water table fluctuation.

Information regarding monsoon recharge in Faridabad District is given in Table 6.1.

Table 6.1: Detailed Calculations of Monsoon Recharge

Name of the Block	*Groundwater Worthy Area (sq. km)* 1	*Specific Yield (%)* 2	*Average Water Table Fluctuation (m)* 3	*Monsoon Recharge (mcm)* 1 × 2 × 3
Faridabad	283.86	14.0	0.84	33.38
Ballabhgarh	319.86	14.0	1.23	55.08
Hathin	234.70	14.0	0.81	26.61
Hodal	898.14	14.0	0.99	55.08
Palwal	375.29	14.0	0.94	49.39
Total	**1611.85**	**14.0**	–	**216.64**

Recharge Due to Non-monsoon Rainfall

The recharge due to non-monsoon rainfall in the study area has been calculated as 25 per cent of the rainfall received (December to March) for the period 1990–1993. The equation used for calculating the non-monsoonal recharge is given below and the calculations are shown in Table 6.2.

Non monsoon rainfall recharge = Area considered groundwater worthy × IMD normal Non-monsoon rainfall × Infiltration index

Table 6.2: Detailed Calculations of Non-monsoon Recharge in Faridabad District

Name of the Block	*Groundwater Worthy Area (sq. km)* 1	*IMD Yearly (mm)*	*Normal Monsoon (mm)*	*Rainfall Non-monsoon (mm)*	*Infiltration Index*	*Non-monsoon Rainfall Recharge (mcm)*
Faridabad	283.86	656	580	76	0.25	5.39
Ballabhgarh	319.86	637	590	47	0.25	8.53
Hathin	234.70	531	470	61	0.25	11.41
Hodal	898.14	508	464	44	0.25	12.55
Palwal	375.29	595	563	32	0.25	11.37
Total	**1611.85**	**2927**	**2667**	**260**	–	**20.11**

Recharge from Surface Water Sources

A dense network of canals (lined and unlined), distributaries and minors dissects Faridabad district. These seepage losses from lined and unlined canals contribute to groundwater storage. The recharge or seepage factor for lined canals is taken as 2 cusecs/million sq. feet. Table 6.3 gives total seepage from canals during both monsoon and non- monsoon periods.

Recharge through Return Flow of Irrigation Water

Water used for irrigating the agricultural land during Rabi and Kharif season contributes to the groundwater storage. The norms given by HAU, Hisar are used for calculating the net recharge from surface water irrigation. The recharge through return flow of irrigation water has been taken as 35 per cent for Paddy in zone B, in which the study area falls. Table 6.4 depicts the data regarding monsoon, non-monsoon and annual recharge through surface water irrigation.

Table 6.3: Calculations of Seepage from Canals in Monsoon and Non-monsoon Period in Faridabad District

Name of the Block	*Seepage through Canals*							
	Unlined			*Lined*			*Total*	
	NM	*M*	*Total*	*NM*	*M*	*Total*	*NM*	*M*
Faridabad	6.69	3.56	10.25	9.64	4.35	13.99	16.33	7.91
Ballabhgarh	5.69	3.37	9.06	6.43	3.48	9.91	12.12	6.85
Hathin	1.99	1.11	3.10	2.35	0.94	3.29	4.34	2.05
Hodal	1.68	0.76	2.44	2.32	1.19	3.51	4.00	1.95
Palwal	5.12	2.07	7.19	4.70	2.74	7.44	9.84	4.81
Total	**21.17**	**10.87**	**32.04**	**25.44**	**12.70**	**38.14**	**46.63**	**23.51**

Table 6.4: Total Recharge through Surface Water Irrigation in Faridabad District

Name of the Block	*Return Seepage from Surface Water Irrigation*		
	Monsoon (mcm)	*Non-monsoon (mcm)*	*Annual (mcm)*
Faridabad	1.31	1.86	3.17
Ballabhgarh	2.34	3.00	5.34
Hathin	2.54	3.09	5.63
Hodal	5.39	4.73	10.12
Palwal	4.27	3.88	8.15
Total	**15.85**	**16.56**	**32.41**

Recharge through Tanks and Ponds

According to the recommended norms for calculating recharge from tanks and ponds, a seepage factor of 44 cm/year has been taken as the annual gross storage. Depending upon the agro-climatic conditions of the area, the losses should be taken into account. It is worth mentioning here that while calculating the gross recharge, potential recharge from the flood prone areas and shallow water table was also taken and it is given along with the recharge from lakes and ponds in Table 6.5.

Total Annual Groundwater Recharge

The following components have been used in calculating the total annual groundwater recharge of the study area.

Total annual groundwater recharge = Monsoon recharge + Non-monsoon Recharge + Potential recharge

Therefore, total groundwater recharge = Normalized monsoon recharge + non monsoon rainfall recharge + seepage from canals during non-monsoon period + return seepage from surface water irrigation during non-monsoon period + recharge from tanks and ponds + potential recharge

Table 6.5: Recharge from Tanks and Ponds along with Potential Recharge from Flood Prone Areas and Shallow Water Table in Faridabad District

Name of the Block	*Recharge from Tanks and Ponds (mcm)*	*Potential Recharge from Flood Prone Areas and Shallow Water Table (mcm)*
Faridabad	0.49	1.73
Ballabhgarh	0.69	9.69
Hathin	1.01	22.2
Hodal	0.36	7.96
Palwal	0.93	8.14
Total	**3.48**	**49.72**

Since the water table fluctuation in an aquifer corresponds to the rainfall of the year of observation therefore, the monsoon rainfall recharge has to be corrected to the long-term normal rainfall of the area as given by IMD.

Normalization Factor = Long term rainfall/Average rainfall of the period under consideration

The normalized monsoon rainfall recharge has been calculated using the following equation:

$$Nmr = Mr + Md - (Sm + Rm + RFm)\,Nf + Sm + Rm$$

where,

Nmr: Normalized monsoon recharge

Mr: Monsoon recharge

Md: Gross monsoon draft

Sm: Seepage from canal during monsoon period

Rm: Return flow during surface water irrigation during monsoon period

RFm: Return flow from groundwater irrigation during monsoon

Nf: Normalization factor.

The average annual groundwater draft along with monsoon and non-monsoon draft are given in Table 6.6. Monsoon draft is assumed to be 45 per cent of the annual draft and remaining 55 per cent, constitutes the non-monsoon draft.

Table 6.6: Calculations Showing Gross Monsoon and Non-monsoon Draft along with Normalized Monsoon Recharge (mcm)

Name of the Block	*Average Draft 1991 to 1993*	*Gross Monsoon Draft*	*Gross Non-monsoon Draft*	*Sm*	*Rm*	*RFm*	*Nf*	*Mr*	*Nmr*
Faridabad	105.97	47.69	58.28	7.91	1.31	14.31	0.881	33.3	59.94
Ballabhgarh	101.58	45.71	55.87	6.85	2.34	13.71	1.015	55.0	88.28
Hathin	40.51	18.23	22.28	2.05	2.54	5.47	1.260	26.6	48.42
Hodal	86.96	39.13	47.88	1.95	5.39	11.74	1.244	55.1	100.93
Palwal	102.69	46.21	56.48	4.81	4.27	13.86	1.242	49.3	99.38
Total	**437.70**	**196.97**	**240.74**	**23.57**	**15.85**	**59.09**	**–**	**219.0**	**396.95**

Table 6.7: Calculations for Annual Groundwater Recharge in Faridabad District (mcm)

Name of the Block	*Nmr + Nr + Sn + Rn + Rtp + Pr*	*Total Annual Recharge*
Faridabad	59.94 + 5.39 + 16.33 + 1.86 + 0.49 + 1.73	85.75
Ballabhgarh	88.28 + 3.76 + 12.12 + 3.00 + 0.69 + 9.69	117.54
Hathin	48.42 + 3.58 + 4.34 + 3.09 + 1.01 + 22.20	82.64
Hodal	100.93 + 4.38 + 4.00 + 4.73 + 0.36 + 7.96	122.36
Palwal	99.38 + 3.00 + 9.84 + 3.88 + 0.98 + 8.14	125.16
Total		**533.45**

The total annual recharge may be called the total groundwater resource. The value of the total annual recharge is the minimum for Hathin block (82.64 mcm) and Faridabad block (85.75 mcm) and maximum for Palwal block (125.16 mcm). These calculations are in agreement with the hydraulic flow direction.

As discussed earlier, 85 per cent of the total groundwater resource is reserved for irrigation purposes while the remaining 15 per cent is left for domestic and industrial uses, though in the entire state the requirement of domestic and industrial purposes is less than 7 per cent Table 6.8 shows utilization of groundwater resources in Faridabad district.

Table 6.8: Utilization of Groundwater Resources for Different Purposes in Faridabad District (mcm)

Name of the Block	*Total Groundwater Resources*	*Utilizable Resources for Agriculture*	*GW Resources for Domestic, industrial and Other Purposes*
Faridabad	85.75	72.89	12.86
Ballabhgarh	117.54	99.91	17.63
Hathin	82.64	70.24	12.40
Hodal	122.36	104.01	18.35
Palwal	125.16	106.39	18.77
Total	**533.45**	**453.43**	**80.02**

Groundwater Draft

The groundwater discharge in the study area is mainly due to the withdrawal for irrigation and domestic purposes through hand pumps, shallow and deep tube wells, dug wells with or without pump sets. The magnitude of withdrawal is the maximum in Rabi season and to a lesser extent during Kharif season. The groundwater losses may also occur as a result of (*i*) outflow to rivers (*ii*) Transpiration by plants and trees (*iii*) evaporation from water table. Evapo-transpiration from deep-rooted trees results in depletion of groundwater equivalent to supplementary water requirements of vegetation for its growth.

Unrecoverable Losses

In the study area, the other avenues of groundwater discharge are through natural discharge through canals, streams and by evapo-transpiration especially in the area with thick vegetation cover and shallow groundwater level. These losses contribute to about 10 per cent of gross annual recharge.

In deep water table areas, both evaporation and transpiration losses are negligible. Table 6.9 gives the details of theses losses for Faridabad district.

Table 6.9: Details of Unrecoverable Losses in Faridabad District

Name of the Block	*Annual Recharge*	*Unrecoverable Losses through Evaporation Evapo-transpiration and Effluent Losses*
Faridabad	84.02	8.40
Ballabhgarh	107.85	10.78
Hathin	60.44	6.04
Hodal	114.40	11.44
Palwal	117.00	11.70
Total	**483.73**	**48.37**

Groundwater Balance

The groundwater balance in an area is the difference between total groundwater recharge and the net annual draft. Table 6.10 shows the details of the net annual draft in the study area. Therefore, the equation employed in groundwater balance analysis is given below:

Groundwater balance = Utilizable resources – Net annual draft

= (85 per cent of the total annual recharge) – (70 per cent of the total annual draft)

Table 6.10: Net Annual Draft Available for Groundwater Development in Faridabad District

Name of the Block	*Annual Groundwater Draft*	*Unrecoverable Losses*	*Total Annual Groundwater Draft*	*Net Groundwater Draft*
Faridabad	105.97	8.40	114.37	80.06
Ballabhgarh	101.58	10.78	112.36	78.65
Hathin	40.51	6.04	46.55	32.59
Hodal	86.96	11.44	98.40	68.88
Palwal	102.69	11.70	114.39	80.07
Total	**437.70**	**48.37**	**486.07**	**340.25**

The results of groundwater balance studies in Faridabad district are summarized in Table 6.11.

Table 6.11: Groundwater Balance in Faridabad District

Name of the Block	*Utilizable Resources*	*Net Groundwater Draft*	*Groundwater Balance*
Faridabad	72.89	80.06	–7.17
Ballabhgarh	99.91	78.65	21.26
Hathin	70.24	32.59	37.66
Hodal	104.01	68.88	35.13
Palwal	106.39	80.07	26.32
Total	**453.43**	**340.25**	**113.18**

Categorization of the Blocks

The level of groundwater development is also taken as the rate of net annual draft to total utilizable resources for irrigation.

Level of development = Net annual draft/Utilizable resources for irrigation

The guidelines for level of evaluation of groundwater resources, appropriate to the level of the groundwater resource development, were adopted as contained in the recommendations of the Groundwater Estimation Committee (NABARD, 1986) and are given below:

1. If the projected net extraction for 5 years is less than 65 per cent of the total utilizable groundwater resource for irrigation, that area is considered to be safe and categorized as white.
2. If this value varies from 65 per cent to 85 per cent of the total utilizable groundwater resource for irrigation, then that area is considered to be semi critical and categorized as grey.
3. If this projected net extraction exceeds 85 per cent of the total utilizable groundwater resource for irrigation, then that area is considered to be critical and categorized as dark.

The categorization of the development blocks in Faridabad district has been shown in Table 6.12.

Table 6.12: Categorization of the Blocks Depending on the Level of Development

Name of the Block (1)	*Level of Development in 1993 (2)*	*Category (3)*	*Level of Development After 5 Years (1.016) × (2)*	*Category*
Faridabad	(80.06/72.89) × 100 = 109.80	Dark	118.91	Dark
Ballabhgarh	(78.65/99.91) × 100 = 78.72	Grey	85.25	Dark
Hathin	(32.56/70.24) × 100 = 46.39	White	50.24	White
Hodal	(68.88/104.01) × 100 = 66.22	Grey	71.71	Grey
Palwal	(80.07/106.39) × 100 = 75.26	Grey	81.50	Grey
Total	**(340.25/453.43) × 100 = 75.27**	**Grey**	**81.51**	**Grey**

Conclusion

The main source of the groundwater recharge in the study area is rainfall and contributes almost more than half of the recharge. The other sources of recharge include seepage from canals, surface water bodies, irrigation return flow etc. The groundwater draft is mainly taking place as a result of withdrawal of groundwater for irrigation and domestic purposes through hand pumps, tube wells and dug wells. The unrecoverable losses of groundwater are through evaporation, evapo-transpiration and natural discharge through canals and streams. The estimation of the groundwater potential revealed that out of five blocks in the study area one falls under critical category (Faridabad Block) and one under safe category (Hathin) and the remaining three namely, Ballabhgarh, Hodal and Palwal are in the semi critical category.

Keeping in view the population growth and ever-increasing demands from agriculture, domestic and industrial sector, Projections for the year 1998 show that except one block (Hathin) all four blocks will fall in the grey to dark category.

The need of the hour demands that immediate steps should be taken to reduce groundwater mining. Instead of adopting the methods of flood irrigation everywhere, sprinkler irrigation should be adopted in over drafted areas.

References

Basu, P.K., 1989. Classification of major Indian sedimentary basins. *Bull. O.N.G.C.*, 24(2): 55–60.

Bhumla, D.R. and Abrol, I.P., 1972. Is your water suitable for irrigation? *Indian Farming*, 22: 15–17.

Dogra, R., 1996. Hydrogeological and hydrogeochemical studies in Karnal and Panipat districts of Haryana state, India, with special reference to groundwater pollution. *Ph.D Thesis*, Panjab University, Chandigarh, 177 p.

GWEC (Groundwater Estimation Committee), 1986. *Groundwater Estimation Methodology*. Ministry of Irrigation. Government of India, New Delhi, 53 p.

NABARD (National Bank for Agriculture and Rural Development), 1986. *Norms of Groundwater Assessment*. Based on the report of the groundwater estimation committee, Mumbai, National Bank for Agriculture and Rural Development, pp. 1–22.

Sharma, M., 1996. Hydrogeological and hydrogeochemical studies in Faridabad district and adjoining areas, Haryana state, India, with special reference to industrial pollution of water. *Ph.D Thesis*, Panjab University, Chandigarh, 166 p.

Walton, W.C., 1970. *Groundwater Resource Evaluation*. McGraw Hill, Kogakusha Ltd., Japan, 664 p.

Chapter 7

Studies on the Effect of Bavistin (Carbendazim) on Seed Germination and Growth of Some Vegetable Crops

P. Sundaramoorthy, K. Sankar Ganesh, L. Baskaran, Al.A. Chidambaram and S. Natarajan

Environmental Biology Laboratory, Department of Botany, Annamalai University, Annamalainagar – 608 002, Tamil Nadu, India

ABSTRACT

Seed treatment is one of the best way to prevent any seed born diseases. Bavistin is used in seed dressing purposes for vegetable crops to avoid certain seed borne pathogens. If the concentration exceeds above the recommended level, it will affect the germination and the growth of crops. So, an attempt has been made to examine the effect of bavistin on some vegetable crops such as tomato (*Lycopersicum esculentum* L.), brinjal (*Solanum melongena* L.) and chilli (*Capsicum annum*). In the present study, the bavistin are used in three doses *i.e.*, recommended level, below recommended level and above recommended level. The seeds soaked in water is treated as control. An inhibitory effect of bavistin on germination was observed on 7th day and other parameters were observed on 30th day of its growth. There was a drastic change in root length, shoot length, total leaf area, number of leaves, fresh weight and dry weight. Vigour index and tolerance index were also observed in different concentrations of bavistin. Brinjal showed higher sensitivity than the other crops tested.

Keywords: *Bavistin, Vegetable crops, Germination, Growth and Phytotoxicity.*

Introduction

Now-a-days, the increasing population demands more food production to solve serious food scarcity problems. A considerable amount of crop losses were caused by insects and pathogens. This can be avoided by using fungicides and pesticides. Pesticides are biologically active chemicals used for killing the pests. They safeguard agricultural production by killing the insects and controlling plant diseases. Most of the pesticides are synthetic organic compounds. They kill the pathogens as well as beneficial microorganisms in the soil. Seed treatment is the cheapest technology for quality seed production and it also protects the seeds against diseases. Among all the methods of application, seed treatment with fungicide is reported to be one of the most promising and economic methods of protecting the crops (Pandurangamurthy and Leelavathy, 2002). Seed treatment with fungicide is essential because of large number of diseases caused by fungi are seed borne. When those seed germinates, the fungi also become active and cause seedling mortality. Bavistin is one of the commonly used fungicide for vegetable crops by farmers. Carbendazim, commonly termed as Bavistin, is basically a seed fungicide and also used for soil treatment. Carbendazim is one of the most effective fungicide against many seed borne fungi like *Sclerotium rolfsil, Rhizoctonia bactaticola, Cercospora* and *Aspergillus.* Seeds treated with carbendazim at 2 g per kg of seed recorded higher germination than untreated seeds (Kamble and Sabale, 1999). At the same time, it will be toxic for the seeds at elevated level (Kamble and Sabale (1999). So, an attempt has been made to explore the effect of different doses of bavistin on germination and growth behaviour of tomato, brinjal and chilli.

Materials and Methods

The seeds of tomato, (*Lycopersicum esculentum* L.) brinjal (*Solanum melongena* L.) and chilli (*Capsicum annum* L.) were procured from private commercial agrocentres, Mayiladuthurai, Tamil Nadu. Bavistin was obtained from an authorized Agro dealer in Mayiladuthurai. The seeds were soaked with recommended dosage (2 g/kg of seeds) for 6 hours. In order to observe the variation, the seeds were also treated with above recommended dosage (25 per cent more) and below recommended dosage (25 per cent less). The water soaked seeds were maintained as control.

The chemical slurry was prepared and seeds were mixed thoroughly and kept for 12 hours. The seeds were sown in the pots containing three kilograms of soil. Germination of seeds was observed on 7th days and germination percentage was calculated. The various morphological parameters such as root length, shoot length, fresh weight, dry weight, number of leaves and total leaf area were measured on 30 DAS. The vigour index and tolerance index were also calculated by using the formula given by Abdul Baki and Anderson (1973) and Turner and Marshal (1972) respectively.

Results and Discussion

The deleterious and adverse effect of the different doses of bavistin on various crops on germination percentage, root length and their dry weight was presented in Table 7.1.

In tomato, the lowest germination percentage (70 per cent), root length (5.92 cm/seedling), shoot length (10.54 cm/seedling), fresh weight (1.452 g/seedling), dry weight (0.620 g/seedling), number of leaves (26.1/plant) and total leaf area (36.8 cm^2/plant) were observed above the recommended level. Similarly, the higher germination percentage (94 per cent), root length (12.80 cm/seedling), shoot length (20.64 cm/seedling), fresh weight (4.780 g/seedling), dry weight (0.989 g/seedling), number of leaves (74.2/plant) and leaf area (73.0 cm^2/plant) were observed at the recommended level (Table 7.1).

Table 7.1: Effect of Bavistin on Morphological Parameters of Tomato (*Lycopersicum esculentum* L.) Plant (30 days)

Concentrations of Bavistin	Germination Percentage	Root Length (cm/ seedling)	Shoot Length (cm/ seedling)	Fresh Weight (g/ seedling)	Dry Weight (g/ seedling)	Number of Leaves/ Plant	Leaf Area (cm²/plant)	Tolerance Index	Vigour Index
Control	90 ±4.5	6.74 ±0.33	19.78 ±0.98	3.786 ±0.18	0.756 ±0.03	45.5 ±2.27	48.2 ±2.41	–	2386.8 119.34
BRL (1.5g/kg)	92 ±4.6	12.24 ±0.61	20.26 ±1.01	3.936 ±0.19	0.786 ±0.03	62.4 ±3.12	65.2 ±3.26	1.816 ±0.09	2990.0 ±149.5
RL (2 g/kg)	94 ±4.7	12.86 ±0.64	20.64 ±1.03	4.780 ±0.23	0.980 ±0.04	74.2 ±3.71	73.0 ±3.65	1.908 ±0.09	3149.0 ±157.4
ARL (2.5 g/kg)	70 ±3.5	5.92 ±0.29	10.54 ±0.52	1.452 ±0.07	0.620 ±0.03	26.1 ±1.30	36.8 ±1.82	0.878 ±0.04	1152.2 ±57.61

RL: Recommended level; BRL: Below recommended level; ARL: Above recommended level.

±: Standard deviation.

In brinjal, there was a reduction in germination percentage (60 per cent), root length (3.8 cm/seedling), shoot length (6.66 cm/seedling), fresh weight (1.92 g/seedling), dry weight (0.720 g/seedling), number of leaves (8.8/plant) and leaf area (96.2 cm^2/plant) at above the recommended level. Similarly, higher germination percentage (92), root length (8.2 cm/seedling), shoot length (10.36 cm/seedling), fresh weight (3.66 g/seedling), dry weight (1.606 g/seedling), number of leaves (19.2/plant) and leaf area (148.8 cm^2/plant) were observed from recommended level (Table 7.2).

Table 7.2: Effect of Bavistin on Morphological Parameters of Brinjal (*Solanum melongena* L.) Plant (30 days)

Concentrations of Bavistin	Germination Percentage	Root Length (cm/ seedling)	Shoot Length (cm/ seedling)	Fresh Weight (g/ seedling)	Dry Weight (g/ seedling)	Number of Leaves/ Plant	Leaf Area (cm²/plant)	Tolerance Index	Vigour Index
Control	80 ±4.0	4.0 ±0.20	7.5 ±0.37	2.13 ±0.10	0.752 ±0.03	13.5 ±0.67	118.5 ±5.92	–	920.0 ±46.00
BRL (1.5 g/kg)	90 ±4.5	5.2 ±0.26	9.38 ±0.46	2.49 ±0.12	0.968 ±0.04	16.4 ±0.82	132.6 ±6.63	1.816 ±0.09	1312.2 ±65.61
RL (2 g/kg)	92 ±4.6	8.2 ±0.4l	10.36 ±0.51	3.66 ±0.18	1.606 ±0.08	19.2 ±0.96	148.8 ±7.44	1.908 ±0.09	1707.5 ±85.37
ARL (2.5 g/kg)	60 ±3.0	3.8 ±0.19	6.6 ±0.33	1.92 ±0.09	0.720 ±0.03	8.8 ±0.44	96.2 ±4.81	0.878 ±0.04	624.0 ±31.2

RL: Recommended level; BRL: Below recommended level; ARL: Above recommended level.

±: Standard deviation.

In case of chilli, the highest germination percentage (92), root length (14.50 cm/seedling), shoot length (21.86 cm/seedling), fresh weight (5.880 g/seedling), dry weight (1.816 g/seedling), number of leaves (42.2/plant) were observed and leaf area (96.2 cm^2/plant) was found to increase at the recommended level when compared to control (Table 7.3).

Table 7.3: Effect of Bavistin on Morphological Parameters of Chilli (*Capsicum annum* L.) Plant (30 days)

Concentrations of Bavistin	*Germination Percentage*	*Root Length (cm/ seedling)*	*Shoot Length (cm/ seedling)*	*Fresh Weight (g/ seedling)*	*Dry Weight (g/ seedling)*	*Number of Leaves/ Plant*	*Leaf Area (cm²/plant)*	*Tolerance Index*	*Vigour Index*
Control	92 ±4.6	7.21 ±0.36	20.51 ±1.02	4.986 ±0.24	0.648 ±0.03	32.5 ±1.62	62.2 ±3.11	–	2550.2 ±127.50
BRL (1.5 g/kg)	96 ±4.8	13.52 ±0.67	21.00 ±1.05	5.168 ±0.25	0.821 ±0.04	38.6 ±1.93	78.5 ±3.92	1.875 ±0.09	3313.9 ±165.60
RL (2 g/kg)	98 ±4.9	14.50 ±0.72	21.86 ±1.09	5.880 ±0.29	1.816 ±0.09	42.2 ±2.11	96.2 ±4.81	2.011 ±0.100	3563.2 ±178.16
ARL (2.5 g/kg)	76 ±3.8	6.28 ±0.60	12.18 ±0.60	2.000 ±0.10	0.628 ±0.03	30.0 ±1.5	48.2 ±2.41	0.871 ±0.04	1402.9 ±70.14

RL: Recommended level; BRL: Below recommended level; ARL: Above recommended level.

±: Standard deviation.

Bavistin promoted the germination and growth of tomato, brinjal and chilli in the recommended level when compared with the control. Similar trend was observed by Utpalnath and Jayapragasam (1993) on rice. Increasing the concentrations of Furadon (Fungicide) from 50 to 500 ppm had more beneficial over the control. The same findings were also noted by using other insecticide, fungicide and pesticide with other crops, *i.e.*, Mote and Gujar (1989) and Mathur *et al.* (1989), on insecticides, Pandurangamurthy and Leelavathi (2002) on Fungicide, Gupta *et al.* (2004a) on pesticide. The increase in pesticide concentrations (above recommended level) had an adverse effect on germination and growth of vegetable crops. The same findings were observed earlier by Reddy and Vidyavathi (1984), Gamble and Sabale (1999) and Gupta *et al.* (2004a and b). The decrease in the rate of germination at higher concentration is attributed to the inhibitory action of fungicide on the metabolic activities (Pandurangamurthy and Leelavathi, 2002).

The fresh and dry weight of tomato, brinjal and chilli was higher in recommended level when compared with control. At the same time, the dry weight decreased in above the recommended level. These results are strongly supported by Pahwa and Prakash (1992). They reported that dry weight of leaves, stem and root per plant were significantly reduced at higher concentration of herbicides. Similar findings were also reported by Kundu and Trimohan (1989), Nova *et al.* (1996), Pandurangamurthy and Leelavathi (2002) and Gupta *et al.* (2004b). The number of leaves and leaf area were higher in recommended level and it decreased at above recommended level. The number of leaves and total leaf area are increased in recommended level. It may be due to the drastic seedling growth at the recommended level of bavistin.

Conclusion

It is concluded that the application of recommended dosage of Bavistin to vegetable seeds have showed a better vegetative growth of crops. If the concentration exceeds the level it will affect the growth and behaviour of the vegetable crops. So the usage of fungicides as prescribed level is good for plant growth and yield.

References

Abdul Baki, A.A. and Anderson J.D., 1973. Vigour determination of soybean seed by multiple criteria. *Crop Sci.*, 3: 630–633.

Gupta, P., Dwivedi, S.K., Sharma, C., Shrivastava, A. and Verma, S., 2004a. Microbiological studies on different doses of pesticides in chickpea, (*Cicer arietinum* L.)–*Rhizobium* symbiosis. *Plant Archives*, 4(2): 413–417.

Gupta, P., Dwivedi, S.K., Jha, S.K. Kumar, S., Malaiya, S. and Sharma, C., 2004b. Effect of different doses of various insecticides and herbicides on Chickpea–*Rhizobium* symbiosis under sterilized condition. *Plant Archives*, 4(2): 487–490.

Kamble, A.B. and Sabale, A.B., 1999. Influence of Bavistin and monocrotophos on seed germination and seedling growth of *Trigonella foenumgraecum* (L.). *Poll. Res.*, 18(1): 61–65.

Kundu, G.G. and Trimohan, 1989. Effect of rhizobium in association with granular insecticides on nodulation and yield in soybean. *Current Science*, 58(2): 1340–1343.

Mathur, S.N., Singh, V.K., Mathur, M. and Srivastava, R.C., 1989. Studies with phorate, an organophosphate insecticide on some enzymes on nitrogen metabolism, in *Vigna mungo* L. Hepper. *Biol. Plant*, 30: 61.

Mote, U.N. and Gujar, S.M., 1989. Influence of new insecticides as seed dressers on germination and initial plant growth characters of *Sorghum hybrid. Pestiology*, 113: 45–46.

Nova, M.C.S.S., Cruz, S.P., Pcreiria, J.C.V.N.A., Nagai, V. and Ambrosio, L.A. 1996. Effect of herbicides on biomass, symbiotic fixation and yield of soybean. *Planta Darinta*, 14(1): 65–81.

Pahwa, S.K. and Prakash, J., 1992. Effect of some herbicides on the growth nodulation and nitrogen fixation in chickpea (*Cicer arietinum* L.). *Ind. J. Plant Physiol.*, 35(3): 207–212.

Pandurangamurthy, G. and Leelavathi, S., 2002. Effect of Gaucho and apron on seed germination, seedling growth and chlorophyll content of two cultivar varieties of sunflower (*Helianthus annuus* L.). *Poll. Res.*, 21(6): 319–329.

Reddy, J.M.K. and Vidyavathi, P. 1984. Effect of fungicide on the growth and seedling metabolism of *Dolichos biflorus. Geobios*, 10: 174–178.

Turner, L.G. and Marshal, C., 1972. Accumulation of zinc by subcellular fraction of root of *Agrostis tennis* sibth in relation of zinc, tolerance. *New Phytol.*, 71: 671–676.

Utpalnath and Jayapragasam, M., 1993. Effect of pesticides on germination of rice IR–50. *J. Ecobiol.*, 5(4): 285–288.

Chapter 8

Seasonal Variations in Ambient Air Quality of Jalgaon Urban Centre

*Nilesh D. Wagh and S.T. Ingle**

School of Environmental Sciences, North Maharashtra University, Jalgaon – 425 001

ABSTRACT

An experimental investigation on urban air atmosphere of Jalgaon city was carried out with special reference to vehicular pollution. The sampling was done from April 2003 to May 2005 at five different stations within the city.

Sulphur dioxide (SO_2), oxides of nitrogen (NOx), Suspended Particulate Matter (SPM) and respirable suspended particulate matter (RSPM) in ambient air was measured. The Air Quality Index (AQI) was calculated and it was observed that at Ajanta sampling stations, the SPM and RSPM air quality index was worst, followed by Icchadevi and Prabhat the values are above the limit. SO_2 and NOx values are also very high, but in summer season the values are coming under limits, this may be due to strong wind current which flushes maximum air pollutant away. The Ganesh colony sampling station is the control area where all the values are within the limits. The emission intensity of line sources shows that the National Highway No 6 is the major source of air pollutants followed by Railway Station to Mahabal road in the city. Ganesh colony to Ajanta road is the minimum line source emission of air pollutants among the major roads in the city.

Proper regular road maintenance, large width roads and compulsory use of unleaded petrol are some of the basic control measures to minimize the vehicular pollution in the Jalgaon city.

Keywords: *SO_2, NOx, SPM, RSPM, Air Quality Index (AQI) and Line source emission (Ep).*

Corresponding Author: E-mail: st_ingle@indiatimes.com; Phone: +91-0257-2258428 Ext. 428; Fax: +91-0257-2258403

Introduction

A larger and more diverse city area is a sign of India's increasingly dynamic economy. Swelling urban population and increased concentration of traffic, domestic activities and refuse burning have resulted in increased air pollution in the city area. Emission from the traffic, domestic activities and refuse burning are threatening the health of the city dwellers, imposing not just a direct economic cost by impacting human health but also threatening long-term productivity. The dispersion and air pollutants emitted by vehicle is one of the most investigated topics in urban meteorology (Theurer *et al.*, 1996 and Clifford *et al.*, 1997). Air pollution has become a serious health hazard to the inhabitants of many mega cities (Raga & Le Moyne, 1999) and its fundamental impact on the environment affect cities of all sizes.

In urban areas mobile or vehicular pollution is predominant and significantly contributes to air quality problems. Road traffic produce volatile organic compounds suspended particulate matter (SPM), sulphur dioxide (SO_2), oxides of nitrogen (NOx), CO and particles, which makes adverse health effects on the exposed population (Shrivastava and Kumar, 2002). The particles emitted from the vehicular exhaust of more than 10-micron size are held in upper respiratory tract and particles less than 10-micron size (PM_{10}) accumulates in the lung and produces respiratory abnormalities (Price *et al.*, 2003). Hence, there parameters are of great concern in air pollution studies.

In India urbanization process is restricted to selected cities. These cities attract migration of population from surrounding rural areas and sometimes even from remote places. Jalgaon is one of the fastest developing cities in North Maharashtra region in India, including all type of population groups (Wagh *et al.*, 2003). Jalgaon City is the trade and commercial centre of North Maharashtra Region, India. City includes all types of population groups. The population of Jalgaon City had grown up by 23 per cent during 1981–91 and by 19 per cent during 1991–2001. Current population of the city is standing at 4 lakhs. With the population, vehicular number is also increasing in the city. The data shows that nearly 400 new vehicles are registered every day at Jalgaon Road Transport Office.

Vehicle population data of Jalgaon District shows that there is a continuous increase of vehicles since 1998 to 2005. Higher incomes, mobility, rapid expansion of the city in the last five years have increased the demand of motorized transport, resulting in the disproportional high concentration of vehicles in the urban center. Irrational distance between homes and places of work, greater incentives for private transport and inadequate and poor quality public transport has further aggravated the problem in the city.

Urban areas have in general been experiencing a higher concentration of air pollution due to extensive vehicular traffic movements and other activities concentrated in comparatively smaller areas. Vehicular traffic is the major source in maximum urban areas (Jain and Saxena, 2002). The Government of India under the supervision of regulatory agencies such as MoEF, CPCB etc. laid down emission norms for petrol and diesel vehicles. The first Indian emission regulations were idle emission limits which became effective in 1989. These idle emission regulations were soon replaced by mass emission limits for both gasoline (1991) and diesel (1992) vehicles, which were gradually tightened during the 1990's, since the year 2000, India started adopting European emission and fuel regulations for four wheeled light duty and for heavy duty vehicles.

The Government of India on the basis of extensive study has prescribed the National Ambient Air Quality Standards (NAAQS) for industrial, commercial and residential areas.

Table 8.1: Indian Emission Standards

For Two Wheelers				gm/km
Sl.No.	*Year*	*Carbon Monoxide*	*HC*	*HC +Nox*
1.	1991	12–30	8–12	–
2.	1996	4.50	–	3.60
3.	**2000**	**2.00**	–	**2.00**
4.	2005 (BS–II)	1.50	–	1.50

For Three Wheelers				**gm/km**
Sl.No.	*Year*	*Carbon Monoxide*	*HC*	*HC + Nox*
1.	1991	12–30	8–1	–
2.	1996	6.75	–	5.40
3.	**2000**	**4.00**	–	**2.00**
4.	2005 (BS–II)	2.25	–	2.00

Cars					
Sl.No.	*Year*	*Carbon Monoxide*	*gm/km*	*NOx*	*PM*
1.	1991	14.30–27.10	2.00–2.00	–	–
2.	1996	8.68–12.40	–	–	3.00–4.36
3.	1998*	4.34–6.20	–	–	1.50–2.18
4.	**2000**	**2.72–6.90**	–	–	**0.97–1.70**
5.	BS–II	2.20	–	–	0.50
6.	BS–III	2.30	0.20	0.15	–

Diesel Vehicles		***Heavy Duty***				*gm/km*
Sl.No.	*Year*	*Carbon Monoxide*	*H.C.*	*NOx*	*HC + NOx*	*PM*
1.	1991	17.30–32.60	2.70	–	3.70	–
2.	1996	5.00–9.00	–	–	2.00–4.00	–
3.	**2000**	**2.72–6.90**	–	–	**0.97–1.70**	**0.14–0.25**
4.	BS–II	1.00–1.50	–	–	0.70–1.20	0.08–0.17
5.	BS–III	0.64–0.95	–	0.50–0.78	0.56–0.86	0.05–0.10

* For catalytic converted fitted vehicles. Values in bold used for the estimation of line source intensity (Ep).

Materials and Methodology

Study Area

Jalgaon is one of the fastest developing cities in the North Maharashtra region. It is also one of the productive agro markets in the Maharashtra State. Fruit sale market is one of the international fruit export centre located near the city. The MIDC area is also well equipped with some well known agro industries near the city. So the major roads going through the city are continuously flowing. Among the various roads in the city National Highway no. 6 (NH-6) has the maximum traffic density and related activities along the roadside. From the point of view of air pollution study total five spots are selected for the monitoring of air in the city.

Monitoring Stations

Five monitoring stations were selected for air quality monitoring throughout two year. These stations are selected keeping in view the general characteristics of the areas *i.e.*, location, traffic density and activities on that station.

Table 8.2: Characterization of Sampling Sites (Indian Standards, 1969)

Sl.No.	*Sampling Stations*	*Nature of the Sampling Station*
1.	Sahstri Tower	Commercial
2.	Ajanta	Industrial and Commercial
3.	Icchadevi	Residential and Commercial
4.	Prabhat	Residential and Commercial
5.	Ganesh Colony	Residential

Assessment of Parameters

Monitoring of air quality on the locations is done throughout year *i.e.* from April 03 to May 05. Sampling period is divided in three seasons that is Monsoon, Winter and Summer. Air quality parameters SPM, RSPM, SO_2, Nøx are monitored by using High Volume Sampler (Envirotech Instrument APM 460) following standard procedures laid down by the CPCB (IS, 1969 and CPCB, 1996).

Air Quality Index

The air quality index is calculated by converting measured pollutant concentrations in to index values. To generate the index values, pollutant concentrations are compared with limit values laid down by National Ambient Air Quality Standards (NAAQS) for residential area.

Table 8.3: National Ambient Air Quality Standards

Sl.No.	*Pollutant*	*Sampling Time*	*Concentration in Ambient Air µg/m³*		
			Industrial	*Residential*	*Sensitive*
1.	SO_2	Annual*	80	60	15
2.		24 hr**	**120**	**80**	**30**
3.	Nox	Annual*	80	60	15
4.		24 hr**	**120**	**80**	**30**
5.	RSPM	Annual*	120	60	50
6.		24 hr**	**150**	**100**	**75**
7.	SPM	Annual*	360	140	70
8.		24 hr**	**500**	**200**	**100**

*: Annual arithmetic mean of all measurements in a year.

**: 24 hr/18 hr. values shall be met 98 per cent of the time in a year. 2 per cent of the time, it may be exceed but not on two consecutive days. Values in bold form are used for the estimation of AQI.

The concentration of the pollutant is measured by air quality monitoring equipment at a monitoring station. This pollutant concentration is then converted to all index values using the equation below:

$$\text{Index Value} = \frac{\text{Pollutant Concentration}}{\text{NAAQ Standard for that pollutant}} \times 100$$

The index value is segregated as follows:

Index Value	*Air Quality*
0–33	Very good
34–66	Good
67–99	Fair
100–149	Poor
> 150	Very poor

Emission Intensity of Line Source (Ep) (Zhongan and Shengan, 2002)

Pollutant emission levels from in-service vehicles vary depending on vehicle characteristics, operating conditions, level of maintenance, fuel quality and ambient conditions. The emission factor is defined as the estimated average emission rate of the given pollutant for a given class of vehicles. Estimates of vehicle emissions are obtained by multiplying an estimate of the distance traveled by the given class of vehicles by an appropriate factor.

The intensity of the line source (road) can be calculated as follows:

$$Ep = \Sigma L \times Ni \times Fpi$$

where,

L: Length of the road researched (Km)
i: type of vehicle
Ni: Traffic flow in Veh./Hr.
Fpi: Emission factor for vehicle type
Ep: Emission intensity of a line segment (gm/hr/km)
p: Type of pollutant.

To study the line source pollutant emission intensity in the Jalgaon City, three major roads are selected, National Highway No. 6, Ganesh colony to Ajanta and Railway Station to Mahabal. These roads are heavy traffic roads carry nearly 75 per cent of the city traffic and cover all the sampling stations in the city. The traffic density was monitored during the study duration and segregated the traffic flow in three sessions that is morning, afternoon and evening. The collected data then used to estimate the line source intensity of that road.

Results and Discussion

Automobiles are mobile polluters and petrol vehicles are the worst. The highest emission rates occur during motor idling, deceleration and during slow speed. Road intersections, especially those that are traffic light controlled and sharp turn in cities slow down the traffic and enhance the pollution emission rates. Nitrogen oxides (NOx), sulphur dioxide (SO_2), Respirable Suspended Particulate Matter

(RSPM) and Suspended Particulate Matters (SPM) are the some general pollutants from automobiles all together make the urban environment unpleasant.

Air pollution is consistently increasing over the past two and half decades. On one hand the population of Jalgaon is growing year after year and on the other hand the vehicular population is also increasing. This is due to the increasing fuel consumption and vehicular use is at a faster rate in the city with growing population.

The air pollution monitoring (Tables 8.4 and 8.5) in the two consecutive years shows that concentration of Suspended Particulate Matter (SPM) and Respirable Suspended Particulate Matter (RSPM) was two to four times greater than the prescribed standard. At Ajanta sampling point the situation is worst; the traffic density monitoring shows that heavy flow of vehicular traffic at this location. The oxides of sulfur and nitrogen were also high and above the standard limit. Decrease in the concentration of oxides of nitrogen and sulfur was observed in the summer season. This is due to higher dispersion due to heavy wind currents observed as during this period. Icchadevi is the second sampling spot of highest air pollution; here also the SPM and RSPM concentration are high. It is observed that the concentration of the suspended particulate matter at this spot was very high due to very large patch of vacant land along both sides of the road. The strong wind current carries the dust for longer distance. Prabhat and Shastri tower were having the moderate air quality during monsoon and summer season. Prabhat is the residential and commercial area, where in winter season the destructed air quality due to cold condition and very low wind currents was observed. Sahstri tower is purely commercial area; it is also the centre place of the city. Very high two and three wheeler traffic is observed here during the study duration. The air quality in this area is within the limits due to less traffic congestion and area is well constructed with good space for ventilation along the road side. Ganesh colony area is purely residential and very low pollution levels was observed. The traffic flow is also low as compared to the rest of the major roads in the city. Rarely heavy traffic was observed at this location. This road is wide and at a few points only the traffic congestions are observed.

Tables 8.6 and 8.7 shows the air quality index of sampling locations in the Jalgaon city. Very high AQI was recorded at Ajanta sampling point; this is due to very high concentration of SO_2, Nox, RSPM and SPM. Icchadevi is the second highest AQI value in the city area followed by Prabhat area. Moderate Air Quality Index was recorded at Shastri tower. Ganesh colony is the controlled area in the city and air quality index shows good air quality during the study period at this location.

Table 8.8 shows traffic densities at air monitoring locations. The traffic densities are recorded in vehicles/hour and vehicles/day. It was observed that at all the sampling locations the heavy traffic flow was observed during morning and evening hours. Among all the sampling locations very high traffic of heavy duty vehicles are observed at Ajanta point and very less heavy duty vehicle traffic flow was observed at Ganesh colony area.

Tables 8.10 and 8.11 shows emission intensity of line source for different sessions and in a day. It was observed that at morning and evening sessions the emission intensity of air pollutants is very high on National Highway and Railway Station to Mahabal road. Ganesh colony to Ajanta road was having very low emission intensity of air pollutants. The National Highway alone emits 352.14 Kg/day of Hydrocarbon + Oxides of Nitrogen (that is 278.62 tons per year of all sources) and 51.786 Kg/day of Particulate Matter (that is 18.90 tons per year) through heavy duty vehicles moving along the road. 4 wheelers cars and 2 + 3 wheelers emit 90.82 Kg/day and 320.4 Kg/day of H.C. + NOx in to the air atmosphere. Very low emission of air pollutants was of Ganesh colony to Ajanta road.

Table 8.4: Seasonal Variations in Air Quality During April 2003 to May 2004 at Different Sampling Stations

Season		Sampling Locations																			
		Shastri Tower				Ajanta				Icchadevi				Ganesh Colony				Prabaht			
		SO_2	NO_x	RSPM	SPM	SO_2	NO_x	RSPM	SPM	SO_2	NO_x	RSPM	SPM	SO_2	NO_x	RSPM	SPM	SO_2	NO_x	RSPM	SPM
Monsoon	June	23	25	81	109	109	91	221	856	98	91	212	751	13	09	79	103	49	46	199	431
2003	July	19	18	70	89	107	90	245	700	101	89	236	801	18	11	82	113	54	51	200	428
	Aug	12	16	79	88	119	108	280	880	105	109	221	790	12	10	91	119	55	57	210	419
	Sept	20	14	64	98	98	101	276	652	93	92	200	777	17	12	90	109	53	48	202	425
Winter	Oct	19	26	80	101	121	110	200	751	120	103	219	856	13	21	98	117	113	96	230	567
2003–04	Nov	22	30	66	103	130	91	207	801	107	108	236	882	10	17	89	122	108	90	237	629
	Dec	24	28	74	115	139	121	213	886	114	96	200	879	11	23	83	113	110	97	242	645
	Jan	20	28	70	123	114	125	198	820	98	110	229	891	13	20	102	137	126	102	245	610
Summer	Feb	21	20	73	99	109	70	290	817	54	81	245	837	19	09	109	192	52	51	249	555
2004	March	12	19	88	105	71	68	300	798	69	89	269	875	12	11	113	181	63	56	265	590
	April	16	12	103	166	78	67	302	819	63	79	251	856	11	10	117	180	57	53	249	623
	May	10	13	127	211	70	74	312	809	59	80	240	861	12	08	129	187	60	63	260	620

Table 8.5: Seasonal Variations in Air Quality During June 2004 to May 2005 at Different Sampling Stations

Season		Sampling Locations																			
		Shastri Tower				Ajanta				Icchadevi				Ganesh Colony				Prabaht			
		SO_2	NO_x	RSPM	SPM	SO_2	NO_x	RSPM	SPM	SO_2	NO_x	RSPM	SPM	SO_2	NO_x	RSPM	SPM	SO_2	NO_x	RSPM	SPM
Monsoon	June	18	21	92	111	78	107	201	703	77	70	211	336	10	09	77	103	79	65	200	569
2004	July	10	23	88	107	89	96	197	690	80	82	197	390	09	11	89	116	63	59	217	545
	Aug	12	20	79	98	80	103	222	693	88	88	201	451	13	08	70	135	69	71	221	512
	Sept	17	18	90	121	83	100	210	657	90	74	213	400	08	03	81	126	60	79	212	503
Winter	Oct	12	20	101	156	101	112	200	617	98	103	227	529	12	08	88	112	63	82	215	511
2004–05	Nov	19	28	98	137	113	110	210	680	93	98	235	570	18	11	72	106	78	88	231	570
	Dec	17	21	107	120	109	107	207	622	109	113	233	621	21	13	91	119	107	91	217	600
	Jan	21	27	100	131	111	99	219	657	100	110	201	603	19	09	89	123	113	90	222	589
Summer	Feb	20	19	96	121	67	59	281	799	64	84	279	706	11	07	79	155	60	45	252	622
2005	March	17	20	101	137	78	69	270	820	69	78	298	753	13	10	81	149	63	53	236	669
	April	18	12	112	129	83	73	303	837	78	80	280	790	10	12	98	171	56	49	261	781
	May	15	19	136	142	92	81	319	845	70	70	282	721	12	10	103	140	49	60	269	769

Table 8.6: Seasonal Variations in Air Quality Index During April 2003 to May 2004 at Different Sampling Stations

Season		Sampling Locations																			
		Shastri Tower				Ajanta				Icchadevi				Ganesh Colony				Prabaht			
		SO_2	NO_x	RSPM	SPM	SO_2	NO_x	RSPM	SPM	SO_2	NO_x	RSPM	SPM	SO_2	NO_x	RSPM	SPM	SO_2	NO_x	RSPM	SPM
Monsoon	June	29	31	81	55	136	113	221	428	122	113	212	375	16	11	79	51	61	57	199	215
2003	July	24	23	70	44	133	112	245	350	126	111	236	400	22	13	82	56	67	63	200	214
	Aug	15	20	79	44	148	135	280	440	131	136	221	395	15	12	91	59	68	71	210	209
	Sept	25	18	64	49	122	126	276	326	116	115	200	388	21	15	90	54	66	60	202	212
Winter	Oct	24	33	80	50	151	137	200	375	150	128	219	428	16	26	98	58	141	120	230	283
2003–04	Nov	28	38	66	51	162	113	207	400	133	135	236	439	12	21	89	61	135	112	237	314
	Dec	30	35	74	57	173	151	213	443	142	120	200	445	13	28	83	56	137	121	242	322
	Jan	25	35	70	61	142	156	198	410	122	137	229	418	16	25	102	68	157	127	245	305
Summer	Feb	26	25	73	49	135	87	290	408	67	101	245	437	23	11	109	96	65	63	249	277
2004	March	15	24	88	52	88	85	300	349	86	111	269	428	15	13	113	90	78	70	265	295
	April	20	15	103	86	97	83	302	409	78	98	251	430	13	12	117	90	71	66	249	311
	May	13	16	127	105	87	92	312	404	73	100	240	432	15	10	129	93	75	78	260	310

Table 8.7: Seasonal Variations in Air Quality Index During June 2004 to May 2005 at Different Sampling Stations

Season		Sampling Locations																			
		Shastri Tower				Ajanta				Icchadevi				Ganesh Colony				Prabaht			
		SO_2	NO_x	RSPM	SPM	SO_2	NO_x	RSPM	SPM	SO_2	NO_x	RSPM	SPM	SO_2	NO_x	RSPM	SPM	SO_2	NO_x	RSPM	SPM
Monsoon	June	22	26	92	55	97	133	201	351	96	87	211	168	12	11	77	51	98	81	200	284
2003	July	12	28	88	53	11	120	197	345	100	102	197	195	11	13	89	58	78	73	217	277
	Aug	15	25	79	49	100	128	222	346	110	110	201	225	16	10	70	67	86	88	221	256
	Sept	21	22	90	60	103	25	210	328	112	92	213	200	10	03	81	63	75	88	212	251
Winter	Oct	15	25	101	78	126	140	200	308	122	128	227	264	15	10	88	56	78	98	215	255
2003–04	Nov	23	35	98	68	141	137	210	340	116	122	235	285	22	13	72	53	97	102	231	285
	Dec	21	26	107	60	136	133	207	311	136	141	233	310	26	16	91	59	133	110	217	300
	Jan	26	33	100	65	138	123	219	328	125	137	201	301	23	11	89	61	141	113	222	294
Summer	Feb	25	23	96	60	83	73	281	399	80	105	279	353	13	8.7	79	77	75	112	252	311
2004	March	21	25	101	68	97	86	270	410	86	97	298	376	16	12	81	74	78	56	236	334
	April	22	15	112	64	103	91	303	418	97	100	280	395	12	15	98	85	70	61	261	390
	May	18	23	136	71	115	101	319	422	87	87	282	360	15	12	103	70	61	75	269	384

Table 8.8: Traffic Densities at Air Monitoring Stations in the Jalgaon City

Sl.No.	Mode of Transport	Name of the Monitoring Stations									
		Shastri Tower		Ajanta		Icchadevi		Ganesh Colony		Pràbhat	
		Veh./Hr	Veh./Day	Veh./Hr	Veh./Day	Veh./Hr	Veh./Day	Veh./Hr	Veh./Day	Veh./Hr	Veh./Day
1.	Heavy vehicles (Truck + Tempo+ Buses)	81	1458	902	16248	766	13788	05	92	800	14412
2.	Passenger cars 4-wheelers	342	6152	330	5952	110	1980	89	1602	214	3852
3.	2 + 3 wheelers Scooters + Mopeds + Autos	462	8316	590	10632	472	8508	352	6348	517	9312

Table 8.9: Major Heavy Traffic Roads in the City

Mode of Transport	Name of the Road with Length in Km								
	National Highway–6 (14 Km)			Ganesh Colony to Ajanta Crossing (08 Km)			R. Station to Mahabal (06 Km)		
	Traffic Density*								
	Morning 06.00 am to 12.00 pm	Afternoon 12.00 pm to 17.00 pm	Evening 17.00 pm to 00.00 am	Morning 06.00 am to 12.00 pm	Afternoon 12.00 pm to 17.00 pm	Evening 17.00 pm to 00.00 am	Morning 06.00 am to 12.00 pm	Afternoon 12.00 pm to 17.00 pm	Evening 17.00 pm to 00.00 am
Heavy Veh.	6232±105	1370±89	7194±124	30±10	25±14	35±08	67±44	22±8	54±21
4 wheelers	1658±98	363±78	1809±141	543±45	445±82	623±104	710±102	480±85	718±88
2 + 3 wheelers	4156±110	1315±56	53l2±101	21l2±78	1760±98	2464±117	2211±132	1010±91	2781±113

*All values are the averages of three monitoring ± SD.

Table 8.10: Emission Intensity of the Line Sources (Ep) in gm/day/km Using the Major Heavy Traffic Roads in Jalgaon City

Mode of Transport	*Name of the Road with Length in Km*								
	National Highway–6 (14 Km)			*Ganesh Colony to Ajanta Crossing (08 Km)*			*R. Station to Mahabal (06 Km)*		
	*HC + NOx**								
	Gm/day km	*Kg/day km*	*Tons/year*	*Gm/day km*	*Kg/day km*	*Tons/year*	*Gm/day km*	*Kg/day km*	*Tons/year*
Heavy vehicle	352144	352.144	128.53	1224	1.224	0.446	1468	1.468	0.535
4 wheelers	90820	90.82	33.1493	21782	21.782	7.95	22896	22.896	8.35
2 + 3 wheelers	320400	320.400	116.94	86169	86.169	31.45	72144	72.144	26.33
Total	763364	763.364	278.62	109175	109.175	39.84	96508	96.508	35.22
	PM*								
Heavy vehicle	51786	51.78	18.89	180	0.18	0.065	216	0.216	0.078

* Indian emission standards 2000 are used.

Conclusion

On one hand the population growth is continuously increasing and on the other hand the lifestyle of the population is also increasing. The demand of vehicles is also increasing, which enhances the air pollution in the urban areas. The current transport system also caused serious traffic congestions and the vehicle exhaust has become major source of air pollution in the Jalgaon City. The current study purely suggest that the mass transport activity must be enhanced for long distance journey and one way system must bė adopted on the major roads in the city.

During the study it is also observed that there are no isolated bus stops along the roadside. City and state transport buses stand on the road, this causes traffic congestions on the roads.

References

Central Pollution Control Board (CPCB), 1996. Ambient Air Quality: Status and Statistics–1996, CPCB Report, Ambient Air Quality Monitoring Series: NAAQSMS/10/1996.

Central Pollution Control Board (CPCB), 1999. Air Quality at Major Traffic Intersections of Delhi–1999, CPCB Report, Ambient Air Quality, Monitoring Series: NAAQSMS/11/1998–99.

Clifford, M.J., Clarke, R. and Riffat, S.B., 1997. Local aspects of vehicular pollution. *Atmospheric Environment*, 31: 271–276.

Indian Standards, 1969. *Indian Standard Methods for Measurement of Air Qualities.* IS: 5182 (Part II, 1969).

Indian Standards, 1969. *Indian Standard Methods for Measurement of Air Qualities.* IS: 5182 (Part IV, 1973).

Jain, Manish Kumar and Saxena, N.C., 2002. Air quality assessment along Dhanbad–Jahira road. *Environmental Monitoring and Assessment*, 79: 239–250.

Price, Monica, Colin Q'Dowd and Marion Dixon, 2003. Interpretation of roadside PM_{10} monitoring data from Sunderland, UK. *Environmental Monitoring and Assessment*, 82: 225–241.

Raga, G.B. and Le Moyne, L., 1999. On the nature of air pollution dynamics in Mexico City–I. Nonlinear analysis. *Atmospheric Environment*, 23: 3987–3993.

Reddy, G.S. and Biswajit, R., 2003. Ambient air quality status in Raniganj–Asansol area, India. *Environmental Monitoring and Assessment*, 89: 153–163.

Shrivastava, Anjali and Rakesh Kumar, 2002. Economic valuation of health impacts of air pollution in Mumbai. *Environmental Monitoring and Assessment*, 75: 135–143.

Theurer, W. Plate E.J. and Hoschele, K., 1996. Semi-empirical methods as a combination of wind tunnel and numerical dispersion modelling. *Atmospheric Environment*, 30: 3583–3597.

Wagh, N.D., Pachpande B.G., Khadare R.D., Attarde S.B., and Ingle S.T., 2003. Carbon monoxide levels in the ambient air at major road sides in Jalgaon city. *Indian Journal of Air Pollution and Control*, 3: 2.

Zhongan, Mao and Gao Shengan, 2002. Traffic Pollution in Xi'an City, P.R. China (BAQ 2002); *Better Air Quality in Asian and Pacific Rim Cities*, 16 December 2002–18 December 2002, Hong Kong, SAR, PS-21-1-8.

Chapter 9

Drought Tolerance of Coriander (*Coriandrum sativum* Linn.) Genotypes in Rainfed Vertisols

Lakshmi Narasmimha Rao Kamineni, Giridhar Kalidasu, C. Sarada
Acharya NG Ranga Agricultural University, Regional Agricultural Research Station, Lam, Guntur - 522 034

ABSTRACT

Coriander is grown traditionally in rain fed vertisols in South India unlike its cultivation as irrigated crop in North India. Short to medium duration varieties and capacity to over come moisture stress during the crop growth period and later, are two pre-requisites, for the development any successful variety in these areas. Varietal development in Coriander for these areas always considered medium duration as panacea for the aforementioned problems. Hence, a study was taken up to evaluate the fifty-germplasm lines available at RARS, Lam, Guntur. Data on RWC at 45 days, RWC at 75 days, Chlorophyll stability index, Proline (μ mole gm^{-1} of fresh leaf) at 45 DAS, Proline (μ mole gm^{-1} of fresh leaf) at 75 DAS were recorded. Among the genotypes evaluated, the Relative Water Content (RWC) at 45 DAS values ranged from 56.74 (LCC–147) to 85.99 (LCC–153) whereas at 75 DAS the RWC ranged from 45.86 (LCC–167) to 79.50 (LCC–157). The Chlorophyll Stability Index (CSI) ranges from 0.18 (LCC–158) to 0.88 (LCC–133). The leaf Proline content at 45 DAS ranged from 58.0 (LCC–147) to 182.0 (LCC–165) whereas at 75 DAS the Proline content values ranged from 75 (LCC–133) to 240 (LCC–136). Thus, the genotypes with relatively high CSI, RWC, and Proline content *i.e.*, LCC–143, LCC–159, LCC–150, LCC–164, LCC–165 may be considered as drought tolerant.

Keywords: Coriander, Drought, Moisture stress.

Introduction

Coriander is a major seed spice crop grown in India and one third of its production is from South India. Coriander is grown traditionally in rain fed vertisols in South India unlike its cultivation as irrigated crop in light soils of North India. Short to medium duration varieties and capacity to over come moisture stress during the crop are two pre-requisites for any successful variety in these areas. Varietal development in Coriander for these areas always considered medium duration as panacea for the aforementioned problems. Until now, identification of suitable genotype, which comes up well with residual soil moisture in vertisols, is the most important research priority. There was little effort in to discerning the underlying physiology that contributes to moisture stress tolerance of this crop. In addition, most of the varieties developed were mostly by selection thus restricting the scope for exploitation of available germplasm in the country. In this scenario, any study regarding the drought physiology of the crop is a welcome move. Keeping this in mind, the authors of this study initiated an evaluation of germplasm available at Regional Agricultural Research Station, Lam, Guntur for their drought physiology.

Materials and Methods

The experiment was conducted during the rabi season of the year 2004–05. The study was carried out in vertisols under residual soil moisture regime at Regional Agricultural Research Station, Lam, Guntur. In this study, fifty genotypes were evaluated in Augmented Block Design with four check varieties. The experimental soil was medium in available N, medium in available P_2O_5 and high in exchangeable K_2O. The recommended dose of fertilizers 30 kg N, 40 kg P_2O_5, K_2O applied as basal dose and necessary cultural operations were taken up periodically in the experimental field. Data on RWC at 45 days, RWC at 75 days, Chlorophyll stability index, Proline (µ mole gm^{-1} of fresh leaf) at 45 DAS, Proline (µ mole gm^{-1} of fresh leaf) at 75 DAS were recorded. In addition to this, data on plant height, number of primary branches, number of secondary branches, number of umbels, number of umbellets per umbel, number of fruits per umbel, days taken to 50 per cent flowering, days taken to maturity and yield were recorded. Data was statistically analyzed for drawing conclusions.

Results and Discussion

The data related to plant and physiological parameters of drought given in Table 9.1. Among the genotypes evaluated, the Relative Water Content (RWC) at 45 DAS values ranged from 56.74 (LCC–147) to 85.99 (LCC–153) whereas at 75 DAS the RWC ranged from 45.86 (LCC–167) to 79.50 (LCC–157). The chlorophyll stability index ranges from 0.18 (LCC–158) to 0.88 (LCC–133). The leaf Proline (µ mole gm^{-1} of fresh leaf) content at 45 DAS ranged from 58.0 (LCC–147) to 182.0 (LCC–165) whereas at 75 DAS the Proline content values ranged from 75 (LCC–133) to 240 (LCC–136).

Several methods have been used to estimate drought tolerance and water use efficiency. Typically, these involve measurement of water potential, relative turgidity, diffusion pressure deficit, proline and chlorophyll stability index (Bates *et al.*, 1973; Turk and Hall 1980; Morgan 1984; Yadava and Patil 1984). In this study Relative Water Content, Proline and Chlorophyll Stability Index were used to study the drought physiology of Coriander.

Most of the reviews (Ashley 1993; Subbarao *et al.*, 1995; Boyer 1996) have brought together the available knowledge on different aspects of drought tolerance in crop plants and options to minimize yield losses due to drought. Major differences among and within crop species have been reported and different strategies to breed drought tolerant varieties have been suggested (Blum 1985; Walker and Miller 1986; Arraudeau 1989; Acevedo and Ceccarelli 1989).

Table 9.1: Drought Tolerance Parameter, Range, and Germplasm Lines with Maximum and Minimum Values

Drought Tolerance Parameter	*Range*	*Germplasm Lines*	
		Low	*High*
RWC at 45 days	56.74–85.99	LCC–147(56.74), LCC–155(61.54)	LCC–153(85.99), LCC–156(85.71)
RWC at 75 days	45.86–79.50	LCC–167(45.86), LCC–130(48.48)	LCC–157(79.5), LCC–143(78.03)
Chlorophyll stability index	0.18–0.88	LCC–158(0.18), LCC–167(0.30)	LCC–133(0.88), LCC–161 (0.78)
Proline micromoles for gram of fresh leaf at 45 DAS	58–182	LCC–147(58), LCC–163(62)	LCC–165(182), LCC–164(176)
Proline micromoles for gram of fresh leaf at 75 DAS	75–240	LCC–133(75), LCC–166(76)	LCC–136(240), LCC–158(237)

Table 9.2: Relative Water Content, CSI, Proline, and Yield of Coriander Germplasm Lines

Sl.No.	*Genotype*	*RWC at 45 DAS*	*RWC at 75 DAS*	*CSI*	*Proline (μ mole gm^{-1} of Fresh Leaf) at 45 DAS*	*Proline (μ mole gm^{-1} of Fresh Leaf) 75 DAS*	*Yield (kg/ha)*
1.	LCC 121	64.80	58.74	0.583	61.45	92.85	683.2
2.	LCC 122	68.50	52.64	0.603	87.45	93.85	441.1
3.	LCC 123	75.39	67.71	0.513	93.45	119.80	683.2
4.	LCC 124	65.14	60.42	0.503	81.45	117.80	694.2
5.	LCC 125	66.53	67.25	0.473	92.45	138.90	819.2
6.	LCC 126	69.16	60.32	0.583	95.45	130.90	808.2
7.	LCC 127	76.72	77.83	0.493	83.45	135.90	822.2
8.	LCC 128	72.41	56.29	0.503	97.45	107.80	822.2
9.	LCC 129	64.06	55.81	0.593	73.45	116.80	872.2
10.	LCC 130	67.27	49.25	0.613	101.40	112.80	779.2
11.	LCC 131	73.35	53.39	0.643	106.20	117.80	789.2
12.	LCC 132	74.34	50.44	0.533	88.20	104.80	728.2
13.	LCC 133	79.49	51.80	0.503	80.20	92.85	913.2
14.	LCC 134	77.35	55.64	0.703	118.20	123.80	853.2
15.	LCC 135	73.42	61.57	0.643	94.20	129.90	842.2
16.	LCC 136	67.82	57.69	0.403	80.20	87.85	664.2
17.	LCC 137	73.48	57.10	0.543	72.20	93.85	592.2
18.	LCC 138	78.04	52.06	0.493	86.20	97.85	778.2
19.	LCC 139	85.02	53.37	0.403	112.20	116.80	842.2
20.	LCC 140	87.12	61.79	0.433	105.20	113.80	821.2
21.	LCC 141	78.74	62.69	0.603	114.20	125.60	842.2
22.	LCC 142	78.26	65.73	0.663	118.20	139.60	714.2

Contd...

Table 9.2–Contd...

Sl.No.	Genotype	RWC at 45 DAS	RWC at 75 DAS	CSI	Proline (μ mole gm^{-1} of Fresh Leaf) at 45 DAS	Proline (μ mole gm^{-1} of Fresh Leaf) 75 DAS	Yield (kg/ha)
23.	LCC 143	85.45	77.08	0.343	124.20	136.60	906.2
24.	LCC 144	81.77	55.67	0.453	98.20	105.60	582.2
25.	LCC 145	79.27	69.05	0.633	112.20	160.60	439.1
26.	LCC 146	82.62	68.47	0.543	102.20	120.60	618.2
27.	LCC 147	59.20	54.37	0.543	54.20	149.60	899.2
28.	LCC 148	84.10	65.72	0.383	90.20	108.60	864.2
29.	LCC 149	83.84	59.98	0.393	108.20	114.60	792.2
30.	LCC 150	80.82	52.63	0.623	129.20	158.60	1092.0
31.	LCC 151	83.59	63.33	0.383	101.70	121.60	961.9
32.	LCC 152	76.35	74.80	0.393	95.70	143.60	943.9
33.	LCC 153	85.61	62.93	0.323	86.70	111.60	879.9
34.	LCC 154	83.46	58.68	0.473	114.70	130.60	461.9
35.	LCC 155	61.16	54.63	0.663	109.70	152.60	961.9
36.	LCC 156	85.33	57.78	0.343	107.70	131.60	925.9
37.	LCC 157	82.30	81.95	0.463	79.70	143.60	897.9
38.	LCC 158	75.44	63.79	0.193	65.70	83.60	1119.0
39.	LCC 159	76.50	76.99	0.763	135.70	181.60	815.9
40.	LCC 160	71.42	60.39	0.433	77.70	102.60	900.9
41.	LCC 161	74.81	52.89	0.778	88.45	99.10	832.7
42.	LCC 162	75.40	56.60	0.438	86.45	101.10	803.7
43.	LCC 163	75.41	54.46	0.588	64.45	78.10	957.7
44.	LCC 164	76.45	58.28	0.738	178.40	243.10	935.7
45.	LCC 165	73.94	57.40	0.668	184.40	240.10	308.6
46.	LCC 166	70.26	50.17	0.498	71.45	79.10	596.7
47.	LCC 167	72.28	45.98	0.298	82.45	95.10	721.7
48.	LCC 168	78.03	63.00	0.388	91.45	111.10	960.7
49.	LCC 169	75.00	51.34	0.538	104.40	126.10	946.7
50.	LCC 170	75.85	53.45	0.558	80.45	99.10	768.7
Means		75.64	59.82	0.5172	97.38	122.80	794.0
Checks							
51.	Swathi	69.96	49.22	0.546	89.00	107.60	842.2
52.	Sindhu	81.46	54.54	0.528	110.40	127.60	858.2
53.	Sadhana	67.10	53.37	0.57	107.80	129.80	870.2
54.	A. Sonalika	68.75	54.82	0.498	102.60	123.40	574.0
Means		71.82	52.99	0.5355	102.40	122.10	786.2
Overall Means		75.36	59.32	0.5186	97.76	122.80	793.4
L.S.D. (5%)		7.43	7.47	0.14	12.15	10.25	141.2
CV.		6.72	9.15	16.74	7.7	5.45	8.28

The germplasm entries with high CS1, stable proline content from flowering to maturity, high proline at the time maturity, high RWC at maturity, stable RWC content from flowering to maturity can be considered considerably tolerant to drought. These entries must be further tested for their stability over different environments to ensure their tolerance to drought is not due to influence of environment but due to their genetic capacity.

Thus, LCC–164 and LCC–165 with relatively high GSI (0.738 and 0.668 respectively), high Proline at 45 DAS (178.40 and 184.40 respectively) and 75 DAS (243.0 and 240.10 respectively); and LCC–143 with relatively high RWC at 45 (85.45) and 75 DAS (77.08) and moderately high Proline at 45 DAS (136.60); and LCC–159 with relatively high RWC at 75 DAS (76.99), CSI (0.763) and high Proline at 45 DAS (135.70); and LCC–150 with high RWC at 45 DAS (80.82), relatively high Proline at 45 DAS (129.20) and 75 DAS (158.60) may be considered as drought tolerant. However, the yield of entry LCC–165 is quite unsatisfactory hence may be only used as a source of drought tolerance. The yield of other entries *i.e.* LCC–164 (935.7 kg/ha), LCC–143 (906.2 kg/ha), LCC–159 (815.9 kg/ha), was on par with the best check Sadhana (858.2 kg/ha). Moreover, LCC–150 (1092.0 kg/ha) recorded significantly higher yield than the best check Sadhana. Hence, LCC150, LCC–143, LCC–164, LCC–159 can be used as source of drought tolerance for the development of drought tolerant varieties.

Acknowledgements

The authors are grateful to Acharya N.G. Ranga Agricultural University, Rajendranagar and AICRP on Spices, Calicut for providing the funds and facilities for conducting this experiment.

References

Acevedo, E. and S. Ceccarelli, 1989. Role of physiologist breeder in a breeding program for drought resistance conditions. In: *Drought Resistance in Cereals*, (Ed.) W.G. Baker, pp. 117–139. CAB International, Wallingford, UK.

Arraudeau, M.A., 1989. Breeding strategies for drought resistance. In: *Drought Resistance in Cereals*, (Ed.) W.G. Baker, pp. 107–116. CAB International, Wallingford, London, UK.

Ashley, J., 1993. Drought and crop adaptation. In: *Dryland Farming in Africa*, (Ed.) J.R.J. Rowland, pp. 46–67. Macmillan Press Ltd, UK.

Bates, L.S., R.P. Waldren, and I.O. Teare, 1973. Rapid determination of free proline in water stress studies. *Plant and Soil*, 38: 205.

Blum, A., 1985. Breeding crop varieties for stress environments. *Critical Reviews in Plant Sciences*, 2: 199–238.

Morgan, J.M., 1984. Osmoregulation and water stress in higher plants. *Annual Review of Plant Physiology*, 35: 299–319.

Subbarao, G.V., C. Johansen, A.E. Slinkard, R.C. Nageswara Rao, N.P. Saxena, and Y.S. Chauhan, 1995. Strategies for improving drought resistance in grain legumes. *Critical Reviews in Plant Sciences*, 14: 269–523.

Turk, K.J. and A.E. Hall, 1980. Drought adaptation of cowpea. Influence of drought on plant water status and relations with seed yield. *Agronomy Journal*, 72: 421–427.

Walker, D.W. and J.C. Miller Jr., 1986. Intraspecific variability for drought resistance in cowpea. *Scientia Horticulturae*, 29: 87–100.

Yadava, R.B.R. and B.D. Patil, 1984. Screening of cowpea (*Vigna unguiculata* L.) varieties for drought tolerance. *Zeitschrift Fur Acker Und Pflanzenbau*, 93: 259–262.

Chapter 10

Comparison of Rate of Copper Ion Induced Oxidation of Lipoprotein in End Stage Renal Diseased and Renal Transplant Patients: An *in vitro* Study

C.S. Parameswari[1]*, B. Vijaya Geetha[2], R. Vijaya Kumar[3]

[1]Reader, [2]Research Scholar
Post Graduate Department of Biochemistry, Bharathi Women's College (Autonomous), North Chennai – 600 108, Tamil Nadu
[3]Professor and Head, Department of Nephrology, Stanley Medical College and Hospital, Chennai – 600 001, Tamil Nadu

ABSTRACT

The Cardiovascular Disease (CVD) accounts for 15–30 per cent of deaths in patients suffering from End Stage Renal Disease (ESRD) and about 47 per cent of deaths in patients having renal transplantation. The increased lipoprotein oxidation is found to be the main risk factor for CVD and thereby the progression of atherosclerosis. The purpose of the present study is to assess the rate of lipoprotein oxidation among the ESRD and renal transplant patients. The level of Malondialdehyde (MDA) and Conjugated Dienes (CD) were estimated in the lipoprotein fraction before and after an *in vitro* copper ion induced oxidation and the rate of formation of CD was also estimated. The levels of lipid peroxides and CD were significantly increased in oxidized LDL + VLDL fractions of renal transplant patients. When compared to normal subjects and ESRD patients, the lag time for CD formation and the time taken to form the maximum level of CD were significantly reduced for renal transplant patients. The shorter lag time of LDL + VLDL

* Corresponding Author: Phone: 044-28487064, 044-28487060; E-mail: vijhmphil_2002@yahoo.com

lipoprotein oxidation in renal transplant patients may be due to high levels of cholesterol and decreased levels of serum antioxidants among these patients. Further it proves that the increased susceptibility of the LDL + VLDL fraction of renal transplant patients to oxidation make them more prone to the progression of atherosclerosis and arteriosclerosis leading to Chronic rejection among these patients.

Keywords: *Cardiovascular disease, Lag time, Lipoprotein oxidation, Antioxidants, Atherosclerosis and Chronic rejection.*

Introduction

Cardiovascular disease is a significant cause of morbidity and mortality in ESRD patients and renal transplant patients (Leskinen *et al.*, 2003). The impaired renal function promotes atherogenesis by increasing the oxidation of lipoproteins in both the ESRD and renal transplant patients (Luc and Fruchart 1992; Parfery *et al.*, 1999). Cyclosporine A contributes significantly to the cardiovascular risk in transplant patients because of its hypertensive and hyperlipidemic effects (Kahan 1989). The oxidative modification of LDL which is most prevalent among ESRD and renal transplant patients is an important factor in the initiation and development of atherosclerosis and arteriosclerosis. The arteriosclerosis leads to chronic rejection in renal transplanted patients (Linton MF and Fazio 2001).

The aim of the present study involves the measurement of lipoprotein oxidation in *in vitro* condition in ESRD and renal transplant patients. The adequate markers of oxidatively modified LDL are studied. The kinetics of formation of CD during copper ion induced lipoprotein oxidation is studied and compared with the normal subjects.

Subjects and Methods

Patients

The blood samples for the present study were collected from Nephrology Department, Stanley Medical College Hospital, Chennai, Tamil Nadu. The study was carried out in 20 ESRD patients with a creatinine level > 5mg/dl of blood who were undergoing hemodialysis using polysulphane membrane and acetate buffered dialysate for two or more sessions of each for at least 4 hours of dialysis per week and in twenty patients who underwent live related renal transplantation since 2 years, at the Nephrology Department, Stanley Medical College Hospital, Chennai. They were under treatment with Cyclosporine A at a dosage of 6 mg/kg body weight initially and adjusted depending on the Cyclosporine A level in blood and tapered the utilization of Cyclosporine A and steroid 1 mg/kg body weight, the level reduced by 6 months with Azathioprine of 1–1.5 mg/kg body weight increased to 1.5–2.4 mg/kg body weight as life long treatment. The patients had no clinical or laboratory evidence of fever, diabetes mellitus, elevated liver enzyme levels and infective disorders. They were non-alcoholic, non-smokers and without antilipidemic drug treatment. The normal healthy volunteers served as control subjects. The patients and the normal subjects were of male in the age group between 20 and 45 years. Informed consent was obtained from each patient before the sample collection. The study was approved by the committee of Ethics at Stanley Medical College Hospital, Chennai.

Blood Sampling

The ESRD patients were inpatients and the renal transplanted patients were treated as the outpatients in the Nephrology Department. From each patient, 10ml of blood was collected after a 12 hours of overnight fasting in sterile tubes and the serum obtained was used for the following studies.

Isolation of LDL + VLDL from Serum

The LDL + VLDL lipoprotein fraction was isolated from the serum according to the method of Burstein and Scholnick (Burstein and Scholnick, 1973). The LDL + VLDL was isolated using sucrose, sodium salt of heparin and Magnesium chloride under the high speed centrifugation of about 6000g for 30 minutes. The isolated LDL + VLDL were subjected to dialysis using Tris-HCI buffer and Barium chloride at 4°C to remove impurities like protein and heparin. The resultant was a clear yellow solution of LDL + VLDL. The protein in LDL + VLDL fraction was estimated according to the method of Markwell *et al.*, 1978. 20 µl of LDL + VLDL fraction was made up to 1 ml using distilled water. Then 3 ml of Markwell reagent was added and the tube was incubated at room temperature for 10 minutes. Then 0.3 ml of Folin Phenol reagent was added and the blue colour developed was read at 660 nm after 45 minutes. The protein content of LDL + VLDL fraction was expressed as mg/ml of LDL + VLDL fraction.

Assay of Lipid Peroxidation in LDL + VLDL Fraction

LDL + VLDL fraction was oxidized in *in vitro* condition by the method of Wallin *et al.* with some modifications (Wallin *et al.*, 1993). The extent of lipid peroxidation in the LDL + VLDL fraction before and after an *in vitro* induction of oxidation was studied by measuring Thiobarbituric Acid Reacting Substances (TBARS) and Conjugated Dienes (CD). The lipid peroxiation in terms of TBARS was quantitated as follows; about 200 µg (in terms of LDL + VLDL protein) of LDL + VLDL isolated from the sample was suspended in 50 µl of 5 µM copper sulphate solution. Then the volume of the tube was made up to 1 ml using Phosphate Buffered Saline (PBS) (0.001 M pH 7.2). At the end of one hour of incubation at room temperature, 100 µl of 50 per cent Trichlroacetic acid was added to arrest the reaction. The TBARS formed was estimated by adding 100 µl of 1.3 per cent of TBA in sodium hydroxide and heated at 60°C for 30 minutes. The tube was cooled and the pink colour developed was extracted using 4ml of n-butanol and pyridine mixture (15 : 1) and the absorbance of butanol layer was read at 535 nm. The amount of MDA formed was calibrated from a standard curve prepared using 1, 1′, 3, 3′-tetramethoxy propane. The CD in the LDL + VLDL fraction was assayed by the method of Esterbauer *et al.*, 1989. 200 µg of LDL + VLDL fraction (in terms of protein) was suspended in 50 µl of 5 µM copper sulphate for *in vitro* oxidation. After 10 minutes, the oxidation was stopped by the addition of 100 µl of 0.1 per cent Butylated hydroxytoluene in alcohol. To this 1.5 ml of cyclohexane was added and the absorbance was read at 233 mm against the cyclohexane blank. The rate of copper ion induced *in vitro* oxidation of LDL + VLDL lipoprotein fraction was determined by estimating CD in oxidized LDL + VLDL fraction as mentioned above at a time interval of 5 minutes for a period of 2 hours. A graph depicting time in minutes against absorbance at 233 nm was plotted and the indices or oxidation in terms or lag time and the time taken for maximum oxidation were calculated.

Statistical Analysis

The numerical data were presented as mean value ± standard deviation. The values were subjected to analysis of normal tests of significance. The statistical significance was evaluated by One-way ANOVA (Analysis of Variance).

Results and Discussion

The death rate due to complications of vascular disease ranges from 5/1000 deaths per patient year in younger transplanted patients to 18.5/1000 deaths in the older age group (Raine and Ledingham, 1984). Renal transplant patients have infact the accelerated atherosclerosis because of arterial hypertension, dyslipidemia and other vascular risk factors (Japichino *et al.*, 2001). In 44 per cent of renal transplant patients the hypercholesterolemia is due to increased hepatic synthesis of apoB containing lipoproteins and is an independent risk factor for kidney graft loss by chronic rejection in male patients with previous acute rejection (Isabel Beneyto, Castello, 2002). The *in vitro* oxidation of lipoprotein using the copper ion exhibits the same scenario us it is present in *in vivo* condition.

The levels of TBARS and conjugated dienes in native and oxidized forms of LDL + VLDL fraction of serum from the normal subjects, ESRD and renal transplant patients were presented in Table 10.1. When compared to normal and ESRD patients, the renal transplant patients showed a significant increase in TBARS and conjugated diene levels.

Table 10.1

The levels of TBARS and Conjugated dienes in the native and Cu^{2+} ion induced *in vitro* oxidized forms of LDL + VLDL fractions from the serum of normal subjects, ESRD and renal transplant patients. Each Group consists of 20 subjects.

Subjects	*TBARS*		*Conjugated Dienes*	
	Native	*Oxidized*	*Native*	*Oxidized*
Normal Subjects	23.6±0.63	43.5±0.76	2.44×10^3±187.06	6.24×103±273.25
ESRD	***A	***A	***A	***A
Patients	29.19±0.65	72.75±1.44	$3.56.10^3$±256.03	10.85×10^3±125.46
Renal	***B	***B	***B	***B
Transplants	***C	***C	***C	***C
	81.4±1.71	116.15±2.89	7.83×10^3±2.89	19.38×10^3±155.16

***F < 0.001–highly significant by ANOVA.

The levels of TBARS are expressed as nanomoles formed/mg of LDL+ VLDL protein.

The levels of Conjugated diene formed are expressed as $\Delta233\times10^3$/mg of LDL + VLDL protein.

The Values are mean ± SD

A: Comparison of normal subjects and ESRD patients

B: Comparison of normal subjects and Renal transplant patients

C: Comparison of ESRD and Renal transplant patients.

Figure 10.1 represented the rate of Copper ion induced *in vitro* oxidation of LDL + VLDL. The graph showed the level of CD formed, when LDL + VLDL fraction isolated from the serum of normal subjects, ESRD patients and renal transplant patients were subjected to 5 μM Copper ion induced oxidation at a time level of 5 minutes for 2 hours. The duration of lag time and the time of maximum lipid peroxidation are obtained for normal subjects and both the patients by kinetic modeling analysis. The lag time of oxidation for normal subjects, ESRD and renal transplant patients were found to be 20 min, 15 min and 10 min respectively. The renal transplant patients had significantly shorter lag time when compared to normal and ESRD patients. Similar changes have also been reported already (McEneny *et al.*, 1997). The time taken to form maximum CD formation was found to be 70 min, 50 min and 25 min for healthy subjects, ESRD patients and renal transplant patients respectively. The shorter duration was utilized for the maximum amount of CD formation in renal transplant patients when compared to ESRD patients and normal subjects.

The lag phase in transplant patients is shorter due to the fact that there is low level of antioxidants in LDL which have been fully used up, not remained to prevent LDL oxidation and hence the lag

The rate of Copper ion induced oxidation of LDL+VLDL in the Healthy volunteers, ESRD patients and Renal Transplant patients.

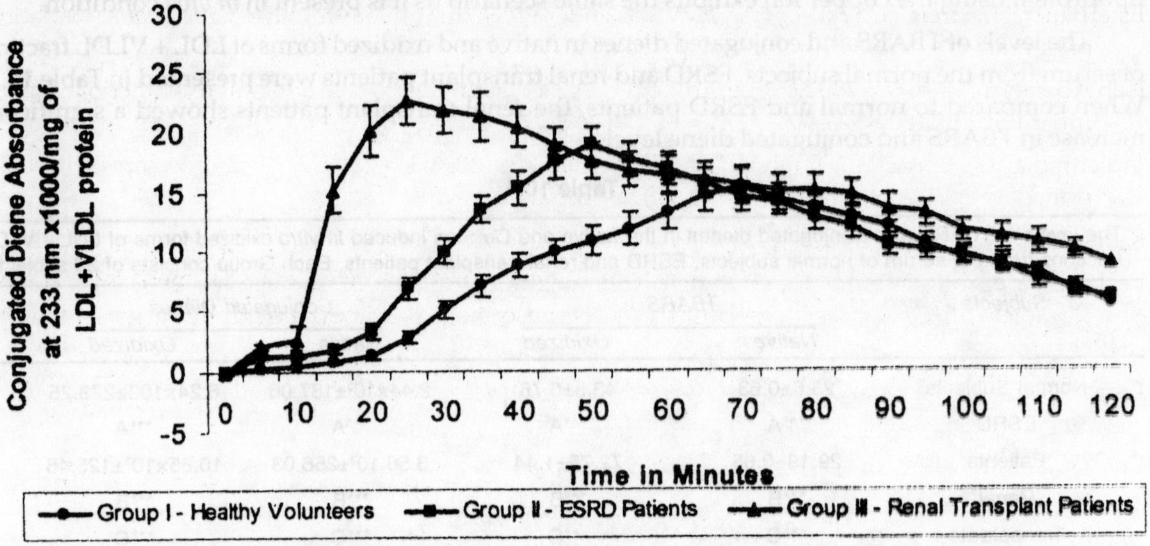

Figure 10.1: Estimation of Rate of Copper Ion Induced Oxidation of LDL + VLDL

The levels of Conjugated diene formed are expressed as absorbance at 233 nm × 1000/mg of LDL + VLDL.

The values are expressed as Mean ± Standard Deviation.

Legend:

Healthy volunteers: The normal healthy male subjects in the age group of 20–45 years.

ESRD Patients: The ESRD patients with blood creatinine level greater than 5 mg/dl of blood

Renal transplant patients: Live related renal Transplant Patients since two years.

phase is shorter in renal transplant patients when compared to ESRD and healthy controls which is depicted in the Figure 10.1. The low level of serum antioxidants in renal transplant patients have been reported in our previous studies (Parameswari *et al.*, 2004). The prolonged dialytic treatment in ESRD patients causes a decrease in vitamin E concentration of LDL and increases their susceptibility to oxidation (Maggi *et al.*, 1994).

Cyclosporine A, the drug used in the immunosuppressive therapy of renal transplants is the glycogenic immunosuppressor that can induce post transplant hyperlipidemia which may contribute to less favorable plasma lipid profile and contribute to high incidence of CVD by facilitating lipid peroxidation of LDL thereby increasing the uptake of LDL by LDL receptors in arterial walls. The renal transplant patients with higher concentrations of Cyclosporine A have significantly higher oxidisability of LDL (Venkiteswaran *et al.*, 2001).

The decreased serum antioxidants level of the ESRD and renal transplant patients mainly contributes to the shorter lag time of lipoprotein oxidation. Hence it may be concluded that the antioxidant therapy for renal transplant patients would extend the lag phase. It may further reduce the mortality and morbidity of renal diseased patients due to CVD and the graft loss caused by chronic rejection among the renal transplants.

References

Burstein, M. and Scholnick, H.R., 1973. Lipoprotein–Polyanion metal interactions. *Adv. Lipid Res.*, 11: 68–108.

Esterbauer, H., Streigl, O., Pulh, H. and M. Rothender, 1989. Continuous monitoring of *in vitro* oxidation of human low density lipoprotein. *Free Radic. Res. Commun.*, 6: 67–75.

Isabel Beneyto, Castello, 2002. Hyperlipidemia: A risk factor for chronic allograft dysfunction. *Kidney Int.*, 61 Suppl. (80): 873–877.

Japichino, G.G., Bonati, L., Rubini, P. and E. Capocasale, 2001. Prevalence of atherosclerosis in renal transplant patients. *Minerva Cardio Angiol.*, 49(4): 229–238.

Kahan, B.D., 1989. Cyclosporine. *N. Engl. J. Med.*, 321: 1725–1738.

Leskinen, Y., Groundstroem, K., Viratenen, V., Letimaki, T., Huhtala, H. and H. Saga, 2003. Risk factors for aortic atherosclerosis determined by transesophageal echocardiography in patients with chronic renal failure. *Am. J. Kidney Dis.*, 42(2): 277–285.

Linton, M.F. and S. Fazio, 2001. Class A: Scavenger receptors, macrophages and atherosclerosis. *Curr. Opin. Lipidol.*, 12(5): 489–495.

Luc, G., and J.C. Fruchart, 1992. Oxidation of lipoproteins and atherosclerosis. *Am. J. Clin. Nutrition*, 53: 2065– 2095.

Maggi, E., Bellazzi, R., Falaschi, F., Frattoni, A., Perani, G., Finardo, G., Gazo, A., Nai, M., Romanini, D. and G. Bellomo, 1994. Enhanced LDL oxidation in uremic patients: An additional mechanism for accelerated atherosclerosis? *Kidney Int.*, 45(3): 876–883.

Markwell, M.A.S., Haas, S.M., Bieber, Z.L. and N.E. Tolbert, 1978. A modification of Lowry procedure to simplify protein determination in membranes and lipoprotein sample. *Anal. Biochem.*, 87: 206–210.

McEneny, J., Loughrey, C.M., Trimble, E.R., McName, P.T., and I.S. Young. Susceptibility of VLDL to oxidation in patients on regular hemodialysis. *Atherosclerosis*, 29(2): 215–220.

Parameswari, C.S., Vijayachamundeeswari, D. and R. Vijaya Kumar, 2004. Antioxidant status in the renal transplant patients with chronic rejection. *SFRR–India Bulletin*, 3(2): 17–22.

Parfery, P.S., Foley, R.N. and C. Rigatto, 1999. Risk issue in renal transplantation: Cardiac aspects. *Transplant Proc.*, 31: 91.

Raine, A.E.G. and J.G.G. Ledingham. Cardiovascular complications after renal transplanation. In: *Morris Kidney Transplanation*, II edition.

Venkiteswaran, K., Sgoutas, C.S., Santana, N. and J.F. Neylan, 2001. Tacrolimus, Cyclosporine and plasma lipoproteins in renal transplant recipients. *Transplant Int.*, 14(6): 405–410.

Wallin, B., Rosengren, B., Shetzer, H.G. and G. Comejo, 1993. Lipoprotein oxidation and measurement of thiobarbituric acid reactive substance formation in a single microtitre plate: Its use for evaluation of antioxidants. *Anal. Biochem.*, 208: 10–15.

Chapter 11

Activation of Green Gram Amylase by Calcium Chloride

T. Devasena, S.K. Chithreswari and J. Christinal*

Department of Biotechnology, Mother Teresa Women's University, Kodaikanal – 624 102, Tamil Nadu

ABSTRACT

Cerelas are major Indian food. Cerelas are rich in starch. Amylase is a starch digesting enzyme. We have investigated amylase activity in green gram seeds germinated for different duration (24, 48, 72, 96 hours). Amylase activity was highest in the seeds germinated for 96 hours, supporting the fact that amylase activity increase with increase in germination time. Germinated Green Gram Seeds (GaGS) (germinated for 96 hours) was used for further *in vitro* investigation. Our *in vitro* study deals with the influence of calcium chloride on amylase activity in GGGS. Amylase activity was greater in GGGS incubated with 10 mM calcium chloride for ½ hour. However, the activity was lesser in GGGS in absence of calcium chloride. Our results show that calcium chloride stimulates and stabilizes amylase enzyme in GGGS. The possible mechanism involved behind our results are discussed.

Keywords: Amylase, Calcium chloride, Green gram, In vitro.

Introduction

Cerelas are primary food crops consumed in major part of our country. Starch, the chief source of carbohydrates in human diet forms the major energy reserves in cereal grains (Lehman and

* Corresponding Author: E-mail; tdevasenabio@yahoo.com.

Schlessimann, 1983). Amylase is an enzyme, which plays a significant role in initial stages of starch degradation and hydrolysis in human begins (Tarrago *et al.*, 1983).

Also, amylase find potential application in food, textile and paper industries and also in many other fields, such as clinical, medical and analytical chemistry. Amylasc taken between meals may be beneficial in case of asthma, hay fever, joints immobility, insect bites, allergies, skin eruption, histamine reaction, sinus conditions and celiac problems.

This, amylase reserves significance not only as a digestive enzyme but also as a industrially and clinically important enzyme. Therefore, stimulation of amylase activity may deserve several socio economic advantages, Previous reports suggest that chloride ions, manganese ions, calcium ions and ferrous ions are stimulators and stabilizers of amylase (Patel *et al.*, 2005). Germinated leguminous seeds are good source of amylase (Sumathi *et al.*, 1995). Among leguminous seeds, Green gram (Mung bean) seeds is a rich source of amylalse (Sumathi *et al.*, 1995). The

aim of this preliminary study is to investigate the effect of calcium chloride on amylase activity in germinated green gram seeds (GGGS) *in vitro*. The duration of germination that shows maximum amylase activity is fixed initially.

Materials and Methods

Green gram was purchased from the local market of Kodaikanal. Calcium chloride was purchased from Qualigens Fine Chemicals, Mumbai.

Fixation of Green Gram Germination Time

Separate portion of green gram was allowed to germinate for 24 hours, 48 hours, 72 hours and 96 hours. After germination period, 500 mg of seeds was washed and ground with 5ml of 0.5 M phosphate buffer and centrifuged for 15 minutes at 5000 rpm in a refrigerated centrifuge at 4°C. The supernatant was analysed for amylase by dinitro salicylic acid method as described by Miller (Miller, 1959)

Seeds germinated for 96 hrs showed maximum amylase activity (Table 11.1). Hence, this germination time is fixed for further *in vitro* study. There after, seeds germinated for 96 hrs was abbreviated as GGGS (Germinated Green Gram Seeds).

Table 11.1: Activity of Amylase in Green Gram Seeds at Different Hours of Germination

Hours of Germination	*Amylase Activity (Mg of Maltose Liberated/Minutes/Litre)*
24 hours	24.12±0.05
48 hours	31.45±0.07
72 hours	41.26±1.01
96 hours	55.00±0.06

Values are mean ± SD (n = 25).

In vitro Study

500 mg of GGGS was washed and ground with 5 ml of 0.5 M phosphate buffer and centrifuged for 15 minutes at 5000 rpm in a refrigerated centrifuge at 4°C. The supernatant was analysed for amylase by dinitrosalicylic acid method as described by Miller (Miller, 1959).

Simultaneously, 500 mg of GGGS was washed and ground with 5 ml of phosphate buffer containing 10mM $CaCl_2$ and incubated for 15 minutes and centrifuged as described above and the supernatant was assayed for amylase.

Statistical Analysis

Values of amylase activity are expressed as Mean ± SD. Statistical analysis was performed using Mann Whitney U- test (Non parametric). The null hypothesis was rejected for $P < 0.05$.

Results

Activity of amylase in green gram seeds at different hrs of germination are shown in Table 11.1. Seeds germinated for 96 hrs showed significantly maximum amylase activity. Effect of $CaCl_2$ on amylase activity in GGGS is shown in Table 11.2. Activity of amylase was higher in GGGS + $CaCl_2$ mixture. The activity of amylase in GGGS alone was significantly lower, when compared to GGGS + $CaCl_2$ mixture.

Table 11.2: Effect of $CaCl_2$ on Amylase Activity in GGGS

Incubation Mixture	*Amylase Activity (Mg of Maltose Liberated/Minutes/Litre)*
GGGS	25.00±0.11
GGGS + $CaCl_2$	37.60±0.13

Values are mean ± SD (n = 25).

Discussion

Germinated Green Gram Seeds (GGGS) are native source of amylase. However, the amylase activity was increased with an increase in time of germination. Our findings are in line with previous report that, amylase activity is directly proportional to time of germination (Sumathi *et al.*, 1995; Devasena and Sudha, 2005). Leguminous seeds belonging to Vigna genotypes, including green gram, contain amylase inhibitors. The activity of the inhibitor decreases during germination (Kokiladevi *et al.*, 2005). Thus, increase in the amylase activity in GGGS germinated for 96 hrs (Table 11.1) could be due to inactivation of amylase inhibitor with increase in time of germination.

Amylase activity of GGGS was higher in the presence of calcium chloride than in the absence of calcium chloride. Enhancement of amylase activity of *Aspergillus oryzae* by 10mM calcium chloride has already been reported (Patel *et al.*, 2005). Levitski and Steer (1974), have reported that the polypeptide chain of amylase possess binding sites for calcium and chloride ions. Granger *et al.* (1975) have reported that the disulphide bridge of the polypeptide chain of amylase has more affinity for calcium ions. Based on these reports, we could suggest that the amylase of GGGS binds to calcium ions and chloride ions at its disulphide moiety. Binding of these ions may induce conformational changes to enhance the enzyme activity. Thus, we speculate that enhancement of amylase activity of GGGS in the presence of 10mM calcium chloride could be due to stabilization and activation of the enzyme induced by binding of calcium and chloride ions to the disulphide moiety.

Conclusion

Commercialization of a new product made out of GGGS and calcium chloride could emerge out as a potent formula for better application as digestive stimulant as well as in clinical, medical and industrial fields.

References

Devasena, T. and Sudha, S., 2005. A study of amylase stimulators. In: *Proceedings of National Conference on Recent Trends in Environmental Science*, pp. 59.

Granger, M. and Abadia, B., 1975. Limited action of trypsin on porcine pancreatic amylase: Characterization of the fragaments. *FEBS. Lett.*, 56: 189.

Kokiladevi, E., Manickam, A. and S. Thayumanavan, 2005. Characterization of a amylase inhibitor in *Vigna sublobata*. *Bot. Bull. Acad. Sin.*, 46: 189–196

Levitski, A. and M. Steer, 1974. The allosteric activation of mammalian a amylase by chloride. *Eur. J. Biochem.*, 41: 171.

Lehman, J. and P. Schlesselmann, 1983. Cereals and Starch. *Carbohyd. Res.*, 113: 93–99.

Miller, G.L., 2005. Use of Dinitrosalicylic acid reagent for determination of reducing sugar. *Anal. Chem.*, 31: 426–429.

Patel, A.K., Nampoothri, K.N., Ramachandran, S., Szaikes, G. and A. Pandey, 2005. Partial purification of α-amylalse produced by *Aspergillus oryzae* using spent brewing graints. *Ind. J. Biotech.*, 4: 336–341.

Tarrago, J., Rodriguez, R., Bujan, M.C. and G. Nicolas, 1978. Starch degradation during germination of *Civer arintinum* L. Seed. *Rev. ESP. Fisiol.*, 34: 87–92.

Sumathi, A., Mallesh, N.G. and S.V. Rao, 1995. Elaboration of amylalse activity and changes in paste viscosity of some common Indian legumes during germination. *Plant. Food. Hum. Nutr.*, 47: 341–347.

Chapter 12

Mite Pest Scenario and their Status Associated with Common Vegetables

Rabindra Prasad[1], Uday Kumar Prasad[2], Sanjay Kumar Sathi[3] and Devendra Prasad[1]

[1]Department of Entomology, Birsa Agricultural University, Kanke, Ranchi – 834 006, Jharkhand

[2]ZRS, Chianki, Palamau, BAU, Ranchi, [3]KVK, Jagnathpur, BAU, Ranchi

ABSTRACT

Findings of a field survey and surveillance conducted through out the year from May 2002 to May 2004 revealed that eleven species of mite pests were found to infest as many as 19 commonly grown vegetables in Ranchi district of Jharkhand. Out of 11 species of phytophagous mites, 7 species belong to Tetranychidae, 2 species belong to Tenuipalpidae and one each comes under Tarsonemidae and Eriophyidae. Four tetranychid mites, *viz., Tetranychius urticae, T. ludeni, T. neocaledonicus* and *T. macfarlanei* appeared as major pest. On cucumber, okra, brinjal, French bean two spotted spider mite (*T. urticae*) appeared as major pest. Red legged spider mite (*T. ludeni*) remained major pest on cowpea, french bean, hyacinth bean and broad bean, T. *neocaledonicus* occurred as major pest on cowpea and French bean. Pumpkin, Bottle gourd, ridge gourd and sponge gourd harbored *T. macfarlanei* as major mite pest during summer. Another mite, *Eutetranychus orienialis* proved to be major mite pest ofhyacinth bean. One tarsonemid mite *Polyphagotarsonemus latus* Banks was found to be severe pest of tomato and shimla mirch *Capsicum frutescence* and extremely severe pest of chilli (C. *anum*). Pest status of these mite pest species was found to be most pronounced during hot summer month (middle of April to middle of June) followed by post monsoon periods (September and October). Colder winter month (December and January) proved to be highly disfavourable for survival of the mite pest species. Rainy season was also not much congenial for mite pest attack.

Keywords: Common vegetables, Mite pest species, Host range, Seasonal cycle, Status.

Introduction

The acceptance of phytophagous mites as pests of economic significance of agricultural crops has now been accepted in India and abroad. Mite infestation proved one of the important limiting factors in the vegetable production in India (Channa Basavanna, 1971 and Prasad, 2002). Gupta (1981) estimated that an average loss in yield of vegetable crops in general in India due to mite pests is to the tune of 25 per cent. During summer it may cause yield loss up to 70- 80 per cent in extreme case (Prasad, 2002). Mite pest spectrum and their status normally varies form place to place, crop to crop and season to season. Practically, nothing has been done so far to explore the information pertaining to seasonal incidence, and status of the mite pest in Jharkhand in general and Ranchi region in particular. The primary objective of the present investigation is to visualize the magnitude of the mite pest problem crop wise along with their seasonal variation in the region in the vegetable agro-ecosystem.

Materials and Methods

Field survey and surveillance was conducted to visualize the incidence, seasonal variation in the pest status of phytophagous mites in common vegetables, crop-wise, grown in different places of Ranchi district of Jharkhand during two consecutive years from May 2002 to May 2004. The plant parts infested with mite pests were collected and placed in the individual polyethylene bags crop and area wise and brought to the laboratory for determining qualitative and quantitative composition of the mites pest species. They were examined under a stereoscopic binocular microscope. The mites collected with the help of a soft and fine camel hairbrush were preserved in 70 per cent ethyl alcohol containing a few drops of glycerol. The mites were mounted in Hoyer's medium and identified for their proper documentation. Depending upon the mite population harbored by the unit area *i.e.*, one square centimeter of leaf surface, the crop plants were categorized as minor or major host plant (Table 12.1).

Results and Discussion

Results of faunistic survey conducted from May, 2002 to May, 2004 for visualizing the mite pest problem and its magnitude associated with nineteen common vegetable crops revealed the prevalence of eleven mites pest species (Table 12.1) Out of them, 7 species belong to tetranychids (spider mites) two species belong to tenuipalids (false spider mite) and one each comes under eriophyids (erineum or gall mite) and tarsonemid (yellow or broad mite) group of mite (Table 12.1).

Tetranychid Mite

Tetranychus urticae Koch

This Two Spotted Spider Mite (TSM) was found as major pest of okra, cucumber, brinjal and french bean. The incidence of the mite was registered almost through the year in different seasons on the respective hosts depending upon the availability of the crop plants in the field. The mite was observed to be extremely severe pest during the hot summer months (May–June) and moderately severe pest during post monsoon period (September–October). The minor pest status of *T. urticae* was also noticed on chilli, tomato, bottle gourd, sponge gourd and ridge gourd. The higher peak period on the major host plants were found during middle of April to middle of June and the lower peak period of incidence of *T. urticae* remained during September–October, in the present studies. Almost similar observation was recorded by Arbabi *et al.* (1994) in the agro climatic condition of Uttar Pradesh.

Table 12.1: Scenario of Mite Pest Fauna Associated with Common Vegetables Grown in Ranchi (Jharkhand)

Mite Pest Species	*Host Plant Species*		*Peak Period of Occurrence*	
	Major	*Minor*	*Upper Peak (1st Peak)*	*Lower Peak (2nd Peak)*
Tetranychus urticae Koch	Okra	Chilli	April–Mid June	Sept–Oct
	Cucumber	Tomato	April–Mid June	Sept–Oct
	Brinjal	Bottle guard	April–Mid June	Sept–Oct
	French bean	Sponge gourd	April–Mid June	Sept–Oct
		Ridge gourd	April–Mid June	Sept–Oct
		Pointed gourd	April–Mid June	Sept–Oct
		Cowpea	May–June	Sept–Oct
Tetranychus ludeni Zacher	Cowpea	Watermelon	April–Mid June	Sept–Oct
	French bean	pumpkin	April–Mid June	Sept–Oct
	Hyacinth bean	Okra	April–Mid June	Sept–Oct
	Broad bean	Sponge gourd	April–Mid June	Sept–Oct
		Ridge gourd	April–Mid June	Sept–Oct
Tetranychus neocaledonicus Andre	French bean	Snake gourd	April–Mid June	Sept–Oct
	Cowpea	Bottle gourd	April–Mid June	Sept–Oct
Tetranychus macfarlanei Baker and Pritchard	Round gourd	–	May–June	Sept–Oct
	Pumpkin	Okra	April–Mid June	Sept–Oct
	Bottle guard	Cucumber	April–Mid June	Sept–Oct
	Ridge guard	Cowpea	April–Mid June	Sept–Oct
	Sponge gourd	French bean	April–Mid June	Sept–Oct
	Ash gourd	–	May–June	Sept–Oct
Eutetranychus orientalis Klein	Hyacinth bean	Okra	March–April	Oct–Nov
		Bitter gourd	March–April	Oct–Nov
		Pointed gourd	March–April	Oct–Nov
		Brinjal	March–April	Oct–Nov
Eutetranychus bredini Baker and Pritchard	N.A.	Brinjal	N.O.	N.O.
	N.A.	Okra	N.O.	N.O.
Schizoteteranychus andropogon Hirst	N.A.	Sponge gourd	May–June	Sept–Oct
	N.A.	Ridge gourd	May–June	Sept–Oct
	N.A.	Bottle gourd	May–June	Sept–Oct
Family: Tenuipalpidae				
Brevipalus phoenicis Geij	N.A.	Okra	Sept–Oct	Feb–March
		Brinjal	Sept–Oct	Feb–March
		Tomato	Sept–Oct	Feb–March
		Bitter gourd	Sept–Oct	Feb–March
		Bottle gourd	Sept–Oct	Feb–March

Contd...

Table 12.1–Contd...

Mite Pest Species	Host Plant Species		Peak Period of Occurrence	
	Major	Minor	Upper Peak (1st Peak)	Lower Peak (2nd Peak)
		Sponge gourd	Sept–Oct	Feb–March
		Ridge gourd	Sept–Oct	Feb–March
		Hyacinth bean	Sept–Oct	Feb–March
		French bean	Sept–Oct	Feb–March
Brevipalus californicus Banks	N.A.	Bottle gourd	Sept–Oct	Feb–March
		Pumpkin	Sept–Oct	Feb–March
		Hyacinth bean	Sept–Oct	Feb–March
		Okra	Sept–Oct	Feb–March
Family: Tarsonemidae				
Polyphagotarsonemus lutus Banks	Chillies	Sponge gourd	May–June	Sept–Oct
	Tomato	Brinjal	May–June	Sept–Oct
	Shimla mirch	Hyacinth bean	May–June	Sept–Oct
		Bitter gourd	May–June	Sept–Oct
		French bean	May–June	Sept–Oct
		Cowpea	May–June	Sept–Oct
Family: Eriophyidae				
Aceria lycopersicae Wolf	N.A.	Brinjal	Feb–April	Sept–Oct
		Tomato	March–April	N.A.
		Chilli	March–April	N.A

Major hosts plants: > 5 mite per square centimeter of leaf area.

Minor hosts plants: < 5 mite per square centimeter of leaf area.

N.A.: Not available; N.O.: Not occurred as pest of economic significance.

Low incidence: < 5 mites/sq. cm of leaf area.

Mild incidence: > 5 and < 10 mites/sq.cm of leaf area.

Severe incidence: > 10 and < 15 mites/sq.cm. of leaf area.

Extremely severe incidence: > 15 mites/sq. cm. of leaf area.

Tetranychus ludeni Zacher

During the course of present study, severe incidence of the mite was recorded on cowpea, french bean, *hyacith* bean, broad bean. (Table 12.1) Hence, these crops were considered as major hosts for (*T. ludeni*). However, minor incidence of the mite pest was recorded on pumpkin, okra, sponge gourd and ridge gourd. The higher (*i.e.* 1st) peak of incidence of the mite was found from middle of April to middle of June, while lower (*i.e.*, 2nd) peak was noticed during September to October (Table 12.2). Prasad (2002) recorded almost similar results on cowpea in Varanasi.

Tetranychus neocaledonicus Andre

This mite pest was mostly found to infest the leguminaceous vegetables, *viz.*, cowpea, French bean, lab-lab and broad bean as preferred and major host plant, whereas the minor and stray occurrence of this mite was recorded on snake gourd and bottle gourd in the present study. Manjunatha and Puttaswamy (1995) also registered severe attack of *T. ludeni* on French bean in Kamataka agro-climatic condition. Singh and Singh (1996) also registered more of less similar results in Varanasi. Seasonal incidence of this mite species was almost similar to that of *T. ludeni* in the present investigation.

***Tetranychus macfarlanei* Baker and Pritchard**

This spider mite was noticed as the major mite pest of cucurbitaceous vegetables *viz.*, round gourd, pumpkin, bottle gourd, ridge gourd, sponge gourd, and ash gourd. Higher (*i.e.*, 1st) peak incidence period remained during hot summer months (middle of April to middle of June) lower (*i.e.*, 2nd) peak was found to exist from September to October. The mite was found to be extremely severe pest of these crops during summer in general with particular reference to late sown crop in the present study (Table 12.1). Prasad (2002) recorded almost similar results on certain vegetable crops in Varanasi region.

***Eutetranychus orientalis* Klein**

Hyacinth bean (lab-lab) was found to be infested with this mite as major host plant. However, minor and stray occurrence of this mite pest was also recorded on okra, bottle gourd and brinjal. Higher (*i.e.*, 1st) peak incidence of this mite was observed during March to April whereas lower peak (*i.e.*, 2nd) occurrence of the mite was found to exist during October in present investigation. Arbabi *et al.* (1994) also found almost similar results in this regard in the agro-climatic condition of Varanasi of Uttar Pardesh.

In addition to these four major spider mite pests on vegetables, two more mite pest species were observed to infest some vegetables in the present studies as minor pest. *Eutetranychus bredine* Baker and Pritchard was also found to infest some vegetable crops *viz.*, brinjal and okra upto very low and stray incidence in the agro-ecosystem.

***Schizoteranychus andropogoni* Hirst**

This mite species was also found to occur on some cucurbitaceous vegetables *viz.*, sponge gourd, ridge gourd, and bottle gourd.

Stray and very low incidence of these two mite pest species, *E. bredine* and *S. andropogoni* were registered on the respective host plants in the agro-climatic condition of Ranchi in the present study (Table 12.1). Findings of Arbabi *et al.* (1994) recorded in the Varanasi region of Uttar Pradesh are almost in the consonance with the results of present investigation.

Tenuipalpid Mites

Two mite species of this group *viz.*, *Brevipalpus phoenicis* Geij and *B. califomicus* was found to infest some vegetable crops up to very low level. *Brevipalpus phoenicis* Geij occurred in very low level on okra, brinjal, tomato, bitter gourd, bottle gourd, sponge gourd, ridge gourd, hyacinth bean and french bean in the stray pattern in the agro-climatic condition of Ranchi district of Jharkhand in the present study. Arbabi *et al.* (1994) and Singh (1996) also obtained more or less similar results. Another mite of this group *viz.*, *B. califomicus* appeared as stray and minor pest of bottle, pumpkin, hyacinth bean and okra in the present study conducted in Ranchi region, though, the incidence of these two tenuipalpid mites pest species were recorded during September to October as compared to February to March unlike other mites recorded in the present field investigation.

Tarsonemid Mite

Only one species of this group of phytophagous mite *i.e.*, *Polyphagotarsonemus latus* Banks was registered as severe pest of tomato and shimla mirch (*Capsicum frutescence*) and extremely severe pest on chilli (*C. anum*) during summer months. Rusetting and curling of tomato and chillies leaves were noticed in the field, which was more pronounced during summer months and post monsoon periods in the present study. Rao *et al.* (1983) and Ahmed *et al.* (2000) also reported that *P. latus* remained extremely severe mite pest of chillies in Andhra Pradesh. Higher (*i.e.*, 1st) peak incidence of the mite remained during May–June, followed by lower (*i.e.*, 2nd) peak occurrence during September to October in the present investigation. Sponge gourd, brinjal, hyacinth bean, bitter gourd, french bean and cowpea were found to behave as minor hosts for *P. latus* in the present study.

Eriophyid Mite

One species of this group of mite *i.e.*, *Aceria lycopersicci* Wolff was found to infest brinjal, chilli and tomato as minor and stray pest in the present study. Arbabi *et al.* (1994) and Singh and Singh (1996) also reported that *A. lycopersici* was noticed to attack brinjal and tomato as minor pest in the agroclimatic condition of Estern Uttar Pradesh. However, Prasad (2000) recorded severe incidence of this mite during summer seasons on brinjal at Varanasi area of Uttar Pradesh.

Based on the survey and surveillance conducted in the different parts of Ranchi district of Jharkhand during May 2002 to May 2004, it is concluded that five tetranychid mite, *T. urticae, T. ludeni T. neocaledonicus, T. macfarlanei* and *E. orientalis* were found to infest some commonly grown vegetables as major mite pest Their higher peak (*i.e.*, 1st) incidence period remained during middle of April to middle of June during both of the years in the present study, *Eutetranychus orientalis* remained the major pest of hyacinth bean. One tarsonernid mite, *Polyphagotarsonemus latus* emerged as severe pest on tomato and shimla mirch and extremely severe pest on chilli. The highest incidence of this mite was recorded during summer (April–June) followed by post monsoon months, September to October. In general, winter season proved to be highly disfavourable for mite pest fauna. Hence, the vegetables remaining almost free from attack of mite pests during winter in general. The findings suggest that special care should be taken to protect the crops against the peak period of attack of mite pest species infesting respective nineteen vegetable crops.

References

Ahmed, Khalid, Rao, P. Pusa Chandra and Rao, N.H.P., 2002. Evaluation of new insecticides against yellow mite, *Polyphagotarsonemus latus* Banks on chillies. *Pestology*, 24(1): 54–57.

Arbabi, Masoud; Singh, R.K. and Singh, J., 1994. Effect of injurious mites on their host plant in Varanasi. *Pestology*, 18: 5–14.

Channa, Basavanna, G.P., 1971. *Bibliography of Indian Plant Food Mites*, Univ. Agric. Sci., 8: 1–24.

Gupta, S.K., 1991. *Mites of Agricultural importance in India and their Management.* Tech. Bull. ICAR, 1: 1–18.

Manjunath, M. and Puttaswamy, 1995. Chemical control of *Tetranychus neocaledonicus* (*Acari : Tetranychidae*) infesting french bean and ridge gourd. *J. Acarol.*, 13 (1 and 3): 91–94.

Prasad, R., 2002. Mite problem associated with common vegetables with particular reference to brinjal and okra in Varanasi. *Ph.D. Thesis*, submitted to Banaras Hindu University, Varanasi.

Rao, B.H.K., Subharathnam, G.V. and Murthy, K.S.R. 1983. Crop losses due to insect pests. Special issue. *Indian J. Ent.*, 1: 2–5.

Singh, R.N. and Singh, J., 1996. Qualitative composition of vegetable mites of Eastern Uttar Pradesh. *J. Insect Sci.*, 9(1): 81–83.

Chapter 13

Screening of Antimutagenic Effects of Green and Black Tea (*Camellia sinensis*) in Reverse Mutation Assay

***K.S. Santhy*[1]*, S. Namitha*[1]*, Sherly P. George*[1] *and P. Arulraj*[2]**

[1]Department of Life Sciences, Avinashilingam Deemed University, Coimbatore, Tamil Nadu, India

[2]Department of Surgical Oncology, Government Royapettah Hospital, Chennai, Tamil Nadu, India

ABSTRACT

Tea (*Camellia sinensis*) is one of the most consumed beverages worldwide. In the present investigation antimutagenic effects of petroleum ether, chloroform, ethanol and water extracts of green and black tea were evaluated in *Salmonella typhimurium* TA–98 and TA–100 strains. Addition of Sodium azide and Daunomycin, two well known mutagens at a concentration of 10 µl and 6 µl per plate respectively resulted in the induction in the histidine revertant colonies. However addition of 10 µl of petroleum ether, chloroform, ethanol and water extracts of green and black tea to 10 µl of Sodium azide and 6 µl of Daunomycin treated plates resulted in the inhibition in the number of histidine revetant colonies. Further more supplementation with all the four extracts of green and black tea at a concentration of 6 µl and 10 µl per plate respectively in the presence of S9 fraction also led to a significant inhibition in sodium azide and Daunomycin induced colony formation. The antimutagenic activity of ethanolic extract of green and black tea was found to be higher than that of the other extracts. Hence the study revealed that green and black tea has protective efficacy in Sodium azide and Daunomycin induced mutagenicity in the test microbial system.

Keywords: Green tea, Black tea, Antimutagenic activity, Ames assay.

Introduction

Plant contains many natural substances that can promote health and alleviate illness. Flavonoids, one of the major constituent of the plants show biological properties that help to reduce the risk of many diseases. Tea plant (*Camellia sinensis*) native to south East Asia is consumed worldwide. Next to water, tea is the most consumed beverage in the world. Green and black tea have many therapeutic uses. It has been found that tea consumption lowers the incidence of skin disorders, guards tooth decay and prevent various diseases.

Flavonoids, a group of phenolic compounds occurring abundantly in vegetables, fruits and green plants attracted special attention as they showed high antioxidant property. The antioxidants are known to prevent cellular damage caused by Reactive Oxygen Species (ROS). Catechins are highly potent flavonoids present in tea and serve perhaps as the best dietary source of natural antioxidants. The fresh tea leaves contains four major catechins as colorless water soluble compounds, Epicatechin (EC), Epicatechin Gallate (ECG), Epigallocatechin (EGC) and Epigallocatechin Gallate (EGCG). Most of the green tea catechins during the manufacture of black tea are oxidized and converted into orange or brown products known as Theaflavins (TF) and Thearubigins (TR). These compounds retain the basic C6-C3-C6 structure and thus are classified as flavonoids.

Reports on potent antimutagenicity of green tea reveals that EGCG is perhaps the most potent antimutagenic agent protecting DNA scissions and non-enzymatic interception of superoxide anions. This leads to the general conclusion that development of cancer is prevented by tea consumption through antimutagenic protection paralleling to their antioxidant efficacy.

In the present investigation an attempt was made to evaluate the antimutagenic effect of green and black tea extracted using four different solvents *viz.*, petroleum ether, chloroform, ethanol and water in Salmonella microsome assay.

Materials and Methods

Green and black tea were procured from a local market. Histidine, biotin, Bactoagar, glucose, sodium ammonium hydrogen phosphate, Daunomycin and Sodum azide were of analytical grade and purity and purchased from Himedia Laboratories Ltd., Mumbai.

Soxhlet Extraction

10 g of the green and black tea powders were weighed using an electrical balance and made into 8 packets using Xerohaze filter paper. Soxhlet extraction of powdered green and black tea were carried out to obtain their extracts. Petroleum ether, chloroform, ethanol and water were used as solvents for soxhlet extraction in the increasing order of polarity. The distillation process was carried out at a low temperature of 40°C. After evaporation of solvents, corresponding residues obtained are stored in the refrigerator for further use. 100 mg of soxhlet extract was dissolved in 2 ml of DMSO and then mixed with 100 ml distilled water and this formed 1000 ppm solution. From this stock solution, solutions of required concentrations were prepared and used in this study.

Bacterial Tester Strains

Salmonella typhimurium tester strains TA-98 and TA-100 were kindly provided by Professor Bruce N. Ames, Berkley, U.S.A. The Strains were checked routinely for Amphicillin resistance, ultraviolet sensitivity and spontaneous revertants.

Preparation of Metabolically Activated Rat Liver S9 Mix

Albino rats (wistar strain) of 200 ± 25 g were obtained from animal laboratory, Food Science and Nutrition Department, Avinashilingam·Deemed University, Coimbatore and kept in plastic cages with husk bedding and a stainless steel lid suitable for feeding and watering. The mouse was fed on by standard rodent diet pellet. Mouse was injected with phenobarbitone at a dose of 1 mg/g body weight intra peritoneally for 3 consecutive days. On day six, no food was provided to the mouse for fasting. The mouse was sacrificed on the seventh day for preparation of liver S9 fraction. All the steps were performed at 0–4°C with cold and sterile solutions and glass wares. The liver was excised out after dissecting the animal. The excised liver was then washed in an equal volume of 0.15 M KCl. Then it was mixed in 0.14M KCl and homogenized with a homogenizer. The homogenate was centrifuged for 10 min. at 9000 g and the supernatant which was so collected, was the S9 mix fraction. The freshly prepared S9 fraction was quickly frozen in dry ice and stored at –20°C.

For plate incorporation assay, top agar (2 ml) was distributed into each small test tubes held in a water bath. In different set groups of experiments in above tubes, 10 µl/plate of petroleum ether chloroform, ethanol and water extracts of green tea/10 µl/plate of petroleum ether, chloroform, ethanol and water extracts of black tea plus the mutagen (Daunomycin at the concentration of 6 µl/plate and Sodium azide at the concentration of 10 µl/plate) and 10 µl of metabolically activated S9 mix plus 10 µl of standardised bacterial cultures of TA-98 and TA-100 strains were added to the top agar and then poured into minimal glucose agar plates. The plates were then inverted and placed in an incubator at 37°C for 48 hours and counted for the number of histidine revertant colonies.

Similar experiments were carried out for positive controls (taking Daunomycin and Sodium azide) and negative controls (Untreated groups) for identifying spontaneous culture for both the strains concurrently.

Statistical Analysis

The mean values of number of histidine revertants/plate of different groups were subjected to statistical analysis using student 't' test.

Results

The present investigation depicts the antimutagenic potential of green and black tea extracts in *Salmonella typhimurium* reverse mutation assay (Tables 13.1 and 13.2). The number of spontaneous revertants were found to be 38 and 144 in TA-98 and TA-100 strains respectively. Addition of Daunomycin and Sodium azide to the minimal glucose plates resulted in significant induction in the number of histidine revertants and were found to be 61 and 184 of TA-98 and TA-100 strains respectively. However in plates supplemented with different extracts of black and green tea resulted in the inhibition of induction of histidine revertant colonies either by Daunomycin or Sodium azide.

The percentage inhibition of Daunomycin 26 per cent, 28 per cent, 33 per cent and 19 per cent for green tea and 23 per cent, 26 per cent, 30 per cent and 19 per cent for black tea in petroleum ether, chloroform, ethanol and water extracts respectively in TA-98 strains. The percentage inhibition of different extracts of green and black tea towards Sodium azide induced histidine reversion was found to be 8 per cent, 9 per cent, 10 per cent and 5 per cent and 3 per cent, 8 per cent, 8 per cent and 5 per cent respectively for petroleum ether, chloroform, ethanol, water extracts in TA-100 strains. The number of histidine revertants per plates for TA-98 and TA-100 tester strains in green tea was found to reduce to 45, 44, 41 and 50 and 171, 169, 167 and 175 respectively. The number of histidine revertants per plates for TA-98 and TA-100 tester stains in black tea was found to be reduced to 47,45, 43 and 50 and 179,

171, 170 and 175 respectively. In the presence of S9 fraction the number of spontaneous revertants for petroleum ether, chloroform, ethanol and water extracts of green and black tea were found to be 106 and 203 in TA-98 and TA-100 strains respectively. On addition of Daunomycin and Sodium azide to the above extracts in TA-98 and TA-100 strains the number of histidine revertant were found to be increased to 155 and 359 respectively. However in plates supplemented with petroleum ether, chloroform, ethanol and water extracts of green and black tea resulted in inhibition of induction of histidine revertant colonies either by Daunomycin or by Sodium azide. The number of histidine revertants/plate of TA-98 and TA-100 tester strains of green tea were found to be reduced to 141, 134, 127 and 136 and 204, 210, 208 and 202 respectively. The number of histidine revertants/plate of TA-98 and TA-100 strains by adding petroleum ether, chloroform, ethanol and water extracts of black tea were found to be reduced to 139, 141, 130 and 138 and 327, 325, 323 and 327 respectively.

Table 13.1: Antimutagenic Effect of Petroleum Ether, Chloroform, Ethanol and Water Extract of Green and Black Tea in *Salmonella typhimurium* TA-98 and TA-100 Strains

Strain	*Treatment*	*Petroleum Ether*	*Chloroform*	*Ethanol*	*Water*
TA-98	SR+GT	39±3.29NS	41±3.23NS	40±2.79NS	37±5.19NS
	SM+GT	45±2.61NS (26%)	44±3.60NS (28%)	41±3.88NS (33%)	50±2.66NS (19%)
	SR+BT	41±3.75**	39±5.01**	39±5.95**	37±2.69**
	SM+BT	47±4.25** (23%)	45±3.57** (26%)	43±4.96** (30%)	50±3.67* (19%)
TA100	SR+GT	146±5.65NS	143±9.08NS	141±10.53NS	145±8.18NS
	SM+GT	171±4.99NS (8%)	169±3.87NS (9%)	167±3.37NS (10%)	175±2.47NS (5%)
	SR+BT	145±7.68**	143±8.48**	139±10.52**	143±6.69**
	SM+BT	179±2.35** (3%)	171±5.23** (8%)	170±3.10** (8%)	175±4.54** (5%)

Results are the average of two independent experiments.

Spontaneous revertant rate for TA-98 was 38±4.1 and TA-100 was 144±3.7.

Standard mutation rate for TA-98 was 61±2.1 and TA-100 was 184±3.2.

NS: Not significant; *: Significant at p = 0.05.

**: Significant at P = 0.01. Per cent inhibition of revertant frequency with the addition of different green and black tea extracts to standard mutagen induced plates is given in the parenthesis.

Discussion

The *Salmonella. typhimurium* reverse mutation assay is most commonly used method to assess mutagenic potential of test chemicals, which may cause base pair and flame shift mutations in the genome of this organism (Maron and Ames, 1983). Its applicability in screening the antimutagenic potential of green and black tea has been performed in the present study. Daunomycin and Sodium azide rule the known genotoxicant in mammalian and microbial test systems. Addition of Dauno mycin and Sodium azide to the minimal glucose plates resulted in the significant induction of histidine revertant colonies. In the present study addition of green and black tea extracts to Sodium azide and Daunomycin treated plates resulted in the significant inhibition of number of colonies formed in TA-100 arid TA-98 strains respectively.

Table 13.2: Antimutagenic Effect of Petroleum Ether, Chloroform, Ethanol and Water Extracts of Green and Black Tea in *Salmonella typhimurium* TA-98 and TA-100 Strains in the Presence of S9 Fraction

Strain	*Treatment*	*Petroleum Ether*	*Chloroform*	*Ethanol*	*Water*
TA-98	SR+GT	108±8.08NS	105±6.48NS	104±6.55NS	112±8.60 NS
	SM+GT	141±8NS9 (9%)	134±6.11NS (14%)	127±3.15NS (18%)	136±4.05NS (13%)
	SR+BT	102±4.60**	108±4.76**	104±5.63**	102±4.89**
	SM+ BT	139±5.65** (10%)	141±4.12** (9%)	130±3.30** (17%)	138±3.42** (11%)
TA-100	SR+GT	204±8.12NS	210±6.84NS	208±5.86NS	202±3.15NS
	SM+GT	316±7.06NS (12%)	315±5.74NS (13%)	311±6.45NS (14%)	338±7.25NS (6%)
	SR+BT	210+4.79**	207±9.34**	211+9.08**	200±7.87**
	SM+BT	327±13.63** (9%)	325±11.31** (10%)	323±13.11** (11%)	327±9.53** (9%)

Results are the average of two independent experiments.

Spontaneous revertant rate for TA-98 was 106±8.6 and TA-100 was 203±5.8.

Standard mutagen rate for TA-98 was 155±4.9 and TA-100 was 359±5.5.

NS: Not significant; **: Significant at p = 0.01.

Percent inhibition of revertant frequency with the addition of different green and black tea extracts to standard mutagen induced plates is given in the parenthesis.

Catechin component including Epicatechin Gallate (ECG) and Epigallocatechin Gallate (EGCG) provide a significant protection against mutagenicity of Trp-P-2 and N-OH-Trp-P-2 using *Salmonella typhimurium* TA-98 and TA-100 (Hayatsu *et al.*, 1992; Kuroda and Hara, 1999). EGCG also have been reported to provide strong inhibitory effect against mutagenicity of Ba P diol epoxide in TA-100 strain (Hour *et al.*, 1999). Using *Salmonella typhimurium* TA-98 and TA-100, the tea catechins ECG and EGCG have been shown to inhibit the mutagenic activity of direct acting mutagens (Okuda *et al.*, 1984). The extracts of both green and black tea decreased the mutagenic activity of N-methyl-N-nitro-N-nitroso guanidine (MNNG) in *Escherichia coli* WP2 in a desmutagenic manner (Kuroda and Hara, 1999; Jain *et al.*, 1989) (Theaflavins from black tea were found to suppress the mutagenicity of H_2O_2 in *Salmonella typhimurium* (TA 104) (Shiraki *et al.*, 1994). The *Antimutagenic* potential of ethanolic extracts of Rheo discofor in *Salmonella typhimurium* TA 102 pretreated with ROS-generating mutagen nor floxacin in Ames test, protests liver cell structures against diethyl nitrosamine (Avila *et al.*, 2003). Procarcinogens like Benzo (a) pyrene and Aflatoxin B, require metabolic activation by cytochrome P-450 dependent enzymes to manifest their mutagenic/carcinogenic response. The antimutagenic potential of black tea in part, relate to their ability to inhibit cytochrome P-450 dependent metabolic activation of mutagens which inturn results in the inhibition of PAH–DNA binding (*Weisburger et al.*, 1996). Catechins arc competitive inhibitors of NADPH–Cytochrome C reductase enzyme (Hernaez *et al.*, 1998; Wang *et al.*, 1988).

The inhibition of PHIr mutagenicity by black and green tea extracts or polyphenols has been observed in the *Salmonella typhimurium* TA-98 assay containing rat S9 fraction. Green tea extracts were also effective against the mutagenicity of PAH, Benzo (a) pyrene, DMBA with S9 activation (Kuroda and Hara, 1999). The antimutagenic effect of tea involves interaction between the reactive genotoxic species of various promutagens and polyphenolic tea component present in the tea (Kuroda and Hara, 1999; Weisburger, 1999a). The antigenotoxic properties of tea include induction of DNA repair and binding of activated carcinogens (Weisburger, 1999b; Yang *et al.*, 2002).

The antimutagenic activity of aqueous tea poly-phenols and black tea poly-phenols towards Benzo (a) pyrene and cyclophosphamide in *Salmonella typhimurium* tester strain TA-98 and TA-100 (Taneja *et al.*, 2003). The inhibition of Aflatoxin B1-2-amino fluorine and 2-aminoanthracene induced mutagenicity by extracts of *Maytenus ilicifolia* and peltastes peltatus was observed in salmonella microsome assay in the presence of S9 fraction (Horn and Vargas, 2003).

Our findings point to higher antimutagenic activity of ethanolic extracts of green and black tea when compared to other four extracts using petroleum ether, chloroform, ethanol and water. This study throws possibility of reduction of mutagenicity and thereby carcinogenicity in people drinking green tea and black tea regularly.

References

Avila, M.G., Alba, M.A., Delagarza, M., Carmen, M.D., Pretelin, H., Oritz, A.D., Fazenda, S.F. and Trevino, S.V., 2003. Antigenotoxic, antimutagenic and ROS scavenging activities of Rheo dicolor ethanolic crude extract. *Toxicology in vivo*, 17(1): 77–83.

Hayastu, H., Inaba, N., Kakutani, T., 1992. Suppression of genotoxicity of carcinogenesis by(–)epigallocatechin gallate. *Prev. Med.*, 21: 370–376.

Hernaez, F.J., Xu, M. and Dashwood, R.H., 1998. Antimutagenic activity of tea towards 2-hydroxyamino 3-Methilimidazo (4,5-F) quinoline effect of tea concentration and brew time on electrophile scavenging. *Mutat. Research/Fundamental Molecular Mechanism of Mutagenesis*, 902(1–2): 299–306.

Horn, R.C. and Vargas, V.M.F., 2003. Antimutagenic activity of extracts of natural substances in the *Salmonella*/Microsome assay. *Mutagenesis*, 18(2): 113–118.

Hour, T.C., Liang, Y.C., Chu, I.S. and Lin, J.K., 1999. Inhibition of eleven mutagens by various tea extracts epigallocatechin-3-gallate, gallic acid and caffeine. *Food Chem. Toxicol.*, 37: 569–579.

Jain, A.K., Shimoi, K., Nakamura, Y., 1989. Crude tea extracts decrease the mutagenic activity of N-methyl N-nitro-N-nitrosoguanidine *in vitro* and intragastric tract of rats. *Mutat. Res.*, 210: 1–8.

Kuroda, T. and Hara, Y., 1999. Antimutagenicity and carcinogenic activity of tea polyphenols. *Mutat. Res.* 436: 69–97.

Maron, D.M. and Ames, B.N., 1983. Revised methods for *Salmonella* mutagenicity test. *Mutat. Res.*, 113: 173–175.

Okuda, T., Mari, K. and Hayatsu, H., 1984. Inhibitory effect of tanins on direct-acting mutagens. *Chem. Pharm. Bull.*, 32: 3755–3758.

Shikari, M., Hara, Y. and Osawa, T., 1994. Antioxidative and antimutagenic effects of theaflavins from black tea. *Mutat. Res.*, 323: 29–34.

Taneja, P., Arora, A. and Shukla, Y., 2003. Antimutagenic effects of black tea in the *Salmonella typhimurium* reverse mutation assay. *Asian Pacific J. Cancer Prev.*, 4: 193–198.

Wang, Z.Y., Das, M., Brickers, D.R. and Mukthar, H., 1988. Intraction of epicatechins derived from green tea with rat hepatic cytochrome P-450. *Drug Metab. Dispos.*, 16: 98–103.

Weisburger, J.H., 1999a. Mechanisms of action of antioxidants exemplified as in vegetables, tomatoes and tea. *Food Chem. Toxicol.*, 37: 943–948.

Weisburger, J.H., 1999b. Tea and health: The underlying mechanism. *Proc. Soc. Exp. Biol. Med.*, 220: 271–275.

Weisburger, J.H., Hara, Y. and Dolan, L., 1996. Tea polyphenols as inhibitors of mutagenicity of major classes of carcinogens. *Mutat. Res.*, 371: 57–63.

Yang, C.S., Maliakal, P. and Meng, X., 2002. Inhibition of carcinogenesis by tea. *Annu. Rev. Pharmocol. Toxicol.*, 42: 25–54.

Chapter 14

Effect of Larval Size and Weight on Pupation Site Preference in Different Species of *Drosophila*

N.B. Vandal and N. Shivanna*

Department of Studies in Zoology, Karnatak University, Dharwad – 580 003, India

ABSTRACT

The effects of larval size and weight in different species of *Drosophila* have been studied to know its influence on pupation site preference. The larvae of media, glass and cotton pupating species show differences in their size and weight. The larval size and weight of *virilis* and *repleta* group species are higher than *melanogaster* and *ananassae* group species. The *melanogaster* and *ananassae* species group larvae have similarity in their size and weight, even then they prefer to pupate on media, glass and cotton. Whereas the *virilis* and *repleta* group species are similar in size and weight, they prefer to pupate maximum on glass. These results and partial correlation analysis revealed that size and weight of the larva has no effect on its pupation site preference in *Drosophila*.

Keywords: Larva, Size and weight, Pupation, Drosophila.

Introduction

The larval Pupation Site Preference (PSP) is an important event in *Drosophila* preadult development, because the place selected by the larva has decisive influence on the subsequent survival as pupae (Sameoto and Miller 1968). The larval PSP has been analyzed by two types of phenotypic characters,

* Corresponding Author: Phone: 0836–2215230; Fax: 0836–747884; E-mail: dmshivanna@rediffmail.com.

one is the pupation height and the other is pupation site preference. The pupation height has been studied by measuring the distance a larva pupated above the surface of the food medium (Sokal *et al.*, 1960; Sameoto and Miller, 1968; Sokolowski, 1985; Casares and Carracedo, 1987; Schnebel and Grossfield, 1986, 1992; Singh and Pandey, 1991, 1993a, 1993b). The larval PSP has also been analysed by measuring the percentage of larva pupated at different sites *viz.*, cotton, glass and medium (Barker, 1971; Shirk *et al.*, 1988; Shivanna *et al.*, 1996; Shivanna and Ramesh, 1997; Vandal *et al.*, 2003). The effect of abiotic factors such as temperature, humidity, water, moisture, resource acidic pH, light and dark on pupation height has been studied in different species of *Drosophila* (Sokal *et al.*, 1960, Sameoto and Miller 1968, Casares and Carracedo, 1987; Rodriguez and Sokolowski, 1987; Schnebel and Grossfield, 1986, 1992; Pandey and Singh, 1993; Hodge *et al.*, 1996; Hodge and Caslaw, 1997) and it reveals that the abiotic factors affect the pupation height.

Biotic factors such as larval density, sex, locomotory path length, digging and developmental time have also been shown to influence the pupation height of *Drosophila*. The increased larval density increases with the pupation height. The males larvae were found to pupate higher than female larvae, early pupating larvae tend to pupate higher than late pupating larvae and early pupating larvae show peripheral pupation than late pupating larvae which pupates at centre of media in *D. melanogaster*. The larvae with longer path length and lesser digging behaviours showed higher pupal height; and the larvae with shorter path length and higher digging behaviours showed pupation on or off the fruit or periphery of the food media (Sokal *et al.*, 1960; de Souza *et al.*, 1970; Sokolowski, 1985; Bauer and Sokolowski, 1985; Mueller and Sweet, 1986; Casares and Carracedo, 1987; Godoy-Herrera, 1986; Sokolowski and Bauer, 1989; Pandey and Singh, 1993; Joshi and Mueller, 1993; Joshi, 1997; Sokolowski *et al.*, 1997).

The percentage of PSP studies revealed that most of the *Drosophila* species, prefers maximum media and few species prefers glass and cotton for pupation (Barker, 1971; Shirk *et al.*, 1988; Shivanna *et al.*, 1996; Vandal *et al.*, 2003). The correlation studies between larval PSP and the quantity of larval salivary gland protein called glue protein revealed that the larvae which secretes larger quantity of glue protein tend to pupate on media and those synthesize half of the quantity of glue protein prefers to pupate on glass wall arid very less or negligible quantity of glue protein prefers to pupate on cotton (Shivanna *et al.*, 1996). The studies of Shivanna and Ramesh (1995) on larval salivary gland secretions (glue proteins) and the gland size in 15 species of *Drosophila* reveals that the quantity of secretions synthesized is independent of size of the salivary glands. Whereas the importance of size and weight of the larva in relation to PSP has not been studied. The present study was undertaken to analyze is there any relation between the size and weight of larvae and its pupation site preference.

Materials and Methods

Following *Drosophila* species were used to study the relationship between size and weight of the larva on PSP. *D.melanogaster, D. simulans, D. yakuba* and *D. mauritiana* are sibling species belong to the *melanogaster* subgroup species, *D. ananassae, D. bipectinata, D. malerkotliana* and *D. rajasekari* are closely related sympatric species and belongs to *ananassae* subgroup of *melanogaster* species group, *D. virilis* and *D. novamexicana* are belongs to *virilis* group and *D. hydei* belongs to repleta species group (Bock and Wheeler, 1972; Ehrman, 1978; Ranganath *et al.*, 1985; Ashburner, 1989; Singh and Pandey, 1991).

In order to maintain uniformity with regard to the age of the larvae, the eggs were collected every 6 hours using the modified technique of Delcour as described by Ramachandra and Ranganath (1988) and allowed to hatch. The culture was maintained at 22±1°C with 80 per cent RH. The late third instar (96 hour old) larvae were used to carryout the experiment. Late third instar larvae were isolated from the cultures, the size of the larva was measured from the anterior spiracles to the posterior spiracles of larva (Length and Breadth). The weight of the larva was measured using electronic balance by individual. The average weight was calculated based on the weight of twenty five larvae. Then the larvae allowed to pupate in the culture vials. The partial correlation analysis was used to correlate the size and weight of the larva with PSP.

Results

Table 14.1 shows the mean of larval size (length and breadth) weight and percentage of PSP in different species of *Drosophila*. Among the media pupating species *D. simulans, D. yakuba, D. mauritiana, D. bipectinata* and *D. malerkotliana* prefers maximum media for pupation (93.4 per cent, 71.4 per cent, 53.2 per cent, 86.6 per cent and 74 per cent). The approximate larval size of these species varies between 3 to 3.5 mm and weight varies between 0.6 to 0.7 mg. The larvae of *D. melanogaster, D. ananassae, D. virilis, D. novamexicana* and *D. hydei* prefer maximum glass for pupation (94.2 per cent, 78 per cent, 95 per cent, 76.6 per cent and 74.25). The larval size of these species varies between 3.3 to 6 mm and weight varies between 0.6 to 1.7 mg. The larvae of *D. rajasekari* prefer maximum cotton for pupation (61.8 per cent). The larval size is 3.5 mm and weight is 0.6 mg.

Table 14.1: Size and Weight of Third Instar Larvae and their Maximum PSP in Different Species of *Drosophila*

Species	*Size (LXB) (mm)*	*Weight (mg)*	*Percentage of Pupation (%)*
Media pupating species			
D. simulans	3.3	0.6	93.4
D. yakuba	3.5	0.6	71.4
D. mauritiana	3.4	0.6	53.2
D. bipectinata	3.5	0.7	86.6
D. malerkotliana	3.0	0.7	74.0
Glass pupating species			
D. melanogaster	3.3	0.6	94.2
D. ananassae	3.5	0.7	78.0
D. virilis	5.0	1.1	95.0
D. novamexicana	6.0	1.7	76.6
D. hydei	5.5	1.7	74.2
Cotton pupating species			
D. rajasekari	3.5	0.6	61.8

Size–Mean length and breadth of larvae includes anterior and posterior spiracles (mm).

Weight–Mean weights of late third instar larvae (mg).

The comparison between the larval size and weight with maximum PSP in different species analyzed shows significantly negative correlation (partial correlation) with their maximum PSP; on media *D. simulans* (r = –0.9545 and r = –0.9981), *D. yakuba* (r = –0.9559 and r = –0.9965), *D. mauritana* (r = –0.9065 and r = –0.9973), *D. bipectinata* (r = –0.9644 and r = –0.9971) and *D. malerkotliana* (r = –0.9979 and r = –0.9458), on glass D. *melanogaster* (r = –0.9605 and r = –0.9984), *D. ananassae* (r = –0.9661 and r = –0.9961), *D. virilis* (r = –0.983 and r = –0.9439), *D. novamexicana* (r = –0.97 and r = –0.9945) and *D. hydei* (r = –0.9769 and r = –0.9924) and on cotton *D. rajasekari* (r = –0.9165 and r = –0.9977).

Discussion

The larvae of different species show differences in the larval size and weight with their pupation site preference. The glass pupating species *D. virilis, D. novamexicana* and *D. hydei* are larger in size and weight than media pupating species, *D. simulans, D. yakuba, D. mauritiana, D. bipectinata* and *D. malerkotliana.* The larvae of glass pupating species *D. melanogaster* and *D. ananassae* and cotton pupating species *D. rajasekari* are more or less similar in their size and weight. Whereas *D. virilis, D. novamexicana* and *D. hydei* have bigger size than the larvae of *D. melanogaster, D. ananassae* and *D. rajasekari* but they prefer to pupate on the glass. The culture conditions were maintained constant for all the species analyzed.

The studies of larval size, developmental stage and age on pupation at different temperatures in different populations of *D. melanogaster* reveals that the weight of the larva within the age is significantly correlates with pupation probability in tropical populations, whereas in temperate populations no relation with larval weight, age and with pupation probability and most of the larvae succeeded in pupating on/in and then produced small adults (Bochdanovitz and de Jong, 2003). The hormonal event leading pupariation are initiated in the third larval instar when critical stage is reached, after which there is a fixed period of post critical feeding growth before pupariation occurs (Riddiford, 1985). In *D. melanogaster,* the critical stage occurs right after the second moult. The size of the larva reaching the critical stage of commitment to pupariation is referred to as its critical weight. The critical weight is symptom of the underlying physiology and need no imply a direct relation between size and decision to pupate. Larval critical weight will partly determine the way age and size at maturity respond to environmental variations and is therefore important life history evolution (Bernardo 1993). The larval developmental period is determined by the time needed to reach the critical weight and the time from the critical stage to pupation and final body weight is determined by the critical body weight and the possibilities for additional growth before the onset of pupariation as determined by the availability of resource (Robertson 1963). The same larval weight or age might have different meaning for different genotype and higher probability of pupating was associated with lower adult size once feeding was stopped and the minimal size is needed to pupate and that might vary between genotypes within population of *Drosophila* (Bakker, 1961; Bochdanovitz and de Jong, 2003).

Shivanna and Ramesh (1995) studied the larval salivary gland and quantity of glue protein and reported that the secretion of larval glue protein is not associated with size of the salivary gland and quantity of the secretion is independent of the salivary gland. The larvae which secrets larger quantity of glue protein tend to pupate on media and lesser was preferred glass for pupation and it reveals that the larval PSP depends on the quantity of glue protein synthesized by the late third instar larvae (Shivanna *et al.,* 1996). The present study reveals that, irrespective of size and weight of the larvae, the species of *D. melanogaster, D. ananassae, D. virilis, D. novamexicana* and *D. hydei* prefer to pupate on glass. *D. rajasekari* having similar size and weight with glass and media pupating species prefer to pupate on cotton. *D. virilis, D. novamexicana* and *D. hydei* are having more size and weight than other species prefers to pupate on glass. The *melanogaster* and *ananassae* group species larvae were found to pupate on glass and media though they are having similar size and weight. The result shows that the pupation site preference is not taxonomically related. Further it is concluded on the basis of the above result that, the size and weight of the larvae has no relationship with their pupation site choice.

Acknowledgement

Thanks are due to Professor H.A. Ranganath *Drosophila* Stock Centre (DSC) Department of Zoology, University of Mysore, 'Manasagangotri' Mysore, for *Drosophila* stocks and UGC-SAP-II and COSIST for financial assistance.

References

Ashburner, M., 1989. *Drosophila.* In: *A Laboratory Handbook.* Cold Spring Harbor Laboratory, Cold Spring Harbor, New York, USA.

Bakker, K., 1961. An analysis of factors which determines success in competition for food among larvae of *Drosophila melanogaster. Arch. Neerland. Zool.*, 14: 200–281.

Barker, J.S.F., 1971. Ecological differences and competitive interaction between *Drosophila melanogaster* and *Drosophila simulans* in small laboratory populations. *Oecologia*, 8: 139–156.

Bauer, S.J., 1984. Larval foraging behaviour in isofemale lines of *Drosophila melanogaster* and *Drosophila pseudoobscura. J. Heredity*, 75: 131–134.

Bauer, S.J. and Sokolowski, M.B., 1985. Larval foraging behaviour in isofemale lines of *Drosophila melanogaster* and *Drosophila pseudoobsura. J. Heredity*, 75: 131–134.

Bemardo, J., 1993. Determinants of maturation in animals. *Trends Ecol. Evol.*, 8: 166–173.

Bock, I.R. and Wheelar, M.R., 1972. *The Drosophila melanogaster Species Group*. Univ. Tex, Publ. No. 7213, 1–102 pp.

Bochdanovits, Z. and de Jong, G., 2003. Temperature dependent larval resource allocation shaping adult body size in *Drosophila melanogaster. J. Evol. Biol.*, 16: 1159–1167.

Casares, P. and Carracedo, M.C., 1987. Pupation height in *Drosophila:* Sex differences and influence of larval developmental time. *Behav. Genet.*, 17: 523–535.

De Souza H.L., Da Cunha, A.B. and Dos Santos, E.P., 1970. Adaptive polymorphism of behaviour developed in laboratory population of *Drosophila willisfoni. Amer. Nat.*, 102: 583–586.

Ehrman, P., 1978. Sexual behaviour. In: *The Genetics and Biology of Drosophila*, Vol. 2b, (Ed) M. Ashburner and T.R.F. Wright. Academic Press, New York, 127–157 pp.

Godoy-Herrera, R., 1986. The development and genetics of digging behaviour of *Drosophila* larvae. *Heredity*, 56: 3–41.

Hodge, S., Campbell-Smith, R. and Wilson, N., 1996. The effect of resources of acidity on the development of *Drosophila* larvae. *Entomologists*, 115: 129–139.

Hodge, S. and Caslaw, P., 1997. The effect of resource pH on pupation height in *Drosophila* (Diptera : Drosophilidae). *J. Insect. Behav.*, 11: 47–59.

Joshi, A. and Mueller, L.D., 1993. Directional and stabilizing density-dependent natural selection for pupation height in *Drosophila melanogaster. Evolution*, 47: 176–184.

Joshi, A., 1997. Laboratory studies of density dependent selection: Adaptation to crowding in *Drosophila melanogaster. Curr. Sci.*, 72: 555–562.

Mueller, L.D. and Sweet, V.F., 1986. Density-dependent natural selection in *Drosophila:* Evolution of pupation height. *Evolution*, 40: 1354–1356.

Pandey, M.B. and Singh, B.N., 1993. Effect of biotic and abiotic factors on pupation height in four species of *Drosophila. Indo J. Expo Biol.*, 31: 912–917.

Ranganath, H.A., Gowda, L.S. and Rajasekarshetty, M.R., 1985. Competition studies between three sympatric species of *Drosophila. Entomon.*, 10: 249–253.

Ramachandra, N.B. and H.A. Ranganath, 1988. Estimation of population fitness of parental races *Drosophila nasuta nasuta* and *Drosophila nasuta albomicana* and of the newly evolved Cytoraces I and II. *Genome,* 30: 58.

Riddiford, L.M., 1985. Cellular and molecular action of juvenile hormone: General considerations and premetamorphic actions. *Adv. Insect. Physiol.*, 24: 213–274.

Rodriguez, L. and M.B. Sokolowski, 1987. The effect of soil moisture and temperature on *Drosophila* pupation behaviour. *Behav. Genet.*, 17: 600–604.

Robertson, F.W., 1963. The ecological genetics of growth in *Drosophila.* 6. The genetic correlation between the duration of the larval period and body size in relation to larval diet. *Genet. Res.*, 4: 74–92.

Sameoto, D.D. and Miller, R.S., 1968. Selection of pupation site by *Drosophila melanogaster* and *Drosophila simulans. Ecology*, 49: 177–180.

Schnebel, E.M. and Grossfield, J., 1986. Pupation temperature range in 12 species *Drosophila* species from different ecological backgrounds. *Experientia*, 42: 600- 604.

Schnebel, E.M. and Grossfield, J., 1992. Temperature effects on pupation height response in four Drosophila species traids. *J. Insect. Physiol.*, 38: 727–732.

Shirk, P.D., Roberts, P.A. and Harn, C.H., 1988. Synthesis and secretion of salivary gland proteins in *Drosophila gibberosa* during larval and prepupal development. *Roux's Arch. Dev. Biol.*, 29: 926–929.

Shivanna, N. and Ramesh, S.R., 1995. Increase in the size of the gland is not always associated with increased secretion: An evidence from the larval salivary glands of a *Drosophila. Curr. Sci.*, 68: 1246–1249.

Shivanna, N., Siddalingarnurthy, G.S. and Ramesh, S.R., 1996. Larval pupation site preference and its relationship to the glue proteins in a few species of *Drosophila. Genome.* 39: 105–111.

Shivanna, N. and Ramesh, S.R., 1997. Intraspecific larval pupation site preference in *D.melanogaster. Dros. Inf. Serv.*, 80: 2–4.

Singh, B.N. and Pandey, M.B., 1991. Intra and interspecies variation in pupation height in *Drosophila. Ind. J. Exp. Biol.*, 29: 926–929.

Singh, B.N. and Pandey, M.B., 1993a. Evidence for polygenic control pupation height in *Drosophila ananassae. Hereditas*, 119: 111–116.

Singh, B.N. and Pandey, M.B., 1993b. Selection for high and low pupation height in *Drosophila ananassae. Behav. Genet.*, 23: 239–243.

Sokal, R.R., Ehrlich, P., Hunter, P. and Schlager, G., 1960. Some factors affecting pupation site in *Drosophila. Ann. Ento. Soc. Amer.*, 53: 174–182.

Sokolowski, M.B., 1985. Genetics and ecology of *Drosophila melanogaster.* Larval foraging and pupation behaviour. *J. Insect. Physiol.*, 31: 857–864.

Sokolowski, M.B. and Bauer, S.J., 1989. Genetic analysis of pupation distance in *Drosophila melanogaster. Heredity*, 62: 177–183.

Sokolowski, M.B., Pereira, H.S. and Hughes, K., 1997. Evolution of foraging behaviour in *Drosophila* by density-dependent selection. *Proc. Nat. Acad. Sci.*, U.S.A., 94: 7373–7377.

Vandal, N.B., Modagi, S.A. and Shivanna, N., 2003. Larval pupation site preference in a few species of *Drosophila. Ind. J. Exp. Biol.*, 41: 918–920.

Chapter 15

Protective Effect of *Mucuna pruriens* Seed on Ethanol Treated Rat Brain ATPases

G. Krishnamoorthy and A. Sivamady

Department of Zoology, K.M. Centre for Post Graduate Studies, Pondicherry – 605 008, India

ABSTRACT

The impact of *Mucuna pruriens* seed on ethanol treated rat brain ATPases was assessed in the present study. A group of rats were given ethanol orally (25 per cent 1 ml) + *Mucuna pruriens* seed extract (15 mg/kilogram body weight) for 30 days (twice daily). The ATPase activities of these rat brain were compared with ethanol treated and control group of rats. Suppressive action of ethanol on these enzymes correlated to the disturbed nerve physiology and functional behaviour. Mucuna seed extract stimulate the brain performance by activating the energy cleaving enzyme ATPase in alcoholic rats. The present study suggest that the *Mucuna pruriens* seed treatment may be beneficial to prevent ethanol induced alterations on ATPase mediated and normal transport functions of brain.

***Keywords**: Mucuna pruriens, Rat, Brain, Ethanol, ATPase.*

Introduction

Ethanol consumption disturbs a variety of physiological and behavioural aspects in the central nervous system. Changes in memory, uncontrolled behaviour and inappropriate confidence are usually associated with chronic alcoholism. Intake of ethanol for a longer period interferes in the electrical and communication properties of nerve cells (Rodrigo *et al.*, 2002). Earlier studies reveals the disturbed neural transport functions and membrane bound enzyme activities of brain after alcoholization (Oner *et al.*, 2002; Mischuk *et al.*, 2003). Further it is stated that ethanol induce injury on astroglial cell by generating free radical species and change its viability (Muscoli *et al.*, 2002).

The poor response of allopathic drugs on alcoholics instigated the researchers to work on some traditional medicines. Moreover, a series of principles isolated from Indian medicinal plants act as a antioxidant and scavengers of free radicals (Sanz *et al.*, 1994; Gyanji *et al.*, 1999). *Mucuna pruriens* a potent herb was used to treat the Parkinson's disease in ancient time. In addition it is the best source of many principles which regulates the neurotransmitters of brain cells (Manyam, 1995) and also known to enhance mental alertness and coordination (Manyam, 2004). The present study was designed to delineate the protective effect of *Mucuna pruriens* seed on rat brain in relation to ethanol toxicity.

Materials and Methods

Healthy adult male albino rats of Wistar strain (*Rattus norvegicus*) weighing 230 to 300 g of body weight were used. The rats were kept in clean cages in a temperature controlled room with 12 hours light/dark scheduled. They were fed with balanced diet with free access to water. Fifteen rats were selected for this study and randomly divided into three groups of five each. Group I includes control, (Rats received an isocaloric quantity of sucrose in the same volume as experimental rats that received ethanol). Group II includes Ethanol treated (Ethanol was administered twice daily at regular intervals by gastric intubation at a dose of as 25 per cent (1 ml) aqueous solution for 30 days. Group III includes Ethanol (1 ml of 25 per cent) + *Mucuna pruriens* seed extract (15 mg/kilogram body weight) treated for 30 days, twice daily at regular intervals by gastric incubation. At the end of the experimental period (30 days) the animals were sacrificed by decapitation. The brain, was removed carefully and cleaned from adjoining tissues. The sodium-potassium (Na^+ K^+ ATPase), magnesium (Mg^{++} ATPase) and calcium (Ca^{++} ATPases) dependent adenosine triphosphatases were estimated according to the method of Takeo and Sakanashi (1985).

Results and Discussion

The activities of Na^+ K^+ ATPase, Mg^{++} ATPase and Ca^{++} ATPases generally shows decreased trend in ethanol treated group than the control rats. The reduction in the activities of ATPases correlated to altered ionic transport and decreased ATP breakdown which drastically impairs the metabolic and vital physiological activities. Previous studies also reported the altered neural membrane function associated with decreased ATPase activities in ethanol treated animals (Kanbak *et al.*, 2001; Babich *et al.*, 2002; Oner *et al.*, 2002). Further ethanol treatment is known to suppress the ATPase activities through activation of lipid peroxidation in the neural membranes (Zamai *et al.*, 2002). The free radicals generated during the catalytic cycle of ethanol would have induced the peroxidation process in membrane lipids (Warner and Gustafsson, 1994).

The combined treatment of *Mucuna pruriens* and ethanol prevents the adverse effect of alcohol on brain ATPases. The activities of different ATPases in brain was found increased in these group compared to ethanol treated animals. *Mucuna pruriens* seed is the best natural source of L-Dopa and easily cross the blood brain barrier (Manyam, 1995). L-Dopa is the precursor for neurotransmitter synthesis and enhance the neuronal activity (Manyam *et al.*, 2004). Besides the L-dopa, the other bioactive agents of Mucuna seed would have acted on brain cells as free radical scavenger/inhibitors of lipid peroxidation and exert stimulatory effect on brain (Sinha,1992). The present study suggest that the bioactive principles of Mucuna seed would have counteracted the ethanol toxicity at molecular level. In addition the increased activities of brain ATPases after Mucuna seed treatment may be the

Table 15.1: Effect of Ethanol and *Mucuna pruriens* Seed on ATPases in Rat Brain

Group	Mg^{++} *ATPase*	Ca^{++} *ATPase*	Na^{+} K^{+} *ATPase*
Control	170.77±8.35	199.27±5.20	124.42±5.13
Ethanol treated (E)	104.44±6.5***	109.35± 8.49***	46.17± 4.80***
Ethanol + *Mucuna pruriens* seed treated (EM)	159.22^{C}±3.53	169.14^{C}±4.82**	101.47^{C}±4.13

Enzyme activities are expressed as μ moles of Pi formed/hr/mg protein.

Each value is Mean±SEM of five animals.

***: $P < 0.001$ = Control Vs Ethanol (E) treated animals.

**: $P < 0.01$ = Control Vs Ethanol + *Mucuna pruriens* seed (EM) treated animals.

C: $P < 0.001$ = Ethanol treated (E) Vs Ethanol + *Mucuna pruriens* seed (EM) treated animals.

basic mechanism for the improvement of mental alertness and coordination in ethanol toxicated animals.

References

Babich, L.G., Shlykov, S.G. and Borisova, L.A. 2002. Effect of ethanol on intracellular Ca^{++} metabolism. *Ukr. Biokhim. Zh.*, 74: 19–26.

Gyanji, M.A., Yonamine, M. and Aniya, Y., 1999. Free-radical scavenging action of medicinal herbs from Ghana: *Thonningia sanguinea* on experimentally-induced injuries. *Gen. Pharmacol.*, 32: 661–667.

Kanbak, G., Akyuz, F. and Inal, M., 2001. Preventive effect of betaine on ethanol induced membrane lipid composition and membranes ATPases. *Arch. Toxicol.* 75: 59–61.

Manyam, B.V., 1995. An herbal alternative. *J. of Alternative and Complement Med.*, 1: 249–255.

Manyam, B.V., Dhanasekaran, M. and Hare, T.A., 2004. Effect of antiparkinson drug HP-200 (*Mucuna pruriens*) on the central mono aminergic neurotransmitters. *Phytother. J. Res.*, 18: 97–101.

Mishchuk, D.O. and Kaplia, A.A., 2003. Structural and functional state of microsomal membranes in the brain cortex during long-term ethanol. *Ukr. Biokhim. Zh.*, 75: 97–100.

Muscoli, C., Fresta, M., Cardile, V., Palumbio, M., Remis, M., Puglisi, G., Paoline, D., Nistoco, S., Rotiroti, D. and Mollace, V., 2002. Ethanol induced injury in rat primary cortical astrocytes involves oxidative stress: Effect of indebenone. *Neurosci. Lett.*, 23: 21–24.

Oner, P., Cinar, F., Kocak, H. and Gurdol, F., 2002. Effect of exogenous melatonin on ethanol induced changes in $Na^{(+)}$, $K^{(+)}$ and Ca^{++} ATPase activities in rat synaptosomes. *Neurochem. Res.*, 27: 1619–1623.

Rodrigo, R., Trujilla, S., Bosco, C., Orellana, M. and Araya, L., 2002. Changes (Na^{+} K^{+}) ATPase activity and ultrastructure associated with oxidative stress: Induced by ethanol intoxication. *Chest*, 121: 589–596.

Sanz, M.J., Ferrandiz, M.L., Ejudo, M., Terencio, M.C., Gill, B., Bustos, G., Ubeda, A., Gunasegaran, R. and Alcaraz, M.J., 1994. Influence of a series of natural flavonoids on free radical generating systems and oxidative stress. *Xenabiotoca*, 24: 689–699.

Sinha, R., 1992. Principle constituents of *Mucuna pruriens*. *J. Res. Educ. Indian Med.*, 11: 15–18.

Takeo, S. and Sakanashi, M., 1985. Characterization of membrane bound adenosine triphosphatase activity of enriched fraction from vascular smooth muscle. *Enzyme*, 34: 152–165.

Warner, S. and Gustafsson, K., 1994. Effect of ethanol on cytochrome P450 in the rat brain. *Prac. Nat. Acad. Sci.*, USA, 91: 1019–1023.

Zamai, T.N., Titova, N.M., Zamai, A.S., Usol'tseva, O.S., Yulenkova, O.V. and Shumkova, D.A., 2002. Effect of alcoholic intoxication on water content and activity of Na, K-ATPase and Ca-ATPase in rat brain. *Bull. Exp. Biol. Med.*, 134: 541–543.

Chapter 16

Efficacy of Rapid H_2S Test for Detection of Fecal Contamination in Drinking Water

D.H. Tambekar[1] *, N.B. Hirulkar[1], S.R. Gulhane[1], Y.S. Banginwar[2] and N.S. Bhajipale[2]

[1]P.G. Department of Microbiology, Amravati University, Amravati - 444 602, India
[2]Institute of Pharmacy, Kaulkhed, Akola, India

ABSTRACT

Study included the assessment of rapid H_2S test with MPN technique for bacteriological analysis of drinking water. A good correlation was recorded between H_2S test, MPN count and Eijkman test. Total 510 drinking water samples were analysed by standard MPN technique, Manja's modified H_2S test and Eijkman test. All the water samples that had MPN count zero were negative for H_2S test. Out of 510 samples analysed, while 269 were positive for MPN test (> 10 coliforms/100 ml), 234 were positive for H_2S test and 220 water samples-were confirmed TTC by Eijkman test. However 234 water samples were positive and 238 were negative by both H_2S and MPN test (< 10 coliforms/100 ml) indicating 92.5 per cent agreement between the results in both methods. The positive test percentage of agreement between. H_2S test and MPN method of coliforms was 87 per cent and 94 per cent with Eijkman test. Thus H_2S test is 92.5 per cent efficient with a standard MPN test and proved to be an alternative method for assessing the water quality of potable water.

Keywords: *Fecal contamination, H_2S method and MPN test, Coliforms.*

* Corresponding Author: E-mail: diliptambekar@rediffmail.com.

Introduction

The water quality and surveillance in most developing countries is inadequate to test all drinking water resource regularly, this is large due to poor laboratory facilities, widely spread water sources and resource crunch. The standard methods, which are available for detection of fecal contamination in drinking water, require trained analyst, bacteriological media and other supporting materials and facilities of microbiology laboratory. In such a scenario, a reliable and easy to use field test can help in effective monitoring of drinking water and water source by-user themselves. In 1982 K.S. Manja (DRDO, Mysore) developed H_2S test based on production of hydrogen sulphide by bacteria that are associated with fecal contamination. This rapid fields method need no technical staff and the cost is lower than conventional bacteriological test for fecal contamination.

Sivaborvorn (1951) tested 705 samples from a variety of water (shallow and deep wells, rainwater, pond water) in Thailand by the original H_2S test and by MPN test. Based on agreement between a positive H_2S test and 10 MPN/100 ml as a coliform or fecal coliform positive, the two tests agreed 85 per cent and 88 per cent of the time, respectively. Kaspar *et al.* (1992) evaluated the modified H_2S test and applied it to 101 water samples and concluded that the test was not suitable for control of surface water and dug well water due to the frequent presence of non-fecal (total) coliform presumed to arise from degradation of plant tissues and poikilothermic animal. Venkobachar *et al.* (1994) developed a modified H_2S test that included cysteine in the medium and was used in an MPN test with five 20 ml samples. The modified test reduced the test time from 23 to 17 hours, was more sensitive than the original H_2S test and was well correlated with total coliform (89 per cent) and fecal coliform (91 per cent) tests when applied to 101 water samples. Genthe and Franck (1999) evaluated the H_2S test of Venkobachar *et al.* (1994), for specificity, sensitivity and interference and non-target bacteria using positive and negative samples and reported favorable result when applied to 413 water samples from various source, including ground and surface water, the H_2S test showed 82 per cent and 86 per cent agree with fecal coliform result when applied to higher quality water test incubation temperatures of 35°C and 22°C respectively.

Pillai *et al.* (1999) evaluated various modification of H_2S test for detection of fecal contamination using 100 ml volume of feces diluted in distilled water to contain different levels of fecal coliform bacteria. The presence of cysteine in the medium and higher incubation temperatures 28–44°C vs. 22°C improved detection, with lower levels fecal contamination (fewer coliforms) detected faster. Rijal *et al.* (2000) compared two versions of the H_2S test, MPN and a membrane filter enumeration on agar medium, to each other and to the occurrence of total coliforms and *E. coli* in samples of rainwater, groundwater and stream water. The MPN, MF version of the H_2S test and *E. coli* achieved similar detection of bacterial contamination, although total coliforms were detected in more samples than either *E. coli* or H_2S bacteria. The H_2S test was compared to total and fecal coliforms and *E. coli* tests to determine efficacy of solar disinfections system similar results for indicator reduction were achieved by all fecal indicator tests used. Ratto *et al.* (1997) evaluated the original H_2S test at incubation temperatures of 22 and 35°C and compared it to MPN and P-A total coliform (TC) and fecal coliform (FC) tests on 20 potable water samples from Lima, Peru. The frequency of positive (unsuitable) samples was similar but not identical for all tests: 9/20 by P-A, 9/20 by H_2S at 35°C, 6/20 by H_2S at 22°C, 8/20 by TC MPN and 6/20 by FC MPN.

Castillo *et al.* (1997) reported that for 622 water samples tested by the H_2S and coliform tests, 168 samples were positive by both tests and 179 samples were negative by both tests. The H_2S test produced about 10 per cent more positive samples than the coliform test but included samples that were positive for *Clostridium* spp. In studies of 54 complete conventionally treated drinking waters and their corresponding raw source waters, Marks *et al.* (2002) found 100 per cent agreement between total coliform and H_2S results for raw waters and 81 per cent agreement for treated waters. In treated waters the H_2S and TC results were significantly positively correlated ($P < 0.0001$ Spearman rank correlation test) but in raw waters they were significantly negatively correlated ($P = 0.0008$).

The H_2S test is simple, sensitive and correlated with traditional indicator bacteria, especially fecal coliform and requiring little laboratory support and well suited for routine quality assessment of rural water sources and can said that the test is an equally or more sensitive test than TC and FC tests and an ideal procedure to screen and measure the hygienic quality water for fecal contamination in the field and considered valuable as an educational and motivational tool for improved water sanitation, because of the color change and foul smell from positive sample, however positive H_2S test results must be confirmed by standard bacteriological tests.

Though various people test the validity of the H_2S test with MPN or MFT. Further validation is required to make the test as standard test for detection of quality of drinking water, moreover WHO and APHA needs standardization of this method for use in developing countries. Hence attempt was made to evaluate the H_2S test with standard water analysis test, where study data were subjected to statistic analysis.

Materials and Methods

In present study, total 510 samples were collected from different hotels, restaurants and schools in sterilized bottle in Amravati city. All water samples were subjected to bacteriological examination by using H_2S method (Manja *et al.*, 2001), (cystiene in the medium), standard MPN procedure and Eijkman test (APHA, 1997). A concentrated H_2S medium (total volume 50-ml) was prepared (Table 16.1). One ml of concentrated H_2S media was added in each 30 ml bottle and sterilized. These bottles were inoculated with 20 ml water sample and incubated at 37°C for 24 to 48 hours to determine the extent of blacking in the bottles.

Table 16.1: Composition of H_2S Medium

Chemicals	*Quantity*
Bacteriological Grade Peptone	20.0 g
Di-potassium Hydrogen	1.5 g
Ferric Ammonium Citrate	0.75 g
Sodium Thio-sulphate, A.R.	1.0 g
L-Cysteine HCl	0.125 g
Teepol or Labolene (Neutral pH)	1.0 ml
Total volume of the medium w/water	50 ml

At the same time all water samples also tested by MPN method for total coliform and fecal coliform (9 tube MPN) using MacConkey double and single strength broth. Water samples those were positive by MPN procedure was inoculated in Brilliant Green Lactose Bile broth and Tryptone broth (indole test) for thermo tolerant fecal coliform by Eijkman test. All the bacteriologIcal culture media were procured from Hi-media Pvt. Ltd. Mumbai. The data were analysed by various statistical methods for H_2S test and standard methods and for each case the percentage correlation was determined.

Results and Discussions

The H_2S method has been extensively studied by a number of investigators in different parts of the world. Such studies include evaluations of the original method, studies on modifications of the method and field-testing, usually with side-by-side comparison to other water quality tests. In some of these comparison studies the data are limited or have not been subjected to rigorous statistical analysis. However, the results of most studies suggest that the H_2S method detects fecal contaminated water with about the same frequency and magnitude as the traditional methods to which it was compared. In general, the sensitivity of the H_2S test appears about the same as other tests for fecal contamination of water, although, this aspect of the test has not been rigorously tested in some of the reported studies. Testing conditions and format, sample size, incubation temperature and incubation time influences test sensitivity. Because these conditions have differed among the different studies reported in the literature, it is difficult to make consistent comparisons and draw overall conclusions. However when comparisons with other methods of detecting fecal contamination were done, the H_2S method appeared to have sensitivity similar to the other methods, based on finding contaminated samples.

When the H_2S test is compared with standard tests to identify FC, the agreement rates ranged from 90 to 94.4 per cent by Grant and Ziel (1996), 111.1 per cent by Castillo *et al.* (1997) and 140 per cent by Ratto *et al.* (1997). Grant and Ziel (1996) also found an 80 per cent agreement with *Clostridium perfringens,* which were known to be of strong fecal origin. These numbers showed that the H_2S test is a very good surrogate (> 90 per cent correlation) for the standard test to identify FC. From the previous studies cited above, it appears that the H_2S test is a more sensitive test than other FC tests. The H_2S test is more likely to overestimate the presence of FC than TC. This is also partly due to the greater specificity of the FC group.

Manja *et al.* (2001) compared H_2S test (with cysteine in the medium, different sample volumes, different incubation time and incubation at different temperature) to MPN test for coliform detecting fecal contamination in 686 water samples in India. The H_2S test gave results comparable to the MPN test (not significantly different), with concordance in 620, (90 per cent) samples, negative H_2S test and positive MPN test (false negative) in 34 samples (4.9 per cent) and positive H_2S test and negative MPN test (false positive) in 32 samples (4.7 per cent). However, 21 of 23 "false positive" (negative coliform MPN) samples had coliforms in H_2S bottles. Agreement of H_2S positive and coliform positive samples increased from 91 per cent at 48 hours to 95 per cent at 72 hours. The H_2S test results were comparable (not significantly different) for sample volumes of 20, 55 and 100 ml. Positive H_2S results were generally obtained in 18–48 hours of incubation at 25–44°C.

In present study a total 510 water samples tested by standard MPN technique, H_2S method and Eijkman test. The results obtained after 24 hrs incubation of H_2S test, presence of coliforms by MPN method and confirmation of Thermo Tolerant Coliform (TTC) fecal contamination by Eijkman test. Out of 510 samples analysed, while 269 were positive for MPN test (> 10 coliforms 100 ml), 234 were positive for H_2S test and 220 water samples were confirmed TTC by Eijkman test. However 234 water samples were positive and 238 were negative by both H_2S and MPN test (< 10 coliforms/100 ml) indicating 92.5 per cent agreement between the results in both methods (Tables 16.2 and 16.3).

Table 16.2: Comparison Between Negative MPN Count and Negative H_2S Test

MPN Test		*H_2S Test*		
Count	*No. of Samples*	*+ve*	*–ve*	*% Concentration*
0	160	0	160	100%
3	22	0	22	100%
4	28	0	28	100%
7	12	0	12	100%
9	19	3	16	84.2%
Total	**241**	**3**	**238**	**98.75%**

Table 16.3: Comparison Between MPN Count, Positive H_2S Test, and Eijkman Test

MPN Count	No. of Sample	H_2S Test			Eijkman Test		
		+ve	−ve	% Correlation	+ve	−ve	% Correlation
11	5	1	4	80%	0	5	80%
14	4	3	1	75%	3	1	100%
15	7	4	3	57%	3	4	75%
21	10	8	2	80%	7	3	87.5%
23	23	18	5	78.2%	18	5	100%
39	3	1	2	33.3%	1	2	100%
43	9	5	4	55.5%	4	5	80%
64	3	2	1	66.6%	2	1	100%
75	5	5	0	100%	5	0	100%
93	17	15	2	88.2%	15	2	100%
150	12	9	3	75%	8	4	88.6%
210	6	5	1	83.3%	4	2	80%
240	19	19	0	100%	18	1	94.7%
460	20	19	1	95%	16	4	84.2%
1100	20	18	2	90%	18	2	100%
2400	106	102	4	96.2%	98	8	92.4%
Total	**269**	**234**	**35**	**87%**	**220**	**49**	**94%**

Out of 510 water samples, 269 samples showed MPN coliforms more than 10 per 100 ml. The positive percentage of agreement between H_2S test and MPN method of coliforms was 87 per cent. Out of positive 234 H_2S test, 220 samples showed fecal contamination by Eijkman test and positive per cent agreement was 94 per cent. (Table 16.3).

The results of H_2S positive samples were compared with the density of coliforms obtained by MPN method and fecal contamination by Eijkman test. It was observed that 99 per cent to 100 per cent correlation was recorded with H_2S test when the MPN test was negative or MPN count less than 10 coliforms/100 ml. As the MPN count increased from 11 to 2400 coliforms per 100 ml water, the percentage correlation with H_2S test was also increased from 67 per cent to 96 per cent (Table 16.4). Further, H_2S test was positive in 79 per cent sample where coliform density exceeds 40/100 ml. Seven samples, which were H_2S test negative, but total coliforms count was more than 210/100 ml. This infers that H_2S producing microorganisms are always present in association with coliforms. The low agreement or disagreement was recorded between H_2S test and standard MPN test when MPN count was between 11 to 210, may be due to lack of precision in the MPN method as quoted earlier by Swaroop (1951) and Manja *et al.* (1994).

The per cent correlation between positive H_2S test and Eijkman was 91 per cent when the MPN count was 11 to 40, 93 per cent when MPN count was between 41 to 210 and it was 95 per cent when the count was above 210 (Table 16.5). There was increase in percentage correlation of H_2S test with TTC coliforms detected by Eijkman test as the coliform count increased. There was higher degree of percentage correlation between H_2S test and Eijkman test when the MPN count was between 11 to 210 as compared to MPN method and H_2S test. This evident that H_2S producing organisms are having coexistence with coliforms especially of fecal origin.

Table 18.4: Comparison of H_2S Test with Coliform Density (MPN Count)

MPN Count	*No. of Samples*	*H_2S Test*		*% Correlation*
		+ve	*−ve*	
< 10	241	3	238	99%
11 to 40	52	35	17	67%
41 to 210	52	41	11	79%
> 210	165	158	7	96%

Table 18.5: Comparison of H_2S Test with Eijkman Test

MPN Count	*H_2S +ve Test*	*Eijkman Test*		*% Correlation*
		+ve	*−ve*	
11 to 40	35	32	20	91%
41 to 210	41	38	14	93%
> 210	158	150	15	95%
Total	**234**	**220**	**49**	**94%**

On these results it was clearly indicated that when MPN count was very low *i.e.* less than 10 coliform per 100 ml or negative MPN, the percentage correlation was almost 100 per cent. When the MPN test was positive or higher MPN count the percentage correlation with H_2S also increased upto 96 per cent. This clearly indicated that more coliforms per 100 ml lead to more accurate H_2S test and good correlation.

Thus authors concluded that the H_2S test is a simple, low cost and versatile test that can be carried out in the field for suitable indicator of potable water quality and for the routine monitoring of water for detection of fecal contamination in the field as well as epidemics of water born diseases and applicable to tropical and subtropical potable waters. It was also found that modified H_2S test was more suitable alternative to conventional MPN method and most useful to detect fecal pollution in drinking water especially at village level. It could be employed for routine testing where time, man power and laboratory facilities are too meager. Therefore, this test is recommended for the routine monitoring of water for recent fecal contamination in the field where technical expertise and incubation equipment are not readily available.

References

American Public Health Association (APHA), 1997. *Standard Method for Examination of Water and Wastewater*, 21st ed. APHA, Washington D.C.

Castillo, G., Castillo, J., Thiers, R., 1997. Evaluation of the coliphage procedure and presence/absence test as simple rapid economical methods for screening potable water sources and potable water supplies in Chile. *IDRC Canada.*

Genthe, B. and M. Franck, 1999. A tool for assessing microbial quality in small community water supplies: An H_2S strip test. WRC Report No. 96171/99, 33 pages, to: Water Research Commission. By: Division of Water, Environment and Forestry Technology, CSIR, Stellenbosch, South Africa.

Grant, M.A. and Ziel, C.A., 1996. Evaluation of a simple screening test for fecal pollution in water. *Journal Water SRT-Aqua.* 45(1): 13–18.

Kaspar, P., I. Guillen, D. Revelli, T. Meza, G. Velazquez, H. Mino de Kaspar, L. Pozolli, C. Nunez and G. Zoulek, 1992. Evaluation of simple screening test for the quality of drinking water systems. *Tropical Medicine and Parasitology*, 43(2): 124–127.

Manja, K.S., 1994. Simple microbiological method for water quality testing and their field application. In: *MICON-94 and 35th AMI Conference*, 9–12 November, 1994.

Manja, K.S., M.S. Maurya and K.M. Rao, 1982. A Simple field tests for the detection at fecal Pollution in drinking water. *Bulletin of the World Health Organizations,* 60: 797–801.

Manja, K.S., R. Sambasiva, K.V. Chandra Shekhara, K.J. Nath, S. Dutta, K. Gopal, L. Iyengar, S.S. Dhindsa and S.C. Parija, 2001. Report of study on H_2S test for drinking water, 96 pages, UNICEF, New Delhi.

Mark, D. Sobsey and Frederic K. Pfaender, 2002. Department of Environmental Science and Engineering School of Public Health-Evaluation of H_2S method for detection of fecal contamination of drinking water, Geneva, WHO.

Pillai, J.K. Mathew, R. Gibbs and G. Ho, 1999. H_2S paper strip method: A bacteriological test for fecal coliforms in drinking water at various temperatures. *Water Sci. Technol.*, 40: 85–90.

Ratto, M.A., Lette, C.V., Lopez C., Mantilla, H., Apoloni, L.M., 1997. Evaluation of the coliphage procedure and the presence absence test as simple, rapid, economical methods for screening potable water sources and potable water supplies in Peru. *IDRC Canada.*

Rijal, G.K., R.S. Fujioka and C.A. Ziel, 2000. Evaluation of the hydrogen sulphide bacterial test: A simple test to determine the hygienic quality as drinking water. Abstracts of the *General Meeting of the American Society for Microbiology,* Abstract Q354, page 622. Amer. Soc. Microbial, Washington, D.C.

Sivaborvorn, 1988. Development of simple test for bacteriological quality of drinking water (Water quality control Southeast Asia). Department of sanitary engineering, Mahidol University. Thailand Center File 3-P-83-0317-03. International Development Research Center, Canada.

Swaroop, S., 1951. The rage of variation of most probable number of organisms estimated the dilution method. *Indian J. Med. Res.*, 39: 107.

Venkobachar, C., D. Kumar, Talreja, A. Kumar and I. Iyengar, 1994. Assessment of bacteriological quality using a modified H_2S strip test. *Aqua* (Oxford), 43(6): 311–314.

Chapter 17

In vitro Sensitivity Study of Phytopathogenic Fungi Against Indian Piper

J. Das, S. Goswami, R. Gupta and M. Begam

Division of Biotechnology, Defence Research Laboratory, Post Bag No. 2, Tezpur – 784 001, Assam

ABSTRACT

In the present investigation 14 methanol extracts obtained from leaf and stem of 6 different species of *Piper* were studied against 4 plant pathogenic fungi *viz., Corynespora cassiicola, Colletotrichum lindemuthianum, Fusarium oxysporum* and *Rhizoctonia solani.* Out of these, four leaf extracts from *P. argyrophyla* and 3 different types of *P. betle* were found to possess antifungal property showing inhibition zone diameter ranging from 10 to 28 mm. *P. betle* (Sathyavaram) and *P. argyrophyla* were found promising in inhibiting the mycelial growth of the most resistant *Fusarium oxysporum,* producing zone diameter of 20 and 19 mm respectively.

***Keywords**: Phytopathogenic fungi, Plant extracts, Antifungal activity, Inhibition zone.*

Introduction

Vegetable crops in northeast India suffer seriously from various fungal diseases due to prevalence of hot and humid climate. Outbreak of diseases incited by fungal infection causes significant losses in many important vegetable crops. A large number of effective commercial synthetic fungicides are available in the market, but their indiscriminate use has led to resurgence of new fungal strains, in the development of resistance, undesirable effects on non-target organisms and promote environmental and human health problems. In view of all these ill effects, the development of safer strategies for effective control of fungal diseases is gaining importance throughout the world. As such a plant-derived fungicide may be one of the solutions, because plants contain a large number of fungicidal compounds (Kavita *et al.*, 2000). The revival of interest in plant-derived fungicides is due to several advantages, such as ecofriendly, biodegradable, target specific, inability of pathogen to develop resistance and broad-spectrum activity.

The *Piper* is one of the valuable genus with a large number of cultivated as well as wild species and types. This region is one of the two centers of species diversity of Indian Piper, besides the Southern Deccan (Rahiman and Nair, 1987). Among the wild species, *P. longum* is the best known for its use in Ayurvedic preparations. A number of species are being traditionally used as medicines for treatment of various ailments. The indigenous people of northeast India commonly use nearly 10 species of *Piper* in traditional medicines (Gajurel *et al.*, 2001). *P. betle* that is commonly known as 'pan' is widely consumed across the Indian subcontinent as a mouth refresher. *P. betle* has been used by the common people for curing various diseases such as fungal infection on nails as revitalizer since long. Medicinally *Piper* species are used commonly for fever, eye and mouth diseases, bronchitis, body pain, paralysis, unconsciousness, asthma, leprosy, indigestion, jaundice, piles, antidotes for snakebite, hair tonic and many other ailments (Gajurel *et al.*, 2001). Very recently, the anticancerous property of *P. betle* has been reported (Anonymous, 2004). The essential oil and extracts of the leaves of *P. betle* possess activity against various pathogenic bacteria and fungi. Basumatary *et al.* (2004) reported that the Bodo people of Assam use juice of *P. betle* as eye drop in painful eyes. Oil coated leaves are used for dressing blistered surface and ulcer. The usage of paste of *P. nigrum* to cure skin diseases of animal was reported by Sharma and Joshi (2004).

Considering the above facts a preliminary *in vitro* investigation was undertaken to evaluate antifungal activity of 14 methanol extracts derived from 6 different species of *Piper* against 4 most potent plant pathogenic fungi *viz.*, *Corynespora cassiicola, Colletotrichum lindemuthianum, Fusarium oxysporum* and *Rhizoctonia solani*, that are responsible for a huge loss to food crops and other economic plants of northeast region.

Materials and Methods

Leaf and stem of 6 different *Piper* species namely *P. longum, P. nigrum, P. betle* (Type–Sathyavaram, Chandana, Sagar bangla), *P. griffitii, P. argyrophyla* and *P. brachystachium* were collected from in and around Tezpur (Assam) during the month of September–October, 2004.

Preparation of Extract

Plants materials *i.e.*, leaf and stem were thoroughly washed and dried under shade and crushed into powder. The powders so obtained were immersed separately in methanol for ten days, shaking vigorously twice every day. The mixtures were filtered through Whatman filter paper No. 1. Standard extracts of 100 per cent conc. were prepared by evaporating the solvent from the filtrate at room temperature. The test solution was prepared by dissolving the extract initially in little amount of Dimethylsulphoxide and then by adding distilled water to obtain 20 per cent (w/v) solution and finally filter sterilized through Millipore filter (0.2 μm pore size).

Preparation of Inoculum

Inoculum was prepared by adding one loop full of pure culture of test pathogen in 50 ml of potato dextrose broth and then incubated at 28±2°C for suitable period depending on their growth rate.

Antifungal Sensitivity Test

Antifungal activity of the plant extracts was determined by employing agar cup diffusion method. Inoculum (500 µl) was spread evenly over the Potato Dextrose Agar (PDA) plate with a sterile glass spreader. Cups of 7mm diameter were cut out in the agar plates (2 cups in each plate) with a sterile cork borer and then each cup was filled with 0.3 ml of 20 per cent test extract. The extracts were allowed to diffuse at room temperature for 2 hours. One set of control was also maintained filling the cups with distilled water. The plates were then incubated at 28±2°C for 2–7 days based on extent of the mycelial growth of each of the fungi. The efficacy of the extracts was determined by measuring the diameter of inhibition zones.

Analysis of Per cent of Inhibition

Net per cent of inhibition was calculated according to the following formula (Vyas *et al.*, 2006).

$$\text{Net\% of Inhibition} = \frac{\text{Inhibition Zone in mm}}{^{*}\text{Control}} \times 100$$

* Growth zone is equal to plate diameter *i.e.*, 80 mm as growth occurs all over the agar plate.

Results and Discussion

From the results it was clear that among the 14 test extracts (Table 17.1), only 4 extracts from leaves of *P. betle* (type–Sagar bangla, Chandana and Sathyavaram) and *P. argyrophyla* were found to possess significant inhibitory property against the tested pathogens.

Table 17.1: Plants Tested for Antifungal Efficacy

Plant Species/Type	*Common Name*	*Part Used*
P. longum	Pipoli	Leaf, Stem
P. nigrum	Jaluk	Leaf, Stem
P. betle (Sathyavaram)	Pan	Leaf, stem
P. betle (Chandana)	Pan	Leaf
P. betle (Sagat bangla)	Pan (Bangla)	Leaf
P. griffitii	–	Leaf, stem
P. argyrophyla	–	Leaf, stem
P. brachystachium	–	Leaf, stem

In the present investigation, the type Sagar bangla of *P. betle* at the concentration of 0.2 g/ml was strongly active against *C. cassiicola,* showing highest inhibition zone diameter of 28 mm followed by 25 and 15 mm against *C. limndemuthianum* and *R. solani* respectively. However *F. oxysporum* was found highly resistant showing no sensitivity to this extract (Table 17.2).

P. betle (Chandana) also showed almost similar results, exhibiting inhibition zone diameter of 20 mm against *C. cassiicola* and 15 mm against *C. lindemuthianum* and *R. solani.* This extract also did not show any activity against *F. oxysporum* (Table 17.3).

In case of *P. argyrophyla* leaf extract, *C. lindemuthianum* showed resistance to the extract, whereas the other 3 test fungi *viz., C. cassiicola, F. oxysporum* and *R. solani* were found susceptible showing inhibition zone diameter 25, 19 and 15 mm respectively (Table 17.4).

Table 17.2: Effect of *P. betle* (Sagar bangla) on Phytopathogenic Fungi

Test Pathogen	*Inhibition Zone with Cup (mm)*	*Inhibition Zone Without Cup (mm)*	*Net % of Inhibition*
C. cassiicola	28	21	26.25
C. lindemuthianum	25	18	22.5
F. oxysporum	–	–	–
R. solani	15	8	10

Table 17.3: Effect of *P. betle* (Chandana) on Phytopathogenic Fungi

Test Pathogen	*Inhibition Zone with Cup (mm)*	*Inhibition Zone Without Cup (mm)*	*Net % of Inhibition*
C. cassiicola	20	13	16.25
C. lindemuthianum	15	8	10
F. oxysporum	–	–	–
R. solani	15	8	10

Table 17.4: Effect of *P. argyrophyla* on Phytopathogenic Fungi

Test Pathogen	*Inhibition Zone with Cup (mm)*	*Inhibition Zone Without Cup (mm)*	*Net % of Inhibition*
C. cassiicola	25	18	22.5
C. lindemuthianum	–	–	–
F. oxysporum	19	12	15
R. solani	15	8	10

Among all the four promising extracts, *P. betle* (Sathyavaram) exhibited broad-spectrum activity against all the test fungi, causing varying inhibition zone diameter ranging from 10 to 20 mm (Table 17.5).

Table 17.5: Effect of *P. betle* (Sathyavaram) on Phytopathogenic Fungi

Test Pathogen	*Inhibition Zone with Cup (mm)*	*Inhibition Zone Without Cup (mm)*	*Net % of Inhibition*
C. cassiicola	10	3	3.75
C. lindemuthianum	10	3	3.75
F. oxysporum	20	13	16.25
R. solani	20	13	16.25

By comparing the net per cent of inhibition displayed by the test extracts against the test pathogens, it was observed that the highest net per cent of inhibition 26.25, produced by *P. betle* (Sagar bangla) against *C. cassiicola* and 22.5 against *C. lindemuthianum*. On the other hand highest net per cent of inhibition 16.25 was recorded against *F. oxysporum* and *R. solani* produced by *P. betle* (Sathyavaram). *P. argyrophyla* showed 22.5 per cent net inhibition against *C. cassiicola* (Tables 17.2–17.5).

In the present experiment, none of the stem extracts was found effective. Although some of the *Piper* species for example *P. longum* and *P. nigrum* are medicinal, in the present study these species did not exhibit efficacy against the test pathogens. Among the pathogens studied, *C. cassiicola* and *R. solani* were found highly sensitive to all the 4 extracts. *F. oxysporum*, although highly resistant, showed sensitivity towards leaf extracts of *P. betle* (Sathyavaram) and *P. argyrophyla*.

Considering the experiences of other workers and outcome of the present study, it is reasonable to infer that the methanol extracts from *P. betle* (type–Sagar bangla, Chandana and Sathyavaram) and *P. argyrophyla* may be tapped for further research to develop an ecofriendly fungicide for combating the fungal diseases of food crops.

Acknowledgement

The authors are thankful to Dr. S. N. Dube, Director, Defence Research Laboratory, Tezpur for his constant support throughout the study period. The authors are also thankful to Ashish Kar, S.R.F. for helping in identification of the plants and Dr. K.N. Bhagabati, Professor, Department of Plant Pathology, Assam Agricultural University, Jorhat for providing the test pathogens.

References

Anonymous, 1969. *The Wealth of India, Raw Materials*. Publications and Information Directorate, CSIR, New Delhi, India, 8: 94.

Anonymous, 2004. *PTI Science Service*, 16–31: 5

Basumatary, S.K., Ahmed, M. and Deka, S.P., 2004. Some medicinal plant leaves used by Boro (tribal) people of Goalpara district, Assam. *Natural Products Radiance*, 3(2): 88–90.

Dutta, B.K., Rahman, I. and Das, T.K., 2004. *Piper betel:* An effective antidermatophytic plant. *Environment and Ecology*, 22(Spl): 480–482.

Dutta, B.K., Rahman, I. and Das, T.K., 2004. Growth inhibition of phytopathogens by the application of plant extracts. *Environment and Ecology*, 22(3): 618–620.

Gajurel, P.R., Rethy, P., Singh B. and Kumar, Y., 2001. Importance of systematic investigation for proper utilization and conservation of *Piper* species of northeast India. In: *Proceedings, Ethno medicines of NEI-National Seminar*, pp. 305–313.

Grammar, A., 1976. *Microbiological Methods*, (Eds.) Collins C.H. and Lyne, P.M., Butterworths, London, pp. 235.

Kavitha, N.S., Hilda, A. and Ramesh, V.M., 2000. Fungicidal activity of plant extracts against the growth of health risk causing fungi. *Geobios*, 27(2–3): 81–84.

Rahiman, B.A. and Nair, M.K. 1987. The genus *Piper* Linn. in Karnataka, India. *J. Bombay Natural History Society*, 84: 66–83.

Sharma, M.C. and Joshi, C., 2004. Plants used in skin diseases of animal. *Natural Products Radiance*, 3(4): 293–299.

Rahman, I., Dutta, B.K. and Das, T.K., 2004. Susceptibility of pathogenic fungi to *Piper betel* extracts, an *in vitro* evaluation. *Environment and Ecology*, 23(Spl-1): 8–11.

Vyas, Y.K., Bhatnagar, M. and Sharma, K.J., 2006. Antimicrobial activity of a herb, herbal based and synthetic dentrifrices against oral microflora. *Cell and Tissue Research*, 6(1): 639–642.

Chapter 18

Integrated Management of Brinjal Fruit Borer (*Leucinodes orbonalis* Guen.) through Varietal Resistance and Judicious Insecticidal Application

Rabindra Prasad[1], Rajesh Kumar[1], Udaya Kumar Prasad[2], Muneshwar Prasad[3] and Devendra Prasad[1]

[1]Department of Entomology, Birsa Agricultural University, Kanke, Ranchi - 834 006
[2]ZRS Chianki, Palamau, Birsa Agricultural University, Ranchi
[3]Department of Horticulture, Birsa Agricultural University, Ranchi

ABSTRACT

An overall result of the field study conducted for the two consecutive years, 2002 and 2003 revealed that the protection measures provided to brinjal plants in the field conditions against fruit borer, *Leucinodes orbonalis* Guen. proved to be highly effective in significantly reducing the fruit borer incidence in all the five promising varieties of the crop under test. The protection to the crop provided by the alternate foliar spray of deltamethrin applied @ 30 g a.i./ha and Btk, Delfin WG @ 1000 g/ha at the three weeks intervals was found to be capable in reducing fruit damage upto significantly lower level *viz.*, 17.89, 6.33, 22.31, 18.70 and 17.84 per cent which in turn substantially enhanced yield of marketable healthy fruits upto 44.71, 28.26, 41.04, 82.44 and 65.55 per cent with the extra production of 63.82, 50.45, 65.12, 99.14 and 84.96 q/ha which resulted to net profit of Rs. 22,567; 17,219; 23,083; 36,695 and 31,023, per hectare alongwith the benefit cost ratio of 7.62, 5.81, 7.97, 12.39 and 10.47 in case of brinjal varieties, Pusa purple long, Pusa purple cluster, Mukta Keshi, Pusa Kranti and Pusa purple round respectively through investing merely as protection cost of Rs. 2960.80/ha. The study revealed that management of fruit borer, *L. orbonalis* through varietal resistance and pesticidal protection remained highly effective and profitable by realising rewarding yield of brinjal and higher net return and benefit cost ratio.

***Keywords**: Brinjal, Fruit borer, Varietal resistance, Insecticides, Yield, Net profit.*

Introduction

Brinjal (*Solanum melongena* Linn.) is one of the most important and popular solanaceous vegetable crops in India. The crop is commonly endangered by fruit borer (*Leucinodes orbonalis* Guen.) in the field, resulting to substantially higher loss in the yield of healthy and marketable fruits of brinjal amounting from 38 to 55 per cent (Tripathi *et al.*, 1996) and even upto 76 per cent (Gupta *et al.*, 1998). The extent of crop loss differs from variety to variety of brinjal as well as from place to place, depending upon the variation in the agroclimatic conditions. Considering the pest status of the fruit borer and lack of information regarding the quantification of loss caused by *L. orbonalis* and profit generated by its control, particularly in Jharkhand state, the present study was undertaken to explore some basic ideas on this aspect and to formulate the cost effective management of the pest problem through the varietal resistance and judicious insecticidal application for sustainable production of brinjal with higher net returns.

Materials and Methods

An experiment was conducted during spring summer season for the two consecutive years, 2003 and 2004 in the farmers field near the main campus of Birsa Agricultural University, Ranchi with the five commonly used promising brinjal varieties grown in protected and unprotected conditions on the randomized block design (RBD) comprising of ten treatments and three replications (Table 18.1). The plot size was kept 4.0 × 3.5 m^2. Row to row and plant to plant distance were maintained 75 and 60 cm for round/oblong variety and that of long brinjal varieties were kept 60 and 45 cm. Transplanting of brinjal seedlings was made in the second week of January during 2003 and 2004. Recommended packages of practices were adopted for raising the crop. Foliar spraying with deltamethrin (30 g a.i./ha) and Btk, Delfin WG @ 1000 g/ha alternating one at three weeks intervals were applied over the standing crop commencing first spray with deltamethrin at the early reproductive stage of the crop with the knap sack sprayer excepting unprotected crop of each variety. As such, three spray with deltamethrin and two spray with Btk (Delfin WG) were applied. Plucking of fruits were done periodically at proper edible stage for recording yield in terms of per plot basis and finally calculated into q/ha. Total weight of healthy and damaged fruits were recorded treatment wise to calculate the percentage of fruit damage due to *L. orbonalis.* Year wise data were pooled to find out pooled mean of two years. Statistical analysis was made year wise and that of pooled values of two years in respect of percentage of fruit damage and fruit yield. Finally economics was worked out on the basis of pooled data of two years for calculating net return and benefit cost ratio. Percentage gain in yield over unprotected crop and avoidable loss in yield (per cent) were calculated by the following formula:

$$\text{Yield gain \%} = \frac{T - C}{C} \times 100$$

$$\text{Avoidable Loss in Yield \%} = \frac{T - C}{T} \times 100$$

where,

T and C are yield obtained from treated and untreated crops respectively.

Results and Discussion

A perusal of the results (Tables 18.1 and 18.2) indicated that protection measures provided to each of the five brinjal variety by foliar spray with deltamethrin @ 30 g a.i./ha and Btk, Delfin (WG)

@ 1000 g/ha alternatively applied at three weeks interval against fruit borer (*L. orbonalis*) gave rise to the significantly more reduction in the fruit damage as compared to the unprotected respective varieties which in turn resulted to the significant corresponding enhancement in fruit yield, net profit and Benefit Cost Ratio (BCR) in the respective varieties of brinjal. However, variation in the increase in the yield were noticed due to the variation in the genetic yield potentiality of the respective varieties coupled with the extent of protection provided against the insect pest. The enhancement in yield of marketable fruits was found to be maximum in Pusa Kranti followed by Pusa purple round, Pusa purple long, Mukta Kehsi and Pusa purple cluster (Tables 18.1 and 18.2).

Table 18.1: Effect of Fruit Borer (*Leucinodes orbonalis* Geun.) Infestation on Some Promising Brinjal Varieties and their Yield Under Protected and Unprotected Conditions, Recorded During 2003 and 2004

Treatment	*Fruit Damage (%) Caused by Fruit Borer*			*Yield of Brinjal (q/ha)*			*Avoidable Yield Loss in Unprotected Over Protected Crops (%)*
	2003	*2004*	*Mean*	*2003*	*2004*	*Mean*	
Pusa purple long (Protected)	9.41 (17.85)	13.63 (21.68)	11.52 (19.76)	208.30	204.80	206.55	–
Pusa purple long (Unprotected)	28.42 (32.23)	30.41 (33.49)	29.41 (32.86)	145.60	139.86	142.73	30.89
Pusa purple cluster (Protected)	2.54 (9.16)	4.06 (11.64)	3.30 (10.41)	231.65	226.30	228.97	
Pusa purple cluster (Unprotected)	8.39 (16.88)	10.87 (19.23)	9.63 (18.05)	180.30	176.74	178.52	22.03
Mukta Keshi (Protected)	4.03 (11.55)	6.41 (14.66)	5.22 (13.10)	225.80	221.76	223.78	–
Mukta Keshi (Unprotected)	26.72 (31.13)	28.35 (32.15)	27.53 (31.64)	160.55	156.77	158.66	29.10
Pusa Kranti (Protected)	13.48 (21.48)	15.23 (22.94)	14.35 (22.21)	221.60	217.18	219.39	–
Pusa Kranti (Unprotected)	31.46 (34.09)	34.64 (36.04)	33.05 (35.06)	122.44	118.07	120.25	45.18
Pusa purple round (Protected)	11.65 (19.94)	14.38 (22.33)	13.01 (21.13)	216.38	212.75	214.56	–
Pusa purple round (Unprotected)	29.63 (32.98)	32.08 (34.46)	30.85 (33.72)	131.70	127.50	129.60	39.59
SEm (±)	(0.72)	(0.84)	(0.46)	3.72	3.45	3.81	–
C.D. (0.05)	(2.21)	(2.73)	(1.44)	11.35	10.74	11.76	–
C.V. (%)	(8.26)	(7.47)	(9.40)	6.89	9.63	7.58	–

Figures in parentheses are angular transformed values.

Table 18.2: Analysis of Economic Loss Caused by Fruit Damaged Due to *L. orbonalis* and Gain from its Control in Some Promising Brinjal Varieties (Based on Pooled Mean of 2003 and 2004)

Sl.No.	Parameters of the Economics	*Pusa Purple Long*		*Pusa Purple Cluster*		*Mukta Keshi*		*Pusa Kranti*		*Pusa Purple Round*	
		Unprotected	*Protected*	*Unprotected*	*Protected*	*Unprotected*	*Protected*	*Unprotected*	*Protected*	*Unprotected*	*Protected*
1.	Fruit damage (%) due to fruit borer	29.41	11.52	9.63	3.30	27.53	5.22	33.05	14.35	30.85	13.01
2.	Reduction in fruit damage (%) over unprotected ones	–	17.89	–	6.33	–	22.31	–	18.70	–	17.84
3.	Yield (q/ha) of marketable brinjal fruits	142.73	206.55	178.52	228.97	158.66	223.78	120.25	219.39	129.60	214.56
4.	Yield increase (q/ha) over unprotected crop	–	63.82	–	50.45	–	65.12	–	99.14	–	84.96
5.	Per cent increase in yield over unprotected crop	–	44.71	–	28.26	–	41.04	–	82.44	–	65.55
6.	Avoidable yield loss (%)	30.89	–	22.03	–	29.10	–	45.18	–	39.69	–
7.	Value of increased produce @ Rs. 400 per q due to protection	–	25528.00	–	20.180.00	–	26048.00	–	39656.00	–	33984.00
8.	Cost of chemical control of fruit borer (Rs/ha) comprising cost of labour plus insecticide	–	2960.88	–	2960.80	–	2960.80	–	2960.80	–	2960.80
9.	Net profit (Rs/ha) due to fruit borer control	–	22567.20	–	17219.20	–	23087.20	–	36695.20	–	31023.20
10.	Benefit cost ration (BCR)	–	7.62	–	5.81	–	7.97	–	12.39	–	10.47

In the present field study, the results (Tables 18.1 and 18.2) revealed that the fruit damage caused by *L. orbonalis* was observed to be reduced upto 17.89, 6.33, 22.31, 18.70 and 17.84 per cent in Pusa purple long, Pusa purple cluster, Mukta Keshi, Pusa Kranti and Pusa purple round respectively. With the help of protection measures provided through foliar sprayings comprising of deltamethrin @ 30 g a.i./ha followed by alternate spray with Btk, Delfin WG @ 1000 g/ha. As a result, additional yield of healthy and marketable fruit upto 63.82, 50.45, 65.12, 99.14 and 84.96 q/ha in the respective brinjal varieties were obtained that in turn gave rise to net returns of Rs. 22,567; Rs. 17,219; Rs. 23,087; Rs. 36,695 and Rs. 31,023 per hectare with benefit cost ratio of 7.62, 5.81, 7.97, 12.39 and 10.47 by enhancing 44.71, 28.26, 41.04, 82.44 and 65.55 per cent yield in the respective varieties of brinjal (Tables 18.1 and 18.2). Avoidable yield loss varying from 30.80, 22.03, 29.10, 45.18 and 39.59 per cent were recorded in the respective brinjal varieties. Tewari and Moorthy (1983) reported that by protecting brinjal against *L. orbonalis* through foliar spraying of cypermethrin applied @ 15 g a.i./ha applied at three weeks intervals, rewarding yield and benefit cost ratio could be obtained. Similarly Vein (1985) and Prasad (2002) obtained higher yield by foliar application of deltamethrin and alphamethrin respectively.

Sharma *et al.* (1998) conducted varietal screening trial on brinjal with 7 varieties against *L. orbonalis* and reported that none of the cultivars were found to be absolutely tolerant to this pest. Arka kusmakar and Pusa purple cluster were ranked as tolerant while Mukta Keshi and BR-112 were rated as moderately susceptible. Pusa Kranti, Pusa purple long, Pusa purple round and Neelum round were found to be highly susceptible to the fruit borer.

Thus, based on the two years results, it is concluded that protection of brinjal against fruit borer (*L. orbonalis*) through alternate foliar spray of deltamethrin @ 30 g a.i./ha and Btk, Delfin WG @ 1000 g/ha applied at three weeks interval proved to be highly effective and profitable, irrespective of the varieties in realising remuneratively rewarding yield, higher net returns and appreciable benefit cost ratio. Though resistant or tolerant varieties suffered the least from the pest attack and as such yield loss in such varieties was found to be almost lesser also.

Acknowledgement

The author are grateful to the Vice-Chancellor, Dean (Agric.) and Director of Research, B.A.U., Kanke, Ranchi for providing the facilities for conducting this experiment.

References

Gupta, R.N., Srivastava, J.P., Gupta, H.K., Mathur, Y.K., 1998. Integrated management of jassids and fruit borer of brinjal. In: *Abstracted Research Papers*, pp. 275, *International Conference on Pest and Pesticide Management for Sustainable Agriculture* (ICPPMSA), held at C.S.A. University of Agriculture and Technology, Kanpur, 11–13 December, 1998.

Prasad, R., 2002. Integrated management of brinjal fruit borer (*Leucinodes orbonalis* Guen.) through interaction of crop association and judicious insecticidal application. In: *Environmental Pollution and Agriculture*. Ashish Publication, New Delhi.

Sharma, V.K., Roshan Singh, Arora, R.K., Gupta Arun, Singh, R. and Gupta, A., 1998. Field respgnse of brinjal cultivars against shoot and fruit borer, *Leucinodes orbonalis* Guen. *Annals of Biology*, Ludhiana, 14(2): 199–201.

Tewari, G.C. and Moorthy, P.N.K., 1983. Effectiveness of synthetic pyrethroids against the pest complex of brinjal. *Entomon.*, 8(4): 365–368.

Tripathi, M.K., Senapati, B. and Patra, R., 1996. Seasonal incidence and population fluctuation of *Leucinodes orbonalis* Guenee at Bubaneshwar, Orissa. *Pest Management and Economic Zoology*, 4(1–2): 15–18.

Yein, B.R., 1985. Field efficacy of some insecticides against shoot and fruit borer (*Leucinodes orbonalis* Guen.) of brinjal. *Journal of Research, Assam Agric. Univ.*, 6(1): 31–34.

Chapter 19

Insect Pests Scenario in Rice Agroecosystem in Ranchi, Jharkhand

***Rabindra Prasad*[1], *Sanjay Kumar Sathi*[2], *Udaya Kumar Prasad*[3], *and Devendra Prasad*[1]**

[1]Department of Entomology, Birsa Agricultural University, Kanke, Ranchi - 834 006
[2]KVK, Jagathpur, Birsa Agricultural University, Ranchi
[3]ZRS Chianki, Palamau, Birsa Agricultural University, Ranchi

ABSTRACT

The plateau region of Chotanagpur and Santhal Parganas including Ranchi area is having a rice based cropping system. Among various reasons, responsible for low production of rice, insect pets complex are major factors for lowering down the yield. Pest spectrum of a crop varies from place to place as per variation in the agro climatic conditions of the locality. Visualization of real pest problem of an area is the pre-requisite for formulating a sustainable IPM strategy. Keeping these points in view, pest. Survey and surveillance was conducted for three consecutive years to reckon the pest scenario of Ranchi region. The results revealed that as many as 19 insect pests belonging to 7 order and 13 families were found to attack paddy crop in the field condition. Based on mode of injuries caused by the pest species, to the crop plants, they could be categorized in 8 groups, such as: (1) Sap suckers: rice green leaf hopper, brown plant hopper, rice thrips, rice mealy bug; (2) Leaf eaters or defoliators: rice skipper, adult of rice hispa, case worm, grass hoppers, leaf folder and black hairy caterpillar; (3) Leaf miner: grub of rice hispa and whorl maggot; (4) Stem borers; (5) Ear cutting pests: swarming caterpillar, army worms and grass hoppers, (6) Gall makers: rice gall fly (gall midge); (7) Grain feeders/suckers: rice gundhibug; (8) Root feeders: termite, white grub and root grub. Based on extent of damage caused to the crop plants they were found to fall into two main groups *i.e.* minor and major pests. As such, rice skipper, rice thrips, rice mealy bug, white grub, brown plant hopper and green leaf hopper were of minor economic importance for Ranchi region and rests of other insect pests were of major economic significance. However, rice hispa, army worm, leaf folder, black hairy caterpillar and swarming caterpillars were found to occur in sporadic in mode of appearance and caused considerable extent ot damage to rice crop in the plateau region, whenever they occasionally occurred.

Keywords: *Rice, Insect pest species, Succession, Status, Mode of injury.*

Introduction

Rice in rainfed agroecosystem forms a major source of livelihood for almost two third population of India. The plateau region of Ranchi is having a rice based cropping system. Among various reasons, which are responsible for low production of rice, insect pest complex are major factors for lowering down the yield. Kalode *et al.* (1985) revealed that grain yield loss in rice due to insect pests in India has been estimated to vary from 21 to 51 percent, varying from area to area as per variation in the agroclimatic conditions. Pest spectrum of a crop also varies from place to place as per accordingly. Visualization of real pest problem of an area is the pre-requisite for formulating a sustainable IPM strategy. Keeping these points in view pest survey and survelliance was conducted for eight consecutive years to reckon the insect pests scenario of rice-ecosystem of Ranchi region.

Materials and Methods

In order to explore information on the insect pests scenario associated with rice in Ranchi region, roving survey and fixed plot survey and survelliance, was periodically conducted for two consecutive years, 2002-03 to 2004–05 during Kharif. For the purpose of conducting fixed plot pests monitoring, farmers field of Bundu, Tamar, Ratu (Kamade), Pithoriya, Piska-Nagari, Thakurgaon, Itaki, Khunti, Sonspatratu, Pali, Bundu, Palandu (Namkum), Ormajhee and Barabatoili of Angaraha Block were undertaken to visualize the pest problems on rice. A pocket lens (10X) and insect collecting net, glass vials and polyethylene bags were used for collection of insect pests for their proper identification in the laboratory with the held of the appropriate technical literature. Some insects were identified on the spot/farm and some of them were brought to the laboratory for detailed study. Periodically, intensity of the respective insect pest (s) were measured in terms of pest population per unit area/row length in some cases, whereas intensity of pest attack were determined by measuring percentage of infested plants with the respective insect species, *viz.*, gall fly, stem borer, leaf folder, rice skipper, case worm, termite, root weevil, whorl maggot and white grub etc. Mean of the population or intensity of injury caused by the pest species recorded at different observations were worked during the respective years. Overall mean of two years of observation were calculated insect wise for the purpose of classifying them into different groups. Based on their abundance, population density, mode of injury and nature of damage, mode of occurrence and pest status (severity as pest) they were properly categorized into different groups (Table 19.2). On the basis of extent of injury made to rice plants by the particular insect species, they were grouped into pest of negligible, minor, mild, major and severe economic importance. Keeping in view their mode of occurrence and frequency, the pest were treated as occasional, regular, sporadic, rare, epidemic, endemic in terms of appearance (Table 19.2). Overall information explored from the field investigation were complied and presented in Tables 19.1 and 19.2.

Results and Discussion

Accounts of scenario of insects pest fauna associated with rice-ecosystem, obtained from the field observation have been presented in Tables 19.1 and 19.2.

Table 19.1: An Account of Insect Pests Scenario Associated with Rice Ecosystem in Ranchi

Sl.No.	*Common Name*	*Zoological Name*	*Order*	*Family*	*Damaging Stage of the Insect Pest(s)*
1.	Yellow rice stem borer	*Scirpophaga incertulas* Walker	Lepidoptera	Pyralidae	Larvae
2.	Rice skipper	*Pelopidas mathias* Fs.	Lepidaptera	Hesperiidae	Larvae
3.	Rice gall fly	*Orseolia oryzae* Wm.	Diptera	Cecidomyiidae	Maggot
4.	Rice hispa	*Dicladispa armigera* Ol.	Coleotera	Chrysomellidae	Adult and grub
5.	Rice case worm	*Nymhula depunctalis* Gn.	Lepidoptera	Pyralidae	Larvae
6.	Rice grass hopper	*Hieroglyphus banian* Fab. *Oxya chinensis* (Thumb)	Orthoptera	Acrididae	Adult and nymph
7.	Rice gundhi bug	*Leptocorisa acuta* Th. *L. varicornis* Th.	Hemiptera	Coredidae	Adult and nymph
8.	Rice leaf folder	*Cnaphalorosis medinalis,* Guen.	Lepidoptera	Pyarlidae	Larvae
9.	Rice green leaf hopper	*Nephotettix nigro pincuts,* Stal; *Nephotettx virescens* (Dist.)	Homoptera	Cicadellidae	Adult and nymph
10.	Brown plant hopper	*Nilaparvata lugens,* Stal.	Homoptera	Delphacidae	Adult and nymph
11.	Rice thrips	*Baliothrips biformis* (Bogn.)	Thysanoptera	Thripidae	Adult and nymph
12.	Rice mealybug	*Heterococous rehi* (Lind)	Homoptera	Pseudococcidae	Nymph and adult
13.	Army worm	*Mythimna unipunctata* Haw; *M. Separata* Wlk.	Lepidoptera	Noctuidae	Caterpillar
14.	Swarming caterpillar	*Spodoptera maruitia* Boisd	Lepidoptera	Noctuidae	Larvae
15.	Black hairy caterpillar	*Nisaga simplex* (Wlk)	Lepidoptera	Eupierotidae	Caterpillar
16.	Whorl maggot	*Hydrellia griseola* (Fall)	Diptera	Ephydridae	Maggot
17.	White grub	*Holotrichia* spp.	Coleoptera	Scarabaeidae	Grub
18.	Termite	*Odontotermes obesus* Ramb.	Isoptera	Termitidae	Adults and Youngs (workers)
19.	Rice root weevil	*Hydronomidius molitor* Faust.	Coleoptera	Curcuiionidae	Grub

Table 19.2: Succession, Nature of Damage and Status of Pest Complex of Rice in Ranchi Area

Sl.No.	*Name of the Insect Pests*	*Stage of the Crop Attacked*	*Nature of Damage of Insect Pests and Symptoms of Injuries*	*Mode of Occurrence*	*Pest Status*
1.	Rice stem borer	Nursery, vegetative and reproductive stages	Larvae were found to bore into the crop stem, resulting into the formation of dead heart (vegetative stage) and white ear head (reproductive stage)	Regular	Major
2.	Rice skipper	Vegetative and reproductive stages	Larvae of the insect were found to cause damage to the crop by defoliating the plants	Sporadic	Minor
3.	Rice gall fly	Nursery and tillering stages	Maggots were seen to damage the growing point, resulting into silvery onion shoot, that is modification of leaf sheath. Affected panicles could not emerge out on such tillers. Heavy loss in yield in seriously affected crop was observed.	Regular	Major
4.	Rice hispa	Vegetative stage, just after transplanting stage	Adults, scraped leaves causing white longitudinal and parallel strips on leaves whereas grub acted as leaf miners living within the epidermis of leaf	Sporadic/ occasional	Mild to severe
5.	Rice case worn	Late vegetative stage	Larvae were able to cut out small pieces of leaves (2.0–2.5 cm) and constructed tubes serving as boat for the caterpillars. As a result leaves become white and papery	Occasional/ Regular	Mild to severe
6.	Rice grass hopper	All stages of the crop, *i.e.* all round the field in the whole season	Adults and nymphs were noticed to feed on leaves from margin inward and defoliation was caused in affected plants	Regular	Minor
7.	Rice gundhi bug	Late vegetative and at reproductive stage	Adult and nymphs were observed to suck sap from young leaves in vegetative stage and from milky grains in reproductive stage of rice plants	Regular	Mild to severe
8.	Rice leaf folder	Vegetative stage	The larvae of the insects were found to make rolls from leaves vertically or longitudinally by bringing together two leaves and feed on them on green tissues living within the fold	Sporadic	Mild to severe
9.	Rice green leaf hopper	Vegetative stage	The adults and nymphs were found to suck the sap from leaves and some times transmitted tungro-virus disease in plants	Regular	Minor to mild
10.	Brown plant hopper	Vegetative stage	The adults and nymphs insects were found to suck the plant sap from the stem as a result circular patch of hopper burn could be noticed in the affected field	Sporadic	Minor
11.	Rice thrips	Vegetative stage	The insect were found to feed on the leaf sap by lacerating the leaf tissues causing longitudinal rolling of leaves as if crop was withering due to lack of moisture	Occasional	Minor

Contd...

Table 19.2–Contd...

Sl.No.	*Name of the Insect Pests*	*Stage of the Crop Attacked*	*Nature of Damage of Insect Pests and Symptoms of Injuries*	*Mode of Occurrence*	*Pest Status*
12.	Rice mealy bug	Vegetative stage, usually occurrence was more pronounced in drought condition	Adult and nymphal stage of the insect were found to suck plant sap causing yellowing of the crop	Occasional	Minor
13.	Army worm	Vegetative and reproductive stage	The caterpillar (larvae) of the insects were observed to defoliate the plants severely and cut our panicles	Sporadic/ epidemic	Mild to severe
14.	Swarming caterpillar	Soon after sowing or transplanting of the crop; may or may not be throughout vegetative stage	The larval stage of the insects were found to cause serious damage to the young crop by causing defoliation of the plants	Sporadic/ epidemic	Mild to severe
15.	Black hairy caterpillar	Vegetative stage	The caterpillars were found to feed voraciously on the leaf. The plants were defoliated badly	Sporadic/ epidemic	Mild to severe
16.	Whorl maggot	Vegetative stage	Larvae (maggot) mined leaves	Rare	Minor
17.	White grub	Early and vegetative stage	Grubs preferred to feed the roots, resulting in withering and killing of plants, when the field remained dry	Rare/ occasional	Negligible
18.	Termite	Seedling and vegetative stage	Termites preferred to feed germinating seeds and seedling within the soil at ground level resulting in drying of plants	Occasional/ Sporadic	Mild
19.	Rice root weevil	Early, vegetative stage	Grubs were found to feed on roots within the soil causing withering and drying off plants	Rare	Minor

Table 19.1 contains information on insect pest fauna. (along with their Taxonomic position) of rice and their respective damaging stage(s).

Table 19.2 comprises of mode of occurrence, succession, nature of damage and status of the insect species as pest. The results revealed that as many as 19 insect pests species belonging to 7 orders and 13 families were found to attack paddy crop in the field condition in Ranchi region. Based on mode of injuries caused by the pest species, to the crop plants, they could be categorized in 8 groups, such as: (1) Sap suckers: rice green leaf hopper, brown plant hopper, rice thrips, rice mealy bug; (2) Leaf eaters or defoliators. rice skipper, adult of rice hispa, case worm, grass hopper, leaf folder and black hairy caterpillar, (3) Leaf miner: grub of rice hispa; (4) Stem borers; (5) Ear cutting insects: swarming caterpillar, army worms and grass hoppers (6) Gall makers: rice gall fly (gall midge); (7) Grain feeders/suckers: rice gundhibug; (8) Root feeders: termite, white grub, root weevil. Based on extent of damage caused to the crop plants they were found to fall into two main groups *i.e.*, minor and major pests. As such, rice skipper, rice thrips, rice mealy bug, white grub, brown plant hopper and green leaf hopper were of minor economic importance for this region and rests of other insect pests were of major economic significance. However, rice hispa, army worm, leaf folder, black hairy caterpillar and swarming caterpillars were found to occur in sporadic in appearance and caused considerable extent of damage to rice crop in the plateau region in the present study.

Root Zone's Insect Pests

It was found that termite, white grub and root weevil were found to damage germinating. plants, root, rootlets and seedling of rice particularly in rainfed upland situation. Of them termites were found as sporadic, occasional in occurrence and mild to severe infesting the crop in the present investigation. Veeresh (1995) reported that pest status of termites in field crops has been gradually changing from minor to major particularly in rainfed upland situation.

Root weevil (*Hydronomidii.Js molitol*) was found as rare pest of minor importance in the region. As a result of larval feeding on roots of young paddy plants, the attacked plants remain stunted and produced a few tillers. The damaged plants in severe infestation first showed withering and then get killed. Singh and Choudhary (1965) also reported that the root weevil prevailed as minor pest of rice in Bihar, occurring as spordically and rarely.

White grubs (*Holotrichia* spp) was rarely and occasionally found to infest paddy plant in rainfed upland situation; the extent of damage was almost negligible in the present study. The incidence was recorded from Madanpur village (near Pithoriya) which seems to be first report from Jharkhand. Yadava (1995) and Singh *et al.* (2003) reported that white grubs (Coleptera : Scarabaidae) are emerging as a pest of economic significance in several rainy season crops grown under rainfed upland conditions.

Sap Sukers

GLH, BPH, thrips and mealy bugs were observed to suck sap from paddy leaves. GLH appeared on regular basis to cause minor to mild damage to the crop in its vegetative stage in the present study. Khanna and Mittal (1972) and Prasad and Prasad (2004) reported that Indian states *viz.*, Uttar Pradesh, Bihar and West Bengal experienced serious economic losses to rice on account of GLH. Present field investigation revealed that BPH and rice thrips appeared as sporadic, occasional in occurrence as minor pest in the plateau region.

Leaf Eaters/Defoliators

Rice skipper appeared in vegetative and reproductive stage of the crop sporadically as minor pest. Rice hispa usually damaged the plant early vegetative stage occasionally and sporadically upto mild to severe extent. Prakash *et al.* (2003) revealed that hispa, rice case worm, grass hopper, leaf folder and swarming caterpillar were pest of major economic importance of rainfed rice ecosystem in India. The present study revealed that among the other major defoliating insects on rice, *viz.*, rice leaf folder, case worm and grass hoppers were found in the plateau region of Ranchi. Black Hairy, caterpillar, *Nisaga simplex* Wlk. emerged as major pest causing mild to sever damage in the vegetative stage of paddy. Though, the pest appeared sporadically but in epidemic form during 2002–03 and 2003–04. Recently, Prasad (2000) and Prasad and Prasad (2004) also opined that *N. simplex* emerged as a new threat to upland rice in Jharkhand.

Leaf Miners

Grubs of rice hispa (*Dicladispa armigera* Ol.) and larvae of whorl maggot (*Hydrellia griseola* Fall.) were found to mine leaves of rice. The former insect remained as the pest of mild to severe pest of sporadic and occasional occurrence while the latter was found to be in rare of minor incidence. Prakash *et al.* (2003) opined that hispa is a major pest on the crop in certain parts of India.

Stem Borers

Larvae of *Scirpophaga incertulus* remained pest of rice of major econornic importance and appeared regularly in both vegetative and reproductive stages of the crop in the plateau region. Earlier, Pradhan (1969) opined that among half a dozen of different species of lepidopterous larvae boring into tissues of paddy plant, yellow stem borer *S. incerlulus* remained the major one in all parts of India in rice growing areas.

Ear Cutting Insect Pests

Swarming, caterpillar, *Spodoptera mauritia* Boisd., army worm, *Mythimna separate* Wlk. and *M. unipunctata* and grass hoppers, *Hieroglyphus banian* Fab. and *Oxya chinensis* (Thumb) were found to cut rice ears in fields (Tables 19.1 and 19.2). Rai and Singh (1995) and Prasad and Prasad (2004) reported that serious out breaks of army worms took place in Uttar Pradesh, Madhya Pradesh and some parts of Jharkhand.

Gall Maker

Rice gall fly (*Orseolia oryzae* Wm) was found as one of the most important pest problem in certain areas of the. plateau area like Simdege, Bundu, Khuntl and Tamar etc. and appeared endemically there. The pest is of regular occurrence right from nursery to tillering stages of the crop causing severe damage. Prakash *et al.* (2003) also opined that the insect pest is causing considerable loss in rice in several parts in India.

Grain Suckers

Stink bug or ear bug of rice (*Leptocorisa acuta* Th. and *L. varicornis*) was found to be a regular and major insect pest, causing mild to severe damage by sucking sap from young leaves in late vegetative stage and milky grains in reproductive stage of rice plants in all-around the Ranchi plateau region. Kalode *et al.* (1995), Prasad and Prasad (2004) reported that rice gundhi bug is commonly occurring major grain sucking insect pest of rice in several parts of India. Kalode *et al.* (1995) opined that out of more than 100 insect pests prevailing in rice ecosystem in India, about 15 insect pests in general could be considered as major pests which are: stem borers, gall midge, leaf hoppers, plant hoppers, leaf folder, whorl maggot, rice hispa, cut worm (army and swarming caterpillars) and ear bug etc.

Foregoing discussion revealed that as many as 19 insect pests have been occurring on rice, out of which at least eleven pests *viz.*, stem borer, gall fly, hispa, case worm, ear bug, leaf folder, green leaf hopper, army worm, swarming caterpillar, black hairy caterpillar and termite were noticed as pest of major concern in Ranchi region.

Acknowledgement

Authors are grateful to the Vice chancellor, Director of Research and the Dean (Agric.) of Birsa Agricultural Universities, Ranchi for providing the necessary facilities for conducting the experiment.

References

Kalode, M.B., Pasalu, I.C., Krishnaiah, N.V. and Bentur, J.S., 1995. Changing insect pest complex in relation to cropping system of rice. In: *Proc. National seminar on Changing Pest Situation in the Current Agric. Scenario of India.* Published by ICAR, New Delhi, pp. 243–255.

Khanna, S.S. and Mittal, M.C., 1972. *Rice in Uttar Pradesh.* Institute of Agricultural Sciences, Kanpur, pp. 51–56.

Pradhan, S., 1969. Pests of paddy. In: *Insect Pests of Crops.* National Book Trust of India, New Delhi, pp. 200.

Prakash, A., Rath, P.C., Rao, J., Dani, R.C., Padhi, G., Sasmal, S., Behera, K.S. and Jena, M., 2003. Insect pests of shallow rainfed low land rice in eastern India and their management. In: *Proc. National Symposium on Frontier Areas of Entomological Research*, held at IARI on 5–7 November 2003, New Delhi, pp. 4–6.

Prasad, D., 2000. Black hairy caterpillar, *Nisaga simplex* Walker: A new threat to upland rice. *B.A.U.J. Res.*, 12(2): 265–266.

Prasad, R. and Prasad, D., 2004. An account of insect pest problem in rice ecosystem in Ranchi. *Abstracted Res. Papers, Nat. Conf. Increasing Rice Production Under Water Limited Environment*, December 3–4, 2004, held at B.A.U., Ranchi (India), pp. 58–59.

Rai, Lallan and Singh, S.P.N., 1995. Analysis of factors for the outbreak of army worms causing national problems, In: *Proc. National Seminar on Changing Pest Situation in the Current Agric. Scenario of India*, published by ICAR, New Delhi, pp. 114–121.

Singh, M.P. Bisht, R.S. and Mishra, P.N., 2003. Survey to explore the natural enemies of white grub (*Holotrichia spp.*) in Garhwal Himalayas. *Indian J. Ent.*, 65(2): 202–210.

Singh, M.P. and Chaudhary, D.P., 1965. Paddy root weevil (*Hydronomidius molitor* Fst.): A new insect pest of paddy in Bihar. *Rice Newsletter*, 13(2): 37–38.

Veeresh, G.K., 1995. Status of termites in the changing agricultural scenario in India. In: *Proc. National Seminar on Changing Pest Situation in the Current Agriculture Scenario in India*, Published by ICAR, New Delhi, pp. 160–162.

Yadava, C.P.S., 1995. Changes in crop cultivation practices responsible for white grub problem in India. In: *Proc. of National Seminar on Changing Pest Situation in the Current Agric. Scenario of India*, Published by ICAR, New Delhi, pp. 256–260.

Chapter 20

In vitro Antimicrobial Activity of Citric Acid Against Multiple Drug Resistant Uropathogens

***A.V. Gomashe*[1] *and P.M. Tumane*[2]**

[1]Head of Microbiology, Shri Shivaji Science College, Nagpur - 440 012, Maharashtra, India
[2]P.G. Department of Microbiology, Rashtrasant Tukadoji Maharaj Nagpur University, Nagpur - 440 033, Maharashtra, India

ABSTRACT

Minimum Inhibitory Concentration (MIC) of citric acid–a new antimicrobial agent was determined for 250 multiple drug resistant uropathogens *viz., E. coli* (100), *Klebsiella sp.* (50), *Proteus sp.* (50) and Coagulase negative Staphylococci (50). MIC range 2000–8000 µg/ml was found against *E. coli* and. *Klebsiella* sp. For *Proteus* sp. and Coagulase Negative Staphylococci (CONS) MIC range was 1000–4000 µg/ml and 1000–2000 µg/ml respectively. The results show that, a newly identified antimicrobial agent, citric acid is highly effective *in vitro* against multiple drug resistant uropathogens.

Keywords: Uropathogens, Citric acid, Minimum inhibitory concentration (MIC).

Introduction

Urinary Tract Infections (UTI) are caused by variety of bacteria. *Escherichia coli* is the most frequent cause of UTI, followed by *Pseudomonas* sp., *Klebsiella* sp., *Proteus* sp., *Staphylococci* sp. etc. (Thomas, 2000).

In recent years, there has been a dramatic increase in antibiotic resistance of uropathogens, which has created serious therapeutic difficulty. Anderson *et al.* demonstrated that there is a close correlation between the clinical introduction of each new antibacterial drug and the emergence of bacteria resistant to it (Anderson, 1974).

Inspite of all efforts made towards a better chemotherapeutic agent, the problem of overcoming the development of resistance has not yet been solved.

Citric acid as a chemotherapeutic agent, active against drug resistant *Ps. aeruginosa* has been reported (Nagoba *et al.*, 1998a; Nagoba *et al.*, 1998b). Considering the chemotherapeutic use of citric acid, an attempt was made to determine antibacterial activity of citric acid against multiple drug resistant uropathogens.

Materials and Methods

Bacterial Strains

A total of 250 multiple drug resistant isolates of urinary pathogen *viz.*, *Escherichia coli* (100), *Klebsiella* sp. (50), *Proteus* sp. (50) and coagulase negative *Staphylococci* (50) were selected to study the minimum inhibitory concentration (MIC) of citric acid. MIC of citric acid was determined by broth dilution method (Baron *et al.*, 1994).

Preparation of Inoculum

Each bacterial inoculum was prepared by inoculating a loopful of test organisms in a 5 ml of Hi-si test broth and incubated at 37°C for 6–8 hrs. till a moderate turbidity was developed. The turbidity was matched with 0.5 McFarland Standards.

MIC Determination

Minimum inhibitory concentration of citric acid was determined by Broth dilution method (Baron *et al.*, 1994).

In broth dilution method, citric acid solution of 32 mg/ml was prepared by dissolving 320 mg of citric acid in 10 ml. Sterile water and two fold dilutions were prepared in test tube containing sterile distilled water (Table 20.1). Then equal amount of double strength Hi-sensitivity broth was mixed in each tube.

Table 20.1: Protocol for Broth Dilution Method for MIC determination of Citric Acid

Sl.No.	*Solution Added*	*Tube No.*									
		1	*2*	*3*	*4*	*5*	*6*	*7*	*8*	*C+*	*C–*
1.	Sterile distilled water (ml)	–	5	5	5	5	5	5	5		
2.	Working citric acid solution (32 μg/ml)	10→	5→	5→	5→	5→	5→	5→	5*	–	–
	Volume in each tube (ml)	5	5	5	5	5	5	5	5	5	5
3.	Double strength Hi-sensitivity broth (ml)	5	5	5	5	5	5	5	5	5	5
	Final volume (ml)	10	10	10	10	10	10	10	10	10	10
4.	Inoculum size, (ml) 10^6 CFU/ml	0.1	0.1	0.1	0.1	0.1	0.1	0.1	0.1	0.1	0.1
	Final citric acid Conc. (mg/ml)	16.0	8.0	4.0	2.0	1.0	0.5	0.25	0.125	0.0625	–
	In μg/ml	16000	8000	4000	2000	1000	500	250	125	62.5	–

C+ → Positive Control, C → Sterility control; * → Discarded.

Inoculation and Incubation

In Broth dilution method 0.1 ml of inoculum was inoculated in 10ml of Hi-sensitivity broth set. All the tubes were incubated at 37°C for 18–24 hrs.

Results and Discussion

Drug resistant *Escherichia coli* were found to be inhibited by citric acid at a concentration range of 2000 µg/ml to 8000 µg/ml with mean MIC value of 2320 µg/ml.

In case of *Klebsiella* sp. effective range of citric acid was found to be 2000 µg/ml to 8000 µg/ml with mean MIC of 2440 µg/ml.

Effective range of citric acid for *Proteus* sp. was found to be 1000 µg/ml to 4000 µg/ml with mean MIC value of 1180 µg/ml.

In multi-drug resistant coagulase negative Staphylococci, effective range of citric acid was found to be 1000 µg/ml to 2000 µg/ml with mean MIC value of 1080 µg/ml (Table 20.2).

Table 20.2: MIC Range and Mean MIC of Citric Acid by Broth Dilution Method

Sl.No.	*Organism*	*MIC Range (µg/ml)*	*Mean MIC (µg/ml)*
1.	*E. coli*	2000–8000	2320
2.	*Klebsiella* sp.	2000–8000	2440
3.	*Proteus* sp.	1000–4000	1180
4.	CONS	1000–2000	1080

The incidence of urinary tract infections has increased because of widespread use of broad spectrum antimicrobial agents. This resulted in development of resistance in uropathogens against commonly used antibiotics and chemotherapeutic agents.

Use of 3 per cent citric acid for the successful treatment of superficial nosocomial infection caused by *Ps. aeruginosa, S. aureus, E. coli, Klebsiella* sp. and *Proteus* sp. has been replied (Nagoba *et al.*, 1998a; Nagoba *et al.*, 1998b; Nagoba *et al.*, 1999; Nagoba *et al.*, 2000) where traditional antibiotic therapy was ineffective.

In the present study, citric acid was tested against 250 multiple drug resistant isolates and found to be effective against all the drug resistant strains. Low concentration of citric acid was required to inhibit coagulase negative Staphylococci (Mean MIC = 1080 µg/ml) and *Proteus* sp. (Mean MIC = 1180 µg/ml) as compared to *E. coli* (Mean MIC = 2320 µg/ml) and *Klebsiella* sp. (Mean MIC = 2440 µg/ml) (Table 20.2).

From the present study, it has been concluded that, a newly identified antimicrobial agent, citric acid is highly effective against multiple drug resistant uropathogens *in vitro* and can be a solution to overcome the problem of development of resistance in bacterial isolates.

References

Anderson, J.S., 1974. The ecological significance of R factor activity. In: *Topic in Infectious Diseases*. I. Drug recepto interaction in antimicrobial chemotherapy. Springer-verlag, New York, pp. 59–76.

Baron, E.J., Peterson, L.R. and Finegold, S.M., 1994. Methods for testing antimicrobial effectivenss. In: *Bailey and Scott's Diagnostic Microbiology*, 9th ed. The C.V. Mosby Company, London, pp. 168–188.

Nagoba, B.S., Deshmukh, S.R., Wadher, B.J., Mahabaleshwar, L., Gandhi, R.C., Kulkarni, P.B., Mane, V.A. and Deshmukh, J.S., 1998b. Treatment of superficial pseudomonal infections with citric acid. *J. Hosp. Infection*, pp. 155–157.

Nagoba, B.S., Gandhi, R.C., Wadher, B.J., Deshmukh, S.R. and Gandhi, S.P., 1998a. Citric acid treatment of severe electric burns complicated by multiple antibiotic resistant *Pseudomonas aeruginosa*, *BURNS*, pp. 481–483.

Nagoba, B.S., Kulkarni, P.B., Wadher, B.J., Kulkarni, U.P. and Mahabaleshwar, L., 2000. Citric acid treatment of Diabetic foot: A simple and effective approach. *J. Asso. Physician of India*, 48(7): 739–741.

Nagoba, B.S., Pathan, H.B. and Wadher, B.J., 1999. Citric acid treatment of superficial nosocomial infectious: A new era in antimicrobial chemotherapy. *Kuwait Medical Journal*, 31(1): 72–74.

Thomas, J.G., 2000. Urinary tract infections. In: *Textbook of Diagnostic Microbiology*, 2nd ed. W.B. Saunders Company, London, p. 1011–1032.

Chapter 21

Enhanced Salinity Tolerance of Tomato [*Lycopersicon esculentum* (L.) Mill.] Plants as Affected by Paclobutrazol Treatment

B. Sankar, R. Somasundaram*, P. Manivannan, A. Kishorekumar, C. Abdul Jaleel and R. Panneerselvam

Division of Plant Physiology, Department of Botany, Annamalai University, Annamalainagar – 608 002, Tamil Nadu, India

ABSTRACT

Tomato [*Lycopersicon esculentum* (L) Mill.] seedlings were treated with 40 mM NaCl and 40 mM NaCl + 2.5 mg l^{-1} paclobutrazol to study the effect of NaCl and the ameliorative effect of paclobutrazol on NaCl stressed seedlings. NaCl stress decreased the growth rates (root, shoot length and total leaf area) protein content and peroxidase activity and increased the amino acid and proline contents, paclobutrazol treatment increased the decreased protein content, amino acid and proline content paclobutrazol treatment ameliorated the deleterious effects of NaCl salinity on tomato seedlings.

Keywords: *Lycopersicon esculentum, Peroxidase, Salinity, Paclobutrazol.*

Introduction

The normal biosynthetic machinery of the plant is disturbed under saline condition. Salinity affects many aspects of plant mechanism and accumulation of various organic solutes (Sudhakar *et al.*

* Corresponding Author: E-mail: kalaisomu_20@rediffmail.com.

1993). Plant bioregulator mediated biochemical changes have been shown to play vital role during salinity stress. Reduced growth rate under salinity stress has been ascribed to altered indigenous levels of hormones. It has been reported that adverse effects of salinity on plants could be to some extent, overcome by treating plants with plant growth regulators (Parashar and Verma, 1993). Triazole compounds are widely used as fungicide arid also have plant growth regulating properties. The biological activities of several triazole derivatives have been reviewed by Fletcher (1985). It has been demonstrated that the triazole can protect plants against various stresses including drought, low and high temperatures, salinity and air pollutants and therefore referred as "plant multiprotectants" (Fletcher *et al.*, 2000). Tomato [*Lycopersicon esculentum* (L.) Mill.] is one of the important vegetable crops. Its productivity is very much affected by soil salinity. The present study was investigate the changes in protein, amino acid, proline content and the activity of peroxidase enzyme under salinity and paclobutrazol treatment during early seedling growth of tomato.

Materials and Methods

The seeds of *L. esculentum* were obtained from Ankur Seeds Pvt. Ltd., Nagpur, India. Seeds were surface sterilized with 0.1 per cent $HgCl_2$ for 5 minutes, followed by thorough washing with deionised water. The seeds were soaked for 12 hours in distilled water, 40 mM NaCl and 2.5 mg l^{-1} paclobutrazol in 40 mM NaCl and sown in 30 × 40 × 7 cms plastic trays containing acid washed sand and grown in a seed germinator maintained at 25±1°C, 80–85 per cent RH and 450 µE $m^{-1}s^{-1}$ of irradiance for 14 hours per day till end of the experiment. Seedling were irrigated with respective treatment solution daily. Ten Days After Sowing (DAS) the seedlings were harvested randomly and washed with deionised water to remove the salt adhering to the seedlings and separated into root, stem and leaves and used for analysis.

Protein was estimated following the method of Bradford (1976). The total free amino acid content was determined using the method of Moore and Stein (1984). Proline was estimated according to the method of Bates *et al.* (1973). Peroxidase activity was assayed using the method of Kumar and Khan (1982) and expressed in units (U) (U = 0.1 absorbance min^{-1} mg^{-1} protein).

Results and Discussion

Sodium chloride stress decreased the protein content in all parts of seedlings. Sodium chloride treatment decreased the protein synthesis and increased its hydrolysis in pea roots and soybean (Klyshev and Rakova, 1964; Durgaprasad *et al.*, 1996). Triazole compounds like paclobutrazol treatment to the NaCl stressed seedlings increased the protein content to the level of control. Similar results were found in triadimefon treated salt stressed peanut seedling (Muthukumarasamy and Panneerselvam, 1997).

Sodium chloride stress increased the total amino acid and proline content in all parts of the seedlings. The accumulation of free amino acids in salt stressed plants may be due to a reduction in the incorporation of amino acid into protein as observed by Hurkman and Tanaka (1987). Amino acid content increased under NaCl stressed soybean seedling (Durgaprasad *et al.*, 1996). Accumulation of proline in plant cell is a stress symptom. Increased proline content was observed under salinity stress in mulberry (Kumar *et al.*, 2000) and mungbean (Nandini Chakrabarti *et al.*, 2002). Accumulation of proline under stress conditions might induced the formation of strong H^+ bonds with water around and protein, there by preserving the native state of the cell bipolymers (Rascio *et al.* 1994). Proline and free amino acid content were slightly lowered by the paclobutrazol treatment in NaCl stressed seedlings, however, it was higher than that of control.

Table 21.1: Effect of Paclobutrazol on the Protein, Amino Acid, Proline Content and Peroxidase Activity in Salt Stressed Tomato Seedlings (Values are mean±SD of 3 samples)

Parameters	*Root*			*Stem*			*Leaf*		
	Control	*40 mM NaCl*	*40 mM NaCl + 2.5 mg l^{-1} Paclobutrazol*	*Control*	*40 mM NaCl*	*40 mM NaCl + 2.5 mg l^{-1} Paclobutrazol*	*Control*	*40 mM NaCl*	*40 mM NaCl + 2.5 mg l^{-1} Paclobutrazol*
Protein (mg g^{-1} FW)	38.820±1.386	25.474±0.980	37.738±1.348	20.487±0.788	15.765±0.631	18.639±0.666	28.889±0.996	12.790±0.474	26.703±0.921
Amino acid (mg g^{-1} FW)	8.438±0.301	20.582±0.762	14.366±0.513	25.932±1.297	34.320±1.271	29.837±1.148	2.013±0.072	5.968±0.213	5.092±0.189
Proline 1.382±0.051 (mg g^{-1} FW)	2.164±0.077	10.260±0.38	9.312±0.32	1	2.477±0.095	9.879±0.353	7.939±0.294	3.029±0.112	2.975±0.110
Peroxidase (U mg^{-1} protein)	1.231±0.047	0.93±0.033	2.234±0.086	1.02±0.036	0.632±0.023	1.68±0.062	1.92±0.069	1.63±0.060	2.063±0.076

The peroxidase activity was inhibited in all parts of the NaCl stressed seedlings. Paclobutrazol treatment to the NaCl stressed seedlings increased the peroxidase activity to a higher extent even above the level of control. Paclobutrazol treatment protected corn seedlings from chilling damage and the stress protection was mediated by an increase in antioxidants and with enhanced activities of *peroxidase* and catalase (Pinhero and Fletcher, 1994). Paclobutrazl treatment increased the protein synthesis, biochemical constituents like amino acid and proline content and thereby ameliorated the NaCl stress in tomato seedlings.

References

Bates, L.S., Waldron, R.P. and Teare, I.D., 1973. Rapid determination of free proline in water stress studies. *Plant and Soil*, 39: 205–207.

Bradford, M.M., 1976. A rapid and sensitive method for the quantitation of microgram quantities of protein utilizing the principle of protein-dye binding. *Anal. Biochem.*, 72: 248–254.

Durgaprasad, K.M.R., Muthukumarasamy, M. and Panneerselvam, R., 1996. Changes in protein metabolism induced by NaCl salinity in soybean seedlings. *Ind. J. Plant Physiol.* 1: 98–101.

Fletcher, R.A., 1985. Plant growth regulating properties of sterol inhibiting fungicides. In: *Hormonal Regulation of Plant Growth and Development*, (Ed.) S.S. Purohit. Agrobotanical Publishers, Bikaner, India, 2: 103–113.

Fletcher, R.A., Gilley, A., Davis, T.D. and Sankhla, N., 2000. Triazoles as plant growth regulators and stress protectants. *Hort. Rev.*, 24: 55–138

Hurkman, W.J. and Tanaka, C.K., 1987. The effects of salts on the pattern of protein synthesis in barley roots. *Plant Physiol.*, 83: 517–524.

Klyshev, L.K. and Rakova, N.M., 1964. Effect of salinisation of the substrate on the protein composition of the roots in pea shoots. *Tr. Bot. Inst. Akad. Nauk. Kaz., SSR*, 20: 156–167.

Kumar, K.B. and Khan, P.A., 1982. Peroxidase and polyphenoloxidase in excised ragi (*Eleusine corocana* cv. PR 202) leaves during senescence. *Indian J. Exp. Bot.*, 20: 412–416.

Kumar, S.G., Madhusudhan, K.V., Sreenivasulu, N. and Sudhakar, C., 2000. Stress responses in two genotypes of mulberry (*Morus alba* L.) under NaCl salinity. *Indian J. Exp. Biol.*, 38: 192–195.

Moore, S. and Stein, W.H., 1984. Photometric method for use in the chromatography of amino acids. *J. Biol. Chem.*, 176: 367–388.

Muthukumarasamy, M. and Panneerselvam, R., 1997. Amelioration of NaCl stress by triadimefon in peanut seedlings. *Plant Growth Regul.*, 6: 1–6.

Nandini Chakrabarti and Subhendu Mukherji, 2002. Growth regulator mediated changes in leaf area and metabolic activity in mungbean under salt stress condition. *Indian J. Plant Physiol.*, 7: 256–263.

Parashar, A. and Verma, S.K., 1993. Effect of gibberellic acid on chemical composition of wheat (*Triticum aestivum* L.) grown under different salinity levels. *National Conf. Plant Physiol.*, 19: 76–89.

Pinhero, R.G. and Feltcher, R.A., 1994. Paclobutrazol and anemidol protect corn seedlings from high and low temperature stresses. *Plant Growth Regul.*, 15: 47–53.

Rascio, A., Plantani, C., Sealfati, G., Tonti, A. and Difonzo, N., 1994. The accumulation of solutes and water binding strength in drum wheat. *Physiol. Plant*, 90: 715–721.

Sudhakar, C., Reddy, P.S. and Veeranjaneyulu, K. 1993. Effect of salt stress on the enzymes of proline synthesis and oxidation in greengram (*Phaseolus aureus* Roxb.) seedlings. *Indian J. Plant Physiol.*, 141: 621–623.

Chapter 22

Seed Invigoration in Indian Bean (*Lablab purpureus* L.)

R.L. Moharana, D.P. Khuntia, S.J. Pramanik and A.K. Basu

Department of Seed Science and Technology, Bidhan Chandra Krishi Viswavidyyalaya, Mohanpur, Nadia – 741 252, West Bengal

ABSTRACT

Locally available five genotypes of Indian bean (*Lablab purpureus* L.) were collected differing distinctly for their plant, flower, pod and seed characters. Seeds kept in cloth bags and stored in ambient condition for six months were subjected to six different invigoration treatments *viz.*, Soaking Drying (SD), 100 ppm GA_3, 50 ppm ascorbic acid, 1 per cent solution of calcium chloride and thio urea and 1 per cent concentrated sulphuric acid. The response of different invigoration treatments was noted to be unique for individual genotypes. Therefore, assessment for improved seed vigour and viability after invigoration treatment was made separately for individual genotypes. At the same time the action of individual treatment was also assessed and found to be varied based on varying nature of genetic constitution of individual genotypes.

Introduction

Indian bean (Sem) is an important leguminous vegetable crop consumed as human food, cattle food and also used as green manure. Tender seeds and pods are cooked as vegetable, while mature and dried seeds are used as pulse, it is a matter of great concern that these seeds need to be preserved for planting in the next season; but due to passage of time, seeds gradually loose their viability. This loss in germination and viability could be protected through different treatments at different stages of seed storage *viz.*, at pre-storage, mid-storage and post storage condition. Some workers have already prescribed a number of seed invigoration treatments specified for crops, crop species or in general such as Dey *et al.* (1998) in Black gram by dry physiological treatments, Jeng and Sung (1984) in peanut seed through hydration effect, Mandal *et al.* (2000) for soybean through both wet treatment and dry-dressing of seeds, etc. But the authors are unaware about any reports on seed invigoration on lablab bean. Keeping this problem in view with all its perspectives, the present experiment was carried out for invigorating post-storage lablab bean seeds prior to next sowing not only to check the further loss but also to improve its viability and vigour status.

Materials and Methods

Five locally available genotypes, distinctly different for their morphological characters and collected from different location of Nadia district, West Bengal, were grown and seeds at field maturity were collected, properly dried at 10–12 per cent moisture content and stored in cloth bag under ambient condition. One year stored seeds were subjected to six seed invigoration, treatments along with untreated control. The details of treatments are: T_1–Control: stored seeds without treatment; T_2–Soaking-drying: five hours soaking in distilled water without chemicals, then air-dried and finally dried back to its original moisture content; T_3–100 ppm GA_3 for 3 hours; T_4– per cent Thio-urea for 3 hours; T_5–1 per cent calcium chloride for 3 hours; T_6–1 per cent concentrated H_2SO_4 for 10 minutes and T_7–50 ppm Ascorbic acid for 3 hrs. After invigoration treatment, (for T_3 to T_7), the seeds were thoroughly washed in running water, surface dried and then dried back to its original moisture content. As per treatment schedule, 50 (fifty) seeds/treatment/replication (three) were placed in germination in glassplate–blotter method (Punjabi and Basu, 1982). Observations were recorded after 10 (ten) days on germination (per cent), root-shoot length (cm), fresh and dry weight (mg) and vigour index of seedlings. Vigour Index was calculated after Kalakannavar *et al.* (1989) as: Vigour index = Germination (per cent) × root length (cm). Data obtained were statistically analysed following Factorial Completely Randomized Design (Gomez and Gomez, 1984).

Results and Discussion

The response of five locally available genotypes against different seed invigoration treatments could be revealed through the tables on germination, root- shoot length, fresh and dry weight and vigour index of seedlings. Significant differences for response of genotypes, influence of invigoration treatments as well as (genotype × treatment) interaction were recorded for all the characters studied excepting root length.

Significantly highest average value was recorded for genotype-2 followed by genotype-5 and 4 for both germination and seedling shoot length (Tables 22.1 and 22.3); whereas for vigour index and seedling dry weight, genotype-2 along with genotype-4 and genotype-1 respectively exhibited best performance (Tables 22.4 and 22.6). But for fresh weight of seedlings, genotype-5 recorded significantly highest average value followed by genotype-4 and genotype-1 (Table 22.5). The change in position of different genotypes for average performance against different parameters indicated uniqueness in their genetic constitution. Kurdikeri *et al.* (1993) also observed variation in germination for five different hybrid types of maize, when they were subjected to invigoration treatments.

Though lablab bean is a member of leguminoceae family, soaking-drying (T_2) was noted to be best suited for germination when averaged over genotypes followed by Thio-urea 1 per cent (T_4). Whereas, it was calcium chloride 1 per cent (T_5) for shoot length and fresh weight of seedlings followed by soaking-drying (T_2) and 1 per cent concentration H_2SO_4 (T_6) respectively. 1 per cent Thio-urea (T_4) was noticed to be best for vigour index and dry weight of seedlings followed by control (T_1) and soaking-drying (T_2) respectively. Though the lowest magnitude of vigour index was exhibited by 50 ppm Ascorbic acid (T_7) preceded by 1 per cent $CaCl_2$ (T_5), they were significantly indifferent from each other. And it is interesting to note that the different invigoration treatments could not be able to induced enhanced vigour over untreated control excepting 1 per cent Thiourea (T_4) (Table 21.4). Kapri *et al.* (2003) noted that Celin containing vitamin C (ascorbic acid) acted as an effective chemical for controlling seed deterioration due to storage in Okra, which is contradictory to the present findings. It may be due to differences in response of different crops against invigoration treatments.

Table 22.1: Effect of Seed Invigoration on Germination (%)

Genotypes	*Treatments*							*Mean*
	T_1	T_2	T_3	T_4	T_5	T_6	T_7	
V_1	58.66 (49.99)	69.33 (56.38)	40.66 (39.62)	64 (53.14)	30.66 (33.62)	31.33 (34.04)	26 (30.65)	45.80
V_2	68.66 (55.67)	88 (69.78)	79.33 (62.97)	97.33 (80.70)	88.66 (70.35)	57.33 (49.22)	74.66 (59.79)	79.13
V_3	56 (48.45)	97.33 (80.74)	48.66 (44.24)	81.33 (64.41)	88.66 (70.45)	76.66 (61.12)	64.66 (53.53)	73.32
V_4	64 (53.14)	80 (6.45)	80.66 (63.92)	81.33 (64.42)	89.33 (71.20)	64 (53.14)	74 (59.36)	76.18
V_5	74.66 (59.78)	80 (64.98)	90.66 (72.23)	75.33 (60.25)	80 (63.45)	84.66 (66.96)	66 (54.34)	78.75
Mean	**64.39**	**82.93**	**67.99**	**79.86**	**75.46**	**62.79**	**61.06**	

	CD (P = 0.05)	CD (P = 0.01)
Genotype	0.9047	1.2012
Treatment	1.0705	1.4213
Genotype × Treatment	2.3937	3.1781

Table 22.2: Effect of Seed Invigoration on Root Length (cm)

Genotypes	*Treatments*							*Mean*
	T_1	T_2	T_3	T_4	T_5	T_6	T_7	
V_1	19.57	12.41	12.87	16.48	37.27	12.77	10.77	17.46
V_2	22.40	17.73	18.73	20.49	8.26	19.00	20.03	18.09
V_3	14.67	10.57	13.70	9.87	16.57	18.70	19.27	14.76
V_4	19.43	16.16	21.60	17.47	17.87	17.60	21.67	18.83
V_5	17.50	13_50	11.80	13.57	13.41	17.20	7.73	13.53
Mean	**18.71**	**14.07**	**15.74**	**15.57**	**18.69**	**17.05**	**15.89**	

	CD (P = 0.05)	CD (P = 0.01)
Genotype	NS	NS
Treatment	NS	NS
Genotype × Treatment	NS	NS

Table 22.3: Effect of Seed Invigoration on Shoot Length (cm)

Genotypes	Treatments							Mean
	T_1	T_2	T_3	T_4	T_5	T_6	T_7	
V_1	20.23	21.27	16.27	39.27	22.60	14.67	11.47	20.83
V_2	21.23	29.96	31.41	23.00	26.50	30.77	27.27	27.16
V_3	22.07	25.17	17.07	18.27	25.56	23.07	25.23	22.35
V_4	17.47	26.02	27.60	10.47	33.63	22.67	24.80	23.24
V_5	23.63	28.77	18.40	24.70	31.80	20.03	29.07	25.20
Mean	**20.93**	**26.24**	**22.15**	**23.14**	**28.02**	**22.24**	**23.57**	

	CD (P = 0.05)	CD (P = 0.01)
Genotype	0.2606	0.3459
Treatment	0.3083	0.4093
Genotype × Treatment	0.6894	0.9154

Table 22.4: Effect of Seed Invigoration of Vigour Index

Genotypes	Treatments							Mean
	T_1	T_2	T_3	T_4	T_5	T_6	T_7	
V_1	1147.93	860.56	523.47	1054.35	290.20	400.13	279.87	650.92
V_2	1538.30	1560.71	1486.27	1994.61	732.33	1089.33	1495.67	1413.89
V_3	821.73	1029.49	666.80	802.40	1469.27	1433.40	1246.00	1067.01
V_4	1243.80	1292.86	1742.27	1420.67	1596.40	1126.53	1603.07	1432.23
V_5	1307.13	1079.69	1072.73	1008.00	1073.00	1457.33	510.57	1072.63
Mean	**1211.78**	**1164.65**	**1098.31**	**1256.01**	**1032.24**	**1101.35**	**1027.02**	

	CD (P = 0.05)	CD (P = 0.01)
Genotype	23.4688	31.1587
Treatment	27.7687	36.8675
Genotype × Treatment	62.0928	82.4382

Genotype × invigoration treatment interaction indicated a peculiar scenario apart from either average genotypic response or treatment influence for both germination and vigour index. Interaction of genotype–2 and thio-urea 1 per cent (T_4) expressed in the best way for both of these two parameters, though genotype–3 interacting with soaking drying (T_2) was also recorded to be significantly indifferent with genotype–2 × Thio-urea 1 per cent for the same. While for other three parameters *viz.*, shoot length, fresh and dry weight of seedlings, the genotype–1 when interacted with Thio-urea 1 per cent (T_4) established itself as the most superior combination for expression of those parameters. If interaction effects are critically analysed, it could be revealed that for germinations genotype–1 interacted in the best way with T_2 (soaking-drying), genotype–2 with T_4 (1 per cent Thio-urea), genotype–3 with T_2 (soaking-drying), genotype–4 with T_5 (1 per cent $CaCl_2$) and genotype–5 with T_3 (100 ppm GA_3); whereas, for vigour index. The scenario was observed to be different to that of germination except in

V_2, *viz.*, genotype–1 in control, genotype–3 with T_5 (1 per cent $CaCl_2$), genotype 4 with T_3 (100 ppm GA_3) and genotypes–5 with T_6 (1 per cent H_2SO_4). This situation could also be noted for other three parameters studied.

Table 22.5: Effect of Seed Invigoration on Fresh Weight (mg)

Genotypes	*Treatments*							*Mean*
	T_1	T_2	T_3	T_4	T_5	T_6	T_7	
V_1	7.797	7.310	7.573	10.817	6.666	7.531	4.348	7.434
V_2	6.216	6.594	8.370	6.345	7.478	9.788	4.860	7.093
V_3	4.572	7.318	8.671	5.963	6.848	8.123	4.837	6.619
V_4	4.605	7.958	7.601	7.668	9.969	6.379	8.563	7.535
V_5	7.193	9.180	6.340	4.660	10.462	.8.348	9.393	7.939
Mean	**6.077**	**7.672**	**7.711**	**7.091**	**8.284**	**8.034**	**6.400**	

	CD (P = 0.05)	CD (P = 0.01)
Genotype	0.0558	0.0741
Treatment	0.0660	0.0877
Genotype × Treatment	0.1477	0.1961

Table 22.6: Effect of Seed Invigoration on Dry Weight (mg)

Genotypes	*Treatments*							*Mean*
	T_1	T_2	T_3	T_4	T_5	T_6	T_7	
V_1	0.8915	0.7543	0.6530	1.3009	0.7062	0.5722	0.6633	0.7916
V_2	0.5849	0.7906	1.0041	0.8024	0.6969	1.0912	0.5733	0.7919
V_3	0.4856	0.8915	0.9274	0.8698	0.7686	0.7134	0.6330	0.7556
V_4	0.4747	0.7405	0.7187	0.8902	0.7094	0.5703	0.7728	0.6967
V_5	0.8423	0.8186	0.6264	0.5188	0.8559	0.6104	0.8866	0.7370
Mean	**0.6558**	**0.7991**	**.0.7859**	**0.8764**	**0.7474**	**0.7115**	**0.7058**	

	CD (P = 0.05)	CD (P = 0.01)
Genotype	0.0247	0.0329
Treatment	0.0293	0.0389
Genotype × Treatment	0.0655	0.0870

All the available information recorded response of single genotype of a particular crop against invigoration treatments, as a result of which variation in, genotypic response towards seed invigoration treatments could not explained with previous works done.

Therefore, the present findings indicated that the response towards invigoration treatments was not only crop specific, but also genotype specific *i.e.*, the genotypes responded against different invigoration treatments in unique mode for individual character, probably due to differences in their genetic background.

References

De, B.K., Mandal, A.K. and Basu, R.N., 1998. Effect of dry physiological seed treatments for improved vigour, viability and productivity of black gram (*Phaseolus mungo* Roxb.). *Indian Agriculturist*, 42: 13–20.

Gomez, K.A. and Gomez, A.A., 1984. *Statistical Procedures for Agricultural Research*. John Willey and Sons, New York.

Jeng, T.L. and Sung, J.M., 1994. Hydration effect on lipid peroxidation and peroxidase-scavenging enzyme activity of artificially aged peanut seed. *Seed Science and Technology*, 22: 531–539.

Kalakannavar, R.M., Shashidhara, S.D. and Kulkarni, G.N., 1989. Effect of grading on quality of wheat seeds. *Seed Res.*, 17: 182–185.

Kapri, B., Sengupta, A.K., De, B.K., Mandal, A.K. and Basu, R.N., 2003. Pre-storage seed invigoration treatments for improved germinability and field performance of Okra (*Hibiscus esculentus*). *Indian Journal of Agricultural Sciences*, 73(5): 276–279.

Kurdikeri, M.B., Aswathiah, B. and Prasad, S.R., 1993. Seed invigoration studies in maize hybrids. *Seed Research*, 21(1): 8–12.

Mandal, A.K., De, B.K., Saha, R. and Basu, R.N., 2000. Seed invigoratron treatments for improved storability, field emergence and productivity of Soybean (*Glycine max* L. Merrill). *Seed Science and Technology*, 28: 201–207.

Punjabi, B. and Basu, R.N., 1982. Testing germination and seedling growth by an inclined glass plate blotter method. *Indian Journal of Plant Physiology*, 25: 289–295.

Chapter 23

Integrated Control of *Rhizoctonia solani* by Leaf Extract of *Argemone mexicana* and *Trichoderma viride*

H.S. Shukla[1]* and P.V. Ramaiah[2]

[1]C.H.C. Arts, S.G.P. Commerce, B.B.J.P. Science College, Taloda, Nandurbar - 425413, Maharashtra, India

[2]Centre for Postgraduate Studies and Research in Botany, G.T.P. College Campus, Nandurbar - 425 412, Maharashtra, India

ABSTRACT

Under laboratory conditions, isolate of *Trichoderma viride was* found to be tolerant up to 70 per cent leaf extract of *Argemone mexicana,* whereas the plant pathogen *Rhizoctonia solani* was susceptible to a dose of less than 60 per cent. Exposure to sub-lethal concentrations of leaf extract had no effect on the *in vitro* antagonistic ability of *T. viride.*

Under greenhouse conditions a combination of *T. viride* and a reduced dose of leaf extract (55 per cent) completely controlled disease incidence of *R. solani* in cauliflower seedlings compared with controls in untreated soils.

Keywords: Antifungal activity, Trichoderma viride, Leaf extract, Rhizoctonia solani.

* Corresponding Author: Kacheri Road, Taloda Dist. Nandurbar – 425 413, Maharashtra.

Introduction

Protection of crop plants from the ravages of fungi by synthetic fungicides and biofungicides has been the usual practice. Angiosperms are reported to possess a reservoir of effective therapeutants and constitute an inexhaustible source of harmless protectants (Grainge and Alvarez, 1987). In recent years attempts were made to screen the antifungal properties of different plants against plant pathogenic fungi (Grayer and Rarborne, 1994).

Biological control is an alternative way to control plant diseases. In recent years members of the genus *Trichoderma* have gained recognition as potential biocontrol agents (Radar *et al.*, 1979; Karthikeyan, 1996; Locke *et al.*, 1985 and Marios and Mitchell, 1981). This article reports experiments, which investigated the integration of leaf extract and biological control agent for controlling the disease, caused by *Rhizoctonia solani* on cauliflower (*Brassica oleracea* L. var. *botrytis* L).

Materials and Methods

Pure cultures of *Trichoderma viride* and also the test organism *R. solani* obtained from M.T.C. C (Microbial type culture collection), Institute of microbial technology, Chandigarh, India, were grown and maintained in the various media as given bellow:

T. viride

Growth condition: Aerobic; Temperature: 30ºC; Incubation time: 7 days; Malt extract Agar (MA) medium containing: Malt extract: 20.0g; Agar: 20.0g; Water: 1000 ml (pH: 6.5).

R. solani

Growth condition: Aerobic; Temperature: 25ºC; Incubation time: 5 days; Potato: Dextrose Agar medium containing: Potato (scrubbed and diced): 200.0g; Dextrose: 20.0g; Agar: 15.0g; Water: 1000 ml. Diced potatoes were boiled in 500 ml water until thoroughly cooked; filtered through cheesecloth and water added to the filtrate to make up to 1000 ml. Agar was added to the filtrate and dissolved by boiling. Glucose was added after cooling. pH was adjusted to 5.6.

Argemone mexicana Linn. (Papavaraceae)

A prickly herb 2–4 fit, high divaricately branched. Leaves sessile, spiny on the margins. The plant has been widely established and is to be met with along roadsides and as a weed in cultivated fields through out India. The natives use the yellow juice medicinally and oil is expressed from the seeds. The weed contains the alkaloid protopine. Its juice is diuretic and alterative; it is given in dropsy, skin diseases and gonnorrhoea. Being mildly corrosive, juice is applied to blisters, rheumatic pains, excoriation, ulcers, scabies and eruptions. The root is alterative and stimulant. Its decoction is given in diarrhoea, gleets, vesicular calculus and skin diseases. The seeds are narcotic, stomachache, emetic, expectorant, cathartic and demulcent.

Leaf Extract Preparation Method

100 gram leaves of *A. mexicana* were collected and washed in running water three times and ground with 80 per cent ethanol. The extract was filtered through Whatman's No. 1 filter paper and centrifuged at 5000 rpm for five minutes. Further, the extract was diluted with 80 per cent ethanol to 45 per cent, 50 per cent, 55 per cent, 60 per cent, 70 per cent and 85 per cent. An isolate of *T. viride* found to be antagonistic to *R. solani* was used throughout this study. It was grown in a wheat bran/peat mixture (1 : 1, v/v) incubated in an illuminated chamber for 14 days at 30ºC, according to Sivan *et al.*

(1984). The preparation was mixed in soil at a rate of 5 g/kg soil. Greenhouse experiment was conducted in a black cotton soil.

Laboratory Experiments

Mycelial disc (5 mm) of *T. viride* and *R. solani* were placed centrally on a synthetic medium (Okon *et al.*, 1973) in 9-cm petridishes. After 24 h, cultures were exposed to mixtures of air and leaf extract in glass desiccators. Three concentrations of leaf extract (45 per cent, 50 per cent and 60 per cent) were obtained by injecting the required volume of leaf extract into each desiccator. After 24 h of exposure to leaf extract, the cultures were removed and colony diameter was measured after every 24 h. The growth of culture untreated with leaf extract was also recorded as check. Cultures were incubated and treated with leaf extract at 30°C. The antagonistic ability of *T. viride* was checked *in vitro* according to Dennis and Webster (1971). Dual cultures of *T. viride* and *R. solani* were exposed to 50 per cent *A. mexicana* extract for 24 h.

Greenhouse Experiment

Total soil, populations of *Rhizoctonia* and *Trichoderma* were determined on Martins rose Bengal medium (Martin, 1950) and *Trichoderma* selective, medium (Elad *et al.*, 1981a) and expressed as Colony Forming Units (CFU) per g dry soil.

Application of leaf extract to the soil for greenhouse experiment was carried out in plastic boxes 20 × 20 × 10 cm covered with a polythene sheet; leaf extract was applied at the required dose. The polyethylene was removed after 48 h. the soil was then aerated for 72 hand washed with 1 litre water per kg soil. In order to estimate changes in soil fungal population due to application of leaf extract, boxes with soil were treated with leaf extract at a dose of different concentrations. Immediately after plant extract application and at 2, 9 and 16 days later samples of soil were taken and the total fungal population and *Trichoderma* population in the samples were estimated. A wheat bran/peat preparation of *T. viride* was mixed with soil (5 g/kg) and the mixture left for 2 weeks. The *Trichoderma* population was then estimated before and after treatment with leaf extract of *A. mexicana.*

Soil in plastic pots (9 × 10 × 6 cm) to which *T. viride* had been added 2 weeks earlier plus boxes of unamended soil were either treated with *A. mexicana* leaf extract or left untreated. A week later *T. viride* was added to some boxes of treated and untreated soil not previously amended with this fungus. Nine days after *A. mexicana* leaf extract treatment; ten cauliflower seeds were sown in each box. Six replicates arranged in six blocks, were maintained in a greenhouse at 26–30°C for 21 days, when disease severity on each hypocotyls was recorded using a scale of 0–5 where 0 represents healthy seedlings and 5 dead seedlings (Sneh *et al.*, 1966).

The ability of *T. viride* to prevent reinfestation of contaminated soil with *R. solani* was tested under greenhouse conditions. Soil infested with *R. solani* was treated with *A. mexicana* leaf extract (60 per cent) and divided into two samples. A week later *T. viride* was added to one sample only and after a further week cauliflower seeds were sown in both samples. After 21 days, plants were uprooted and their *R. solani* disease index was determined. Soil infested with *R. solani* was then mixed (1 : 20, v/v) with all the soil samples, which were again sown with cauliflower seeds, twice successively. Disease index was determined on each sample.

Results

Laboratory Experiments

Effect of *A. mexicana* leaf extract on linear growth of fungi on agar, neither *R. solani* nor *T. viride* grew during exposure to the *A. mexicana* leaf extract treatments. When colonies were aerated, *T. viride* treated with 60 per cent and 70 per cent concentration of *A. mexicana* leaf extract continued to grow, whereas *R. solani* did not grow even after exposure to 60 per cent concentration of *A. mexicana* leaf extract (Figure 23.1). Mycelial samples taken from colonies which did not continue growing after exposure to *A.mexicana* leaf extract were inoculated on fresh SM plates and were incubated at 30°C for 7 days in order to test viability. *T. viride* was killed only after exposure to 85 per cent *A. mexicana* leaf extract. *R. solani* survived after exposure to *A. mexicana* leaf extract lower than 50 per cent concentrations.

Effect of *A. mexicana* Leaf Extract on Dual Culture of *R. solani* and *T. viride*

Dual culture of *T. viride* and *R. solani* were exposed to leaf extract of *A. mexicana* at 50 per cent concentration for 24 h after colonies met on SM plates. *R. solani* was alive after this exposure. In non-exposed cultures, *T. viride* grew into *R. solani* and colonized all its mycelium within 27 h. During

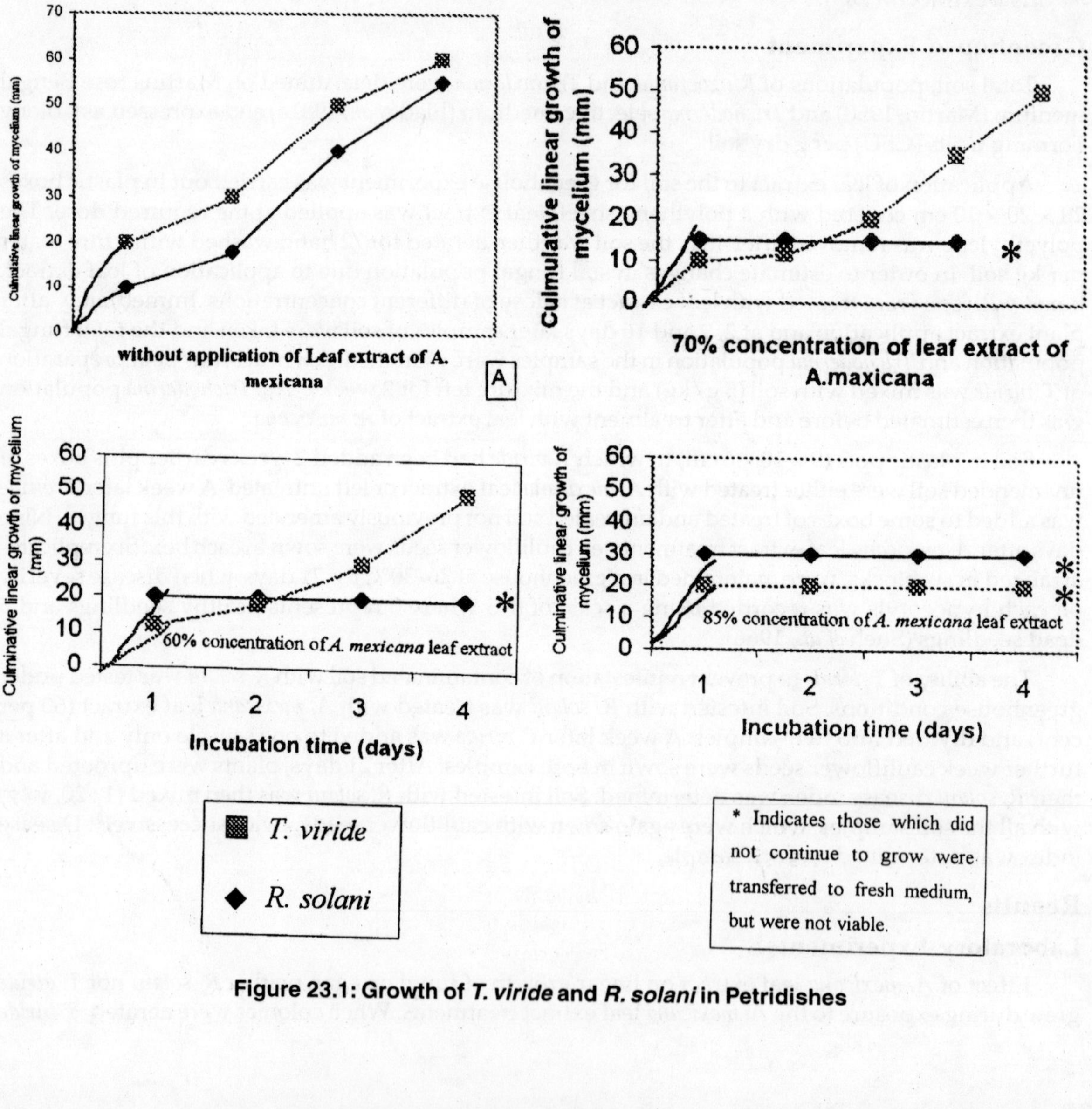

Figure 23.1: Growth of *T. viride* and *R. solani* in Petridishes

exposure to leaf extract, *T. viride* did not colonize the mycelium of *R. solani* but after aeration of plates it grew over the pathogens mycelium at a rate similar to that of non-exposed cultures.

Greenhouse Experiments

Trichoderma sp. and general fungal populations in fumigated soils: The total fungal population in a wet black cotton soil was 4×10^3 CFU/g soil, whereas the *Trichoderma* population was 2.4×10^2 CFU/g soil. Treatment with *A. mexicana* leaf extract at a dose 70 per cent reduced the fungal population to 3.2×10^2 CFU/g soil. However *Trichoderma* was not affected at this concentration of leaf extract and its relative amount in the general population in soil increased from 6 per cent before. The population of *T. viride* in amended non- treated soil was 5.2×10^6 CFU/g and 4.6×10^6 CFU/g soil after the treated with *A. mexicana* leaf extract.

Integrated Control of *R. solani*

Table 23.1 shows that leaf extract of *A. mexicana* at rate equivalent to 60 per cent concentration was more effective in reducing the *R. solani* disease index than with a reduced rate. *T. viride* reduced disease incidence with leaf extract of *A. mexicana* when it was applied either a week before or a week after soil application.

Table 23.1: The Influence of Leaf Extract of *A. mexicana* and *T. viride* (5 g/kg soil) on the *R. solani* Disease Index of Cauliflower under the Greenhouse Conditions

A. mexicana Leaf Extract (%)	*Trichoderma Application Time*		
	None Applied	*2 Weeks Before Application*	*1 Week After Application*
0	1.2 A	0.3 A	0.7 A
60%	0.3 B	0 A	0.1 A
85%	0 C	0 A	0 A

Discussion

Mycelium of the biocontrol agent *T. viride* showed tolerance to higher concentration of leaf extract of *A. mexicana* than mycelium of *R. solani*. More ever, exposure to leaf extract of *A. mexicana* in sub-lethal concentrations did not appear to affect the antagonistic activity of *T. viride* in culture.

Leaf extract of *A. mexicana* considerably decreased the total fungal population whereas it did not reduce *Trichoderma* population. More ever mixing a preparation of *Trichoderma* with soil before leaf extract application did not result in decline of this fungus after treatment. The antagonistic colonized and leaf extract applied oil was better than a non-applied one, within the 2 weeks of testing.

Therefore, it was concluded that either natural or artificial populations of *Trichoderma* in soil are resistant to leaf extract of *A. mexicana* at a different concentrations and leaf extract of *A. mexicana* could give an added advantage to *A. Trichoderma* as a biocontrol agent.

Application of leaf extract to the soil at different concentrations, reduced the *R. solani* disease index from 1.2 to 0.7, where as addition of *Trichoderma* preparation after the application of leaf extract totally reduced disease incidence. Thus it is advisable to apply *Trichoderma* soon after application of leaf extract of *A. mexicana*, to control disease caused by *R. solani*.

Acknowledgements

We are thankful to the U.G.C., New Delhi, India for financial support.

References

Dennis, C. and Webster, I., 1971. Antagonistic properties of species groups of *Trichoderma.* III. Hyphal interaction. *Transactions of the British Mycologica Society*, 57: 363–369.

Elad, Y., Chet, I. and Henis, Y., 1981a. A selective medium for improving quantitative isolation of *Trichoderma* spp. *Soil Phytoparasitica*, 9: 59–67.

Grainge, M.D and Alvarez, A.M., 1987. Antibacterial and antifungal activity of *Artobotrys hexapetalus* leaf extracts. *International Journal Tropical Plant Diseases*, 5: 173–179.

Grayer, R.J and Harborne, I.B., 1994. A survey of antifungal compounds from plants. *Phytochemistry*, 37: 19–42.

Hadar, Y., Chet, I. and Henis, Y., 1979. Biological control of *Rhizoctonia solani* damping-off with wheat bran culture of *Trichoderma harzianum. Phytopathology*, 69: 64–68.

Karthikean, A., 1996. Effect of organic amendments, antagonist *Trichoderma viride* and fungicides on seed and collar rot of ground nut. *Plant Disease Research*, 11. 72–74.

Locke, I.C., Marois, J.J. and Papavizas, G.C., 1985. Biological control of *Fusarium* wilt of greenhouse grown *Chrysanthemum. Plant Disease*, 69: 167–169.

Marois, J.J and Mitchell, D.J., 1981. Biological control of *Fusarium* crown rot of tomato under field condition. *Phytopathology*, 71: 1253–1260.

Martin, I.P., 1950.Use of acid, rose-bengal and streptomycin in the plate method of estimating soil fungi. *Soil Science*, 69: 215–205.

Okon, Y., Chet, I. and Hems, Y., 1973. Effect of lactose, ethanol and cyclohexamide on the translocation pattern of radioactive compounds and on *sclerotium rolfsii. Journal of General Microbiology*, 74: 251–258.

Sivan, A., Elad, Y. and Chet, I., 1984. Biological control of *Pythium aphanidermatum* by a new isolate of *Trichoderma harzianum. Phytopathology*, 74: 498–501.

Sneh, B., Katan, I., Henis, Y. and Wahl, Y., 1966. Methods of evaluating inoculum density of *Rhizoctonia* in naturally infested soil. *Phytopathology*, 56: 74–78.

Chapter 24

Disease Related Laser Use Survey at Indore

Varsha Jain[1], K.N. Chaturvedi[1] and M.M. Prakash[2]

[1]Department of Electronics, [2]Department of Zoology
Government Holkar Science College, Indore

ABSTRACT

The present article deals with the study of disease related LASER use survey conducted at Indore during 2003–04. The results obtained reveals that in eye related disease LASER use was maximum (50.17 per cent) and in kidney related disease was minimum (2 per cent). Study also discusses the various kinds of LASERs and their uses in various diseases.

Keywords: Laser, Laser therapy.

Introduction

Laser application in medical science is now well established. Day by day its utility in medicine and surgery is tremendously increasing. Ruby laser was first applied in the eye therapy (Kukreja, 1990). Now with the invention of various kinds of laser it is entering deeper and deeper in the various sections of medical science. In the present scenario it is not only limited to the diagnosis and treatment processes of various diseases, but also able to find effective path in the field of RNA and DNA Polymerize transcription, gene therapy, reproductive biology and antigen-antibody reaction etc. (Mohanti, 2002).

According to Oshiro and Calderhead (1991) laser has great potential in ophthalmology and Dermatology etc. Low reactive level laser bio activation has stimulated a rapidly expanding use of lasers in laser therapy as against the conventional laser surgery (Oshiro and Ca!derhead, 1991 and Oshiro, 1993). Bhatia *et al.* (1994) clinically demonstrated the effectiveness of low average power N_2 laser irradiation in the treatment of resistant pulmonary tuberculosis while Chalnania and Oza (1994) described its utility in the treatment of burn wounds. But laser use in the treatment of various diseases is still limited and least popular among the patient in comparison to the traditional methods, though scientific progress in this field is very much impressive. Looking to the importance of laser in the medicine present study was undertaken to study and analyze laser applications in the treatment of various diseases at various hospitals and clinic centers of Indore (M.P).

Materials and Methods

Present study was carried out in the medically advanced city of Madhya Pradesh. Data were collected from the 14 leading hospitals and 7 clinic centers through questionnaire during 2003–04. The hospitals and clinic centers visited for the proposed study were M. Y. Hospital, Govt. Cancer Hospital, Bombay Hospital, Choithram Hospital, Indore Eye Hospital, Hardia Eye Hospital, Hardia Eye and Child Care Center, Dr. Kishan Eye Care and Laser Surgery Center, Choudhary Eye and Retina Research Center, Maharshi Skin Medicure Center, EILAMS Center, Dr. R. Agrawal Clinic and New Look Laser Clinic. 40 doctors, 20 nurses, 20 technicians and 50 patients were contacted for filling of questionnaire.

Results and Discussion

Patient suffering from the different diseases under laser treatment were analyzed. Results obtained (Table 24.1) reveals that in eyes related diseases laser use was maximum (50.17 per cent) followed by skin (12.5 per cent) and wound (10.59 per cent) treatment, while in ulcer, heart, cancer, lungs, chronic pain and kidney treatment percentage were: 10.0 per cent, 6.5 per cent, 6.5 per cent, 4.17 per cent, 4.17 per cent and 2 per cent respectively. The reason is quite obvious that laser treatment for eyes was available in the city for a long time, whereas history of use of laser in other diseases is in initial stage. The one field where laser treatment getting popularity at an extremely fast rate was skin disease including cosmetic treatments. The level of awareness in this field has increased tremendously due to the extensive advertisement by the clinics / Doctors using them. In cosmetic use of laser, it was observed that a number of beauty parlors started using laser for removing acne and unwanted spots, scars and hair (specially of female's face). According to these centers, increase in customer-cum-patient was due to adopting aggressive marketing strategy.

Table 24.1: Percentage of Patients Suffering from Different Diseases Using Laser Treatment

Sl.No.	*Diseases*	*Percentage of Patients*
1.	Eye disease	50.17
2.	Skin diseases	12.50
3.	Wound (Non healing)	10.59
4.	Ulcer	10.00
5.	Heart	6.5
6.	Cancer	6.5
7.	Lungs	4.17
8.	Chronic Pain	4.17
9.	Kidney	2.00

The number of patients offering themselves for laser treatment was very less as compared to the facilities available at these centers. Table 24.2 provides the number of patients benefited by laser procedure per year. This showed that New Look Laser clinic was on top (3600 patients per year) followed by Rohit Eye Hospital and Child Care Center (1000 patients per year). Rest 12 hospitals and clinic centers position were not very much impressive. Thus in our opinion for the benefits of patients and medical centers a joint advertising strategy is needed which can attract patients from other cities and states besides the internal one (Indore city). Increasing number of patients offering laser treatment will certainly reduce the treatment cost in long term.

Table 24.2: Patients (Approximate) Benefited by Laser Therapy in Different Hospitals

Sl.No.	*Hospitals/Clinics/Medical Centers*	*Number of Patient per Year*
1.	M.Y. Hospital, Indore	200
2.	Government Cancer Hospital, Indore	270
3.	Bombay Hospital, Indore	464
4.	Choithram Hospital, Indore	500
5.	Indore Eye Hospital, Indore	360
6.	Hardia Hospital, Indore	100
7.	Hardia Eye Surgery and Research Center, Indore	105
8.	Rohit Eye Hospital and Child Care Center, Indore	1800
9.	Dr. Kishan Eye Care and Laser Surgery Center, Indore	455
10.	Choudhary Eye and Retina Research Center, Indore	10
11.	Maharshi Skin Medicure Center, Indore	349
12.	EILAMS Center, Indore	143
13.	Dr. R. Agrawal Clinic, Indore	400
14.	New Look Laser Clinic, Indore	3600

When patients were contacted for observing their awareness level about the laser procedure that lasers operations/uses are generally blood-less, less time consuming and patient friendly. We came to know that 50 per cent patients have an idea about these things. 41.66 per cent know these things through doctors and 8.33 per cent know about these things by surroundings. This also reveals that popularization level of laser therapy and treatment record is not much impressive thus need further improvement for getting better results. During the course of study remarks given by patients regarding laser were as follows:

1. It is very good procedure. After taking the laser treatment patients were feeling better.
2. Laser treatment in the case of heart is very good. It is the process through which blockage in the heart can be treated. Patients of this group were most comfortable with this treatment.
3. When there is no remedy in medicine, laser helps the patients. For some patients laser provided an alternative of operation, when they were not fit for surgery.
4. The procedure is non-invasive and less expensive.
5. Laser therapy is effective, time reducing, totally successful and painless.

This showed that patients accepted this therapy in positive way. The over all study reveals that looking to the facility available in the various medical centers of Indore the input of patients is very less, may be due to less awareness of patients, least advertisements by hospitals and misconception in the society that laser treatment is comparatively costly and not long lasting and effective.

Acknowledgement

The authors are thankful to the Principal of the College and Head of the Departments of Physics Electronics and Zoology for encouragement of such type of field based research.

References

Bhatia, G.C., Bhagwani, N.S., Sharma, N. and Palsule, V, 1994. Low-level laser therapy in pulmonary tuberculosis. In: *Proceedings of the National Laser Symposium*, CAT, Indore, pp. 329–330.

Baxter, G.D., 1994. *Therapeutic Laser: Theory and Practice.* Churchill Livingstone, Edinburgh.

Chamania, S. and Oza, N., 1994. Effect of nitrogen laser in infected non-healing wounds. In: *Proceeding of National Laser Symposium, CAT, Indore*, pp. 327–328.

Chopra, S. and Chawla, H.M., 1992. *Laser in Chemical and Biological Sciences.* Wiley Eastern Limited.

Kukraja, L.M., 1990. Role of laser in Medicine and Surgery (in Hindi). *Vagayanik*, 22(1): 36–38.

Mohanti, S.K., 2002. Use of laser forceps (twizer) in medicine (in Hindi). *Pragati*, CAT, Indore, pp. 10–12.

Oshiro, T., 1993. Light and Life: A review of low reactive level laser therapy following 13 years experience in over 12,000 patients. *Laser Therapy* 5: 5–22.

Oshiro, T. and Calderhead, R.G., 1991. *Low-level Laser Therapy: A Practical Introduction.* John Willey, Chichester.

•

Chapter 25

Spontaneous Positive Geotropic Shoot Development in Onion

M. Babu Rao

Department of Botany, P.G.C.S Saifabad (O.U.), Hyderabad - 500 004

Generally in all plants the root shows positive geotropism and the shoot shows negative geotropism. But in this case positive geotropism of shoot was observed. The same is reported.

During the past several years onion bulbs are being used for harvesting root tips for studying Mitosis. Normally the bulbs are kept in glass containers filled with water so as to dip the basal portion of the bulb in water. Within 24-48 hrs roots begin to grow downwards. Few days later the shoot development begins in the opposite direction. In other words roots are positively geotropic and shoots are negatively geotropic.

However in the present case positive geotropic development of shoot occurred (Figures 25.1 and 25.2). A survey of literature showed that such a phenomenon has been observed in certain Lilliaceae members such as Tulips, *Erythroniun* and *Gagea* as reported by Arbar (1925), who described the peculiarity as "Dropper Formation".

This is an interesting specialization in certain bulb geophytes. This has been explained as the developmental sequence that forms an interesting parallel to the sequence by which the plumule is buried by the geotropic action of the cotyledonary tube. Where a young axillary bud becomes adnate to the base of the leaf mesophyll, which then elongates with positive geotropism and forms a long tube that buries the bud farther in the ground. This bud then forms new bulb scales and adventitious roots and develops into a new bud. The adaptive value of this complex mechanism is obvious, since it affords additional protection for the young bulb from both desiccation and attacks of animal predators. One is tempted to speculate the genetic mechanism for dropper development is actually homologous to the early seedling growth and involves the same sequence of activation and inhibition of growth substances (Stebbins, 1974).

Figure 25.1

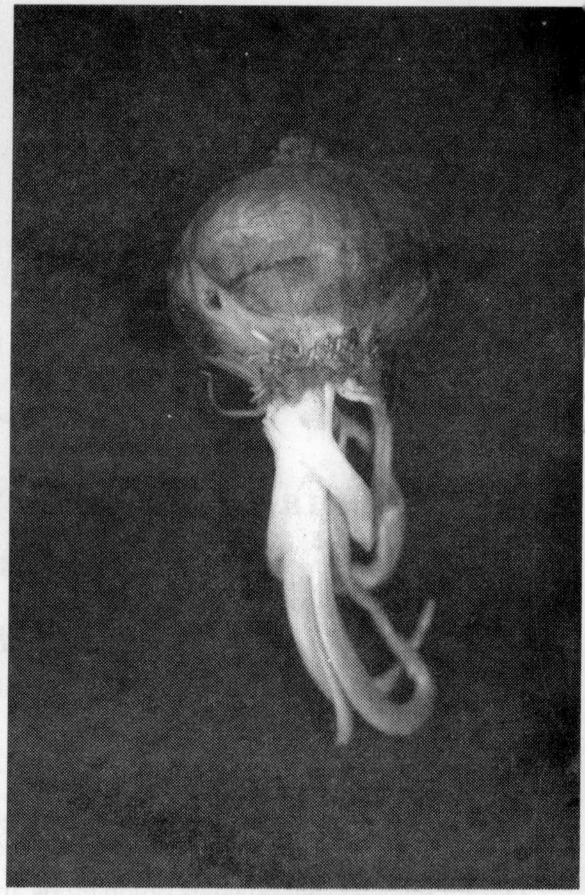

Figure 25.2

The method of growth of adult plant is distinctive evolutionary feature of the monocotyledons. A series of vegetative specialization in monocotyledons are the consequence of presence of numerous vascular bundles particularly in the leaf bases. This condition can serve as initial modification that permits evolution of bulb and corm geophytes in response to highly seasonal climate that has been a long period of drought or cold. Thus most of the members of Lilliales possess bulbs or corms. The present observation serves as a pointer to the fact the bulbs are ordained with additional adaptive trait for the purpose of perennation.

References

Arber, A., 1925. *Monocotyledons: A Morphological Study*, Cambridge University Press, Cambridge, England.

Stebbins, G.L., 1974. *Flowering Plants Evolution above the Species Level*. Edward Arnold Publishers, London.

Chapter 26

Ethnoveterinary Practices by Santhal Tribe in Jamtara District of Jharkhand

A.K. Mandal and B.B. Dutta

P.G. Department of Botany, P.K. Roy Memorial College, Dhanbad

ABSTRACT

Traditional methods of veterinary treatment using plants are predominant in rural folk of Jharkhand. A total formulations from 24 plant species used to treat various diseases of domestic animals are described. The method of preparation, dose and duration of each plant preparation are discussed. The plants are described with botanical name, family and santhali (local) names.

Keywords: Santhal, Ethnoveterinary, Herbal medicine.

Introduction

Jharkhand is one of the tribal states of the country. Among the tribals, santhal tribe is dominant. The state, particularly the hilly regions provide many species of wild plants with potent medicinal properties. Apart from all the modern medical systems, even today man and their pets are dependant on several plants for primary healthcare. This dependency on medicine plants is still more in rural areas. Although a good number of plant species have been identified and reported from tribal regions of state (Pal and Jain, 1998; Hembrun and Verma, 1995; Bodding, 1925) a large number of plant species found in unexplored areas yet to be reported. Among the tribals of Jharkhand, santhals are more social and they live in rural areas along with other castes besides their preferred habitats near forests. Santhals have their own age old material culture. They have a clear understanding of the forest and forest resources. They use a number of wild plant species not only to meet their day to day requirements but also to treat their cattle and pets.

Materials and Methods

A list of herbal healers and witch doctors was prepared by gathering information from local people. The knowledge about medicinal plants and uses of plants in the treatment among the tribal groups are rather specialized and limited to a few people in the community who are recognized as herbal healer, or witch doctor or vaidya. In some localities, there are several individuals who, do not practice on herbal medicine but possess medical knowledge and act as reliable informants. Information were collected through interactions and discussions with informants and local herbal healers. Preliminarily the people were unwilling to disclose the secrets but the help of village head and some educated people among them solved the problem of their unwillingness.

Regular field trips were undertaken to different locations preferably santhal dominated areas during the period of 2001–2003. Each locality was visited in different seasons and information were collected.

During field trips, help was taken from the local people to identify the plants for their use and local name. The local name and uses of each plant were collected on the spot. Habit, habitat and distribution status of each plant was recorded based on field observation. All collected plant species were preserved as herbarium specimen. Identification and taxonomic classification of these plants have been made with the help of Flora of British India (Hooker, 1872–79) Botany of Bihar and Orissa (H.H. Hanes, BSI 1961) and by consulting herbarium at BSI, Shibpur, Howrah.

Available literature indicate that many of these plants are not used at least for same purpose everywhere in India. (Chopra *et al.*, 1956; Pal and Jain, 1981, 1998).

Results

Important medicinal plants used as veterinary medicine are enumerated with their botanical names, local name method of use are given in Table 26.1

Table 26.1: List of Medicinal Plants Used by Santhals

Sl.No.	*Name of the Plant, Fls. and Frts.*	*Local Name in Santhali*	*Traditional Uses*
1.	*Alangium salvifolium*, (L) Wang (Alangiaceae) Fls. and Frts. April–May	Dhela	Paste of Stem bark with goat milk is given to dogs in fever and intestinal disorder for a week. Also applied to treat madness.
2.	*Alstonia scholaris*, Linn (Apocynaceae) Fls. and Frts. Nov.–July	Kunumung	Latex with decoction of black pepper is used to treat dysentery of cattle.
3.	*Amorphophalus bulbifer*, Roxb. (Araceae) Fls and Frts. May–Sept.	Kachuhada	Paste of corm with Kusum (*Schleichera oleosa*) seed oil on wounds of cattle. It is very common in the case where wound is caused by ploughshare.
4.	*Anthocephalus chinensis*, (Lank), Rich cx Walp. (Rubiaceae) Fls. and Frts July–Oct.	Kadam	About 15 ml. of decoction of stem bark is given thrice a day for 2–3 days to cure dyspepsia.
5.	*Argemone maxicana*, Linn (Papavaraceae) Fls. and Frts. Nov. –July	Sundi-Sapka	One part stem juice with three parts of onion paste is applied to kill ectoparasites on the body of cattle.

Contd...

Table 26.1–Contd...

Sl.No.	*Name of the Plant, Fls. and Frts.*	*Local Name in Santhali*	*Traditional Uses*
6.	*Bambusa balcooa*, Roxb. (Poaceae) Fls. and Frts. Rarely seen	Bora bans	For quick delivery of foetus fresh green leaves are given as fodder to the cattle. It is also used to check loose motion of goats and cattle.
7.	*Butea monosperma*, (O. Kuntz), Taub. (Fabaceae) Fls. and Frts. March–July	Polar-baha	Seed powder is used to cure worm infested wounds of cattle.
8.	*Calotropis gigantica*, Linn (Asclepiadaceae) Fls. and Frts. Dec.–July	Parkha	Latex of the plant is used to cure septic wounds of cattle.
9.	*Dendrocalamus strictus*, (Roxb) Nees. (Poaceae) Fls. and Frts. Rarely seen	Buru-mad	Fresh green leaves are given as fodder for quick delivery of foetus and rapid expulsion of placenta.
10.	*Dendrophthoe falcate*, (Linn. f) Etting (Loranthaceae) Fls. and Frts. Nov.–Mar.	Sum	Decoction of stem bark with black pepper is prepared for a narcotic. Simply decoction of bark is used to cure wounds of cattle.
11.	*Diospyros melanoxylon*, Roxb. (Ebenaceae) Fls. and Frts. Mar.–May.	Kend	Decoction of stem bark is given to cure diarrhoea.
12.	*Dolichus biflorus*,. (L) Hore (Fabaceae) Fls. and Frts. Nov.–Mar.	Kurthi	Decoction of seed is given to cure diarrhoea.
13.	*Eclipta alba* (Linn) Hassk (Asteraceae) Fls. and Frts. Aug.–Mar.	Bonda-Kanda	Leaf juice is applied on wounds of cattle as an antiseptic drug.
14.	*Euphorbia nerifolia* (Linn) (Euphorbiaceae) Fls. and Frts. Nov.–Mar. Jan.–Apr.	Monsa-Kanta	Latex of the plant is used in snake bite or any poisonous insect bite. The plant is a symbol of serpent goddess.
15.	*Evolvulus alsinoides*, Linn. (Convolvulaceae) Fls. and Frts. Nov.–Mar.	Jungli-ba	Root paste with black pepper is used to cure pain on neck region of cart pulling oxen.
16.	*Ficus benghalensis* (Linn) (Moraceae) Fls. and Frts. Mar.–Aug.	Bar-gachha	Paste of aerial root with stem bark of nux-vomica is applied to set dislocated joints (of leg bones)
17.	*Gmelina arborea*, Roxb. (Verbenaceae) Fls. and Frts. Jan.–Apr.	Kasmar-daru	Paste of stem bark is applied on septic wounds of cattle. Leaf paste is used to treat swelling of throat.
18.	*Moringa oleifera*, Lamk (Moringaceae) Fls. and Frts. Jan.–Mar.	Munga-sag	Santhals give decoction of stem bark with salt to cure dyspepsia. Fresh root bark paste is applied locally to worm infested wounds of cattle.
19.	*Ocimum basicilicum* (Linn) (Lamiaceae) Fls. and Frts. Sept.–March.	Dimbu-buha, Ban-tulsi	Dried leaf powder is applied on the body of cattle to remove lica.
20.	*Oryza sativa* (Linn) (Poaceae) Fls. and Frts. Sept.–Nov.	Dhan	Rice bran with molasses in the ratio of 2 : 1 is applied as plaster on fractured bone. The plaster is supported by bamboo sticks.

Contd...

Table 26.1–Contd...

Sl.No.	Name of the Plant, Fls. and Frts.	Local Name in Santhali	Traditional Uses
21.	*Pongamia glabra* (Linn) Merre (Fabaceae) Fls. and Frts. May–Jan.	Karanj	Seed oil is used to cure skin disease. Leaf paste is applied locally to cure worm infested wounds.
22.	*Semecarpus anacardium* (Linn) (Anacardiaceal) Fls. and Frts. Oct.–Dec.	Bhelwa	Tar like oil is extracted from seeds which is used to cure hoof-sores of cattle. It is also used to cure sprain of leg and inflammation of any part of the body.
23.	*Terminalia bellirica* (Gaertn) Roxb. (Combretaceae) Fls. and Frts. Jan.–Mar.	Behra	About 50 ml of fruit infusion is given to cure dysentery of cattle.
24.	*Vitex negundo*, Linn. (Verbenaceae) Fls. and Frts.–Most of the year.	Sinduari, Lunguni	Leaf-decoction is used to cure septic wounds of cattle

Discussion

24 plants belonging to 18 families are discussed here. Among these, uses of *Euphorbia nerifolia*, Linn, *Ficus benghalensis* Linn., *Alstonia scholaris* Linn., *Terminalia Billerica* Roxb., *Vitex negundo*, Linn. have been reported earlier as potent ethnoveterinary medicines. Similarly *Oryza sativa*, Linn., *Pongamia glabra* Linn. are used by other people of the locality as well, Ethnoveterinary, claims on rest plants are probably new in the district.

The noteworthy claims are those used to treat worm infested wounds of the cattle and also foot and mouth diseases, which are, common in the rainy season. *Moringa oleifera* Lamk., *Semecarpus anacardium*, Linn. show miraculous effect in the treatment of the above diseases. Formulation of medicines, their methods of preparation varies in different locality and villages. These formulations need further investigation for the effective treatment of different diseases of domestic animals.

References

Hains, H.H., C.I.E., E.C.H., F.L.S., 1961. *The Botany of Bihar and Orissa*, BSI, Calcutta.

Harsh, V.H., Hebbar, S.S., Shripathi and Hedge, G.R., 2003. Ethnorobotany of Uttara Kannada, *J. Ethronopharm* Ltd., 84: 37.

Jain, S.K. and Pal, D.C., Banerjee, D.K., 1973. Medicinal plants among certain adibasi in India. *Bull. Bot. Survey of India*, 15: 85.

Kirtikar, K.R. and Basu, B.D., 1984. *Indian Medicinal Plants*, Vols. I–IV (Allahabad), India.

Varma, S.K. and Hembrum, P.P., 1981. An anthrobotanical studies or Santhal pargana. *Ind. For.*, 107(1): 30–41.

Witch doctors and medicine man of the locality.

Chapter 27

Hydrophytic Plants Used as Vegetable in Dharawad District of Karnataka

N.M. Rolli, M.G. Nadagouda, R.H. Ratageri, H.C. Lakshman

Post-graduate Department and Research in Botany, Karnatak University, Dharwad – 580 003

ABSTRACT

Thirty hydrophytic plants have been screened in Dharwad district of Karnataka. Plants were commonly used as vegetables. Seasons of produced flowers and fruits have been recorded other than their main part used.

Keywords: *Seasons, Families, Hydrophytic Vegetables.*

Introduction

Finding enough land water and plant to support, the world's food needs occupies the top slot. It is other than cereals, nuts and fruits. Vegetable constitute an important part of our daily diet. A good number of hydrophytic plants are the source of vegetables. These plants commonly seen, on a wide range of habitats depending on the available source of moisture and minerals in the soil. Reports on hydrophytic vegetable are very meager except a few reports (Satyanarayan, 1962; Islam, 1986; Pathak, 1996). No reports on hydrophytic vegetables of this region. Therefore, the present article recorded on hydrophytic plants which are commonly used as vegetables in Dharwad district in Southwestern part of Karnataka.

Materials and Methods

Screening of hydrophytes mainly used for vegetable has been undertaken in Dharwad district. The area is situated approximately between 14°78′ and 15°5′ North latitude and 74°48′ and 76° East latitude. General configuration of the area is plan with low-lying Sayadri hills and agricultural land found scattered. The collected geographical area is 758 sq.km. It comprising the chief permanent water bodies, ponds, pools, ditches, lakes, tanks, water falls, rivers mud sludges and moist places. Besides, there are many low-lying areas including paddy fields where water logging is a common feature during rainy seasons. The uses of few plants were practically used by the authors. Some plants uses were clarified by interviewing, elderly people of the villages. Plant samples were compared for confirmation from the post graduate department of Botany Karnatak University Dharwad. The voucher specimens have been deposited in the herbarium of regional research laboratory Coimbatore.

Table 27.1: Showing the Checklist of Hydrophytic Plants Used as Vegetables in Dharwad

Family Name of the Sps	*Flowers and Fruit*	*Part Used*
Amaranthaceae		
Alternanthera philoxenoides (Mark) Griseb.	During rainy days flowering, fruits not seen	Young leaves, tender-shoots cooked as vegetables
A. sessils (L) R.Br Ex.Dc.	Almost throughout the year	Young leaves, tender-shoots cooked as vegetables
Amaranthus spinosa L.	April–Nov., July–May	Young leaves, tender-shoots cooked as vegetables
A. paniculata L.	Almost throughout the year	Young leaves, tender-shoots cooked as vegetables
Achryanthus aspera L.	March–July	Young leaves, tender-shoots cooked as vegetables
Glomphera globosa L.	Almost throughout the year	Young leaves, tender-shoots cooked as vegetables
Apiaceae		
Centella asiatica L. Urban	Throughout the year	Juice of the whole plant taken raw or cooked 4 gm/lt water
Hydrocotyl sibthorpiodes, R.Br.L.	Feb.–July	Whole plant cooked as veg
Oenaathe javanica	June–Sept.	Young leaves and tender shoots
Asteraceae		
Eclipta prostrate L.	April–Nov.	Juice of leaves taken raw or cooked
Enhydra fluctuans Lour.	March–July	Tender shoots and leaves cooked as vegetables
Araceae		
Lasia spinosa (L) Thw.	Jan.–April	Tender, leaves, cooked as vegetables
Brassicaceae		
Borippa aquaticum (L) Heyek Bon Sorioh.	Mar.–May	Tender shoots and leaves cooked as vegetables

Contd...

Table 27.1–Contd...

Family Name of the Sps	*Flowers and Fruit*	*Part Used*
Caryophyllaceae		
Stellaria media (L) Vill.	Nov.–May	Whole plant
Commelinaceae		
Cynotis axillaries R and S.	Jan.–April	Tender stem and leaves
Convolulaceae		
Ipomea aquatica Fersk.	Sept.–May	Tender and leaves
Chenopodium		
Chenopodium album Linn.	March–Oct.	Tender stem and leaves
Spinacia olrraceae Linn.	Jan.–April	Whole plant except root system
Nelumbonaceae		
Nelumbo nucifera Gaertn.	April–Oct.	Rhizome and young petiole
Gentianaceae		
Nymphaceae hydrophyllum (Lour) (Kuntze)	Almost throughout the year	Whole plant
Nymphaceae		
Furyale ferox Salisb.	Almost throughout the year	Young leaves
Nymphaea nouchali N.L. Burm.	Almost throughout the year	Whole plant
N. stellata Willd.	March–Oct.	Whole plant
Hydrocharitaceae		
Ottelia alismoides (L) Pers.	Jan.–Dec.	Young leaves and Fruits
Nyctaginaceae		
Boerhavia repand (Willd)	June–Oct.	Tender leaves
Onagraceae		
Jussia repens L.	Jan.–Dec.	Tender leaves
Ludwiga parviflora Roxb.	March–Oct.	Tender leaves
Oxalidaceae		
Oxalis corniculata L.	Almost throughout the year	Whole plant
Pontederiaceae		
Monochoria hastata (L). Solms	May–Sept.	Tender shoots
Portulacaceae		
Portulaca oleraceae (L)	Almost throughout the year	Tender shoots

Results and Discussions

Families are arranged alphabetically and plant species with their botanical names. Seasons in the production of flowers and fruits. The use of edible portion of the plant aquatic angiospernls are very remarkable plants due to the habitat in which they spend most of lives. But a good number of them remain unused by human beings. Most of the people in remote habitats of the surveyed region depend on at their doorstep native edible plants. People discovered many hydrophytic plants for various ailments. In India a few workers reported some hydrophytic vegetative of different parts of the country (Virendra Singh *et al.*, 1995; Madhav Chetty *et al.*, 1998).

Further studies are deserved and needed to assess the potential of these newly reported plants and their chemical analysis to understand both in primary health care and as source of new drugs.

Acknowledgments

The authors are thankful to the Chairman P.G. Department of Botany, Karnataka University, Dharwad for providing necessary facilities to carryout the work. First three authors are thankful to the UGC for Teacher Fellowship under X plan FIP programme.

References

Islam, M., 1986. Certain hydrophytes of Assam. In: *Aquatic Weeds of North East India*. Dehradun.

Madhava Chetty, Lakshmipathi Chetty, Sudhakar, A. and Ramesh, C., 1998. Ethnomedico botany of some aquatic Angiospermae in Chittoor district of Andhra Pradesh, India. *Ficotera pia*.

Pathak, K.C., 1996. Hydrophytic plants used as vegetable in Southern district, Assam. *World Weeds*, 3: 81–84.

Satyanarayan, G., 1962. Hydrophyte vegetation of Jalakbari. *Bull. Bot. Surv., India*, 4: 217–218.

Virendra Singh, B.K, Kapathi, T.N. and Srivastava, 1995. *Medicinal Herbs of Ladhakh Especially Used in Home Remedies*.

Chapter 28

Preparation of Value Added Products by Utilizing Low Value Deep Sea Fish Bull's Eye (*Priacanthus hamurur*)

L. Suragihali Siddappa, C.V. Raju, Jayanaik, M.H. Bhandari and Basavakumar

College of Fisheries, Hoige Bazar, Mangalore – 575 002, Karnataka
Karnataka Veterinary, Animal and Fisheries Sciences University, Bidar, India

ABSTRACT

Bull's eye one of the underutilized deep-sea fish fetching low market value due to its fairly thick skin and large eyes. An attempt has been made to prepare a kneaded, broiled Japanese style fish paste product (chikuwa) using low cost technologies. The technology for product preparation was standardized to suit common fisher folk to develop small scale or cottage business, which would ultimately bring financial benefits. The quality changes and acceptability study of the product indicates that chikuwa stored at 0–5°C was acceptable upto 12 days and those at –20°C was good upto 120 days.

Keywords: Processing, Salting and Curing

Introduction

Bull's eye commonly known as disco fish in Mangalore is a deep sea underutilized species found all along the west coast of India. During 1999, its catch along Mangalore Coast was 957.5 tonnes (CMFRI, 2000). This species is comparatively addition to our fishery. It fetch low market price but it can be compared with croaker and Pink perch in chemical composition, meat yield and quality. Due to its thick skin and large eyes, physical appearance and other characteristics it is not preferred even for salt curing. Hence, an attempt was to utilize its de-boned meat for the preparation of Chikuwa, a Ready-to-Eat (RTE) product and to develop appropriate technology for the preparation of minced meat products, this would ultimately bring financial benefits to fisherfolk.

Materials and Methods

Fresh fish Bull's eye was procured from the landing centre was to processing hall in iced condition. Fishes were dressed to remove head, entrails; fins were washed to remove blood and peritoneal membrane. After draining, fishes were fed to the meat-picking machine to meat separate. The picked meat was the fed to meat mincer. Later the minced meat was mix with additives (Table 28.1) in silent cutter for 15 minutes. The resultant paste from silent cutter was taken for the preparation of Chikuwa.

Table 28.1: Recipe Used for the Preparation of Chikuwa Paste

Sl.No.	*Materials*	*Weight, gm/l*
1.	Minced meat	700
2.	Sodium chloride	15
3.	Sugar	15
4.	Poly phosphate	2
5.	Monosodium glutamate	2
6.	Starch	100
7.	Spice Mixture	4
	(*a*) Chilly Powder	14
	(*b*) Pepper powder	2
	(*c*) Coriander	4
	(*d*) Water	100
	(*e*) Oil	50

Approximately 15 g was spread over to the bamboo sticks to make cylindrical shape, of about 20 cm length, using two halves of the pipe (when two halves of the pipe was closed, it appears as hallow tube) and kept for 10 minutes for setting and then boiled for about 20 minutes using charcoal oven. Then the broiled paste or Chikuwa was separated and the temperature was noted down. The separated Chikuwa was packed in high-density polyethylene bags and heat sealed. The product was divided in to two batches and one batch was frozen at –20°C and the other batch was stored at refrigerated (0–5°C) temperature.

During the processing, about 200g. Raw paste was collected for proximate, bio-chemical and microbiological analysis. The biochemical, microbiological and Organoleptic changes of the product stored at refrigerated (0–5°C) and three days and cold storage (–20ºC) temperature were analyzed once in fortnight respectively upto 150 days.

Results and Discussion

The decrease in pH was noticed in the product stored at refrigerated temperature, as increase in PH was noticed in products stored at cold storage. The changes in pH during storage of sausage may due to microbial activity in the product during storage. The increase in titratable acidity is due to the production of acids from sugars by microorganisms and may be due to the formation of free fatty acids and some amino acids due to hydrolysis of lipids and proteins respectively. Both TMA-N and TVB-N is increased steadily up to ninety days in case of product stored at cold storage temperature and increased steadily up to twenty-one days in case of products stored at refrigerated temperature. The increase in TMA-N and TVB-N may be due to microbial activity in the products. No rancid odour was observed until the storage, PV in both temperatures increased steadily but well within the limits of acceptability throughout the storage periods. Freshly prepared Sausage paste had a TPC of 8.01×0^{-7} cfu/gm that reduced to 7.6×10^{-6} cfu/gm, which may be due to the boiling process.

In the product stored under cold storage temperature. TPC steadily increased up to 21 days storage, when the product was considered spoiled. The sensory score gradually decrease during storage from 8.2–6.3 in 12 days of storage at 0–5°C and from 8.1–5.7 during frozen storage at 150 days of storage.

As the storage period increase there was a gradual reduction in mean panel scores of all the attributes and this reduction was significant at 5 per cent level. However, between the attributes there was no significant difference, which means that there was uniform reduction in scores of all attributes during storage. Srinivas *et al.* (1999) have also made similar observations when fish sausage was stored in cold storage.

During frozen storage white discoloration was noticed after 120 days but not before 90 days, which was spread throughout the storage period. The emergence of fast foods in India has provided immense opportunity for marketing innovative products such as Sausage, a value added product from underutilized and low priced fish. Bull's eye fish a deep- sea variety can effectively be utilized for the preparation of Japanese styled fish product.

Table 28.2: Raw Material Characteristics of Bull's Eye (*P. hamurur*)

(A)	**Physical Characteristics**	
	Total length (cm)	18.50
	Standard length (cm)	15.00
	Total weight (g)	83.50
	Dressed yield (%)	65.00
	Picked meat yield (%)	39.80
	Minced meat yield (%)	31.50
(B)	**Biochemical Characteristics**	
	Moisture (%)	75.53
	Protein (%)	17.87
	Total lipids (%)	01.40
	Total ash (%)	01.20
	pH	06.50
	Total volatile base nitrogen (Mg %)	07.10
	Trimethyle amine nitrogen (Mg %)	02.77
	Peroxide value (Millimoles of oxygen/kg fat)	14.87
	Free fatty acid (% of Oleic acid)	02.37
(C)	**Microbiological Characteristics**	
	Total plate count (cfu/gm)	3.2 × 1
	Yeast and mold count (cfu/gm)	—
(D)	**Organoleptic Characteristics**	
	Appearance	08.70
	Colour	08.20
	Odour	08.20
	Texture	08.10
	Overall acceptability	08.30

*Mean of hedonic scores as assessed by 10 panelists.

Table 28.3: Change in Physical, Biochemical and Microbiological Characteristics of Sausage Stored at Refrigerated Temperatures (–5°C)

Parameters	*Days*						
	0	*6*	*9*	*12*	*15*	*18*	*21*
Expressible water (%)	8.72	7.83	8.18	8.67	8.99	9.44	9.86
Folding test (Grades)	A	A	B	C	C	D	D
pH	6.72	6.70	6.64	6.61	6.53	6.47	6.41
Total titratable acidity (%)	0.108	0.189	0.247	0.247	0.310	0.351	0.382
TMA–N (%)	1.67	1.80	2.40	3.82	4.17	5.92	9.48
TVB–N (%)	6.46	8.43	11.42	14.71	17.30	22.36	25.92
FFA (% of oleic acid)	2.91	4.26	5.30	6.39	8.25	9.46	10.48
PV (millimoles of oxygen/kg fat)	8.39	10.58	13.57	14.52	16.47	20.23	23.17
TPC (cfu/gm)	7.7×10^6	4.0×10^{-6}	8.21×10^{-6}	1.02×10^8	5.45×10^8	1.2×10^9	9.2×10^9
Overall acceptability	8.29	7.71	7.20	6.42	–	–	–

Table 28.4: Changes in Physical, Biochemical and Microbiological Characteristics of Sausage Stored (–20°C)

Parameters	*Days*						
	0	*15*	*30*	*45*	*60*	*90*	*120*
Expressible water (%)	7.72	8.39	9.21	10.48	11.63	12.69	14.49
Folding test (Grades)	A	A	A	B	B	C	D
pH	6.72	6.75	6.77	6.81	6.84	6.88	6.92
Total titratable acidity (%)	0.108	0.126	0.139	0.153	0.166	0.180	0.216
TMA–N (%)	1.672	3.442	4.242	5.402	6.415	7.81	8.40
TVB–N (%)	6.457	8.030	10.49	11.28	12.72	14.84	17.33
FFA (% of oleic acid)	2.91	3.82	4.83	5.55	5.81	6.31	8.05
PV (millimoles of oxygen/kg fat)	8.39	10.69	12.17	13.78	14.55	16.89	20.09
TPC (cfu/gm)	7.7×10^6	1.02×10^6	8.66×10^5	2.30×10^5	9.13×10^4	3.45×10^3	6.9×10^3
Overall acceptability	8.26	8.07	7.86	7.16	6.98	6.79	5.81

References

AOAC, 1984. *Official Methods of Analysis* 12th ed. AOAC, Washington D.C., pp. 109.

APHA, 1976. *Compendium of Methods for the Microbiological Examination of Foods*. APHA, New York, pp. 701.

James, D., 1984. The future of fish in nutrition, info fish marketing digest, 4: 41–44.

Kim, J.M. and Lee, C.M., 1987. Effect of Starch on textural properties of Surimi gel. *J. Food Sci.*, 52: 722.

Kinsella, J.E., 1987. *Sea Foods and Fish Science in Human Health and Diseases*. Marcel Dekker Inc., New York.

Lee, C.M., Wu, M.C. and Okada, M., 1992. Ingredients and formulation technology for Surumi based products. In: *Proceeding of the International Symposium in Engineered Seafood including Surumi,* National Fisheries Institute, Washington, D.C., pp. 168.

Ravindran, K., 2004. Utilization Fisheries resources of the Indian Exclusive Economic zone. In: *Large Marine Ecosystems: Exploration and Exploitation for Sustainable Development and Conservation on Fish Stocks,* (Ed.) V.S. Somavamshi. Fishery Survey of India, Mumbai, pp. 252–262.

Sikorski, Z.F., Kolakowaski, A. and Pan, B.S., 1990. The nutritive composition of the major groups of Marine foods organisms In: *Sea Food: Resources, Nutritional Composition and Preservation,* (Ed.) Z.E. Sikoriski. CRC press. Boca Raton, Florida, pp. 29–54.

Srinivas, T.V., Bhandari, M.H. and Raju, C.V., 1999. Standardisation of colour of sausage using chilly, turmeric and by smoking process. *Mysore J. Agric. Sci.,* 33: 253–260.

Whittle, K.J., 1984. A vital role for aquabe resources in feeding a hungry world. *Infofish Mark Dig.,* 5: 20–24.

Chapter 29

Study of Algal Flora in Rice Fields of University Campus, Bhagalpur, and Bounsi, Banka (Bihar)

Braj Nandan Kumar

University Department of Botany, Environmental Biology Research Laboratory, T.M. Bhagalpur University, Bhagalpur – 812 007, Bihar

ABSTRACT

32 algal taxa were recorded from two rice fields (University campus, Bhagalpur and Bounsi, Banka). This was the first attempt to explore the algal flora ofrice fields in this region. The following genera were reported: *Oscillatoria* (3), *Lyngbya* (2), *Anabaena* (1), *Nostoc* (2), *Spirulina* (1), *Cylindrospermum* (1), *Aulosira* (1), *Scytonema* (1), *Gloeotrichia* (1), *Rivularia* (1), *Closterium* (2), *Zygnemopsis* (1), *Spirogyra* (2), *Scendesmus* (1), *Synedra* (3), *Naviala* (1), *Nitzschia* (1), *Gomphonema* (2), *Cymbella* (1), *Pleurosigma* (1), *Pinnularia* (1), *Phacus* (1), *Euglena* (1).

***Keywords**: Rice field, Algal flora.*

Introduction

The occurrence of large number of algae in different parts of India has been reported by various workers. Algal inoculation to rice crop was reported to be effective in different agroclimatic conditions and soil types (Gopal and Venkataraman, 1971; Kannaiyan, 1983). Keeping the importance of algae in nitrogen fixation of rice field in view present investigation was undertaken at University Campus, Bhagalpur and Bounsi, Banka (87°02′ east longitude and 25°15′ north latitude). Though algal flora of rice fields have been studied in different parts of India extensively but this part has not been explored.

Keeping this into consideration the present work aims to record the diversity of algae in rice fields, which have been listed below.

Results

Oscillatoria ornata Kutz. ex Gomont
Desikachary, T.V. 1959, P. 206, Pl. 37, Fig. 12
Trichome breadth 9–11μ, Length 2.3–2.5μ.

Oscillatoria obscura Bruhl et Biswas
Desikachary, T.V. 1959, P. 207, Pl. 37, Fig. 2
Trichome breadth 3.4–4.6μ, Cells 1–1.5μ long.

Oscillatoria curviceps Ag.ex.Gomont.
Desikachary, T.V. 1959, P. 209, Pl. 39, Fig. 10
Trichome breadth 14.2–16.7μ, Cells 2–4μ long.

Lyngbya major Menegh. ex Gomount.
Desikachary, T.V. 1959, Pl. 52, Fig. 11, P. 320
Cells 11–15μ broad, 2-3.2μ long.

Lyngbya allorgei Fremy.
Desikachary, T.V. 1959, Pl. 54, Fig. 6, P.313
Trichome 3.6μ broad, cells 4.6–8.2μ long.

Anabaena naviculoides Fritsch.
Desikachary, T.V. 1959, P. 410, Pl. 72, Fig. 2
Trichome elongate more or less, Cells breadth 3.5–5μ
Length 3.2–4.5μ, Heterocyst breadth 5–6μ, Length 6–7μ.

Nostoc carneum Ag. ex Born. et Flah.
Desikachary, T.V. 1959, P. 381, Pl. 69, Fig. 6
Trichome breadth 3.5–4.0μ length 7.0–8.2μ
Heterocyst ablong, breadth 6.1μ, Length 5–10μ.

Nostoc ellipsosporum (Desm.) Rabenh. ex Born. et Flah.
Desikachary, T.V. 1959, P. 383–384, Pl. 69, Fig. 5
Trichome breadth 3.9μ, Cells Length 6–14μ
Heterocyst breadth 6–7μ, Length 6–13.5μ.

Spirulina major Kutz. ex Gomont.
Desikachary, T.V. 1959, P. 195–197, Pl. 36, Fig. 13,
Breadth 1.7μ, regularly spirally coiled, Spirals, breadth 2.3–4.1μ and, 2.6–4.1μ distant.

Cylindrospermum indicum Rao, C.B, orth. mut. DeToni
Desikachary, T.V. 1959, P. 369, Pl. 64, Fig. 11
Trichome cells quadrate, breadth 3.4–7.9μ, Length 3.6–6.1μ.

Aulosira jertilissima Ghose
Desikachary, T.V. 1959, P. 341, Pl. 80, Fig. 6
Trichome cells 6–11.5μ and Length 7.2–10μ
Cylindrical when young, breadth 8.5–9.5μ, Length 10–14μ

Scytonema simplex Bhardwaja
Desikachary, T.V. 1959, P. 455, Pl. 89, Fig. 1,
Trichome breadth 15.4 μ, hetrocyst cylindrical breadth 9.2–11.5 μ, Length 11.4–45.1 μ.

Gloeotrichia raciborskii woloszynska
Desikachary, T.V. 1959, P. 562–563, Pl. 118, Fig. 4,
Trichome breadth 7.0–8.0 μ, hetrocyst length 46.7 μ, breadth 5.2–6.0μ.

Rivularia beccariana (De Not) Born. et. Flab.
Desikachary, T.V. 1959, P. 551, Pl. 106, Figs. 8, 9,
Trichome breadth 3.1–7.9 μ

Closterium arcuatum Breb
Turner, William Barwell, 1892, P. 19, Tab. 1, Fig. 17 × 400,
Long 218 μ, Lat. 19 μ.

Closterium ehrenbergii Meneghi
Turner, William Barwell, 1892, P. 19, Tab. 1, Fig. 16 × 450
Long 281 μ, Lat. 56 μ.

Spirogyra decimina (Mull) Kutz.
Randhwa, M.S. 1959, P. 325, Fig. 309 a-b,
Vegetative cell 33–42 × 66–150 μ, zygosp. 31–40 × 41–68 μ.

Spirogyra biformis Jao
Randhwa, M.S. 1959, P. 317, Fig. 293 a-b
Vegetative cell 34–47 × 65–130 μ, zygosp. 36–51 × 60–83 μ

Zygnemopsis indica Randhwa
Randhwa; M.S. 1959, Fig. 129 a–b, P. 197–198
Vegetative cell 11–15μ broad, 38–43μ long. zygosp. 37–45μ broad

Scenedesmus obliquus (Turb.) Knetz.
Hosetti, B.B. 2002, Fig. 11, 12, P. 71
Length 39μ, width 6.5μ

Synedra ulna (Nitz.) Ehr.
Gandhi, H.P. 1967, P. 269, Fig. 63
Length 213μ, breadth 6μ.

Synedra ulna V. danica (Kuetz.) Grun.
Gandhi, H.P. 1967, P. 269, Fig. 69
Length 201μ, breadth 4.1μ.

Synedra acus Kuetz. *V. radians* (Kuetz.) Hustedt.
Sarode and Kamat, 1984, P. 31, Pl. 2, Fig. 34
Valves 51–60μ long, 2–2.5μ broad

Navicula minuta (Cleve) A.cl.
Gandhi, H.P. 1958, P. 497, Fig. 38
Valves 19μ long and 7μ broad

Nitzschis gracilis Hantzsch.
Sarode and Kamat, 1984, Pl. 25, Fig. 593, P. 217
Valves 113–116μ long, 3.2–3.5μ broad

Gomphonema parvulum Kutz.
Gandhi, H.P. 1967, P. 258, Fig. 24
Length 17μ, breadth 5μ

Gomphonema parvulum var. exilissima Grun.
Gandhi, H.P. 1967, P. 258, Fig. 25
Length 23μ, breadth 6μ

Cymbella jurgida (Greg.) Cl.
Gandhi, H.P. 1967, P. 256, Fig. 32
Length 37μ, breadth 9.0μ

Pleurosigma salinarum Grun.
Sarode and Kamat, 1984, Pl. 8, Fig. 157, P. 70
Valves 71–132μ long, 12–14μ broad

Pinnularia cardinaliculus (Cleve) Lund.
Sarode and Kamat, 1984, Pl. 16, Fig. 361, P. 138
Valves 65–73μ long, 11–12μ broad

Euglena acus Var. rigida Hueb.
Hosetti, B.B., 2002. Fig. 5, 9, P.74
Length 156μ, Width 65μ

Phacus curvicauda Swirenko
Hosetti, B.B., 2002, Fig. 5, 13, P. 74
Length 52μ, Width 26μ

Acknowledgement

The author is grateful to professor S.K. Chaudhary, University Department of Botany, T.M. Bhagalpur University, Bhagalpur – 812 007, for encouragement and suggestions. I am also thankful to University Department of Botany for providing laboratory facilities.

References

Desikachary, T.V., 1959. *Cyanophyta*, ICAR, Delhi.

Gandhi, H.P., 1958. Freshwater diatoms from Kolhapur and its immediate environs. *J. Bom. Nat. Hist. Soc.*, 55(3): 493–511.

Gandhi, H.P., 1967. Notes on the diatomaceae from Ahmedabad and its environs. *Hydrobiologia*, 30(3): 248–272.

Gyaatiiri, V. and Anand, N., 2002, Role of cyanobacterial association in the improvement of rice crop. *J. Indian Bot. Soc.*, 81: 41–46.

Hosetti, B.B., 2002. *Wetland Conservation and Management.* Pointer Publishers, Jaipur (Raj), India, pp. 71, 74.

Randhawa, M.S., 1959. *Zygnemaceae*, ICAR, New Delhi, p. 197–325.

Saha, L.C., 1986. Algae of Bhagalpur ponds: Bacillariophyceae. *Phykos*, 25: 136–143.

Sarode, P.T. and Kamat, N.D., 1984. *Freshwater Diatoms of Maharashtra.* Saikirpa Prakashan, Aurangabad, p. 70–217.

Turner, W.B., 1892. *The Freshwater Algae (Principally Desmidiae) of East India.* Royal Swedish Academy of Sciences, pp. 19.

Chapter 30

Marine Actinomycetes: A Potential Source for L-asparaginase

P. Dhevagi and E. Poorani

Assistant Professor, Department Environmental Sciences, Tamil Nadu Agricultural University, Coimbatore – 3, Tamil Nadu

Introduction

Microorganisms are miniature chemical factories as they have the capacity to convert a variety of raw materials into a series of value added products. The main products are antibiotics, polysaccharides, proteins, oils, fatty acids, enzymes, pigments etc. The success and effective exploitation of microbes to large extent rely on the diversity of microorganisms in the environment. Particularly the pharma industry recognizes that diversity is an essential and potentially important element in the development of new drugs for the disease control. Actinomycetes occur in a wide range of environment producing a variety of scientifically interesting and commercially useful high value metabolites. The actinomycetes produce about 67 per cent of total 1200 microbial metabolites. The marine environment is a potential source for new actinomycetes and novel antibiotics (Mathew *et al.*, 1994). There are very few reports on antimicrobial activity from marine actinomycetes from west coast of India. In the last decades a few novel bioactive substances have been isolated from marine strains of Streptomycetes and other actinomycetes (Ravel *et al.*, 1998 and Canedo *et al.*, 2000). Work on diversity of marine actinomycetes is very much limited around the world. Only few institutions are working in this field as this type of research is more laborious and difficulties in isolating the actinomycetes. Keeping this in view, the review on actinomycetes has been given.

Biodiversity of Actinomycetes

Actinomycetes were first discovered by Cohn in 1875 and studies on actinomycetes have been numerous then. Erikson (1940) found that the anaerobic Actinomycetes *Antinomyces Israelli* settledout as compact bread 'crump' 'cauliflower' or puffball colonies in static culture. Laksman (1950) reported 21 recommended media in which four are frequently used for isolation of Actinomycetes. Kuster and Williams (1964) and Kriss *et al.* (1967) suggested that some actinomycetes might be terrestrial forms that have adapted to the salinity of seawater and sediments. Early work on marine actinomycetes was given by Baam *et al.*, 1966 and Okami and Okazaki (1972). Sambamurthy and Ellaiah (1974) isolated a new species called *Streptomycetes marinesis* from water of Palm Beach. Lakshmanaperumalsamy (1978) reported that out of 518 strains isolated from the marine sediments of Porto Novo, 85 per cent were *Streptomyces* species and 15 per cent were *Micromonospora* and *Nocardia*.

Postmaster and Freitas (1975) and Walker and Colwell (1975) reported that the *Streptomycetes* species showed high antibiotic activity. Vanajakumar (1979), Vanajakumar *et al.* (1981), Ellaiah and Reddy (1987) and Balagurunathan (1992) found that the isolated strains of actinomycetes (386 from different molluscs, 140 from marine sediments of Vishakapattinam coast and 51 from marine sediment of Parangipetti) were antagonistic against bacteria and fungi. Cross (1982), Wetzel (1983), Takizawa *et al.* (1993), Schallenberg and Kalff (1993) and Jiang and Xu (1996) reported that generally actinomycetes are abundance in the sediment.

Good fellow and Haynes (1984) and Ellaiah and Reddy (1987) reported that the marine sediments are potent sources for the isolation or actinomycetes with good antimicrobial activity. A high concentration of morphological form tends to produce a dispersed form of growth whilst a low concentration normally results in pellet formation (Lawton *et al.*, 1989). Jiang and Xu (1996) and Murphy and Hill (1998) reported that the actinomycetes are traditionally considered being soil bacteria but increasingly they are being isolated from sediments obtained from very deep waters and in the vicinity of hydrothermal vents.

Sivakumar (1998) isolated more than fifty strains of actinomycetes from mangrove sediments of Pitchavaram and more than 30 per cent were active against pathogenic microbes in which, more than 10 per cent showed broad spectrum of antagonistic activity and he also isolated some rare forms. Dhevendran and Annie (1999) and Balagurunathan (2000) found that in the marine and coastal ecosystems must be rich in gene pool possibly containing isolates, capable of producing useful metabolites. Mangroves, by virtue of fluctuating physico-chemical conditions can harbour actinomycetes of high genetic potential.

Gomathinayagam and Lakshmanaperumalsamy (2001) observed that the density of actinomycetes population in water and sediment varied monthly. A systematic and significant difference in population was observed in water and sediment. Higher density of actinomycetes population appeared in the period of pre-monsoon and relatively low population was recorded during post monsoon.

Whol and McArthur (2001) studied that the biomass and organic matter decomposition of actinomycetes-fungal interactions differ from those of individual isolates. Dhevendaran and Anithakumari (2002) isolated *Streptomyces* spp. from the gut of fish exhibiting L-asparaginase activity under growing conditions in a liquid broth. Similar trend was noticed with sodium chloride in the estuarine strains,

Mincer *et al.* (2002) and Kokare *et al.* (2004) studied that the sediment samples from Alibag, Janjira and Goa are potent sources for the isolation of bioactive actinomycetes. Most of the isolates from the sediment samples were identified as *Streptomyces*. Poorani (2005) isolated actinomycetes from the sediments of Southeast and Southwest coastal regions of India.

The followings are the attempts on the Indian marine actinomycetes

Authors	Year	Places
Chandramohan	1972	Sediments of Bay of Bengal
Postmaster and Freitas	1975	Marsh sediments of Bombay waters
Laksmanaperumalsamy	1978	Sediments of Parangipettai area
Vanajakumar	1979	Various parts of molluscs
Ellaiah and Reddy	1987	Sediments of Vizag
Balagurunathan	1992	Sediments of Parangipettai and mangrove area
Rathnakala	1995	Sediments of Cochin
Sivakumar	1998	Sediments of Pitchavaram
Devendaran and Annie	1999	Sediments of estuarine Veli lake
Dhevagi and Poorani	2006	Sediments of Pitchavaram

Isolation of Actinomycetes

Kanagawa and Kelly (1987) reported that the actinomycetes were isolated from sludge acclimate to thiophene-2-carboxylic (T2C) or 5-methyl-thiophene-2-carboxylic acid (T5M2C) and were identified as *Rhodococcus*.

Herron and Wellington (1990) reported a new method for the isolation and enumeration of *Streptomyces* spores from soil. Rathnakala and Chandrika (1993) observed that out of many recommended media for selective isolation of actinomycetes from soil, Glucose asparagine agar, Grein and Meyer's agar, Oat meal agar and Kuster's agar were found suitable for isolation of actinomycetes from mangrove sediments. In Kuster's agar when acetic acid was used, the colonies were countless showing selective enrichment of actinomycetes over control medium.

Whol and McArthur (1998) found that aquatic actinomycetes may have important differences from their terrestrial counterparts and a wide array of isolation techniques was most suitable for collection of aquatic actinomycetes (Figure 30.1). Lateef and Oloke (2003) observed that Lactose minimal agar is adjusted to be good for the isolation of actinomycetes, as it inhibited the growth of bacteria and fungi. Kuster and Williams (1964), Shirling and Gottlib (1966) and Parson *et al.* (1984) used sea water complex broth for culturing the actinomycetes.

Poorani (2005) isolated actinomycetes from the sediments of the Southeast and Southwest coastal regions of India and screened for their potential L-asparaginase activity using starch casein agar, Kuster's agar, seawater complex agar, Kenknight agar and glucose asparagine agar.

Importance of Actinomycetes

Actinomycetes have provided many important bioactive compounds of high commercial value and continued to be routinely screened for new bioactive compounds. Rainbow and Rose (1963) reported that the actinomycetes play a major role in producing antibiotics and other metabolites such as intracellular enzymes, pigments and growth promoting factors.

Okami and Okazaki (1972) and Chandramohan *et al.* (1972) reported that the actinomycetes may occur not only as a part of the marine ecosystem but also may contribute significantly to the economy of the sea. Young and Smith (1975) and Willoughby (1976), obtained many extra cellulase enzymes,

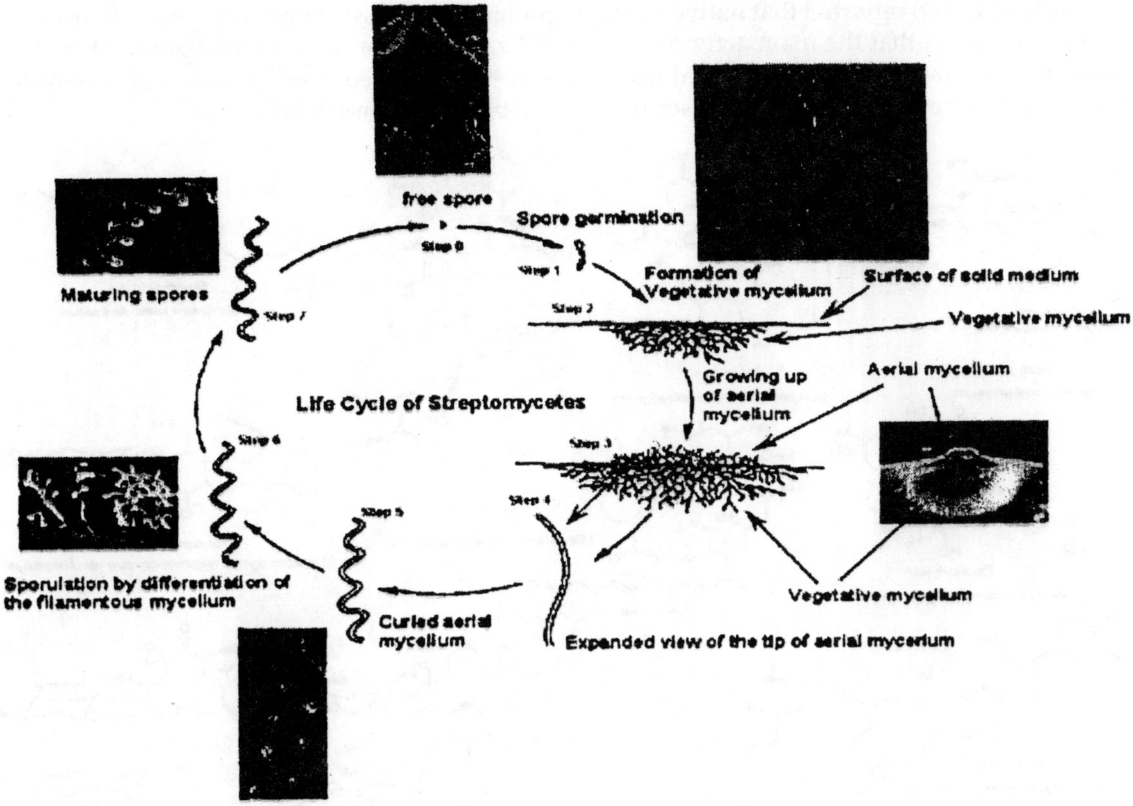

Figure 30.1: Complex Life Cycle of Streptomyces

which degrade cellulose, chitin, keratin and lignin from actinomycetes. They suggested that the marine actinomycetes might also take an active role in the deterioration of cellulosic substances in the marine environment.

Stastna *et al.* (1977), Metz *et al.* (1979) and Shomura *et al.* (1979) reported that production of antibiotic by some actinomycetes is affected by the morphological form of that organism. They found that the antibiotics are produced by filamentous growth forms, but not in fragmented mycelium. Balasubramanian *et al.* (1979) and Ishaque (1980) reported that the cellulase from the *Streptomycetes* isolates required 1–3 per cent sodium chloride for maximum activity and when the concentration was increased to 10–15 per cent there was no considerable loss in activity.

Kanagawa and Kelly (1987) reported that actinomycetes capable of complete degradation of thiophene derivatives and of their use by it as sole substrates for growth and they reported that thiophene-2- carboxylic acid and its 5-methyl derivative can be metabolized by some actinomycetes. Okami and Hotta (1988) reported that the actinomycetes have provided many important bioactive compounds successfully and approximately two-thirds of naturally occurring antibiotics of medical importance, which have high commercial value and continue to be routinely screened for new bioactive substances from Actinomycetes.

Ball *et al.* (1989) reported that native lignin degradation was associated with primary growth in actinomycetes and that the main activity was solubilization rather than mineralization. Ford *et al.* (1990) and Parthiana *et al.* (1991) and Takizawa *et al.* (1993) observed that the marine actinomycetes have received increasing attention as a source of novel bioactive compounds.

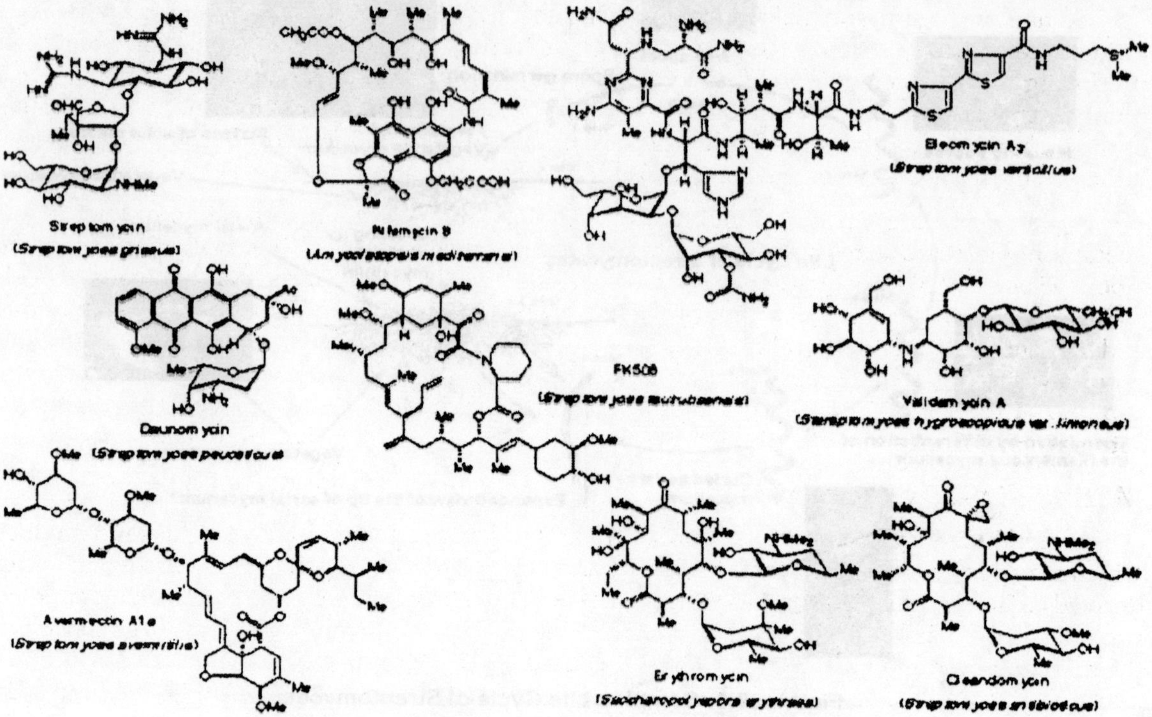

Figure 30.2: Antibiotics Produced by Streptomycetes

Jiang and Xu (1996) reported that the aquatic actinomycetes play a significant role in the decomposition of organic substances including some toxic compounds such as phenol in these lakes. Mercer *et al.* (1996) found that the actinomycetes are potentially rich sources of peroxidases for introduction into a market that was substantial and almost totally dominated Horse Radish Peroxidases (HRP) which was both well characterized and well active.

Murphy and Hill (1998) reported that a single group of bacteria produces over 70 per cent or all naturally occurring antibiotic drugs. Dhevenduran and Annie (1999) reported that the *Streptomycetes* associated with fish and shellfish have potential pharmaceutical value as they showed considerable antagonistic activity against fish and human pathogens.

Balagurunathan (2000) reported that the actinomycetes are well known for the production of high value metabolites such as nutrients, antibiotics, vitamins, enzymes, pigments etc. Today the value of antibiotic production from actinomycetes is > 1010 billion dollars/year. Novel strains of actinomycetes are registered as patents and sold at about 25–50 US dollar/strain from countries other than India. The biotechnological industries of developed countries are in need of potential strains of actinomycetes especially from the tropical areas that are blessed with rich microbial diversity.

Mieguelez *et al.* (2000) reported that the colony growth of the *Streptomycetes* provides an excellent prokaryotic experimental system for the study of the mechanism of cell death and its role in development. Zheng *et al.* (2000) reported novel antismoke agents from actinomycetes. Lazzarini *et al.* (2000) and Stach (2003) reported that currently Actinobacteria, particularly spore forming Actinomycetes represent the most economically and biotechnologically valuable organisms in the bioactive compounds.

Gomathinayagam and Lakshmanaperumalsamy (2001) observed the continuous success of actinomycetes in production of bioactive compounds. Various sources are being explored for antibiotic producing actinomycetes to cater the world demand for new antibiotics. It was found that very high numbers of actinomycetes are capable of producing broad spectrum compounds and are distributed in throughout length of river. A high incidence of bioactive compounds producing actinomycetes indicated the existence of invaluable potent organisms in the fresh water.

Ranjekar and Sridhar (2002) reported that among the microorganisms, actinomycetes gained special importance due to their capacity to produce bioactive secondary metabolites and enzymes. About 95 per cent of the isolates out of 64 isolates tested exhibited enzyme activity. Lateef and Oloke (2003) reported that isolates of actinomycetes sp was screened for the production of β-galactosidase and they showed potential β-galactosidase activity for lactose hydrolysis. Mishra and Oebnath (2003) reported that the *Streptomyces griseus NCIM2020* was used for glucose isomerase production in submerged fermentation. Balaguranathan (2004) and Kokare *et al.* (2004) reported that the marine actinomycetes isolated from sediments possessed higher antimicrobial and antifungal activities.

Marine Therapeutic Enzymes

Currently, marine microorganisms are considered as untapped sources of metabolites and products, which may possess novel properties. Murphy and Hill (1998) reported that there are several marine derived compounds in clinical trials, other on the development pathway and a number of commercial products on the market. "Didemnin B" a compound from a Caribbean tunicate has long been considered the marine compound most likely to be the first used clinically as an anti cancer drug. In addition to anti cancer and anti AIDS activities marine compounds have a wide range of other activities, including neuro and immuno modulation, antibiotic activity and anti-inflammation.

Mellado and Ventosa (2003) and Sabu (2003) reported that the halophilic adaptation of enzymes from halophilic microorganism would permit a wide range of industrial applications. For these reasons, very recently extensive attempts to isolate different types of salt adapted enzymes from halophilic microorganisms have been performed. The use of salt tolerant enzymes from marine bacteria provides an interesting alternative for therapeutic purpose (Table 30.1). The major potential therapeutic application of enzymes is in the treatment of cancer (Table 30.2). Asparaginase has proved to be particularly promising for the treatment of acute lymphocytic leukaemia. Its ac;tion depends upon the fact that tumour cells are deficient in aspartate ammonia ligase activity, which restricts their ability to synthesize the normally non-essential amino acid, L-asparagine. Poorani (2005) reported that the partially purified L-asparaginase from marine actinomycetes showing potential growth inhibition on tumour cell lines.

L-asparaginase Enzyme from Microorganisms

Wide range of bacteria, fungi, yeast, actinomycetes and algae are very efficient producers of L-asparaginase. Mashbern and Wriston (1964) and Yellin and Wriston (1966) were successfully purified and demonstrate the tumourcidal activity of *E. coli* L-asparaginase. The partially purified two isoforms of L-asparaginase having the therapeutic potential by using salt precipitation, starch block electrophoresis and DEAE-Cellulose column chromatography. Oettegen *et al.* (1967) studied the efficacy of L-asparaginase in human beings with leukemia.

Table 30.1: Microbial Sources of Therapeutic Enzymes

Enzyme	*Source*
L-Glutaminase	*Beauveria bassiana, Vibrio coslicoia, Zygosaccharomyces rouxii,*
L-asparaginase	*Pseudomonas acidovorans, Acinetobacter* sp.
β-lactamase	*Citrobacter freundii, Serratia marcescens, Klebsiaiia neumonia*
Serratia peptidase	*Serratia marcescens*
Lipase	*Candida liipolytica, C. rugosa, Aspergillus oryzae*
Alginate lyase	*Pseudomonas aeruginosa*
L-arabinofuranosidase	*Aspergillus niger*
Protease	*Bacillus polymyxa, Beauveria basssiana*
Superoxide dismutase	*Mycobacterium* sp., *Nocardia* sp.
Glucosidase	*Aspergillus niger*
Amylase	*Aspergillus oryzae, Bacillus* sp.
Serrapeptase	*Serratia marcescens*
Penicillin acylase	*Penicillium* sp.
Laccase	*Trametes versicolor*

Source: Sabu, 2003.

Table 30.2: Some Important Therapeutic Enzymes and their Applications

Enzyme	*Application*
L-asparaginase	Antitumour
L-Glutaminase	Antitumour
Superoxide dismutase	Anti-oxidant, anti-inflammatory
Serratia peptidase	Anti-inflammatory
Penicillin acylase	Synthetic antibiotic production
Collagenase	To treat Skin ulcers
Lipase	Digests lipids
Streptokinase	Anticoagulant
Urokinase	Anticoagulant
Laccase	Detoxifier
L-arginase	Antitumour
L-Tyrosinase	Antitumour
Glucosidase	Antitumour
Galactosidase	Antitumour
β lactamase	Penicillin allergy
Ribonuclease	Antiviral

Source: Sabu, 2003.

Broome (1968) studied the effects of the L-asparaginase enzyme on asparagine levels in the blood, normal tissues and 6C3HED Lymphomas of mice. Heinemann and Howard (1969) reported that *Serrutia murcescens* ATCC 60 is a high potential strain to produce tumour inhibitory L-asparaginase in submerged fermentation for large scale production. Angeli *et al* (1970) and Berenbaum (1970) found that the *A. terreus* asparaginase is not inactivated either at the pH of the peritoneal fluid or by the ascetic fluid. The weak activity on solid tumours may be correlated with the low diffusibility of this enzyme preparation from the peritoneal cavity into the blood stream.

Boyd and Phillips (1971) and Wade *et al.* (1971) reported that L-asparaginase and L-glutaminase are very common among bacteria. An automated modification of the test tube method was used to determine the asparaginase activities of about 200 strains from 78 species and the glutaminase activities of 46 strains from 13 species. Both the enzymes were widely distributed and at pH 8.5, asparaginase was generally the more active. Asparaginase was exceptionally active in some species of *Erwinia*. The tumour inhibitory L-asparaginase from *Serratia marcescens* showed a 365-fold purification and 15 per cent recovery of the enzyme, with specific activity of 250 IU per mg of protein.

Kafkewitz and Goodman (1974) and Wills and Woolfolk (1974) reported that asparagine requiring auxotroph of *Escherichia coli K-12* that have an active cytoplasmic asparaginase do not conserve asparagines supplements for use in protein synthesis. They reported that the rumen anaerobe *Vibrio succinogens* possesses a constitutive L-asparaginase. The compound supplied to the organism to generate the fumaric acid (affects the amount of enzyme produced.

Bascomb *et al.* (1975) and Gaffer and Shethna (1975) studied the purification, antitumour properties and large scale production in an inexpensive medium. The highest enzyme yield was obtained in corn-steep liquor medium (9.2 per cent w/v) at 37°C, the specific activity of the purified preparation was 45 IU/mg protein. The stimulation of L-asparaginase activity in *Azotobacter vinelandii* has been attempted using a variety of carbon and nitrogen sources, though the tested carbon sources failed to induce the enzyme, nitrogen sources such as ammonium salts, urea, L-aspartic acid and L-glutamic acid were found to be good inducers. The partially purified enzyme preparation possesses antitumour activity against Yoshida ascites sarcoma in rats.

Distasio *et al.* (1976) found that *V. succinogens* produced an L-asparaginase enzyme which showed higher L-asparaginase activities. Balakrish Nair *et al.* (1977), Barnes *et al.* (1977) and Selvakumar *et al.* (1977) reported that the details of the occurrence and activity of asparaginase in marine sediments. They suggests that marine sediments may be a good sources for active asparaginase producing fungi and found that the fungi isolated from the marine environment exhibit low asparaginase activity and their activity mainly restricted to the members of the genus *Aspergillus*.

Albanese and Katkewitz (1978) reported that the asparaginase synthesis by *Vibrio succinogens* is induced by ammonium ions. Kitto *et al.* (1979) described the isolation of two asparaginase enzyme from *P. geniculata* using a relatively straightforward purification procedure. The two enzymes were found to differ markedly both in their physicochemical properties and in their ability to affect the growth of murine neoplasms.

Mostafa (1979) reported that like bacteria, actinomycetes are also good source of L-asparaginase. Streptomyces in synthetic media with asparagine as a nitrogen source will stimulate more enzyme production than natural media. They found that the five genus of *Streptomycete* are capable of producing detectable amounts of L-asparaginase. Among them most potent L-asparaginase producers were identified as *Streptomyces collines, S. karnatakensis* and *S. venezulae* under different environmental and nutritional conditions. Cells grown on L-asparagine showed amidase activity with other amides but at a reduced rate.

Abuchowski *et al.*, 1979; Yashimoto *et al.*, 1986 and Jurgens *et al.* (1988) were reported that the biochemical properties of PEGylated asparaginase markedly differ from the native enzyme and its molecular weight is higher. The SDS is unable to separate the subunits of the enzyme due to cross-linking by PEG and having antitumour activity as clinically both in animals and humans. Arst and Bailey (1980) reported that the genetic evidence for a second asparaginase in *Aspergillus nidulans*.

Schemer and Holcenberg (1981) observed that L-asparaginase is the first enzyme with antitumour activity to be intensively studied in human beings. It is an enzyme drug of choice for acute lymphoblastic leukuemia in children used in combination therapy. Paul (1982) reported that L-asparaginase has been purified from a marine *Chlamydomonas* species, the first such enzyme to be purified from marine algae. The purified enzyme (mol.wt. 275000) possessed a km for asparagines of 1.34×10^{-4} M and showed limited antitumour activity in an antilymphoma assay *in vivo* and properties of the enzyme are contrasted with those of asparaginase from prokaryotic and eukaryotic sources.

Mostafa and Ali (1983) isolated the crude extract of L-asparaginase from *Thermoactinomycetes vulgaris* 13 MES by grinding the cells with sand and glass beads and followed by rapid freezing, thawing and exposure to ultrasonic waves. Wriston (1985) found that the purified asparaginase peak was pooled and usually found to be homogenous on analytical disc electrophoresis, although some preparations still show a second faint band. Gilbert *et al.* (1986) observed the expression of the cloned L-asparaginase gene was subject to glucose repression in *E. coli* but was not significantly repressed by glycerol. Recombinant plasmids, containing the asparaginase gene, when introduced into *Erwinia carotovora*, caused increased synthesis of the enzyme.

McEwen *et al.* (1987) and Leo *et al.* (1988) reported that the two L-asparaginase enzymes possess different immunological specifications. They confirmed that the L- asparaginase have immunogenicity in highly sensitized children *in vivo* with multiple acute lymphoblastic leukemia.

Asselin *et al.* (1989), Gallagher *et al.* (1989) and Masao (1989) reported that the L-asparaginase treatment for acute lympoblastic leukaemia is a major breakthrough in modern oncology because it induces complete emissions in over 90 per cent children with in weeks. The treatment with L-asparaginase as a single agent have kill the cells as both *in vitro* and *in vivo* in patients with acute lymphoblastic leukemia and besides these specific effects can exert immunosuppressive effects in general. This therapy got attention as a specific and favourable therapeutic idea which represents the inhibition of the leukemic cell growth without damaging the normal cells. Mesas *et al.* (1990) reported that the L-asparaginases are intracellular, the pH and the temperature for optima for L-asparginase production are the same as that for the growth of the enzyme producing organism.

Benny and Kurup (1991) and Selvakumar *et al.* (1991) attempted to screen L-asparaginase producing microorganisms from the estuarine sediments. The marine *Vibrio* isolates from the gut regions of *T. telescopium* showed the highest L-asparaginase activity and found that the bacterial isolates from different origins in the marine environment could yield potent strains for L-asparaginase production. The microbial population increased with increase of organic carbon content and decreased with increase of phosphate and nitrate. Percentage of L-asparaginase positive strains decreased with increase of organic carbon.

Benny and Ayyakkannu (1992) and Ramaiah and Chandramohan (1992) reported that the quantitative determination of L-asparaginase from the marine luminous bacteria and found the secretion of L-asparaginase by marine luminous bacteria did not seem to be influenced by the habitats. However, strains isolated from seawater particularly from the offshore regions appear to be potential sources of asparaginases. The total percentage of L-asparaginase positive population was slightly higher in sediments (66.6 per cent) than from fishes (62.8 per cent).

Maya *et al.*, (1992), Maladkar *et al.* (1993) and Annie *et al.* (1994) reported that the, preferably NaCl are essential for the enzyme activity and growth of Streptomycetes. The purified L-asparaginase enzyme showed significant antitumor activity on experimental animal models. Kil *et al.* (1995) and Mohapatra *et al.* (1997) found that the halophilic nature of marine bacteria can be exploited industrially. The most of the microbial L-asparaginase is intracellular in nature except few.

Gulati *et al.* (1997) demonstrated that pH and dye-based procedure for screening L- asparaginase producing microorganisms. This procedure is suitable for bacterial and fungal screening and the results are obtained within 24 and 48 hours for bacteria and fungi respectively. Dhevendran and Annie (1999) screened *Streptomycetes* isolate's from fish, shellfish and sediment of estuarine Veli Lake, for antibiotic production and L-asparaginase activity. Shome and Shome (2001) reported that the random screening in the mangrove dominated areas of Andaman showed good proportion of L-asparaginase harbouring bacteria.

Dhevendaran and Anithakumari (2002) studied the L-asparaginase activity of antagonistic *Streptomycetes* associated with the gut of the fish, under different cultural conditions like temperature, pH, sodium chloride, carbon sources, amino acids, heavy metals, inorganic phosphate and sulfate and found that it is possible to optimize the growth conditions and maximum L-asparaginase enzyme synthesis under laboratory conditions.

Sabu (2003) and Savitri and Azmi (2003) reported that the L-asparaginase catalyzes the hydrolysis of L-asparagines into L-aspartic acid and ammonia. Certain tumour cells are deficient in their ability to synthesize the non-essential amino acid, L-asparagine and are forced to extract it from body fluids; by contrast, most normal cells can produce their own L-asparagines.

Poorani (2005) isolated the L-asparaginase from marine actinomycetes and it is partially purified for characterization of the enzyme. It was a molecular weight of 140 K Da and showed maximum activity at pH 8 and 60°C.

L-asparaginase Enzyme from Marine Actinomycetes

Marine actinomycetes have provided a number of biologically active substances, metabolites, antibiotics and enzymes for industries especially pharmaceutical industries. Imada *et al.* (1973) reported that 25 strains of *Streptomyces* sp. were cultivated in 40 ml of ST-2 medium in 200 ml Erlenmeyer flasks for 3 days with shaking, L-asparagines and L-glutamine deamidating activities were found in the sonicated preparations from such cultures. Selvakumar *et al.* (1977) observed that the asparaginase of *Streptomyces griseus* has a pH-optimum of 8.5 and it is interesting to note that the marine sediments harbour potential L-asparaginase enzyme producers.

Dhevendaran and Annie (1999) and Dhevendaran and Anithakumari (2002) reported that minimum concentration of salts, preferably NaCl are essential for the L-asparaginase enzyme activity and growth of *Streptomycetes*. Savitri and Azmi (2003) found that like bacteria, actihomycetes are also good source of L-asparaginase. Three most potent enzyme producers were identified as different strains of *Streptomyces cyllinus* and presence of L-asparagine in the culture medium induces the enzyme production but it is not essential for the enzyme biosynthesis.

Dhevagi and Poorani (2006) isolated the tumour inhibiting L-asparaginase from marine actinomycetes (Figures 30.3 and 30.4). They suggested that the enzyme from marine actinomycetes was more in starch casein broth.

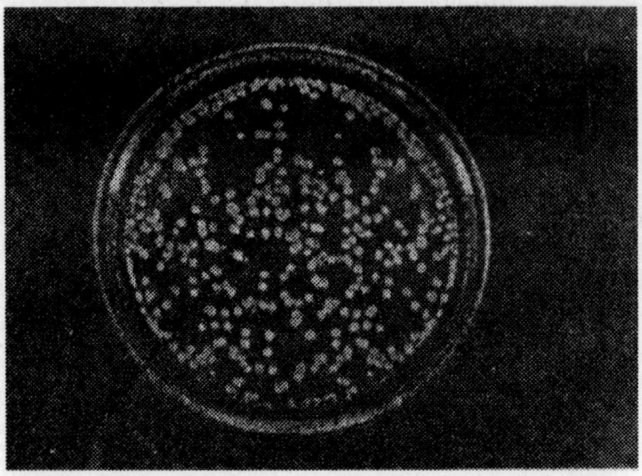

Figure 30.3: Actinomycetes Isolated from Pitchavaram Sediment

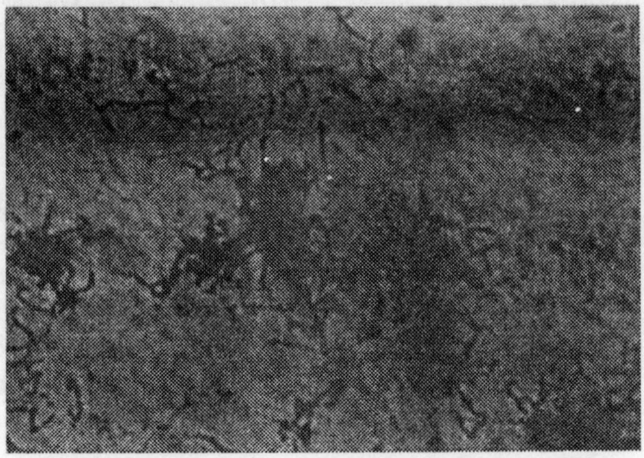

Figure 30.4: Microscopic View of Actinomycetes Isolated from Pitchavaram Sediment

Antitumour Activity of L-Asparaginase Enzyme

L-asparaginase is the first enzyme with antitumour activity to be intensively studied in human beings, rats and mice tumour cell lines. Angeli *et al.* (1970) and Berenbaum (1970) demonstrated the antitumour activity of L-asparaginase enzyme preparation on Walker 256 carcinosarcoma growing in ascetic form in the peritoneal cavity of the rat. They found that the preparation of *A. terreus* asparaginase has a greater careinostatic effect on the ascitic tumour and a smaller effect on those solid tumours that frequently develop in the subcutaneous at the inoculation site. The asparaginase effects the cells mediating the immune response and the effectiveness is lost once the cells begin to multiply rapidly, which may be relevant to the action of asparaginase in acute leukaemia.

Boyd and Phillips (1971) described the purification and properties of tumour inhibitory L-asparaginase enzyme from *Serratia marcescens.* It shows the inhibition of the Gardner lymphosarcoma 6C3HED in C3H mice. Complete regression of this tumour was obtained with a smaller dose of the enzyme from *S. marcescens* than with enzyme from *Escherichia coli.* The reason for this difference as not evident from a comparison of several properties of the two enzymes.

Bascomb *et al.* (1975) reported the properties and large scale production of an intracellular L-asparaginase with antitumour activity from a strain of *Citrobacter.* The anti-lymphoma activity of the enzyme was demonstrated with Gardner lymphosarcoma and was found only slightly less potent than Crasnitin, the most active asparaginase so far in this system. Gaffer and Shethna (1975) studied that the production, partial purification and antitumour activity of L-asparaginase from *Azotobacter vinelandii.* The partially purified enzyme preparation possesses antitumour activity against Yoshida ascites sarcoma in rats. The administration of 2,000 units/kg body weight, of L-asparaginase provided maximum protection against the tumour. It can also be seen that administration of increasing units of the enzyme results in a decrease in the survival period. This could be due to the toxicity of the enzyme preparation at high concentrations.

Distasio *et al.* (1976) and Barnes *et al.* (1977) reported the antitumour activity of purified L-asparaginase enzyme from *V. succinogens.* It possessed a potent antilymphoma activity in 6C3HED mice. The L-asparaginase therapy, alone or in combination with other drugs, is finding increased success in the management of acute lymphocytic leukemias. Selvakumar *et al.* (1977) screened for new strains from different ecological niches for asparaginase having antitumour and antileukaemia properties. Albanese and Kafkewitz (1978) found that the effect of medium composition on the growth and asparaginase production of *Vibrio succinogenes* and found that the properties of the *Vibrio* enzyme suggest that it may prove to be a clinically useful enzyme.

Kitto *et al.* (1979) reported that the tumour inhibitory and non-tumour inhibitory L-asparaginase from *Pseudomonas geniculata* and found that the asparaginase A was found to be devoid of antitumour activity in mice, whereas the asparaginase AG was effective in increasing the mean survival times of both C3H mice carrying the asparagines requiring Gardner 6C3HED tumour line and Swiss mice bearing the glutamine requiring Ehrlich ascites tumour line. These differences in antitumour activity were related to differences in the Km values for L-asparagine for the two enzymes.

Paul (1982) reported that the *Chlamydomonas* L-asparaginase possessed little ability to inhibit the growth of the Gardner lymphosarcoma in C3H mice. Benny and Kurup (1991) recommended *Aeromonas* isolated from estuarine mollusc for industrial production to meet the increasing demand of the enzyme in the treatment of lymphatic leukemia.

Selvakumar *et al.* (1991) reported that the L-asparaginase of marine *Vibrio*, isolated from the gut of *T. telescopium*, was found to be effective in suppressing Yoshida ascites sarcoma in Wistar rats. Benny and Ayyakkannu (1992) observed that the tumour cell requires an extra cellular source of L-asparagines and in its absence protein synthesis fails to occur in cancer. L-asparaginase hydrolyzes L-asparagine to aspartic acid and ammonia. When asparaginase from *Escherichia coli* was injected into mice suffering from certain types of leukaemia, marked important and often apparent cures occurred. Ueno *et al.* (1997) obtained the cell cycle arrest and apoptosis of leukemia cells induced by asparaginase. He found that the apoptotic cell death of murine leukemia cells was induced by *E. coli* L-asparaginase.

Savitri and Azmi (2003) and Sabu (2003) reported that the L-asparaginase (LA) can be effectively used for the treatment of lymphoblastic leukemia and tumour cells. Interest in this enzyme arose few decades ago when it was discovered that the antilymphoma activity of the guinea pig was due to LA. For pharmacologically and clinical tests, microbial sources are best for the bulk production of LA. Initially this drug failed to fall in antineopalstic category due to the immunogenic reactions caused by the foreign protein. With the development of protein engineering, modifications carried out in purified LA either reduced or completely eliminated the immunogenicity of LA in test model. The improved therapeutic activity and decreased immunogenicity of LA can be immensely used as an antineoplastic agent.

Poorani (2005) reported that the partially purified L-asparaginase isolated from marine actinomycetes showed maximum activity at 60°C and pH 8 and Stable upto 80°C. The enzyme has molecular weight of 140 K Da. The enzyme showed cytostatic and cytotoxic effects on tumour cell lines of American Type Culture Collections at 24 hours and 48 hours growth inhibition studies respectively.

Conclusion

It is interesting that the world's oceans, which cover 70 per cent of the earth's surface and include some of the most biodiverse ecosystems on the planet, have not been widely recognized as an important resource for novel actinomycetes. In fact, the distributions of actinomycetes in the sea remain largely undescribed and even today, conclusive evidence that these bacteria play important an ecological role in the marine environment has remained elusive. Speculation regarding the existence of indigenous populations of marine actinomycetes arises because these bacteria produce resistant spores that are known to be transported from land into the sea where they can remain viable but dormant for many years. Thus, it has been frequently assumed that actinomycetes isolated from marine samples are merely of terrestrial origin. The marine derived actinomycetes can be metabolically active and physiologically adapted to growth in seawater. Although some work has been done in the past 20 years on the marine actinomycetes not much work has been done in South Indian marine areas which themselves present a unique habitat and hence potentially new species and novel properties. Little information is available on the marine actinomycetes and its novel metabolites. Marine actinomycetes are new potential source of novel drugs and enzymes especially anti cancer enzyme and drugs. Therefore we report here the review on Marine actinomycetes and its potential anti leukeamic L-asparagmase.

References

Abuchowski, A. *et al.*, 1979. Treatment of L5178Y tumour bearing BDf mice with a non-immunogenic L-glutaminase-asparaginase. *Cancer Treat. Rep.*, 63: 1127–1129.

Asselin, B.L. *et al.*, 1989. *In vitro* and *in vivo* killing of all cells by L-asparaginase. *Cancer Res.*, 49: 4363–4369.

Albanese, E. and Kafkewitz, D., 1978. Effect of medium composition on the growth and asparaginase production of *V. succinogens. Appl. Env. Microbiol.*, 36(1): 25–30.

Angeli, L.C.D., Pocchiari, F., Russi, S., Tonolo, A. and Zurita, V.E., 1970. Effect of L-asparaginase from *Aspergillus terrus* on Ascites sarcoma in the rat. *Nature*, 225: 549–550.

Annie, K., Maya, J.S. and Devendaran, K., 1994. Antibiotic activity of *Streptomces* isolated from sediments. *Indian J. Mar. Sci.*, 17: 213–217.

Arst, H.N. and Bailey, C.R., 1980. Genetic evidence for a second *Aspergillus nidulans. J. of General Microbial.*, 121: 243–247.

Baam, R.B., Gandhi, N.M. and Freitas, Y.M., 1966. Antibiotic activity of marine microorganisms. *Helgoander Wiss. Meeresunters*, 13: 181–187.

Balagurunpathan, R., 1992. Antagonistic actinomycetes from shallow Sea sediments with references to alpha and beta unsaturated gamma-lactone type of antibiotic from *Streptomyces griseobrunneus* (p. 33). *Ph.D. Thesis*, Annamalai University, pp. 82.

Balagurunathan, R., 2000. *Actinomycetes* in mangrove ecosystems. In: *Flora and Fauna in Mangrove Ecosystems: A Manual for Identification*, pp. 148–152.

Balagurunathan, R., 2004. Marine actinomycetes: A promising future of pharmaceutical industry. *Advanced Biotech.*, 20(4): 16–21.

Balakrishna Nair, G., Selvakumar, N., Chandramohan, D. and Natarajan, R., 1977. Distribution and activity of L-asparaginase producing fungi in the marine environment of *Porto novo. Indian J. Mar. Sci.*, 6: 172–173.

Balasubramanian, T., Lakshmanaperumalsamy, P., Chandramohan, D. and Natarajan, R., 1979. Cellulolytic activity of *Streptomycetes* isolated from the digestive tract of a marine borer. *Indian J. Mar. Sci.*, 8: 111–114.

Ball, A.S., Betts, W.B. and McCarthy, A.J., 1989. Degradation of lignin-related compounds by *Actinomycetes. Appl. and Env. Microbiol.*, 55(6): 1642–1644.

Barnes, W.R., Dorn, G.L, and Vela, G.R., 1977. Effect of culture conditions on synthesis of L. asparaginase by *E. coli* A-1. *Appl. and Env. Microbiol.*, 33(2): 257–261.

Bascomb, S., Banks, G.T., Skarstedt, M.T., Fleming, A. and Bettelheim, K.A., 1975. The properties and large scale production of L-asparaginase from *citrobacter. J. General Microbiol.*, 91: 1–16.

Benny, A. and Ayyakkannu, 1992. L-asparaginase activity of benthic marine bacteria and of the muricid Gasteropod *chicoreus ramosus*, East coast of India. *Phuket. Mar. Biol. Spec. Publ.*, 11: 137–140.

Benny, P.J and Kurup, M., 1991. L-asparaginase activity in bacteria from estuarine sediments and mollusc. *Indian J. Mar. Sci.*, 20: 36–39.

Berenbaum, M.C., 1970. Immunosuppression of L-asparaginase. *Nature*, 225: 550–552.

Boyd, J.W. and Phillips, A.W., 1971. Purification and properties of L-asparaginase from *S. marcescens. J. Bacteriol.*, 106(2): 578–587.

Broome, J.D., 1968. Studies on the mechanism of tumour inhibition by L-asparaginase. *Br. J. Cancer*, pp. 1055–1072.

Canedo, L.M., Fernandez Puentes, J.L. and Baz, J.P., 2000. IB-G6212 a novel cytotoxic macrolide produced by a marine *Micramanospora* (II) physico-chemical properties and structure determination. *J. Antibiot.*, 53: 479–483.

Chandramohan, D., Ramu, S. and Natarajan, R., 1972. Cellulolytic activity of marine *Streptomycetes. Curr. Sci.*, 41(7): 245–246.

Cross, T., 1982. Aquatic actinomycetes: A critical survey of the occurrence, growth and role of actinomycetes in aquatic habitats. *J. Appl. Bacteriol.*, 50: 397–423.

Dhevagi, P. and Poorani, E., 2006. Isolation and characterization of actinomycetes from marine sediments. *J. Microb. World*, 8(1): 59–65.

Dhevendaran, K. and Annie, K., 1999. Antibiotic and L asparaginase of *Streptomycetes*.isolated from fish, Shellfish and sediments of veli estuarine along Kerala Coast. *Indian. J. Mar. Sci.*, 28: 335–337.

Dhevendaran, K. and Anithakumari, Y.K., 2002. L-asparaginase activity in growing conditions of *Streptomyces* spp. Associated with *Therapon jarbua* and *Villoritacyprinoids* of Veli lake, South India. *Fish. Technol.*, 39(2): 155–159.

Distasio, J.A., Niderman, R.A., Kafkewitz, D. and Goodman, D., 1976. Purification and characterization of L-asparaginase with anti-lymphoma activity from *Vibrio succinogens. The J. Biol. Chem.*, 251(22): 6929–6933.

Ellaiah, P. and Reddy, A.P.C., 1987. Isolation of *actinomycetes* from marine sediments of Vishakapatnam East coast of India. *Indian J. Mar. Sci.*, 16: 134–135.

Erikson, D., 1940. *Pathogenic Anaerobic Organisms of the Actinomyces Group*. Special report series, No. 240. Medical Research Council, London.

Ford, L.M., Eaton, T.E. and Godfrey, O.W., 1990. Screening of *St. ambofaciens* mutants that produce large quantities of spiramycin and determination of optimal conditions for spiramycin production. *Appl. and Env. Microbiol.*, 56(11): 3511– 3514.

Gaffar, S.A. and Shethna, Y.I., 1975. Partial purification and antitumour activity of L-asparaginase from *Azotobacter vinelandi. Curr. Sci.*, 44(20): 727–729.

Gallagher, M.P., Breuerjammli, M. and Mahro, B., 1989. L-asparaginase a drug for treatment of acute lymphoblastic leukemia. *Essays Biochem.*, 24: 1–40.

Gilbert, H.J., Blazek, R., Bullman, H.M.S. and Minton, N.P., 1986. Cloning and expression of *Erwinia chrysanthemi* asparaginase gene in *Escherichia coli* and *Erwinia carotovora. J. General Microbiol.*, 132: 151–160.

Gomathinayagam, P. and Laksmanaperumalsamy, P., 2001. Occurrence, distribution and antimicrobial activity of freshwater *actinomycetes. Asian J. Microbiol. Biotech. and Env.*, 3(3): 157–166.

Goodfellow, M. and J.A. Haynes, 1984. Actinomycetesin marine sediments. In: *Biological Biochemical Aspects of Actinim*, (Eds.) Oritz-Oritz, L., F. Bojatil and V. Yakoleff. Academic Press, London, pp. 453–472.

Gulati, R., Saxena, R.K. and Gupta, R., 1997. A rapid screening for L-asparaginase producing microorganisms. *Letters in Appl. Microbiol.*, 24: 23–26.

Heinemann, B. and Howard, A.J., 1969. Production of tumour inhibitory L–asparaginase by submerged growth of *Serratia marcescnes. Appl. Microbiol.*, 18(4): 550–554.

Herron, P.R. and Wellington, E.M.N., 1990. New method for extraction of *Streptomycetes* spores from soil and application to the study of lysogeny in sterile amended and nonsterile soil. *Appl. and Env. Microbiol.*, 56(5): 1406–1412.

Imada, A., Igarasi, S., Nakahama, K. and Isono, M., 1973. Asparaginase and glutaminase activities of microorganisms. *J. General Microbiol.*, 76: 85–99.

Ishaque, M. and Kluepfel, O., 1980. Cellulose complex of a mesophilic *Streptomyces* strain. *Can. J. Microbiol.*, 26: 183–189.

Jiang, C.L. and Xu, L.H., 1996. Diversity of aquatic *actinomycetes* in lakes of the middle plateau, Yunnan, China. *Appl. and Env, Microbiol.*, 62(1): 249–253.

Jurgens, H., Gibson, T.J., Plewniak, F. and Jeanmougin, F., 1988. Klinische erfahrungen mit polyathylengekoppelter *E. coli* asparaginase bei patuntenmit ALL-Mehrfachrezidiv klin. *Padiatr.*, 200: 184–191.

Kafkewitz, D. and Goodman, O., 1974. L-asparaginase production by the rumen anaerobe *V. succinogens. Appl. Microbiol.*, 27(1): 206–209.

Kanagawa, T. and Kelly, D.P., 1987. Degradation of substituted thiophenes by bacteria Isolated from activated sludge. *Microb. Ecol.*, 13: 47–57.

Kil, J.O., Church, D.M., Lash, A.E. and Leipe, D.D., 1995. Extraction of extracellular L-asparaginase from *Candida utilis. Biosci. Biotechnol. Biochem.*, 59: 749– 750.

Kitto, J.B., Smith, G., Thiet, T.Q., Mason, M. and Davidson, L., 1979. Tumour inhibitory and non-tumour inhibitory L-asparaginase from *P. geniculata. J. Bacteriol.*, 137: 204– 212.

Kokare, C.R., Mahadik, K.R., Kadam, S.S. and Chopade, B.A., 2004. Isolation of bioactive marine actinomycetes from sediments isolated from Goa and Maharashtra coastlines (West coast of India). *Indian J. Mar. Sci.*, 33(3): 248–256.

Kriss, A.E., Mishustina, J.E., Mitskevich, J.N. and Zemtsova, E.V., 1967. *Microbial Populations of Oceans and Seas.* Arnold, London, pp. 76–127.

Kuster, E. and Williams, S.T., 1964. Selection of media for the isolation of *Streptomycetes. Nature*, 202: 928–929.

Laksman, K., 1950. Isolation of marine microorganisms. *Appl. Environ. Microbiol.*, 36: 25–30.

Laksmanaperumalsamy, P., 1978. Studies on actinomycetes with special reference to antagonistic *Streptomycetes* from sediments of Porto Novo coastal zone. *Ph.D. Thesis*, Annamalai University, pp. 192.

Lateef, A. and Oloke, J.K., 2003. Enzymatic synthesis of oligosaccharides by *actinomycessp. Asian J. of Microbiol. Biotech. Env. Sci.*, 5(3): 291–295.

Lawton, P., Whitaker, A., Odell, D. and Stowell, J.D., 1989. *Actinomycetes* morphology in shaken culture. *Can. J. Microbiol.*, 26: 881–889.

Lclzzarini, A., Cavaletti, L., Toppo, G. and Marinelli, F., 2000. Rare genera of actinomycetes as potential producers of new antibiotics. *Antonie van Leeuwenhoek*, 78: 399–405.

Leo, H.T., Rappe, M.S., Hanada, Y. and Baden, D., 1988. Liposomal palmitoyl L-asparaginase; characterization and biological activity. *Cancer Chemother. Pharmacol.*, 34: 230–241.

Maladkar, N.K., Rainey, F.A. and Geobel, B.M., 1993. Fermentative production and isolation of L-asparaginase from *Erwinia carotovora*, EC-113. *Hindustan Antibiotic Bull.*, 35: 77–86.

Masao, N., 1986. Process for producing immobilized L-asparaginase preparations for the therapy of leukemia. *US Pat.*, 4: 617–627.

Mashbem, L.T. and Wriston, J.C., 1964. Tumour inhibitory effect of L-asparaginase from *E. coli. Arch. Biochem.*, 105: 450–458.

Mathew, A., Dhevendaran, K., Georgekutty, M.I. and Natarajan, P., 1994. L-asparaginase activity in antagonistic Streptomycetes associated with *Clam villorrita* cyprinoides (Hanley). *Indian J. Mar. Sci.*, 23: 204–208.

Maya, J.S., Devendaran, K. and Annie, K., 1992. L-asparaginase activity of *Streptomyces* sp. *Indian J. Mar. Sci.*, 12: 147–150.

McEwan, E.G., Lucon, C.M.M. and Rimmer, D.L., 1987. A preliminary study on the evaluation of asparaginase. *Cancer*, 59: 2011–2020.

Mellado M.E. and Ventosa, A., 2003. Biotechnological potential of moderately and extremely halophilic microorganisms. *Morgs for Healthcare, Food and Enz. Produc.*, pp. 233–256.

Mercer, D.K., Iqubal, M.P., Miller, G.G. and McCarthy, A.J., 1996. Screening *actinomycetes* for extra cellular peroxidase activity. *Appl. and Env. Microbiol.*, 62: 2186–2190.

Mesas, J.M., Ward, A.C. and Roux, K.H., 1990. Characterization and partial purification of L-asparaginase from *Cornebacterium glutamicum. J. Gen. Microbiol.*, pp. 136.

Metz, B., Kossen, N.W.F. and Van Suijdam, J.C., 1979. The morphology of actinomycetes. *Adv. Biochem. Eng.*, 11: 103–156.

Mieguelez, E.M., Hardisson, C. and Manzanal, M.B., 2000. *Streptomycetes:* A new model to study cell death. *Internatl. Microbiol.*, 3: 153–158.

Mincer, T.J., Jensen, P.R., Kauffman, C.A. and Fenical, W., 2002. Widespread and persistent populations of a new marine actinomycete taxon in Ocean sediments. *Appl. Environ. Microbiol.*, 68(10): 5005–5011.

Mishra, A. and Debnath, M., 2003. Studies on effect of nutrients on Glucose isomerase production by *St. griseus. NCIM* 2020. *Asian J. of Microbial. Biotech. Env. Sci.*, 5(1): 91–96.

Mohapatra, B.R., Rheims, H., Wolterink, A. and Stackebrandt, E., 1997. Production and properties of L-asparaginase from *Mucor* sp. associated with a marine sponge (*Spirastrella* sp.). *Cytobios*, 92: 165–173.

Mostafa, S.A., 1979a. Activity of L-asparaginase in cells of *Streptomyces karnatakensis. Zentralbl Bacteriol.*, (Naturwiss), 134: 343–351.

Mostafa, S.A., 1979b. Production of L-asparaginase by *Streptomyces karnatakensis* and *Streptomyces venezuelae. Zentralbl Bacteriol* (orig A), 134: 429–436.

Mostafa, S.A. and Ali, O.A., 1983. L-asparaginase activity in cell free extracts of *Thermoactinomyces vulgaris* 13 M.E.S. *Zbl. Microbiol.*, 5: 397–404.

Mostafa, S.A. and Salama, M.S., 1979. L-asparaginase producing *Streptomyces* from soil of Kuwait. *Zentralbl Bacteriol* (Naturwiss), 134: 325–334.

Murphy, P. and Hill, R.T., 1998. Marine vision becomes reality: Drugs from the sea. *Biofuture*, 119: 34–49.

Oettegen, H.F., P.A. Stephensen, M.K. Schwartz, R.D. Leeper, L. Tallal, C.C. Tan, B.D. Clarkson, R.B. Golbey, I.H. Krakoff, D.A. Karnofsky, M.L. Murphy and J.H. Burchenal, 1967. Toxicity of *E. coli* L-asparaginase in man. *Cancer*, 25: 253–278.

Okami, Y. and Hotta, 1988. Search and discovery of new antibiotics. In: *Actinomycetes in Biotechnology*. Academic Press, London, pp, 34–67.

Okami, Y. and Okazaki, T., 1972. Studies on marine microorganisms and its isolation from the sea. *J. Antibiot.*, 25: 456–460.

Parsons, T.R., Maita, Y. and Lalli, C.M., 1984. *A Manual of Chemical and Biological Methods for Seawater Analysis*. Pergamon Press (1st Edition), pp. 157–161.

Pathirana, C.D.M., Tapiolas, P.R., Jensen, R. Dwight and Fenical, 1991. Structure determination of madurakide: A new 24-membered ring macrolide glycoside produced by a marine bacterium (Actinomycetales). *Tetrahedron Lett.*, 32: 2323–2326.

Paul, J.H., 1982. Isolation and characterization of a *Chlamydomonas* L-asparaginase. *Biochem. J.*, 203: 109–115.

Poorani, E. and Dhevagi, P., 2005. Characterization of L-asparaginase from marine actinomycetes and checking its antitumour activity. *M.Phil. Thesis*, Bharathiar University, Coimbatore.

Postmaster, C. and Freitas, Y.M., 1975. An antibiotic producer from Marsh sediment. *Hindusthan Antibiot. Bull.*, 17: 118–120.

Rainbow, S.W. and Rose, H., 1963. Metabolites and antibiotics from Actinomycetes. *Microbiol Ecology*, 4: 24–27.

Ramaiah, N. and Chandramohan, D., 1992. Production of L-asparaginase by the marine luminous bacteria. *Indian J. Mar. Sci.*, 21: 212–214.

Rathnakala, R. and Chandrika, V., 1993. Effect of different media, for isolation growth and maintenance of *actinomycetes* from mangrove sediments. *Indian J. Mar. Sci.*, 22: 297–299.

Ravel, J. Schrempfu and Hill, R.T., 1998. Mercury resistance is encoded by transferable giant linear plasmids in two Chesapeake Bay Streptomycetes Strains. *Appl. Environ. Microbiol.*, 64: 3383–3388.

Renjekar, M.K. and Sridhar, K.R., 2002. Occurrence Find extracellular enzyme potential of *actinomycetes* of a thermal spring, Southern India. *Asian J. Microbial. Biotech. Env. Sci.*, 4(1): 59–64.

Sabu, A., 2003. Sources, properties and applications of microbial therapeutic enzymes. *Indian J. Biotechnol.*, 2: 334–341.

Sambamurthy, K. and Ellaiah, P., 1974. A new *Streptomycete* producing neomycin CB and W Complex. *S. marinenzis* (Part 1). *Hindustan. Antibiot. Bull.*, 17: 24–28.

Schemer, G. and Holcenberg, J.S., 1981. *Enzymes as Drugs*, (Eds.) J.S. Holcenberg and J. Roberts. Wiley Inter Science, New York, pp. 455–473.

Shomura, T., Yoshida, J., Amano, S., Kjima, M., Inouye, S. and Niida, T., 1979. Studies on actinomycetales producing antibiotics only on agar culture. I. Screening, taxonomy and morphology-productivity relationship of *S. halstedii* strain. *J. Antibiot.*, Tokyo, 52: 427–435.

Sivakumar, K., 1998. Research on marine *Actinomycetes*. In: *Flora and Fauna in Mangrove Ecosystems: A Manual for Identification*, pp. 47–51.

Savitri Asthana, N. and Azmi, W., 2003. Microbial L-asparaginase: A potent antitumour enzymes. *Indian J. Biotechnol.*, 2: 184–194.

Schallenberg, K.W. and Kalff, D.W., 1993. Ecology of actinomycetes. *Ann. Rev. Microbiol.*, 37: 189–216.

Selvakumar, N., Chandramohan, D. and Natarajan, R., 1977. L-asparaginase activity in marine sediments. *Curr. Sci.*, 46(9): 287–291.

Selvakumar, N., Vanajakumar and Natarajan, R., 1991. Partial purification, characterization a antitumour properties of L-asparaginase (Anti-leulkaemic agent) from *vibrio. Bioactive Compounds from Microorganisms*, pp. 289–300.

Shirling, E.B. and Gottlieb, D., 1966. Methods for characterization of *Streptomyces species. Internatl. J. Systematic Bacteriol.*, 6(3): 313–340.

Shome, R. and Shome, B.R., 2001. Microbial L-asparaginase from mangroves of Andaman Islands. *Indian J. Mar. Sci.*, 30: 183–184.

Sivakumar, K., 1998. Research on marine *Actinomycetes*. In: *Flora and Fauna in Mangrove Ecosystems: A Manual for Identification*, pp. 47–51.

Stach, J.E.M., Maldonado, L.A., Ward, A.C., Goodfellow, M. and Bull, A.T., 2003. New primers for the class actinobacteria application to marine and terrestrial environments. *Env. Microbiol.*, 5(10): 828–841.

Stastna, J., Caslavska, P., Wolf, A., Vinter, V. and Mikulik, K., 1977. Origin and morphology of a typical forms of *Streptomyces granaticolor. Folia Microbiol.*, 22: 339–345.

Takizawa, M., Colwell, R.R. and Hill, R.T., 1993. Isolation and diversity of *actinomycetes* in the Chesapeake Bay. *Appl. and Env. Microbiol.*, 59(4): 997–1002.

Ueno, T., Ohtawa, K., Mitsui, K., Kodera, Y., Hiroto, M., Matsushima, A.Y. and Nishimura, H., 1997. Cell cycle arrest and apoptosis of leukemia cells induced by asparaginase. *Leukemia*, 11(11): 1858–1861.

Vanajakumar, 1979. Studies on actinomycetes associated with molluscs from Porto novo coastal waters. *Ph.D. Thesis*, Annmalai University, pp. 236.

Vanajakumar, Selvakumar N. and Natarajan, R., 1981. Antagonistic Properties of *Actinomycetes* isolated from mollusks of Porto Novo Region, South India. In: *Bioactive Compounds from Marine Organisms: Emphasis on the Indian Ocean*, pp. 265–273.

Wade, H.E., Robinson, H.K. and Phillips, B.W., 1971. Asparaginase and Glutaminase activities of bacteria. *J. General Microbiol.*, 69: 299–312.

Walker, J.D and Colwell, R.R., 1975. Factors affecting enumeration and isolation of actinomycetes from Chesapeake Bay and southeastern Atlantic Ocean sediments. *Mar. Biol.*, 30: 193–201.

Wetzel, D.F., 1983. Enumeration, isolation and some physiological properties of actinomycetes from sediment and water. *Syst. Appl. Microbiol.*, 10: 85–91.

Whol, D.L. and McArthur, J.V., 1998. *Actinomycetes*-flora associated with submerged freshwater macrophytes. *FEMS Microbiol. Ecol.*, 26: 135–140.

Whol, D.L. and McArthur, J.L., 2001. Aquatic *actinomycetes:* Fungal interactions and their effects on organic matter decomoposition. *Microb. Ecol.*, 42: 446–457.

Wills, R.C. and Woolfolk, C.A., 1974. Asparagine utilization of *Escherichia coli*. *J. Bacteriol.*, 118(1): 231–241.

Willoughby, A.W., 1976. A continuing source of new metabolites. *Develop. Indust. Microbiol.*, 23: 1–7.

Wriston, J.C., 1985. *J. Methods in Enzymology,* 113, (Eds.) S.P Colowick and N.O. Kaplan. Academic Press, New York, pp. 608.

Yashimoto, T. *et al.*, 1986. Characterization of polyethylene glycol-modified L-asparaginase from *E. coli* and its application to therapy of leukemia. *Lap. Cancer. Res.*, 77: 1264–1270.

Yellin, T.Y. and Wriston, J.C., 1966. Antagonism of purified asparaginase from guinea pig serum towards Lymphoma. *Science*, 151: 998–1004.

Young, W.D. and Smith, P.M., 1975. Actinomycetes nature, distribution activities and importances. *Appl. Environ. Microbiol.*, 24: 17–22.

Zheng, W. and Crawford, D.L., Pometto, A.L. and Rafii, F., 2000. Survival and effects of wild-type, mutant and recombinant *Streptomyces* in a soil ecosystem. *Can. J. Microbiol.*, 35: 535–543.

Chapter 31

Biological Treatment of Azodyes

P. Dhevagi[1] and K. Sujatha[2]

[1]Department of Environmental Science, Tamil Nadu Agricultural University, Coimbatore – 3

[2]Kongu Nadu Arts and Science College, Coimbatore – 29

Introduction

Textile mill uses raw water about 61–646 1/kg of cloth with an average of 172 1/kg of cloth processed (50–81 per cent of water consumed, Bal 1999). Colored effluents are continuously released into sewage and adjoining water resources which render a catastrophic effect on the environment. The wastewater generated contains dyes at concentration of 10 to 200 mg/l and about 10 to 20 per cent goes along with other organic materials such as fats, waxes, pectin solid fragment, starch derived from the cloth during its processing and constitute major source of pollution (Zollinger, 1961; Anliker, 1979; Chudgar, 1985; Lewis, 1991 and Ashoka *et al.*, 2002). Soluble reactive dyes which are being used in increasing quantities are known to hydrolyze during application without a complete fixation results in larger proportion of these dyes being released into the environment (Carliell *et al.*, 1996). The recalcitrance of the azodyes to biolobrical degradative processes results in severe contamination of the rivers and groundwater in those areas of the world with a high concentration of dyeing industries (Namasivayan and Yamuna, 1992).

Azo dyes are largely used in textile industries, can also be found in the food, pharmaceutical, paper and printing, leather and cosmetics industries (King-Thom Chung *et al.*, 1978 and Sudhakar *et al.*, 2002). Many of these dyes find their way into the environment via wastewater facilities. These compounds retain their colour and structural integrity under exposure to sunlight, soil, bacteria and sweat; they also exhibit a high resistance to microbial degradation in wastewater treatment systems. The development of synthetic fabrics such as nylon, Lycra, rayon and polyester has required the production of new dyes that can effectively bond to these materials. Azo dyes must be continually updated to produce colors that reflect the trends dictated by changing social ideas and styles. Brighter, longer lasting colors are often necessary to satisfy this demand. There are more than 8000 chemical products associated with the dyeing process listed in the Colour Index (1998). While over 1,00,000 commercially available dyes (7×10^5 metric tons) are produced annually (Zollinger, 1987).

A multitude of dyes were used in textile industry are usually aromatic and heterocyclic (Vyas and Motiforis, 1995) and some are toxic and carcinogenic different classes of dye include azo, acid, reactive, metal complex, disperse, vat, mortant, direct, basic, suphur etc. (Vijaya *et al.*, 2003).

Effective and economic treatment of a diversity of effluents containing azo group has become a problem. No single treatment system is adequate for degrading the various dye structures. Physico-chemical and biological process has been investigated extensively for treating dye-bearing effluents. Even though chemical coagulation appears to be effective in treating the dye bearing effluents (Venkata Mohan *et al.*, 1999), the toxic sludge handling problem associated and the chemical cost retarded its usage. Adsorption employing activated carbon and various other adsorbents has been quite widely studied; however, the cost of carbon and the regeneration limited its application. Chemical oxidation is sometimes coupled with UV light exposure to increase the color removal. Other techniques involve electrochemical or wet oxidation, activated carbon adsorption, reverse osmosis, or coagulation/flocculation (Edwards, 2000). Many of these technologies are cost prohibitive, therefore are not viable options for treating large waste streams. Therefore, scientists have been forced to become very creative in the development of effective treatment technologies for the Azo dye removal.

Now the science and technology comes handy with nature's waste disposer the microbes, in cleaning up the environmental pollutants. Bioremediation of pollution is mandatory for an ecofriendly environment. Recent stress is on microbial based biological methods which are considered to be sustainable, ecofriendly, cost effective and also easy manageable effluent treatment system.

Understanding the basic composition of azo dyes and specifically fiber-reactive azo dyes is necessary to envision how these molecules can be destroyed. By understanding the general chemical structure of these compounds, considerati6n can be given to the toxic potential that they pose to the environment.

Azo Dyes and its Intermediates

Azo dyes contain a least one nitrogen-nitrogen (N=N) double bond, however many different structures are possible (Cripps *et al.*, 1990 and Zollinger, 1991). Monoazo dyes have only one N=N double bond, while diazo and,triazo dyes contain two and three N=N double bonds, respectively. The azo groups are generally connected to benzene and naphthalene rings, but can also be attached to aromatic heterocyclic or enolizable aliphatic groups (Zollinger, 1991). These side groups are necessary for imparting the color of the dye, with many different shades and intensities being possible. A common example of an azo dye can be seen in Figure 31.1 (Emitiazi, 2000). When describing a dye molecule, nucleophiles are referred to as *auxochromes*, while the aromatic groups are called *chromophores*. Together, the dye molecule is often described as a *chromogen*. The absorption and reflection of visible and UV irradiation is ultimately responsible for the observed color of the dye. Synthesis of most azo dyes involves diazotization of a primary aromatic amine, followed by coupling with one or more nucleophiles. Amino- and hydroxyl-groups are commonly used coupling components (Zollinger, 1991). Because of the diversity of dye components available for synthesis, a large number of structurally different azo dyes exist and are used in industry (McCurdy, 1991).Worldwide production of organic dyes is currently estimated at nearly 4,50,000 tons, with 50,000 tons being lost in effluents during application and manufacture (Lewis, 1999).

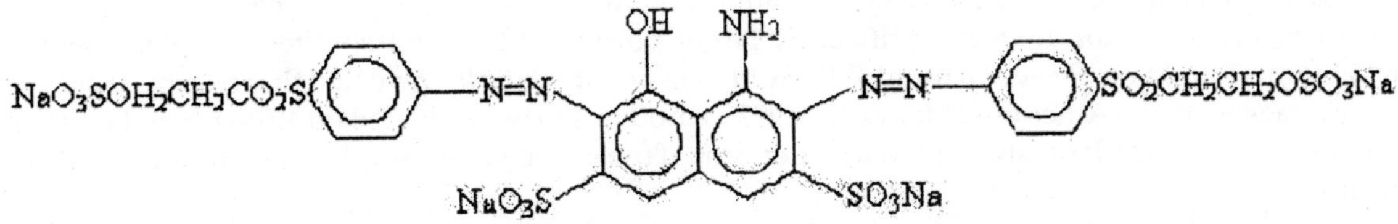

Figure 31.1: Example of an Azo Dye Structure (Remazol Black 5) (Emitiazi, 2000)

Eighty to ninety-five per cent of all reactive dyes are based on the azo chromogen (Zollinger, 1991 and Edwards, 2000). Reactive dyes are colored compounds that contain one or two functional groups capable of forming covalent bonds with the active sites in fibers. A carbon or phosphorous atom of the dye molecule will bond to hydroxyl groups in cellulose, amino, thiol and hydroxyl groups in wool, or amino groups in polyamides. Most fiber-reactive azo dyes are used for dyeing cellulosic materials, such as cotton and are a major source of dye waste in textile effluents. Fiber-reactive azo dyes exhibit a high wet-fastness, due to their ability to covalently bond to substrates. However, dyes that hydrolyze in solution prior to bonding to a substrate are often lost in the washing processes (Loyd, 1992). Schematic diagram of fiber reactive azo dyes is given in Figure 31.2.

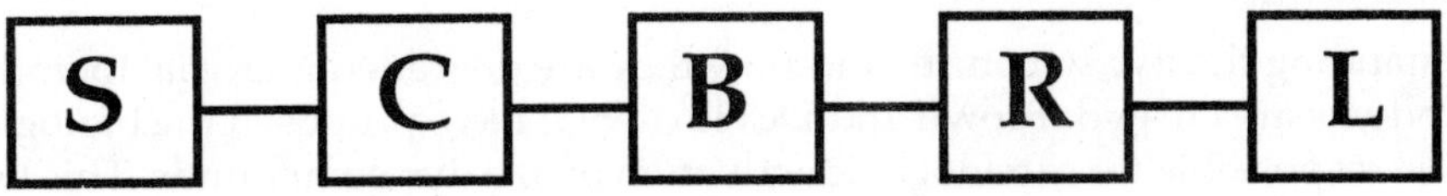

Figure 31.2: Schematic Diagram of Fiber Reactive Azo Dye

where,
S: Water solubiling group; C: Chromogen; B: Bringing group (can be part of chromogen); R: Reactive group; L: Fiber reactive group

The bridging group serves to combine the chromogen with the reactive group of the dye molecule. The bridging group must be stable, soluble in water and exhibit a certain degree of flexibility. Amino and alkylamino groups are generally used for this purpose. The reactive group serves to bond the dye molecule to a substrate via nucleophilic substitution or addition. Mono-, di- and trichlorotriazinyl are all examples of reactive functional groups. Approximately 200 different reactive groups are listed in the patent literature. Twenty-two new reactive azo dye structures were submitted for patent in early 1998, which was nearly five times as many from other classes of azo dyes (Freeman and Sokolowska, 1999). With such a disproportionate production rate, it is not 'surprising that a large percentage of dye pollution problems are related to fiber-reactive azo dyes.

Toxicity Considerations

The potential for toxic effects to the environment and humans, resulting from the exposure to dyes and dye metabolites, is not a new concem. As early as 1895 increased rates in bladder cancer were observed in workers involved in dye manufacturing (Rehn, 1895 and Rehn *et al.*, 1994). Since that time, many studies have been conducted showing the toxic potential of azo dyes. A complete review of these studies is beyond the scope of this paper; however, a broader understanding of the problem can be found in the works of Levine (1991) as well as Brown and DeVito (1993). Both papers indicate that the problem associated with azo dyes is created by the dye metabolites.

Azo dyes have been identified as potentially carcinogenic agents (IARC, 1996). While most azo dyes themselves are non-toxic a significantly larger portion of their metabolites are toxic (Ganesh, 1992). An investigation of several hundred commercial textile samples revealed that nearly 10 per cent were mutagenic in the Ames test (McCarthy, 1997). Another study conducted on 45 combined effluents from textile finishing plants showed that 27 per cent of the wastewater samples were mutagenic in the Ames test.

Many textile effluents contain heavy metals that are complexes in the azo dyes. Little *et al.*, 1974 reported that all cationic dyes are more toxic and vat dyes are less toxic. High concentrations of salt are often used to force fiber-reactive dyes out of solution and onto substrates (Zollinger, 1991). The azo dyes reduced by cytoplasmic reductases, results in the formation and accumulation of aromatic amines (Chung and Stevens, 1993). These reduction products may be toxic, mutagenic and/or carcinogenic to animals and humans (Levine, 1991) and reduces photosynthesis in plants (Saranaik and Kanekar, 1995). Reduced compounds can cause high electrolyte and conductivity concentrations in the dye wastewater, leading to acute and chronic toxicity problems equal to that of other metals (Venkata Mohan *et al.*, 2002).

Aromatic amines, which are known to be human carcinogens, have been found in the urine of dyestuff workers and test animals following the administration of azo dyes. Azo dye compounds are linked to bladder cancer in humans and to hepato carcinoma and nuclear anomalies in intestinal epithelial cells in mice.

Understanding the dye structures and how they are degraded is crucial to understanding how toxic by-products are created. Brown and DeVito (1993) have proposed the biological mechanisms thought to be responsible for carcinogenic activation of azo dye compounds. This list is based on an extensive review of the literature regarding azo dye toxicity. Brown and DeVito (1993) postulate that:

1. Azo dyes may be toxic only after reduction and cleavage of the azo linkage, producing aromatic amines.
2. Azo dyes with structures containing free aromatic amine groups that can be metabolically oxidized without azo reduction may cause toxicity.
3. Azo dye toxic activation may occur following direct oxidation of the azo linkage producing highly reactive electrophilic diazonium salts.

An example of a reductive pathway that is mediated by intestinal anaerobic bacteria and leads to the formation of benzidines is shown in Figure 31.3 (Brown and DeVito, 1993).

Similar reactions and by-products would be possible in an anaerobic treatment system. Examples of toxic aromatic amines, which could be created from the degradation of azo dye compounds and its human effects (Cartwright, 1983, Levine, 1991, Brown and Devito, 1993 and Chung, 2000), were given in Table 31.1.

Treatment Options

The treatment of textile effluents is of interest due to their toxic and esthetic impacts on receiving waters. While much research has been preformed to develop effective treatment technologies for wastewater containing azo dyes, no single solution has been satisfactory for remediating the broad diversity of textile wastes. Despite being aware of the problem, many textile manufactures have failed to adequately remove azo dye compounds from their wastewaters. Until dye and textile manufactures are able to develop efficient technologies, allowing for increased dye-fiber bonding and lower dye house losses (Lewis, 1999), the problem of treating these types of wastes will fall to the wastewater treatment facilities.

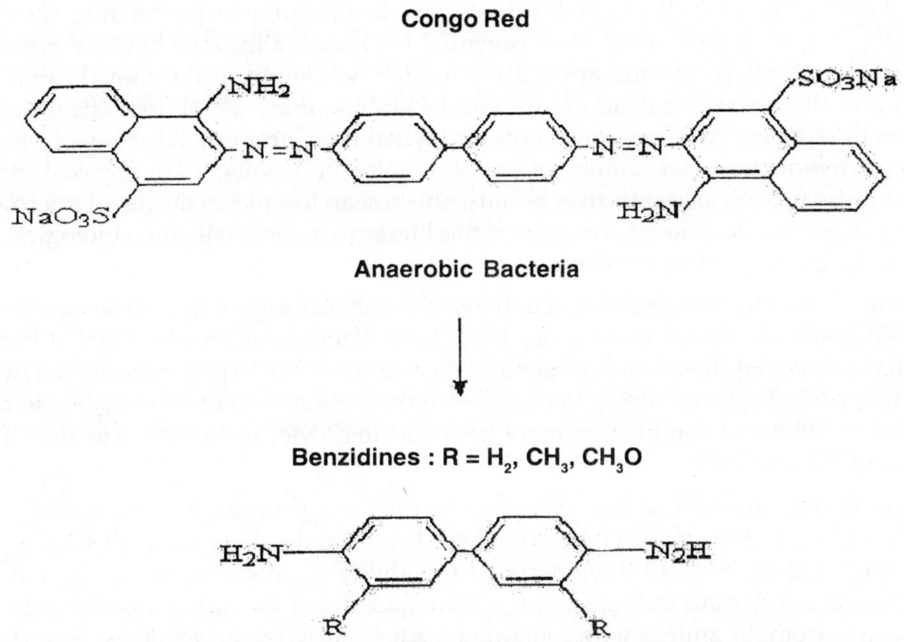

Figure 31.3: Example of Azo Dye Reduction via Anaerobic Bacterium

Table 31.1: Effect of Aromatic Amines and Potential Dye Metabolites

Sl.No.	*Compound*	*Human Effect*
1.	1-Napthylamine	Slight/mixed
2.	2-Napthylamine	Good
3.	2,5-Diamiotoluene	Slight
4.	3,3'-Dichlorobenzidine	Slight/mixed
5.	3,3'- Dimethoxy benzidine	Slight /mixed
6.	3,3'-Dimethylbenzidine	Slight
7.	4-Biphenylamine	Good
8.	4-Nitrobiphenyl	Slight/mixed
9.	4,4'-Methylenebis(2-chloroaniline)	Slight
10.	Auramine	Slight
11.	Benzidine	Good
12.	N,N-Bis(2-chloroetlhyl)-napthylamine	Good
13.	Magenta	Slight

To ensure the safety of effluents, proper technologies need to be used by treatment facilities when degrading fiber-reactive azo dyes. Azo dyes usually resist biodegradation in conventional treatment methods (Pagga and Brown, 1986, Shaul *et al.*, 1991 and Willmott *et al.*, 1998). Previous research efforts have focused on various biological, chemical and physical techniques for treating azo dye wastes. There is evidence that all three areas have potential for remediating dye house wastes. However, chemical treatment is often cost and application limited, while physical removal can lead to extra solid wastes and increased overhead (Yamini and Lalithakumari, 2001). Biological treatment has been effective in reducing dye house effluents and when used properly has a lower operating cost than other remediation processes. Combinations of chemical and biological or physical and biological treatment have also proven to be effective. Because this research explores the use of microbial sludges for the treatment of a textile effluent, the focus of this literature review will be on biological techniques used for degrading wastewaters containing azo dyes.

Because of their recalcitrant nature, azo dyes often pass through activated sludge facilities with little or no reduction in color (Cariell *et al.*, 1995, 1996; Pagga and Brown, 1986). Although some researchers have observed slight color reductions, their findings are largely outweighed by those who have not (Loyd, 1992, Zissi *et al.*, 1997). Reductions in the carbon content and oxygen demand of azo dye wastewaters following aerobic treatment are well cited (McCurdy, 1991, Horning 1977, Loyd, 1992, Pagga and Brown, 1986).

The anaerobic reduction of azo dyes to simpler compounds has been well researched (Chinwetkitvanich *et al.*, 2000, Razo-Flores *et al.*, 1997, Brown and Laboureur, 1983, Chung *et al.*, 1978). These and other studies, have all demonstrated the ability of anaerobic microbes and sludges to effectively reduce azo dyes to their structures, thus destroying the apparent color. Many of these intermediates are aromatic amines with constituent side groups. By reducing the dye compounds to their intermediates, the problem of aesthetic pollution is solved, but a larger and more deleterious problem may be created. Most azo dyes are non-toxic, but a higher percentage of their intermediates have been identified as carcinogens (Brown and DeVito, 1993,Wong and Yuen, 1996). Because of the toxic potential of many aromatic amines, further degradation of the dye compound is necessary if toxicity is to be eliminated or reduced (Levine, 1991and Brown and DeVito, 1993).

Aerobic Treatment

Conventional activated sludge treatment of wastes is often an effective and highly economic system for reducing organic pollutants in wastewater. A fair amount of research has been conducted assessing the viability of using activated sludge to treat textile effluents (Pagga and Brown, 1986, Shaul *et al.*, 1991, Loyd, 1992, Brown and DeVito, 1993 and Zissi *et al.*, 1997). However, aerobic treatment of azo dye wastes has proven ineffective in most cases, but is often the typical method of treatment used today (Edwards, 2000, Yang *et al.*, 1998). Because aerobic microbes cannot reduce azo linkages, their ability to destroy dye chromogens is less than anaerobic bacterium. However, aerobic sludges have been successfully used to stabilize dye metabolites (Brown and Laboureur, 1983). Pagga and Brown (1983) conducted a study on 87 commercial dye stuffs. Some of the dye stuffs were in a technically pure form, while others were in a sales form containing organic substances such as wetting agents. The tests were performed in a reactor designed to simulate the conditions of and adapted activated sludge wastewater treatment plant. The samples were tested for color and DOC removal following 42 days of treatment. Kumar *et al.*, 2006 studied the decolorisation, biodegradation and detoxification of Direct Black-38, a benzidine based azo dye, by a mixed microbial culture isolated from an aerobic bioreactor treating textile wastewater. Pagga and Brown indicated that the primary mechanism for removal of dyes in activated. sludge systems may occur by adsorption into the cell walls (Knapp *et al.*, 1995 and Banat *et al.*, 1996). In an earlier study by Brown and Laboureur (1983a), the aerobic biodegradability of aniline, o-toludine, p-anisidine, p-phenetidine, o-dianisidine and 3,3′-

dichlorobenzidine, was investigated. These compounds are all lipophilic aromatic amines and possible by-products of azo dyes. Because many aromatic structures are non biodegradable in anaerobic environments hydrophilic, they can accumulate in the adipose tissues of organisms.

Brown and Laboureur (1983) indicated that azo dyes may be broken down to their intermediate structures in a reductive environment, but were not amenable to further degradation by anaerobes. Brown and Laboureur (1983a) concluded that aniline, p-anisidine, p-phenetidineand o-toludine were readily biodegradable by aerobes, while o-dianisidine and 3,3'-dichlorobenzidine were inherently biodegradable. They suggested that these compounds could be stabilized if released into the environment or directly from a dye house into a conventional wastewater treatment plant. Shaul *et al.* (1991) conducted a study on 18 dyes to determine their fate in the activated sludge process. Of these dyes, 15 were acid azo dyes and three were direct azo dyes. The dyes were spiked into pilot-scale treatment systems. Eleven of the dyes passed through the activated sludge system substantially untreated, four were significantly absorbed into the sludge and three were apparently biodegraded.

Loyd (1992) also performed activated sludge treatment tests on two wastewaters. The first was a textile dyeing and finishing process water that contained Reactive Navy 106 and the second was a municipal wastewater consisting predominately of textile effluents. Both effluents were fed to laboratory-scale activated sludge reactors. Loyd concluded that aerobic treatment of the azo dye wastewaters provided significant biodegradation with minimal decolorization and the biodegradation did not include the azo dyestuffs.

Moosvi *et al.*, 2005 developed consortium exhibited 94 per cent decolourization ability within, 37 h under a wide pH range from 6.5 to 8.5 and temperature ranging from 25 to 40 °C. The bacterial consortium was able to grow and decolourize RV5 under static conditions in the presence of glucose and yeast extract and also showed an ability to decolourize in the presence of starch in place of glucose. Maximum decolourization efficiency was observed at 200 ppm (mg/l) concentration of RV5. Bacterial consortium RVM11.1 had the ability to decolourize 10 different dyes tested.

Idaka *et al.*, 1987 described the reductive fission of azo bonds by *P. cepacia* and aerobic reduction of simple azo compounds by *Aeromonas hydrophilia.* The ability of bacteria to utilize simple azo dye compounds as sole source of carbon and energy was shown by Dykes *et al.*, 1994 and Yatome *et al.*, 1993 and *Pseudomonas* K22 strain capable of utilizing carboxy orange II was well established by Kulla 1981, Zimmermann *et al.*, 1982, Kulla *et al.*, 1983 and Coughlin *et al.*, 1997 and 1999.

Finally, Zissi *et al.* (1997) investigated the biological oxidation of p-aminoazobenzene (pAAB) by *Bacillus subtilis* and results proved that *Bacillus subtilis* could cometabolize pAAB in the presence of glucose, breaking the N=N double bond and producing aniline and p-phenylenediamine. The degradation of the dye was the direct result of an oxygen insenstive azo reductase enzyme found to be present in the soluble I. fraction of the biomass. This enzyme was also synthesized independently of the presence of pAAB.

Bacterial cultures namely *Vibrio logei* and *Pseudomonas nitroreducens* from a wastewater treatment plant degraded a toxic azo dye (methyl red) by decolourization. Complete decolourization using a mixed-culture was achieved at pH 6, 30°C within 6 h at 5 mg/l methyl red concentration and 16 hat 20–30 mg/l (Adedayo *et al.*, 2004).

Azo Dye Degradation by Fungi

The inappropriate disposal of dyes in wastewater constitutes an environmental problem and can cause damage to the ecosystem. Altemative treatments have been reported that fungi are particularly effective in the decolorization of textile effluents.

The wood degrading whit rot basidiomycete *Phanerochaete chrysosporium* was found to degrade a number of Azo dyes (Glenn and Gold, 1983 and Paszczynski *et al.*, 1992, Spadaro *et al.*, 1992,). The extra cellular peroxidases produced by *P. chrysosporium*, Laccase produced by *pyricularia orison*, Mn peroxidase produced by *Aspergillus terreus* were found to initiate azo dye degradation (Glenn *et al.*, 1986, Chivukula Cripps *et al.*, 1990 and Renganathan, 1995). The degradation pathway of copper-pthalocyanine dyes by *P. chrysosporium* was given by spectrometry and polarography (Conneely *et al.* 1999). Anthraquinone dye degradation by *Geotricum candidum* was reported by Kim *et al.*, 1995 and Kim and Shoda, 1999.

The decolorization of dyes with different molecular structures by *Cunni.nghamella elegans* was evaluated under several media conditions. The decolorization profile was highly dependent upon the incubation time, the molecular structure of the dye and presence or absence of co-substrates. The presence of sucrose or both sucrose and peptone significantly increased the decolorization of the solutions, however, the presence of only the nitrogen source suppressed it (Ambrosio and Campos-Takaki 2004).

Basidiomycete PV 002, a recently isolated white-rot strain from decomposed neem waste displayed high extracellular peroxidase and rapidly decolorized azo dyes. White rot strain PV 002 efficiently decolorized Ranocid Fast Blue (96 per cent) and Acid Black 210 (70 per cent) on day 5 and 9 respectively under static conditions. The degradation of azo dyes under different conditions was strongly correlated with the ligninolytic activity. The optimum growth temperature of strain PV 002 was 26°C and pH 7.0 (Pradeep Verma and Datta Madamwar 2005).

Algal Biodegradation

The commonly available algal spirogyra species was found to degrade decolorize the aromatic basic dye-stuff containing azine group in batch scale operation (Venkata Mohan *et al.*, 2002). The decrease in aqueous phase pH below 3 during initial phase reduces the surface charge of algal cell, which sorbed the dye molecule in the aqueous environment through diffusion. This was observed in the initial stages of the study and about 10 per cent of the dye removal may be attributed to this mechanism (Biosorbtion). Once the dye molecules adsorbed onto the surface of the cell diffuses into the cell and stored in vacuole and participate in the respiration/photo conversion and subsequently releases polysaccharides and related organic compounds (bioconversion). The released metabolic intermediates possess excellent coagulation capacity and the dye remaining in the aqueous phase tend to absorb on the surface of the polymers and settles (Biocoagulation).

Actinomycete Biodegradation

A variety of actinomycetes like *Streptomyces viridosporrns* (Ramachandra *et al.*, 1988), *Thermomonospora mesophila* and *Streptomyces badius* (Godden *et al.*, 1992) and *Streptomyces chromofuscus* A11 (Pasti-Grigsby *et al.*, 1996) involving in azo dye degradation have been reported. These *Streptomycetes* sp. produce extra cellular peroxidases that contribute to their ability to de colorize the dyes. Evidence does show that the aerobic biodegradation of azo dye intermediates is possible and is perhaps an effective treatment process for stabilizing these compounds after anaerobic reduction.

Anaerobic Treatment

Anaerobic reduction of azo dyes using microbial sludges can be an effective and economic treatment process for removing color from dye house effluents. Previous studies have demonstrated the ability of anaerobic bacteria to reductively cleave the azo linkages in reactive dyes (Chung *et al.*,

1978; Brown and Laboureur, 1983; Brown and Hamburger, 1987; Loyd, 1992; Ganesh, 1992; Razo-Flores *et al.*, 1997 and Chinwetkitvanich, 2000). Although this effectively alters the chromogen and destroys the observed color of the dye, many aromatic groups are not susceptible to anaerobic reduction. However, there is evidence that some azo dye metabolites may be fully stabilized in anaerobic environments (Weber and Wolfe, 1987 and Razo-Flores, 1997).

During anaerobic treatment, it is expected that the dye molecules would cleave via reduction of the azo bonds. While this is often effective for reducing the color of the dye, it does not usually lower the carbon content (Loyd, 1992; Ganesh, 1992). Brown *et al.* (1993) studied the degradability of various azo dyes in both anaerobic and aerobic systems. In the first study, Brown and Laboureur (1983) investigated the anaerobic degradability of 22 commercial dyes. Of the dyes studied, four monoazo and six diazo-dyes showed substantial biodegradation, while two polyazo dyes showed moderate to Hamburger's confirmed the findings from earlier research, showing decolorization of the azo dyes. Confirming the cleavage of azo linkages, the production of metabolites was also observed, but at less than theoretical concentrations.

Brown and Hamburger (1987) Loyd (1992) and Ganesh (1992), who all reported good color losses, but low carbon removals following the anaerobic treatment of various azo dyes. It is hypothesized that the dye molecules undergo only partial degradation, limiting the carbon loss, but not the color removal. More recently, Razo-Flores *et al.* (1997) investigated the fate of Mordant Orange 1 (MO1) and Azodisalicylate (ADS) under methanogenic conditions using continuous Upflow-Anaerobic-Sludge-Blanket. (UASB) reactors and demonstrated the ability of an anaerobic consortium to completely mineralize some azo dye compounds. Razo-Flores *et al.* (1997) observed the complete mineralization of ADS with and without a co substrate, indicating the possibility for aromatic amine destruction in methanogenic environments. The compound, 1,4-phenylenediamine was not observed to degrade in either test reactor, indicating the specificity of aromatic amine utilization by anaerobes.

In studies conducted by Loyd (1992) and Ganesh (1992), the anaerobic reduction of textile mill effluents and the azo dyes Reactive Black 5 and Navy 106 were investigated, respectively. In both cases, good decolorization with minimal nutrient removal was observed. Chinwetkitvanich *et al.* (2000) performed a study on various reactive dye bath effluents concluded that higher initial color concentrations might be deleterious to acid forming bacteria, resulting in a lower dye removal. Additionally, the authors suggest that sulfate-reducing bacteria might out-compete other anaerobic microorganisms for available organic carbon, but contribute minimally to decolorization. This could serve to limit the reduction equivalents necessary for dye degradation.

Anaerobic/Aerobic Sequential Step-Treatment

Anaerobic bacteria are often able to reduce the azo linkages, but are generally unable to further stabilize the dye metabolites; it would seem advantageous to follow anaerobic treatment processes with an aerobic treatment step. As mentioned previously, aerobic organisms can oxidize aromatic ring compounds to simpler-molecules. A substantial amount of research has been conducted on ANA/AER sequential step-treatment systems used for degrading textile wastewaters (Brown and Hamburger, 1987; Loyd, 1992; Seshadri and Bishop, 1994; Fitzgerald and Bishop, 1995 and O'Neill *et al.*, 2000). Brown and Hamburger (1987) conducted a study on the ultimate biodegradability of various dye stuffs. Fourteen azo dyes and two other dye types were studied using lab-scale anaerobic and activated sludge reactors. Metabolite production was observed following anaerobic treatment, indicating the presence of eight identifiable aromatic amines. Results from the aerobic treatment phase corresponded with the work performed by Brown and Laboureur (1983a), showing reductions in DOC for most of the dyes. Some sulphonated aromatic amines were found to be non- biodegradable during this test.

Seshadri and Bishop (1994) investigated the fate of azo dyes Acid-Orange 7, Acid-Orange 8, Acid-Orange 10 and Acid-Red 14 in an ANA/AER sequential step- treatment system in a bench-scale Fluidized-Bed Anaerobic Reactor (FBR) followed by a bench-scale activated sludge reactor as a sequenced second stage treatment step. Their results indicated that the transformation of all the dyes to intermediates was readily achieved via anaerobic reduction; and was assumed to be the result of azo bond cleavage. Complete mineralization was not observed, however, COD and color removals were greatest at HRT's of 12 and 24 hours, with one hour being the shortest HRT tested and 24 hours the longest. However, the largest cumulative removals occurred in the first two hours of treatment. This would be expected based on the higher nutrient concentrations available for biodegradation during that period. The Acid-Orange 10 appeared to inhibit dye removal at concentrations of 15 mg L^{-1}. The authors believed the production of aromatic amines was responsible for the toxicity, citing the work of Chakrabarti *et al.* (1988). All other dyes tested did not exhibit inhibition at a concentration of 15 mg L^{-1}. COD removal was variable depending on the dye, but reductions were seen in both the anaerobic and aerobic phases. Aerobic oxidation of dye intermediates was necessary to decrease COD levels to an acceptable range.

Results from Zissi and Lyberatos (1996) conf1rIned that the anoxic biodegradation of p-aminobenzene, a simple azo dye, is effective in removing its apparent color. The findings from this research suggest that an ANA/AER sequential step-treatment system is the most effective method for biologically treating textile wastewaters.

Fitzgerald and Bishop (1995) used three lab-scale reactor systems to study the degradation of the azo dyes Acid-Orange 10, Acid-Red 14 and Acid-Red 18. The reactor system included an anaerobic fluidized bed system in the first stage, which was followed by an aerobic swisher reactor in the second stage. Their results indicated a high degree of degradation of the Acid Red 18 and Acid Red 14 in the anaerobic stage, with decolorization greater than 90 percent. Acid Orange 10 was only decolorized by 70 percent, however. Furthermore, analysis of the dye intermediates suggested a high degree of removal in the anaerobic stage. This is interesting, as most of the literature reports pool metabolite reduction in anaerobic environments. Low color loss and COD removal was measured in the aerobic stage. The authors do state that further investigation is necessary to verify if the dye intermediates biodegraded in the anaerobic reactor.

Recently, O'Neill *et al.* (2000) conducted a study on degradation of reactive azo dye Procion Red H-E7B in an ANA/AER sequential step-treatment system comprised of a lab-scale UASB reactor and an activated sludge tank. Based on this research, O'Neill concluded that Procion Red H-E7B could be qualitatively shown to degrade to aromatic amine derivatives after anaerobic treatment with subsequent oxidation of these derivatives following aerobic treatment.

Factors Affecting Azo Dye Biodegradation

Due to the highly variable nature of biological treatment systems and especially textile effluents, there are a number of factors that may affect the biodegradation rate of azo dyes. Non-dye related parameters such as temperature; pH, dissolved oxygen or nitrate concentrations, type and source of reduction equivalents, bacteria consortium and cell permeability can all affect the biodegradation of azo dyes and textile effluents. Dye related parameters such as class and type of azo dye (*i.e.*, reactive-monoazo), reduction metabolites, dye concentration, dye side groups and organic dye additives could also affect the biodegradability of azo dye wastewaters.

Wuhrmann *et al.* (1980) investigated the effects of pH, temperature, type and concentration of respiration substrates and oxygen tension on the rate of biological reduction of a variety of azo dyes.

A consortium of microbes was used, including *Bacillus cereus, Sphaerotilus natans* and two others isolated from sewage-activated sludge. Also, activated sludge was used in experiments with mixed biocenoses. Temperatures, which are too high or too low, can result in the exclusion of a particular group of microorganisms. Using activated sludge, Wuhrmann *et al.* (1980) determined that temperature has an increasing liner relationship with the reduction rate of Orange II and Lanasyl violet up to 28°C. In general however, most studies have been conducted at set temperatures, offering minimal data on temperature effects. The wastewater pH can affect the proper functioning of both anaerobic and aerobic organisms (Grady *et al.*, 1999). Wuhrmann *et al.* (1980) also investigated the effect of pH on dye reduction rates, but were unable to conclusively establish a relationship. However, they did state that an exponential increase in the decolorization rate was observed by decreasing the pH, but this relationship depended on the dye being tested. Loyd (1992) observed an indirect increase in the rate of decolorization of Navy-106, with decreased pH values in anaerobic batch tests. No statistical data was performed to verify this result; however Nitrate and especially oxygen may play an important role in determining the rate of dye reduction. The presence of oxygen generally inhibits the degradation of azo dye chromogens. Interestingly, Wuhrmann *et al.*, demonstrated that obligate aerobes might actually de colorize azo compounds under temporary anoxic conditions. However, high nitrite or nitrate concentrations in the mixed liquor of activated sludge plants could significantly inhibit dye removal. Zissi and Lyberatos (1996) observed *Bacillus subtilis* to degrade p-aminoazobenzene under anoxic conditions.

Without the necessary reduction equivalents to optimize bacterial respiration and growth, dye reduction may be inhibited. Often, bacterial cultures are unable to proliferate when an azo dye is the sole carbon and nitrogen source. Therefore, additional, readily biodegradable sources may be necessary. Wuhrmann *et al.* (1980) indicated that in the absence of oxygen an azo compound will act as the sole oxidant, and its reduction rate will be governed by the rate of formation of the electron donor. This may be a problem in WWTPs that receive a high loading of dye waste with a low, readily available, organic carbon content. Gingell and Walker (1971) state that the presence of oxygen may compete with the azo dye as the preferred oxidizer of reduced electron carriers in the respiration chain and thus limit the reduction of azo linkages. The type of bacteria or consortium used for dye biodegradation will undoubtedly affect the reduction rate. In general however, aerobic microbes do not have the ability to substantially decolorize azo dyes, but can oxidize the dye metabolites. Ganesh (1992) concluded that very little of the dye added to a biological reactor will be leached from the biomass when placed in a landfill. This might suggest that the dye is effectively reduced after adsorption to the cell wall or that very little dye is actually adsorbed. Cell permeability might play an important role in dye biodegradation.

Jo-Shu Chan *et al.*, 2004 reported that the addition of supernatants containing metabolites from growth and decolorization cultures triggered an enhancement of decolorization rates. Although extracellular metabolites play a crucial role for stimulating decolorization, they still cannot enable decolorization alone without involvement of biodecolorizers (*E. coli* strain NO_3).

In the study conducted by Wuhrmann *et al.* (1980), all dyes that were not reduced by whole cells were effectively degraded by cell extracts from both facultative, anaerobes and obligate aerobes. This suggests that many cells might be capable of dye biodegradation, but are limited by the permeability of their cell walls. The azo dye structure can play a significant role in the dye biodegradation rate. Depending on the number and placement of the azo linkages, some dyes will biodegrade more rapidly, than others. In general, the more azo linkages that must be broken will cause the reduction rate to be slower. Brown and Laboureur (1983) observed that two poly-azo dyes showed only moderate to variable biodegradation as compared to four monoazo and six diazo dyes. The authors indicate that poly-azo dyes are less likely to degrade than mono- or diazo dye types. Fiber-reactive azo dyes often contain solubilizing side groups, as well as a nucleophilic reactive group. Depending on the nature of these groups, biodegradation might be inhibited.

According to Ganesh (1992), sorption of dye to sludge depends on the type, number and position of the constituents in the dye molecule. Hydrophilic sulfo groups reduce the dye removal through sorption and conversely, sorption is increased by the presence of hydroxyl, nitro and azo groups in the dye molecule. The production of toxic by products or the presence of toxic dye additives may also inhibit biodegradation. High, salt concentrations are not uncommon in textile effluents and may result in adverse conditions for biodegradation. Dispersing and solubilizing agents may also create inhibitory conditions for dye reduction (Carliell, *et al.*, 1994).

In various studies (Wuhrmann *et al.*, 1980; Donlagic and Levec, 1998, and O'Neill *et al.*, 2000) the production of inhibitory dye metabolites is cited as causing a decrease in biodegradation. O'Neill *et al.* concluded from respiration-inhibition testing that anaerobic degradation of simulated textile effluent generated metabolites that were, toxic to some aerobic organisms, Donlagic' and Levec concluded that the distribution of dye intermediates plays an important role in determining the aerobic biodegradability of Orange II. They further state that low dye removal may be attributed to the presence of intermediates that are less susceptible to microbial degradation or that act as inhibitory agents. Wurhmann *et al.* (1980) attributes a decline to the accumulation of reduction products in the test medium. Inhibition of various microorganisms to dye metabolites is frequently cited throughout the literature and is assumed to be a key factor when treating wastewaters containing azo dyes.

A final and important factor to evaluate is the initial dye concentration of the wastewater. Seshadri and Bishop (1994) performed a study investigating the effect of different influent dye concentrations on the color removal efficiency. They concluded that elevated dye concentrations may cause a drop in per cent dye removal. Furthermore, the inhibition may be directly related to the effects of increased dye formation due to higher dye concentrations. Less pronounced reductions at lower concentration levels. It should be noted that tolerable influent concentrations are likely specific to individual or related groups of dyes. Cariell *et al.* (1995) also states that toxicity assays showed that C.I. Reactive Red 141 was inhibitory to anaerobic organisms at concentrations greater than 100 mg/l, however biomass adaptation increased their resistance to elevated dye concentrations.

The Research Need

Biodegradation of azo dyes by a single species of microorganism requires that species to possess all the necessary enzymes involved in the pathway and also genetic information. Continual exposure of microbes to azo dyes can result in the evaluation of novel metabolic processes which enables the microorganisms to wholly or partially degrade the azo dyes. There are two possible ways by which the microbes acquire new traits. They are (1) Natural mutation and natural gene transfer and (2) Artificial gene transfer. Natural mutations occur at the rate of 1 mutation per 100 cell divisions, mostly non beneficial to the cell. Many genes that encode key the catabolism of azo dyes are plasmid encoded. Such plasmids can be one cell to another by the processes of conjugation and transformation. In cells possessing plasmids which only encode for a few enzymes for azo dye degradation must be complemented with chromosomal genes so that plasmid encoded pathway is linked to a metabolic pathway. Encoding of degradative genes on plasmids gives the possibility for the construction of microbes by genetic engineering with the metabolic requirements for the treatment of azo dye containing wastes.

References

Adedayo, O.S., Javadpour, C., Taylo: Anderson, W.A. and Moo-Young, M., 2004. Decolourization and detoxification of methyl red by aerobic bacteria from a wastewater treatment plant. *World J. Microbiol. Biotechnol.*, 20(6): 545–550.

Ambrosio, S.T. and Campos-Takaki, G.M., 2004. Decolorization of reactive azo dyes by *Cunninghamella elegans* UCP 542 under co-metabolic conditions. *Biores. Technol.*, 91(1): 69–75.

Anliker, R., 1979. Ecotoxicology of dyestuffs: A joint effort by industry Ecotox. *Environ. Safety*, 3: 59–74.

Ashoka, C., Geetha, M.S. and Sullia, S.B., 2002. Biobleaching of compost textile dye effluent using bacterial consortia. *Asian J. Microbiol. Biotech. Env. Sci.*, 4: 65–68.

Bal, A.S., 1999. Waste water management for textile industry: An overview. *Indian J. Env. Hlth.*, 41: 264–290.

Banat, I.M., Nigan, P., Singh, D. and Marchanto, R., 1996. Microbial decolourisation of textile dye containing effluents: A review. *Biores. Technol.*, 58: 217–227.

Brown, D. and Hamburger, B., 1987. The degradation of dyestuffs, Part III: Investigations of their ultimate degradability. *Chemosphere*, 16(7): 1539–1553.

Brown, D. and Laboureur, P., 1983. The degradation of dyestuffs, Part I: Primary biodegradation under anaerobic conditions. *Chemosphere*, 12(3): 397–404.

Brown, D. and Laboureur, P., 1983a. The aerobic biodegradability of primary aromatic amines. *Chemosphere*, 12(3): 405–414.

Brown, Mark A. and Stephen C. DeVito, 1993. Predicting azo dye toxicity. *Crit. Rev. Environ. Sci. Tech.*, 23(3): 249–324.

Brown, M.S. and Devito, S.C., 1993. Predicting azo dye city. *Crit. Rev. Environ. Sci. Tech.*, 23: 249–342.

Cariell, C.M., Barclay, S.J. and Buckley, C.A., 1996. Treatment of exhausted reactive dye bath effluent using anaerobic digestion: Laboratory and full scaletrials. *Water SA*, 22(3): 225–233.

Cariell, C.M., Barclay, S.J., Naidoo, N., Buckley, C.A., Mulholland, D.A. and Senior, E., 1994. Anaerobic decolorisation of reactive dyes in conventional sewage treatment processes. *Water SA*, 20(4): 341–344.

Canell, C.M., Barclay, S.J., Naldoo, N., Buckley, C.A., Mulholland, D.A. and Senior, E., 1995. Microbial decolourisation of a reactive azo dye under anaerobic conditions. *Water SA*, 21(1): 61–69.

Cartwright, R.A., 1983. Historical and modern epidemiological studies on populations exposed to N-substituted aryl compounds. *Env. Health Perspect.*, (49): 13.

Chakrabarti, T., Subrahmanyam, P. and Sundarsan, B., 1988. Biodegradation of recalcitrant industrial wastes. *Biotreatment Systems Vol. II.*, (Ed.) D. Wise. CRC Press, Inc., Boca Raton, FL.

Chinwetkitvanich, S., Tuntoolvest, M. and Panswad, T., 2000. Anaerobic decolorization of reactive dye bath effluents by a two-stage UASB system with tapioca as a co-substrate. *Water Research*, 34(8): 2223–2232.

Chivukula, M. and Renganathan, V., 1995. Phenolic azo dye oxidation by laccase from *Pyricularia oryzae*. *Appl. Environmental Microbiol.*, 61: 4374.

Chudgar, R.J., 1985. Azo dyes. In: *Kirk–Othmer Encyclopedia of Chemical Technology*, 4th edn, (Ed.) Kroschwitz. Wiley, New York, pp. 821–875.

Chung, King-Thom and Stevens, S.E., 1993. Degradation of azo dyes by environmental microorganisms and helminthes. *Environ. Toxicol. Chem.*, 12: 2121–2132.

Chung, King-Thom, Fulk G.E. and Egan, M., 1978. Reduction of azo dyes by intestinal anaerobes. *Appl. Environmental Microbiol.*, 35(3): 558–562.

Chung, K.T., 2000. Mutagenictiy and carcinogenicity of aromatic amine metabolites produced from azo dyes. *Enviro Carcino. and Ecotox. Rev.*, 18: 51–74.

Colour Index International: Additions and Amendments. 1998. *The Society of Dyers Colourists*, 109: 2860–2895.

Conneely, A., Smyth W.F. and McMullan, G., 1999. Metabolism of the pthalocyanine textile dye turquoise blue by *Phanerochaete chrysosporium. FEMS Microbiol. Lett.*, 179: 333–337.

Coughlin, M.F., Kinkle, B.K. and P.L. Bishop, 1999. Degradation of azo-dyes containing aminonaphthol by *Spingomonas* sp. strain ICX. *Indian J. Microbiol. Biotechnol.*, 23: 341–346.

Coughlin, M.F., B.K-.Kinkle, K. Tipper and P.L. Bishop, 1997. Characterisation of aerobic azo-dye degrading bacteria and their activity in biofilms. *Water Sci. Tech.*, 36: 215–220.

Cripps, C., J.A. Bumpus and S.D. Aust, 1990 Biodegradation of azoheterocyclic dyes by *Phanerochaete chrysosporium. Appl. Environ. Microbiol.*, 56: 1114–1118.

Donlagic, Jelka and Janez Levec, 2000. Comparison of catalyzed and noncatalyzed oxidation of azo dye and effect on biodegradability. *Environ. Sci. Technol.*, 32: 1294–1302.

Dykes, G.A., Timm, R.G. and Von Holy, A., 1994. Azo reductase activity in bacteria associated with the greening of instant chocolate pudding. *Appl. Environ. Microbiol.*, 60: 3071–3074.

Edwards, Jesscia C., 2000. Investigation of color removal by chemical oxidation for three reactive textile dyes and spent textile dye wastewater. *Masters Thesis*, Virginia Polytechnic Institute and State University, 56 pp.

Emitiazi, G., 2000. Decolorisation and biodegradation of dyes by *Aspergillus terreus* grown on wheat straw with Mn peroxidase activity. *Poll. Res.*, 19: 31–35.

Fitzgerald, Sean W. and Paul L. Bishop, 1995. Two stage aerobic/aerobic treatment of sulfonated azo dyes. *J. Environ. Sci. Health*, 30(6): 1251–1276.

Freeman, Harold S. and Sokolowska, J., 1999. Developments in dyestuff chemistry. *Review of Progress in Coloration and Related Topics*, pp. 29.

Ganesh, R., 1992. Fate of azo dyes in sludges. *Masters Thesis*, Virginia Polytechnic Institute and State University. 193 pp.

Gingell, R. and Walker, R., 1971. Mechanisms of azo reduction by *Streptococcus faecalis* II: The role of soluble flavines. *Xenobiotica*, 1: 231–239.

Glenn, J.K. and Gold, M.H., 1983. Decolorisation of several polymeric dyes by the lignin degrading basidiomycete *Phanerochaete chrysosporium. Appl. Environ. Microbiol.*, 45: 1741–1747.

Glenn, J.K., Akileswara, L. and Gold, M.H., 1986. Mn (II) oxidation is the principal function of the extra cellular Mn peroxid from *Phanerochaete chtysosporium. Arch. Biochem. Biophys.*, 251: 688–696.

Godden, B.A., S. Ball, Helvenstein, P.A., Carthy J. Mc and Penninckx, M.J., 1992. Towards elucidation of the lignin degradation pathway in actinomycetes. *J. Gen. Microbiol.*, 138: 2441–2448.

Grady, C.P.L. Jr., Daigger, G.T., Lim, H.C., 1999. *Biological Wastewater Treatment*. Marcel Dekker, Inc., New York, NY, 1076 pp.

Homing, R.H., 1977. Characterization and treatment of textile dyeing wastewaters. *Textile Chemist and Colorist*, 9(3): 73–76.

IARC, World Health Organization International Agency for Research on Cancer. 1982 Monographs on the Evaluation of the Carcinogenic Risk of Chemicals to Humans. *Some Industrial Chemicals and Dyestuffs*, Vol. 29, Lyon, France. Jager, I., *et al.*, 1996. *Melliand Textilber*, 77: 72.

Idaka, E., Ogawa, T. and Horitsu, H., 1987. Some properties of azo reductase produced by *Pseudomonas*. *Bull. Environ. Contam. Toxicol.*, 39: 982–989.

Jo-Shu Chan, Bor-Yann Chen and Yung Sheng Lin, 2004. Stimulation of bacterial decolorization of an azo dye by extracellular metabolites from *Escherichia coli* strain NO_3. *Biores. Technol.*, 91(3): 243–248.

Kim, S.J. and M. Shoda, 1999. Purification and characterization of a novel peroxidase from *Geotrichum candidum* December 1 involved in decolorisation of dyes. *Appl. Environ. Microbiol.*, 65: 1029–1035.

Kim, S.J., Ishikawa, K., Hirai, M. and Shoda, M., 1995. Characteristics of a newly isolated fungus, *Geotrichum candidum* December 1 which decolorizes various dyes. *J. Fermentation and Bioengineering*, 79: 601–607.

King-thom, Chung, George E. Fulk and Mary Egan, 1978. Reduction of azodyes by intestinal anaerobes. *Appl. Env. Microbiol.*, pp. 558–562.

Knapp, J.S. and Newby, P.S., 1995. Decolourization of dyes by wood rotting basidiomycete fungi. *Water Research*, 29: 1807–1809.

Kumar, K., Saravana Devi, S., Krishnamurthi, K., Gampawar, S. Nilesh Mishra, Pandya G.H. and Chakrabarti, T., 2006. Decolorisation, biodegradation and detoxification of benzidine based azo dye. *Biores. Technol.*, 97(3): 407–413.

Kulla, H.G., Klausner, U. Meyer, B., Ludeke B. and Leisinger, T., 1983. Interference of aromatic sulfo groups in the microbial degradation of the azo dyes Orange I and Orange II. *Arch. Microbiol.*, 135: 1–7.

Kulla, H.G., 1981. Aerobic bacterial degradation of azo dyes in microbial degradation of xenobiotics, recalcitrant compounds, (Eds.) T. Leisinger, A.M. Cook, J. Nuesh and R. Hutter. Academic Press, London, pp. 387–399.

Levine, Walter G., 1991. Metabolism of azo dyes: Implications for detoxification and activation. *Drug Metabolism Reviews*, 23(3–4): 253–309.

Lewis, David M., 1999. Coloration for the next century. *Review of Progress in Coloration and Related Topics*, 29: 23–28.

Longbottorn, J.E. and J.J. Lichtenberg, 1982. *EPA Test Methods*. EPA–600/4–82–057.

Little, L.W.J., Lamd, C., Chillingworth, M.A and Durkin, W.B., 1974. Acute toxicity of selected commercial dyes to the fathead minnow and evolution of biological treatment for reduction of toxicity. In: *Proc. 29th Purdue Ind. Waste Conf.* Ann. Arbor Science, Ann Arbor, Michigan.

Loyd, Chapman K., 1992. Anaerobic/aerobic degradation of a textile dye wastewater. *Masters Thesis*, Virginia Polytechnic Institute and State University, 184 pp.

McCarthy, B.J., 1997. Biotechnology and Coloration. *Review of Progress in Coloration and Related Topics*, 27: 26–31.

McCurdy, Michael W., 1991. Chemical reduction and oxidation combined with biodegradation for the treatment of a textile dye wastewater. *Masters Thesis*, Virginia Polytechnic Institute and State University, pp. 181.

Moosvi, S., Haresh Keharia and Datta Madamwar, 2005. Decolourization of textile dye Reactive Violet 5 by a newly isolated bacterial consortium RVM 11.1. *World J. Microbiol. Biotechnol.*, 21(5): 667–672.

Namasivayam, C. and Yamuna, R.T., 1992. Removal of congored from aqueous solution by biogas waste slurry. *J. Chem. Tech. Biotechnol.*, 53: 153–157.

O'Neil, C., Lopez, A., Estevez, S., Hawkes, F.R., Hawkes, D.L. and Wilcox, S., 2000. Azo-dye degradation in an anaerobic-aerobic treatment system operating on simulated textile effluent. *Appl. Microbiol. Biotech.*, 53: 249–254.

Pagga, U. and Brown, D., 1986. The degradation of dyestuffs, Part II: Behaviour of dyestuffs in aerobic biodegradation tests. *Chemosphere*, 15(4): 479–491.

Pasti-Grigsby, M.B., Burke, N.S., Goszezynski S. and Crawford, D.L., 1996. Transformation of azo dye isomers by *Streptomyces chromofuscus*. *Appl. Environ. Microbiol.*, pp. 1814–1817.

Paszcezynski, A., Pasti-Grigsby, M., Goszceynski, S., Crawford, R. and Crawford, D.L., 1992. Mineralization of sulfonated azo dyes and sulfanilic acid by *Phanerochaete chxysosporium* and *Streptomyces chromofuscus*. *Appl. Environ. Microbiol.*, 58: 3598–3604.

Pradeep Verma and Datta Madamwas, 2005. Decolorization of azo dyes using Basidiomycete strain PV 002. *World J. Microbiol. Biotechnol.*, 21(4): 1573.

Ramachandra, M., Crawford, B.L. and Hertel, G., 1988. Characterization of extra cellular lignin peroxidase of the lignocellulose actinomycetes *Streptomyces viridosporus*. *Appl. Environ. Microbiol.*, 54: 3057–3063.

Razo-F1ores, E., Luijten, M., Donlon, B., Lettinga, G. and Field, J., 1997. Biodegradation of selected azo dyes under methanogenic conditions. *Water Sci. Technol.*, 36(6–7): 65–72.

Rehn, L., 1895. Blasengeschwulste bei Fuchsin Arbeitem. *Arch. Klin. Chir.*, 50: 588.

Saranaik, S. and Kanekar, P., 1995. Bioremediation of colour of methyl violet and phenol from a dye industry waste emuent using *Pseudomonas* sp. isolated from factory soil. *J. Appl. Bacteriol.*, 79: 459–469.

Seshadri, S., Bishop, P.L. and Agha, A.M.1994. Anaerobic/aerobic treatment of selected azo dyes in wastewater. *Waste Management*, 14(2): 127–137.

Shaul, Glenn M., Holdsworth, T.J., Dempsey, C.R. and Dostal, K.A., 1991. Soluble azo dyes in activated sludge process. *Chemosphere*, 2(1–2): 107–119.

Spadaro, J.T., Gold, M.T. and Renganathan, V., 1992. Degradation of azo dye by the lignin degrading fungus *Phanerochaete chtysosporium*. *Appl. Environ. Microbiol.*, 58: 2391–2401.

Sudhakar, P., Palaniappan, R. and Gowrishankar, R., 2002. Degradation of azo dye (Blach E) by an indigenous bacterium *Pseudomonas* sp. BSP-4. *Indian J. Microbiol. Biotech. Env. Sci.*, 4: 203–208.

Venkata Mohan, S., Charidrasakar Rao, N. and Krishna Prasad, K., 2002. Biological decolorisation of stimulated basic dye effluents by algal Spirogyra species. *Asian J. Microbiol. Biotech. Env. Sci.*, 4: 107–111.

Vijaya, P., Padmavathy, P. and Sandiya, S., 2003. Decolourisation and biodegradation of reactive azodyes by mixed culture. *Indian J. Biotech.*, 2: 259–263.

Vyas, B.R. and Molitoris, H.P., 1995. Involvement of an extracellular H_2O_2-dependent lignolytic activity of the white-rot fungus, *Pleurotus ostreatus* in the decolorization of Remazol Brilliant Blue R. *Appl. Environ. Microbiol.*, 61: 3919–3927.

Weber, Eric J. and Lee Wolfe, N., 1987. Kinetic studies of the reduction of aromatic azo compounds in anaerobic sediment/water systems. *Environmental Toxicology and Chemistry*, 6: 911–919.

Willmott, N., Guthrie, J. and Nelson, G., 1998. The biotechnology approach to colour removal from textile effluent. JSDC, 114: 38–41.

Wong, P.K. and Yuen, P.Y., 1996. Decolourization and biodegradation methyl red by *Klebsiella pneumomae* RS-13. *Water Research*, 36: 1744–1746.

Yamini, R. and Lalithakumari, D., 2001. Aerobic treatment of textile mill effluent and decolorisation of commercial azo dyes. *Asian J. Microbiol. Biotech. Env. Sci.*, 3: 353–358.

Yang, Y., Wyatt, D.T. II and Bahorshky, M., 1998. Decolorization of dyes using UV/H_2O_2 photochemical oxidation. *Textile Chemist and Colorist*, 30: 27–35.

Yatome, C., Matsufuru, H., Taguchi, T. and Ogawa, T., 1993. Degradation of 4-dimethylamino azobenzene-2-carboxylic acid by *Pseudomonas stuzeri*. *Appl. Microbiol. Biotechnol.*, 39: 778–781.

Zimmermann, H., Kulla, H.G. and Leisinger, T., 1982. Properties of purified orange li azo reductase enzyme initiating azo dye degradation by *Pseudomonas* KF46. *Env. J. Biochem.*, 129: 197–203.

Zissi, U. and Lyberatos, G., 1996. Azo-dye biodegradation under anoxic conditions. *Wat. Sci. Tech.*, 34(5–6): 495–500.

Zissi, U., G. Lyberatos and S. Pavlous, 1997. Biodegradation of p-aminobenzene by *Bacillus subtilis* under aerobic conditions. *J. Industrial Microbiol. Biotechnol.*, 19: 49–55.

Zollinger, H., 1961. *Azo and Diazo Chemistry Aliphatic and Aromatic Compounds*. Interscience Publishers, New York, London.

Zollinger, H., 1987. *Colour Chemistry: Synthesis Properties and Applications for Organic Dyes and Pigments*, pp. 92–102. VCH Publishers, Inc., New York,

Zollinger, Heinrich, 1991. *Color Chemistry: Syntheses, Properties and Applications of Organic Dyes and Pigments*. 496 pp.

Chapter 32

Groundwater Quality of Bhadravathi Town, Karnataka State

Vijaya Kumara, J. Narayana, K. Harish Babu, Devidas Kamath and E.T. Puttaiah

Department of PG Studies and Research in Environmental Science, Kuvempu University, Shankaraghatta – 577 451, Karnataka

ABSTRACT

A hydro chemical study of the groundwater of Bhadravathi town, Karnataka state, India has been carried out to examine the suitability of water for drinking purposes. Water samples representing the groundwater of the region were collected during pre-monsoon and post-monsoon seasons during the years 2000–2001 and 2001–2002 respectively. A total of 46 water samples collected from different sites of the town were analysed for water quality parameters. The data was analysed with reference to BIS and WHO standards. Ionic relationships were studied. The results of the study provide information needed for groundwater quality management in the region.

Keywords: *Groundwater quality, Bhadravathi town, Physico chemical parameters, Correlation, E. coli.*

Introduction

Water is the life blood of every living creature on earth. Through the wonders of nature, water can take many forms. It is easy to understand the significance of surface water that plays in our lives but it may be difficult to understand the water that exists below the earth's surface. Fresh water, for human consumption is a fragile and finite resource. It is vital for many aspects of economic and social development, for agriculture, energy production, domestic, industrial supply and. is a critical component of global environment (Jain *et al.*, 2000). Hydrosphere is the most important factor for the life on earth and its sustainable development. Good quality of water is inadequate even for the normal living and is getting polluted due to industrial discharge including those of paper, textile, pesticides, fertilizers, detergents, oil refineries and photo films. A perusal of the available literature on the groundwater quality assessment, has revealed that, no scientific investigation has been carried out in respect of groundwater source of Bhadravathi town. It is with this background, the present work was taken up.

Materials and Methods

Study Area

Bhadravathi city is a taluk headquarters, situated about 16 kms from Shimoga district, Karnataka state (South India). Bhadravathi is the removed center of industries had a population of 1,63,784. There are 25 major and minor industries situated in the vicinity. The Mysore Paper Milk and Visweswaraya Iron and Steel Limited are the major industries and minor industries cover manufacturing units like rice mills, oil mills, cement pipes, chemicals, machinery parts and poultry farms. The geographical location of Bhadravathi city lies between the latitude of 13°49' to 13°54' north and longitude of 75°40' to 75°45' east m about mid southwestern part of the Karnataka state (Figure 32.1). It is situated at an altitude of 581.55 meters above Mean Sea Level (MSL) and the city covers an area of 67.08 sq. km. The average rainfall of the area is 1029 mm and Temperature varies from 8.9 to 40 °C. Geologically the study area consists of schists and gneisses of Archaean age and forms a part of Dhaewar super group.

Sampling locations in Bhadravathi town have been made using random grid or spatial network method on the basis of geographical ground map of Bhadravathi town. The ground map has been divided into 2 segments and m each segment an average of 23 samples from 23 different localities have been selected so that 46 water samples from 46 localities were collected (Table 32.1). Water samples from different locations were collected as per the guidelines of random sample technique. Borewells fitted with motors for water lifting were allowed to run the water for 5 minutes and the other fitted with hand pump were allowed to run 15 minutes in order to flush out stationary water. As soon as the collection of water, temperature and pH were measured immediately. The physico-chemical analysis were made adopting the standard methods (APHA, 1995)

Results and Discussion

The objective of present study was to assess the quality of fresh water in the study area with respect to physico-chemical parameters, to classify the groundwater on the basis of hydrochemical parameters in order to determine the suitability of water for various uses and to study the statistical correlation analysis and its interpretation, in order to evaluate quality of groundwater.

Colour (Col)

Generally the colour of water is due to degradation of organic matter and oxidation of divalent metal ion species such as Fe^{2+} and Mn^{2+} as were as untreated wastewater percolation or seepage (Sawyer, 1978; APHA, 1985 and Kotaiah, 1994). In the present investigation colour values varied from a minimum of 0 to a maximum of 100 Hazen units in pre-monsoon season (Table 32.3) and minimum of 5 to a maximum of 100 Hazen units in post-monsoon season (Table 32.2). The HIS acceptable limit for colour is 25 Hazen units. In the present study 26 per cent water samples in post-monsoon season and 17.4 per cent water samples in pre-monsoon season cross the BIS (1998) acceptable limit for

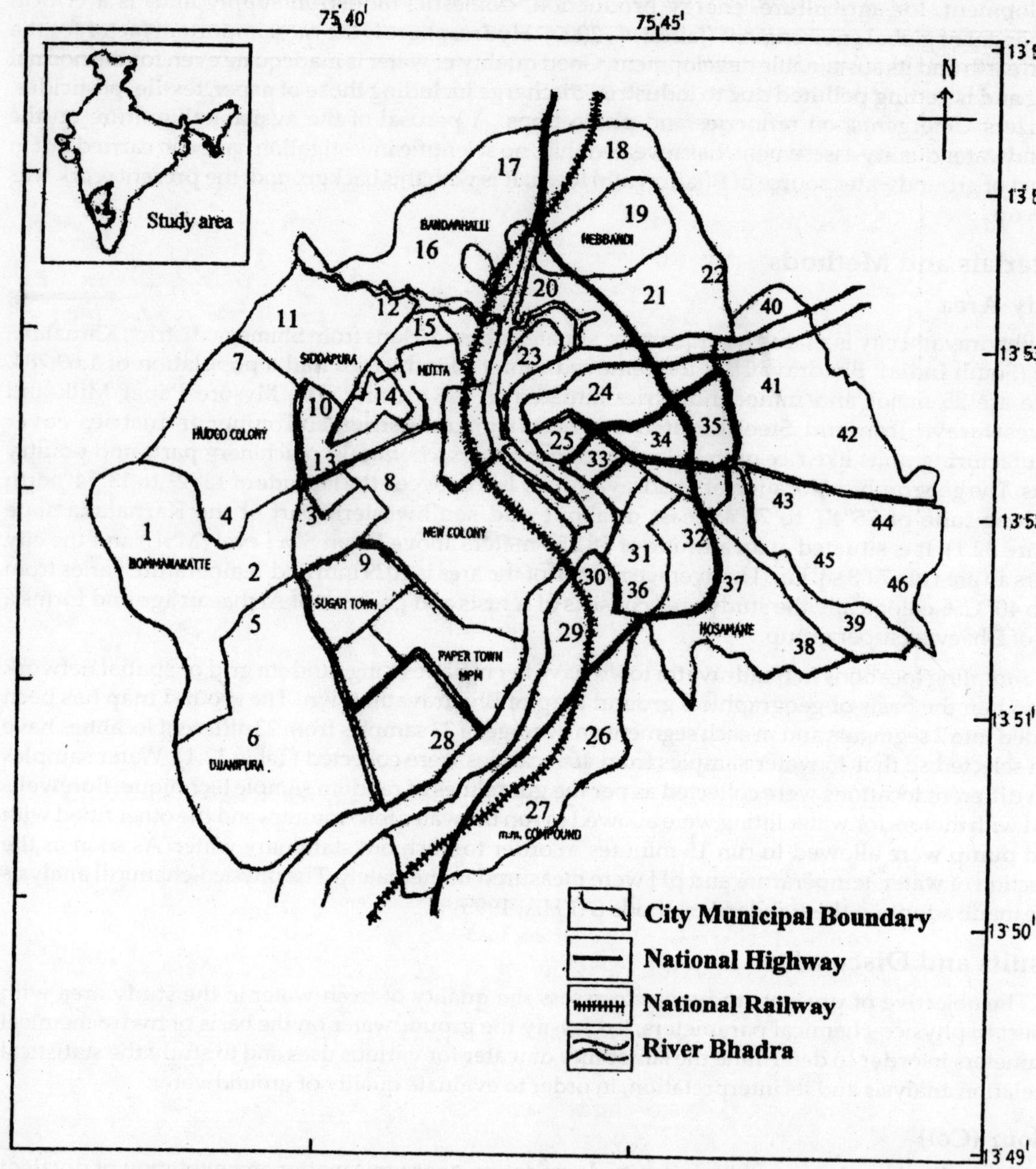

Figure 32.1: Map Showing Groundwater Sampling Locations in Bhadravathi Town

drinking water. Further, the colour has established a positive highly significant correlation with turbidity and iron in both pre and post-monsoon seasons (Tables 32.4 and 32.5). This is in agreement with the findings of Halck *et al.* (1963) and Kotaiah (1994), who made similar observation in their studies.

Table 32.1: Groundwater Sampling Locations of Bhadravathi Town

Sl.No.	Sample No.	Location	Depth of the Borewell in Feet
1.	B1	Bommanakatte, near Baptist Church	225
2.	B2	Bommanakatte, near Bommanakatte pond	180
3.	B3	Cooli block shed, near public toilet	231
4.	B4	Cooli block shed, Slum area, near Vinayaka Balasubramanya temple	250
5.	B5	Coli block, opposite to masjid	281
6.	B6	Ralappa shed, opposite to Manasa fancy center	231
7.	B7	Ganesha colony, opposite to Inchara beauty parlor	287
8.	B8	Jannapura, opposite to Jayashree Kalyana mantapa	293
9.	B9	Jannapura, beside Sridevi nilaya	290
10.	B10	Jannapura, near Karnataka dwaja sthamba	291
11.	B11	Kuvempu Badavane, Jannapura, opposite to Malleswara plastic stores	257
12.	B12	Rosa Siddapura, 8th cross	188
13.	B13	Zinc line, near public toilet and solid waste dumping site	175
14.	B14	Zinc line, slum area, opposite to Sapthagiri nivas	231
15.	B15	Caval gundi, opposite to Keshava nilaya	254
16.	B16	Bandarahathi, beside Shakthi nivas	265
17.	B17	Bandarahathi, opposite to Anganawadi Kendra	241
18.	B18	Kadada Katte, opposite to Nava chetana kannada school	255
19.	B19	Hebbandi Road	245
20.	B20	Caval gundi, opposite to ITI	235
21.	B21	Caval gundi, opposite of Narayanappa stores	268
22.	B22	Bhadravathi, Near bus stand, opposite to Shankara service station	281
23.	B23	Lower hutta, near Tirumala temple	245
24.	B24	Halappa circle, near Shankar film theater	276
25.	B25	Halappa circle, opposite to Viswa Swarupini Mariyamma Temple	282
26.	B26	Nehru Nagar, after railway gate, Tarikere road	255
27.	B27	Nehru Nagar, Tarikere road	268
28.	B28	M.M. compound, Tarikere road	245
29.	B29	Madavanagar, near Agricultural field	256
30.	B30	Bhutanagudi, old town, opposite to Shaneswara devalaya	275
31.	B31	Old town, opposite to Venkateswara nilaya	198
32.	B32	Bhutanagudi, opposite to Venkateswara nilaya	231
33.	B33	Bhutanagudi, near Kiran house	225
34.	B34	Basaweswara circle, OSM road, old town	254
35.	B35	Madavachar Circle, opposite to telephone exchange office	281
36.	B36	Old town, opposite to police station	264

Contd...

Table 32.1–Contd...

Sl.No.	Sample No.	Location	Depth of the Borewell in Feet
37.	B37	Bhrahmanara beedi, opposite to Srinivasa vanijya shale	253
38.	B38	Haladammaa beedi, near Grama devate temple	275
39.	B39	Hosamane, near Harish house	285
40.	B40	Gowdarahalli, oposite to bus stand	265
41.	B41	Gowdarahalli, near agricultural field	231
42.	B42	Hale Seegebagi, opposite to Hindu rudrabhoomi	241
43.	B43	Hale Seegebagi, near Laxmi samil	238
44.	B44	Azad nagar, near Budan Shab house	265
45.	B45	Anwar colony, near Urdu residency school	245
46.	B46	Anwar colony, near masjid	264

Turbidity (Tur)

Most of the suspended matter which may be colloidal or coarse size like clay, silt, organic matter and hydrolyzed metals, together with phytoplankton are responsible for turbidity in water (Knight, 1951). The values of turbidity ranged between 0.1 to 73.45 NTU in post-monsoon season (Table 32.2) and 0.05 to 47.3 NTU in pre-monsoon season (Table 32.3). Further, it is observed that the turbidity values of water samples during post- monsoon season have indicated an increasing trend when compared to pre-monsoon season. However except 3 samples most of the water samples in the present investigation are well within the safe limit of drinking water standards (25 NTU). Turbidity has indicated a significant positive correlation with iron in both pre and post-monsoon seasons (Tables 32.4 and 32.5). Nevertheless, most of other parameter shows insignificant correlation with turbidity.

pH

pH is one of the important parameters of water whose determination facilitates a quick evaluation of acidic or alkaline nature of water. In the present investigation, pH values varied from a minimum of 6.9 to a maximum of 8.35 with a mean value of 7.43 in post-monsoon season (Table 32.2). In pre-monsoon season it ranged between 6.6 to 8.25 with a mean value of 7.25 (Table 32.3). It indicates that the waters under study are alkaline in nature. The recommended value of pH for drinking purposes is between 6.5–8.5 (BIS, 1998). In the present study all the water samples analyzed are all well with in the safer limits. As has been reported here, the water quality of most of the groundwater resources has been found to be alkaline except on a few occasion as per the studies made by Somashekara Rao, 1989 and 1993; Narayana and Suresh, 1989; Govardan, 1990; Gill *et al.*, 1993; Mehta and Trivedi, 1993 and Mittal *et al.*, 1994. pH shows positive correlation with nitrate in pre-monsoon season and with sulfate and potassium in post-monsoon season. However, other parameters studied have exhibited an inverse relationship with pH (Tables 32.4 and 32.5). Observations of present study are in total agreement with the findings of Narayana and Suresh (1989).

Electrical Conductivity (EC)

In the present study, the values of EC ranged between 460–1480 μmhos/cm in pre-monsoon season (Table 32.3) and 456–1566 μmhos/cm in post-monsoon season (Table 32.2). It is observed that the EC values have exhibited an increasing trend in post-monsoon seasons owing to the fact that

Table 32.2: Water Quality Data (Average Values) of Bhadravathi Town During Post-monsoon Season for the Year 2000–2001

Sl.No.	Col.	pH	Tur	EC	TDS	TH	DO	COD	Ca^{2+}	Mg^{2+}	Na^{+}	K^{+}	Cl^{-}	HCO_3^{+}	SO_4^{2-}	NO_3^{-}	PO_4^{-}	F^{-}	E. coli
B1	75	7.10	37.55	1084	650	328	4.15	7.85	93.47	65	75.60	21.10	317	280	204	5.55	0.01	0.585	–
B2	32.50	7.15	4	1057	634	292	3.55	7	99.90	54.27	27.40	18	344	287	112	26.50	0.17	0.265	–
B3	50	7.35	6.30	916	550	306	3.50	3.25	77.90	43.39	32.05	13.20	244	287	123	3.40	0.03	0.86	–
B4	100	7.50	16.55	640	384	251	3.65	2.85	69.60	42.80	54.95	12.75	114	389	86.75	2.70	0.03	0.395	–
B5	7.50	7.20	3.90	1116	670	462	4.05	5.10	113	70.43	55.05	9.20	200	272	70	0.75	0.035	0.28	10
B6	75	7.20	38.90	789	474	364	4.40	11	125	41.78	56.45	12.85	109	407	82.50	1.05	0.015	0.345	25
B7	5	6.95	0.10	1131	679	450	3.85	12.50	124	63	70.55	16.45	228	520	89	4.50	0.01	0.515	–
B8	2.50	6.90	0.30	1016	610	379	3.70	10.15	131	62.80	116	30.05	223	627	111	3.60	0.125	0.38	–
B9	37.50	8.35	3.20	775	465	320	3.90	14.10	100	51.47	13.90	9.05	107	344	258	3.65	0.02	0.265	–
B10	5	7.40	0.55	535	321	195	4.20	6.10	58.10	25.11	58.30	4.35	108	507	312	6	0.01	0.385	–
B11	5	6.95	0.15	764	459	318	2.95	5.70	66.60	50.43	20.60	4.85	117	422	72.35	2	0.015	0.405	–
B12	2.50	7.25	0.30	787	472	327	4.35	11.70	93.15	80.15	13.75	1.80	121	406	42.50	37.50	0.225	0.60	–
B13	2.50	7.25	0.20	854	512	313	5.35	12.30	49.23	37.14	14.40	3.45	195	264	57.30	50	0.125	0.74	–
B14	2.50	7.25	0.10	907	544	346	5.90	11.55	116	43.21	55.90	6.66	171	467	163	23.50	0.135	0.61	–
B15	10	6.95	2.50	1237	742	465	3.30	11.80	161	64.56	62.30	11.80	245	690	163	23.25	0.15	0.80	–
B16	7.50	8.10	1.65	921	553	364	3.30	9.25	120	63.66	33.65	12.20	171	387	114	5.75	0.045	0.83	–
B17	5	7.50	0.60	1042	625	416	2.90	12.25	126	50.15	60.65	15.30	187	264	109	46.75	0.315	0.91	–
B18	7.50	7.36	0.20	1195	717	495	3.50	7.50	107	78.84	60.70	16.80	202	302	123	4.60	0.135	0.385	–
B19	5	7.45	0.25	970	582	412	4.45	6.80	111	54.91	55.90	11.16	167	267	69.50	12.75	0.01	0.426	–
B20	7.50	7.40	0.70	989	594	360	4.75	5.65	91.98	49.22	49.15	10.76	204	172	90.80	6	0.055	0.435	–
B21	12.50	7.25	2	811	487	309	4.30	3.40	74.90	47.68	32.80	5.30	160	365	96.20	3.35	0.01	0.56	–
B22	12.50	8.25	1.76	602	361	287	3.62	8.05	152	44.38	14.15	43	85.55	272	111	31.80	0.27	0.425	–
B23	5	7.20	0.20	585	351	209	2.90	6.25	60.20	29.15	19.30	3.70	83.40	387	154	45.45	1.7	0.36	–
B24	2.50	7.20	0.10	702	421	320	5.Z5	7.25	70	48.04	13.65	2.30	67.84	362	72.80	2.70	0.145	0.575	–
B25	2.50	7.40	0.15	774	464	372	3.70	4	63.50	66.33	25.30	6.15	81.18	475	80.30	2.15	0.035	0.575	–

Contd...

Table 32.2–Contd...

Sl.No.	Col.	pH	Tur	EC	TDS	TH	DO	COD	Ca^{2+}	Mg^{2+}	Na^{+}	K^{+}	Cl^{-}	HCO_3^{+}	SO_4^{2-}	NO_3^{-}	PO_4^{-}	F^{-}	*E. coli*
B26	32.50	7.10	0.70	1076	646	442	4.35	3	87.68	71.66	50.80	5.40	208	387	67.50	0.95	0.075	0.91	–
B27	15	7.95	2.50	1073	644	425	5.10	3.25	50.65	85.12	67.80	6.70	154	367	92.05	1.70	0.025	0.33	–
B28	5	7.30	0.15	949	569	383	3.85	6.40	70.21	63.60	35.30	7.50	149	362	82.30	2.16	0.015	0.285	–
B29	12.50	7.70	1.06	456	274	201	3.55	4.45	45.05	29.70	64.95	8.30	54.16	215	96.10	33	0.145	0.615	–
B30	100	7.35	73.75	874	525	233	5.35	6.50	33.37	43.51	43.40	11.60	57.67	282	117	3.85	0.025	0.80	–
B31	10	7.55	1.30	1006	604	463	2.90	11.90	122	61.41	35.30	4.20	195	257	154	6	0.01	0.76	–
B32	5	7.40	0.20	807	489	346	3.40	8.90	52.50	64.10	44.80	12.40	158	387	171	8.50	0.03	0.90	–
B33	45	7.50	9	1037	622	531	3.40	7	52.70	95.64	60.20	17.50	172	297	232	12.80	0.795	0.59	–
B34	20	7.95	3.90	986	592	382	4	10.90	80.51	61.31	41.90	13.80	205	364	302	11	0.045	0.585	–
B35	0.25	8.25	0.10	1024	615	431	4.10	6.95	60.28	98.33	38.30	16.10	183	327	280	42.50	0.70	0.515	–
B36	0.25	7.20	0.10	1566	940	752	3.70	6.55	127	113	60.80	12.40	205	562	101	5.65	0	0.52	–
B37	0.50	7.65	2.55	1012	607	472	3.60	7.45	92.09	74.37	70.30	13	140	457	70.15	13	0.055	0.59	–
B38	50	7.40	13.40	989	593	458	2.85	12	67.38	88.50	114	15.30	169	337	80.10	12.85	0.11	0.445	–
B39	32.50	7.50	9.40	904	543	342	3.25	5.30	116	32.25	13	13	207	427	77.35	14.8	0.10	0.575	–
B40	12.50	7.40	3.55	971	583	357	4.30	6.95	69.06	58.74	13.80	11	102	272	86.45	5.70	0.015	0.59	–
B41	10	7.05	0.55	608	365	286	4.20	7.65	56.84	47.64	26.50	8.35	65.58	280	69.15	5.65	0.01	0.56	–
B42	2.50	7	0.45	631	379	290	3.70	7.10	57.30	47.18	34.95	10.65	75.70	262	140	6.35	0.01	0.685	–
B43	5	7.45	0.40	601	361	210	5.90	11	87.40	19.67	46.35	12.75	122	252	58.70	31.10	0.03	1.07	–
B44	32.50	7.45	3.15	711	425	299	3.85	5.25	117	49.67	35.75	14	127	347	43.85	45.10	0.225	0.63	–
B45	50	7.90	19.16	976	586	379	3.55	5.60	130	64.55	34.85	5.55	175	376	38.95	2.65	0.055	0.47	–
B46	25	8.25	10.16	811	487	342	4.15	8.20	100	40.34	70	19.65	152	262	80.40	3.10	0.105	0.71	–
Min	5	6.90	0.10	456	274	195	2.85	2.85	33.37	19.67	13	2.30	54.16	172	38.95	0.75	0	0.265	10
Max	100	8.35	73.75	1566	940	752	5.90	12.50	152	113	116	30.05	344	690	312	46.75	1.70	1.07	25
Mean	20.56	7.43	6.02	897	408	362	3.96	7.73	89.98	57.36	45.56	11.77	159	359	115	13.55	0.139	0.566	–
SD	25.65	0.37	13.26	211	137	100	0:"75	2.99	31.08	19.60	23.95	7.28	64	106	69	14.70	0.284	0.195	–

Note: All parameters are expressed in mg/l (ppm) except pH, colour (Hazen units), Turbidity (NTU) and conductivity (μmohs/cm).

Table 32.3: Groundwater Quality Data (Average Values) of Bhadravathi Town During Pre-monsoon Season for the Year 2001–2002

Sl.No.	Col.	pH	Tur	EC	TDS	TH	DO	COD	Ca^{2+}	Mg^{2+}	Na^+	K^+	Cl^-	HCO_3^+	SO_4^{2-}	NO_3^-	PO_4^-	F^-	E. coli
B1	32.50	7	11.25	1064	638	307	3.50	7	92.50	52.40	60.65	11.50	291	207	160	5.75	0.05	0.50	–
B2	12.50	7.25	2.95	954	572	278	3	5.75	78.85	48.51	27.70	7.45	315	299	102	17.50	0.12	0.35	–
B3	50	7.55	5.10	774	464	287	3.55	2.40	62.60	54.65	30.80	12.80	212	303	123	7.50	0.001	0.74	–
B4	100	7.05	47.30	622	373	239	3.65	2.95	67	41.79	26.80	5.40	113	355	95.90	3.45	0.056	0.29	–
B5	5	7.15	0.10	986	591	402	4.35	3.80	73	80.06	37	16.35	170	258	67	0.65	0.01	0.245	10
B6	45	6.90	21.25	863	518	357	4.35	14	123	56.86	34.95	11.50	126	394	79	1.40	0.065	0.325	25
B7	2.50	7.25	0.15	1124	674	421	3.90	13	116	74.23	63.30	7.75	226	492	87	3	0.005	0.57	–
B8	5	6.95	0.30	960	576	366	3.40	9.85	158	50.60	113	37.25	202	632	102	3	0.08	0.475	–
B9	25	7.25	1.65	851	510	361	4.15	11	99.60	63.64	12.45	12	113	336	173	3.85	0.015	0.32	–
B10	5	7.15	0.80	580	348	227	3.85	5.90	47.25	43.64	36.30	2	107	515	246	6.55	0.005	0.34	–
B11	5	6.70	0.30	687	412	312	2.70	5.25	114	48.23	25.85	7.75	99.60	407	69.50	1	0.005	0.56	–
B12	5	7.15	0.40	734	441	341	6.40	15	118	54.18	13	12.50	112	362	23.60	40	0.155	0.57	–
B13	2.50	7.15	0.15	972	584	311	3.50	12	96.75	52.06	14.40	1.25	167	247	47.30	51.50	0.095	0.68	–
B14	7.50	7.55	0.15	915	549	324	6.35	16	71.80	61.40	43.20	1.65	261	437	157	15.75	0.095	0.43	–
B15	5	7.55	0.25	1144	686	404	4.35	14	112	70.77	35.30	2.40	231	637	123	21.90	0.10	0.605	–
B16	5	7.25	0.25	881	529	358	3.40	9.10	126	56.37	44.15	3.60	199	322	107	0.50	0.10	0.87	–
B17	5	7.15	0.50	1004	603	404	3.70	4	123	68.23	30.50	5.45	194	262	102	51	0.32	0.90	–
B18	5	6.95	0.10	1110	666	437	3.85	6.40	103	81.11	60.30	5.05	172	302	118	30.50	0.06	0.30	–
B19	5	6.85	0.25	801	481	381	3.55	5.45	101	68.15	31.80	4.05	204	255	86.50	2	0.30	0.51	–
B20	32.50	7.20	5.45	836	502	352	3.95	4.85	86.90	64.28	26.10	4.25	176	168	90.25	1.25	0.075	0.52	–
B21	12.50	7.15	4.05	782	469	299	4.05	4.20	75.65	59.25	27	7	146	314	86.40	3.40	0.01	0.67	–
B22	5	6.95	1.50	611	367	281	3.60	8.25	108	40.54	7.85	3.40	70.80	305	96.40	30.40	0.05	0.40	–
B23	0	8.10	0.25	537	322	261	3.40	5.45	129	31.95	15.30	2.80	67.65	380	110	66.50	0.36	0.445	–
B24	0	7,20	0.10	699	420	319	5.75	6.35	69.50	60.74	16	1.45	70.95	359	66.80	0.60	0.275	0.65	–
B25	7.50	7.15	0.95	762	457	331	3.85	2.50	82.15	60.58	25.60	5	82	435	73.80	1.50	1.175	0.615	–

Contd...

Table 32.3–Contd...

Sl.No.	Col.	pH	Tur	EC	TDS	TH	DO	COD	Ca^{2+}	Mg^{2+}	Na^+	K^+	Cl^-	HCO_3^+	SO_4^{2-}	NO_3^-	PO_4^-	F^-	E. coli
B26	15	6.95	0.20	1148	689	419	3.95	3.15	57	87.96	44.30	11.30	216	366	67.35	1	0.02	0.50	–
B27	5	7.15	1.50	1058	635	408	3.85	3.45	191	52.66	80.30	14	174	364	87.80	2.75	0.085	0.46	–
B28	2.50	8.50	0.60	916	550	382	4.15	6.50	73	75.07	36.30	6.50	171	364	52.80	11.50	0.015	0.33	–
B29	10	7.20	4.45	460	276	204	3.40	4.40	73	31.82	46.15	5.85	40.40	188	29.30	43.15	0.01	0.65	–
B30	47.50	7.30	27.75	901	541	270	5.05	5.65	45.40	54.66	43.45	10.30	57.90	266	106	8.80	0.01	0.15	–
B31	5	7.10	3.15	1004	602	505	3.20	10	120	93.51	37.30	3.25	193	267	92.65	6	0.02	0.75	–
B32	15	7.20	0.08	812	487	329	2.75	5.65	54.95	66.59	48	9.50	140	375	99	3	0.01	0.9	–
B33	22.50	7.30	0.10	1070	642	479	3.85	5.80	65	100	41.20	10.50	159	317	193	6.85	0.025	0.59	–
B34	12.50	7.25	1.25	926	556	317	3.65	14	70.30	60.06	40.70	1	202	347	219	7.70	0.005	0.34	–
B35	2.25	8.10	5	1021	613	404	4.55	5.75	63.80	82.66	32.50	15	177	331	241	52	0.41	0.61	–
B36	7.50	7	0.68	1480	888	652	3.90	4.90	179	114	47.50	12.20	204	550	116	6.70	0.05	0.595	–
B37	5	7.25	0.40	1049	630	450	3.70	6	117	80.85	76.30	6.50	135	454	75.35	11.50	0.10	0.45	–
B38	40	7.25	16.80	999	599	405	3.35	17	69.50	81.60	117	52.50	159	317	108	12.60	0.01	0.47	–
B39	25	7.35	9.50	883	530	336	3.55	5.25	129	50.06	1.20	0.70	187	400	66.40	10.30	0.25	0.54	–
B40	5	7.25	1.60	947	568	315	4.55	6.65	66.10	60,47	15.30	1.85	96.30	256	97.15	6.85	0.15	0.55	–
B41	5	7	0.10	595	357	290	4.25	8.05	66.20	54.38	25.50	8.65	50.40	259	58.25	3.65	0.01	0.63	–
B42	5	7.05	0.15	602	361	270	3.85	5.45	53.90	52.50	26	6.15	66.20	236	122	5.40	0.01	0.68	–
B43	0.25	6.95	0.10	562	337	215	3.75	5.35	60	38.27	26.50	10	123	259	69	32.65	0.05	1.11	–
B44	22.50	7.20	2.70	683	410	330	3.65	6.35	63.80	64.80	39.20	12.10	112	307	110	42.70	0.10	0.55	–
B45	40	7.65	11.95	944	566	373	3.65	3.6	136	57.46	33.40	4.35	147	352	46.70	1.70	0.05	0.64	–
B46	17.50	8.25	2.85	816	490	330	3.55	8.7	104	54.69	75.95	15.30	140	261	26.70	3.25	0.01	0.73	–
Min	0	6.70	0.05	460	276	204	2.70	2.4	45.40	31.82	1.20	0.70	40.40	168	23.60	0.50	0.001	0.245	10
Max	100	8.25	47.30	1480	888	652	6.40	17	191	114	117	37.25	315	632	246	66.5	1.175	1.11	25
Mean	15.50	7.25	4.26	872	523	349	3.91	7.41	93.50	62.16	38.99	8.89	154.2	344	101	14.14	0.109	0.558	–
SD	18.70	0.36	8.72	200	120	81.44	0.75	4	34.04	17.16	23.89	9.02	63	102	50.26	17.34	0.19	0.182	–

Note: All parameters are expressed in mg/l (ppm) except pH, colour (Hazen units), Turbidity (NTU) and conductivity (μmohs/cm).

Table 32.4: Correlation Matrix Between Different Physico-chemical Parameters During Post-monsoon Season for the Year 2000–2001

Sl.No.	Col.	pH	Tur	EC	TDS	TH	DO	COD	Ca^{2+}	Mg^{2+}	Na^{+}	K^{+}	Cl^{-}	HCO_3^{+}	SO_4^{2-}	NO_3^{-}	PO_4^{-}	F^{-}	Fe^{2+}
Col.	1																		
pH	0.051	1																	
Tur	**0.826**	–0.024	1																
EC	–0.045	–0.133	0.013	1															
TDS	–0.046	–0.133	0.012	**0.999**	1														
TH	–0.046	–0.037	–0.170	**0.869**	**0.869**	1													
DO	0.003	–0.036	0.183	–0.129	–0.129	**–0.238**	1												
COD	–0.169	0.036	–0.040	0.114	0.114	0.120	0.033	1											
Ca^{2+}	–0.101	0.036	–0.122	**0.411**	**0.410**	0.120	**–0.217**	0.356	1										
Mg^{2+}	–0.096	0.056	–0.095	**0.733**	**0.734**	**0.838**	**–0.231**	0.008	0.092	1									
Na^{+}	0.136	–0.141	0.141	**0.362**	**0.362**	**0.352**	–0.089	0.128	0.150	**0.306**	1								
K^{+}	0.148	**0.234**	0.115	0.129	0.128	0.095	–0.208	0.135	**0.414**	0.092	**0.334**	1							
Cl^{-}	0.047	–0.174	–0.060	**0.708**	**0.708**	**0.419**	–0.166	0.127	**0.417**	**0.327**	**0.308**	**0.247**	1						
HCO_3^{-}	–0.153	–0.301	–0.125	**0.285**	**0.285**	**0.303**	–0.158	0.135	**0.343**	**0.235**	**0.258**	–0.022	0.133	1					
SO_4^{-2}	0.015	**0.281**	0.003	0.023	0.024	–0.01	–0.108	**0.208**	–0.151	0.091	0.057	0.113	0.136	0.101	1				
NO_3^{-}	–0.252	0.106	–0.227	**–0.210**	**–0.211**	–0.223	0.007	0.276	0.038	–0.174	**–0.197**	0.075	–0.020	–0.148	0.013	1			
PO_4^{-}	–0.102	0.063	–0.114	–0.140	–0.140	–0.087	**–0.246**	–0.026	–0.144	0.012	–0.127	0.022	–0.107	–0.024	**0.241**	**0.545**	1		
F^{-}	–0.040	–0.028	0.039	–0.038	–0.037	–9.064	0.133	0.163	–0.038	–0.154	–0.053	–0.078	0.009	–0.108	–0.074	**0.213**	–0.108	1	
F^{2+}	**0.356**	–0.152	**0.249**	**0.194**	**0.194**	–0.063	0.133	–0.110	0.080	0.075	0.048	0.027	**0.462**	0.121	–0.041	–0.076	**–0.211**	–0.068	1

Note: Bolded values shows significant correlation.

Table 32.5: Correlation Matrix Between Different Physico-chemical Parameters During Pre-monsoon Season for the Year 2001–2002

Sl.No.	*Col.*	*pH*	*Tur*	*EC*	*TDS*	*TH*	*DO*	*COD*	*Ca^{2+}*	*Mg^{2+}*	*Na^+*	*K^+*	*Cl^-*	*HCO_3^+*	*SO_4^{2-}*	*NO_3^-*	*PO_4^-*	*F^-*	*Fe^{2+}*
Col.	1																		
pH	−0.041	1																	
Tur	**0.898**	−0.051	1																
EC	−0.074	0.023	−0.101	1															
TDS	−0.074	0.023	−0.101	**0.999**	1														
TH	−0.182	−0.007	**−0.223**	**0.840**	**0.840**	1													
DO	−0.083	0.134	0.002	0.026	0.026	0.005	1												
COD	−0.100	0.029	−0.046	0.163	0.162	0.111	**0.325**	1											
Ca^{2+}	−0.184	−0.066	−0.139	**0.398**	**0.398**	**0.502**	−0.150	0.095	1										
Mg^{2+}	−0.122	0.021	−0.190	**0.775**	**0.775**	**0.906**	0.080	0.077	0.092	1									
Na^+	0.041	0.003	0.045	**0.390**	**0.390**	**0.323**	**−0.214**	**0.214**	**0.227**	**0.262**	1								
K^+	0.179	−0.034	0.152	0.192.	0.191	0.196	−0.117	0.245	0.068	0.193	**0.724**	1							
Cl^-	−0.014	0.055	−0.126	**0.664**	**0.664**	**0.401**	−0.112	0.193	**0.224**	**0.357**	**0.280**	0.086	1						
HCO_3^-	−0.142	0.035	−0.108	**0.316**	**0.316**	**0.317**	0.090	**0.249**	**0.393**	0.175	**0.260**	0.121	0.184	1					
SO_4^{-2}	0.027	0.063	−0.024	0.159	0.159	0.060	0.017	0.122	**−0.244**	0.185	0.043	−0.001	**0.238**	0.182	1				
NO_3^-	**−0.264**	**0.255**	−0.154	0.159	−0.188	−0.173	0.051	0.071	0.011	**−0.209**	**−0.219**	−0.092	−0.138	−0.147	0.030	1			
PO_4^-	−0.180	0.090	−0.103	−0.078	−0.078	−0.006	0.094	**−0.214**	0.064	−0.041	**−0.224**	−0.151	−0.122	0.117	−0.023	0.185	1		
F^-	−0.167	−0.009	−0.175	−0.119	−0.119	−0.079	−0.106	−0.161	−0.066	−0.051	−0.074	−0.070	−0.117	**−0.210**	**−0.229**	0.137	0.076	1	
Fe^{2+}	**0.325**	−0.018	**0.226**	0.176	0.176	−0.113	0.089	0.064	0.084	−0.157	0.012	0.123	**0.361**	0.072	−0.031	−0.144	**−0.237**	−0.164	1

Note: Bolded values shows significant correlation.

during post-monsoon season the dissolution of salts, minerals and other soil constituents increases due to increase in the groundwater table (Shivasankaran, 1997).

Most of the inorganic salts such as sodium chloride, potassium sulfate and potassium nitrate are responsible for increasing the EC values of groundwater systems. Sharma *et al.* (1995) classified the groundwaters based on electrical conductivity values as indicated below:

Excellent	000–333
Good	333–500
Permissible	500–1000
Brackish	1000–1500
Saline	1500–10,000

The results obtained revealed that more than 65 per cent of water belongs to permissible, 30.43 per cent of water belongs to brackish and 2.1 per cent belongs to excellent and saline category.

The statistical correlation of conductivity with other parameters is presented in correlation matrix (Table 32.4 and 32.5). Electrical conductivity showed a significant positive correlation with total dissolved solids, total hardness, calcium, magnesium, sodium, chloride and bicarbonates. The correlations established for electrical conductivity in the present work are similar to those observed by Kaza Somashekara Rao (1994) and Basavarajappa (2002).

Total Dissolved Solids (TDS)

The term solid refers to the matters either filterable or non filterable that remain as a residue in water *i.e.* TDS of water includes all soluble materials in solutions whether ionized or non-ionized. It does not include suspended sediments, colloids or dissolved gasses. TDS values are estimated by pursuing the empirical relationship (USSLS, 1954; Hem, 1985; Kotaiah *et al.*, 1994; Rambabu *et al.*, 1996 and Chandankeri, 1996).

In the present study TDS values ranged from a minimum of 276 mg/l to a maximum of 888 mg/l in pre-monsoon season (Table 32.3) and a minimum of 274 mg/l to a maximum of 940 mg/l in post-monsoon season (Table 32.2). It is observed that the its values have exhibited an increasing trend in post-monsoon seasons owing to the fact that during post-monsoon season dissolution of more quantity of constituents of soil particles as groundwater table increases during post-monsoon season. In the present study almost all water samples are well with in the limit of drinking water standards.

Carrol, 1962 classified fresh water based on TDS values as indicated below.

Fresh	0–1000 ppm
Brackish	1000–10000 ppm
Saline	10000–100000 ppm
Brine	Above 100000 ppm

The results obtained revealed that water in the study area belongs to the fresh category.

Total dissolved solids showed positive correlation with total hardness, calcium, magnesium, sodium, chloride and bicarbonates in both the seasons (Table 32.4 and 32.5). Narayana and Suresh (1989) also observed similar correlation in their study.

Total Hardness (TH)

In the present investigation, total hardness values varied from a minimum of 204 mg/l to a maximum of 652 mg/l in pre-monsoon season (Table 32.3) and a minimum of 195.5 mg/l to a maximum of 752.5 mg/l in post-monsoon season (Table 32.2).

Das Gupta (2000) and Shivasankaran (1997) are of the opinion that the concentration of hardness increases towards the post-monsoon season and decreases towards pre-monsoon season. In the present study also a similar behavior of hardness is noticed.

The degree of hardness in ppm has been classified in terms of equivalents of calcium carbonate concentration (APHA, 1995; Kotaiah, 1994) as:

Soft	0–50 mg/l
Medium	50–150 mg/l
Hard	150–300 mg/l
Very Hard	Greater than 300 mg/l

The results obtained revealed that more than 75 per cent of water samples belongs to the very hard category.

The statistical correlation of total hardness shows a highly significant correlation with electrical conductivity, total dissolved solids, calcium, magnesium, chloride and bicarbonates (Tables 32.4 and 32.5). This is conformity with the findings of Hussain (2001).

Chemical Oxygen Demand (COD)

In the present investigation COD values ranged from a minimum of 2.4 mg/l to a maximum of 17.5 mg/l in pre-monsoon season (Table 32.3) and a minimum of 2.85 mg/l to a maximum of 12.5 mg/l in post-monsoon season (Table 32.2). The WHO permissible limit for COD is 10 mg/l. In the present study the sample numbers 8, 9, 12, 13, 14, 16, 31 and 34 in post-monsoon season and sample numbers 6, 7, 9, 12, 14, 15, 31, 34 and 38 in pre-monsoon season showed higher concentration of COD than the standards prescribed for drinking water.

The statistical correlation of chemical oxygen demand shows a positive correlation with dissolved oxygen, sodium, potassium, bicarbonates and negative correlation with phosphate in pre-monsoon season (Table 32.5).

Calcium (Ca^{2+}) and Magnesium (Mg^{2+})

In the present study, calcium values ranged from a minimum of 33.37 mg/l to a maximum of 152.6 mg/l in post-monsoon season (Table 32.2) and a minimum of 45.4 mg/l to a maximum of 191.25 in pre-monsoon season (Table 32.3). However, the magnesium values ranged from a minimum of 31.82 mg/l to a maximum of 114.7 mg/l in pre-monsoon season (Table 32.3) and a minimum of 19.67 to a maximum of 113.08 mg/l in post-monsoon season (Table 32.2). In the present investigation the calcium and magnesium values are were with in the maximum permissible limit of drinking water standards.

Further, it is important to note that both calcium and magnesium have indicated strong significant correlation with total hardness, total dissolved solids, electrical conductivity, sodium, chloride but inverse correlation is found with sulfate and nitrate (Tables 32.4 and 32.5). Garg *et al.* (1988) has also expressed a similar opinion on correlation of calcium and magnesium.

Sodium (Na^+) and Potassium (K^+)

In the present investigation thè sodium values are ranged from a minimum of 1.2 mg/l to a maximum of 117 mg/l in pre-monsoon season (Table 32.3) and a minimum of 13 mg/l to a maximum of 116 mg/l in post-monsoon season (Table 32.2). However, the potassium ranged from a minimum of 0.7 to a maximum of 37.25 mg/l in pre-monsoon season (Table 32.3) and a minimum of 2.3 mg/l to a maximum of 30.05 in post-monsoon season (Table 32.2). The values of sodium and potassium are well with in the drinking and domestic water standards prescribed by BIS.

Sodium shows positive correlation with electrical conductivity, total dissolved solids, chemical oxygen demand, calcium, magnesium, potassium, chloride, bicarbonates and inverse correlation with dissolved oxygen, nitrate and phosphate (Tables 32.4 and 32.5). The above correlations are in total agreement with those observed by Hussain *et al.* (2001).

Chloride (Cl)

Chloride ion is generally present in natural waters and its presence can be attributed to the dissolution of salt deposits, discharge of effluents from chemical industries, oil were operations, sewage discharges, irrigation drainage, contamination from refuge leachates. The salty taste produced by chloride ion depends on chemical composition of the water (Vijaya Kumara *et al.*, 2002). In the present study, chloride values ranged from a minimum of 54.16 mg/l to a maximum of 344.3 mg/l in post-monsoon season (Table 32.2) and a minimum of 40.4 mg/l to a maximum of 315.5 mg/l in pre-monsoon season (Table 32.3). It is observed that the concentration of chloride ions has shown increased trend during post-monsoon season. This may due dissolution of chloride containing substances in soil during infiltration or percolation of rain water (Shivasankaran, 1997).

The correlation matrix indicates that chlorides have a strong positive correlation with electrical conductivity, total dissolved solids, calcium, magnesium, sodium, sulfate and iron. However, it shows insignificant correlation with nitrate and fluoride (Tables 32.4 and 23.5).

Bicarbonate (HCO_3^-)

In the present study, the bicarbonate values ranged from a minimum of 172.5 mg/l to a maximum of 690 mg/l in post-monsoon season (Table 32.2) and a minimum of 168.5 mg/l to a maximum of 632.5 mg/l in pre-monsoon Season (Table 32.3). The results revealed that all the water samples are well with in the standards prescribed for drinking water.

Bicarbonates establish a positive correlation with electrical conductivity, total dissolved solids, total hardness, chemical oxygen demand, calcium, sodium and inverse correlation with fluoride (Tables 32.4 and 32.5). However, Narayana and Suresh (1989) have indicated that bicarbonate shows positive correlation with total dissolved solids, total hardness, calcium, sodium and also showed inverse correlation with dissolved oxygen.

Sulfate (SO_4^-)

The sulfate content of natural water is an important parameter in determining the suitability of water for residential use or public use. Higher concentration of sulfate (> 250 ppm) cause cathartic action and miss functioning of alimentary canal and gastrointestinal irrigation (ISI, 1982) in human beings. Hence, determination of sulfate in fresh water becomes essential. In the present investigation, sulfate values ranged from a minimum of 38.95 mg/l to a maximum of 312.5 mg/l in post-monsoon season (Table 32.5) and 23.6 mg/l to a maximum of 246 mg/l in pre-monsoon season (Table 32.3). The study reveals that the concentration of sulfate is high during post-monsoon season as compared to pre-monsoon season. Alexander (1961) and Miller (1979) are of the opinion that the break down of organic substances in soil, leachable sulfates present in fertilizers and other human interference's are the expected causes for high concentration of sulfate.

The statistical correlation revealed that the sulfate is negatively correlated with fluoride, colour, magnesium, sodium and positive correlation with pH (Table 32.4 and 32.5).

Fluoride (F)

In the present study, the fluoride values ranged from a minimum of 0.245 mg/l to a maximum of 1.11 mg/l in pre-monsoon season (Table 32.3) and a minimum of 0.265 mg/l to a maximum of 1.07 mg/l in post-monsoon season (Table 32.2). In the study area the fluoride concentration is well with in the limit of drinking water standards.

Nitrate (NO_3)

In the present study, the nitrate values ranged from a minimum of 0.75 mg/l to a maximum of 46.75 mg/l in pre-monsoon season (Table 32.3) and a minimum of 0.50 mg/l to a maximum of 66.50 mg/l in post-monsoon season (Table 32.2).

Laksmanan *et al.* (1986) reported that human wastes also contains nitrogen for about 5 kg/person/year (WHO, 1984). Further, fertilizers, animal wastes, municipal and industrial untreated wastes are considered as important sources of nitrate contamination in groundwater (WHO, 1984 and Handa, 1983). Even in the absence of fertilizer applications and geological deposits, the high level nitrates were observed in urban regions of Hyderabad and Secunderabad in some groundwaters owing to the lack of good sanitary systems and proper drainage management (Davina *et al.*, 1999). Percolation of sewage increases the concentration of nitrate in groundwater (Vijaya Kumara, *et al.*, 2002). The same opinion can also be considered in some sampling locations of the study area. Therefore the nitrate levels in the sample number 13, 17, 23 and 44 revealed that the waters of the particular location are unsuitable for drinking purposes with respect to nitrate concentration in the water.

Phosphate (PO_4^-)

In the present study, the phosphate values ranged from a minimum of 0.001 mg/l to a maximum of 1.17 mg/l in pre-monsoon season (Table 32.3) and a minimum of 0 mg/l to a maximum of 1.07 mg/l in post-monsoon season (Table 32.2). Rajmohan *et al.* (2000) have reported phosphorous concentration at a minimum of 0.03 ppm to a maximum of 0.70 ppm in their study area owing to the intensively irrigated area of Kanchipuram Taluk of Tamil Nadu.

E. Coli

The examination of water samples for *E. coli* contamination has revealed that the bacterial count was minimum of zero count in the almost all the samples except sample nos. 5 and 6 where the *E. coli* number was recorded to be 10/100 ml and 25/100 ml respectively (Tables 32.2 and 32.3). This is attributed to the percolation of untreated municipal sewage and solid waste leachate in to the borewell water.

Conclusion

Following conclusions could be drawn from this study:

1. From the results of the seasonal samples, it is observed that the concentration of major physico-chemical parameters have exhibited an increasing trend during post-monsoon season compared to the pre-monsoon season. This is attributed to the dissolution of salts

and minerals in soil through the recharge of groundwater by rainfall and rising the groundwater table during post-monsoon season.

2. It is observed that 30 per cent of water samples investigated are non-potable and 70 per cent of the samples are potable and it is in accordance with that of BIS for drinking water.
3. The present study has revealed that the fluoride content in the study area is well with in the prescribed limits.
4. In five sampling locations, the nitrate content is higher than the prescribed standards of BIS for drinking water. This is attributed to the percolation of untreated municipal sewage and industrial effluents.
5. The examination of water samples for *E. coli* contamination has revealed that the bacterial count was minimum of zero count in almost all the samples except in water sample numbers 5 and 6 where the *E. coli* number is 10/100 ml and 25/100 ml respectively. This is attributed to the percolation of untreated municipal sewage and solid waste leachate.
6. In the study area, the total hardness content of 75 per cent of water samples belongs to the very hard category.
7. The cations and anions concentration in ppm is in the order of relative dominance in the following sequences. $Ca^{2+} > Mg^{2+} > Na^{+} > K^{+}$, $HCO_3 > Cl > SO_4^{2-} > NO_3 > F > PO_4^{3-}$.
8. The nitrate concentration is in the order of higher magnitude than phosphate.

Further this study has given the criteria that help in providing important information for implementation of water quality control practices. It is expected that the criteria should serve the public interest at large and it is based upon scientific facts.

References

Alexander, M., 1961. *Introduction to Soil Microbiology*. Wiley, New York, London, pp. 472.

APHA, 1985. *Standard Methods for the Examination of Water and Wastewater*, 17th edn. American Public Health Association, AWWA, WPCF, Washington D.C., New York.

APHA, 1995. *Standard Methods for the Examination of Water and Wastewater*, 18th edn. American Public Health Association, Washington D.C., New York, pp. 208.

Basavarajappa, B.E., 2002. Studies on the impact of environmental pollution on groundwater quality in and around Davanagere. *Ph.D. Thesis*, Kuvempu University, Jnanasahyadri, Shankaraghatta.

Black, 1963. *Water Pollution Technology*. Reston, Virginia.

Bureau of Indian Standards, 1998. *Specification for Drinking Water*, New Delhi.

Chandankeri, G.G., 1996. An integrated approach to groundwater studies of Kumudavathi River lower Basin. *Ph.D. Thesis*, Karnataka University, Dharwad.

Davina, V. Gonsalves and Joe D'Souza, 1999. Impact of the tourism industry on groundwater in Calangute of Goa. *Ecology, Environment and Conservation*, 5(1): 19–24.

Garg, V.K., Dahiya, Sudhir, Chaowdhary, Arti and Deepshika, 1998. Fluoride distribution in underground of Gind district of Haryana (India). *Ecology, Environment and Conservation.*

Gill, S.K., Sahota, S.K., Sahota G.P.S., Sahota, B.K. and Sahota, H.S., 1993. Comparisons of physico-chemical parameters of groundwater from shallow aquifer near 2 thermal power plants in Punjab. *Indian Journal of Environmental Protection*, 13: 584–587.

Govardan, V., 1990. Groundwater pollution hazardous to human life: A case study of Nalgonda district. *Indian Journal of Environmental Protection*, 10: 54–61.

Handa, B.K., 1983. Effect of fertilizers use on groundwater quality in India. In: *Groundwater in Water Resource Planning*, UNESCO, IAH-IAHS, Koblenz.

Hem, J.D., 1985. *Study and Interpretation of the Chemical Characteristics of Natural Water*, 3rd edition. U.S. Geological Survey Water Supply Paper, 2254: 263.

Hussain, J., Sharma, K.C., Hussain, I. and Ojha, K.G., 2001. Physico-chemical characteristics of water from borewells of an industrial town Bhilwara, Rajasthan: A correlation study. *Asian J. Chemistry*, 13(2): 470–476.

Jain, C.K., Sharma, M.K., Bhatia, K.K.S. and Seth, S.M., 2000. Groundwater pollution: Endemic flurosis. *Pollution Research*, 4(19): 505–509.

Kaza, Somashekara Rao, Raju, V.A., Singanan, M., Someshwara Rao, B., Sheshagiri Rao, P.V. and Chakravarti, K.R., 1994. Studies on the quality of water supplied by the municipality of Kakinanda and groundwater of Kakinanada town. *Indian Journal of Environmental Protection*, 14(3): 167–169.

Knight, A.G., 1951. The photometric estimation of colour in turbid waters. *Journal of Institution of Water Engineering*, 5: 623.

Kotaiah, B. and Kumaraswamy, N., 1994. *Environmental Engineering Laboratory Manual*. Charotar Publishing House, Anand–388 001 (India).

Lakshmanan, A.R., Krishnarao, T. and Viswanathan, S., 1986. Nitrate and fluoride levels in drinking waters in the twin cities of Hyderabad and Secunderabad. *Indian Journal of Environmental Health*, 28(1): 39–47.

Mehta, S.B. and Trivedi, V.H., 1993. Groundwater contamination. *Indian Journal of Environmental Protection*, 13: 577–579.

Miller, J.C., 1979. Nitrate contamination of the water table aquifer by septic tank systems in the coastal plain of Dilaware. *Rural Environmental Conference*, Warren V.P.

Mittal, S.K., Rao, A.L.J., Singh, S. and Kumar, R., 1994. Groundwater quality of some areas in Patiala city. *Indian Journal of Environmental Health*, 31: 228–236.

Narayana, A.C. and Suresh, G.C., 1989. Chemical quality of groundwater of Mangalore city in Karnataka. *Indian Journal of Environmental Health*, 31(3): 228–236.

Rajamohan, N.L., Elango, S., Ramachandran and Natarajan, M., 2000. Major ion correlation in groundwater of Kancheepuram region (South India). *Indian Journal of Environmental Protection*, 20(3): 188–193.

Rambabu, C. and Somashekara Rao, K., 1996. Studies on the quality of borewell water of Nuzvid. *Indian Journal of Environmental Protection*, 16(7): 41–47.

Sawyer, N.C. and MeCarty, P.L., 1978. *Chemistry for Environmental Engineers*, 3rd Edition, McGraw-Hill Book Company.

Sharma, D.K. *et al.*, 1998. Studies in quality of water in and around Jaipur. *IWWA (Indian Waste Water Analysis)*, 20(3).

Sharma, Sanjay, Jain, P. C. and Mathur, R., 1995. Quality assessment of groundwater in municipal and fringe areas near Gwalior. *Indian Journal of Environmental Protection*, 15(7): 534–538.

Shivashankaran, M.A., 1997. Hydrological assessment and current status of pollutants in groundwater of Pondicherry region of South India. *Ph.D. Thesis*, Anna University, Chennai.

Somashekara Rao, K., 1989. Quality and assessment of groundwaters. *Indian Journal of Environmental Protection*, 6: 483–444.

Somashekara Rao, K., 1993. Correlations among water quality parameters of groundwater of Nuzvid town and Nuzvid Mandalam. *Indian Journal of Environmental Protection*, 4: 261–266.

USSLS, 1954. Diagnosis and improvement of saline alkali soils. U.S. Salinity Laboratory Staff, U.S. Department of Agriculture Handbook, 60: 164.

Vijaya Kumara, Narayana, J. and Puttaiah, E.T., 2002. Assessment of groundwater quality of Bhadravathi town, Karnataka. *Geobios*, 29: 217–220.

Vijaya Kumara, Narayana, J. and Puttaiah, E.T., 2002. Evaluation of groundwater quality in urban and rural regions of Bhadravathi taluk, Shimoga district, (Karnataka). *Science Journal*, Kuvempu University, 2(1): 61–66.

WHO, 1984. *Guidelines for Drinking Water Quality*, WHO recommendations, Vol. 2.

Chapter 33

Phycological Aspects and Water Quality Assessment in the Rivers of Andhra Pradesh, India

P. Manikya Reddy and V. Venkateswarlu

Department of Botany, Osmania University, Hyderabad – 500 007, India

ABSTRACT

Phycological aspects in the rivers has been discussed based upon the data collected on algae from a number of rivers in Andhra Pradesh. Diatoms constituted the dominant group in benthic flora. Their generic and species sequential analysis gave some interesting results. The diatom flora appears to be more or less uniform at unpolluted stations of different results. It is concluded that benthic diatoms serve as good indicators of water quality and pollution in flowing water.

Keywords: Phycological, Diatoms, Rivers, Generic and species sequential analysis indicators.

Introduction

The study of river ecosystems/lotic habitats is quite different in many ways when compared to that of lentic environments, perhaps, due to (1) the fickle and unstable nature of the medium and substratum, (2) the insecurity of an organism in water current, (3) continuous nutrient supply and (4) considerable physiological and mechanical stress (Blum, 1960). The floristic and ecology of river algae have been reviewed by Blum (1956), Hynes (1970a) and the examples of benthic and epiphytic algae widespread in flowing waters are given by Whitton (1975). Algae in lotic habitats could be epilithic, epipelic, epizoic, epiphytic and planktonic. The lotic species exhibit very effective attaching devices. They show structural adaptations and Cedergen (1938) pointed out 4 such types. According to Symoens (1951) the communities of algae in rivers exhibit no constant composition of species from place to place and frequently their composition changes rapidly.

Venkateswarlu (1986) and Manikya Reddy and Venkateswarlu (1992) have collected lot of data on the algae of the rivers of Andhra Pradesh and the present study aims at incorporating the various aspects concerning river algae. It also deals with the critical analysis of different species present in different situations. The species which serve as indicators of river water quality and pollution have been identified.

Materials and Methods

The river Moosi has its source in Ananthagiri hills near Vikarabad in the Ranga Reddy district of Andhra Pradesh. It runs through the city of Hyderabad and after traversing a course of about 250 km, it joins the river Krishna at Wazeerabad. In the thickly populated areas of the city, the river receives domestic wastes. The river Manjira originates in Balaghat range hills in Maharashtra State. After flowing through the states of Maharashtra and Karnataka it enters the Andhra Pradesh State in Medak district and finally joins the river Godavari. The river Thungabhadra rises in the Western ghats on the border of Karnataka State. It is composed of the rivers Tunga and Bhadra. The river after traversing a course of about 640 km joins the river Krishna at Sangameshwar near Alampur in the Mahabubnagar district ofAndhra Pradesh. The river Tungabhadra receives effluents from Rayalaseema paper mills near Kurnool.

The river Kagna originates near Vikarabad in the Ranga Reddy district of Andhra Pradesh and after flowing in westernly direction through the states of Andhra Pradesh and Karnataka it joins the river Bhima near Wadi. The river Godavari is the largest river of the peninsula and has a total length 1500 km. It rises in the Western ghats in the Nasik district of Maharashtra state and receives a number of tributaries. It receives treated effluents from Bhadrachalam paper board mills near Bhadrachalam and from a fertilizer factory at Ramagundam. The river Krishna rises near Mahabaleshwar in the western ghats. Its length is about 1300 km. It flows through the Maharashtra and Andhra Pradesh and receives a number of tributaries.

Methods

Four stations were selected in each river for the collection of water and algal samples. Surface water samples were collected from all the rivers at monthly intervals and analyzed for various chemical, parameters by following standard methods (APHA, 1971). Simultaneously benthic algae were collected by the technique of Blum (1956) and Venkateswarlu (1969). For determining the frequency and percentage of different groups and different species of algae, the numbers of individuals per 120 high power fields of the microscope were recorded and percentages of different groups were calculated.

Results

The percentages of different groups of benthic algae, total algae, species number and number of diatom species recorded in all the rivers are given in Tables 33.1a,b, and 33.2a,b. The average concentrations of some important nutrients present at unpolluted and polluted stations of different rivers are given in Tables 33.3 and 33.4.

In all the rivers diatoms dominated the algal populations except in the river Manjira where Cyanophyceae are dominant. Even in the sequence of algae diatoms occupy first position followed by Cyanophyceae and Chlorophyceae. Diatoms constitute the major bulk of algal populations in the river benthos. In general, Pennales are dominant over Centrales (*Cyclotella* only).

Table 33.1a: Percentages of Different Lithophytic Algal Groups in the Rivers of Andhra Pradesh Unpolluted Stations

Algal Groups	*Moosi*	*Manjira*	*Tungabhadra*	*Kagna*	*Tungabhadra*	*Godavari*	*Krishna*
	1961–63	*1979–81*	*1981–83*	*1982–84*	*1984–85*	*1984–85*	*1985–86*
Bacillariophyceae	90.8	46.8	70.9	74.5	74.9	61.2	77.4
Chlorophyceae	4.83	9.5	6.6	6.5	6.5	6.2	2.3
Cyanophyceae	4.3	39.4	22.3	19.2	18.5	30.6	19.9
Euglenophyceae	0.06	3.5	–	0.12	–	22	0.5

Table 33.1b: Percentages of Different Lithophytic Algal Groups in the Rivers of Andhra Pradesh at Polluted Stations

Algal Groups	*Moosi*			*Tungabhadra*	*Tungabhadra*	*Godavari*
	1961–63	*1973–74*	*1981–82*	*1981–83*	*1984–85*	*1984–85*
Bacillariophyceae	81.55	15.4	8.1	67.9	59.7	24.9
Chlorophyceae	2.95	75.9	8.01	2.0	5.9	4.5
Cyanophyceae	11.7	5.5	6.4	38.5	31.8	68.1
Euglenophyceae	3.8	3.4	5.3	1.3	2.5	2.3

Table 33.2a: Total Algae Total Number of Species and Total Number of Diatoms Species in the Rivers of Andhra Pradesh at Unpolluted Stations

Algal Groups	*Moosi*	*Manjira*	*Tungabhadra*	*Kagna*	*Tungabhadra*	*Godavari*	*Krishna*
	1961–63	*1979–81*	*1981–83*	*1982–84*	*1984–85*	*1984–85*	*1985–86*
Total algae	5464	18445	15225	10455	15268	13565	5620
Total number of species	58	56	57	64	62	62	65
Total number of diatom species	25	26	32	37	29	36	42

Table 33.2b: Total Algae Total Number of Species and Total Number of Diatoms Species in the Rivers of Andhra Pradesh at Polluted Stations

Algal Groups	*Moosi*		*Tungabhadra*	*Tungabhadra*	*Godavari*
	1961–63	*1973–74*	*1981–83*	*1984–85*	*1984–85*
Total algae	4602	9231	16165	18189	15692
Total number of species	45	23	42	41	47
Total number of diatom species	15	8	26	23	22

Table 33.3: The Average Concentrations of Some Important Nutrients in the Rivers of Madhya Pradesh at Unpolluted Stations (in mg/l except pH)

Nutrient Parameters	*Moosi*	*Manjira*	*Tungabhadra*	*Kagna*	*Tungabhadra*	*Godavari*
	1961–63	*1979–81*	*1981–83*	*1982–84*	*1984–85*	*1984–85*
pH	8.3	8.4	8.4	8.5	8.5	8.5
CO_3	9.99	22.76	25.7	30.45	17.13	15.95
HCO_3	232.95	186.79	197.2	252.36	200.0	171.54
Cl	18.1	27.98	86.48	19.54	88.91	34.62
DO	7.9	7.6	7.3	7.6	7.5	7.8
Org. matter	1.23	0.88	1.95	1.22	1.22	0.81
F.NH_3	0.64	0.93	0.75	0.72	1.20	0.94
NO_3	1.12	1.59	1.29	1.13	0.29	0.48
NO_2	0.01	0.01	0.02	0.004	0.003	0.002
PO_4	0.001	0.01	0.015	0.067	0.007	traces
SiO_2	16.95	7.5	6.15	9.8	2.7	3.8

Table 33.4: The Average Concentrations of Some Important Nutrients in the Rivers of Andhra Pradesh at Polluted Stations

Chemical Parameters	*Moosi*			*Tungabhadra*	*Tungabhadra*	*Godavari*
	1961–63	*1973–74*	*1981–82*	*1981–83*	*1984–85*	*1984–85*
pH	7.9	7.2	7.4	8.0	8.2	8.1
CO_3	2.8	–	–	11.92	2.14	3.75
HCO_3	331.15	–	447.4	202.4	206.1	236.6
Cl	40.75	146.4	208.0	149.0	154.6	104.1
DO	3.0	0.6	nil	4.3	3.2	3.9
Org. matter	5.0	2.5	30.5	7.74	9.70	9.73
F.NH_3	2.62	14.7	20.1	1.09	2.2	1.09
NO_3	0.39	0.13	0.7	0.97	1.12	1.37
NO_2	0.05	0.06	–	0.002	0.001	0.001
PO_4	0.85	0.32	11.5	0.2	0.06	0.22
SiO_2	16.7	8.7	15.6	9.6	5.7	7.7

The generic and species sequential analysis of diatoms exhibited interesting phenomena and are given in the following:

Generic Sequential Analysis

1. River Moosi (1961–63): *Achnanthes* > *Cymbella* > *Synedra* > *Anomoeoneis* > *Navicula* > *Caloneis.*
2. River Moosi (1973–74): *Nitzschia* > *Cymbella* > *Synedra* > *Navicula.*
3. River Manjira: *Synedra* > *Cymbella* > *Navicula* > *Achnanthes.*

4. River Tungabhadra (1981–83): *Cymbella > Navicula > Synedra > Nitzschia > Mastogloia > Caloneis.*
5. River Tungabhadra (1984–86): *Cymbella > Synedra > Navicula > Nitzschia.*
6. River Godavari: *Synedra > Cymbella > Achnanthes > Navicula > Caloneis > Nitzschia.*
7. River Krishna: *Synedra > Cymbella > Gomphonema > Nitzschia > Achnanthes > Cocconeis.*
8. River Kagna: *Cymbella > Synedra > Achnanthes > Navicula > Gomphonema > Nitzschia.*

Species Sequential Analysis

River Moosi

Unpolluted

(1961–63): *Achnanthes microcephala > Cymhella microcephala > Synedra ulna > A. minutissima v. cryptocephala.*

1973–1974: *Nitzschia amphihia > Cymbella affinis > Synedra tabulala > Navicula cryptocephala v. veneta.*

Polluted

(1961–63): *Nitzschia palea > Achnanthes exigua > Cyclotella meneghiniana > Navicula pupula. f. capitata > Pinnularia biceps > Navicula pigmaea.*

1973–74: *Nitzschia palea > Gomphonema sphaerophorum > Pinnularia bicep > Achnanthes exigua > Cyclotella meneghiniana.*

River Tungabhadra

Unpolluted

Cymbella affinis > Navicula cryptocephala > Synedra ulna > Nitzschia denticula v. curta > Mastogloia smithii amphicephala > Caloneis silicula > Achnanthes microcephala.

Polluted

Nitzschia patea > Gomphonema parvulum > Achnanthes exigua > Gomphonema lanceolalum > Nitzschia hungarica.

River Manjira

Synedra ulna v. aequalis > Cymbella cymbiformis v. jimboi > Cymbella affinis > Nitzschia denticula curta > Gomphonema constrictum v. capitata > Achnanthes minutissima v. cryptocephala.

River Kagna

Cymbella affinis > C. Cymbiformis > Synedra ulna > Achnanthes minutissima > Navicula rhynchocephala > Nitzschia denticula v. curta.

River Krishna

Synedra ulna v. aequalis > Cymbella aspera > Achnanthes minutissima v. cryptocephala > Cocconeis placentula.

River Godavari

Unpolluted

Synedra ulna v. aequalis > *Cymbella aspera* > *Achnanthes minutissima v. cryptocephala* > *Navicula bacillum* > *Caloneis silicula v. trancatula* > *Nitzschia denticula v. curta.*

Polluted

Nitzschia obtuse v. scalpelliformis > *Syndera ulna* > *Achnanthes exigua* > *Nitzschia hungarica.*

Discussion

From the literature survey and also from the data on different rivers of Andhra Pradesh, it is quite evident that diatoms constitute the major bulk of benthic populations. Perhaps, the substratum, the composition of the medium and the effective attaching mechanism of various species are the possible reasons for their dominance.

Hustedt (1957), Cholnoky (1968), Schoeman (1973) and Lowe (1974) have "used diatoms as indicators of water quality and pollution. Prasad and Singh (1982) made a preliminary attempt on diatoms as indicators of water pollution. Trivedy (1986) surveyed the literature on the use of algae in biomonitoring of water pollution. However, these authors could not make a critical analysis of diatom species which represent the dominant flora in rivers and streams.

The generic analysis reveals that *Cymbella, Syndera, Navicula and Achnanlhes* are the most predominant algae in the benthic communities at unpolluted stations of the rivers. Besides, *Epithemia, Rhopalodia* and Amphora are also found only in unpolluted waters. The genus *Cymbella* appears to occupy either the first or second place in most of the rivers investigated. Even the species analysis shows that the populations include a number of species belonging to this diatom. *Cymbella cymbiformis v. jimboi, C. affinis, C. microcephala, C. aspera, Cynedra ulna v. aequalis, Achnanthes microcephala, Nitzschia denticula v. cura* and *N. amphibia* are the most dominant/common species in almost all the rivers investigated. Certain genera like *Achnanthes, Navicula, Pinnularia, Gomphonema* and *Nitzschia* occur both in unpolluted and polluted habitats

The diatom species sequential analysis in order of their abundance indicates that although certain species are common in different rivers investigated, their order of sequence is not uniform, especially at the unpolluted stations. However, in the polluted areas there appears to be some uniformity in their sequence. In the former it is mainly due to the large variety of species, the abundance of which depends upon the composition of the medium, type of substratum and physical conditions. On the other hand in polluted waters the species number is limited and perhaps, the less the number of species the more the uniformity in their sequence.

In polluted habitats species belonging to Araphidae group are not present as they can not exhibit any movement due to the absence of raphe. On the other hand the species with raphe can evade the areas which are toxic by way of movement within the habitat. So the species with raphe have advantage over raphe-less forms specially in the polluted environments.

Benthic Algae as Indicators of River Water Quality

It is quite evident from the data certain species of algae playa role in assessing the quality of water. They are given in the following:

Name of the Species	*Water Quality*
Achnanthes microcephala *A. minutissima v. cryptocephala* *Cymbella cymbiformis v. jimboi* *Navicula pupula f. rectangularis* *Rhopalodia gibba* *Nitzschia amphibia* *N. denticula v. curta* *Spirogyra adnata* *Coelosphaerium kuetzingianum*	Clean, dissolved oxygen > 5.0 mg/l., low BOD, organic matter, ammonia chlorides and phosphates. More number of species
Achnanthes exigua *Navicula pygmaea* *N. pupula f. capitata* *N. muralis* *Pinnularia biceps v. amphicephala* *Nitzschia palea* *Cyclotella meneghiniana* *Stigeoclonium tenue* *Chlorella vulgaris* *Oscillatoria chalybea* *Euglena acus*	Highly polluted (organically) High organic matter, BOD, ammonia, chlorides and phosphates and very low D.O. or nil, less number of species, more number of individuals.
Large Populations of *Nitzschia kutzingiana* *N. palea* *N. thermalis*	High concentration of organic nitrogenous materials (Cholnoky, 1968)
Abundance of *Nitzschia thermalis* and **Disappearance of** *Achanthes minutissima*	Anaerobic conditions (Schoeman, 1973)
Spirogyra adnata *Euastrum bombayense* *Navicula pupula f. rectangularis* *Anomoeoneis exilis f. lanceolata* *Stigeoclonium tenue*	Clean, fast flowing water, Polluted turbulent water.

Name of the Species	*Water Quality*
Large growths of *Cladophora glomerata*	Relatively high nutrient levels (Whitton, 1970) Heavy metals in low levels.
Abundant growth of *Stigeoclonium tenue*	High levels of heavy metals with relatively high nutrient levels.
Chlamydomonas botryopara	
Chlamydomonas suhcaudata	
Carteria ovata	Chemical effluents from
S. obliquas	pharmaceutical industries mixed
Spharellopsis fluviatilis	with sewage water
Scenedesmus incrassulatus	
Lepocinclis salina f. pachyderma	

Important Environmental Parameters

Water current is one of the most important factor in river ecology. For the growth of certain algae water movement is desirable. The benthic algae are some how benefited by moderate current whereas the fast currents cause mechanical danger to plankton (Blum, 1956). The size surface texture and chemical composition of the substratum may influence the distribution of algae in rivers. The natural substrata provide more reliable data than the artificial ones (Venkateswarlu and Manikya Reddy, 1985).

In lotic environments the nutrient supply will be continuous, because no nutrient gradient is established due to continuous agitation of water. The climatic conditions such as rainfall, temperature and light play an important role in river ecology. The distribution of the flora depends upon fluctuations in temperature, light regime and age of the water. Temperature determines the nutrient load because of its influence on evapotranspiration. In most of the rivers the fluctuations in temperature are minimum. The benthic flora gets mostly the reflected and refracted light (Witford and Schumacher, 1963).

Conclusions

On the basis of the literature survey and the critical analysis of the data on the rivers of Andhra Pradesh it can be concluded that benthic algae are abundant than plankton. In the former diatoms are dominant, may be due to the effective attaching adaptations shown by a number of species. Water current is the most important parameter in river ecology along with the substratum and climatic conditions. The diatom generic and species analysis reveal interesting phenomena. The abundance of diatoms frustules may give some clue to explore the oil deposits in different river basins.

References

APHA, AWWA and WPCF, 1971. *Standard Methods for the Examination of Water and Wastewater,* 13th ed. Washington U.S.A.

Blum, J.L., 1956. Ecology of river algae. *Bot. Rev.,* 22(5): 291–341.

Blum, J.L., 1960. Algal populations in flowing waters in the ecology of algae. *The Pymatu Symposia in Ecology.* Spl. Publ. No. 2, Univ. Pittasburgh, pp. 11–21.

Cedergren, G.R., 1938. Reofila eller det rinnands vattnets algamhallen, Sveensk. Bot. Tidskr., 32: 363–373.

Cholnoky, B.J., 1968. Die Okologie der Diatomeen in Sinnengewassem. T. Cramer Publishers, pp. 699.

Hustedt, F., 1957. Die Diatomeenflora des Fluss systema der weser in Gebiet der Hansestadt Brement. Abh. Naturw. Ver. Bremen., 34: 181–440.

Hynes, H.B.N., 1970. *The Ecology of Running Waters*. Liverpool Univ., Toronto Press, Canada.

Lowe, R.L., 1974. Environmental requirements and pollution tolerance of fresh water diatoms. *Envi. Monit. Ser.,* EPA 670/4-74-005. Nat. Env. Res. Centre. Res. and Dev., U.S. Env. Prot. Agency, Cincinnati, Ohio, 334 pp.

Manikya Reddy, P. Venkateswarlu, V., 1992. The impact of paper mill effluents on the algal flora of the river Tungabhadra. *J. Indian. Bot. Soc.*, 71: 109–114.

Prasad, B.N. and Singh, Y., 1982. On diatoms as indicators of water pollution. *J. Indian Bot. Soc.*, 61: 326–336.

Schoeman, F.R., 1973. A systematic and ecological study of the diatom flora of Lesotho with special reference to the water quality. V& H Printers, Pretoria, 365 pp.

Symeoens, J.J., 1951 Esquise s'um systeme des associations algales s'ean douce. Verh. Inst. *Ver. Theoret.* Angew. Lin. 11: 395–408.

Trivedy, R.C., 1986. Role of algae in biomonitoring of water pollution. *Asian Environment*, 8(3): 31–42.

Venkateswarlu, V., 1969. An ecological study of the algae of the River Moosi, Hyderabad (India) with special reference to water pollution. I. Physico-chemical complexes. *Hydrobiologia*, 33(1): 117–143.

Venkateswarlu, V., 1986. Ecological studies on the rivers of Andhra Pradesh with special reference to water quality and pollution. In: *Proc. Indian Acad. Sci. (Pl. Sci.)*, 96(6): 495–508.

Venkateswarlu, V. and Manikya Reddy, P., 1985. Algae as biomonitors in river ecology. In: *Symp. Biomonitoring State Environ. Poll.*, pp. 183–189.

Whitford, L.A. and Schumacher, G.J., 1963. Communities of algae in North Carolina streams and their seasonal relations. *Hydrobiologia*, 22(1–2): 137–167.

Whitton, B.A. (Ed.), 1975. *River Ecology*. Blackwell Scientific Publ., London.

Whitton, B.A., 1970. Toxicity of heavy metals to Chlorophyta from flowing waters. *Arch. Microbial.*, 72: 353–360.

Whitton, B.A., 1984 Algae as monitors of heavy metals in freshwaters. In: *Algae as Ecological Indicators*, (Ed.) L. Elliot Shubert. Academic Press Inc., London Ltd., pp. 257–280.

Chapter 34

Determining the Genetic Variability in *Dioscorea alata* L. in Tirunelveli Hills in Tamil Nadu

A. John De Britto, N. Nirmal Kumar and R. Mahesh

Plant Molecular Biology Research Unit, Department of Plant Biology and Biotechnology, St. Xavier's College (Autonomous), Palayamkottai - 627 002, Tamil Nadu, South India

ABSTRACT

Dioscorea alata commonly known as "*Winged yam*" belonging to the family Dioscoreaceae is one of the most important medicinal herbs used in Indian medicine for asthma, rheumatism and food for catteles. The distribution of genetic variation as revealed by *RAPD* markers was examined in population of this species from Tirunelveli District. It was observed that this medicinal plant possesses a considerable degree of genetic variation. Random Amplified Polymorphic *DNA* (*RAPD*) fingerprints were analyzed by Polymerase Chain Reaction (*PCR*) of genomic DNA using random primers. The *RAPD* fragments were scored for presence/absence, to calculate Jaccard's similarity index. Clustering based on similarity index was done following unweighted pair group with arithmetic mean method and a dendrogram was constructed and analyzed.

Introduction

Wild yams make a significant contribution both as root crops and vegetables to the diets of tribal people of India, particularly in rural areas where they are freely available. Many different forms and cultivars of the wild edible yam species are available in different areas and it is likely that these differ in composition and nutritional values. *Dioscorea alata* L. commonly known as "Winged Yam" belonging to the family Dioscoreaceae is one of the most important species used in Indian medicine for asthma, rheumatism and Food for catteles. The yams, are used as a food for the Kani peoples. Hence *Dioscorea* alata was selected for the genetic variation study.

DNA markers (RAPD) were used to compare genetic differentiation within the *Dioscorea alata* species. The utility of RAPD markers in estimating genetic divergence has been demonstrated in several studies, which have reported close correspondence between RAPD and other molecular data sets (Anil Kant *et al.*, 2006 and Timro *et al.*, 2005). Because RAPD detect multiple loci per primer in many cases and can conveniently generate a large set of genetic markers, they have become increasingly common for analyzing genetic differentiation with in the species. Although population studies of several medicinal plants species have been examined genetically since the early 1990 using RAPD technique, the amount of genetic data concerning *Dioscorea alata* is relatively limited.

Genetic variation can undermine the ability of the plant species to respond to the natural selection.

The small populations are often subject to the loss of alleles, through genetic drift (or) random fluctuations is allele frequency. Hence genetic diversity measurement are important for selection of superior genotypes with respect to longevity and for considering conservation of that particular species. This study facilitates to identify the variants of *Dioscorea alata* and for the selection of superior genotypes.

Materials and Methods

Plant Material

Samples of *Dioscorea alata* were collected from hilly areas like Manjolai, Kothayar, Papanasum, Karaiyar and courtallum in Tirunelveli hills in Tamilnadu. Five plant specimens from each accession were collected. The collected plant materials were transferred to plastic bags for transport from field to laboratory. Permanent storage was at –70°C until DNA isolation and RAPD analysis was carried out.

Table 34.1: Collected Area and the Accession ID

Collection Area	*Accession*
Manjolia	Pop1
Kothayar	Pop2
Papanasum	Pop3
Karaiyar	Pop4
Courtallum	Pop5

DNA Method

Individual young top fresh leaves were removed from plants, washed with sterile distilled water. The tissue sample was placed in a porcelain mortor chilled with liquid, nitrogen and ground with a pestle to a fine powder. Total genomic DNA extracted using the CTAB technique of Doycle and Doycle (1987). The A 260/280 reading of DNA ranged from 1.5 to 2.0.

Amplification reactions of the RAPD method were conducted in a 25 µl volume reactions mixture containing 10MM Tris HCL pH 8.3, 50 mm KCL, 15 mm $Mgcl_2$, 0.001 per cent gelatin, 100 µm each of dATp, dGTP and dTTP, 0.2 µm of random primers, 25 mg of genomic DNA and 0.5 unites of Tag polymerase (Williams *et al.*, 1990).

Amplification was performed in eppendorf Thermal cycler for 45 cycles of 1 min at 94°C, min at 36°C, 2 min 72°C and a final extension for 7 minutes at 72°C using the fastest available transitions between each temperature. Amplification products were analyzed by electrophoresis, in 1.20 per cent agorse gels and detected by staining with Ethidium Bromide. Preliminary screening with 8 RAPD primers from operon Technologies was conducted. In the final analysis, 5 RAPD primers were used (Table 34.3) which all produced reproducible landing patterns.

Table 34.2: Oligonucleotides Used as Random Primers in *Dioscorea alata* and their Sequence

Primer	*Sequence 5'–3'*	*Number of Bands*
OPB–13	TTCCGCCACC	8
OPB–8	TGGCGCAGTG	7
OPB–5	CCGCTACCGA	5
OPB–20	CCCAGCT AGA	10
OPB–5	CCGCT ACCGA	5

Table 34.3

POPID	*1*	*2*	*3*	*4*	*5*
1.	*****	0.6275	0.2215	0.3512	0.3231
2.	0.2157	*****	05522	0412	04322
3.	0.3212	0.7623	*****	0.3799	0.5011
4.	0.5215	0.6122	0.6222	*****	0.3818
5.	0.2151	0.2522	0.6111	0.3799	*****

Data Analysis

Based on the primary data [Presence (or) absence of bands], pair wise genetic distance between samples were calculated using Pop gene package version 1.31.

Results and Discussion

The five primers used to analayze genetic variation is *Dioscorea alata* resulted in a total of 35 polymorphic bands (loci). The same type of bands occurred at different frequencies is all populations. There was many additional bands neglected which were irreproducible. The genetic distance between the population ranged from 0.2157 to 0.7623 and the genetic identity ranged from 0.3231 to 0.6275. The overall observed and effective number of alleles is about 2 and 1.58 respectively. The overall genetic diversity according to Neis's index is 0.4022.

In the UPGMA dendrogram based upon Nei's genetic distance, the populations were highly differentiated by their own genetic distance. By analyzing the RAPD data they are invented as dominants although the banding patters can be used to analyze the gene diversity (Esselmanetal *et al.*, 2004). This is the first record describing the genetic diversity in *Dioscorea alata* using RAPD markers in Tirunelveli hills.

The use of RAPD markers to identify generic variations was preferred over convention morphological and biochemical markers since these are completely devoid of any interference from environmental effect and growth stages of experimental material; thus making them highly reliable. The absence of origin of genetic variation with in the species and the clustering the result of different accessions suggests that *Dioscorea alata* under go major part of genetic variation by environmental factors. The present findings make a strong point to enlarge the scope and size of collection through out the distribution area of this plant in order to detect and quantify the prevalent genetic diversity existing with in this species at molecular level. Data generated from the present study as well as from same studies in future would go a long way in conserving district genotypes of this species. It would also help in identifying genetically valuable in the management of genetic resources in this economically important species.

Figure 34.1

Acknowledgement

The authors are very thankful to University Grants Commission, New Delhi for their financial assistance.

References

Anilkant, G., Sharma, D. and Briquet, M., 2006. Molecular analaysis of genetic variability in *Pinus gerardiana* in Kinnaur (HP). *Ind. J. Biotech.*, pp. 6267.

Doycle, J.J. and Doycle, J.L., 1987. A rapid DNA isolation of fresh leaf tissue phytochem. 19: 11–15.

Esslemen, E.J. and D.J. Crawford, 2004. RAPD marker diversity with in and divergence among species of Dendroseris. *Amer. J. Bot.*, 87: 591–596.

Nei, 1987. Estimation of average heterozygosity and genetic distance from a small number of individuals. *Genetics*, 89: 583.

Timro, A.J. and Peakal, T. Huff. Dr., 2000. RAOD variation in *Buchloe dactylodies. Mol. Ecol.*, 4: 95–99.

Williams, G.K. and Anne R. Kubelit, 1990. DNA polymorphism amplified by arbitrary primers of genetic markers. *Nucleic and Research*, pp. 6531–6535.

Chapter 35

Effect of Colchicine on Various Morphological Characters in *Cucumis pubscens* Willd.

M. Babu Rao

Department of Botany, P.G.C.S (O.U.), Hyderabad - 500 004

ABSTRACT

Dry seeds of *Cucumis pubescens* willd. were presoaked in distilled water for 24 hours and were treated with 0.1 per cent and 0.25 per cent of colchicine for 24 hours and after the treatment they were thoroughly washed under tap water and sown in the field. The various morphological characters like vine length number of days to flower, number of fruits per plant, fruit size, yield per plant and pollen fertility, total yield were studied for two generations M1 and M2 and the results of the same were reported.

Keywords: *Colchicine, Yield, Cucumis pubescens.*

Introduction

Since the discovery of colchicine as a polyploidising agent, experimental production of polyploids became an additional tool for plant improvement programmes. It was observed by Kumar and Abharam (1942) in *Phaseolus radiatus*, Sen and Chada (1958) in *P. mungo* in *Capsicum fruitescens* by Raghuvanshi and Joshi (1964), Roy and Singh (1968) in *Trigonella* Roy *et al.* (1968) in *Luffa acutangula*, Roy and Ghosh (1971) in *L. echinata*. There were instances where polyploidy decreases the size of the leaflets as reported by Bhattacharya (1956) in autotetraploid *Cajanus cajan*. The present investigation was done with a view to study the effect of colchicine on various parameters like vine length, number of lateral branches, days to flower, number of fruits per plant and pollen fertility.

Materials and Methods

Dry seeds of *Cucumis pubescens* willd., were presoaked in distilled water for 24 hours prior to treatment with different concentrations of colchicine. The concentrations used were 0.1 per cent and 0.25 per cent for 24 hours. After completion of the treatment the seeds were washed thoroughly under tap water for about 20 minutes, comparable controls were also maintained. All the treatments were carried out at room temperature. The data was recorded for two generations.

Results and Discussion

From the Tables 35.1 and 35.2, it was clear that the Vine length in MI was increased in the treated material when compared to the control the increase was highest at 0.25 per cent colchicine concentration. The same trend was observed at M2 also but it was lower than the control. The number of lateral branches does not show a regular pattern. In M1 the number of lateral branches was more at 0.25 per cent concentration which was higher than the control. But in M2 it was lower. The 0.1 per cent colchicine concentration showed the same value as control at M1 and this increases slightly at M2. Flowering was delayed at M1 in the treated material when compared to control in both the generations. Maximum delay was observed at 0.25 per cent concentration. In M1 the number of fruits per plant was decreased in the treated material. But in M2 an increase was observed in the treated material. 0.1 per cent colchicine recorded highest number of fruits per plant. As far as size of the fruit is concerned, maximum fruit length was observed at 0.25 per cent colchicine, minimum length was observed at 0.1 per cent concentration. Yield per plant was higher in control at M1 it decreased with an increase in concentration of colchicine. Maximum yield per plant was observed at 0.25 per cent colchicine. Pollen fertility was decreased with an increase concentration of colchicine. In the treated material 0.1 per cent recorded highest yield in both the generations 0.25 per cent recorded minimum yield. Some floral abnormalities like flowers with different number of petals, irregularly shaped flowers and some leaf abnormalities like irregular leaves, trilobed leaves were observed. There was however no increase in the size of the leaves, stomata or pollen grains indicating the absence of gigas characters. The root tip squash and P.M.C also do not record any multiplication in the chromosome number. Increase in the length of vine in the treated material with an increase in concentration of colchicine was observed in both the generations. According to Tamakshimamura (1939), the effect of colchicine on the cells is not uniform. It differs in the same tissue of same root tip depending upon the different stages of nuclear division. Secondly on whether the affected cells belong to the tissue that is growing vigorously or lone that is dominant. According to Shambhulingappa *et al.* (1965), when the seeds are treated with colchicine all the cells are not equally affected and some deep seated cells are left untouched. These cells may divide at a faster rate during the growth of the plant and thus dominate the tetraploid cells which cannot keep pace with diploid cells in their multiplication thus, there may be diplontic selection. The present results are in agreement with above workers. With regard to an increase in size of the fruit at Ml, according to a report by Goswami *et al.* (1978), colchicine can also act as a growth promoting substance in addition to its mutagenic effect. In both the generations control recorded maximum yield in the present case decrease in the yield may be due to one or more factors. It may be due to lesser number of lateral branches or production of less number of female flowers or low pollen fertility due to various meiotic abnormalities. All of these cumulatively might have caused production of less number of fruits per plant and ultimately resulted in the decrease in the yield per plant. The reduction in pollen fertility was also observed by Bose and Mukherjee (1948), Roy and Ghosh (1971), Singh and Roy (1971). Maximum yield was recorded in control in both the generations, but in the treated material 0.25 per cent colchicine recorded maximum yield. The plants obtained from seeds treated with colchicine do not show any polyploidy. They are more or less similar to the control. From the results it is clear the colchicine treatment to the seeds do not give good results as far as the polyploidy is concerned. Sometimes the seed treatment with colchicine may be lethal. Similar results were obtained by Shambhulingappa *et al.* (1965) in *Trigonella*, Bose and Banerjee (1968) in tomato Roy *et al.* (1968) in *Luffa*, Roy and Mishra (1979). According to Bose and Banerjee (1968), the absence of any induced polyploidy type after tomato seed treatment with colchicine and combination with X-rays may be due to the treatment which was of short duration. Another factor which might have been in operation is the diplontic selection, may be an effect similar to that observed by Shambhulingappa (1965) in which the diplontic selection has resulted in absence of polyploidy in the colchicine treated *Trigonella* plants. The same may be true in the present case also.

Table 35.1: Effect of Colchicine on Various Morphological Characters in *C. pubsceus* in M1 Generation

Character	*Control*	*0.1%*	*0.25%*
Vine length in cm	97.00±1.28	102.00±1.50*	142.20±2.50**
No. of lateral branches	6.40±0.49	6.42±0.46	7.12±0.91
No. of days taken to produce first male flower	33.00±2.00	67.00±4.00**	68.00±3.00**
No. of days taken to produce first female flower	39.00±2.00	75.00±4.00**	78.00±2.00**
No. of fruits/plant	9.41±0.55	6.84±0.35**	7.88±0.71
Fruit length in cm	9.08±0.25	10.36±0.31**	14.61±0.72**
Fruit diameter in cm	13.72±0.41	9.29±0.29**	14.24±0.38
Yield/plant in grams	587	579	525
Pollen Fertility %	95	73	68
Total yield in kg	7.684	7.389	4.687

**: Significant at 1 per cent level; *: Significant at 5 per cent level.

Table 35.2: Effect of Colchicine on Various Morphological Characters in *C. pubsceus* in M2 Generation

Character	*Control*	*0.1%*	*0.25%*
Vine length in cm	221.60±0.68	195.00±2.00**	198.00±2.80**
No. of lateral branches	7.12±0.32	7.33±0.52	5.50±0.62*
No. of days taken to produce first male flower	36.00±3.00	44.75±3.00*	49.50±3.00*
No. of days taken to produce first female flower	39.00±3.00	61.00±4.00**	65.00±2.00**
No. of fruits/plant	6.33±0.55	10.69±0.32**	9.40±0.48**
Fruit length in cm	12.55±0.65	9.90±0.17**	10.76±0.42**
Fruit diameter in cm	17.16±0.32	13.67±0.65**	16.93±0.52
Yield /plant in grams	832	597	793
Pollen Fertility per cent	95	75	72
Total yield in kg	10.037	8.366	2.795

**: Significant at 1 per cent level; *: Significant at 5 per cent level.

References

Bhattacharya, S.K., 1956. Study of autotetraploid *Cajanus cajan* L. *Caryologia*, 9: 149–159.

Bose, S. and Banerjee, H., 1968. Effect of treatments of X-rays and colchicine on tomato. *Nucleus*, 11(2): 160–169.

Bose, S. and Mukherjee, R.K., 1968. Colchipliody in *Impatiens balsamina* L-II. Studies in the C2 Generation. *Cytologia*, 32: 324, 350–353.

Kumar, L.S. and Abraham, A., 1942. Induction of polyploidy in crop plants. *Curr. Sci.*, 11: 112–113.

Raghuvanshi, S.S. and Joshi, Shiela, 1964. Cytological studies in colchiploids of, *Capsicum fruitescems* L. *Cytologia*, 29: 61–78.

Roy and Mishra, U., 1979. Studies in colchicine induced tetraploids of *Phaseolus acountifolius*. *J. Ind. Hort. Soc.*, 58.

Roy, Ghosh Jaya, 1971. Experimental polyploids of *Luffa echinata* Roxb. *Nucleus*, 14(2): 111–115.

Roy, R.P. and Sinha, A., 1968. Cytomorphological studies of colchicine induced tetraploid *Trigonella foenumgraceum* L. *Genet Iberica*, 20: 37.

Roy, R.P., Sinha, B.M. and Dutt, B., 1968. Cytomorphological sin the colchicine induced autotetraploids of *Luffa acutangula* Roxb. *Proc. 55th Ind. Sci. Cong.*

Shambhulingappa, K.G. and Channaveeraiah, M.S., and Patel, S.R., 1965. Artificial induction of polyploidy in *Trigonella foenum-graceum*. *Cytologia*, 30(2): 205–212.

Sen, N.K. and Chada, H.R., 1958. Colchicine induced tetraploids of five varieties of Black gram. *Ind. J. Genet. Plant Breed.*, 18: 238-248.

Singh, Avatar and Roy, R.P., 1971. Studies on the colchiploids of four species of *Trigonella*. *Cytologia*, 36(1): 133–142.

Chapter 36

Diversity of Phytoplankton in Mani Reservoir, Hosanagar, Karnataka

D.N. Veerendra S. Manjappa[1] *and E.T. Puttaiah*[2]

[1]Department of Chemistry, UBDT Engineering College, Kuvempu University, Davanagere

[2]Department of Environmental Science, Kuvempu University Shankaraghatta - 577 451

ABSTRACT

This article deals with the phytoplanktonic and physico-chemical composition of the Mani reservoir. A total of 34 species of phytoplankton were identified under 4 classes. Among these maximum density was recorded under Bacillariophyceae, Chlorophyceae Cyanophyceae and Euglenophyceae. Based on the results of the study it has been deduced that the reservoir is less in productivity.

Keywords: Mani reservoir, Phytoplankton, Productivity.

Introduction

Phytoplankton, the floating inconspicuous plant life plays a major role in the food chain of aquatic ecosystem by biosynthesis the organic matter and thus act as the primary producers of food on which other life forms depend. The status of the aquatic ecosystem is dependent on the abiotic propertied of water and biological diversity of the ecosystem.

Evaluation of the potentiality of an aquatic ecosystem is nothing but the estimation of the rate of its primary production, where it involves the primary fixation and its subsequent transfer of higher trophic levels. It is a well established fact that, the pollution of aquatic habitats is assessed by using algae as indictors (Patrick, 1973).

In view of the above thoughts, the present study was carried out which comprises the data on morphological features of the reservoir, physico-chemical characteristics of water and diversity of phytoplankton community. Based on this data an attempt has also been made to evaluate the trophic status of the reservoir.

Morphometric Features of the Reservoir

The Mani reservoir originates at near Mani village, located at 13°34′ to 13°45′ East and 74°52′ and 75°11′ North. It is situated about 95 km from Shimoga city.

Morphometry

1. Water spread area (sq km) : 163
2. Maximum height of the dam (mt) : 59
3. Maximum length of the dam (mt) : 585
4. Storage capacity (M cum) : 960

Materials and Methods

For the qualitative estimation of phytoplankton, water samples were collected with the help of plankton net of mesh size 50 microns during February 2004 to January 2005 Further these samples were fixed in 4 per cent formaldehyde and brought tó the laboratory for identification was made with the help of available literature (Hegde and Bharathi, 1985; Vaishya and Adoni, 1992). Further distribution pattern of the phytoplankton recorded in, Table 36.2.

The physico-chemical characteristics of water samples were analyzed from each tank at an interval of 30 days with help of black colored carboys can of 2 liters capacity. Key waters quality parameters like temperature, DO, free CO_2, BOD, pH, total hardness, total alkalinity, chloride, calcium, TDS, total acidity, sulphate and electrical conductivity was estimated by adopting the method given in APHA (1998).

Results and Discussion

The physico-chemical characteristics that are responsible for the abundance of phytoplankton. The temperature is one of the vital factors which control the abundance of phytoplankton in lentic ecosystem (Nazneen, 1980). In the present investigation temperature ranges between 25° C to 30° C favouring the growth of phytoplankton.

The data indicates that, the water in reservoir is slightly alkaline. Verma and Mohanthy (1995) are of the opinion that, higher pH values promote the growth of the algae and results in blooms. In the present investigation the pH value ranges from 6.5 to 8.5, Robert *et al.* (1974) suggested that, pH 5 to 8.5 is ideal for phytoplankton growth. The range in which the reservoir water under study also lies. Vashiya and Adoni (1992) have stated that, the alkaline pH favors the population of diatoms. The observations of the present investigation agrees with this.

Higher concentration of dissolved oxygen and low temperature favours the dominance of Chlorophyceae. In the present investigation dissolved oxygen ranges between 1.62 to 13.68 mg/l. Venkteshwaralu (1969). Dhakar (1979) also, observed that, green alga prefer water with higher concentration of dissolved oxygen. In the present study members of the Chlorophyceae dominated the other groups. This is also agreement with the findings of the Khatri (1987).

Table 36.1: Monthly Variation of Physico-chemical Characteristics of Mani Reservoir, February 2004 to January 2005

Parameter	*Feb*	*Mar*	*Apr*	*May*	*Jun*	*July*	*Aug*	*Sept*	*Oct*	*Nov*	*Dec*	*Jan*	*Range*
AT	31	32	33	30.5	31	29	28.5	34	26.0	30	28	33	26–33
WT	27	27	30	29.5	28	28	26	28	25.0	29	26	27	25–30
pH	8.4	8.5	8.2	7.6	8.0	7.1	6.5	7.2	8.0	6.5	8.3	7.5	6.5–8.5
EC	120	129	138	92	135	76	68	62	57.0	63	66	63	57–138
TDS	76.8	82.5	88.32	58.88	89.1	48.64	43.52	39.68	36.48	37.12	42.24	40.32	37.12–89.1
Tur	20	17.2	20.01	17.1	19.1	20.1	21.1	19.1	15.1	10.9	24	32	17.1–21.1
D.O	8.10	9.97	8.10	1.62	7.29	6.08	3.24	2.43	5.67	16.2	13.78	5.39	1.62–13.78
Free CO_2	8.8	8.8	8.8	8.8	8.8	4.4	8.8	8.8	4.4	13.2	4.4	4.4	4.4–13.2
Cl_2	12.75	15.60	19.85	19.85	18.43	19.85	14.18	8.50	14.18	12.75	15.60	9.92	8.50–19.85
Ca^{++}	6.73	12.0	11.78	6.73	12.62	3.87	5.30	6.73	5.05	4.20	10.10	5.05	3.87–12.62
Mg^{++}	2.24	3.89	4.53	2.24	4.02	2.8	4.57	0.78	1.31	2.31	3.61	2.92	0.78–4.57
TH	32	46	48	26	48	21.33	32	20	40	18.0	20.40	24.6	18–48
BOD	3.64	3.49	3.64	4.06	3.65	3.06	5.4	3.2	0.3	6.09	6.08	1.09	0.3–6.09
Total alkalinity	40	50	So	40	50	40	20	20	40	10	40	40	20–50
PO_4	0.01	0.03	0.18	0.18	0.14	0.06	0.01	0.09	0.03	0.001	0.001	0.001	0.001–0.18
NO_3	0.21	0.11	0.12	0.11	0.14	0.21	0.26	0.18	0.13	0.17	0.16	0.18	0.11–0.26
SO_4	22.04	22.87	24.57	22.04	24.96	2.04	11.13	11.53	11.1	13.44	41.0	25.15	2.04–25.15
Na^+	2.4	3.1	3.0	3.2	2.8	3.2	2.4	3.1	2.4	1.4	3.2	2.8	1.4–3.2
K^+	1.6	2.3	1.9	2.4	1.1	1.4	1.6	2.0	1.6	1.2	1.6	I.4	1.1–2.0

Note: All the parameters are in mg/l except pH, Temperature (°C), Turbidity (NTU) and Electrical conductivity (µmhos/cm).

Table 36.2: Diversity of Phytoplankton in Mani Reservoir

Chlorophyceae	*Bacillariophyceae*	*Cyanophyceae*	*Euglenophyceae*
Ankistrodesmus acicularis	*Acnathes exilis*	*Apanocapsa stagnina*	*Euglena minuta*
Ankistrodesmus convolutes	*Diatoma vulgare*	*Gleocapsa minutus*	*Phacus caudatus*
Ankistrodesmus falcatus	*Gomphonema gracile*	*Merismopedia tenuissima*	*Phacus tortus*
Closterium lunula	*Melosira granulate*	*Microcystis aeruginosa*	
Cosmarium sp.	*Navicula digitotadiata*	*Nostoc* sp.	
Crucigenia uadrata	*Navicula punctata*	*Phormidium* sp.	
Crucigenia tetrapedia	*Pinnularia nobilis*	*Oscillatoria pseudogeminata*	
Pediastrum simples	*Rhopalofia gibba*		
Scenedesmus quadricuada	*Surirella biseriata*		
Selenastrum gracile	*Surirella ovata*		
Staurastrum arachne	*Synedra acus*		
Staurastrum sp.			
Ulothrix sp.			

Generally Calcium concentration in natural fresh water falls below 10 mg/l. calcium concentration in the vicinity of lime stone ranges between 30–100 mg/l. Zafar (1964) has stated that, the calcium is one of the important elements influencing the distribution of Bacillariophyceae, in the present investigation calcium ranges between 3.67 to 12.68 mg/l, favoring the growth of Bacillariophyceae. This is agreement with the findings of Zafar.

Nitrate is an important source of nitrogen for controlling the occurrence of and abundance of phytoplankton. Nanadan and Patel (1992) have stated that, rainfall is responsible for increasing the nitrates in water. Higher concentration of nitrate is an indication of organic pollution. In the present study nitrate ranges between 0.1 to 0.26 mg/l. Based on the results the investigation concluded that, the water body is oligotrophic.

Phosphate is considered as one of the important nutrients limiting the growth of phytoplankton (Welch *et al.*, 1978). In the present study the phosphate ranges between 0.001 to 0.18 mg/l.

In all 34 species of phytoplankton belonging to four different classes of algae were recorded. The qualitative analysis showed that, Chlorophyceaee had 13 species, Bacillariophyceae 11 sp., Cyanophyceae 7 and Euglenophyceae 3 depicted in Table 36.2.

References

APHA, 1998. *Standard Methods for the Examination of Water and Wastewater*, 20th edition. Washington, D.C.

Dhakar, M.L., 1979. Studies in some aspects of the hydrobiology of Indrasagar tank (South Rajasthan). *Ph.D. Thesis*, University of Udaipur, Udiapur

Hegde, G.R. and S.G Bharathi, 1985. Comparative phytoplankton ecology of fresh water ponds and lakes of Dharward, Karnataka State, India. In: *Proc. Nat. Symp. Pure and Appl. Limnology*. Bull. Bot. Soc. Sagar, 32: 24–29.

Khatri, T.C., 1987. Seasonal distribution of phytoplankton in Indukki reservoir of Kerala (India). *Environ. Ecol.*, 5: 71–73.

Nandan, S.N. and Patel, R.S., 1991. Ecological studies of algae. In: *Aquatic Ecology*, (Eds.) S.R. Mishra and D.N. Saksena. Ashish Publishing House, New Delhi, pp. 69–99.

Nanzeen, S., 1980. Influence of hydrological factors on seasonal abundance of phytoplankton in Kinjhar lake, Pakistan. *Int. Rev. Ges. Hydrobiol.*, 65(2): 269–282.

Vaishya, A.K. and Adoni, A.D., 1992. Phytoplanktonic seasonality and their relationships with physico-chemical properties in a hypereutrophic central Indian lake. *Proc Indian. Sci. Acad.*, 59(B): 153–160.

Venkateshwaralu, V., 1969. An ecological study of the algae of the river Mosi, Hyderabad (India) with special reference to water pollution. IV periodicity of some common species of algae. *Hydrobiol.*, 36: 45–65.

Verma, J. and Mohanty, R.C., 1995. Phytoplankton and its correlation with certain physico-chemical parameters of Danmukundpur pond. *Poll. Res.*, 14(2): 233–242.

Welch, E.B., Staurtevant, P. and Perkins, M.A., 1978. Dominance of phosphorus over nitrogen as the limiter of phytoplankton growth rate. *Hydrobiologia*, 57(3): 209–215.

Zafar, A.R., 1964. The ecology of algae in certain fish ponds of Hyderabad, India: Physico chemical complex, *Hydrobiolgia*, 23: 176–196.

Chapter 37

Water Pollution and its Effect: An Overview

Rajendra Prasad Singh[1], M.T. Dan[2] and Umapati Sahay[3]

[1]Department of Zoology, Marwari College, Ranchi

[2]Retired Professor, Department of Zoology, Ranchi Women's College, Ranchi

[3]Former HOD of Zoology, Ranchi University, Ranchi

ABSTRACT

Water is one of the most important natural resources. Clean water is essential for the survival of living organisms. Unfortunately, the quality of water in lentic and lotic systems has tremendously deteriorated due to rapid industrialization and human interventions. Unconscious indiscriminate use of insecticides (organochlorides, organophosphates etc.) and thermal pollution have aggravated in reversing the water conditions, *i.e.*, changes in physiochemical characteristics of water.

In the present article, the authors have discussed the toxic effects of organochlorides, organophosphates and many other chemicals.

Water Pollution: Present Scenario

Water is being polluted everywhere (sea, rivers, lakes, ponds, ditches etc.) and every day is evident from the Tables 37.1 and 37.2.

Pesticides which Polluted Water

Organochlorides

These include DDT, *Endrin, Dieldrin, Chlordane, Aldrin, Endosulphan, Isobenzan, Heptachlor, Epoxide, Camphechtor* (*Toxaphene*), *Methoxychlor, Lindane,* BHC etc.

Table 37.1: Selected Indian Rivers and their Major Source of Pollution

River	*Major Source of Pollution*
Bhadra (Karnataka)	Pulp, Paper and Steel Industries.
Cauvery (Tamil Nadu)	Sewege, Tanneries, Distillaries, Paper and Rayon Mills
Cooum, Adyar and Buckingham Canal (Madras)	Domestic sewage, Automobile Workshops etc.
Dajora in Bareilly (UP)	Synthetic Rubber Factories
Damodar (between Bokaro and Panchet) Jharkhand	Fertilizer, Fly-ash from Steel Mills, Suspended coal from Washeries and Thermal Power Stations
Godawari	Paper Mills
Gomati (Lucknow)	Paper and Pulp Mills, sewage
The Ganga* (near Kanpur)	Jute, Chemicals, Metal and Surgical Industries, Tanneries, Textile Mills and great bulk of domestic sewage of organic maters from all cities touching the Ganges
Hoogly (near Kolkata)	Power Stations, Paper, Pulp, Jute, Textile, Chemical Mills, Paint, Varnishes, Metal, Steel, Hydrogenated vegetable oils, Rayon, Soap, Match, Shellac and Polythene Industries and sewage
Jamuna (near Delhi)	DDT factories, sewage (contains 7.500 coliform organisms), Indraprasth Power Station etc.
Kali (Meerut)	Sugar Mills, Distilleries, Paint, Soap, Rayon, Silk yarn, Tin and Glycerine Industries
Koshi	Sewage, Paper, Sulphur, Sugar Mills
Kulu (at Dalmianagar)	Cement, Pulp, Paper Mills
Suwa (at Balrampur)	Sugar Industries etc.

* Hardwar, Kannauj, Kanpur, Allahabad, Varanasi and Patna dump millions of tons of untreated sewage, 120 Industries along its bank pump effluents.

Table 37.2: Industrial and Agricultural Pollutants Discharged in World's Oceans (after Southwick, 1976)

Pollutant	*Estimated Annual Discharge (1970–75) in Metric Tons*	*Source*
Air borne lead	350,000	Vehicles
Aldrin-Toxaphene (converted to dieldrin)	25,000	Agricultural and public health operations
Benzene hexachloride	50,000	Agricultural and public health operations
DDT	25,000	Agricultural and public health operations
Hydrocarbons (air borne)	15,00,00	Vehicles, Industries and Power plants
Petroleum and industrial hydrocarbons	3,405,000	Offshore wells, oil tankers and industrial wastes
Polychlorinated Biphenols (PCB)	25,000	Plastic Industries

DDT has been found to affect central nervous system, increased excitability; muscular tremors and convulsions have been observed in certain water inhabiting animals. Presumably DDT residues accumulate in fatty acid tissues (subcutaneous fat and fatty tissues of the mesenteries, heart, liver, thyroid and gonads).

DDT impairs oxygen diffusion through gill membranes in fishes.

Organophosphates

These include *Parathion, Malathion, Ethion, Fenthion, Trithion, Monocrotophos, Dimethoate, Diazion, Durban, Azinophos-methyl, Phosdrin, Fonofos, Disulfoton, Forate, Demeton-methyl, Thionazin, Metasystox, Menazon* etc.

Pesticides Versus Physio-chemical Characteristic of Water

Pesticides contaminate water bodies to a great extent and reduce dissolved oxygen content. Sommani (1985) also found that pesticides like DDT, *Chlordane* and *Lindane* reduce dissolved oxygen level. Yadav and Kumari also found changes in free CO_2 level and total alkalinity level of water. They found that increased rate of respiration in polluted water (stress condition) is the causative factor in the reduction of dissolved oxygen.

Testing Toxicity of Chemicals (in Fishes)

The usual screening method is to test the aqueous concentration of the chemical LC50, which would kill 50 per cent of the test fishes within 24, 48 and 96 hours (Holden, 1973). Acute toxicity of various pesticides have been studied by Amminikutty (1977), Basak and Konar (1977), Verma *et al.* (1979,1981); Manuel molero and Pibano (1986); Kumari and Yadav (1987).

The acute toxicity is measured as median lethal concentration (LC) which kills 50 per cent of the test population (Sprague, 1969).

96 hour LC 50 value of different pesticides of organophosphate group as worked out by various authors is shown ni Tables 37.3 and 37.4.

Table 37.3: Toxic Effect of Organochlorides

Chemical	*Fishes*	*LC50 mg/l*	*Authors*
Thiodan	*M vittatus*	0.00024	Reddy and Gomathy, 1977
Thiodan	*Puntius sophore*	0.0012	Arora *et al.*, 1971 a&b
Thiodan	*H. fossilis*	0.00157	Basak and Konar, 1977
Thiodan	*Cyprinus carpio*	0.00092	Basak and Konar, 1977
Endrin	*O. puctatus*	0.003	Sharma *et al.*, 1976
Aldrin	*Cyprinus carpio*	0.0037	Rao *et al.*, 1975
Aldrin	*H. fossilis*	0.85	Singh and Singh, 1981
DDT	*H. fossilis*	2.95	Mustafa and Murad, 1984
DDT	*C. batrachus*	25.00	Kumari, M., 1987
Lindane	*S. fossilis*	0.537	Verma *et al.*, 1979
Lindane	*C. batrachus*	0.003	Kumari, M., 1987

The Biological Magnification of Pesticides

DDT when introduced during 2nd World War proved boon as it controlled malaria bearing mosquitoes, yet in later years when sprayed proved dangerous for wild life and environment; it showed biological magnification via food chain.

Table 37.4: Toxic Effect of Organophosphates

Chemical	*Fishes*	*LC50 mg/l*	*Authors*
Diazinon	*O. punctatus*	3.10	Sastry and Sharma, 1980
Cythion	*C. batrachus*	18.00	Kumari, M., 1987
Metacid	*C. batrachus*	12.00	Kumari, M., 1987
Diahlorovos	*S. fossilis*	6.61	Verma *et al.*, 1981
Diahlorovos	*M. vittatus*	0.45	Verma *et al.*, 1981
Diahlorovos	*C. mrigala*	0.29	Verma *et al.*, 1981
Fensulfothion	*S. fossilis*	15.17	Verma *et al.*, 1981
Fenitrothion	*S. fossilis*	12.55	Verma *et al.*, 1981
Fenitrothion	*Cyprinus carpio*	2.30	Toor and Kaw, 1974
Parathion	*H. fossilis*	32.00	Singh and Singh, 1981
Parathion	*M. cavasius*	5.90	Murty *et al.*, 1984
Malathion	*H. fossilis*	15.00	Verma *et al.*, 1979a
Malathion	*Cyprinus carpio*	3.15	Arora *et al.*, 1971b
Malathion	*Labeo rohita*	5.05	Arora *et al.*, 1971
Malathion	*Channa punctatus*	2.50	Dubale and Shah, 1971
Malathion	*Cirrhina mrigala*	0.88	Verma *et al.*, 1981

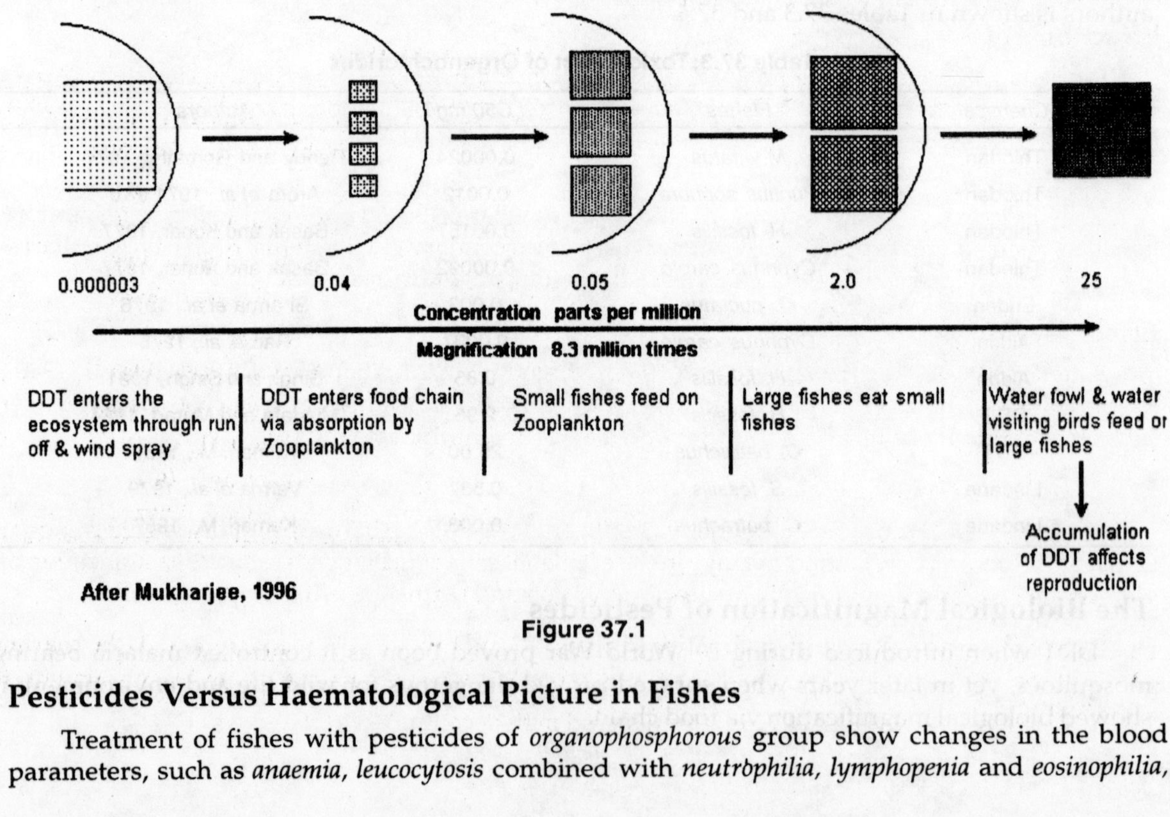

Figure 37.1

Pesticides Versus Haematological Picture in Fishes

Treatment of fishes with pesticides of *organophosphorous* group show changes in the blood parameters, such as *anaemia, leucocytosis* combined with *neutrophilia, lymphopenia* and *eosinophilia, monocytosis* and *basophilia* (Eisler and Edmunds, 1966; Srivastava and Mishra, 1983; Kumari and Yadav, 1987, 1989).

When treated with pesticides of organochloride group *polycythaemia, leucocytosis, lymphocytosis, eosinopenia, monocytopenia* and *basophilia* have been observed by Mahajan and Juneja, 1978; Dhillon and Gupta, 1983; Kumari, 1987.

Furguson *et al.*, 1966 reported that mosquito fish when were exposed to *Endrin*, showed a marked decrease in oxygen consumption rate.

The pollution of Mississippi by *Endrin* (USDA, 1966) and Rhine by *Endosulphan* (Greve, 1972) are worth mentioning.

The accumulation of minute quantity of DDT–0.005 to 0.026 mg/l, *Dieldrin*–0.007 to 0.018 mg/l could prove fatal to certain organism. Exp. Trace amount of pesticides were found in fatty tissue of seals and penguins in Antarctic (Moran *et al.*, 1973).

Terriere *et al.* (1966) found that *Camphechlor* persisted for about one year in shallow lake but up to 5 years in deeper lake.

Weiss and Gakstatler (1964) observe in certain water fishes inhibition in *acetylcholinesterase* activity when organophosphorus pesticides were mixed in water.

Changes in glucose and cholesterol level in fishes due to pesticides in water have been observed by Frank (1980), Mukhopadhya and Dehadrai (1980), Singh and Singh (1980), Awasthi *et al.* (1984), Dange (1986), Van Vuren (1986), Pandey *et al.*, 1987, Kumari and Yadav (1989 and 1990).

Pesticides Versus Histopathological Changes in Fishes

Effect on Gills

Pesticides in water are in touch with gills and consequently the blood vascular system. Works related to the effect of pesticides on gills have been studied by Mukhopadhya and Dehadrai (1980), Dieter (1982), Drewett and Abel (1983), Studnicka (1984), Konar (1985), Virtanen (1987) and Kumari (1987).

They found degenerative changes in the interlamellar cells and epithelial lining of respiratory lamellae, necrosis and exudation of erythrocytes from secondary gill filaments, rupture of capillaries in supporting gill axis and colour changes in the colour of gill filaments and gills.

Effect on Liver

King (1962), Mathur (1962, 1965 and 1976), Konar (1970), Mukhopadhya and Dehadrai (1980), Rashatwara and Iliyas (1984) and Kumari (1984) worked and found that pesticides damage liver cells, degeneration of cytoplasm due to vacuolization and haemorrhage of blood sunusoids.

Effect on Kidney

King (1962), Mathur (1962), Kennedy (1970), Shaft (1980), Rashatwara and Iliyas (1984), Konar (1985) and Kumari (1987) found damage in the epithelial cells of uriniferous tubules, vacuolization of glomerular cells and defects in the nuclear orientation and shrinkage in haemopoietic cells.

Pesticides Versus Reproduction in Fishes

1. Macek (1968 a)–observed in fishes fewer ova + heavy mortality of fish fry when a dose of 2 mg/kg per week of DDT is administered in fish–continued for 156 days.

2. Allison *et al.* (1964)–observed volume and number of ova is unaffected but mortality of fries higher in DDT exposed cut throat trout in water for 24 hours.
3. Konar (1970)–found that fries were more susceptible to *heptachlor* than adults.
4. Lenon (1967)–observed newly fertilized eggs of rainbow trout sensitive and toxic to exposure of *thiodon* when exposed for 29 days at 0.2 mg/L

Table 37.5: The Toxic and Pathological Effects of Heavy Metal Water Pollutants

Metal	*Pathogenic Effects on Man/Animals*
Arsenic	Disturbed peripheral circulation, mental disturbance, liver *cirrhosis, hyperkeratosis,* lung cancer, ulcer in gastro-intestinal tract, kidney damage etc.
Barium	Excessive salivation, vomiting, diarrhoea, paralysis, colic pain etc.
Cadmium	Diarrhoea, growth retardation, bone deformation, kidney damage, atrophy of testis, anaemia, injury, hypertension
Cobalt	Diarrhoea, low blood pressure, lung irritation, deformation of bone, paralysis
Copper	Hypertension, *uremia,* coma and sporadic fever
Hexavalent chromium	*Nephritis,* ulceration-of gastro-intestinal tract, diseases of central nervous system, cancer
Mercury–a byproduct of the production of vinyl chloride and some incinerator power plants, laboratories and hospitals	Results into Minamata diseases (Aaronson, 1971) Abdominal pain, headache, diarrhoea, haemolysis, chest pain etc.
Selenium	Liver damage, kidney damage, nervousness, fever, vomiting, low blood pressure, blindness and death
Zinc	Vomiting, renal cell damage, cramps etc.

Suggested Remedies for Sustenance of Life

1. Mass awareness about the effects of polluted water versus health be brought into effect–involvement of NGOs for the purpose would be effective.
2. Strict legislation and its implementation at several levels.
3. Avoidance of dumping sewage directly into rivers, ponds, lakes, estuaries and sea- this is only possible if sewage treatment plants are erected at proper places.
4. Biological control of insects/pests/predators be made effective in places of use of pesticides.
5. Radio active (Phosphorous-32) pollution can be removed by treating the radio active effluent through beds of aluminium turnings (Olsen, 1961).
6. Methods for sewage treatment as suggested by NERI should be made applicable wherever possible.
7. Development of new ideas/machinery and immediate researches be done to purify the polluted water.
8. Precipitation of Ca^{++} and Mg^{++} by electrolysis.

References

Arora, H.C., Srivastava, S.K. and Seth, A.K., 1971(a). Bioessay studies of some commercial organic insecticides Part I. Studies with a exotic carp *Puntius sophore. Indian J. Environ. Health,* 13.

Arora, H.C., Srivastava, S.K. and Seth, A.K., 1971(b). Bioessay studies of some commercial organic insecticides Part II. Trials of malathion with exotic and indigenous carp. *Indian J. Environ. Health,* 13.

Awasthi, M.P., Shah, M.S. Dubale and P. Gadhia, 1984. Metabolic changes induced by organophosphates in the piscine organs. *Environ. Res.,* 35(1).

Basak, P.K. and Konar, S.K., 1977. Estimation of safe concentrations of insecticides. A new method tested on DDT and BHC. *J. Inland. Fish. Soc., India,* 9.

Dange, A.D., 1986. Changes in carbohydrate metabolism in *Tilapia ereochromis mossambicus* during short term exposure to different types of pollutants. *Environ. Pollut. Ser. A. Ecol. Biol.,* 41: 2.

Eisler, R. and Edmunds, P.M., 1986. Effects of *endrin* on blood tissue chemistry of a marine fish. *Trans. Am. Fish. Soc.,* 95.

Frank, J., 1980. Haematological studies on rainbow trout (*Salmo gairdneri*) and carp (*Cyprinus carpio*) after application of sublethal concentrations of pesticides, rogor, benomyl, pomuran and damatol species. *Z. Aangews. Zool.,* 66: 4.

Holden, A.V., 1973. Effects of pesticides on fish. In: *Environmental Pollution by Pesticides,* (Ed.) C.A. Edward. Plenum Press, London, N.Y.

Hayes, H.B.N., 1960. *The Ecology of Polluted Waters.* Liverpool University Press, Liverpool.

Hynes, H.B.N., 1971. *The Biology of Polluted Waters.* Liverpool University Press, Liverpool.

Kendeigh, S.C., 1961. *Animal Ecology.* Prentice Hall.

Konar, S., 1970. Some effects of sublethal levels of heptachlor on rohu (*Labeo rohita*). *J. Inland Fish. Soc., India,* 2.

Kumari, M. and Yadav, S.C., 1987. Comparative toxicity and behavioural effect of *organophosphate* and *organochlorine* insecticides on *Clarias batrachus* (Linn). *Mendel,* 43.

Kumari, M., 1987. Effects of pesticides on the blood and certain tissues of a catfish, *Clarias batrachus* (Linn). *Ph. D. Thesis,* Magadh University, Bodh Gaya.

Kumari, M. and Yadav, S.C., 1989. The effect of DDT on freshwater Teleost fish *Clarias batrachus.* A biochemical and histopathological study. *Fishcoops,* 1: 4.

Kumari, M. and Yadav, S.C., 1990. Study of cholesterol content of blood in fresh water Teleost fish *Clarias batrchus* (Linn) exposed to *organophosphate* pesticides. In: *Proc. 77th Ind. Sc. Cong. Part II Abstr.,* pp. 73.

Lenon, R.E., 1967. U.S. Bull. Sport. Fish. Wild. Resource Pub. No. 39.

Macek, K.J., 1975. Acute toxicities of pesticides mixture to blue gills. *Bull. Environ. Contain. Toxicol.,* 14: 6.

Macek, L.L. *et al.,* 1975. *Bull. Environ. Contain. Toxicol.,* 14: 6.

Mahajan, C.L. and Juneja, C.J., 1978 *Proc. Ind. Sc. Cong. Assoc.* 65th Session.

Mathur, D.S., 1962. Studies on the histopathological changes induced by DDT in the liver, kidney and intestine of certain fishes. *Expermentia*, 18.

Mathur, D.S., 1965. Histopathological changes in the liver of certain fishes induced by *Dieldrin. Sc. and Cult.*, 31.

Mathur, D.S., 1967. Histopathological changes in the liver of fishes resulting from exposure to *Dieldrin* and *Lindane.* In: *Animal, Plant and Microbial Toxin.* Plenum Publishing Corporation, N.Y.

Moore, J.W. and Ramamoorthy, S., 1984. *Heavy Metals in Natural Waters.* Springer Verlag, N.Y.

Mukherjee, B., 1996. *Environmental Biology.* Tata McGrew Hill Publishing Co. Ltd., N.D.

Mukherjee, B., Sinha, A., Mahanty, Roy S., Chatterjee, P. and Sinha, P., 1992. The influx of detergents and their effect on the oxygen and carbon budgets in fresh water systems. *J. Ecobiol.*, 4(1): 47–53.

Mukhopadhya, P.K. and Dehadrai, P.V., 1980. Biochemical changes in the air breathing catfish, *Clarias batrachus* exposed to malathion. *Environ. Pollut. Ser. A Ecol. Biol.*, 22.

Murty, A.S., Ramni, A.V., Christopher, K. and Rajabhushanam, B.R., 1984. Toxicity of *methyl parathion* and *fensulphothion* to fish *Mystus cavasius. Pollut. Ser. A. Ecol. Biol.*, 34.

Mustafa, S. and Murad, A., 1984. Survival, behavioural response and haematological profile of catfish *Heteropneustes fossilis* exposed to DDT. *Japan J. Ichthyl.*, 31: 1.

Pandey, B.N., Perveen, R., Prasad, S.S., Yasmin, A. and Sinha, D.P., 1987.

Quantitative estimation of protein and caloric values in *Clarias batrachus* (Linn) as an indicator of water quality and extent of polluted load. *Proc. Nat. Nem. Environ. Conser. & Management* Abs. pp. 33.

Rashatwara, S.S. and Ilyas, R., 1984. Effect of *phosphomidon* in fresh water teleost fish *Nemachelius denisonil* (Day). Histopathological and biochemical studies. *J. Environ. Biol.*, 5: 1.

Reddy, T.G.K. and Gomathy, S., 1977. Toxicity and respiratory effects of pesticide *thiodan* on catfish *Mystus vittatus. J. Environ. Health*, 19.

Sahay, Umapati, Bakshi, R., Sah, H.C.P., Dan, M.T. and Sahay, Sarojini, 2002. Water pollution, laws and remedies. In: *Ecology of Polluted Waters,* (Ed.) Arvind Kumar. 24: 257–285.

Sastry, K.V. and Sharma, K., 1980. *Diazinon* effect on the activity of brain enzymes from *Ophiocephalus punctatus. Bull. Environ. Contam. Toxicol.*, 24.

Sastry, K.V. and Shukla, V., 1993. Uptake and distribution of cadmium in tissues of *Channa punctatus. J. Environ. Biol.*, 14(2): 137–142.

Singh, H. and Singh, T.P., 1981. Effect of *Parathion* and *Aldrin* on survival of ovarian 32P uptake and gonadotrophic potency in fresh water catfish *Heteropneustes fossilis. Endocrinologie*, 77.

Toor, H.S. and Kaur, K., 1974. Toxicity of pesticides to fish *Cyprinus carpio communis. Indian J. Expl. Biol.*, 12.

Van, Vuruen, J.H.J., 1986. The effect of toxicants on the haematology of *Labeo umbratus* (Telostei : Cyprinidae). *Comp. Biochem. Physiol. Comp. Pharmocol. Toxicol.*, 83: 1.

Verma, S.R., Bansal, S.K., Gupta, A.K. and Dalela, R.C., 1979. Pesticide induced haematological alteration in a fresh water fish *Saccobranchus fossilis. Bull. Environ. Cotam. Toxicol.*, 22.

Chapter 38

Control of Cabbage Butterfly, *Pieris brassicae* Linn. with Some Recently Developed Neem Extracts

M. Bhubaneshwari Devi

Department of Zoology Manipur College, Imphal

ABSTRACT

Pieris brassicae Linn. (the cabbage butterfly) is the serious pest of cabbage in Manipur. For the control of this pest three neem extracts namely Nimbecidine of T. Stanes and Co. Ltd., Achook of Godrej Agrovet Ltd. and Nimola of New Agro Seeds Company which are available in the local market were adopted. To test the effectiveness of the extracts, analysis of two way classification with three observations per cell is adopted. Achook is found to be more effective than other two extracts on the cabbage pest in both field and laboratory conditions.

Keywords: *Pieris brassicae, Neem extracts, Mortality, Treatment.*

Introduction

Of all the vegetables, cabbage is taken to be one of the most delicious items of foods for human being. It has a peculiar taste which is like by all sections of the people. It is a good source of vitamins A, B, C, protein, carbohydrates, fat, minerals etc. On the other hand, it is a leading vegetable of winter season. In its season, there is no homestead land from small to big without growing cabbage. Thus it plays an important role in family economy. But such nutrient and inevitably important vegetable is facing from insect pest incidence. The insect pests commonly found in Manipur are cabbage butterflies *viz.*, *Pieris brassicae* Linn., *Pieris napi* Linn., *Pieris rapae* Linn. and *Pieris canidia*. The incidence of *Pieris brassicae* Linn. is found to be very high in Manipur. Therefore, it is felt necessary to make a comprehensive study of the incidence and bionomics of the insect pest to adopt certain control measures.

In the present study, an attempt is made to study the control measure of the insect pest by applying plant extracts. The experiment of using chemical insecticides is not carried out. Since the application of such insecticides would be on commonly consumed edible vegetable, the high effectiveness of the chemical insecticides outweigh its side effects but the less side effect of the plant extracts comes into the limelight. For this study, after considering all these things, the method of using chemical insecticides is dropped and the method of using plant extracts is adopted.

Materials and Methods

The main problem in our hand is to select a plant extract which is more effective than others to the control of the cabbage butterfly. Different varieties of plant extracts are not available easily in plenty as chemical insecticides in the market. Some of the neem extracts are available in market. So, for this study three neem extracts are adopted. These are:

1. Nimbecidine of T. Stanes and Co. Ltd.
2. Achook of Godrej Agrovet Ltd.
3. Nimola of New Agro Seeds Company.

To test the effectiveness of the extracts on the pest the experiment is carried out in both field and laboratory conditions. The appropriate dose of the extracts is chosen with a trial before carrying out the actual experiment. In this study the extracts are applied to the pest in both fields and laboratory conditions at different doses *viz.*, 0.5 per cent, 1.0 per cent, 1.5 per cent and 2.0 per cent respectively. In this case 20 insects of each stage namely first, second, third, fourth, fifth instars and pupa are taken and the extracts are applied on them. The observations are taken for one week time. The number of mortal insects is noted. It is found that at 2.0 per cent, all the extracts are considerably effective to all different stages of the pest. Hence 2.0 per cent dose of the extracts is adopted to test their effectiveness on cabbage pest.

To carry out a statistical analysis to test the effectiveness of the extracts on one hand and their effectiveness on different stages of the insect on the other hand, analysis of variance of two way classification is adopted. The experiment is repeated three times by taking 20 insects of each stage as done above in an experiment.

The layout of the experiment for testing the effectiveness of the extracts in both field and laboratory conditions is given in Table 38.1.

Table 38.1

Treatment	*Number of Individuals*	*Duration of Observation*	*Mortality Rate at Different Stages of Insect*					
			1st Instar	*2nd Instar*	*3rd Instar*	*4th Instar*	*5th Instar*	*Pupa*
Achook	20	1 week	20,20,20	20,20,20	20,20,20	20,20,20	20,20,20	20,20,20
Nimbecidine	20	1 week	20,20,20	20,20,20	20,20,20	20,20,20	20,20,20	20,20,20
Nimola	20	1 week	20,20,20	20,20,20	20,20,20	20,20,20	20,20,20	20,20,20

Results and Discussion

Field Condition

The observation of the Analysis of variance of two way classification with three observations per cell for testing the effectiveness of the extracts in this case is given in Table 38.2.

Table 38.2

Treatment	*Number of Individuals*	*Duration of Observation*	*Mortality Rate at Different Stages of Insect*					
			1st Instar	*2nd Instar*	*3rd Instar*	*4th Instar*	*5th Instar*	*Pupa*
Achook	20	1 week	20,20,20	20,20,20	20,20,19,	17,15,16	16,16,15	18,18,19
Nimbecidine	20	1 week	20,20,19	17,17,16	16,16,16	16,16,17	16,17,17	17,17,18
Nimola	20	1 week	19,19,18	16,15,16	11,10,9	6,6,5	5,6,6	4,6,5

In this experiment, our interest is to find out the most effective plant extract among the three. For this we set up the null hypothesis: The plant extracts are equally effective.

We can also consider the effectiveness of the plant extracts at different stages of the insect. But it is sidelined since it is secondary in this context.

To test the above hypothesis we adopt the Analysis of variance of two way classification and the result shown in Table 38.3.

Table 38.3: Anova Table

Source of Variation	*Sum of Squares*	*d.f.*	*Mean Sum of Squares*	*Variance Ratio*	$F_{5\%}$
Treatment	662.49149	2	331.240745	813.04528	Between 3.23 and 3.32
Different stages of insects	349.20371	5	69.840742	171.427237	Between 2.45 and 2.53
Interaction	249.51851	10	24.951851	61.245439	
Residual	14.66667	36	0.407408		
Total	**1275.87038**	**53**			

From the Table 38.3, it is seen that the null hypothesis Ho is rejected at 5 per cent level of significance for (2, 36) d.f. As such it may be concluded that the plant extracts are differently effective on the pest *Pieris brassicae*.

Here, since Ho is rejected, it is needed to examine which plant extract is more effective. For this the value of Critical Difference (C.D) is calculated from the relation:

$$CD = t_{5\% \text{ for residual d.f.}} \times \sqrt{\frac{2S_E^{\,2}}{r}}$$

where,

S_E^2: Mean sum of squares due to residual

r: Number of observation per cell.

Here, $t_{5\% \text{ for } 36 \text{ d.f.}} = 1.96$

$$\text{Now, CD} = 1.96 \times \sqrt{\frac{(2 \times 0.407408)}{3}} = 1.02$$

In this case, the mean effects of the treatments namely, Achook, Nimbecidine and Nimola are 54.83, 51.33 and 31.00 respectively. By comparing the difference between the mean effects for different treatments with the Critical Difference (C.D.), it is found that the first treatment is significantly effective than others. That is, the neem extract Achook is more effective than the other extracts under consideration to cabbage pest.

Laboratory Conditions

The observations of the Analysis of variance of two ways classification with three observations per cell for testing the effectiveness of the extracts in this case is given in Table 38.4.

Table 38.4

Treatment	Number of Individuals	Duration of Observation	Mortality Rate at Different Stages of Insect					
			1st Instar	2nd Instar	3rd Instar	4th Instar	5th Instar	Pupa
Achook	20	1 week	20,20,20	20,20,20	20,20,20	20,20,20	20,20,20	20,19,20
Nimbecidine	20	1 week	20,20,20	18,17,19	18,17,18	17,17,16	15,16,16	17,17,18
Nimola	20	1 week	17,17,17	16,14,15	11,10,9	6,6,5	3,5,4	2,3,3

For this we set up the null hypothesis Ho: The plant extracts are equally effective. To test the above hypothesis we adopt the Analysis of variance of two way classification and the result shown in Table 38.5.

Table 38.5: Anova Table

Source of Variation	Sum of Squares	d.f.	Mean Sum of Squares	Variance Ratio	$F_{5\%}$
Treatment	1179.14815	2	589.574075	1675.63114	Between 3.23 and 3.32
Different stages of insects	264.59260	5	52.918520	150.39996	Between 2.45 and 2.53
Interaction	299.07407	10	29.907407	84.99998	
Residual	12.66667	36	0.351852		
Total	**1755.48149**	**53**			

In this case also, from the Table 38.5, it is seen that the null hypothesis Ho is rejected at 5 per cent level of significance for (2, 36) d.f. As such it may be concluded that the plant extracts are differently effective on the *Pieris brassicae*.

Since the null hypothesis Ho is rejected, it is needed to examine which plant extract is more effective. For this, the value of Critical Difference (C.D.) is calculated from the relation:

$$\text{CD} = t_{5\% \text{ for residual d.f.}} \times \sqrt{\frac{2S_E^2}{r}}$$

where,

S_E^2: Mean sum of squares due to residual

r: Number of observation per cell.

Here, $t_{5\% \text{ for } 36 \text{ d.f.}} = 1.96$

$$\text{Now, CD} = 1.96 \times \sqrt{\frac{(2 \times 0.351851944)}{3}} = 0.95$$

The mean effects of the treatments namely, Achook, Nimbecidine and Nimola are 53.83, 52.87 and 27.17 respectively. The difference between the mean effects of different treatments compare with the C.D. It is found that the first treatment is significantly effective than others. Hence the treatment Achook is the most effective of all the extracts under consideration on the cabbage pest *Pieris brassicae.*

The results obtained in present findings are in conformity with those reported earlier by Singh, *et al.* (1985) and Pandey, *et al.* (1981) who have done in different test insects.

The recent findings are in lines with Singh, *et al.* (1997) who have reported the increase of mortality of test insects with the increase in concentration and time. Many reasearchers such as Rataul (1975), Ram and Pathak (1971) and Sachan and Srivastava (1975) used insecticides for the control of cabbage pests but less work is done in the control of cabbage pests by using Neem extracts. From the ecological point of view Neem extracts are better than the chemical insecticides for the control measures because these do not cause any health hazard.

References

Pandey, U.K., Pandey, M. and Chuahan, S.P.S., 1981. Insecticidal properties of some plant material extracts against painted bug, *Bagrada cruciferarum* Kirk. *Indian J. Ent.*, 43 (4): 404–407.

Rataul, H.S., 1975. Cabbage butterfly and its control. *Indian Farming*, 24(12): 29–30.

Ram, S. and Pathak, K.A., 1971. Insecticidal control of cabbage butterfly, *Pieris brassicae* Linn. (Pieridae : Lepidoptera) in Manipur. *Indian J. Ent.*, 54(3): 353–355.

Singh, R.P., Singh, Y. and Singh, S.P., 1985. Field evaluation of neem (*Azadirachta indica* A. Juss.) seed kernel extracts against the pod borers of pigeon pea, *Cajanus cajan* (L) MILLSP. *Indian J. Ent.*, 47(1): 111–112.

Singh, S.V., Pandey, S., Guddewar, M.B. and Malik, Y.P., 1997. Response of neem extractives against red cotton bug, *Dysdercus koenigii* on cotton seed. *Indian J. Ent.*, 51(1): 41–44.

Sachan, J.N. and Srivastava, B.P., 1975. Studies on the insect pests of cabbage II, Insecticidal control. *Indian J. Ent.*, 37(4): 344–352.

Chapter 39

Studies on the Pollen Foraging Behaviour of Rock Bee, *Apis dorsata*, at Mannampandal, Nagai District, Tamil Nadu

S. Thiripurasundari[1], M. Varadharajan[2] and V. Mathivanan[1]

[1]Department of Zoology, Annamalai University, Annamalainagar – 608 002, Tamil Nadu, India

[2]A.V.C. College, Mannampandal – 609 305, Mayiladuthurai, Tamil Nadu, India

ABSTRACT

Honeybees play an important role in the conservation of forest and grassland ecosystem. Since, the invasion of rockbee in human dwellings, they started foraging on several agricultural and horticultural crops as evidenced in the present study. In view of this, the present study has been undertaken to analysis the pollen foraging behaviour of rock bee, *Apis dorsata* at Mannampandal. Nagai District, Tamil Nadu. The study was carried out from September 2002 to February 2003. The results are discussed in detail.

Keywords: Honey Bee, Apis dorsata, Pollen foraging behaviour.

Introduction

Honeybees are the most important pollinating insects for commercial fruit production. They are the fascinating social insects; for they produce not only honey and wax but also act as effective pollinators of many Angiosperm plants (Mishra, 1996). They are the only managed insects available for pollination of variety of wild as well as cultivated plants throughout the world.

The forage availability of honeybees is not constant and it differs from day to day and season to season. Such changes in forage availability is better understood by the analysis of pollen or honey collected from the hive. The pollen analytical data provide interesting information regarding the bee flowering changes of the plants in the locality also (Thiripurasundari, 2003).

Since pollen is the only source of protein for the entire colony (Seeley, 1995), the selective foraging behaviour upon specific pollen with high nutritive content would support the larval development of the colony in a better way. Hence, the honeybees should exhibit preference to pollen types. Similar to protein, minerals in the pollen also play a vital role in the developmental stages of the honeybees (Thiripurasundari, 2003).

Apis dorsata is very meager because of its wild nature. Hence, an attempt has been made in the present study to find out the forage sources of the rock bee *A. dorsata* collected from Mannampandal village near Mayiladuthurai, Nagai district, Tamil Nadu. The study was carried out from September 2002 to February 2003 with the following objectives.

1. To enlist the bee flora of *Apis dorsata* based on the comb pollen analysis, and
2. To find out the floral preferences based on the percentage composition of pollen loads.

Materials and Methods

Method of Collection and Rearing of Honey Bee

Study Area

Mannampandal is a nearby village of Mayiladuthurai in Nagapattinam district. The study area is rich in agricultural and horticultural activities. Main agricultural crops of this area includes paddy, sugarcane, cotton, brinjal and gingelly. The area is dominated by trees like coconut, mango, tamarind etc. and also rich in different types of herbs and shrubs. Many of the plants located in the study area act as forage sources of honeybees serving as pollen sources or nectar source of both.

Collection of Comb Pollen

Pollen loads were collected from comb of *Apis dorsata* and simply scrapped out with a sharp needle. After collection of the pollen loads, they were weighed using electronic balance of 1 mg sensitivity.

Identification of Pollen Types

The pollen types present in various collections were identified by comparing to reference-slides of the local flora and relevant literature. (Brian, 1983).

Results and Discussion

Bee Flora

The analysis of hundred comb pollen loads from *Apis dorsata* colonies revealed the presence of 28 pollen types collected by worker bees. The list of bee plants recovered from the comb pollen loads has been given in Table 39.1.

The bee plants identified were representing 20 families. The family *Asteraceae* contributed a maximum of five plants (17.85 per cent) in the bee flora of *A. dorsata*, followed by *Arecaceae* (10.73 per cent) and *Fabaceae* (10.73 per cent) each with three plants. The remaining families were represented by single species of plant.

Table 39.1: List of Bee Plants (Species) Identified from the Comb Pollen Loads of *Apis dorsata* in the Study Area

Sl.No.	Name of the Plant Species	Local Name	Family	Nature of the Plant	Other Uses
1.	*Allium cepa*	Onion	LILIACEAE	Tuber	Vegetable
2.	*Ageratum conyzoides*	Mookuthi Poondu	ASTERACEAE	Herb	Not known
3.	*Amaranthus spinosus*	Mullukkirai	AMARANTHACEAE	Herb	Leaves as vegetables
4.	*Areca catechu*	Pakku	ARECACEAE	Tree	Seed as masticant
5.	*Aspidopterys indica*	Not known	MALPIGHIACEAE	Shrub	Not known
6.	*Cajanus cajan*	Tuvarai	FABACEAE	Shrub	Pulse crop
7.	*Capparis grandis*	Mudkondai	CAPPARIDACEAE	Tree	Not known
8.	*Citrus lemon*	Elumitechai	RUTACEAE	Tree	Fruit
9.	*Cocos nucifera*	Thennai maram	ARECACEAE	Tree	Fruit edible, edible oil
10.	*Eupatorium odoratum*	Not known	ASTERACEAE	Herb	Not known
11.	*Evolvulus alsinoides*	Vishnukiranthi	CONYOLVULACEAE	Herb	Not known
12.	*Helianthus annuus*	Sunflower	ASTERACEAE	Shrub	Oilseed, ornamental
13.	*Lagerstoreemia parviflora*	Chennangi	LYTHRACEAE	Tree	Timber
14.	*Mangifera indica*	Maamararn	ANACARDIACEAE	Tree	Fruits and vegetables
15.	*Momordica charantia*	Bitterguard	CUCURBITACEAE	Twiner	Fruits and vegetable, medicinal
16.	*Ocimum basilicum*	Tulsi	LAMINACEAE	Herb	Aromatic plant and medicinal
17.	*Pangamia pinnata*	Pungam	FABACEAE	Tree	Timber, oil from seed and medicinal
18.	*Phoenix sylvestris*	Icham	ARECACEAE	Tree	Fruits edible
19.	*Phyla nodiflora*	Podudhalai	VERBENACEAE	Herb	Medicinal
20.	*Samnaea saman*	Thoongumoonji	MIMOSACEAE	Tree	Avenue tree
21.	*Sapindus emarginatus*	Pounanga	SAPINDACEAE	Tree	Soapnut
22.	*Sesbania grandiflora*	Agati	FABACEAE	Tree	Vegetable, hedge
23.	*Solanum torvum*	Sundai	SOLANACEAE	Shrub	Vegetable and medicinal
24.	*Sterculia urens*	Kavalam	STERCULIACEAE	Tree	Vegetable and medicinal
25.	*Terminalia alata*	Marudarn	COMBRETACEAE	Tree	Timber, tannin
26.	*Tridax procumbens*	Vettukayapoondu	ASTERACEAE	Herb	Medicinal
27.	*Vernonia cinerea*	Not known	ASTERACEAE	Tree	Medicinal
28.	*Zea mays*	Makka cholam	POACEAE	Herb	Corn

The plants were also classified as trees, shrubs, herbs, twiner and tuber as given in Table 39.1 and Figure 39.1. The tree species dominated the bee flora with 14 plants contributing 50 per cent followed by herb types of plants with 28.57 per cent followed by shrub type with 14.28 per cent and the remaining twiner and tuber represented by 3.57 per cent each. The study area was rich in tree species and hence their representation was also more. The tree species like *Areca catechu*, *Capparis grandis*, *Citrus lemon*, *Cocos nucifera*, *Lagerstoreemia parviflora*, *Mangifera indica*, *Pongamia pinnata*, *Phoenix sylvestris, Samaea saman, Sapindus emarginatus* and *Terminalia alata* etc., were abundant in the study area and included in the list of bee flora.

Table 39.2: Other Uses of Bee Forage Plants of *Apis dorsata*

Sl.No.	Name of the Plant Species	Other Uses
1.	*Allium cepa*	Vegetable
2.	*Ageratum conyzoides*	Not known
3.	*Amaranthus spinosus*	Leaves as vegetables
4.	*Areca catechu*	Seed as masticant
5.	*Aspidopterys indica*	Not known
6.	*Cajanus cajan*	Pulse crop
7.	*Capparis grandis*	Not known.
8.	*Citrus lemon*	Fruit
9.	*Cocos nucifera*	Fruit edible, edible oil
10.	*Eupatorium odoratum*	Not known
11.	*Evolvulus alsinoides*	Not known
12.	*Helianthus annuus*	Oilseed, ornamental
13.	*Lagerstoreemia parviflora*	Timber
14.	*Mangifera indica*	Fruits and vegetables
15.	*Momordica charantia*	Fruits and vegetable, medicinal
16.	*Ocimum basiilicum*	Aromatic plant and medicinal
17.	*Pongamia pinnata*	Timber, oil from seed and medicinal
18.	*Phoenix sylvestris*	Fruits edible
19.	*Phyla nodiflora*	Medicinal
20.	*Samnaea saman*	Avenue tree
21.	*Sapindus emarginatus*	Soapnut
22.	*Sesbania grandiflora*	Vegetable, hedge
23.	*Solanum torvum*	Vegetable and medicinal
24.	*Sterculia urens*	Vegetable and medicinal
25.	*Terminalia alata*	Timber, tannin
26.	*Tridax procumbens*	Medicinal
27.	*Vernonia cinerea*	Medicinal
28.	*Zea mats*	Corn

Shrub species like *Cajanus cajan, Helianthus annus, Solanum torvum* etc., were cultivated in this study area. Herb species like *Ageratum conizoides, Amaranthus spinosus, Evolvulus alsinonides, Ocimum basilicum, Phyla nodiflora* etc., were also very common. *Zea mays* was cultivated in vast area in the agricultural tract which was also identified from pollen analysis. The only representation under shrub, tuber and twiner category were *Aspidopterys indica, Allium cepa* and *Momordica charantia*, respectively.

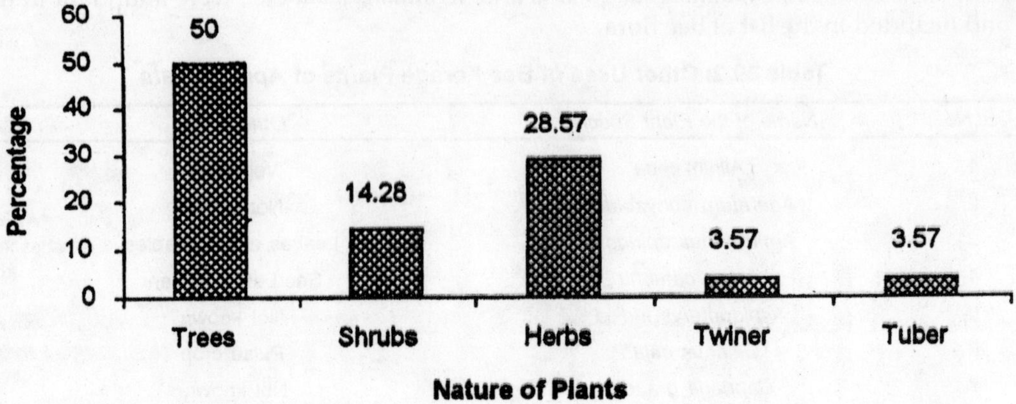

Figure 39.1: Classification of Bee Flora of *Apis dorsata* Based on the Nature of Plants

The plants were also categorized based on their human uses as given in Table 39.1 and Figure 39.1. The results indicated that the major contribution of bee flora was from medicinal plants, since, the number of plants represented in this type was minimum with 8 plants. The important medicinal plants identified from the pollen analysis were *Momordica charantia, Ocimum basilicum, Pongamia pinnata, Phyla nodiflora, Solanum torvum, Sterculia urens, Tridax procumbens* and *Vernonia cinerea.*

The vegetable category was next to medicinal plants with 6 plants. The important vegetables contributing pollen to *A. dorsata* were *Allium cepa, Amaranthus spinosus, Mangifera indica, Momordica charantia, Sesbania grandiflora* and *Solanum torvum.* The fruit yielding plants that served as pollen flora were the 5 species of plants such as *Citrus lemon, Cocos nucifera, Mangifera indica, Momordica charantia* and *Phoenix sylvestris.* The timber yielding plants were 3 species such as *Lagerstoreemia parviflora, Pongamia pinnata* and *Terminalia alata* and all other categories like pulses, oil seeds, ornamental plants, avenue tree, soap nut, aromatic plant and corn were less in number and were represented by single plant each.

Percentage Composition of Floral Types

The relative representation of each plant species in the overall pollen analysis is given in and Figure 39.2. *Cocas nucifera* was the predominant pollen source for *Apis dorsata* as it contributed the maximum of 7.84 per cent in the pollen pellets. *Mangifera indica* was the net predominant plant in the pollen flora with 7.0 per cent. Plants with almost equal representation were *Citrus lemon, Momordica charantia, Evolvulus alsinoides* etc. Remaining plants contributed very less in the pollen composition of *A. darsata* as for *e.g. Capparis grandis* and *Ocimum basilicum* represented only 1.36 per cent and 1.04 per cent, respectively.

Discussion

The present study clearly indicated the availability of rich forage sources for the rock bee *A. dorsata* in the study area. The presence of 28 plant species of 20 families showed the suitability of the study area for the survival of *A. dorsata.* Rock bee, being the wild species of honeybees started invading the plains as they were reported to colonize in tall buildings from several parts of India and other countries (Schmidt *et al.*, 1985 and Varadharajan *et al.*, 2001). As such in the present study also, the

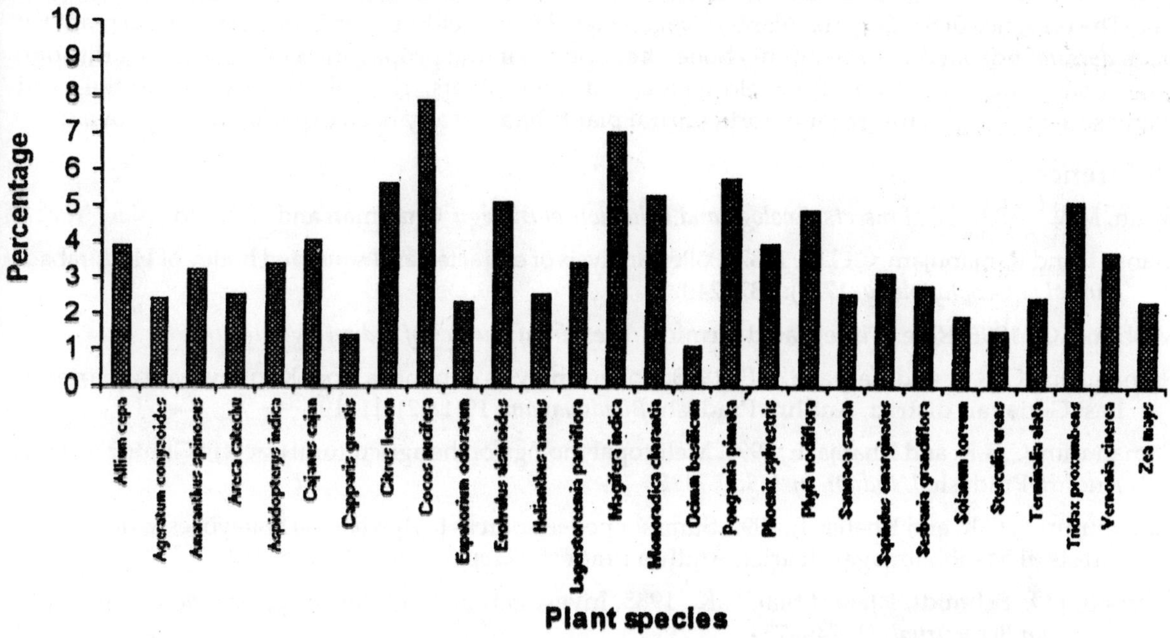

Figure 39.2: Relative Representation of Plant Species in the Comb Pollen Analysis of *Apis dorsata*

colony was found in the sun shade area. Since the invasion of rock bee in human dwellings, they started foraging on several agricultural and horticultural crops as evidenced in the present study.

Plants like *Cocos nucifera, Sapindus emarginatus, Phoenix sylvestris, Tridax procumbens* etc. were earlier reported as forage sources for the rock bee (Ramanujam and Kalpana., 1990; Vaissiera and Vinson, 1994) and the results of the present study was also in accordance with the previous reports. The study also revealed the importance of *Asteracea* as the major plant family contributing more number of plant species as a forage source for which *A. dorsata*. Similar observation of *Asteracea* as a major plant family, had been reported by Jhansi and Ramanujam, (1987).

Among 28 plants identified from the comb pollen analysis, *Cocos nucifera* dominated with 7.84 per cent of the overall occurrence. Similar observation indicating the importance of *Cocas nucifera* in the pollen flora of rock bee had been reported by Ramanujam and Khatija (1991), Ramanujam and Kalpana (1993) and Singaravelan (1998). Since the coconut plantations were more among the human dwellings and also due to the availability of bloom throughout the year in *Cocos nucifera*, this species had been revealed as the major bee flora of *Apis dorsata*.

The study also indicated the major contribution to bee flora from the tree sources since 14 tree, species were identified. The presence of trees as major category of forage source of the rock bee had been reported by Ramanjum and Khatiji (1992) and Singh (1997). Among the three species of honeybees available in the study area, the rock bees are larger in size and their dependence on tall trees may be related to the nutritive requirements in large quantity due to the enormous size of the colony. Since trees provide large bloom, occurrence of trees as in the bee flora of major category rock bee had been referred. (Thiripurasundari, 2003).

The presence of 8 medicinal plants, 6 vegetables, 7 fruit yielding plants etc., in the floral plant list of *A. dorsata* indicated the role of this honey bee species in the propagation of these plants through cross pollination and also in the yield increase of these plants. The role of rock bees in the yield increase in many agricultural and horticultural plants had already been experimentally proved.

References

Brain, M.V., 1983. *Social Insects: Ecology and Behavioural Biology.* Chapman and Hall Ltd., New York.

Jhansi, P. and Ramanujam, C.G.K., 1987. Pollen analysis of extracted and squeezed honey of Hyderabad. *Journal of Geophytology*, 17(2): 237–240.

Mishra, R.C., 1996. Role in integrated farming. *The Hindu, Survey of Indian Agriculture.*

Ramanujam, C.G.K. and Kalpana, T.P., 1993. Pollen analysis of honeys from Kondevaram apiaries of East Godavari district, Andhra Pradesh. *Biovigyanam*, 19(1&2): 11–19.

Ramanujam, C.G.K. and Khatija, F., 1991. Melittopalynology of the agricultural tracts in Guntur district, Andhra Pradesh. *J. Indian. Inst. Sci.*, 71: 25–34.

Ramanujam, C.G.K. and Khatija, F., 1992. Summer pollen sources to *Apis dorsata* honeybees in deciduous forests of Mahboobnagar district, Andhra Pradesh. *Geophytology*, 21: 155–161.

Schmidt, J.O., Schmidt, P.J. and Star, C.K., 1985. Investigation giant honeybee *Apis dorsata* in Sabh. *American Bee Journal*, 11: 749–751.

Seeley, T.D., 1995. *Honeybee Ecology.* Princeton University Press, Princeton.

Singaravelan, N., 1998. Habitat selection for colonisation and pollen foraging in the rock bee *Apis dorsata* in a part of Dharmapuri district, Tamil Nadu. Dissertation submitted to A.V.C. College, Mannampandal, Mayiladuthurai.

Singh, B., 1997. Role of honeybees in farm production, agricultural growth and rural reconstruction in India. *Indian Bee Journal*, 56(1): 24–30.

Singh, S., Jain, K.L. and Saini, Kavitha, 1998. Comparison of nutritional value as determinant of honeybee preference for pollen sources. *Indian Bee Journal*, 60(3): 137–140.

Thiripurasundari, S., 2003. Bee flora and biochemistry of honey and pollen of the rock bee, *Apis dorsata*, at Mannampandal, Tamil Nadu. *M.Phil Thesis*, A.V.C. College, (Autonomous) Tamil Nadu.

Vaissiere, E.E. and Vinson, S.B., 1994. Pollen morphology and its effect on pollen collection by honeybees, *Apis mellifera* L. (Hymenoptera : Apidae), with special reference to upland cotton, *Gossypium hirsutum* L. (Malvaceae). *Grana*, 33: 128–138.

Varadharajan, M., Thiyagesan, K., Singaravelan, N. and Paulra, S., 2001. Nest-site selection by the rock bee *Apis dorsata*. *Indian Bee Journal*, 5(2): 369–374.

Chapter 40

Mosquitocidal Effect of the Plant Extract Against the Yellow Fever Mosquito, *Aedes aetypti* L.

***Renugadevi Arasappan*[1]* *and T. Thangaraj*[2]**

[1]11, Murungappalayam, South, I Street, Tirupur - 641 603, Tamil Nadu
[2]Reader, PG and Research Department of Zoology, Kongunadu Arts And Science College, GN Mills Post, Coimbatore - 641 029, Tamil Nadu, India

ABSTRACT

The plant extracts of *Croton sparsiflorus, Luffa cylindrica, Solanum elaeagnifolium* and *Synadenium grandi* were tested against the hatching of eggs, larval-larval and larval-pupal transfonnations of the mosquito, *Aedes aegypti.* Among the plants tested, *Solanum elaeagnifolium* and *Luffa cylindrica* were found to be active and the LC50 values were ranged between 0.33 mg/ml to 31.88 mg/ml in the crude fractions and LC50 values for silica gel fractions were found between 0.059 to 0.81 mg/ml. I instar larval stages was found more susceptible than the other stages such as egg, IV instar and pupa.

Keywords: Solanum eleaegnifolium, Luffa cylindrica, Aedes aegypti, Plant extracts, Silica gel fractions.

Introduction

Mosquitoes are the vectors for the dreadful diseases of mankind. The yellow fever mosquito, *Aedes aegypti* causes dengue fever and yellow fever by transmitting the arbo virus and togo virus respectively. Yellow fever is not endemic to India. Dengue fever continues recurrent epidemics afflicting millions

* Corresponding Author: E-mail: a_renuqadevire@yahoo.co.in.

and causing death annually. Almost 1.2 million dengue fever cases were reported in America from 1976 to 1985 and an epidemic in Cuba in 1987 involved 350,000 cases of dengue (Gubler, 1988). In order to control the vector mosquito, chemical pesticides are being used from past. But the indiscriminate use of the chemical insecticides lead to the abrupt changes in the environment and their biota. The repeated application of synthetic insecticides has also develops resistance among the mosquitoes. Therefore this situation warranted in search of compounds from plant materials, which are non-toxic, environmentally safe, biodegradable and non-target species-specific compounds. Efforts are being made to isolate, screen and develop phytochemicals possessing pesticidal property. These categories of pesticides are known as Biopesticides (Mulla, 1997). Beerenbaum (1989) envisaged over 20,000 species of North American plants especially belonging to Rutaceae, Solanaceae, Verbenaceae and Cucurbitaceae as having potential insecticidal activity. In the present study, the effect of plant materials as crude and partially isolated have been used to observe insecticidal property on mosquito developments such as egg, I–instar, II–instar and pupal forms of *Aedes aegypti*.

Materials and Methods

Rearing of Mosquito

Fresh eggs of *A. Aegypti* were collected from the enamel trays contained 4 liters of water which was kept along the sides of the compound wall at college campus and allowed to hatch in laboratory conditions (28±2°C). Larval forms were maintained in plastic trays by providing yeast and fish food (composed of glutamine, spirulin, white fish meal, shrimp meal, soya bean, wheat flour, wheat germ, dried yeast and squid) in the ratio of 1 : 1. Eggs, I and IV instar larval and pupal stages were sacrificed when ever required.

Preparation of Plant Extracts

The plants, *Croton sparsiflorus* (aerial), *Luffa cylindrica* (leaf), *Solanum elaeagn!folium* (fruit) and *Synadenium grandi* (leaf) were collected from the places of Tirupur (Coimbatore District), Coimbatore and Kunnathur (Erode District), India and identified taxonomically. The plants were washed with tap water followed by distilled water. Necessary parts of the plants were air dried under shade, powdered and extracted with technical grade methanol in the ratio of 1 : 10 (w : v) as detailed by Muthukrishnan *et al.* (1997). The extracts were concentrated at 45°C under low pressure and dissolved in methanol, defated with an equal volume of petroleum ether and fractionated in ethyl acetate as detailed by Al-Sharook *et al.* (1991). Fractions obtained from petroleum ether and ethyl acetate were taken as the stock solution.

Fractionation of Active Principle

Leaves of *L. cylindrica* and fruits *S. elaeagnifolium* were taken based on the effect of crude extracts tested to purify on silica gel column. Sufficient quantity of powdered plant materials were dissolved in 80 per cent acetone and extracted for 48 hrs. Clear supernatant was air-dried, concentrated and dissolved in 1 per cent acetone (50 mg/100 ml). Column was packed with silica gel (60 × 120 mesh) (ACME Synthetic Chemicals, Mumbai, India) and washed with 1 per cent acetone several times. Sample was centrifuged at 5000 rpm for 2 minutes. The clear supernatant applied over the column and eluted with 1 per cent acetone. Fractions collected at the rate of 3 m;/minute and were air dried and used for bioassay.

Bioassay

To obtain the different concentrations of test medium for crude extract 1 to 10 gm of stock powder and for silica gel fractions 0.001 mg to 1 mg of dried powder were dispensed in 100 ml of 0.02 per cent acetone. Crude samples were tested and LC50 values were obtained in the plants, *Solanum eleaegnifolium* and *Luffa cylindrica* in all the stages of development, *i.e.*, egg, I and IV instars and pupa. To test the effect of the extracts each trail contained minimum of 25 eggs, larvae and pupae. Extracts fractionated using silica gel was, tested against I–instars only. Appropriate control was maintained. The effect of crude and silica gel fractions was noticed for a period of 24 hrs. LC50 values were calculated by the method of Finney (1971).

Results

Plants extracted with the organic solvents such as petroleum ether and ethyl acetate was tested on the development of egg, larvae and pupal stages. The results revealed that *L. cylindrica* and *S. elaeagnifolium* showed good results on the developmental stages of *A. aegypti*. Mortality in control was negligible. Exposure of the eggs to plant extracts of Petroleum ether (PE) and Ethyl acetate (EA) for 24 hours, the plant *S. elaeagnifolium* showed more effect on the egg hatching and the LC50 value in PE soluble fraction was 31.88 mg/ml and for EA fractions it was 18.94 mg/ml (Tables 40.1 and 40.2). *L. cylindrica* did not show effect on egg stage even at higher concentration. In the case of I–instar larval treatment, the order of LC50 values of PE soluble fractions were 0.78 and 3.37 mg/ml in the plants *S. elaeagnifolium* and *L. cylindrica* respectively and LC50 values for EA fractions was 0.33 and 25.15 mg/ml in *S. laeagnifolium* and *L. cylindrica* (Tables 40.1 and 40.2). In the fourth instar larvae, the order of LC50 concentration for PE fraction was 9.16 and 3.96 mg/ml in the plants *S. elaeagnifolium* and *L. cylindrica* respectively and LC50 value for EA fractions was 0.44 and 30.24 mg/ml in the plants, *S. elaeagnifolium* and *L. cylindrical* respectively (Tables 40.1 and 40.2). When pupal stages were treated with the PE extract of the plants, LC50 values were 31.06 and 21.18 mg/ml in the plants, *S. elaeagnifolium* and *L. cylindrica* respectively and LC50 value for EA fraction was 1.99 mg/ml in the plant, *S. elaeagnifolium* (Tables 40.1 and 40.2). *L. cylindrica* did not show effect on pupal stage even at higher concentration.

Table 40.1: Effect of Crude Extracts (Petroleum Ether Fractions)

Plant Name	*LC50 in mg/ml*			
	Egg	*I Instar*	*IV Instar*	*Pupa*
S. elaeagnifolium	31.88	0.78	9.16	31.06
L. cylindrical	–	3.37	3.96	21.18

* 1 to 10 gm of plant extract was dissolved in 100 ml of 0.02 per cent acetone. Mortality rate was, observed for a period of 24 hrs.

Table 40.2: Effect of Crude Extracts (Ethyl Scetate Fractions)

Plant Name	*LC50 in mg/ml*			
	Egg	*I Instar*	*IV Instar*	*Pupa*
S. elaeagnifolium	18.94	0.33	0.44	1.99
L. cylindrical	–	25.15	30.24	–

* 1 to 10 gm of plant extract was dissolved in 100 ml of 0.02 per cent acetone. Mortality rate was observed for a period of 24 hrs.

Fractions of silica gel column showed that the active principles were found between 4th to 9th fractions. Among the four plants tested, *S. elaeagnifolium* and *L. cylindrica* showed more toxic effect when the first instar of *A. aegypti* was treated for 24 hours. The LC50 values noticed in the cases of *S. elaeagnifolium* and *L. cylindrica* were 0.0586 and 0.812 mg/ml respectively (Table 40.3). Prolongation of egg hatchability, larval and pupal period was noticed. During the egg hatching, first instar larvae were unable to, emerge from the egg case and the egg case was attached with the first instar's head region leading to the death of the larvae. The life span was exceeded when exposed to lower concentration of the plant extract. However, exposure in the lethal concentrations, mortality was noticed. The abnormalities observed were, arresting of melanization, molting and formation of cuticle. Retardation of growth rate, discontinuous melanization in the larval and pupal stages, shrinkage and enlargement of larval abdominal segments were also noticed. Larvae died at the stage of larval-pupal transition resulting larval-pupal intermediate. In the case of pupal stages, adults could not emerge from the pupal exuvium. In some cases during adult emergence, the appendages in the head region and thoracic region were attached with the pupal exuvium.

Table 40.3: Effect of Silica Gel Fractions on the First Instar

Plant Name	*Weight of Sample (in mg)*		*Recovery (in mg)*	*LC50 Values (in mg/ml)*	
	Crude	*Silica Gel*		*Crude*	*Silica Gel*
S. elaeagnifolium	60.0	10.0	16.6	8.0	0.0586
L. cylindrica	50.0	23.2	46.4	20.0	0.8118

* 0.001 to 1 mg of plant extract was dissolved in 100 ml of 0.02 per cent acetone and tested for its effect.

Discussion

Very few reports are available on the egg hatchability of mosquitoes and the lethal values were ranging from 0.0025 mg/ml (Zebitz, 1987) and 2.5 mg/ml (Sagar and Sehgal, 1997) in neem products. The reports available on the LC50 values for I-instar larval susceptibility to the plant extracts was found between 0.53 to 0.19 mg/ml in *Vetiveria sisinoides* (Murty and Jamil, 1987) and *Solanum nigrum* (Singh *et al.*, 2001). LC50 values noticed in the fourth instar larva by various authors showed between the ranges of 0.0004 to 0.32 mg/ml. It is interesting to note that the concentration of the plant extract required to cause 50 per cent mortality of *A. aegypti* fourth instar was found between 0.000031 to 0.003549 mg/ml in *Quaj'sia amara* (Evans and Raj, 1991) and *Ca/ophyllum inophyllum* (Pushpalatha and Muthukrishnan, 1999). In general, treatment of plant extracts against various stages of development, I instar larva were more susceptible than other stages. Pupa and egg were more resistant to plant extracts than the larval stages. Generally, among all plants tested in the present study against the developmental stages of mosquito, a higher lethal effect was observed in the Solanaeceous plant, *S. elaeagnifolium*. In most of the treatments the petroleum ether extracts only showed higher effect. The susceptibility of the developmental stages was found in the order of first instar > fourth instar > pupa > egg, when treated with the plant extracts. LC50 values on pupal stages of *Culex quinijuefasciatus* and *Culex pipiens* while treating with the various plant extracts fall between 0.005 to 3.0 mg/ml in the plants *Haplophyllum tuberculatum* (Mohsen *et al.*, 1989), *Melia azedarach* and *Melia volkensi* (Al-Sharook *et al.*, 1991). Plant extracts are capable of producing multiple effects in insects such as antifeedancy, growth regulation, fecundity suppression and sterilization, ovipositional changes, repellency or attractancy and change in biological fitness. The biological fitness of many insect species was substantially reduced at plant extract dosages below those interfering with the molting process. Changes in biological fitness include reduced life span, loss of flying ability and low absorption of nutrients (Wilps, 1989), high mortality (Dom *et al.*, 1987), immuno depression (Azambuja and Garcia, 1992), enzyme inhibition (Naqvi, 1987) and disruption of biological synthesis (Smietanko and Engelmann, 1989). According to these observations it has been suggest that phytochemicals have subtle effects on a variety of tissues and cells, especially those with rapid mitosis, for example, epidennal cells, midgut epithelial cells, ovary and testis. Various active principles have been localized in different plants, which caused deleterious effects on the developmental stages of mosquitoes. In general, the Solanaeceous and Cucurbitaceous plants are reported to contain the secondary metabolites such as solanin, cucurbitacin and luffin which may cause the mortality of *A. aegypti* as observed in the present study. Further analysis is required to isolate the active principle, which is responsible for the toxicity to the developmental stages of the mosquito.

Acknowledgment

Thanks are due to the Department of Collegiate Education, Tamil Nadu, India, for financial assistance to Miss. A. Renugadevi.

References

Al-Sharook, Z., Balan, K., Jiang, Y. and Rembold, H., 1991. Insect growth inhibitors from two tropical Meliaceae. Effect of crude seed extract on mosquito larvae. *J. Appl. Entomol.*, 111: 425–430.

Azambuja, P. and Garcia, E.S., 1992. Effects of Azadirachtin on *Rhodnius prolixus.* Immunity and *Trypanosoma* interaction. *Memb. Inst. Oswaldo Cruz Rio de J.*, 87 (Suppl. V): 69–72.

Beeranbaum, M.R., 1989. North American ethanobotanicals as a source of novel plant based insecticides. *ACS Symp. Ser.*, 387: 11–24.

Dom, A., Rademacher, J.M. and Sehn, E., 1987. Effects of Azadirachtin on reproductive, organs and fertility in the large milk weed bug, *Oncopeltus fasciatus.* In: *Proc. 3rd. Int. Neem Conf.* (Nairobi, Kenya), (Eds.) Schmutterer, H. and Ascher, K.R.S. GTZ, Eschbom, Germany.

Evans, D.A. and Raj, R.K., 1991. Quassin: A mosquito larvicide with selective toxicity. *J. Ecotoxicol. Environ. Monit.*, 1: 243–249.

Finney, D.G., 1971. *Probit Analysis*, 3rd edition. Cambridge University Press, Cambridge, pp. 245

Gubler, D.J., 1988. Dengue. In: *The Arboviruses: Epidemiology and Ecology*, V. II. (Ed.) T. Monath. CRC Press, Florida, pp. 223–261.

Mohsen, Z.H., Abdul Latiff, M.J., Al Chalabi, B.M. and Al Naib, A., 1989. Insecticidal activity of *Vinca rosea* against *Culex quinquefasciatus. J. Biol. Sci. Res.*, 20: 437– 446.

Mulla, M.S., 1997. Nature and scope of biopesticides. In: *Proc. 1st Int. Symp. Boipesticides* (Phitsanulok, Thailand), (Eds.) Rodcharoen, J. Wongsiri, S. and Mulla, M.S. Chulalongkom University Press, Bangkok, Thailand, pp. 5–9.

Murty, U.S. and Jamil, K., 1987. Effect of the South Indian vetiver oil [*Vetiveria sisinoides* (L.) Nash] against the immatures of *Culex quinquefasciatus* Say. (Diptera : Culicidae). *Int. Pest Control*, 29: 8–9.

Muthukrishnan, J., Pushpalatha, E. and Kasthuribhai, A., 1997. Biological effects of four plant extracts on *Culex quinquefasciatus* Say larval stages. *Insect Sci. Applic.*, 17: 389–394.

Naqvi, S.N.H., 1987. Biological evaluation of fresh neem extracts and some neem components, with reference to abnormalities and esterase activir in insects. In: *Proc. 3rd Int. Neem Conference* (Nairobi, Kenya), (Eds.) Schmutterer, H. and Ascher, K.R.S. GTZ, Eschbom, Germany, pp. 315–330.

Pushpalatha, E. and Muthukrishnan, J., 1999. Efficacy of two tropical plant extracts for the control of mosquitoes. *J. Appl. Entomol.*, 123: 369–373.

Sagar, S.K. and Sehgal, S.S., 1997. Toxicity of neem seed coat extract against mosquitoes. *Indian J. Entmol.*, 59: 215–223.

Singh, S.P., Raghavendra, K., Singh, R.K. and Subbarao, S.K., 2001. Studies on larvicidal properties of leaf extract of *Solanum nigrum* Linn. (Family : Solanaceae). *Current Science*, 81: 25–26.

Smietanko, A. and Engelmann, W., 1989. Splitting of circadian rhythm of *Musca domestica* flies with Azadirachtin. *J. Interdiscip. Cycle Res.*, 20: 71–80.

Wilps, H., 1989. The influence of Neem Seed Kernal Extract (NSKE) from the neem tree *Azadirachta indica* on flight activity, food ingestion, reproductive rate and carbohydrate metabolism in the Diptera *Phormia teraenovae* (Diptera : Muscidae). *Zool. Jahrb. Physiol.*, 93: 271–282.

Zebitz, C.P.W., 1987. Potential of neem seed kernal extract in mosquito control. In: *Proc. 3rd Int. Neem Conference* (Nairobi, Kenya), (Eds.) Schmutterer, H. and Ascher, K.R.S. GTZ, Escheuberg, Germany

Chapter 41

Effect of Ethanol and *Mucuna pruriens* Seed on Rat Liver

G. Krishnamoorthy and A. Sivamady
Department of Zoology, K.M. Centre for Post Graduate Studies, Pondicherry - 605 008, India

ABSTRACT

Alcoholics are often associated with several hepatic diseases and liver damages both, functionallyand structurally. The present study was aimed to find out the impact of *Mucuna pruriens* seed on liver of ethanol treated male adult rats. A group of rats were given 25 per cent ethanol (1 ml/100 gm b.wt.) twice daily for 30 days, another group of rats treated 25 per cent ethanol (1 ml/100 gm.b.wt.) + *Mucuna pruriens* seed extract (15 mg/kilogram body weight) twice daily for 30 days. These two group of experimentally treated animals were compared with that of control rats. The dosage of ethanol and *Mucuna pruriens* seed extract were designed for treatment, without disturbing the optimal level of blood glucose. The ethanol treatment exhaust the liver glycogen content and it was restored to safer level by this herbal seed. The toxic effect of ethanol on liver was assessed by the supra physiological level of serum transaminases like Serum Glutamate Oxaloacetate Transaminase (SGOT) and Serum Glutanlate Pyruvate Transaminase (SGPT). The restoration of glycogen and the declined activities of these enzymes in ethanol + Mucuna combined treatment suggest the protective effect of this plant seed containing active principles against alcohol induced liver damage.

Keywords: *Ethanol, Liver, Mucuna pruriens, Rat.*

Introduction

The liver is the largest glandular structure in the body consists of epithelial glandular cells (hepatocytes). Liver is the major metabolic site, stores excess glucose as glycogen (Cherrington and Steiner.,1982) and regulates the synthesis of phospholipids, triglycerides and cholesterol (Ekles *et al.*, 1955; Byers and Friedman, 1960). Liver is not only a metabolic organ but also neutralizes toxins (Meyer and Kulkarni, 2001). Alcoholics are often associated with several hepatic diseases and liver damages both functionally and structurally. Alcoholic liver disease continues to be the most serious liver disorder throughout the world. The levels of specific alcohol metabolizing enzymes in rat hepatocytes were found to be reduced following alcohol intoxication (Saraswat *et al.* 1999). Further, the production of oxygen radicals during the catalytic cycle of ethanol leads to lipid peroxidation and destruction of cell membranes (Bhaduria *et al.*, 2002). Recently, scope in medicinal plant research has increased all over the world. A review of literature highlights the medicinal values of plants curing various diseases. Side effects and expenses associated with allopathic drugs, the plant ingredients are without the side effects, especially those belonging to the traditional system of medicine. A series of principles isolated from Indian medicinal plants act as a antioxidant system and scavengers of free radicals (Sanz *et al.*, 1994; Gyanji *et al.*, 1999). *Mucuna pruriens* belonging to the family Fabaceae, is a potent medicinal herb available in India. The seeds of this plants are rich in some bioactive principles and aphrodiasic tonic, nervine and nutritive. Therefore, the present study was designed to delineate the protective effect of *Mucuna pruriens* seed on liver in relation to ethanol toxicity.

Materials and Methods

Healthy adult male albino rats of Wistar strain (*Rattus norvegicus*) weighing 230 to 300 g of body weight were used. The rats were kept in clean cages in a temperature controlled room with 12 hours light/dark scheduled. They were fed with balanced diet with free access to water. Fifteen rats were selected for this study and randomly divided into three groups of five each. Group I includes control (Rats received an isocaloric quantity of sucrose in the same volume as experimental rats that received ethanol). Group II includes Ethanol treated (Ethanol was administered twice daily at regular intervals by gastric incubation at a dose of 25 per cent (1 ml) aqueous solution for 30 days. Group III includes Ethanol (1 ml of 25 per cent) + *Mucuna pruriens* seed extract (15 mg. Per kilogram body weight) treated for 30 days, twice daily at regular intervals by gastric incubation.

At the end of the experimental period (30 days) the animals were sacrificed. Blood was collected and sera separated and stored at –20°C for further analysis. The liver was removed carefully and cleaned from adjoining tissues. These organs were processed and preserved for further histological and biochemical studies. Liver glycogen was estimated by the method of Hassid and Abraham (1957). The serum glucose concentration was measured by the enzymatic method (Trinder, 1969) and Serum Glutamate Pyruvate Transaminase (SGPT) and Serum, Glutamate Oxalate Transaminase (SGOT) activities were determined by the 2, 4 DNPH method (Reitman and Frankel, 1957) using reagent kit (Span Diagnostics, India). The student's 't' test was used to analyse the data.

Results and Discussion

Table 41.1 reveals the data on liver glycogen and serum glucose levels in control, ethanol treated and ethanol + Mucuna seed combined treated rats. The quantity of liver glycogen was found lesser in ethanol alone and ethanol + Mucuna combined treated rats than control animals. Significant reduction of glycogen was noticed in ethanol treated group, however the effect was moderate in combined treated rats. Ethanol + Mucuna combined treatment shows a significant ($p < 0.05$) raise of glycogen content than the ethanol alone treatment. The serum glucose level was measured in all three groups reveals the absence of wide fluctuation. In general, the data obtained in control, ethanol alone and ethanol + Mucuna treated groups were statistically insignificant.

Table 41.1: Effect of Ethanol and *Mucuna pruriens* Seed on Liver Glycogen and Serum Glucose level in Rat

Group	*Liver Glycogen mg/100 mg Tissue*	*Blood Glucose mg/dl*
Control	0.496±0.011	35.83±3.02
Ethanol treated (E)	0.101±0.004***	33.19±1.20
Ethanol + *Mucuna pruriens* seed treated (EM)	0.198±0.018***[a]	30.7±3.76[b]

Each value is Mean±SEM of five animals.

***: $P < 0.001$ = Control Vs Ethanol treated (E) and Control Vs Ethanol + *Mucuna pruriens* seed treated (EM) animals.

[a]: $P < 0.05$; [b]: $P < 0.01$ = Ethanol treated (E) Vs Ethanol + *Mucuna pruriens* seed treated (EM) animals.

Table 41.2 show the activities of serum transaminases (SGOT and SGPT) in control, ethanol alone and ethanol + Mucuna treated rats. The activities of SGOT and SGPT enzymes were found to be high in ethanol treated animals when compared to control rats ($p < 0.001$). However these enzyme activities in ethanol + Mucuna combined treated animals were reduced than the ethanol ($p < 0.001$) treated group. The activities of these enzymes in ethanol + Mucuna group were parallel to control rats.

Table 41.2: Effect of Ethanol and *Mucuna pruriens* Seed on Serum Transaminases (SGOT and SGPT) Levels in Rat

Group	*SGOT*	*SGPT*
Control	132.78±2.98	69.6±2.72
Ethanol treated (E)	208.4±4.32***	141.86±3.30***
Ethanol + *Mucuna pruriens* seed treated (EM)	143.50±2.94[c]	75.14±2.33[c]

Each value is Mean ± SEM of five animals.

Enzyme activities are expressed as unit/ml.

***: $P < 0.001$ = Control Vs Ethanol treated animals (E).

c: $P < 0.001$ = Ethanol treated (E) Vs Ethanol + *Mucuna pruriens* seed (EM) treated animals.

The liver section from ethanol treated rats documents the presence of some abnormal histoarchitecture and degenerative changes, congested, narrowed sinusoids and enormous infiltrating leucocytes in the central vein. Besides, the hepatocytes shows the presence of vacuole and displaced nuclei [Figure 41.1(c and d)]. Sections taken from Ethanol + *Mucuna pruriens* seed treated rats shows the regenerative cells rather than degeneration. No vacuolization was seen within hepatocytes and the sinusoids were normal. In general, the section shows densely packed new hepatocytes especially in the central focal region [Figure 41.1(e and f)].

(A) Hepatocytes (H) in Control Rat

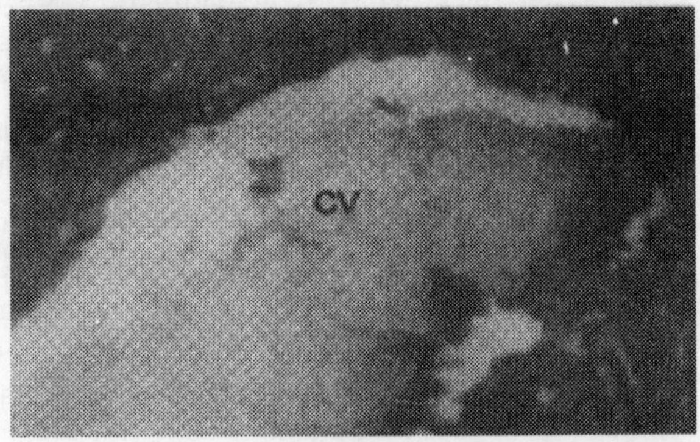

(B) Control Vein (CV) in Control Rat

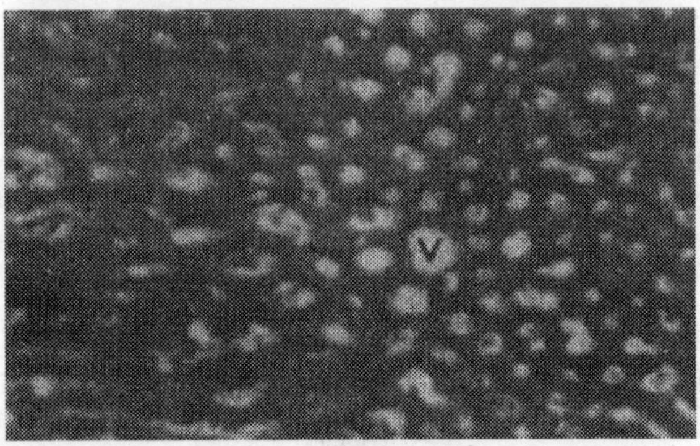

(C) Vacuoles (V) in Ethanol Treated Rat

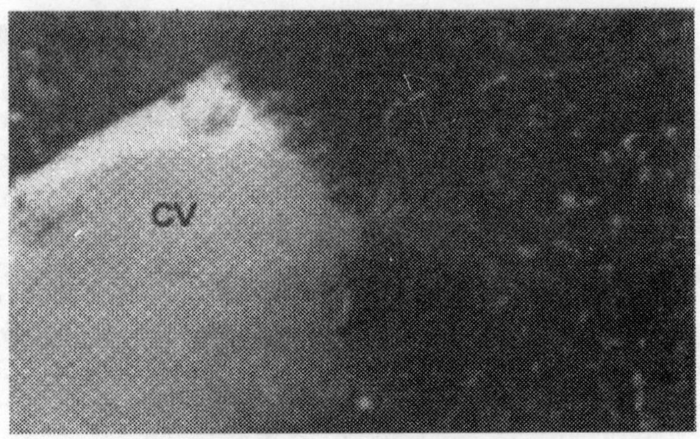

(D) Infiltrated Leucocytes (IL) in Ethanol Treated Rat

(E) No Vacuoles in Ethanol + Mucuna Treated Rat

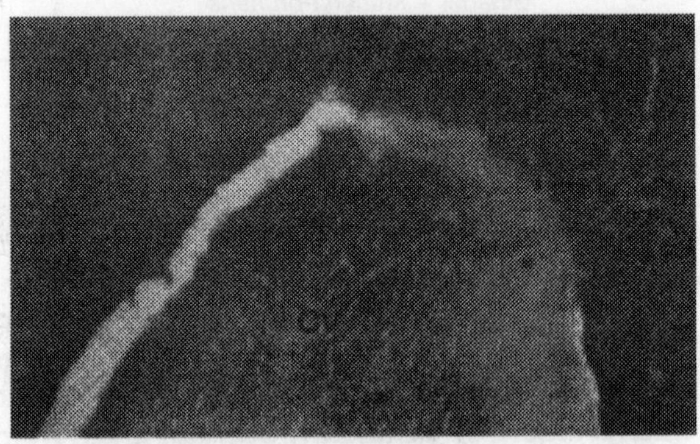

(F) Absence of Leucocytes in Ethanol + Mucuna Treated Rat

Figure 41.1: Histology of Rat Liver

In the present study the liver glycogen content and blood glucose level were assessed in ethanol and *Mucuna pruriens* seed treated rats and compared with control rats. In ethanol treated rats the glycogen level was drastically reduced, this shows the adverse effect of ethanol on liver glycogen. Earlier studies on experimental animals revealed similar effect of ethanol on liver glycogen, (Kaminskii and Kosenko, 1987; Kubota *et al.*, 1992). The decreased level of glycogen in liver may be due to increased rate of glycogenolysis and inhibition of glycogenesis (Winston and Reitz, 1984). The selective activation and suppression of enzymes involved in glycogenesis and glycogenolysis by Mucuna seed would have resulted in moderate raised level of glycogen.

Optimal level of blood glucose was managed by the balance reaction of these glycogenolysis, gluconeogenesis and glycolysis process. Imbalance in these reactions affects the glucose level in circulation. This is in confirmation with the present study and supported by the previous reports, that glucose turnover is maintained constant in ethanol treated rats by accelerating glycogenolysis and inhibiting gluconeogenesis (Kubota *et al.*, 1992; Siler *et al.*, 1998). The level of serum glucose in Mucuna + ethanol group is also insignificant. In spite of its (Mucuna) antidiabetic effect (Manyam *et al.*, 2004) the Mucuna along with ethanol did not disturb much of the glucose level. This result suggests that the active agents present in the Mucuna would have reduced the inhibitory effect of ethanol on gluconeogenesis, which results in safe level of serum glucose.

Histological observation made in the present study is in agreement with serum biochemical changes. Rats intoxicated with ethanol causes an increase in the activities of Serum Glutamate Oxalate Transaminase (SGOT) and Serum Glutamate Pyruvate Transaminase (SGPT) in the blood. Many reports available on elevated enzymatic activities of serum transaminases in alcoholic liver disease in experimental and human models (Skrzydlewska *et al.*, 1990; Yin *et al.*, 1998; Rajagopal *et al.*, 2003). In severe liver damage, serum transaminases level parallel to those of the organs indicating that both cellular and mitochondria membranes have been damaged. Since, the membrane integrity is linked with intra cellular metabolic states, disturbance in latter results in membrane lesion with concomitant increase in enzyme leakage. So, the large doses of ethanol results in cell lysis and cytoplasmic hepatic enzymes are released in blood circulation.

Administration of ethanol on rats resulted in mild degeneration of liver and infiltration of leucocytes in the focal central vein and narrowing of sinusoids was noticed in this study. The toxic effect of ethanol either directly or through its metabolite, acetaldehyde acts on liver cells cause damage to the structure and function (Coon and Koop, 1987). Further the free radicals generation during chronic ethanol exposure may also be an additional factor in liver damage (Wheeler *et al*, 2001). The rats fed with ethanol + *Mucuna pruriens* shows a moderate protective effect on liver. Combination with ethanol did not alter the structure and function of hepatic cells. Congestion of sinusoids and inflammatory vein were also relieved from ethanol toxicity due to Mucuna seed combined treatment. In addition the serum transaminase levels also brought to parallel to control levels. Further the histological studies of liver also confirmed the beneficial role of Mucuna on ethanol toxicity and diminished the number of infiltrating leucocytes and necrotic cells. The result indicate that Mucuna contains certain active principles expedites the process of recovery from ethanol induced liver injury and may be applied therapeutically to alcoholic liver damage.

References

Bhadauria, M., Jadon, A., Sharma, A. and Shukla, S., 2002. Effect of proprietry herbal formulation against chronic carbon tetra chloride induced hepatotoxity. *Ind. J. Exp. Biol.*, 40: 1254–1259.

Byers, S.O. and Friedman, M., 1960. Observations concerning the production and excretion of cholesterol in mammals. Role of chylomicra in transport of cholesterol and lipid. *Am. J. Physiol.*, 179: 79–84.

Cherrington, A.D. and Steiner, K.E., 1982. The effect of Insulin on carbohydrate metabolism *in vivo. J. Clin. Endocrinol. Metab.*, 11: 309–316.

Coon, M.J. and Koop, D.R., 1987. Effect of ethanol on cytochrome P450. *Arch. Toxicol.*, 60: 16–21.

Eckles, N.E., Taylor, C.B., Campbell, D.J. and Gould, R.C., 1955. The origin of plasma cholesterol and the rate of equiliberation of liver plasma and erythrocyte cholesterol. *J. Lab. Ctin. Med.*, 46: 359–371.

Gyanji, M.A., Yonamine, M. and Aniya, Y., 1999. Free-radical scavenging action of medicinal Herbs from Ghana: *Thonningia sanguinea* on experimentally-induced injuries. *Gen. Pharmacol.*, 32: 661–667.

Hassid, W.Z. and Abraham, S., 1957. Determination of glycogen and starch. In: *Methods in Enzymology,* (Eds.) Colowick, S.P and Kaplan N.O. Academic Press, New York, 3: 34–36.

Kaminskii, I.U.G. and Kosenko, E.A., 1987. Diurnal changes in the glucose and glycogen level of the blood and liver of rats in chronic consumption of alcohol and after its with drawal. *Ukr. Biokhim. ZH*, 59: 47–51.

Kubota, M., Virkamaki, A. and Yki-Jarvinen, H., 1992. Ethanol stimulates glycogenolysis in liver from fed rats. *Proc. Soc. Exp. Biol. Med.*, 201: 114–118.

Manyam, B.V., Dhanasekaran, M. and Hare, T.A., 2004. Effect of antiparkinson drug HP-200 (*Mucuna pruriens*) on the central Mono aminergic neurotransmitter. *Phytother. Res.*, 18: 97–101.

Meyer, S.A. and Kulkarni, A.P., 2001.Hepatotoxicity. In: *Introduction to Biochemical Toxicology*, 3rd edn., (Eds.) Hodgson and R.C. Smart. John Wiley and Sons, Inc., New York, pp. 487.

Rajagopal, S., Manickam, P., Periyasamy, V. and Namasivayam, N., 2003. Activity of *Cassia auriculata* leaf extract in rat with alcoholic liver injury. *J. Nutr. Biochem.*, 14: 452–458.

Reitman, S. and Frankel, S., 1957. A colorimetric method for the determination of serum glutamic oxloacetic and glutamic pyruvic transaminases. *Am. J. Clin. Pathol.*, 28: 53–56.

Sanz, M.J., Ferrandiz, M.L., Ejudo, M., Terencio, M.C., Gill, B., Bustos, G., Ubeda, A., Gunasegaran, R. and Alcaraz, M.J., 1994. Influence of a series of natural flavonoids on free radical generating systems and oxidative stress. *Xenobiotoca*, 24: 689–699.

Saraswat, B., Visen, P.K., Patnaik, G.K. and Dhawan, B.N., 1999. *Ex vivo* and *in vivo* investigations of picroliv from *Picrorhiza kurroa* in and alcohol intoxication model in Rats. *J. Ethnopharmacol.*, 66: 263–269.

Siler, S.Q., Neese, R.A., Christiansen, M.P. and Hellerstein, M.K., 1998. The inhibition of gluconeogenesis following alcohol in humans. *Am. J. Physiol.*, 275: 897–907.

Skrzydlewska, E., Worowski, K. and Chyczewski, L., 1990. Zakladu Analizy Instrumentalnej, Akademii Medycznej, Bialymstoku: Effect of cysteine on protein metabolism in the liver or Rats with ethanol induced liver damage. *Rock. Akad. Med. Bialymst.*, 35: 129–141.

Trinder, P., 1969. Enzymatic method of serum glucose estimation. *Ann. Clin. Biochem.*, 6: 24–28.

Wheeler, M.D., Nakagamin, M., Bradford, B.U., Uesugi, T., Mason, R.P., Connor, H.D., Dikalova, A., Kadiiska, M. and Thurman, R.G., 2001. Over expression manganese superoxide dismutase prevents alcohol-induced liver injury in the rat. *J. Biochem.*, 276: 36664–36672.

Winston, G.W. and Reitz, R.C., 1984. Effects of chronic ethanol ingestion on male and female rat liver glycogen phosphorylase phosphatase. *Alcohol. Clin. Exp. Res.*, 8: 277–282.

Yin, M., Ikejima, K., Arteel, G.E., Seabra, V., Bradford, B.U., Kono H., Rusyn, I., and Thurman, R.G., 1998. Glycine accelerates recovery from alcohol-induced liver injury. *J. Pharmacol. Exp. Thel.*, 286: 1014–1019.

Chapter 42

Diurnal Variation in Ayyanakere Lake, Western Ghat Region of Chikmagalore, Karnataka

S. Thirumala, B.R. Kiran, E.T. Puttaiah, Vijayakumara, K. Harish Babu and D. Basavaraja

Department of Environmental Science, Biosciences Complex, Kuvempu University, Shankaraghatta – 577 451, Karnataka, India

ABSTRACT

The present study was carried out for diurnal variations of water quality parameters in Ayyanakere lake of Western Ghats for 24 hour at 3 hour interval commencing from 6.00 A.M. of 3rd February 2006 to 6.00 A.M. of 4th February 2006. Large fluctuations were noted in dissolved oxygen, pH, carbonate and bicarbonate concentrations. The lake water was over saturated with oxygen during daytime (13.9 ppm) and oxygen was depleted during night (3.5 ppm). pH was increased at day time and decreased at night time. However, phytoplankton did not show any apparent diurnal variation except *Microcystis* species. Among zooplankton, *Daphnia* and *Cyclops* showed diurnal variation but other, zooplankton species did not show any diurnal movements.

Keywords: *Ayyanakere lake, Diurnal fluctuation, Western Ghats.*

Introduction

Freshwater ecosystems are highly dynamic and more complex than other types of the ecosystems. Many workers have reported that the water quality and zooplankton movement undergo rapid changes due to diurnal variation (Rana *et al.*, 1982 and Ahamad and Singh, 1991).

Dissolved oxygen is a state variable, which is an indication of the general health of the aquatic ecosystem. The present study reports the diurnal variations of a freshwater lake of Chikmagalore district, India. It also showed diurnal effect in plankton. Literature shows this kind of work deals with observations on tropical ecosystem (Dunn, 1967 and Khan *et al.*, 1970). In the present study an attempt was made to assess the diurnal variations of Ayyanakere lake of Western Ghat region in Karnataka.

Materials and Methods

Study Area

This water body is situated between 13°14'42" North latitude and 75°04'46" eastern longitude. It is a deep lake having an area of 15 square kilometers facilitating to about 1500 hectares of land for irrigation. The average depth is 20 meters.

Water Analysis

The water samples were collected from the fixed location for 24 hour at 3 hour interval starting from 6.00 A.M. for estimation of water quality parameters. Water temperature was measured by mercury thermometer. Dissolved oxygen was estimated by Winkler's method as given by Strickland and Parson (1968). pH was measured by pH digital pen. Bicarbonate and carbonate concentrations were determined by titrating with 0.02 N sulphuric acid solution using phenolphthalein and methyl orange as indicators.

Phytoplankton was enumerated by counting concentrations obtained by fixing 100 ml of water with 1 ml of Lugol's solution. Zooplankton were collected by filtering 50 liters of water with a 20 mesh sieve and counting were done in a Sedge wick-Rafter counting cell.

Results and Discussion

The diurnal variations in physico-chemical parameters and plankton behaviour are depicted in Tables 42.1 and 42.2.

Table 42.1: Diurnal Variations in Physico-chemical Characteristics of Ayyanakere Lake

Sl.No.	*Time (hr)*	*Air Temperature (°C)*	*Water Temperature (°C)*	*pH*	*DO (mg/l)*	*Oxygen Saturation (%)*	*CO_2 (mg/l)*	*Carbonates (mg/l)*	*Bicarbonates (mg/l)*
1.	0600	23.8	23.5	7.4	4.9	65.31	Nil	54.8	203.0
2.	0900	25.2	24.6	7.9	8.1	110.3	Nil	26.3	183.1
3.	1200	27.8	26.8	8.2	11.9	165.12	Nil	46.8	164.1
4.	1500	29.3	27.3	8.4	13.9	188.60	Nil	55.0	145.0
5.	1800	28.8	27.0	8.1	11.9	168.50	Nil	83.4	132.0
6.	2100	28.0	26.6	8.0	9.2	123.34	Nil	70.2	180.0
7.	2400	27.5	25.4	8.0	7.8	105.38	1.2	Nil	197.0
8.	0300	26.4	24.8	8.0	3.5	66.15	1.3	Nil	201.0
9.	0600	23.2	22.0	7.9	5.0	54.27	Nil	52.4	202.0

Air temperature on the day of observation was varied from 23.2 to 29.3°C (Table 42.1) and the water temperature fluctuated accordingly from the minimum of 22.0°C to the maximum of 27.3°C. The maximum temperatures of air and water were noticed during afternoon at 1500 hours and the minimum during dusk at 0600 hours. This fluctuation was because of intense solar heating during daytime.

Owing to the depth of the waterbody, thermal stratification was detected. The difference between air and water temperatures was never more than 1.8° C at any sampling time.

Table 42.2: Diurnal Variation of Plankton in Ayyanakere Lake (Hours)

Sl.No.	Name of the Plankton	Hours			
		0600	1200	1800	2400
(A)	**Chlorophyceae**				
1.	*Microspora* sp.	20	28	46	30
2.	*Spirogyra* sp.	8	10	18	02
3.	*Cosmarium* sp.	20	32	42	20
4.	*Chlorella* sp.	25	40	58	26
5.	*Chlamydomonas* sp.	03	10	18	05
(B)	**Cyanophyceae**				
1.	*Anabaena* sp.	5	8	09	04
2.	*Microcystis* sp.	40	58	80	68
(C)	**Bacillariophyceae**				
1.	*Navicula* sp.	06	15	15	09
(D)	**Euglenophyceae**				
1	*Euglena* sp.	04	09	08	05
Total of the Phytoplankton		**133**	**210**	**294**	**169**
(A)	**Rotifers**				
1.	*Brachionus* sp.	1200	2890	2350	1250
2.	*Keratella tropica*	120	110	135	112
(B)	**Copepod**				
1.	*Cyclops* sp.	350	1210	380	368
2.	*Diaptomus* sp.	46	54	60	80
(C)	**Cladocera**				
1.	*Daphnia* sp.	4830	4115	3918	5894
2.	*Diaphanosoma* sp.	710	640	390	450
(D)	**Ostracoda**				
1.	*Cypris* sp.	04	10	12	05
(E)	**Immature stages**				
1.	Eggs	590	1530	2100	2810
2.	Nauplii	210	218	810	1450
Total of the Zooplankton		**8060**	**10777**	**10155**	**12419**

Dissolved Oxygen (DO) concentration was varied from 3.5 to13.9 mg/L, the maximum concentration was found at 1500 hours and the minimum at 0600 hours. Most of the time sunlight was available when an over saturation in dissolved oxygen of the lake water was noticed. 1800 hours onwards DO concentration gradually decreased. At night the oxygen was consumed by the organisms as has been reported by George (1961). pH of the lake water was found to be ranged from 7.4 to 8.4. pH of the water were found to be directly related to changes in carbonate concentration as pH of the water increased (8.4) during the daytime and decreased in the night (7.4). The difference in the maximum and minimum pH of the lake water during the 24 hours of observation was 0.7, less than the variation recorded by Khan *et al.* (1970).

In the current study, free CO_2 was found to accumulate during night (Table 42.1). Maximum concentration was found at 0300 hours. Carbonate concentration was found to vary from 0.0 to 83.4 mg/l. the highest carbonate concentration was recorded in the sampling made at 1800 hours and the minimum at 0900 hours. Bicarbonate concentration showed a trend inverse to carbonate concentration. Maximum bicarbonate concentration was recorded at 0600 hours and the minimum at 1800 hours.

Plankton Analysis

Phytoplankton was composed of *Spirogyra, Microcystis, Scenedesmus, Navicula, Euglena, Cosmarium, Chlorella* and *Chlamydomonas* species (Table 42.2). While, zooplankton were consisted of *Brachionus, Cyclops, Daphnia, Moina, Keratella, Diaptomus, Cypris,* Egg and Nauplii. A large number of immature stages of the zooplankton was also present.

Profuse heating by the sun during daytime raises the temperature of air and water. In the absence of it, temperature go down at night. Day time activity by phytoplankton makes the water over saturated with O_2 (O_2 is withdrawn in this process from the bicarbonates as the carbon source). Bicarbonate ions decreases and as a result there is an increase in carbonate ion concentration and pH. A direct relationship between pH and carbonate as shown were also been reported by Lauff (1953) in Roger's lake. Dissolved oxygen is liberated during photosynthesis as the by-product. Excess of oxygen goes on accumulating in the day time reaching to 13.9 mg/l, while, respiration in the night exhausts it. DO concentration drops down to minimum and free CO_2 accumulates during night due to absence of sunlight and photosynthesis. An over saturation with oxygen during daytime and its depletion at night are due to abundance of *Microcystis* and other phytoplankton. Such a super saturation with oxygen has been reported by George (1961) in a fish tank at Delhi.

Microcystis formed the water bloom and was more abundant at 1800 and 2400 hours. Whereas other phytoplankton did not show any apparent diurnal variation. Khan *et al.* (1970) also reported similar phenomenon for *Microcystis* and other phytoplankton. Contrary to the observations of Vaas and Sachlan (1953) *Brachionus* was more abundant in the collection of 1200 and 1800 hours. This is in agreement with the findings of Sasmal *et al.* (2005). *Daphnia* and *Keratella* were more numerous at the surface in the morning. Khan *et al.* (1970) reported that there was no *Keratella* at 1800 and 2400 hours. *Daphnia* also showed diurnal behaviour, being more abundant in the morning and night. *Nauplii* were abundantly found at night. Similar observation was made by Tash and Armitage (1960). In the above study it may be concluded that diurnal variation changes the plankton movement.

References

Ahamad, S.H. and A.K. Singh, 1991. Diurnal rhythm of zooplankters and their correlations in a freshwater pond of Dhoti, Bihar. *Ecol.*, 9(1): 23–28.

Dunn, I.G., 1967. Diurnal fluctuations of physico-chemical conditions in a shallow tropical pond. *Limnol. Oceanog.*, 12: 151–153.

George, M.G., 1961. Diurnal variations in two shallow ponds in Delhi, India. *Hydrobiologia*, 18: 165–273.

Khan, A., Siddiqui, A. and M. Nazir, 1970. Diurnal variations in a shallow tropical freshwater fish pond in Shahjanpur, Uttar Pradesh. *Hydrobiologia*, 35: 297–304.

Lauff, G.H., 1953. A contribution to the water chemistry and the phytoplankton, relationships of Rogers Lake, Flathead Country, Montana. *Proc. Montana. Acad. Sci.*, 13: 5–19.

Rana, K.S., Gupta, J.M. and M.P. Singh, 1982. Diurnal variations in physico-chemical components in Keetham lake, Agra. *J. Environ. Res.*, 3(2): 10–13.

Strickland, J.D.H. and T.R. Parson, 1968. *A Practical Handbook of Sea Water Analysis.* J. Fish Res. Bd. Canada, Ottawa, 167: 311–313.

Tash, J.C. and K.B. Armitage, 1960. A seasonal survey of the vertical movements of some plankters in Leaven worth country state lake, Kansas. *Kans Univ. Sci. Bull.*, 41: 657–690.

Vaas, K.F. and M. Sachlan, 1953. Limnological studies of fluctuations in shallow ponds in Indonesia. *Verh. Int. Ver. Limnol.*, 12: 309–319.

Sasmal, S., Chari, M.S. and S. Singh, 2005. Diurnal variations in a tropical freshwater pond. *Environment and Ecology*, 235(3): 503–507.

Chapter 43

A New Species of *Retractocephalus* Haldar and Chakraborty, 1976 (Apicomplexa : Conoidasida) from a Coleopteran Insect in West Bengal, India

Monali Chatterjee[1*] *and T.K. Kundu*[2]

[1]Guest Lecturer, Ranaghat College, Ranaghat, West Bengal, India

[2]Reader, Ranaghat College, Ranaghat, West Bengal, India

ABSTRACT

In 1976, Haldar and Chakraborty established a new genus *Retractocephalus* to accommodate the cephaline gregarine inhabiting the midgut of *Raphidopalpa* (*Aulacophora*) *foveicollis* Lucas. Five named species of *Retactocephalus* have so far been obtained from West Bengal, India. Another new species *Retractocephalus monoleptae* sp.n. discovered from *Monolepta nigrobilineata* was collected from Ranaghat in Nadia district of West Bengal.

Keywords: Coleoptera, Monolepta nigrobilineata, Gregarinicae : Hirmocystidae : Retractocephalus : New species.

Introduction

The septate gregarines (Apicomplexa : Conoidasida) are one of the most common endoparasites of insects. They may occur in the host's alimentary canal, some in the malpighian tubules, hepatic caeca, adipose tissue and other tissues, developing intracellularly or extracellularly. Lipa (1967) pointed out that the parasites *i.e.* the septate gregarines often cause hypertrophy, resulting in the rupture of the

* Corresponding Author: E-mail: dr_monali02@hotmail.com.

tissues involved and infected insects may have untimely death. The five species of *Retactocephalus* Haldar and Chakraborty, 1976 obtained from insects in and around Kalyani, West Bengal, India are:

1. *R. raphidopalpae* Haldar and Chakraborty, 1976 type species from *Raphidopalpa foveicollis.*
2. *R. aulacophorae* from *A. intermedia*
3. *R. spatulatus* from *Lema* sp.
4. *R. spinosus* from *Monolepta signata* and
5. *R. halticus* from *Haltica* sp.

Materials and Methods

Monolepta nigrobilineata (Mots) was collected from Ranaghat in Nadia district in West Bengal for the cephaline gregarine parasites. The collection of host insects were started in June 1998 and continued till August 2000.

Host insects were decapitated and dissected under a dissecting binocular. The entire gut was taken out and placed on a glass slide with 0.5 per cent normal saline solution and gently teased with needles for the parasites to come out of the gut lumen. Thin smears prepared on glass slides containing gregarines were fixed in Schaudinn's fluid, mordanted overnight in 3 per cent iron alum and stained in Heidenhain's haematoxylin for 20 minutes. Differentiation of staining was done with 1 per cent iron alum.

Culture of Cysts

Cysts were collected from the mid or hindgut of heavily infected hosts or from faecal pellets of the host immersed in water for a few minutes. The technique of Sprague (1941) with slight modifications has been followed: two pieces of blotting paper were placed on both sides of a moist chamber and cysts were placed in a drop of 0.5 per cent normal saline on a glass slide and kept within the moist chamber for at least 24 hours. Mode of dehiscence of the cysts was then observed. Oocysts were examined at regular intervals and stages of development were then observed.

Figures were drawn with the aid of a camera lucida and measurements were calculated with an ocular micrometer calibrated to a stage micrometer (Bosch and Lomb, U.S.A).

The following abbreviations have been used:

TL: Total length
LE: Length of epimerite
LP: Length of protomerite
LD: Length of deutomerite
LN: Length of nucleus
WE: Width of epimerite
WP: Width of protomerite
WD: Width of deutomerite
WN: Width of nucleus
LP : TL: Length of protomerite : Total length
WP : WD: Width of protomerite : Width of deutomerite.

Etymology: The specific epithet has been derived from the generic name of the host.

Results

Taxonomic Diagnosis

The gregarine *R. monoleptae* sp. n. parasitizing *Monolepta nigrobilineata* belongs to the family Hirmocystidae with the following characteristics:

Family Hirmocystidae Grassé, 1953

1. Epimerite ordinary, papilla-like or simple, knob-like.
2. Garnetocysts dehisce by simple rupture.
3. Oocysts ellipsoidal, prismatic, fusiform, ovoid or even spherical.

Genus *Retractocephalus* Haldar and Chakraborty, 1976

1. Epimerite globular, retractile into protomerite.
2. Initial development intracellular.
3. Association head to tail (caudo-frontal); oocysts dolioform, liberated from the garnetocyst in small chains by simple rupture.
4. Five named species.

***Retractocephalus monoleptae* sp.n.**

Development of Trophozoite

Examination of stained.sections of the host gut reveals intracellular stages of development of this gregarine which takes place within the epithelial cells of the midgut of the insect. The earliest intracellular stage of the parasite is a spherical body measuring 10.6 µm in diameter. The cytoplasm is finely granulated and the nucleus measures 7.4 µm in diameter. The parasite develops a halo around it inside the parasitized epithelial cell. The second stage is characterized by a two-segmented organism having a hemispherical protomerite, 10.6 µm long and 12.7 µm broad and a cylindro-conical deutomerite 11.6 µm long and 13.8 µm broad. At this stage the cytoplasm of both the protomerite and deutomerite is somewhat vacuolated. The nucleus is deeply stained body with some indentations of the nuclear membrane.

Trophozoite

(72.5 µm) The total length of the trophozoite reaches a maximum of 91.4 µm approximately. Epimerite is simple, globular (9.6 µm × 9.2 µm in dimensions), retractile into protomerite and surrounded by a characteristic triangular hyaline membrane. Nucleus spherical or elliptical in shape. Epicyteal striations lacking. The trophozoite is solitary and found inside the midgut lumen. A fully-grown trophozoite is elongated in structure and appears opaque white in living condition.

Gamont

(143.6 µm) Solitary and/or biassociative. The length of a solitary gamont exceeds upto 204.0 µm approximately. The protomerite retains the scar of the shedded epimerite, sub-conical, greater in length than width. The anterior tip of the protomerite has a deep concavity to receive the occasionally retractile protomerite during trophozoite stage, a very diagnostic feature of the genus. Deutomerite is cylindrical and its posterior end is rounded. Nucleus elliptical in shape and may be situated anywhere in the deutomerite.

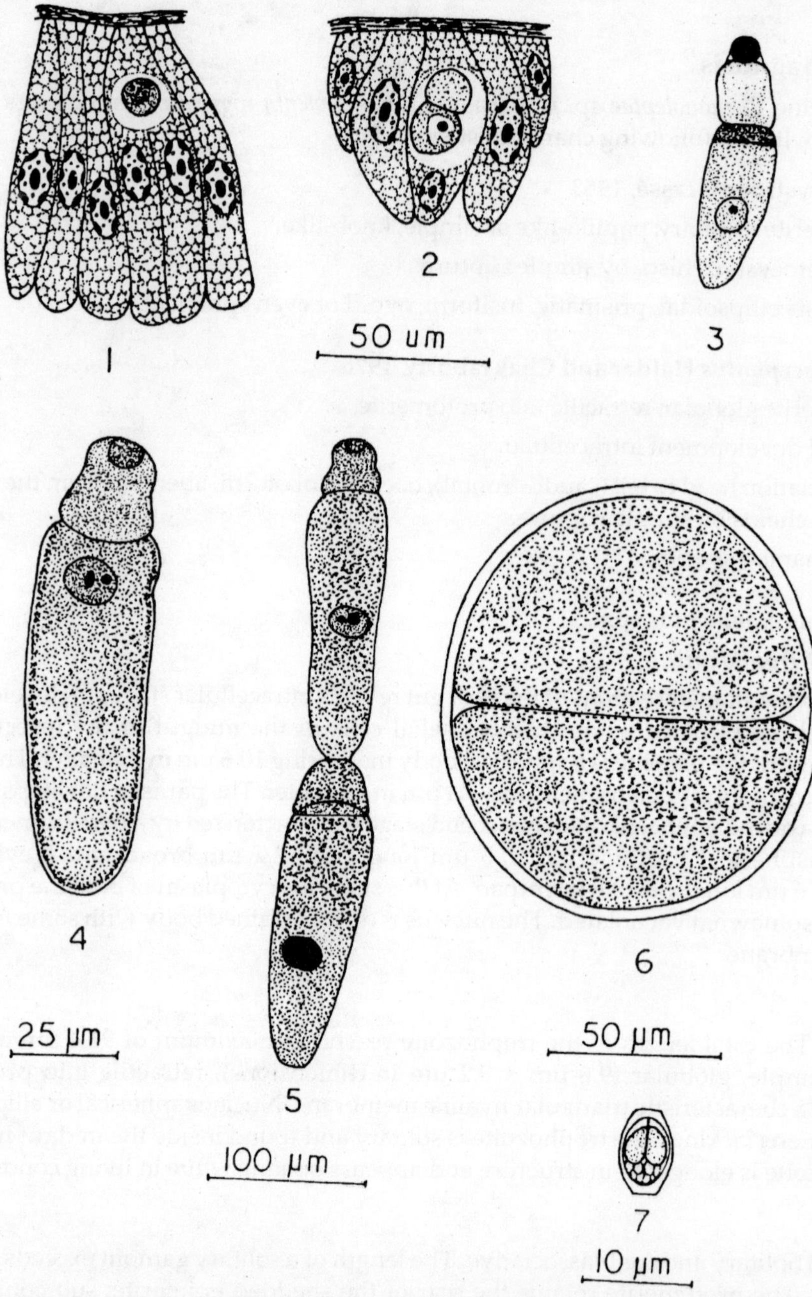

Figures 43.1: Line Drawings of the Different Stages of the Life Cycle of *Retractocephalus monoleptae* sp. n. from *Monolepta nigrobilineata*

(1) First intracellular stage of development within the midgut epithelium (iron-alum haematoxylin; from a section); (2) Second intracellular stage, from a section; formation of two segments in the body may noted (iron-alum haematoxylin); (3) Fully grown trophozoite; (4) Fully grown sporadin; (5) Sporadins in syzygy; (6) A freshly formed cyst; (7) A semi-polar view of oocyst.

Association

(210 μm) The two gamonts associate caudo-frontally reaching a total length of 210 μm approximately. The posterior tip of the primite fits firmly in a concavity of the protomerite of satellite. Gradually the anterior tip of the primite and the posterior tip cf the satellite come closer and ultimately the two organisms lie side by side. They secrete a true cyst membrane around them and a gametocyst 18 formed.

Gametocyst

Cysts are commonly encountered during the winter months and collected from the hindgut of the infected hosts. Opaque white, almost spherical; measures 127.5 μm × 110.5 μm–190.0 μm × 144.5 μm approximately in dimensions with almost equal size of gametocytes within the cyst wall. In a moist chamber, oocysts are liberated at about 60 hours of development by simple rupture in short chains of three to four.

Oocyst

7.2 μm × 4.9 μm in dimensions, double-walled, barrel- shaped in outline. The formation of eight sporozoites occurs which are concentrated at one end of the oocyst in clusters.

Type Specimen

Hapantotype

Trophozoite on slide no. TL1 prepared from the smear preparation of the contents of the midgut of *Monolepta nigrobilineata* collected from Ranagbat in Nadia district, West Bengal, India by Dr. Tarun K. Kundu in October 1998. Slides containing the hapantotype and syntype material have been deposited in the collection museum of the Protozoology Laboratory, Department of Zoology, University of Kalyani.

Ecological Consideration

Seasonal Intensity and Seat of Infestation

The host insects have been collected from Ranaghat, West Bengal from light trap during the month of June 1998 to August 2000. On an average 54.5 per cent of the insects are infected with this gregarine. Maximum infection is found during the months of October and November, while during the other months it declines considerably. The seat of infestation is the midgut.

Summary of measurements of 25 specimens of trophozoites and gamonts with the mean within parenthesis is given below:

Measurements (in microns)

Trophozoite

TL: 52.6–91.4 (72.5); LE: 6.9–13.8 (9.6); WE: 8.3–13.8 (9.2); LP: 11.0–19.3 (15.7); WP: 13.8–18.0 (15.2); LD: 33.2–60.9 (47.0); WD: 16.6–22.1 (18.9); LN: 8.3–13.8 (10.5); WN: 8.3–11.0 (9.1).

Gamont

TL: 51.0–204.0 (143.6); LP: 12.7–38.2(28 6); WP: 12. 7–46.7(31.4); LD: 38.2–170.0 (115.0); WD: 17.0–63.7(43.3); LN: 10.6–25.5 (18.7); WN: 8.5–19.1 (15.1).); LP : TL : 1 : 3.7–7.0 (1 : 4.8); WP : WD : 1 : 1.0–1.6 (1 : 1.3).

Comparative Discussion

The gregarines inhabiting the midgut of the beetles belonging to the family Chrysomelidae possesses simple globular retractile epimerite, gamonts in syzygy, gametocysts without ducts and barrel-shaped oocysts extruded in chains (Haldar, Chakraborty and Kundu, 1982). In *R. raphidopalpae, R. aulacophorae, R. spatulatus* and *R. monoleptae* sp. n. the epimerite in trophozoite is simple, globular, 8.1 µm in diameter. *R. spinosus* described from *M. signata* has an epimerite which is simple, knob-like and 10.0 µm in length. The deutomerite in gamont is cylindrical in *R. raphidopalpae, R. spinosus. R. halticus* and obese in *R. aulacophorae* and *R. spatulatus* but elongated in the newly described species. Distinct epicyteal striations are observed in *R. raphidoplapae, R. aulacophorae, R. spatulatus* and *R. spinosus* but absent in *R. halticus* and *R. monoleptae* sp. n. Gamonts are biassociative in *R. raphidopalpae, R. aulacophorae, R. spatulatus, R. spinosus* and the newly described species but is rarely observed in *R. halticus.* Gametocyst are spherical in *R. aulacophorae, R. spinosus* and *R. halticus;* oval in *R. raphidopalpae* and *R. spatulatus,* but almost spherical in *R. monoleptae* reaching a dimension of 127.5 µm × 110.5 µm–190.0 µm × 144.5 µm which dehisces at about 60 hours of development and oocysts liberated in short chains of 3–4 are barrel-shaped as in all the previously described species. One distinguishing feature in the oocyst is that the eight sporozoites formed are clustered at one pole of the oocyst.

Though *R. monoleptae* sp. n. and *R. spinosus* have been obtained so far from different species of the same host *Monolepta* sp. there are dissimilarities in morphological structures as well as there are similarities and dissimilarities with the other four previously described species. On the viewpoint of such comparison, *R. monoleptae* sp. n. can be conferred a new species status.

References

Clopton, R.E., 2006. Phylum Apicomplexa, Order Eugregarinorida. Systematic arrangement of Septate Gregarines. Laboratory for Parasitology, Department of Natural Science, Peru State College, Nebraska, USA.

Grassé, P.P., 1953. Classe des Gregarinomorphes. In: *Traité de Zoologie.* Mason, et. Cie., Paris, 1: 550–690.

Haldar, D.P. and Chakraborty, N., 1976. *Retractocephalus*: A new genus of cephaline Gregarine (Protozoa: Sporozoa) from insects. *Curr. Sci.*, 45: 668–669.

Haldar, D.P., Chakraborty, N. and Kundu, T.K., 1982. Studies in cephaline gregarines (Protozoa: Sporozoa) from insects: Life history of *Retractocephalus raphidopalpae* Haldar and Chakraborty, 1976 and four new species of the genus *Retractocephalus. Arch. Protistenk,* 125: 41-62.

Haldar, D.P., Sengupta. T. and Ghose, S., 1985. An annotated list of septate gregarines (Apicomplexa: Sporozoea) from Indian arthropods. *J. Beng. Nat. Soc.*, New Series, 4: 20–39.

Lipa, J.J., 1967. Studies on Gregarines (Gregarinomorpha) of arthropods in Poland. *Acta Protozoologica,* 5: 97–179.

Sprague, V., 1941. Studies on *Gregarina blattarum* with particular reference to the chromosome cycle. Ill. *Biol. Monogr.*, 18: 5–57.

Chapter 44

Evaluation of Ginger Varieties for High Altitude and Tribal Area of Andhra Pradesh

M. Mutyala Naidu, M. Padma, K.M. Yuva Raj and P.S.S. Murty

Regional Agricultural Research Station, Chintapalle - 531 111, Andhra Pradesh, India

ABSTRACT

An experiment was conducted to evaluate five Ginger varieties for high altitude area of Visakhapatnam district at Regional Agricultural Research Station, Chintapalle for three crop seasons. Accession-64 released as IISR Varada was significantly superior in its productivity of fresh rhizome 21.54 t/ha (1996–97), 25.0 t/ha (1997–98) and 23.37 t/ha (1999–2000) followed by SG–554 (20.04 t/ha and 18.5 t/ha during 1996–97 and 1999–2000 respectively). Further, it was noted that the characters such as plant height, number of tillers/plant, leaf length and leaf breadth varied significantly among the varieties. The variety IISR Varada is highly suitable for the high altitude areas of Visakhapatnam district.

Introduction

Ginger (*Zingiber officinale* Rosc.) is a rhizomatous herbaceous perennial, usually grown as an annual. Ginger of commerce is the dried rhizome. India is the largest producer of dry ginger in the world accounting for more than half of the world production. In India Ginger is cultivated in an area of 58,008 ha with an annual production of 1.89 lakh tones (Velappan, 1994). In Andhra Pradesh, it is cultivated in an area of 2508 ha. In the agency areas of Visakhapatnam district, it is mostly grown by the tribals and they cultivate Ginger using local varieties. As a result the productivity of Ginger is low in these parts thus making Ginger cultivation less remunerative. Systematic efforts on introduction and evaluation of improved varieties of Ginger were not undertaken in the high ranges of

Visakhapatnam district of Andhra Pradesh. Hence the present study was carried out to evaluate suitable variety for this area.

Materials and Methods

The investigation was carried out at the Regional Agricultural Research Station, Chintapalle in Visakhapatnam district of Andhra Pradesh (17°N 80°22′, E, Alt. 900 m). The trial was laid out in Randomized Block Design with four replications using five varieties namely V_1S_1–8, V_3S_1–8, V_1E_8–2, SG–554 and IISR Varada with Chintapalle local as check. Rhizome weighting 15 to 20 gm each were planted in spacing of 30 cm × 20 cm at a depth of 5 cm in a plot size of 3m × 1 m. The trial was started during 1996–97 and repeated in 1997–98 and 1999–2000 crop seasons. Standard package of practices recommended by Indian Institute of Spices Research, Calicut was followed and five clumps from each plot were selected at random for studying various growth parameters (Plant height, number of tillers/ plant, number of leaves/plant, leaf length, leaf breadh, Rhizome weight/clump and Rhizome yield).

Results and Discussion

The results of growth parameters and yield attributing characters are presented in the Tables 44.1 and 44.2. It is evident from the tables that the cultivars differed significantly among themselves in all the parameters studied.

Table 44.1: Morphological and Yield Attributing Characters of Ginger Varieties

Variety	*Plant Height (cm)*	*Tillers/Plant*	*No. of Leaves/ Plant*	*Leaf Length (cm)*	*Leaf Breadth (cm)*	*Rhizome Weight/Clump (gms)*
SG–554	54.30	5.95	82.50	17.95	2.30	130.0
Acc–64 (IISR Varada)	63.32	7.85	80.50	18.92	2.00	176.8
V_3S_1–8	56.82	8.70	88.60	16.50	2.37	160.5
V_1E_8–2	46.60	7.55	90.50	16.37	2.00	140.2
V_1S_1–8	57.97	9.57	82.00	17.55	2.30	120.8
Chintapalle Local	51.62	7.62	75.80	14.42	2.22	109.5
CD at 5%	3.46	0.96	6.80	0.63	0.21	15.0

Table 44.2: Fresh Rhizome Yield (t/ha) of Ginger Varieties

Variety	*Source*	*Fresh Rhizome Yield in Tonnes/ha*		
		1996–97	*1997–98*	*1999–2000*
SG–554	Solan, H.P.	20.04	16.67	18.50
Acc–64 (IISR Varada)	IISR, Calicut	21.54	25.00	23.37
V_3S_1–8	HARS, Pottangi	9.15	26.62	15.45
V_1E_8–2	HARS, Pottangi	5.50	20.83	8.25
V_1S_1–8	HARS, Pottangi	13.93	9.17	14.19
Chintapalle Local	Chintapalle	16.67	15.40	13.25
CD at 5%		2.49	1.62	2.38

The variety, IISR Varada was significandy superior with a plant height of 63.32 cm. This was followed by V_1S_1–8 (57.97 cm) and V_3S_1–8 (56.82 cm) and were on par. The number of tillers per plant were maximum in V_1S_1–8 (9.57) and V_3S_1–8 (8.70) which were significantly superior to other varieties followed by IISR Varada (7.85). Significantly higher number of leaves/plant were recorded in V_1E_8–2 (90.5) and V_3S_1–8 (88.6) whereas maximum leaf length was recorded in IISR Varada variety (18.92 cm). The varieties *viz.*, V_3S_1–8 SG–554 and V_1S_1–8 recorded maximum leaf breath and were on par with each other. Significant variation in rhizome yield of ginger was also noticed among varieties IISR Varada recorded significantly higher rhizome weight per clump of 176.8 g followed by V_3S_1–8 (160.5 g). This was followed by V_1E_8–2 (140.2 g) and SG–554 (130 g) which were on par with each other.

IISR Varada was significantly superior in its productivity of fresh rhizome yield of 21.54 t/ha (1996–97), 25.0 t/ha (1996–97) and 23.37 t/ha (1999–2000) followed by SG–554 which recorded 20.04 t/ha and 18.5 t/ha during 1996–97 and 1999–2000 respectively (Table 44.2). The varieties, SG–554 and V_3S_1–8 were on par with IISR Varada in respect of rhizome yield during 1996–97 and 1997–98. The higher yields in IISR Varada variety were also reported by Sasikumar *et al.* (1996). The lowest yield was recorded by V_1E_8–2 during 1996–97 and 1999–2000. The higher yields in IISR Varada could be attributed to higher weight of rhizome per clump. The variety is characterized by plumpy rhizomes with flattened fingers.

In the present study all the characters studies varieties significantly among the varieties. In ginger such phenotypic variations in growth and yield attributing parameters have been reported by Nybe and Nair (1979), Rattan *et al.* (1988) and Ravindran *et al.* {1994). These differences in varieties under uniform conditions may be due to genetic factors.

From the present study, the ginger variety, IISR Varada is identified as most suitable for cultivation in the high altitude areas of Visakhapatnam district, Andhra Pradesh, because of its optimum growth and higher productivity during all the three years of study.

References

Nybe, E.V. and Nair, P.C.S., 1979. Studies on the morphology of ginger types. *Indian Cocoa, Arecanut and Spices J.*, 3(1): 7–13.

Rattan, R.S., Korea, B.N. and Dehroo, N.P., 1988. Performance of ginger varieties in Solan area of Himachal Pradesh. In: *Proc. of National Seminar on Chilies, Ginger and Turmeric*, January 1988, Hyderabad, pp. 71–73.

Sasikumar, B., Johnson, K. George and Ravindran, P.N., 1996. IISR Varada: A new high yielding ginger variety.

Valappan, 1994. Integrated programme for the development of spices in India during VIII five year plan. *Indian Cocoa, Arecanut Species J.*, 18(1): 1–4.

Chapter 45

Performance of Different Cluster Bean Varieties

M.M. Naidu, K.P. Pathy, V. Ganesh Babu and R. Sreenivsulu

Agricultural College, Bapatla – 522 101

ABSTRACT

Ten cluster bean varieties differing in growth and pod characters were tested at Agricultural College, farm, Bapatla during kharif 1987 to select suitable high yielding varieties. Higher plant height and more number of branches were recorded with variety Durgapur ـafed. Flowering was early in pusa naubahar while it was late in sharad bahar. The number of pod/plant were maximum in NC_4/P_2^{-1}, E.C. 36952 and Durgapur safed while it was minimum in Naveen and pusa Naubahar. Green pod yield per ha was maximum in sharad bahar and pusa naubahar and these two varieties are suitable and recommended for commercial cultivation in areas around Bapatla, Guntur District.

Introduction

Cluster bean [*Cyamposis tetragonoloba* (L.) Taub.] is a popular vegetable crop particularly of peninsular India, because of its low cost of cultivation and lesser attention it demands. By nature, it is a drought tolerant hardy legume. Besides, rich in protein, cluster bean pods are also a good source of Iron. Vitamin A and C. Protein content varies from 21 to 43 per cent with 'methionine' an essential amino acid and also contain considerable amounts of fats and carbohydrates.

Singh and Sikka (1955) reported that the varieties pusa sadabahar and pusa mausauami gave 92 q/ha of green pod yield. It was reported that in trials conducted at different locations by Dabas *et al.* (1981) sharad bahar gave significantly higher pod yield than pusa 'Naubahar' the percentage of increase ranging from 27.8 per cent to 44.0 per cent.

Several varieties of cluster bean differing in pod characters and growth habits are being grown in India. Little information is available on the morphological and physiological characteristics of several varieties grown in Andhra Pradesh. The vegetable growers around Bapatla are cultivating local varieties and popular varieties of other regions are not grown. Keeping this in view, the present investigation was carried out to select suitable high yielding varieties of cluster bean.

Materials and Methods

The experiment was laid out in randomized block design replicated thrice at the college farm, Bapatla during Kharif season of 1987. Eleven promising varieties of cluster bean *viz.*, pusa naubahar, Durgapur safed. EC 36952, Sharad bahar, Naveen, Bapatla local, NCK selection. NC_4/P_2^{-1}, Guara–80, Ag 112 and PLG 119 were tried under Bapatla agro-climatic conditions. The crop was dibbled on 14th August, 1987 at a spacing of 45 cm × 20 cm. The gross plot size was 3.15 × 2.2 m² and net plot was 2.25 × 1.85 m² Nitrogen, phosphorus and potassium were applied at the rate of 20 kg, 70 kg and 50 kg/ha respectively. The soil of the experimental site was sandy loam.

Results and Discussion

From the data presented in Table 45.1, it is revealed that higher plant height and more number of branches were recorded with varieties Durgapur safed and minimum plant height was recorded with pusa naubahar.

Table 45.1: Growth and Yield Characters of Different Cluster Bean Varieties

Varieties	*Height (cm)*	*No. of Branches/Plant*	*Days to 50% Flowering*	*No. of Clusters/ Plant*	*No. of Pods/Plant*	*Pod Length (cm)*	*Green Pod Yield (t/ha)*
Pusa Naubahar	93.73	1.0	24.5	15.9	70.73	11.88	111.51
Durgapur safed	135.30	15.4	30.23	21.5	99.46	5.43	77.78
EC 36952	135.16	13.56	29.9	18.8	105.53	5.68	69.79
Sharad bahar	126.86	13.70	33.30	17.50	87.20	8.76	129.41
Naveen	118.10	11.06	26.76	15.6	71.86	6.08	54.78
Bapatla local	130.13	13.76	28.00	18.93	88.60	6.89	52.05
NCK selection	113.20	1.00	25.06	17.50	83.86	6.50	59.90
NC_4/P_2^{-1}	115.23	1.00	25.13	21.50	105.53	6.45	62.93
Guara–80	126.10	14.76	30.0	20.50	95.06	5.87	62.03
AG 112	127.0	1.00	25.83	19.56	93.53	6.28	60.05
PLG 119	112.00	1.00	26.00	17.50	85.20	5.64	64.80
SEM ±	2.65	0.168	0.254	0.439	3.13	0.1064	1.16
CD at 5%	7.83	0.495	0.75	1.296	9.25	0.3139	4.76

Flowering was early in pusa naubahar while it was late in sharad bahar. The varieties NC_4/P_2^{-1}, Durgapur safed and Guara–80 produced highest number of clusters per plant and the lowest number of clusters per plant was observed in pusa Naubahar and Naveen.

Higher number of clusters per plant in Durgapur safed were also reported by Gill and Singh (1981) and Taneja (1982). Significant and positive correlation was observed between number of clusters and pods per plant. But in the variety EC 36952, although the number of clusters per plant were less as compared to Guara–80. The number of pods/plant were more due to more number of pods per cluster.

The number of pods/plant were maximum in NC_4/P_2^{-1}, EC 36952 and Durgapur sated, while it was minimum on Naveen and pusa naubahar. The variety pusa naubahar produced lengthy pods where as sharad bahar and Bapatla local produced medium sized pods. Green pod yield per ha was maximum in sharad bahar and pusa naubahar. Eventhough pusa naubahar has recorded less number of clusters and pods per plant, the yields were very high due to its higher pod length and pod weight. Although the yield was lower in Guara–80 when compared to sharad bahar and pusa naubahar due to lesser pod length and pod weight, it has recorded highest number of clusters and pods per plant. Significant and positive correlation was observed for green pod yield with no. of pods and pod length. Similar correlation was also reported by Menen *et al.* (1973) in cluster bean.

From the economic point of view, shared bahar and pusa naubahar gave higher green pod yield and are suitable for commercial cultivation in areas around Bapatla in Guntur District. The varieties sharad bahar and pusa naubahar can be recommended for cultivation for green pods. as they have ideal plant type, smooth, long and succulent pods.

References

Dabar, B.S., T.S. Thomas, S.P. Mital and D.P. Chopra, 1981. Sharad bahar: A new cluster bean. *Indian Horticulture*, 25(4): 17–18.

Gill, P.S. and Kanwar Singh, 1981. Effect of fertilization on yield contributing characters and grain yield or cluster bean [*Cyamopsis tetragonoloba* (L.) taub]. *Haryana Agri. Univ. Journal Res.*, 11(3): 333–338.

Meon, V., M.M. Dubey and R.P. Chandola, 1973. Genetic variability and correlation studies in vegetable 'cluster beans [*Cyamopsis tetragonoloba* (b) Tamb]. *Rajasthan J. Agric. Sci.*, 4(2): 67–73.

Singh, H.B. and S.M. Sikka, 1955. If it is guar, here are two new pusa strains. *Indian Farming*, 5: 8–11.

Taneja, K.D., P.S. Gill and B.D. Sharma, 1982. Effect of row-spacings intra-row spacings on seed yield of guar cultivars. *Forage Res.*, 8(2): 111–115.

Chapter 46

Performance of Different Turmeric Varieties in High Altitude Area of Andhra Pradesh, India

M. Mutyala Naidu, M. Padma, K.M. Yuva Raj and P.S.S. Murty

Regional Agricultural Research Station, Chintapalle - 531 111, Andhra Pradesh, India

ABSTRACT

Seven turmeric (*Curcuma longa*) varieties were evaluated under rainfed conditions for three crop seasons in the high altitude area of Chintappalle in Visakhapatnam district of Andhra Pradesh. The varieties differed in their production potential and growth characters (plant height, number of tillers per plant, leaves per tiller, leaf length and leaf breadth). Among varieties tested, BSR–1 exhibited maximum productivity of fresh rhizome 34.84 t/ha (1996–97), 32.23 t/ha (1997–98) and 36.5 t/ha (1998–99) and it was at par with the productivity of the selection PTS–62 (32.72 t/ha, 34.43 t/ha and 27.36 t/ha during 1996–97, 1997–98 and 1998–99 respectively. These two varieties, BSR–1 and PTS–62 were significantly superior to other varieties during all the three seasons and are suitable for cultivation in the agency areas of Visakhapatnam district of Andhra Pradesh.

Introduction

Turmeric is one of the important spices and a dye of moderate importance which has good demand in India and other oriental countries. India is the largest producer and exporter of turmeric in the world. In India it is grown mainly in the states of Andhra Pradesh, Tamil Nadu, Kerala, Bihar, Orissa and Maharashtra. However, Andhra Pradesh and Tamil Naidu contribute nearly 50 per cent of the production. Crop improvement studies undertaken at various research organizations have resulted in the release of twelve improved varieties (Edison *et al.*, 1991). Systematic efforts on introduction and evaluation of improved varieties of turmeric were not undertaken in the high ranges of Visakhapatnam district of Andhra Pradesh where inferior local clones are under cultivation resulting in low productivity thus making turmeric cultivation less remunerative. Hence the present study was carried out to evaluate the performance of different varieties of turmeric, so as to find out the best variety suitable for this area.

Materials and Methods

The field experiment was carried out under rain fed conditions at the Regional Agricultural Research Station, Chintapalle of Visakhapatnam district, Andhra Pradesh (17°19′ N 80°22′ E, Alt. 900 m). The trial was laid out in RED with three replications using four varieties and three selections of turmeric *viz.*, IISR Prabha, IISR Prathibha, PTS–12, PTS–43, PTS–62, Rajendra Sonia and BSR–1 procured from various research organizations during 1996–97 and repeated in 1997–98 and 1998–99 crop seasons. The net plot size was 3 m × 1 m and a spacing of 30 cm × 20 cm was adopted. Standard package of practices recommended by Indian Institute of Spices Research, Calicut was followed. Observations on plant height, number of tillers per plant, number of leaves per plant, leaf length, leaf breadth and yield attributes were recorded.

Results and Discussion

The mean performance of the varieties in relation to growth characters is presented in Table 46.1. Results indicated that there is significant variation among the turmeric varieties in respect of growth characters such as plant height, number of tillers per plant, number of leaves per plant, leaf length and leaf breadth. BSR–1 was found to be the tallest (70.4 cm) with more number of tillers per plant among the varieties studied. The number of leaves per plant were maximum in IISR Prathibha (15.2) whereas maximum leaf length and leaf breadth were recorded in PTS-62. Rajendra Sonia showed poor growth in terms of plant height, leaf length and leaf breadth. Similar variation in the growth parameters among different cultivars were reported by Shah *et al.* (1982), Reddy *et al.* (1989) and Choke (1993) under different agro-climatic conditions.

Table 47.1: Morphological and Yield Attributing Characters of Turmeric Varieties

Variety	*Plant Height (cm)*	*Tillers/Plant*	*No. of Leaves/ Plant*	*Leaf Length (cm)*	*Leaf Breadth (cm)*	*Rhizome Weight/Clump (gms)*
IISR Prabha	51.50	2.80	15.00	29.73	11.20	277.70
IISR Prathibha	43.40	2.93	15.20	32.30	12.33	239.80
PTS–12	40.50	1.93	10.26	31.33	14.53	232.30
PTS–43	48.40	2.00	11.20	33.66	14.20	299.30
PTS–62	52.35	3.26	14.73	43.86	16.40	284.40
Rajendra Sonia	25.30	2.86	11.80	24.13	8.60	241.50
BSR–1	70.40	3.50	9.80	31.60	14.53	350.50
CD at 5%	6.75	0.54	1.87	4.55	1.11	30.13

Significant variation in fresh yield of rhizomes was noticed among varieties (Table 46.2). Significantly higher rhizome weight, per clump was recorded by BSR–1 (350.5 g) followed by PTS–43

Table 47.2: Fresh Rhizome Yield (t/ha) of Turmeric Varieties

Variety	*Source*	*Fresh Rhizome Yield in Tonnes/ha*		
		1996–97	*1997–98*	*1999–2000*
IISR Prabha	IISR, Calicut	19.47	26.76	26.60
IISR Prathibha	IISR, Calicut	26.77	28.56	19.61
PTS–12	HARS, Pottangi	17.67	33.56	25.99
PTS–43	HARS, Pottangi	23.32	33.33	24.88
PTS–62	HARS, Pottangi	32.72	34.43	27.36
Rajendra Sonia	Dholi, Bihar	19.16	27.23	14.10
BSR–1	RARS, Bhavani Sagar	34.84	32.23	36.50
CD at 5%	5.93	3.59	9.89	

(299 g), PTS–62 (284.4 g) and IISR Prabha (277.7 g) which were on par with each other. BSR–1 exhibited maximum productivity of fresh rhizome 34.84/t/ha (1996–97), 32.23 t/ha (1997–98) and 36.5 t/ha (1998–99) and it was on par with PTS–62 which recorded 32.72 t/ha, 34.43 t/ha and 27.36 t/ha during 1996–97, 1997–98 and 1998–99 respectively. Maximum yield in BSR–1 variety was also reported by Patil *et al.* (1995). The higher yields in BSR–1 and PTS–62 could be attributed to higher number of tillers per plant and large size of mother rhizomes. These two varieties are characterized by bigger sized mother rhizomes and medium sized fingers with bright yellow colour. Positive and significant association of rhizome yield with height of pseudostem, number of tillers and weight of rhizome were reported by Nambiar (1979). The variation in yield and growth attributes among turmeric varieties grown under some agroecological conditions can be attributed to the genetic factors (Aiyadurai, 1966; Subharayadu *et al.*, 1976 and Jalgaonker *et al.*, 1988). It is suggested that BSR–1 and PTS–62 are suitable for cultivation in the high altitude areas of Visakhapatnam district of Andhra Pradesh and the same can be cultivated extensively to enhance the production and productivity of the crop in this region.

References

Aiyadurai, S.G., 1966. Curing quality in turmeric: A review of research on spices and cashewnut.

Choke, S.M., 1993. Performance of turmeric (*Curcuma longa* L.) cultivars. *M.Sc. (Agril.) Thesis*, University of Agricultural Sciences, Dharwad.

Edision, S., Jhony, A.K., Nirmal Babu, K. and Ramadasan, A., 1991. Spices varieties. A compendium of morphological and agronomic characters of improved varieties of spices in India. NRCS, Kerala.

Jalgaonkar, R., Patil, M.M. and Rajput, J.C., 1988. Performance of different varieties of turmeric (*Curcuma longa* L.) under Konkan conditions of Maharashtra. In: *Proc. National Seminar on Chilies, Ginger and Turmeric.* Andhra Pradesh Agricultural University, Hyderabad and Spices Board, Cochin, pp. 102–105.

Patil, D.V., 1995. Performance of turmeric (*Curcuma longa*.L.) varieties in lower pulney hills of Tamil Nadu, India. *Journal of Spices and Aromatic Crops*, 4(2): 156–158.

Reddy, M.L.N., Rao, D.V.R. and Reddy, S.A., 1989. Screening of short duration turmeric varieties suitable for Andhra Pradesh. *Indian Cocoa, Arecanut and Spices J.*, 12(3): 87–89.

Shah, H.A., Seemanthini, R., Arumagam, R., Muthuswamy, S. and Khadar, J.B.M., 1982. Co-1 turmeric: A high yielding mutant. *South Indian Horti.*, 30(4): 276–277.

Subbarayudu, M., Reddy, R.K. and Rao, M.R., 1976. Studies on varietal performance of turmeric. *Andhra Agric. J.*, 23(588): 195–198.

Nambiar, M.C., 1979. Morphological and cytological investigations in the genus curcuma Linn. *Ph.D Thesis*, University of Bombay, pp. 95.

Chapter 47

Rapid Composting of Irrigated Pearl Millet Straw

***J. Kannan*[1] *and P. Singaram*[2]**

[1]Krishi Vigyan kendra, Pechiparai

[2]Department of Environmental Sciences, TNAU, Coimbatore – 3

ABSTRACT

One experiment was conducted to fasten the composting of pearl millet straw with different combination of microorganisms. The microorganisms used were *Bacillus* sp., *Pseudomonas* sp., *Trichoderma* sp., *Pleurotus* sp. and *Streptomyces* sp. Among the different combination of microorganisms utilized, the combination of microbes *Trichoderma* sp. and *Pleurotus* sp. decomposed the straw rapidly and fully matured compost was obtained within sixty (60) days. The nitrogen and potassium content of the matured compost was highest in T_2, T_4 and T_5, all the fungi inoculated treatments. In the fungi inoculated treatments, the total nitrogen content was 15 per cent more than control and the total phosphorus and total potassium contents were 13 per cent and 33 per cent more than control.

***Keywords**: Compost, Microorganisms and Matured compost.*

Introduction

The disposal of organic materials through burning can vanish valuable resources and contribute to environmental problems. When applied properly and adequately, these products can positively impact our environment by improving soil and plant health, conserving water, reducing erosion and minimising the use of fertilizers and pesticides. Composting is a biological process in which biological wastes are stabilized and converted into a product to be used as a soil conditioner and organic manure. Composting is considered to be a part of recycling in which the nutrients are put back into the soil and plant life.

Pearl millet is the fourth important food crop in India next to rice, wheat and sorghum and also the second major coarse cereal grain after sorghum. Pearl millet is extensively cultivated in poor fertile and water-deficit soils, mostly with low and erratic rainfall. India is the largest producers of pearl millet in the world and in Tamil Nadu, the pearl millet is cultivated in about 215 thousand hectares (Balasubramaniyan and Palaniappan, 2003). The pearl millet straw contains lot of nutrients and these nutrients can be recycled, through proper composting. Generally, it takes six to sevn months to obtain good, finished compost from agricultural wastes and one of the important fields of research is to reduce the period of composting of agricultural residues through rapid composting. The quick composting process may be a great boon to the fanners for sustaining the soil fertility.

Materials and Methods

A heap method of composting experiment was carried out in order to quicken the composting of irrigated pearl millet straw at the department of Environmental Sciences, TNAU, Coimbatore, Tamil Nadu. Treatments fixed were six replicated four times. The composting was carried out for a period of 105 days, during February–May, 2004. The size of the heap uniformly was 250 × 95 × 55 cm as length, width and height. The cultures used for composting are as follows:

Cultures used: Bacteria–*Bacillus* sp., *Pseudomonas* sp.

Fungi–*Trichoderma* sp., *Pleurotus* sp.

Actinomycetes–*Streptomyces* sp.

Treatments

T_1: Pearl millet straw + cowdung + *Bacillus* sp. + *Pseudomonas* sp.*

T_2: Pearl millet straw + cowdung + *Trichoderma* sp. + *Pleurotus* sp.*

T_3: Pearl millet straw + cowdung + *Streptomyces* sp.*

T_4: Pearl millet straw + cowdung + Existing microbial inoculum**

T_5: Pearl millet straw + cowdung + mixed microbial inoculum*

T_6: Pearl millet straw + cowdung (control)

Preparation of Inoculants

The cultures were isolated from the compost pits by the standard serial dilution plate technique and by streak plate method. The isolated cultures were purified by single hypal tip method and by streak plate method.

Table 47.1

Sl.No.	Cultures	Broth Used
1.	*Bacillus* sp. and *Pseudomonas* sp.	Nutrient broth, Kings broth
2.	*Trichoderma* sp. and *Pleurotus* sp.	Potato dextrose broth
3.	*Streptomyces* sp.	Kusters broth

* Cultures were isolated during mesophilic and thermophilic stages of composting from the compost pits of Regional Research Station, Aruppukottai. Mixed microbial inoculum consists of *Bacillus* sp., *Pseudomonas* sp., *Trichoderma* sp., *Pleurotus* sp. and *Streptomyces* sp.

** Existing microbial inoculum contains *Bacillus* sp., *Pseudomonas* sp. and *Pleurotus* sp.

The purified cultures were inoculated in the conical flask containing concerned sterilized broth. Then the bacterial cultures were kept in the electrical shaker for two days, whereas the fungal and actinomycetes cultures were kept for eight days for multiplication.

Composting Methodology

The pearl millet straw was chopped into bits of 10 to 15 cm length. One hundred kilograms of straw on wet weight basis was heaped for each treatment which was then sprayed with water to maintain the moisture content of 75 to 80 per cent. Cultures of different organisms were inoculated at 1 per cent level, as per the treatments. Accurately 10 kg of fresh cowdung was prepared as slurry by mixing with 10 litres of water and sprinkled over each heap. The pearl millet straw was allowed to decompose by maintaining the moisture content of 75 to 80 per cent during the period of composting. The second time of inoculation of cultures at 1 per cent level was done on 15th day of composting. Every fortnight, all the compost heaps were turned upside down. The samples were collected from five different spots of each heap and composite samples were obtained for the initial, 7th day of composting and at fortnight interval starting from 15th day of composting. The samples were analysed for their physico-chemical and biochemical properties by following standard procedure. The statistical analysis of data was carried out by completely randomised block design.

Results and Discussion

Table 47.2: Characteristics of the Fresh Irrigated Pearl Millet Straw

Sl.No.	*Characters*	*Pearl Millet Atraw*
1.	pH	6.23
2.	Electrical Conductivity (dSm^{-1})	0.98
3.	Organic carbon (per cent)	38.18
4.	Total nitrogen (per cent)	0.51
5.	C : N ratio	74.86
6.	Total Ca (per cent)	0.49
7.	Total Mg (per cent)	0.20
8.	Cellulose (per cent)	33.80
9.	Hemicellulose (per cent)	25.60
10.	Lignin (per cent)	12.40
11.	Silica (per cent)	8.20
12.	Total phosphorus (per cent)	0.018
13.	Total potassium (per cent)	1.14
14.	Manganese (ppm)	58.96
15.	Zinc (ppm)	25.42
16.	Iron (ppm)	18.74
17.	Copper (ppm)	23.80
18.	Total solids (per cent)	81.75
19.	Ash content (per cent)	9.20
20.	Moisture (per cent)	18.25

Table 47.3: Characteristics of the Cowdung

Sl.No.	Characters	Cowdung
1.	pH	8.18
2.	Electrical Conductivity (dSm^{-1})	1.94
3.	Total nitrogen (per cent)	0.83
4.	Total phosphorus (per cent)	0.09
5.	Total potassium (per cent)	0.24
6.	Total calcium (per cent)	3.12
7.	Total magnesium (per cent)	0.48
8.	Organic carbon (per cent)	17.10

Application of immatured compost with high C : N ratio, can result in immobilization of available nitrogen, causing an nitrogen deficiency in plants (Bannick and Joergensen, 1993). So, testing the maturity and quality of compost is essential. C : N ratio of the compost should be less than 20. Final C : N/Initial C : N ratio should be less than 0.6.

Table 47.4: Compost Maturity Test Conducted

Treatments	Tests Conducted (60th Day of Composting)					Tests Conducted (75th Day of Composting)				
	pH		CEC	C : N Ratio	Final CN/ Initial CN Ratio	pH		CEC	C : N Ratio	Final CN/ Initial CN Ratio
	Before Incubation	After Incubation	Cmol $(p+)kg^{-1}$			Before Incubation	After Incubation	Cmol $(p+)kg^{-1}$		
T_1	7.40	6.43	51.2	21.78	0.29	7.39	7.14	59.4	20.48	0.27
T_2	7.33	7.08	60.1	19.94	0.27	7.32	7.20	60.4	18.15	0.24
T_3	7.54	6.53	52.4	22.65	0.30	7.48	7.27	59.5	20.63	0.28
T_4	7.41	7.11	60.3	19.94	0.27	7.40	7.21	61.0	18.35	0.25
T_5	7.45	7.09	60.5	19.81	0.26	7.44	7.18	60.8	17.61	0.24
T_6	7.21	6.30	50.7	34.42	0.46	7.18	6.61	58.2	25.60	0.34

Table 47.5: Compost Maturity Tests Conducted During 90th Day of Composting

Treatments	Test Conducted				
	pH		CEC	C : N Ratio	Final C : N/Initial C : N
	Before Incubation	After Incubation	Cmol (p+) kg^{-1}		
T_1	7.39	7.31	62.7	16.52	0.22
T_2	7.25	7.14	643	15.23	0.20
T_3	7.44	7.36	63.8	17.27	0.23
T_4	7.38	7.29	64.5	15.50	0.21
T_5	7.42	7.34	63.9	15.62	0.21
T_6	7.15	6.91	59.3	19.80	0.26

T_1: T_6 + Bacterial culture; T_2: T_6 + Fungal culture; T_3: T_6 + Actinomycetes culture; T_4: T_6 + Existing microbial inoculum; T_5: T_6 + Mixed microbial inoculum; T_6: Pearl millet straw + cowdung (control).

Wide C : N ratio and higher amounts of resistant constituents like lignin are responsible for the slow degradation of cereal residues (Bharadwaj and Gaur, 1985). The fresh pearl millet straw had a C : N ratio of 74.86 and lignin content of 12.4 per cent. In irrigated pearl millet straw composting, the treatments T_2, T_4 and T_5 matured on 60th day. The treatment control T_6 (with no microbial inoculation) had not matured completely, even after 90 days of composting [Table 47.5 showing CEC of 59.3 C mol (P+) kg^{-1} which is less than 60). The treatments T_2 and T_5 matured earlier as they were inoculated with *Pleurotus* sp. and *Trichoderma* sp. This is in accordance with the results of Nandi *et al.*, 2000 in which they reported that the inoculation of lignin degrading fungi along with cellulose decomposing fungi deserves its application in disposing of cereal residues by rapid composting.

According to Kalaiselvi and Ramasamy (1996), none of the parameters are 90 per cent sure of deciding the quality. Combination of methods is required to test the quality standards. Hence, four parameters *viz.*, C : N ratio, CEC, final C : N/initial C : N ratio and pH of the water extract before and after incubation at 55°C, under anaerobic condition for 24 hours were tested to confirm the maturity of the compost. During composting of irrigated pearl millet straw the C : N ratio was reduced to 14.08 after 105 days. In contrast, Talashilkar *et al.*, (2002) reported that the C : N ratio of farm wastes reduced to 10 after 105 days of composting with *Trichoderma* sp. The microbial inoculants containing *Pleurotus* sp. and *Trichoderma* sp. were applied twice at an interval of 15 days. The treatments that received the above mentioned cultures T_2, T_4 and T_5 were matured during 60th day itself. This is in accordance with the study conducted by Kumaresan *et al.* (2003), in which they revealed that sugarcane trash, coirpith and pressmud can be composted with microorganisms *Pleurotus sajor-caju* and *Trichoderma viride* along with 1 per cent urea and 10 per cent cowdung slurry within 60 days. In contrast, Singh and Amberger (1998) reported that wheat straw compost enriched with nitrogen, molasses and rock phosphate should be used only after 120 days of decomposition for sustainable crop production. During composting of irrigated pearl millet straw, the treatments (T_2, T_4 and T_5) with fungal inoculum registered significantly higher nitrogen and potassium contents than the treatments not applied with fungal inoculants (Table 47.7). This was in confirmation with the reports of Nakas and Klein (1980) and they indicated that mineralization was high in fungal treatments because of their capacity to produce enzymes capable of polymeric cleavage.

Table 47.6: Chemical Characteristics of the Matured Pearl Millet Straw Compost

Treatments	*pH*	*EC (dSm^{-1})*	*Organic Caron (%)*	*Total N (%)*	*C : N Ratio*	*CEC Cmol (p+) kg^{-1}*	*Heavy Metals (ppm)*		
							Lead	*Cadmium*	*Chromium*
T_1	7.36	0.78	19.04	1.19	16.0	70.9	5.00	0.98	17.80
T_2	7.24	0.88	17.73	1.24	14.3	73.6	5.25	1.26	23.08
T_3	7.43	0.85	18.54	1.13	16.41	70.2	6.75	1.15	16.90
T_4	7.37	0.87	17.61	1.23	14.32	72.9	5.75	1.23	24.56
T_5	7.40	0.85	17.32	1.23	14.08	73.1	6.25	1.29	25.78
T_6	7.11	0.82	19.16	1.05	18.25	67.2	5.00	0.95	15.50
SED	0.14	0.02	0.35	0.02	0.29	1.23	0.02	0.02	0.02
CD (P = 0.05)	0.31	0.03	0.75	0.05	0.63	2.64	0.04	0.05	0.04

T_1: T_6 + Bacterial culture; T_2: T_6 + Fungal culture; T_3: T_6 + Actinomycetes culture; T_4: T_6 + Existing microbial inoculum; T_5: T_6 + Mixed microbial inoculum; T_6: Pearl millet straw + cowdung (control).

Table 47.7: Nutrients Content of the Matured Pearl Millet Straw Compost

Treatments	*Total N (%)*	*Total P (%)*	*Total K (%)*	*Total Ca (%)*	*Total Mg (%)*
T_1	1.19	0.35	2.11	0.60	0.29
T_2	1.24	0.37	2.51	0.69	0.32
T_3	1.13	0.35	1.96	0.61	0.29
T_4	1.23	0.36	2.51	0.69	0.30
T_5	1.23	0.39	2.49	0.67	0.32
T_6	1.05	0.32	1.67	0.55	0.26
SED	0.02	0.02	0.05	0.01	0.006
CD (P = 0.05)	0.05	0.04	0.10	0.03	0.012

T_1: T_6 + Bacterial culture; T_2: T_6 + Fungal culture; T_3: T_6 + Actinomycetes culture; T_4: T_6 + Existing microbial inoculum; T_5: T_6 + Mixed microbial inoculum; T_6: Pearl millet straw + cowdung (control).

References

Balasubramaniyan, P. and Palaniappan, S.P., 2003. *Principles and Practices of Agronomy*, pp: 29–30.

Bannick, C.G. and Joergensen, R.G., 1993. Changes in N fractions during composting of wheat straw. *Biol. Fert. Soils*, 16: 269–274.

Bharadwaj, K.K.R. and Gaur, A.C., 1985. *Recycling of Organic Wastes*, ICAR, New Delhi, pp. 104.

Kalaiselvi, T. and Ramasamy, K., 1996. Compost maturity: Can it be evaluated? *Madras Agric. J.*, 83: 609–618.

Kurnaresan, M., Shanmugasundaram, V.S. and Balasubramanian, T.N., 2003. Biocomposting, of organic wastes. *Agric. Sci. Digest*, 23: 67–68.

Nakas, J.P. and Klein, D.A., 1980. Mineralisation capacity of bacteria and fungi from the rhizosphere-rhizoplane of a semiarid grassland. *Appl. Environ. Microbiol.*, 39: 113–117.

Nandi, N., Rahman, F.R., Sinha, N.B. and Hajra, J.N., 2000. Compatibility of lignin degrading and cellulose decomposing fungi during decomposition of Rice straw. *J. Indian Soc. Soil Sci.*, 48: 387–389.

Singh, C.P. and Amberger, A., 1998. Organic acids and phosphorus solubilization in straw composted with rock phosphate. *Siores. Technol.*, 63: 13–16.

Talashilkar, S.C., Dosani, A.A.K. and Chatterjee, A., 2002. Soil fertility and organic recycling. *Indian J. Agric. Chem.*, 35: 1–31.

Chapter 48

Plankton Diversity at Gopnath, Gulf of Khambhat, Gujarat

Kauresh D. Vachhrajani[1]* and Pradeep C. Mankodi[2]

Department of Zoology, Faculty of Science, The Maharaja Sayajirao University of Baroda, Vadodara – 390 002, India

ABSTRACT

Coastal planktonic diversity was studied at Gopnath, Bhavnagar district, located at juncture of Gulf of Khambhat and Arabian Sea. 38 phytoplankton and 25 zooplankton species were identified. Pinnularia, Biddulphia, Asterionella, Bacillaria and Aphanocapsa dominated phytoplankton. The zooplanktons were dominated by Protozoan and Arthropod species. A few species of Cnidaria, Mollusca, Annelida and one Chaetognatha were also encountered. Overall density of phytoplankton was much less while among zooplankton Protozoan and Arthropod population exhibited some variation at different sampling sites that may be correlated to physical, physico-chemical characters and prey-predator relationships. Planktonic diversity with details of characteristic features of the area is discussed.

***Keywords**: Plankton, Bacillariophyta, Cyanophyta, Protozoa, Arthropods.*

Introduction

Gopnath, in Bhavnagar district, is located at the juncture of Gulf of Khambhat and Arabian Sea. This area is least influenced by anthropogenic activities. However, it is suspected that it might be

* Corresponding Author. E-mail: [1]kdv_zdmsu@yahoo.com; [2]kauresh123-zoo@msubaroda.ac.in.

influenced by activities along the gulf that is continuously enriched by pollutants through various rivers and effluent channels (Nanda, 2001 and Sharma, 1995). At present there is no data available on the biota of this region of gulf. Therefore, present studies were carried out during 2003–2004 to generate a base-line data, which may be utilized in future for ecological and ecotoxicological studies.

Methods

The Study Area

The coastal belt studied stretches over nine villages. The land takes a sharp curvature towards west and, western and eastern shores are divided by a long rocky strip which distinguishes the characteristic features of these regions.

Sampling Sites

The sampling sites were around 1.5 and 3 nautical miles (nm) away from the coast. Seven transects perpendicular to the shore were defined. On each of the transect sampling sites were located at around 1.5 to 3 nm distance.

Sampling Procedure

A mechanized boat was used for sample collection, 20 μm mesh size plankton net was used for sampling. Three samplings were done from around 100 sqm areas at each site and pooled for studies. Each sample comprised of 25 liter water drained through plankton net. Plankton were collected in 100 ml water, properly narcotized, preserved and brought to laboratory. The samples were concentrated by centrifugation and transferred to 10ml distilled water added with preservative. The identification was done using descriptive and illustrative keys (Todd and Laverack, 1991; Westpal, 1974). Quantification of plankton was done for major species. To avoid error in derivation of indices, occasional species were recorded but not considered for quantification, particularly in case of zooplankton. The data were subjected to analysis for population indices (Smith, 1995; Berger and Parker, 1970).

Results

A total of 38 phytoplankton and 25 zooplankton species were identified from all the samples (Tables 48.1–48.3). Twenty Bacillariophyta and 18 Cyanophyta species were recorded where density of the earlier was comparatively higher. Pinnularia, Biddulphia, Aphanocapsa, Microcystis and Marssoniella exhibited high frequency of occurrence (> 70 per cent) followed by Nitzschia, Asterionella, Grammatophora, Bacillaria, Diatoma and Anacystis (50–70 per cent) (Table 48.1). Species like Favus, Chaetocerous, Fragillaria, Schizothrix and Holopedia were occasional and were found at one or two sites out of 14 sampling sites (Table 48.1–48.3). Pinnularia, Biddulphia, Asterionella, Bacillaria and Aphanocapsa were high in number. The overall density of phytoplanktqn was higher at sites 7–14 as compared to those at sites 1–6 (308 no/l and 194 no/l, respectively). The distribution pattern of phytoplankton was much irregular and the similarity indices suggested around 40–50 per cent similarity between different sampling areas (Table 48.4).

The zooplanktons were dominated by Protozoan and Arthropods. Among Protozoans, the species recorded were Lagena, Ceratium, Globigerina, Patellina, Textularia, Saccorhiza, Orbulina, Acanthometra, Actinosphaerium, Actinophrys, Acanthocystis, Clathrulina, Dinoflagellates and Mallomonas (Tables 48.5–48.7). Obelia, Muggiaea and Ephyra larva represented the Cnidarians.

Table 48.1: Phytoplankton Population Dynamics for Sites 1–7

Phytoplankton Species	*1*		*2*		*3*		*4*		*5*		*6*		*7*	
	D	*A*	*D*	*A*	*D*	*A*	*D*	*A*	*D*	*A*	*D*	*A*	*D*	*A*
Bacillariophyceae														
Pinnularia	2.6	10.3	2.5	11.3	2.4	10.7	5.4	10.8	2.0	9.4	4.9	9.4	2.6	7.0
Bidduphia	–	–	–	–	2.3	10.2	5.2	10.4	–	–	5.0	23.6	2.8	7.5
Synedra	2.5	9.9	–	–	–	–	–	–	–	–	–	–	2.4	6.4
Nitzschia	2.8	11.1	2.7	12.2	–	–	–	–	–	–	–	–	–	–
Cylindrotheca	–	–	–	–	–	–	4.6	9.2	4.2	22.2–	–	–	–	–
Asterionella	–	–	2.6	11.8	2.4	10.7	5.0	10.0	–	–	5.0	8.5	2.3	6.2
Grammatophora	–	–	–	–	3.0	13.3	5.0	10.0	2.4	11.3	–	–	–	–
Isthima	–	–	–	–	–	–	–	–	–	–	4.4	7.5	–	–
Bactillaria	3.0	11.9	–	–	–	–	–	–	2.6	4.0	5.4	9.2	3.5	9.4
Triceratium	–	–	–	–	–	–	–	–	–	–	–	–	–	–
Favus	–	–	–	–	–	–	–	–	–	–	2.2	3.7	–	–
Chaetoceros	–	–	–	–	–	–	–	–	–	–	–	–	–	–
Melosira	–	–	–	–	–	–	2.0	4.0	–	–	2.5	4.2	2.0	5.4
Rhizosolenia	–	–	–	–	1.5	6.6	–	–	–	–	–	–	–	–
Coscinodiscus	–	–	–	–	–	–	–	–	–	–	–	–	–	–
Frustulla	–	–	–	–	–	–	–	–	–	–	–	–	–	–
Cocconeis	–	–	–	–	–	–	–	–	–	–	–	–	1.7	4.5
Amphiprora	–	–	–	–	–	–	–	–	–	–	–	–	1.0	2.7
Frgilaria	–	–	–	–	–	–	–	–	–	–	–	–	1.0	2.7
Diatoma	2.5	9.9	2.4	10.9	–	–	–	–	–	–	–	–	–	–
Cyanophyceae														
Tolypothrix	–	–	–	–	–	–	–	–	–	–	2.5	4.2	–	–
Oscillatoria	–	–	1.2	5.4	–	–	–	–	–	–	–	–	1.6	4.3
Phormidium	–	–	–	–	–	–	–	–	–	–	–	–	1.4	3.7
Spirulina	–	–	–	–	–	–	–	–	1.5	10.8	–	–	1.7	4.5
Aphanocapsa	3.0	11.9	2.5	11.3	3.0	13.3	5.4	10.8	2.5	11.8	6.0	10.2	3.2	8.6
Microcystis	2.91	11.5	2.8	12.7	2.5	11.1	5.7	11.4	–	–	2.3	3.9	3.1	8.3
Stigonema	–	–	–	–	–	–	–	–	1.6	7.5	–	–	–	–
Dactylococcopsis	2.8	11.0	–	–	–	–	–	3.5	7.0	–	–	1.8	3.0	–
Marssorriella	3.1	12.3	3.01	3.6	2.6	11.6	4.8	9.6	2.1	9.9	3.4	5.8	3.0	8.1
Wollea	–	–	–	–	–	–	–	3.4	6.8	–	–	2.7	4.6	–
Anabaena	–	–	–	–	–	–	–	–	–	–	2.6	4.4	1.7	4.5
Aphanizomenon	–	–	–	–	–	–	–	–	–	–	–	–	–	–
Schizothrix	–	–	–	–	–	–	–	–	–	–	–	–	–	–
Raphidopsis	–	–	–	–	–	–	–	–	–	–	2.6	4.4	2.0	5.4
Coelosphaerium	–	–	–	–	2.7	12.0	–	–	–	–	–	–	–	–
Chroococcus	–	–	–	–	–	–	–	–	–	–	1.9	3.2	–	–
Anacystis	–	–	2.3	10.4	–	–	–	–	1.7	8.0	2.4	4.1	–	–
Holopedia	–	–	–	–	–	–	–	–	–	–	0.7	1.2	–	–
Biomass (mg l)	170		160		150		235		100		350		170	

D: Density in number × 10^3/L; A: Abundance (in percentage).

Table 48.2: Phytoplankton Population Dynamics for Sites 8–14

Phytoplankton Species	8		9		10		11		12		13		14	
	D	A	D	A	D	A	D	A	D	A	D	A	D	A
Bacillariophyceae														
Pinnularia	–	–	2.5	7.0	–	–	–	–	–	–	5.0	8.2	4.5	6.6
Bidduphia	2.9	9.7	2.8	7.9	2.0	11.9	4.5	8.5	–	–	5.3	8.7	5.4	7.9
Synedra	–	–	–	–	–	–	3.7	7.0	0.5	5.5	–	–	–	–
Nitzschia	2.3	7.7	2.5	7.0	1.7	10.1	–	–	–	–	4.5	7.4	4.5	6.6
Cylindrotheca	–	–	–	–	–	–	–	–	0.4	4.4	–	–	4.5	6.6
Asterionella	–	–	–	–	–	–	4.0	7.6	–	–	–	–	4.5	6.6
Grammatophora	3.0	10.0	2.6	7.3	2.3	13.7	4.3	8.2	–	–	5.4	8.9	5.4	7.9
Isthima	–	–	–	–	–	–	–	–	0.3	3.3	4.7	7.7	–	–
Bactillaria	3.0	10.0	2.9	8.2	–	–	5.0	9.5	0.6	8.8	–	–	5.3	7.8
Triceratium	–	–	–	–	–	–	1.5	2.8	–	–	2.0	3.3	–	–
Favus	–	–	–	–	–	–	–	–	–	–	–	–	–	–
Chaetoceros	–	–	–	–	–	–	0.5	0.9	–	–	–	–	–	–
Melosira	–	–	–	–	–	–	–	–	0.2	2.2	–	–	–	–
Rhizosolenia	–	–	1.0	2.8	–	–	1.5	2.8	0.2	2.2	–	–	1.7	2.5
Coscinodiscus	–	–	–	–	–	–	–	–	–	–	2.2	3.6	–	–
Frustulla	1.0	3.3	1.0	2.8	–	–	–	–	–	–	2.5	4.1	–	–
Cocconeis	–	–	–	–	–	–	2.2	4.1	0.7	7.7	–	–	–	–
Amphiprora	–	–	–	–	–	–	–	–	–	–	–	–	1.5	2.2
Frgilaria	–	–	–	–	–	–	–	–	–	–	–	–	–	–
Diatoma	2.0	6.7	1.5	4.2	–	–	3.0	5.7	–	–	3.5	5.7	3.1	4.5
Cyanophyceae														
Tolypothrix	–	–	22.0	6.2	–	–	–	–	–	–	–	–	2.3	3.4
Oscillatoria	1.5	5.0	–	–	–	–	–	–	–	–	2.0	3.3	–	–
Phormidium	1.6	5.3	–	–	–	–	1.8	3.4	0.7	7.7	–	–	–	–
Spirulina	–	–	2.4	6.7	0.9	5.3	–	–	–	–	2.8	4.6	2.6	3.8
Aphanocapsa	–	–	3.8	10.7	–	–	4.5	8.5	1.2	13.3	6.0	9.9	4.0	5.9
Microcystis	4.0	13.4	–	–	2.5	14.9	3.0	5.7	1.5	16.6	2.5	4.1	–	–
Stigonema	–	–	–	–	1.3	7.7	2.8	5.3	–	–	3.0	4.9	2.6	3.8
Dactylococcopsis	2.0	6.7	1.6	4.5	–	–	–	–	–	–	–	–	2.0	2.9
Marssorriella	3.7	12.4	–	–	2.4	14.3	–	–	1.6	17.7	3.5	5.7	3.0	4.4
Wollea	–	–	2.2	6.2	–	–	2.4	4.5	–	–	–	–	2.1	3.1
Anabaena	–	–	–	–	–	–	–	–	–	–	2.8	4.6	3.0	4.4
Aphanizomenon	–	–	1.9	10.1	2.1	4.0	–	–	–	–	–	–	–	–
Schizothrix	1.2	4.0	–	–	–	–	–	–	–	–	1.7	2.8	–	–
Raphidopsis	–	–	–	–	–	–	–	–	–	–	–	–	2.2	3.2
Coelosphaerium	–	–	2.2	6.2	–	–	2.8	5.3	–	–	–	–	2.4	3.5
Chroococcus	1.6	5.3	–	–	–	–	–	–	0.9	10.0	1.9	3.1	–	
Anacystis	–	–	2.2	6.2	1.9	11.3	2.8	5.3	–	–	2.6	4.3	–	–
Holopedia	–	–	–	–	–	–	–	–	–	–	–	–	1.0	1.4
Biomass (mg l)	185	160	115	290	50	365	290							

D: Density in number × 10^3/L; A: Abundance (in percentage).

Table 48.3: Phytoplankton Population Dynamics

Phytoplankton Species	*F*	*RF*	*RD*	*RD/RF*
Bacillariophyceae				
Pinnularia	71.0	5.26	6.77	1.28
Biddulphia	71.0	5.26	7.51	1.42
Synedra	29.0	2.10	1.79	0.85
Nitzschia	50.0	3.68	4.13	1.12
Cylindrotheca	29.0	2.10	2.79	1.32
Asterionella	50.0	3.68	5.27	1.435
Grammatophora	64.0	4.73	6.57	1.38
Isthima	21.0	1.57	1.85	1.17
Bactillaria	64.0	4.73	6.19	1.30
Triceratium	14.0	1.05	0.68	0.64
Favus	0.7	0.50	0.43	0.86
Chaetoceros	0.7	0.50	0.09	0.18
Melosira	29.0	2.10	1.31	0.62
Rhizosolenia	36.0	2.63	1.16	0.44
Coscinodiscus	0.7	0.50	0.43	0.86
Frustulla	21.0	1.57	0.88	0.56
Cocconeis	21.0	1.57	0.90	0.57
Amphiprora	17.0	1.05	0.49	0.46
Fragilaria	0.7	0.50	0.19	0.38
Diatoma	50.0	3.68	3.54	0.96
Cyanophyceae				
Tolypothrix	21.0	1.57	1.37	0.87
Oscillatoria	29.0	2.10	1.23	0.58
Phormidium	29.0	2.10	1.08	0.51
Spirulina	43.0	3.15	2.34	0.74
Aphanocapsa	86.0	6.30	8.87	1.40
Microcystis	79.0	5.78	6.45	1.11
Stigonema	36.0	2.63	2.22	0.84
Dactylococcopsis	43.0	3.15	2.69	0.85
Marssorriella	86.0	6.30	7.12	1.13
Wollea	36.0	2.63	2.51	0.92
Anabaena	29.0	2.10	1.98	0.94
Aphanizomenon	21.0	1.57	1.12	0.71
Schizothrix	14.0	1.05	0.57	0.54
Raphidopsis	21.0	1.57	1.33	0.84
Coelosphaerium	29.0	2.10	1.98	0.94
Chroococcus	29.0	2.10	1.23	0.58
Anacystis	50.0	3.68	3.12	0.84
Holopedia	14.0	1.05	0.33	0.31
Biomass (mg/l)				

All values are in percentages.

F: Frequency; RF: Relative frequency and RD: Relative density.

Table 48.4: Similarity Indices of Phytoplankton

(A) Between Sampling Sites **(Values are in %)**

1 and 2	*3 and 4*	*5 and 6*	*7 and 8*	*9 and 10*	*11 and 12*	*13 and 14*
66	70	37	40	48	46	50

(B) Between Sampling Stations

	B	*C*	*D*	*E*	*F*	*G*
A	31	35	45	41	29	37
B	–	46	36	40	44	40
C		–	49	53	38	41
D			–	40	36	48
E				–	47	65
F					–	48

Table 48.5: Zooplankton Population Dynamics for Sites 1–7

Zooplankton Species	*1*		*2*		*3*		*4*		*5*		*6*		*7*	
	D	*A*	*D*	*A*	*D*	*A*	*D*	*A*	*D*	*A*	*D*	*A*	*D*	*A*
Protista														
Foraminifera	200.0	20.0	250.0	20.0	200.0	16.0	150.0	14.0	200.0	18.0	200.0	13.8	250.0	15.9
Radiolaria	300.0	30.0	325.0	26.5	400.0	32.0	250.0	23.0	300.0	27.0	425.0	29.3	350.0	22.2
Others	100.0	10.0	75.0	6.1	175.0	14.0	100.0	9.3	50.0	4.5	50.0	3.4	75.0	4.7
Chidaria														
Larval form	50.0	5.0	25.0	2.0			50.0	4.6			50.0	3.4	50.0	3.2
Hydroid polyp							25.0	2.3	25.0	2.3				
Mollusca														
Larval form			25.0	2.0			100.0	9.3	75.0	6.8	100.0	6.8	100.0	6.4
Annelida														
Trochophor larva			50.0	4.0			25.0	2.3	25.0	2.3	125.0	8.6		
Polychaete larva	100.0	10.0	75.0	6.1	50.0	4.0	100.0	9.3	4.5	175.0	12.0	25.0	1.6	
Arthopoda														
Calanus			25.0	2.0			75.0	6.9			50.0	3.2		
Cyclops	25.0	2.5			25.0	2.0			25.0	2.3				
Eucalanus					25.0	2.0	25.0	2.3	50.0	4.5				
Nauplius larva	50.0	5.0	100.0	8.1	100.0	8.0	50.0	4.6	50.0	4.5	125.0	8.6	150.0	9.5
Cyprid larva	50.0	50.0	50.0	4.0			25.0	2.3	50.0	4.5	25.0	1.7	125.0	7.9
Mysis larva			25.0	2.0			25.0	2.3	25.3	2.3			150.0	9.5
Zoeae larva	100.0	10.0	150.0	12.2	200.0	16.0	50.0	4.6	11.3	11.3	125.0	8.6	250.0	15.9
Echinodermata														
Larval forms	25.0	2.5			50.0	4.0	25.0	2.3	50.0	4.5	50.0	3.4		
Chaetognatha														
Sagitta			50.0	4.0	25.0	2.0								
Total	**1000.0**		**1225.0**		**1250.0**		**1075.0**		**1100.0**		**1450.0**		**1575.0**	

D: Density in number × 10^3/l; A: Abundance (in percentage).

Table 48.6: Zooplankton Population Dynamics for Sites 8–14

Zooplankton Species	*8*		*9*		*10*		*11*		*12*		*13*		*14*	
	D	*A*	*D*	*A*	*D*	*A*	*D*	*A*	*D*	*A*	*D*	*A*	*D*	*A*
Protista														
Foraminifera	300.0	15.6	200.0	13.1	350.0	16.7	325.0	17.7	300.0	17.7	300.0	17.4	225.0	9.6
Radiolaria	325.0	17.0	325.0	21.3	325.0	15.5	300.0	17.7	350.0	17.7	350.0	20.3	400.0	17.2
Others	125.0	6.5	125.0	8.2	125.0	6.0	125.0	5.0	75.0	5.0	75.0	4.3	150.0	6.4
Chidaria														
Larval form	100.0	5.2			25.0	1.2					50.0	2.9	75.0	3.2
Hydroid polyp	50.0	2.6			50.0	2.4			50.0	2.5			25.0	1.1
Mollusca														
Larval form	100.0	5.2	75.0	4.9	150.0	7.1	75.0	2.5	100.0	5.0	125.0	7.2	175.0	7.5
Annelida														
Trochophor larva	50.0	2.6			25.0	1.2	50.0	3.2	50.0	2.5	50.0	2.9	125.0	5.3
Polychaete larva	75.0	3.9	50.0	3.3	50.0	2.4	100.0	6.4	25.0	1.2	50.0	2.9	100.0	4.3
Arthopoda														
Calanus	25.0	1.3	25.0	1.6	25.0	1.2	50.0	3.2	50.0	2.5	25.0	1.4	100.0	4.3
Cyclops	25.0	1.3			25.0	1.2			100.0	5.0	50.0	2.9	25.0	1.1
Eucalanus	125.0	6.5			50.0	2.4	50.0	3.2	100.0	5.0.	125.0	7.2	100.0	4.3
Nauplius larva	200.0	10.4	150.0	9.8	300.0	14.3	125.0	8.0	175.0	8.9	150.0	8.7	250.0	10.7
Cyprid larva	50.0	2.6	125.0	8.2	100.0	4.7	50.0	3.2	100.0	5.0	50.0	2.9	75.0	3.2
Mysis larva	100.0	5.2	175.0	11.5	125.0	6.0	175.0	11.3	100.0	5.0	250.0	14.5	125.0	5.3
Zoeae larva	300.0	15.6	250.0	16.4	300.0	14.3	175.0	11.3	250.0	12.6	150.0	8.7	300.0	12.8
Echinodermata														
Larval forms	75.0	3.9	25.0	1.6	100.0	4.7	50.0	3.2	75.0	3.8			125.0	5.3
Chaetognatha														
Sagitta					25.0	1.2								
Total	**2025.0**		**1525.0**		**2150.0**		**1650.0**		**1975.0**		**1800.0**		**2375.0**	

D: Density in number × 10^3/l; A: Abundance (in percentage).

A few Molluscan, Annelid and Echinoderm larval forms were also recorded. All the samples were dominated by Arthropods where Cyclops, Calanus and Eucalanus were found in more than 70 per cent samples. Other genera recorded where Eurytemora, Acartia, Centropagus, Paraunas and Carcinus along with several larval forms.

The zooplankton density was almost double at sites 7–14 as compared to sites 1–6 (Tables 48.5–48.7). At sites 7–14 Arthropod density extensively increased while Protozoan density was higher at sites 1-6 while 60- 70 per cent similarity was noted between sites 7–14 (Table 48.8).

Table 48.7: Zooplankton Population Dynamics

Zooplankton Species	*F*	*RF*	*RD*	*RD/RF*
Protista				
Foraminifera	100.0	7.50	16.00	2.13
Radiolaria	100.0	7.50	22.00	2.93
Others	100.0	7.50	7.10	0.94
Chidaria				
Larval form	64.3	4.80	2.20	0.46
Hydroid polyp	42.8	3.20	1.00	0.31
Mollusca				
Larval form	85.7	6.40	5.50	0.86
Annelida				
Trochophor larva	71.4	5.40	2.60	0.48
Polychaete larva	100.0	7.50	5.10	0.68
Arthopoda				
Calanus	71.4	5.40	2.00	0.37
Cyclops	57.1	4.30	1.40	0.32
Eucalanus	64.3	4.80	3.00	0.62
Nauplius larva	100.0	7.50	9.00	1.20
Cyprid larva	92.8	7.0	4.00	0.57
Mysis larva	78.6	5.90	5.80	0.98
Zoeae larva	100.0	7.50	12.00	1.60
Echinodermata				
Larval forms	78.6	5.90	3.00	0.51
Chaetognatha				
Sagitta	21.4	1.60	0.40	0.25

F: Frequency; RF: Relative frequency and RD: Relative density are all in percentage.

Discussion

The study area is at the outer most region of gulf and at the mouth of river Shetrunji which opens into gulf near Sartanpur. Enormous amount of silt deposit at this part of shore. The rocky strip and prominent curvature of land towards Nava Rajpara greatly reduce the silt deposits westward. The water current circulates in north-east direction towards Sartanpur and north-west towards Methla during high tides. The rocky barrier diverts northwardly current to west. During low tide when the rocky barrier is exposed, the southwardly current is diverted to east. The specific pattern of circulation of water may play an important role in the deposition of silt and also availability of nutrients in western and eastern parts of the study area. At Pipavav, in the west of Gopnath, the highest high tide levels are 3.19 m and lowest low tide levels are 0.50 m. Towards east, inside the gulf, at Ghogha these levels are 10.18 m and 1.43 m, respectively. During tidal fluctuations, the shallow bottom of gulf is vigorously agitated making water more turbid. The phytoplankton density was comparatively much less which greatly reduce primary productivity of the area. Several Protozoan and Arthropods feed upon these phytoplankton (Azam *et al.*, 1983; Hwang and Heath, 1997). Comparatively, the density of zooplankton was much less at sites 1–6 which may be due to environmental factors and low density of phytoplankton. At sites 7–14 the Arthropods reached their peak with marginal decrease in Protozoan and an increase in phytoplankton. The Protozoan and Arthropods exhibit distinct prey-predator relationship (Hansen *et al.*, 2000); and variation in their densities may be the outcome of such relationships. Possibly, several small interlinked food chains exists in the system which is indicated by species diversity.

Table 48.8: Similarity Indices of Zooplankton

(A) Between Sampling Sites **(Values are in %)**

1 and 2	*3 and 4*	*5 and 6*	*7 and 8*	*9 and 10*	*11 and 12*	*13 and 14*
69.59	64.00	80.00	81.48	81.48	92.80	3.33

(B) Between Sampling Stations

	B	*C*	*D*	*E*	*F*	*G*
A	37.50	46.70	51.62	46.70	46.70	51.61
B	–	43.75	36.37	41.17	50.00	42.43
C	–	–	51.61	56.25	66.67	58.06
D	–	–	–	60.60	64.51	68.75
E	–	–	–	–	68.75	60.60
F	–	–	–	–	–	77.42

A great deal of information is yet to be generated to understand the animal associations at this site and strengthen the data on biodiversity. A study is planned to comprehensively look into coastal biodiversity and ecotoxicology.

References

Azam, F., Fenchel, T., Field, J.G., Mayer-Reil, L.A. and Thingstad, F., 1983. The ecological role of water column microbes in the sea. *Mar. Ecol. Prog. Ser.*, 10: 257–263.

Berger, W.H. and Parker, F.L., 1970. Diversity of Planktonic foraminifera in deep sea sediments. *Science*, 168: 1645–1647.

Hansen, B.W., Hygum, B.H., Brozen, M., Jenson, F. and Rey, C., 2000. Food web interactions in a *Calanus finmarchicus* dominated pelagic ecosystem–mesocosm study. *J. Plankton Res.*, 22: 569–588.

Hwang, S. and Heath, R., 1997. The distribution of protozoa across trophic gradient, factors controlling their abundance and importance in the plankton food web. *J. Plankton Res.*, 19: 491–518.

Nanda, A., 2001. Studies on the impact of pollution on the invertebrate diversity of Mahi river. *Ph.D. Thesis*, The Maharaja Sayajirao University of Baroda, Vadodara, India.

Sharma, A.H., 1995. Environmental impact assessment along the effluent channel from Baroda to Jambusar and at its confluence with Mahi estuary at the Gulf of Cambay with reference to heavy metals. *Ph.D. Thesis*, The Maharaja Sayajirao University of Baroda, Vadodara, India.

Smith, R.L., 1995. *Ecology and Field Biology*. Harper Collins Pub., New York, USA.

Todd and Laverack, 1991. *Coastal Marine Zooplankton*. Cambridge University Press, Cambridge UK.

Westpal, 1974. *Protozoa*. Blackie Glasgo, London.

Chapter 49

Studies on the Status of Drinking Water Quality of Bharatpur Area in Rajasthan

***Deepshikha Garg*[1], *R.V. Singh*[1]* and *Sunita Goyal*[2]**

[1]Department of Chemistry, University of Rajasthan, Jaipur – 302 004, India

[2]Department of Chemistry, Jaipur Engineering College, RIICO Industrial Area, Kukas, Rajasthan

ABSTRACT

Deep studies have been made for testing the drinking water quality of the Bharatpur area in Rajasthan. To start these studies eight spots were selected and samples of water were collected from open wells, hand pumps and borings in the area. The various parameters such as temperature, pH, turbidity, colour, total alkalinity, carbonate and non-carbonate hardness, nitrate, fluoride, DO, BOD and COD were monitored and compared with different standard parameters. The analysis reveals that the water at home places is not suitable for drinking purpose. Water of almost all the sampling points is highly contaminated with total dissolved solids except sampling points-1 and 2. High content of total dissolved solids may cause gastrointestinal irritation. In some places nitrate level is also found in higher concentration. High nitrate level in residential water is an immediate health concern for infants and pregnant women because nitrate in drinking water has been linked to 'methamoglobinemia' or 'blue baby' syndrome, in which the oxygen-carrying capacity of an infant's blood is greatly reduced, sometimes leading to death. A link to some types of cancer is also suspected. The findings have been discussed in details.

Keywords: *Bird sanctuary, Keoladeo, Bharatpur, Water pollution physico-chemical analysis.*

* Corresponding Author: E-mail: rvsjpr@hotmail.com; Fax: 0141–2704677.

Introduction

Bharatpur, eastern gate of Rajasthan is situated between 26°22′ to 27°83′ north latitude and 76°53′ to 78°17′ east longitude. It is situated 100 meters above the sea level. It is 184 km. away from Delhi in south east. Northern border of the district touches the district Gurgaon of the state Haryana. Eastern border touches the district Mathura while, southern boarder touches the district Agra of state U.P. and district Dholpur of Rajasthan. It also touches the district Dausa in south west and district Alwar in north west.

Bharatpur is well known place because of Keoladeo Ghana National Park, a paradise of the avian world and the pilgrimage for the bird lovers. The geographical location is ideal as it is on the main north-south avian route of India. Although small in size, 29 km only (Shukla and Dubey, 1996), it boasts to house more than 375 species of beautiful birds and more than 132 of them breed inside the Keoladeo Ghana National Park and nearly every year new ones are added to the list. The sanctuary not only attracts the birds from India but also from places like Europe, Siberia, China and Tibet. About 11 sq. km area of the park is covered with water, the remaining portion is rich with Kingfisher, Red vented and white cheeked Bulbuls, Babblers, Quails, Partridges, Sunbirds, Sparrows and Parakeets which live in the bushes and burrows.

Annual rain fall in Keoladeo Ghana National Park is approximately 690 mm, the climate in summer founds with maximum temperature 42°C and minimum 29°C whereas in winter these remains as 25°C and 8°C, respectively.

Keoladeo Ghana National Park has been famous for the last visiting pair of the western race of the Siberian crane. Unfortunately, the pair did not come in winter in Bharatpur for two years in the sessions 2003 and 2004 and it is likely that this species is now extinct in India (Pain, Gargi, Cunningham, Jones and Prakash, 2004).

Keoladeo National Park is the only largest bird sanctuary in India where 113 species of migrated birds and 392 species of Indian and Monsoon breeds can be seen together. The animal populace also shown their presence although they are thoroughly dominated by feathers, wings and beaks. The animals include the black buck and sambhar.The largest Indian antelope, spotted deer and nigais and python can also be observed at some places lazing in the sun.

Ajan bandh is the main water source to fill the various lakes and ponds of the park besides a well at the "Sitaramji Bagichi" in the park which is approximately 75–80 feets deep. Many people of nearby villages and Bharatpur use this water for drinking purpose. Also there is a hand pump which is approximately 65 feet deep.

Water is the most precious material for the life on the earth without which life on earth would not exist. Because of various pollution conditions, water gets unfit for drinking. Water pollution involves the release into lakes, streams, rivers and oceans, substances that become dissolved or suspended in the water or get deposited upon the bottom and accumulate to the extent of damaging aquatic ecosystems. The chief source of water pollution is the increasing use of chemical fertilizers and pesticides letting in of untreated sewage and industrial effluents into rivers and streams running close to cities and other lowland is yet another cause (Murugesan, Dhamodhar, Rajan, Chandrika, 2004 and Shukla, 1998). Water pollution endangers aquatic birds of both fresh water and marine ecosystems.

During the last 15 years, many towns of Rajasthan have grown up as industrial cities. Various studies have shown that groundwater is contaminated with hazardous substances particularly in industrial one. The industrial and domestic wastes not only affect the water bodies of the area but also exert an impact on the physico-chemistry of the groundwater. The present study of the physico-chemical characteristics of Bharatpur area and groundwater of surrounding area has therefore been taken up.

Experimental

Area selected to find out the drinking water quality is Bharatpur district in Rajasthan. For these studies eight different sites at the distance of approximately, 3–5 km were selected for the collection of water samples. The physico-chemical quality of drinking water was assessed during the month of November 2005. Area which were selected include Ghana, Bus Stand, Railway Station, Ranjeet Nagar, Namak Katra and Jawahar Nagar.

Care has been taken during the collection of the samples so as to avoid accidental contamination. All the samples were properly labeled as 1, 2, 3, 4, 5, 6, 7 and 8 and a record was prepared indicating the sources of the samples, depth of the source and date of collection. Parameters like DO, residual chlorine, temperature and, H_2S paper strip test have been made immediately. For collection of water samples firstly bottle was rinsed thoroughly with water to wash out the local impurities. The parameters and methods employed in the chemical examination are detailed in Table 49.1.

Table 49.1: Parameters, Methods and Standard Values Selected in the Physico-chemical Examination of Samples

Sl.No.	*Parameters*	*Methods*	*Standard Values as Guided by Bureau of Indian Standards*	*Unit*
1.	Colour	By sight	–	–
2.	Odour	Smelling	–	–
3.	Temperature	Thermometric	–	°C
4.	pH	pH meter	6.5–8.5	–
5.	Nitrate	Ionmeter	100	mg/L
6.	Flouride	Ion selective electrode	1.5	mg/L
7.	Total alkalinity	Titrimetric	600	mg/L
8.	DO	Azide modification	7.0 to 9.0 mg/L at 20°C–30°C	mg/L
9.	Total hardness	Titrimetric	600	mg/L
10.	Carbonate hardness	Titrimetric	600	mg/L
11.	Non-carbonate hardness	Titrimetric	600	mg/L
12.	Calcium hardness	Titrimetric	200	mg/L
13.	Magnesium hardness	Titrimetric	100	mg/L
14.	Caicium	Titrimetric	–	mg/L
15.	Magnesium	Titrimetric	–	mg/L
16.	Total dissolved solids (TDS)	Conductivity bridge	2000	mg/L
17.	Chloride	Argentometric	1000	mg/L
18.	Sulphate	Gravimetric	400	mg/L

Table 49.2: The Physico-chemical Characteristics of the Various Sample Stations

Parameters	*Point 1*	*Point 2*	*Point 3*	*Point 4*	*Point 5*	*Point 6*	*Point 7*	*Point 8*
Colour	Colourless	–	–	–	–	–	–	–
Odour	Odourless	–	–	–	–	–	–	–
Temperature	27.1°C	27.0°C	30.0°C	29.5°C	30.0°C	30.0°C	30.1°C	30.1°C
pH	7.8	7.8	7.8	7.9	7.5	8.0	7.7	7.7
Nitrate	1.2	1.2	1.2	22	34	28	136	208
Flouride	0.22	0.17	0.84	0.75	0.15	2.53	0.69	1.50
Total alkalinity	390	410	570	390	300	650	140	660
DO	7.5	7.2	2.8	2.8	2.2	3.1	2.4	4.5
Total hardness	340	440	190	690	1410	560	1140	590
Carbonate hardness	340	410	190	390	300	560	640	590
Non-carbonate hardness	Nil	30	Nil	300	1110	Nil	500	Nil
Calcium hardness	240	270	60	230	980	180	370	150
Magnesium hardness	240	270	60	230	980	180	770	440
Calcium	40	44	48	80	408	40	182	28
Magnesium	74.4	69.6	24	117.6	129.6	120	172.8	127.2
Total dissolved solids (TDS)	672	880	1840	2880	3600	2880	4080	3440
Chloride	20	30	550	650	1050	890	940	1030
Sulphate	8	8	32	616	276	340	704	568

Values are in mg/L.

Results and Discussion

The results of the study area are given in Table 49.2.

Colour

Colour in water may result because of the presence of natural metallic ions (iron, manganese), humus and peat materials, plankton and weeds. Iron oxide causes reddish water and manganese oxide causes brown or blackish water.

Coloured water is not aesthetically acceptable to the general public. The water samples of the study area are colourless.

Odour

When water comes into the contact of many substances in nature and of human use, then it may change its taste and odour. These substances may be minerals, metals and salts from the soil. Some species of the algae produce substances which affect the taste and odour of the water. Water samples of the studied area were found odourless.

Temperature

The various chemical and biological reactions in water depend to a great extent on the temperature. The variation of water temperature depends upon the variations of the atmospheric temperature and variation of temperature' having more effect directly or indirectly on all life processes. The temperature range of the water samples is 27.1°C to 30.1°C. No major variation was noted in the water temperature.

pH

pH is the negative logarithm of the hydrogen (H^+) ion concentration, more precisely hydrogen ion activity. The pH increases during the day time due to the photosynthetic activity whereas it declines during the night due to respiratory activity. The hydrogen ion concentration affects the taste of the water. A pH range is acceptable from 6.5 to 8.5 (USEPA, 1974). The low pH of this range causes corrosion, while high pH causes taste of water soapy feel. The pH value of water in the study area is ranged from 7.7 to 8.0 and thus reveals that the pH of the water samples is absolutely in the desirable range and the samples are slightly alkaline in nature.

Nitrates

Nitrate nitrogen is the highest oxidisable form of nitrogen and occurs in trace quantities in surface waters but may attain high levels in some ground water. Concern about elevated concentrations of nitrate in drinking water is growing especially in rural areas where runoff from nitrate-rich fertilizers and animal manures often finds its way into the water supply. The maximum permissibility of NO_3^- in the drinking water is 100 mg/L (IS–1991). In the present study the NO_3^- was found in the range of 1.2–208. So in some places NO_3^- level is high than the permissible limit. High nitrate level in residential water are an immediate health concern for infants and pregnant women. High level of nitrate in drinking water have been linked to 'methamoglobinemia' or 'blue baby syndrome (Sooch, Kapoor, Singh and Grewal, 2005), in which the oxygen carrying capacity of an infant's blood is greatly reduced, sometimes leading to death. Certain bacteria commonly found in the intestinal tract of infants can convert nitrate (NO_3^-) to highly toxic nitrites (NO_2^-). Nitrites have a greater affinity for haemoglobin in the blood stream than does oxygen (Kumar, Gupta, 2002; Majumdar and Gupta, 2000) and replace that needed oxygen, a condition known as methamoglobinemia. In extreme cases, the victims may die from suffocation. Nitrate forms nitrosamines in stomach which causes gastric cancer. Contamination of drinking water with nitrate is along term problem because once nitrate reaches groundwater, national processes are very slow in removing it.

Fluorides

The guideline value of 1.5 mg/L in drinking water has been proposed by IS (1991). Fluoride is more common in groundwater than in surface water. The main sources of fluorides in groundwater are different fluoride bearing rocks. The excessive amount of fluorides causes disfigurement of teeth known as mottled enamel (dental fluorides) However, presence of less than 0.8 mg/L fluoride in water causes dental caries in children (Kulshretha, Chaturvedi, Dave, Dhindsa and Singh, 2004). The fluoride in water samples of the study area ranged from 0.15 to 2.53 mg/L. So in most of the spots of the study area the, fluoride level is less than the desired limit and it is in higher concentration at point-6 than the pennissible limit.

Total Alkalinity

The alkalinity of water is a measure of its capacity to neutralise acids. Alkalinity is a measure of the water ability to absorb H^+ without significant pH change. That is, alkalinity is measure of buffering capacity of water. It is the sum of all the titrable bases. The major portion of alkalinity in natural waters is caused by hydroxide, carbonate and bicarbonate. In natural water, most of the alkalinity is caused due to CO_2. The free CO_2 dissolves in water to form carbonic acid (H_2CO_3), which further dissociates into H^+ and HCO_3^-. The HCO_3^- thus formed further dissociates into H^+ and CO_3^{2-}.

$$CO_2 + H_2O \rightarrow H_2CO_3 \text{ (dissolved } CO_2 \text{ and Carbonic acid)}$$

$$H_2CO_3 \rightarrow H^+ + HCO_3^- \text{ (bicarbonate)}$$

$$HCO_3^- \rightarrow H^+ + CO_3^{2-} \text{ (carbonate)}$$

The desirable limit for the total alkalinity is 200–600 mg/L (IS–1991). Beyond this limit the taste of the water becomes unpleasant. The total alkalinity of water in the study area was found in the range of 390–660 mg/L. Thus the alkalinity of the studied water samples is mostly in the permissible range.

Dissolved Oxygen (DO)

DO is one of the most important water quality parameter. DO is the amount of dissolved oxygen present in the water. The DO level in the natural and waste water depends on the physical, chemical and biological activities in the water body. The solubility of the O_2 in water is related to the pressure and temperature. A good potable water should have the level of saturated DO 7.0 to 9.0 mg/L at 20–30°C. In the waters of the study area DO ranged between 2.2 to 7.5 mg/L at 27-30°C. Thus DO in most of the water samples is not in good amount and the lowest value indicates the presence of bacteria in very large amount. As DO level falls, undesirable odours, tastes and coloures reduce the acceptability of water. DO is very essential part of the water for maintenance of desire aquatic life. As dissolved oxygen (DO) drops, fish and other aquatic life are threatened which in the extreme case killed.

Total Hardness

Hardness is defined as the concentration of multivalent metallic cations in solution. The hardness of waters varies from place to place. In general, surface waters are softer than groundwaters. The hardness of water reflects the nature of geological formation with which it has been in contact. The maximum permissible value of total hardness in drinking water according to IS–10500 (1991) is 600 mg/L. The total hardness in studied samples were found from 190 to 1410 mg/L out of which three water samples cross the maximum permissible limit of the total hardness.

Carbonate and Non Carbonate Hardness

The carbonate values varied from 190–640 mg/L and non carbonate values varied from nil to 1110 mg/L. The desirable limit is 300 mg/L and permissible limit in the absence of alternate source is 600 mg/L. Thus the non-carbonate hardness exceeds very much than the permissible limit. Carbonate hardness was formerly called temporary hardness, because it can be removed by boiling and it caused by dissolved Ca and Mg bicarbonates. Removal process of Ca and Mg bicarbonates is as follows:

$$Ca(HCO_3)_2 + \text{Heat} \rightarrow CaCO_3 \text{ (precipitate)} + CO_2\uparrow + H_2O$$

$$Mg(HCO_3)_2 + \text{Heat} \rightarrow MgCO_3 \text{ (precipitate)} + CO2\uparrow + H_2O$$

Carbonate hardness is especially important since it leads to scaling. Non-carbonate hardness was formerly called permanent hardness, because it cannot be removed by boiling. Cations, which cause non-carbonate hardness, are associated with the sulphates, chlorides and nitrates of Ca and Mg.

Calcium Hardness

Calcium is common constituents of natural water and has important contribution to the hardness of water. In water Ca reaches from the leaching of the rocks. Because it is an important contributor of hardness, it reduces the utility of water for domestic use. Some $CaCO_3$ is desirable for domestic use of water because it provides a coating in the pipes, which protects them against corrosion. The maximum permissible limit of calcium hardness according to IS (1991) is 200 mg/L in drinking water and experimental values ranged from 60 to 980 mg/L. The highest value of calcium hardness in the study area is very much out of range of the permissible limit.

Magnesium Hardness

Magnesium is also common part of the water and the main sources of the magnesium are the rocks. Magnesium is considered as non-toxic to human being at the concentration expected in water. Magnesium salts have a laxative and diuretic effect particularly for individuals not accustoms to high dosage. The maximum allowable level of Mg according to IS is 100 mg/L. In the present study the Mg level ranged from 60 to 980 mg/L. Except point-3, it is found in higher concentration in all the selected points of the study area.

Chloride

Chlorine is added to the potable water to eliminate or reduce the growth of microorganisms in water and to destroy or modify decomposable organic substances so as to reduce the biochemical oxygen demand of water. Chloride concentration above 100 mg/L gives salty taste of water.

Conclusion and Recommendations

The present studies and data were compared with the standard data and the conclusion made is that the concentration of nitrate is more in some areas of Bharatpur than the permissible limit. Total dissolved solids have been found more than that of permissible limit. In particular areas (point-6) fluoride concentration is high. It was also found that water of Bharatpur area is hard and it is contaminated with calcium and magnesium hardness. Therefore; there is need to improve the water quality, specially with respect to the total dissolved solids due to which many people of Bharatpur area suffering from gastro-intestinal troubles.

Acknowledgement

The authors are thankful to Dr. S.S. Dhindsa and Shri H.S. Devenda P.H.E.D., Jaipur, for helpful discussions. One of the authors Sunita Goyal is grateful to Shri Lalit Kumar Sarogi, Jaipur Engineering College, Kukas, for encouraging to do the applied work.

References

Kulshrestha, S., Chaturvedi, S., Dave, S., Dhindsa, S.S., and Singh, R.V., 2004. Important studies on the Assessment and impact of industrial effluents of Sanganer town of Jaipur city on the quality of soil and water. *Indian J. Environ. Ecoplan.*, 8(2): 485.

Kumar, S., Gupta, A.B. and Gupta, S., 2002. Need for revision of nitrate standards for drinking water: A case study of Rajasthan. *Indian J. Environ. Health*, 44(2): 168.

Majumdar, D. and Gupta, N., 2000. Nitrate pollution of groundwater and associated human health disorders. *Indian J. Environ. Health*, 42(2): 168.

Murugesan, S., Kumar, S. Dhamodhar, Rajan, S. and Chandrika, D., 2004. Comparative study of groundwater resources of east to west region of Chennai, Tamil Nadu. Nat. *Environ. Poll. Techno.*, 3(4): 495.

Pain, D.J., Gargi, R., Cunningham, A.A., Jones, A. and Prakash V., 2004. Mortality of globally threatened Sarus Cranes Grus Antigon from monocrotophos poisoning in India. *Science of the Total Environment*, 326: 55.

Shukla, J.B. and Dubey, B., 1996. Effect of changing habitat on species: Application, to Keoladeo National Park, India. *Ecological Modelling*, 86: 91.

Shukla, V.P., 1998. Modelling the dynamics of wetland macrophytes: Keoladeo National Park Wetland, India. *Ecological Modelling*, 109: 99.

Sooch, S.S., Kapoor, B.S., Singh, B. and Grewal, N.S., 2005. Prediction of nitrate pollution of groundwater: A case study. *Indian J. Environ. Ecopaln.*, 10(2): 357.

Chapter 50

Alterations in Kidney Transaminases After Combined Exposure to Sulphur Dioxide and Nitrogen Dioxide in Albino Rat

Asha Agarwal and Shaista Parveen

Department of Zoology, School of Life Sciences, Dr. B.R. Ambedkar University, Khandari Campus, Agra - 282 002, U.P., India

ABSTRACT

The present study was undertaken in order to assess the impact of (20 + 20) ppm and (40 + 40) ppm combined exposure to sulphur dioxide and nitrogen dioxide gas on kidney transaminases in albino rat for 15 and 30 days for one hour per day. The results show that a highly significant increase in kidney glutamic oxaloacetic transaminase and glutamic pyruvic transaminase activities after (20 + 20) ppm and (40 + 40) ppm combined exposure to sulphur dioxide and nitrogen dioxide gas.

Keywords: *SO_2, NO_2, GOT, GPT, Albino rat, Kidney.*

Introduction

Air pollution evolved as a problem of regional or global dimension. The oxides of sulphur and nitrogen are major threat to social, economic development and even to man's survival. Sulphur dioxide and nitrogen dioxide are the highly toxic pollutants and their chief sources are automobile emission, power plants, combustion of fuel or coal etc. These toxic gases when absorbed leading various disorders in respiratory system and most noticeable biochemical changes observed in tissue. Health effects of air pollution has been suggested by Bernstein *et al.* (2004). Kidney is one of the complex organ of the five major organs of the body and it is finally regarded as a common target of toxic chemicals. Transaminases are important for diagnostic and prognostic purpose. The work of Glutamic Oxaloacetic Transaminase (GOT) and Glutamic Pyruvic Transaminase (GPT) in different tissues of rats and guinea pigs exposed to varying levels of altitude stress for different periods of time observed by Mukherjee and Ghosh (1987). There is no much data concerning the effect of air pollution on the activities of kidney enzymes.

Therefore, the object of present investigation is to observe the adverse consequences of combined sulphur dioxide and nitrogen dioxide on kidney enzymes of albino rat, *Rattus norvegicus* (Berkenhout).

Materials and Methods

Thirty adult and healthy albino rats of almost equal size and weight ranges from 90–120 gms were selected for the present study. Rats were bred at the animal house of Zoology Department. They were kept in polypropylene cages, provided with Gold Mohar Brand rat and mice feed, Hindustan Lever Ltd. India and, water *ad libitum*. Rats were acclimated for one month prior to experiment.

Nitrogen dioxide gas was generated in generator according to the method described by Saltzman (1954) and modified by Levaggi *et al.* (1972). The sulphur dioxide gas was generated in the generator according to the method described by Singh and Rao (1979).

Three sets one control (A) and two experimental sets (B and C) were taken of ten rats each. Experimental rats were exposed to (20 + 20) ppm and (40 + 40) ppm combined sulphur dioxide and nitrogen dioxide gas exposure for one hour per day, while control rats to ambient air in fumigation chamber for 15 and 30 days. Five rats from each set 'A', 'B' and 'C' were sacrificed after 15 days exposure and remaining five rats of each set after 30 days exposure to combined gas for kidney tissue collection.

Kidney glutamic oxaloacetic transaminase and glutamic pyruvic transaminase were determined by the method described by Reitman and Frankel (1957). The readings so obtained were subjected to the formulae for different statistical calculations (Fisher and Yates, 1950).

Results and Discussion

The results obtained for kidney glutamic oxaloacetic transaminase (GOT) and Glutamic Pyruvic Transaminase (GPT) after combined exposure to sulphur dioxide and nitrogen dioxide are shown in Table 50.1.

An elevation in the activities of kidney transaminases is the indication of impaired kidney function due to inflammatory action of the combined gas. An inflammatory process characterized by increased membrane permeability at the loss of soluble enzyme through the membrane might act as a stimulus to increase enzyme synthesis (Chatterjee and Shinde, 1994). In accordance to present findings, Rahman *et al.* (2001) have reported an elevation in kidney transaminases activity due to leakage of enzymes into blood following reservoir tissue damage or dysfunction. Mukherjee and Ghosh (1987) have also observed that both glutamic oxaloacctic transaminase and glutamic pyruvic transaminase activities were significantly increased in different tissues including kidney of both rats and guinea pigs during short period of exposure. A rise in the level of tissue glutamic pyruvic transaminase and glutamic oxaloacetic transaminase activities have also been observed by Whitehead *et at.* (1996) in men with increasing consumption of cigarette smoking.

Table 50.1: Values of Kidney GOT (Units/ml) and GPT (Units/ml) After Combined Exposure to Sulphur Dioxide and Nitrogen Dioxide Gas in Albino Rat

Parameters	*Exposure Days*	*Control Set (5)*	*Experimental Set (5)*	
			Concentrations of Combined Gas (Sulphur Dioxide + Nitrogen Dioxide	
			20 ppm + 20 ppm	*40 ppm + 40 ppm*
		Range Mean±S.Em	*Range Mean±S.Em*	*Range Mean±S.Em*
Kidney GOT (units/ml)	15	50.00–54.50	53.80–56.10	57.70–60.20
		53.00±0.79	55.24±0.42*†	60.062±0.87**†
	30	52.10–55.10	56.80–60.00	60.10–63.00
		53.94±0.57	58.24±0.57***†	61.722±0.47***†
Kidney GPT (units/ml)	15	64.30–68.50	68.20–78.10	70.00–89.40
		66.66±0.74	73.98±2.21*†	78.80±3.13**†
	30	66.50–69.00	69.00–72.00	79.00–83.40
		67.80±0.46	70.16±0.54**†	81.02±0.80***†

PPM: Parts per million; S.Em: Standard error of mean; 5: No. of rats; †: Increase; *: Significant; **: Highly significant; ***: Very highly significant.

Present findings are also supported by Gupta (1998) who reported an increase in the level of SGOT and SGPT activities in albino rats after combined exposure to sulphur dioxide and nitric oxide. Further, Mederios *et al.* (1983) in humans, Shimizu *et al.* (1986) in rats and Bree *et al.* (1992) in rats and guinea pigs have also reported an increase in the level of SGOT and SGPT activities after exposure to air pollutants.

In the present study, a very highly significant elevation in the level of kidney transaminases with increase in concentration and exposure time indicates that the tissue injury became more pronounced due to inflammatory response of toxic gases.

Present study reveals that combined action of sulphur dioxide and nitrogen dioxide gas could affect the renal tissues and impaired kidney functions.

References

Bernstein, J.A., Alexis, N., Barnes, C., Bernstein, I.L., Bernstein, J.A., Nel, A., Peden, D., Diaz-Sancher, D., Tarlo, S.M., Williams, P.B., 2004. Health effects of air pollution. *J. Allergy Clin. Immunol.*, 114: 1116–1123.

Bree, L.V., Marra, M. and Peter, J.A., 1992. Differences in pulmonary biochemical and inflammatory responses of rats and guinea pigs resulting from day time and night time, single and repeated exposure to ozone. *Toxicol. Appl. Pharmacol.*, 116: 209–216.

Chatterjee, C. and Shinde, R, 1994. *Textbook of Medical Biochemistry*. Arun Publishers, Medical Allied Agency, Kolkata.

Fisher, R.A. and Yates, F., 1950. *Statistical Methods for Research Workers*, 12th edition. Oliver and Boyd, Edinburgh, pp. 365.

Gupta, D., 1998. Combined effect of sulphur dioxide and nitric oxide on the serum enzymes in albino rat. *M.Phil. Dissertation*, Dr. B.R. Ambedkar University, Agra.

Levaggi, D.A., Wayman, S. and Feldstein, M., 1972. Method for the production of nitric oxide. *Environ. Sci. Technol.*, 6: 250.

Mederios, M., Bechana, H.G., Naoum, E.J.H. and Mourao, C.A., 1983. Oxygen toxicity and haemoglobinemia in subjects from highly polluted town. *Arch. Environ. Hlth.*, 38: 11–16.

Mukherjee, K. and Ghosh, N.C., 1987. GOT and GPT activities in different tissues of rats and guinea pigs exposed to varying levels of altitude stress for different periods of time. *Aviat. Space Environ. Med.*, 58(1): 18–23.

Rahman, M.F., Siddiqui, M.K.J. and Jamil, K., 2001. Effects of Vepacide (*Azadiracta indica*) on aspartate and alanine aminotransferase profiles in a sub-chronic study with rats. *Human Exp. Toxicol.*, 20: 243–249.

Reitman, S. and Frankel, F., 1957. A colorimetric method for the determination of glutamic oxaloacetic and glutamic pyruvic transaminases. *Am. J. Clin. Path.*, 28: 56–63.

Saltzman, B.E., 1954. Colorimetric microdetermination of nitrogen dioxide in the atmosphere. *Anal. Chem.*, 26: 1949–1955.

Shimizu, T., Sotokawa, H., Hatano, M., Izumiyama, M., Otomo, H. and Kogure, K., 1986. Effects of 50 ppm nitrogen dioxide gas exposure on physiological functions of rats. *Toxicol. Hlth. Camst.*, 32(1–2): 29–36.

Singh, N. and Rao, D.N., 1979. Studies on the effects of sulphur dioxide on Alfa red plants especially under condition of natural precipitation. *Ind. Air Poll. Contr.*, 2(2): 55–59.

Whitehead, T.P., Robinson, D. and Allaway, S.L., 1996. The effects of cigarette smoking and alcohol consumption on serum liver enzyme activities: A dose related study in men. *Ann. Clin. Biochem.*, 33: 530–535.

Chapter 51

Plant Diversity Status of Constructed and Sewage Polluted Pond, Dharwad, Karnataka

R.H. Ratageri and T.C. Taranath

Environmental Biology Laboratory, Department of Botany, Karnatak University, Dharwad – 580 003, Karnataka, India

ABSTRACT

Phytoplankton and macrophytes are the main primary producers of the aquatic ecosystem. Phytoplankton plays a key role in the freshwater ecosystem, because they function as a primary producer in the food chain of the water body and maintaining proper equilibrium between biotic and abiotic components in the aquatic ecosystem. The source of water pollution mainly consists of sewage, industrial waste, detergents, automobiles wastes. These pollutants adversely affects the structure and functions of biotic components, environmental quality and aesthetic value of the freshwater ecosystem. Field investigations were undertaken to study the plant diversity status of constructed and sewage polluted pond. Phytoplankton enumeration revealed a total of twenty-one species of which six species belonging to Cyanophyceae, seven species to Bacillariophyceae, five species to Chlorophyceae and three species to Euglenophyceac. Cyanophyceae and Bacillariophyceae were dominant when compared to other families and a total of thirteen species of aquatic macrophytes were recorded from the constructed pond which includes two fern sps. Six monocots belonging to five families and five dicots belonging to five families. While, sewage polluted pond reveals that there are nineteen species of phytoplankton were enumerated which includes five species of Cyanophyceae, four species of Bacillariophyce and six species of Euglenophyceae and twelve species of aquatic macrophytes of which one fern species and six monocots representing six families and two dicots representing two different families. *Microcystis* and *Euglenoids* are found to be dominant which indicate organic pollution of sewage pond. Results shows plant diversity is low in Sewage Polluted pond.

Keywords: *Phytoplankton, Macrophytes, Constructed, Sewage, Microcystis, Euglenoids.*

Introduction

Phytoplankton and macrophytes are the main primary producers of the aquatic ecosystems. Phytoplankton plays a key role in the freshwater ecosystems because they function as a primary producer in the food chain of the water body and maintaining proper equilibrium between biotic and abiotic ecosystem.

Aquatic macrophytes occur in almost all freshwater bodies which are enriched by natural process or as a result of nutrient loading from urban, agricultural or industrial activities. Most of them are considered as weeds since, they deprive the humans of all facets of efficient use of water and cause harmful effects. It is reported that aquatic weeds alter the quality of water by accumulating various minerals and nutrients from the medium in which they thrive. Most of the studies, on aquatic plants were found to be accumulated by these weeds. In natural ecosystem, macrophytes witnessed to remove both toxic and non toxic elements in the sediment and water (Narayana and Somashekar, 1997). Trophic status is mainly influenced by the variety of communities and indicator species. Moreover, metabolic activities of macrophytic communities accelerate the physico-chemical condition of the system. Aquatic macrophytes play a key role in biogeochemical cycles and food webs of living things in the lentic water bodies.

The study on the pollution status of any water body is important because it ultimately affect the water quality and biodiversity status. Biological production may be used as an indice of trophic status and aquatic resource potential (Jhingran, 1991). The present field investigation aims to know the pollution and plant diversity status of constructed and sewage polluted pond.

Materials and Methods

Study Area

Dharwad (Karnataka State, India) is an inland city, located at about 650 to 700 m above sea level on the Deccan Plateau of India at latitude between 140 78′ and 150 5′ North latitude and 740 48′ and 760 00 East longitude. It receives an average rainfall of 380 mm. Constructed freshwater pond is located within Karnataka University Campus, Dharwad and sewage polluted pond is situated in Sringar of Dharwad city. The pond is bordered by roads on all the sides. The pond is shallow with maximum depth of two meters. It has a thick growth of macrophytic vegetation. It receives out flowing water from Jayanager pond. Near the inlet there is confluence of a sewage line carrying from Saptapur area.

Physico-chemical Parameters

Water samples were collected from different sites of the pond during morning hours. (6 AM to 7 AM) and analysis for physico-chemical parameters as per the standard procedures (APHA, 1998) were made and expressed in mg/L. An EC–TDS analyzer (Elico–India) was used to measure conductivity and total dissolved solids. Phytoplankton enumeration was made as per the procedure given by Adoni, 1985; APHA, 1998. Ten liters of pond water was sampled in poly propylene can and sedimentation was carried out overnight after the addition of 30 ml Lugol's solution (3 per cent) Standard manuals were used for the identification and enumeration of phytoplankton by using Carl Zeiss research microscope with 40x, 100x magnification. (Desikachary, 1959; Philipose, 1967; Fritsch, 1975; APHA, 1998). The simple quadrate method was followed for vegetation analysis of macrophytes. The material was collected and brought to laboratory in poly bags and carefully identified by using standard books and manuals (Subramaniam, K., 1962; Cook, 1974; Fasset, 1975).

Results and Discussion

Results are presented in Tables (51.1-51.3). Data on the physico-chemical parameters of the constructed and sewage polluted pond water are presented in Table 51.1. Quality of an aquatic ecosystem is dependent on the physico-chemical characteristics of waters and also on the biological diversity of the system. Cairns and Dickson (1971) stated that analysis of biological materials along with chemical factors of water forms a valid method of water quality assessment, pH, total solids, calcium, nitrate, phosphate and organic matter are important factors influencing the growth of algae. In constructed pond, phytoplankton enumeration revealed a total of twenty one species of which six species of belonging to Cyanophyceae, seven species to Bacillariophyceae, five species to Chlorophyceae and three to Euglenophyceae, Cyanophyceae and Bacillariophyceae were dominant when compared to other families. While sewage polluted pond reveals nineteen species of phytoplankton which include five species of Cyanophyceae, four species of Bacillariophyceae and six species of Euglenophyceae (Table 51.2). Euglenophyceae and Cyanophyceae were dominant. Our investigation indicate that Euglenoids are dominant which indicate high degree of organic pollution.

Table 51.1: Physieo-chemical Parameters of Constructed Pond and Sewage Polluted Pond

Sl.No.	*Parameters*	*Constructed Pond*	*Sewage Pond*
1.	Temperature	19°–28° C	23°–29° C
2.	pH	7.66	7.73
3.	EC	618 µs	7140 µs
4.	Total dissolved solid (TDS)	311	586
5.	Dissolved oxygen (DO)	5.0	4.0
6.	Salinity	0.3	0.6
7.	Free CO_2	33	68
8.	Chloride	72.42	206
9.	Calcium	41.6	71.0
10.	Magnesium	0.486	18.33
11.	Carbonates	0	2.70
12.	Bicarbonates	260	315
13.	Sodium	71.00	127.33
14.	Potassium	16.20	29.67
15.	Sulphate	2.15	8.33
16.	Phosphate	2.35	5.23

All values are expressed in mg/L except pH and Temperature.

Wetlands have been called the biological supermarkets for their excessive food chains and rich biodiversity they support. Macrophytes particularly emergents acts as nutrient pumps. The discharge of domestic and industrial effluents to fresh water bodies have enriched them with nutrients thereby deteriorating water quality. Macrophytes, because of their potential ability to reduce the nutrient level of waste (Reddy *et al.*, 1982; Tripathi *et al.*, 1999; Trivedy and Nakate, 1999) have become the subject of great interest since last two decades. The biomass can be used as non conventional energy resource for the production of gaseous fuel (Shiralipur and Smith, 1984) and water treatment. Pollution of water by organic wastes results in decline of Dissolved Oxygen (Butcher, 1947). The factors dissolved oxygen

Table 51.2: Phytoplankton of Constructed Pond and Sewage Pond

Sl.No.	Class	Constructed Pond	Sewage Pond
(A)	**Cyanophyceae**		
1.	*Microcyslis* sp.	+	+
2.	*Oscillatoria princeps*	+	+
3.	*Anabaena planclonica*	+	+
4.	*Anacystis cyanea*	+	–
5.	*Agmenellu quadriduplicatum*	+	–
6.	*Chlorococcum humicola*	+	–
7.	*Phormidium*	–	+
8.	*Lyngbya*	–	+
9.	*Rivularia*	–	+
(B)	**Bacillariophyceae**		
1.	*Navicula graciloides*	+	+
2.	*Gomphonema parvulum*	+	–
3.	*Fragillaria crolonensis*	+	+
4.	*Nitzschia palea*	+	+
5.	*Pinnularia nobilis*	+	+
6.	*Stauroneis phoenicenteron*	+	–
7.	*Meridion Criculare*	+	–
(C)	**Chlorophyceae**		
1.	*Scytonema* sp.	+	–
2.	*Oedogonium* sp.	+	–
3.	*Spirogyra* sp.	+	+
4.	*Cosmarium* sp.	+	–
5.	*Desmidium* sp.	+	–
6.	*Pediastrum*	+	+
7.	*Sceneclesmus*	–	+
8.	*Chlorella*	–	+
9.	*Ankistrodesmus*	–	+
(D)	**Euglenophyceae**		
1.	*Euglena acus*	+	+
2.	*Phacus* sp.	+	+
3.	*Rhodomonas*	+	–
4.	*Paramecium*	–	+
5.	*Trachelomonas*	–	+
6.	*Astasia*	–	+
7.	*Lepeocinelis*	–	+

+: Recorded; –: Not recorded.

and biological oxygen demand are seen to be inversely proportionate to each other. The fresh water ponds which receive nutrient rich sewage turns into eutrophic ponds. If this algal water is not exploited properly for fishery then due to the ageing, the algae die and under go decomposition which exert biological oxygen demand on the aquatic systems. This leads to an unhygienic condition, bad odour and growth of undesirable larvae of flies and midges. Such a condition make the water body unfit for recreation and represents an aquatic desert. Hosmani (1975) and Rajendra Nair (1999) reported that nitrates and phosphates are important for the growth of diatoms. Naganandini and Hosmani (1990) and Goel *et al.* (1992) have stated that Bacillariophyceae occurs commonly in all types of waters. In the present investigation, the diatoms were almost equal in both the water bodies Cyanophyceace were the most abundant algae. Mannawar (1970), Hosamani (1975), Hegde and Sujatha (1997) were reported that there is a direct relation between nitrates, phosphates, biological oxygen demand and chemical oxygen demand to the abundance of blue-green algae.

Table 51.3: Aquatic Macrophytes of Constructed Pond and Sewage Pond

Sl.No.	*Name of Plant*	*Class*	*Family*	*Type*	*Constructed Pond*	*Sewage Pond*
1.	*Marsilea quadrifolia*	Fern	Marasileaceae	Marginal, Submerged	+	–
2.	*Salvinia molesta Mitchell*	Fern	Salviniaceae	Floating	–	+
3.	*Eichhornia crassipes* (Mart) Solms	Monocot	Pontederiaceae	Floating	+	+
4.	*Hydrilla verticellata* (L F Royal)	Monocot	Hydrocharitaceae	Submerged	+	–
5.	*Vallisnaria spiralis* L.	Monocot	Hydrocharitaceae	Submerged	+	–
6.	*Lemna gibba* L.	Monocot	Lemnaceae	Floating	+	+
7.	*Potamegeton crispus* L.	Monocot	Potamogetonaceae	Floating	+	–
8.	*Cyperus alopecuroides*	Monocot	Cyperaceae	Marginal, Submerged	+	–
9.	*Nymphaea stellata* Willd	Dicot	Nymphaceaceae	Emerged	+	–
10.	*Ipomoea cornea*	Dicot	Convoluvlaceae	Floating, Marginal	+	–
11.	*Ceratophyllum demersum* L	Dicot	Caratophyllaceae	Submerged	+	–
12.	*Trapa bispinosa* (L) Roxb	Dicot	Hydrocharitaceae	Emerged	+	–
13.	*Utricularia exoleta*	Dicot	Lentibulariaceae	Submerged	+	–
14.	*Alternanthera sessilis* DC.	Dicot	Amaranthaceae	Rooted, Emergent	–	+
15.	*Typha angustata* Bory	Monocot	Typhaceae	Rooted	–	+
16.	*Spirodela polyrhiza* L. Schleid	Monocot	Lemnaceae	Free floating	–	+
17.	*Jussiaea suffruticosa*	Dicot	Onagraceae	Rooted	–	+
18.	*Bacopa monnieri* L Pennell	Dicot	Scrophulariaceae	Rooted	–	+
19.	*Polygonum glabrum* Willd	Monocot	Polygonaceae	Rooted	–	+
20.	*Colocassia antiquorum*	Monocot	Araceae	Rooted	–	+
21.	*Phragmites maximus* (Forsk) Chiov	Monocot	Poaceae	Rooted	–	+

+: Recorded; –: Not recorded.

The occurrence of euglenoids indicates that they respond to changes in the physical and chemical conditions of the ecosystem. Organic pollution often regulate the production of blooms that may cause drastic effects on the life in water. Phosphates, iron and lower concentrations of oxygen favour the growth of Euglenoid blooms. Euglenoid species were observed in both the water bodies under investigation. Paravateesam and Mishra (1993), Tripathy and Pandy (1990) and Hegde and Sujatha (1997) reported that high water temperature, phosphate, nitrate and low dissolved oxygen and carbon dioxide supports the growth of Euglenoids. Cyanophyceae are ubiquitous in waters and occur as permanent blooms in some of the water bodies. Munnawar (1970) considered that calcium is more important and observes that higher calcium supports more Cyanophyceae. Ganapati (1940) points out that low pH and low concentrations of dissolved oxygen favors an abundance of certain species of Cyanophyceae. The ammonia content released by the enormous growth of *Microcystis aeruginosa* and the activity of phosphatase enzyme in producing certain unknown auto toxins. The build up of ammonia in the water creates difficulties in maintaining in acceptable environment for production and maintenance of aquatic life.

Phytoplankton reported from sewage-polluted pond found to be tolerant to organic pollution. The genera includes *Oscillatoria, Spirogyra, Nitzschia, Euglena,* etc. Diversity of phytoplankton is low in sewage-polluted pond and contain some bloom forming algae which includes *Microcystis, Phormidium. Anabaena* etc. Aquatic macrophytes reported from the constructed pond includes, 4 species of submerged, 3 species of emergent and 4 species of free floating macrophytes while sewage polluted pond contain 4 species of free floating and 6 species of rooted aquatic plants (Table 51.3). Thus plant diversity status is low in sewage-polluted pond in comparison to constructed pond.

Acknowledgement

The authors are thankful to the Chairman P.G. Department of Botany, Karnataka University, Dharwad for providing necessary facilities to carryout the work and University Grants Commission, New Delhi for financial assistance under UGC-SAP-DRS-II and COSIST programme. One of the authors (R. H. Ratageri) is thankful to the UGC for Teacher Fellowship under X plan FIP programme.

References

APHA, 1998. *Standard Methods for Examination of Water and Wastewaters*, 20th edn. American Public Health Association, Washington, USA.

Butcher, R.W., 1947. Studies on ecology of rivers. VII the algae of enriched water. *J. Ecology*, 35: 186–191.

Cairns, J. (Jr) and Diskson, K.L., 1971. A Simple method for the biological of waste discharge on aquatic bottom, Dwelling organism. *J. Water Poll. Control Fed.*, 43: 122–275.

Cook, C.D.K., 1924. *Water Plants of the World: A Manual for the Identification of the Genera of Freshwater Macrophytes.* W. Junk. B.V. Publishers, The Hauge.

Desikacharya, T.V., 1959. *Cyanophyta*. Indian Council of Agricultural Research, New Delhi.

Fasset, 1975. *A Manual of Aquatic Vascular Plants*. The University of Wisconsin press, Madison.

Fritsch, F.E., 1975. *The Structure and Reproduction of the Algae*. The Syndics of Cambridge University Press, Euston Road, London.

Goel, P.K., Kulkarni, A.Y., Khatavakar, S.D. and Trivedy, R.K., 1992. Studies on diurnal variation is some physico-chemical characteristics and phytoplankton of fresh water polluted pond. *Indian Jr. Environ. Prot.*, 12(97): 503–508.

Hegde, G.R. and Sujatha, T., 1997. Distribution of planktonic algae is three freshwater lentic habitats of Dharwad. *Phykos*, 361(1 and 2): 49–53.

Hosmani, S.P., 1975. Limnological studies in pond and lakes of Dharwad. *Ph.D. Thesis*, Karnataka University.

Munawar, M., 1970. Limnological studies on fresh water ponds of Hyderabad, India. I. The Biotope. *Hydrobiologia*, 35: 127–162.

Naganandini, M.M. and Hosmani, S.P., 1990, Ecology of certain inland waters of Mysore district: Occurrence of Cynophyceae bloom at Hosakere lake. *Poll. Res.*, 17(2): 123–125.

Narayana, J. and Somashekar, R.K., 1997. Heavy metal composition in the sediment and plants of the river Cauvery. *Journal of Environment and Pollution*, 4: 325–328.

Parvateesam, M. and Mishra, Maneesha, 1993. Algae of Pushker lake including pollution indicating forms. *Phykos*, 32(1 and 2): 27–39.

Philipose, M.T., 1967. *Chlorococcales*. Indian Council of Agricultural Research, New Delhi.

Rajendra Nair, M.S., 1999. Seasonal variation and physico-chemical factors and their impact on the ecology of a village pond at Imalia (Vidisha). *Jr. Ecobiol.*, 12(1): 21–27.

Reddy, K.R., Sacco, P.D., Graetz, D.A., Campbell, K.L. and Sinclair, L.R., 1982. Water treatment by an aquatic system nutrient removed by reservoirs and flooded field. *Environ. Mangmt.*, pp. 261–270.

Shralipour, A. and Smith P.H., 1984. Conversion of biomats in methane gas. *Biomass*, 6: 85–94.

Subramaniam, K., 1962. *Aquatic organisms*, pp. 190, Botanical monograph No. 34. Coun-Sci. Indst. Res., New Delhi.

Tripathy, A.K. and Pandey, S.N., 1990. *Water Pollution*. Ashish Publishing House, pp. 1–326.

Trivedy, R.K. and Nakate, S.S., 1999. Aquatic heleds based wastewater treatment plants in India. *Journal of Ind. Pollut. and Control*, 15(2): 275–279.

Chapter 52

Alterations in the Carbohydrate Metabolism of *Vigna mungo* (L.) Hepper as Affected by Cobalt Stress

K. Jayakumar and P. Vijayarengan

Division of Environmental Biology, Department of Botany, Annamalai University, Annamalainagar – 608 002, Tamil Nadu, India

ABSTRACT

A study was carried out to understand the alterations in the biochemical constituents of *Vigna mungo* (L.) Hepper by cobalt treatment. Blackgram were raised in soils amended with different concentrations of (0, 50, 100, 150, 200 and 250 mg/kg) cobalt. Biochemical constituents such as reducing sugar, non-reducing sugar, total sugar, starch and protein contents were analysed on 30th day. All the biochemical constituents were increased at 50 mg/kg cobalt level in the soil to considerable extent, when compared with control. Further increase in the cobalt level (100–250 mg/kg) in the soil decreased all the biochemical constituents of blackgram plants.

Keywords: *Cobalt, Blackgram, Sugar, Starch, Protein.*

Introduction

Heavy metal contamination affects the biosphere in many places worldwide (Raskin and Ensley, 2000). Metal concentrations in soil ranges from less than 1 mg/kg (ppm) to high as 10,000 mg/kg, whether due to the geological origin of the soil or as a result of human activity (Blaylock and Haung, 2000). Excess concentrations of some heavy metals in soils such as Cd, Cr, Cu, Ni and Zn have caused the disruption of natural aquatic and terrestrial ecosystems (Meagher, 2000).

Heavy metal stress causes multiple direct and indirect effects on all physiological process (Woolhouse, 1983). The cobalt as a heavy metal pollutant in plants has been studied by Terry (1981). The present investigation has been carried out to evaluate the hazardous effects at heavy metal cobalt on the carbohydrate metabolism of *Vigna mungo* (L.) Hepper.

Materials and Methods

The seeds of blackgram [*Vigna mungo* (L.) Hepper var. ADT-3] were obtained from Pulses Research Division, Tamil Nadu Rice Research Institute, Tamil Nadu Agricultural University, Aduthurai. The seeds with uniform size, colour and weight were chosen for experimental purpose and sown in pots containing 3 kg air dried soil each. The inner surface of pots were lined with a polythene sheet. The experiment was conducted in Completely Randomized Block Design (CRBD) method with 5 replicates in pots. Plants were grown in untreated soil (control) and in soil to which cobalt had been applied (50, 100, 150, 200 and 250 mg/kg soil). The cobalt as finely powdered cobalt chloride ($CoCl_2$) was applied to the surface soil and thoroughly mixed with soil. Ten seeds were sown in each pot. All the pots were watered to field capacity daily. Plants were thinned to a maximum of six per pot, after a week of germination.

The biochemical constituents such as reducing sugar, non-reducing sugar, total sugar, starch and protein content of leaves were analysed on 30th day. The reducing, non-reducing and total sugar contents were analysed by the standard method of Nelson (1944), Starch (Summner and Somers, 1949) and protein (Lowry *et al.*, 1951).

Results and Discussion

The increase in cobalt concentration in the soil decreased the biochemical constituents of *V. mungo* over control (Table 52.1). Cobalt treatment at 50 mg/kg soil level proved to be favourable for the biochemical constituents of blackgram. Further increase in cobalt concentration in the soil (100–250 mg/kg) decreased the biochemical constituents of *V. mungo* over control.

Table 52.1: Effect of Cobalt on Sugar, Starch and Protein Content (mg g^{-1} fresh weight) of *Vigna mungo* (L.) Hepper (30th day)

Cobalt Added in the Soil (mg kg^{-1})	*Reducing Sugar*	*Non-reducing Sugar*	*Total Sugar*	*Starch*	*Protein*
Control	1.2364	1.5891	2.8255	3.520	4.1246
50	1.3217 (–6.899)	1.8139 (-14.14)	3.1356 (–10.97)	3.786 (–7.556)	4.6217 (–12.05)
100	1.2248 (0.938)	1.3449 (15.36)	2.5667 (9.159)	3.099 (11.96)	3.1123 (24.54)
150	1.1976 (3.138)	1.2984 (18.29)	2.4960 (11.66)	2.884 (18.06)	2.9876 (27.34)
200	0.9612 (22.25)	1.2829 (19.26)	2.2441 (20.57)	2.162 (38.57)	2.6418 (35.95)
250	0.9418 (23.82)	1.1434 (28.04)	2.0852 (26.20)	1.964 (44.20)	2.3467 (43.10)

Per cent over control values are given in parentheses.

Sugar (reducing, non-reducing and total sugar) and starch content of blackgram plants showed a decreasing trend with progressive increase in cobalt level in the soil. However, 50 mg/kg cobalt level produced positive effect on the reducing, non-reducing, total sugar and starch content which is in consonance with the findings of Mahadeshwaraswamy and Theresa (1992) in *Phaseolus mungo*. The accumulation of reducing, non-reducing, total sugar and starch decreased with increase in cobalt level. The response is similar to that reported by Greger and Lindberg (1986) in sugar beets.

The protein content in leaves reduced with cobalt treatment in blackgram. Nitrogen is a precursor for the synthesis of amino acid (Devlin, 1975). Since the nitrogen content of the metal treated plants was found reduced, ultimately protein contents of plants were also reduced (Mayz and Carturight, 1984) because there was only limited availability of nitrogen for the synthesis of amino acid. Cobalt at high concentrations decreased the protein content. These results are in accordance with the findings in copper, nickel, chromium, cobalt and manganese (Kim *et al.*, 1978), in lead, cadmium, copper and zinc (Kastori *et al.*, 1992) and in cadmium and lead (Battacharjee and Mukherjee, 1994).

References

Bhattacharjee, S. and Mukherjee, A.K., 1994. Influence of cadmium and lead on physiological and biochemical responses of *Vigna unguiculata* (L.) Walp. seedlings I. Germination behaviour, total protein, proline content and protease activity. *Poll. Res.*, 13(3): 269–277.

Blaylock, M.J. and Ruang, J.W., 2000. Phytoextraction of metals. In: *Phytoremediation of Toxic Metals: Using Plants to Clean Up the Environment*, (Eds.) I. Raskin and B.D. Ensley. John Wiley and Sons, Inc., Toronto, Canada, p. 303.

Daviln, R.M., 1975. *Plant Physiology*, 3rd Edn. Litton Educational Publishing, Inc., New York.

Greger, M. and Lindberg, S., 1986. Effects of Cd^{2+} and EDTA on young sugar beets (*Beta vulgaris L.*) Cd^{2+} uptake and sugar accumulation. *Physiol. Plant*, 66: 69–74.

Kastori, R., Petrovic, M. and Petrovic, N., 1992. Effect of excess lead, cadmium, copper and zinc on water relations in sunflower. *J. Plant Nutr.*, 15(11): 2427–2439.

Kim, B.Y., Kim, K.S., Kim, B.J. and Ran, K.M., 1978. Uptake and yield of heavy metal Cu, Ni, Cr, Co and Mn. *Rep. Off. Rural Dev.* p. 1–10.

Lowry, O.H., Rosebrough, N.J., Farr, A.L. and Randall, 1951. Protein measurement with folin-phenol reagent. I. *Biol. Chem.*, 193: 265–275.

Mahadeshwaraswamy and Theresa, Y.M., 1992. Chromium(III) induced biochemical changes in the seedlings of *Phaseolus mungo* L. *Geobios*, 19(6): 242–246.

Mayz, D.M.J. and Cartwright, P.M., 1984. The effect of pH and aluminium toxicity on the growth and symbiotic development of cowpea (*Vigna unguiculata*). *Plant Soil*, 80: 423–430.

Meagher, R.B., 2000. Phytoremediation of toxic elemental and organic pollutants. *Plant Biol.*, 3: 153–162.

Nelson, N., 1944. A photometric adaptation of the Somogyi's method for the determination of reducing sugar. *Anal Chem.*, 31: 426–428.

Raskin, I. and Ensley, B.D., 2000. *Phytoremediation of Toxic Metals: Using Plants to Clean Up the Environment*. John Wiley and Sons, New York, p. 303.

Summner, J.B. and Somers, G.F., 1949. *Laboratory Experiments in Biological Chemistry*, 2nd ed. Academics Press, New York, p. 173.

Terry, N., 1981. Physiological of trace element toxicity and its relation to iron stress. *J. Plant Nutr.*, 3: 561–578.

Woolhouse, H.W., 1983. Toxicity and tolerance in the response of plant to metals. In: *Physiological Plant Ecology*, (Eds.) O.L. Langa, P.S. Nobel, C.B. Osmand and H. Ziegler. III. Encyclopedia of Plant Physiology, (New series) Vol. 12C: 245–300, Springer-Verlag, New York.

Chapter 53

Effect of Chronic Exposure of Cadmium on Histology of *Sarotherodon mossambicus*

D.V. Muley, R.B. Patil, R.S. Dabhole and D.S. Redekar

Department of Zoology, Shivaji University, Kolhapur – 416 004, Maharashtra

ABSTRACT

Histology has been successfully used as a diagnostic to 1 in medical and veterinary sciences ever since mid 19th century. The present investigation was carried out to study the effect of chronic exposure of cadmium on the cellular architecture. The freshwater fish *Sarotheradon mossamblecus* was exposed to 0.20 ppm and 0.40 ppm concentrations of cadmium for 30 days. The effect of cadmium on different tissues like liver, intestine, ovary and testis was observed under Leica Galen III microscope.

From the present study, the histopathological changes caused due to two sub lethal concentrations of cadmium chloride are severe as compared to control. Similarly the damage to different target organs studied were more at 0.40 ppm than 0.20 ppm which shows that the effect of cadmium chloride is dose dependent.

Keywords: *Chronic exposure, Cadmium, Sarotheradon mossambicus and Histology.*

Introduction

Freshwater fishes hold a strategic position in the food web as they serve as staple food for human beings. Studies are mostly on acute toxicity, which has significant limitations in revealing the occurrence of adaptation of fishes to the toxicants. Hence, sub lethal toxicity studies gained more importance

(Perkin, 1979). The survival and productivity of freshwater fishes in sub lethal concentrations, however, depend on their adaptability. The long term exposure of living organisms to low levels of toxicants has been associated with a wide range of metabolic disorders and is believed to the responsible for sub clinical poisoning in several organisms.

Histology has been successfully used as a diagnostic tool in medical and veterinary sciences ever since mid 19th century. According to Virehow, the German pathologist, the normal function of any organ is possible when its structure is normal. Histopathology deals with the study of pathological changes induced in the microscopic structure of tissues. Any particular attention of cell may indicate the presence of disease or toxic substance. Brown (1968) suggested that there is clear correlation between pathological condition of cell or tissues and its affected functions. Thus, the study of histology provides a very important and useful data, concerning changes in cellular or sub cellular structure of an organ much earlier than external notification. The extent of damage induced by the toxicant to a particular organ can also be judged at a cellular level. These studies proved beneficial to investigate the extent of pollution and the nature of lethality of pollutants.

There are limited evidences on histopathological changes due to metal toxicity to aquatic organisms. Gupta and Rajbanshi (1979) showed lethal and sub lethal concentrations of copper sulphate, developed severe damage to the gills, kidney and liver followed by cartilage necrosis, tubular rhexis and hypoxic necrosis respectively in *Heteropneustis fossilis.* Sodium and ammonium sulphate stress caused damage to certain tissues of *Esomus dandricus* (Srivastava and Tripathi, 1981). Haniffa and Sundaravadhanam (1984), showed the effects of distillery effluents on histopathological changes in the gills, intestine and kidney of a freshwater fish, *Barbus stigma.*

Perusal of literature though reveals considerable work on various aspects of metal toxicity to fish, there appears to be paucity of information on the freshwater fishes, from this region where industrial and agricultural operations are intensive. Therefore the present work was undertaken on freshwater teleost *Sarotheradon mossambicus* inhabiting the freshwater bodies around Kolhapur city. In the present study the effects of sub lethal Concentration of Cadmium Chloride ($CdCl_2$) on histopathological aspects of various target organs were studied after chronic exposure (30 days) using static renewable method.

Materials and Methods

The freshwater fish *Sarotheradon mossumbicus:* (8±1 cm in length) were collected from the local tank near Kolhapur and were kept in glass aquarium for 1 week acclimation. Where aerarted water was changed after every 24 hr and the fishes were fed with a fixed diet (Hitachi fish food). Feeding was stopped one day prior to experimentation.

For the chronic toxicity study (30 days) two sub lethal concentrations (0.2 and 0.4 ppm) were selected from the predetermined LC_{50} values of cadmium chloride to the test fish *Sarotheradon mossambicus.* During this period, fishes from control and experimental sets were fed with a fixed dose of diet, once a day at the time of renewal of toxic medium, after every 24 hr. After 30 days, live fishes were sacrificed to obtain liver, intestine, testis and ovary belonging to control and two sub lethal concentrations and tissues were fixed in aqueous Bouin's fixative for 48 hr, washed under tap water, dehydrated in ethyl alcohol grades, cleared in xylol and embedded in wax. They were sectioned at 5–6 μ and stained with Harri's Haematoxylin and alcoholic Eosin and mounted in DPX. All the observations for microphotography are made under Leica Galen III microscope.

Results and Discussion

Liver

Control of Chronic Test

Shape and size of hepatic cells was normal with prominent and normal nuclei. The hepatic cells were arranged in a cord like structure. Blood vessel containing blood cells were observed (Plate 53.1a).

Cadmium Chloride (0.20 ppm)

30 days exposure of fishes to 0.20 ppm of cadmium chloride showed marked changes in the liver. By the end of 30 days the liver manifested extensive damage *i.e.* resulted in loss of their polygonal appearance and rupture of cell membrance and also blood cells are spilled. Nuclei were normal in many cells with few exceptions (Plate 53.1b).

Cadmium Chloride (0.40 ppm)

The severity of damage in the liver tissue was more in 0.40 ppm than 0.20 ppm of cadmium chloride. Almost all the nuclei were swollen showing pyknotic condition. Due to rupture and vaccuolation of the hepatic cells degenerative changes were observed (Plate 53.1c).

Intestine

Control of Chronic Test

Unexposed fishes from the control group showed normal histological structure of intestine. Innermost layer of mucosa comprised of absorptive epithelial mucosa secreting goblet cells, the mucosal layer was thrown into folds of villi. The muscularis was thin layer composed of circular and longitudinal muscles serosa the outer most layer was uniformly thick (Plate 53.1d).

Cadmium Chloride (0.20 ppm)

Marked histological changes were observed in intestine of fish exposed to 0.2C ppm of cadmium chloride. Mostly in mucosa and submucosa marked changes were observed. Degeneration of cells at few places of muscosal layer (Plate 53.1e).

Cadmium Chloride (0.40 ppm)

Damage to fish intestine due to 0.4 ppm was more severe than 0.20 ppm of cadmium chloride. The submucosal cells showed degenerative changes and there was disorganization of submucosal cells and pyknotic nuclei were noticed in many mucosal cells (Plate 53.1f).

Ovary

Control of Chronic Tests

The histological structure of ovary of *Sarotherodon mossambicus* for chronic control was showed various stages of development including oogonic, secondary oocyte and mature oocyte. It also showed stroma. The oogonic contained clear cytoplasm. Primary oocytes were larger than the later. Granulosa and Zona radiata were normal. The mature and ripe oocyte occupied most of the space in the organ due to their large sizes (Plate 53.2a).

Cadmium Chloride (0.20 ppm)

Considerable damage to the ovary of fish *Sarotherodon mossambicus* was caused by 0.20 ppm of cadmium chloride. The cadmium chloride suppressed almost all the stages of oocytes in the ovary due

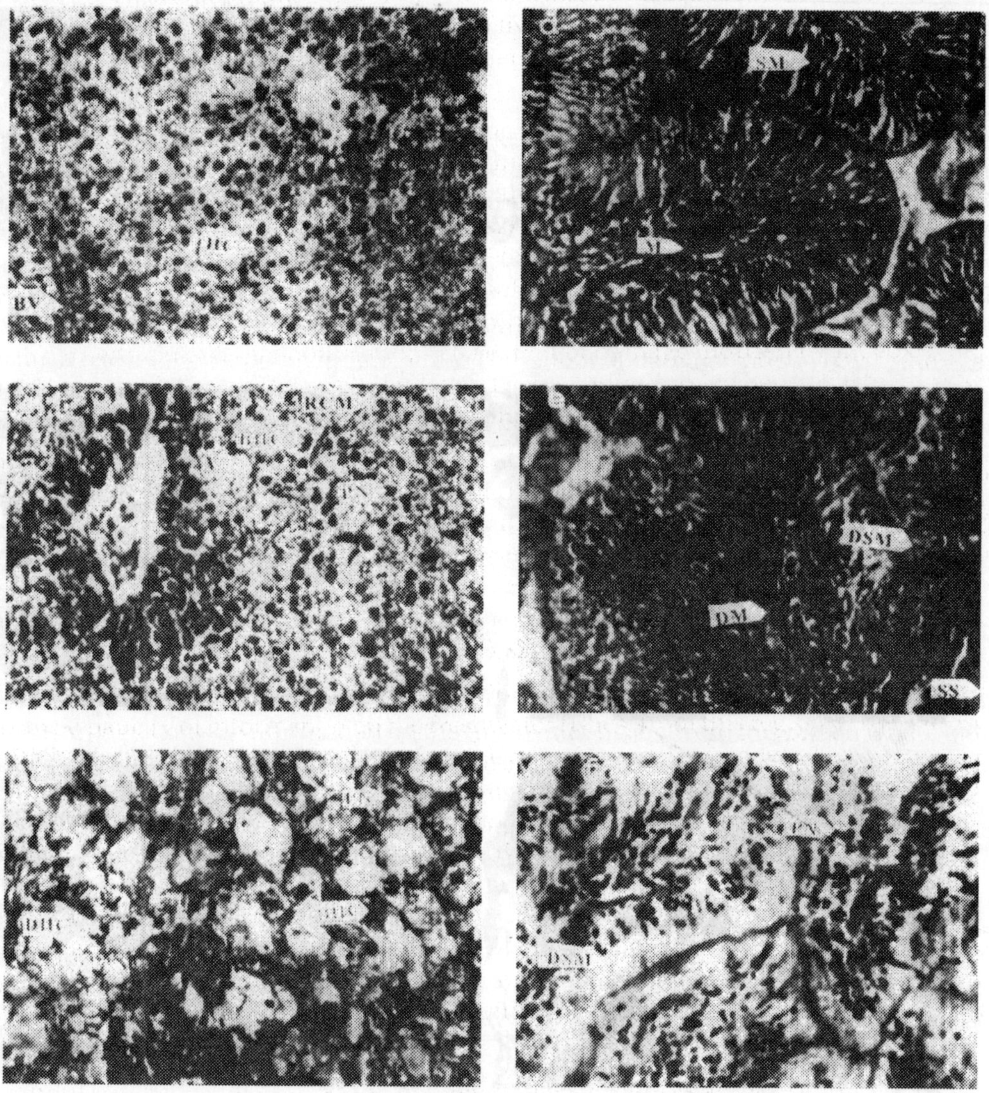

Plate 53.1

Liver

(a) Control liver showing normal structure; (b) Microphotograph showing the effect of 0.20 ppm CdCl2 on liver; (c) Microphotograph showing the effect of 0.40 ppm CdCl2 on liver.

HC: Hepatic cells; N: Nucleus; BV: Blood vessel; RCM: Ruptured cell membrane; PN: Pyknotic nucleus; DHC: Degenerating hepatocytes; V: Vacuole; BHC: Binucleated hepatocyte.

Intestine

(d) Control intestine showing normal structure; (e) Microphotograph showing the effect of 0.20 ppm CdCl2 on intestine; (f) Microphotograph showing the effect of 0.40 ppm CdCl2 on intestine.

M: Mucosa; SM: Sub mucosa; MM: Muscularis mucosa; S: Serosa; DM: Degenerating mucosa; DSM: Degenerating sub mucosa; SS: Separated serosa; V: Vacuole; PN: Pyknotic nucleus; LS: Lost serosa.

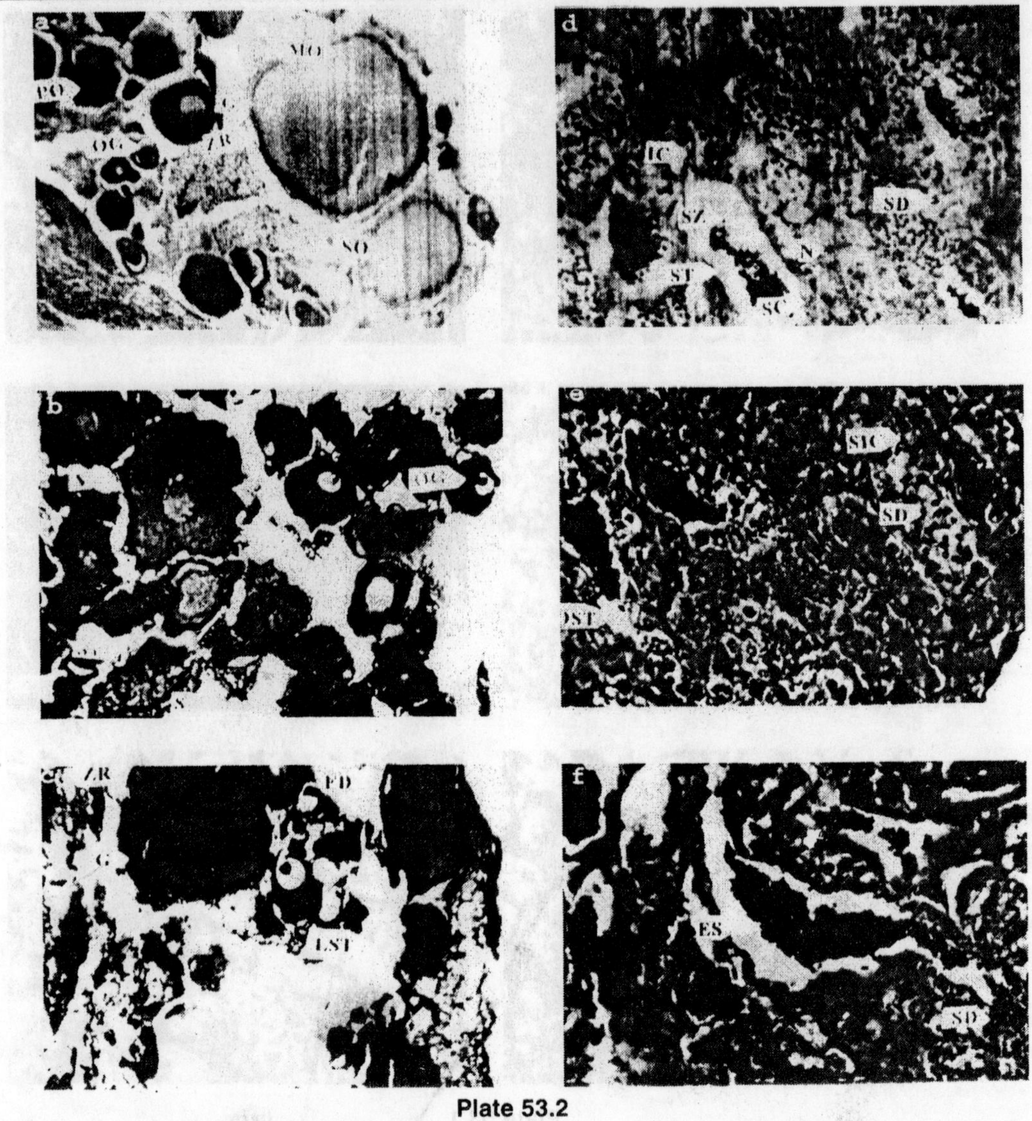

Plate 53.2

Ovary

(a) Control ovary showing normal structure; (b) Microphotograph showing the effect of 0.20 ppm CdCl2 on ovary; (c) Microphotograph showing the effect of 0.40 ppm CdCl2 on testis.

OG: Oogonium; PO: Primary oocyte; SO: Secondary oocyte; ST: Stroma; G: Granulosa; ZR: Zona radiate; S: Space; MO: Mature oocyte; FD: Follicular distoration; LST: Loss of stroma; V: Vacuole.

Testis

(d) Control testis showing normal structure; (e) Microphotograph showing the effect of 0.20 ppm CdCl2 on testis; (f) Microphotograph showing the effect of 0.40 ppm CdCl2 on testis.

ST: Seminiferous tubules; SIC: Shrunken intestitial cells; ES: Empty space; Sc: Sertoli cells; SZ: Spermatozoa; SD: Spermatid; N: Nucleus; IC: Interstitial cells; SG: Spermatogonium; DST: Distorted seminiferous tubules.

to which there was increased mass of stroma. Degeneration of stroma followed by large spaces and shape of the follicles are changed *i.e.*, shrinkage (Plate 53.2b).

Cadmium Chloride (0.40 ppm)

The severity of damage in the architecture of ovary was more in 0.40 ppm than 0.20 ppm of cadmium chloride. Degeneration of stroma was the most shrinking effect of 0.40 ppm of cadmium chloride. Follicular distortion was evident. Zona radiata and granulose of follicle become thin when compared to the control (Plate 53.1c).

Testis

Control of Chronic Test

The histological structure of testis for chronic control showed seminiferous tubules and interstitial cells. Seminiferous tubules enclosing cyst of spermatocytes, spermatids and sperms in the lumen. Size of interstitial cells and germ cells was normal. The sertoli cells were also observed with good number of spermatid attached. Nuclei in the germ cells sertoli cells and interstitial cells were normal and centrally located (Plate 53.2d).

Cadmium Chloride (0.20 ppm)

Marked histological changes were observed in the testis of fish exposed to 0.20 ppm of cadmium chloride for 30 days. Primary effect of cadmium chloride intoxication on fish was much reduction in the size of testis, when compared to control. Interstitial cells were shrink and nuclei pushed towards periphery and somniferous tubules were distorted. Degeneration of spermatocytes was initiated along with spermatozoa and spermatid (Plate 53.2e).

Cadmium Chloride (0.40 ppm)

Damage of fish testis due to 0.40 ppm was more severe than 0.20 ppm of cadmium chloride. Necrosis in interstitial cells was frequently seen with pyknotice nuclei. Degeneration of germ cells was the indication of cadmium chloride intoxication which resulted into the development of large and empty spaces (Plate 53.2i).

Long term (chronic) effects of heavy metals have also been studied by various workers abroad and in India. Sastry and Verma (1980) observed the effect of sub lethal concentration of mercuric chloride (0.3 mg/l) on the blood of a teleost fish *Ophiocephalus punctatus.* Sastry and Rao (1982) studied the intestinal absorption to a sub lethal concentration (3 mg/l) of mercuric chloride for 15 and 30 days. Sastry and Subhadra (1982) observed the chronic toxic effects of cadmium (026 mg/l) on the carbohydrate metabolism of a teleost fish, *Heteropneustes fossilis* after 15, 30 and 60 days of exposure.

Gill *et al.* (1988) observed the effects of sub lethal concentrations, 630 and 840 micrograms/liter (0.05 and 0.066 fraction of the 96 h LC_{50}), of cadmium chloride on the gills of a freshwater fish, *Puntius conchonius.* Usha and Ramamurthi (1989) studied histopathological alterations in the liver of freshwater teleost *Tilapia mossambica* in response to cadmium toxicity when exposed to sub lethal (5 ppm) concentration of cadmium chloride. Radhakrishnaian *et al.* (1993) studied exposure of a freshwater fish *Cyprinus carpio* to the sub lethal concentration of mercury (0.1 mg/l) and zinc (6.0 mg/l) which resulted in distinct changes in the energy metabolism of gill, liver and muscle at 1.15 and 30 days.

In the present study the histopathological changes caused due to two sub lethal concentrations (0.2 and 0.4 ppm) of cadmium chloride are severe as compared to control, similarly the damage to different target organs studied were more at 0.4 ppm than 0.2 ppm *i.e.*, the effect of cadmium chloride is dose dependent. The above results on cadmium toxicity and its impact at cellular level, particularly in liver, intestine, male and female gonads of the freshwater fish *Sarotheradon mossambicus* after chronic exposure, reveals the toxic nature of cadmium at very low concentration.

References

Brown, D.A. and T.R. Parsons, 1978. Relationship between cytoplasmic distribution of mercury and toxic effects to zooplanktons and chum salmon (*Oncorhynchus kets*) exposed to mercury in controlled ecosystem.

Gill, T.S. and J.C. Pant, 1985. Erythrocytic and leucocytic responses to cadmium poisoning in a freshwater fish, *Puntius conchonius. Environ. Res.*, 36(2): 327–337.

Gupta, A.K. and D.V.K. Rajbanshi, 1979. Pathological changes resulting from bioassay of copper to *Heteropneustis fossilis* (Bloch). *Proc. Symp. Environ. Biol.*, p. 7–13.

Haniffa and Sundarvadhanam, 1984. Effect of distillery effluent on histopathological changes in certain tissues of Barbus stigma. *J. Environ. Biol.*, 5(1): 57–60.

Perkin, E.J., 1979. Need for sub lethal studies. *Phil. Trans. R. Soc. London*, 286: 425–432.

Radhakrishnaian, K., Suresh, A. and Sivaram Knshnas, B., 1993. Effect of sublethal concentration of mercury and zinc on the energetics of a freshwater fish *Cyprinus carpio* (Linnacus). *Aqua. Biol. Hung.*, 44(4): 438–447.

Sastry, K.V. and Rao, D.R., 1982. Effect of mercuric chloride on the intestinal absorption of an amino acid, glycine in freshwater mullet *Channa punctatus. Toxicol. Lett.*, 11(1–2): 11–15.

Sastry, K.V. and Subhadra, K., 1982. Effect of cadmium on some aspects of carbohydrate metabolism in a freshwater catfish *Heteropneuestis fossilis.*

Shrivastava, V.M.S. and R.S. Tripathi, 1981. Histopathological changes in tissues of *Esomus dandricus* (Ham) under sodium and ammonium sulphate stress. *Comp. Physiol. Ecol.*, 6(4): 236–238.

Usha, R. and Ramamurthi, R., 1989. Histopathological alteration in the liver of freshwateer Teleost *Tilapia mossambica* in response to cadmium toxicity. *Eco. Toxicol.*, 17(2): 221–226.

Chapter 54

Population Dynamics and Bioefficacy of *Raphidopalpa* (Aulacophora) *foveicollis* (Lucas) (Coleoptera : Chrysomelidae) on *Lagenaria vulgaris* Ser. in Barak Valley of Assam

Dilip Nath and D.C. Ray*

Department of Ecology and Environmental Science, Assam University, Silchar – 788 011, Assam, India

ABSTRACT

The study of population dynamics of *Raphidopalpa foveicollis* (Lucas) (Coleoptera : Chrysomelidae) on *Lagenaria vulgaris* was conducted during July, 2004 to April, 2005 in Katigorah and Alenpur of Cachar district, Barak valley. During autumn, maximum population ($5.4/m^2$) recorded on first part of August, 04 in Katigorah and $2.6/m^2$ on first part of September, 04 in Alenpur whereas minimum ($1.4/m^2$) was recorded in the beginning of July, 04 in Katigorah but no population recorded during middle of December, 04 in Alenpur. During winter maximum population ($1.8/m^2$) recorded on last week of February, 05 in Katigorab and $5.2/m^2$ on last part of February, 05 in Alenpur whereas minimum ($0.2/m^2$) was recorded in the beginning of December, 04 in Katigorah and $1.0/m^2$ in last part of March, 05 in Alenpur. A multiple correlation (F-test) was employed with temperature, rainfall and R.H., which indicated non-significant ($P < 0.05$) with all the abiotic factors in autumn for both the study sites. During winter it was significant ($P < 0.01$) in Katigorah whereas insignificant ($P < 0.05$) in Alenpur. The partial correlation (t-test) indicated significant ($P < 0.05$) in autumn and during winter temperature and R.H. were

* Corresponding Author: E-mail: raydulal@yahoo.co.in.

significant (P < 0.05) whereas rainfall showed insignificant (P < 0.05). Bioefficacy of two biopesticides and three synthetic pesticides were tested. Out of two biopesticides, Calpaste (0.4 per cent) afforded cent per cent mortality only after one day whereas Deltamethrin (0.00 I per cent) gave cent per cent mortality after 5 days of application. ANOVA was employed which indicated significant performance (P < 0.05) after one day in case of biopesticides whereas in other cases of biopesticides and synthetic pesticides it was recorded insignificant.

Keywords: *Raphidopalpa foveicollis, Lagenaria vulgaris, Population dynamics, Bioefficacy, Pesticides.*

Introduction

Red pumpkin beetle, *Raphidopalpa* (*Aulacophora*) *foveicollis* (Lucas) (Coleoptera : Chrysomelidae) is a major and serious insect-pest of bottle gourd (*Lagenaria vulgaris* Ser.) and other cucurbitaceous crops. This important pest is widely distributed in the tropical, sub-tropical and temperate regions of the world (Melamed-Madjar, 1960; Bogawat and Pandey, 1967 and Al-Ali *et al.*, 1982) including India (Butani and Jotwani, 1983). The adults feed on leaves by making regular and irregular holes (Ray, 2000) including flower, stems, fruits of cucurbit crops and larvae to roots, stems below the ground and fruits contact with the soil (Kadam and Patel, 1957). In Assam the problem of red pumpkin beetle is acute and causes considerable economic loss. A good number of reports are available on the population dynamics on cucurbit crops (Shinde and Purohit, 1978 and Pande *et al.*, 1987), nature of damage (Saini, 1959; Singh *et al.*, 2000; Johri and Johri, 2003a) and bioefficacy (Krishnaiah *et al.*, 1979; Thomas and Jacob, 1994; Mehta and Sandhu, 1992; Ray, 2000; Khan and Wasim, 2001; Rajak and Singh, 2002 among others). But no published works are available on the population dynamics and bioefficacy of the pest on *L. vulgaris* from Barak valley a southern part of Assam. Considering the economic importance of the pest the present study has been undertaken on population dynamics and bioefficacy with bio pesticides and synthetic pesticides.

Materials and Methods

The experiments were carried out at cultivators, field in Cachar district of Barak valley. Population dynamics was conducted in Katigorah and Alenpur during July, 2004 to April, 2005. A quadrat (lm^2) was used randomly to record the insect species from foliage of bottle gourd. Five quadrats were considered from each site in each sampling period for studying population dynamics. The management practices has been carried out by RBD method with bio and synthetic pesticides at cultivators' field.

Results and Discussion

Population dynamics indicated the maximum (5.4/m^2) during the first part of August, 04 and minimum (1.4/m^2) in the beginning of July, 04 in Katigorah during autumn. In Alenpur maximum population (2.6/m^2) recorded on first part of September, 04 but no population recorded during middle of December, 04. A multiple correlation (F-test) of population fluctuation was employed with temperature, rainfall and R.H., which showed non-significant (P < 0.05) effect *i.e.* all the abiotic factors together have no any influence on population fluctuation in autumn for both the study sites. The partial correlation (t-test) indicated significant in Katigorah (P < 0.05) and Alenpur (temperature and R,H at P < 0.01, rainfall at P < 0.05) with all the abiotic factors (Tables 54.1 and 54.2; Figures 54.1 and 54.2).

Table 54.1: Seasonal Incidence of *R. foveicollis in* Katigorah on *Lagenaria vulgaris* (Bottle gourd) During July, 04–September, 04

Date of Sampling	*No of Pop^n*	*Temperature (°C)*	*Rainfall (mm)*	*RH (%)*
4/7/2004	1.4+	27.66++	23.81++	90.7++
21/7/2004	2.0	28.06	18.63	86.78
8/8/2004	5.4	28.80	9.25	77.93
25/8/2004	5.2	29.69	11.59	83.44
10/9/2004	2.8	27.35	17.93	90.23
25/9/2004	2.8	28.24	7.12	88.37

'F'-test: 3.80 (NS)

't'

Temp: –71.83**

Rainfall: –3.65*

RH: –32.021**

+: Based on 5 quadrates; ++: Data collected from Meteorological Deptt. (Guwahati); *: Significant at 5 per cent level; **: Significant at 1 per cent level; NS: Non-significant.

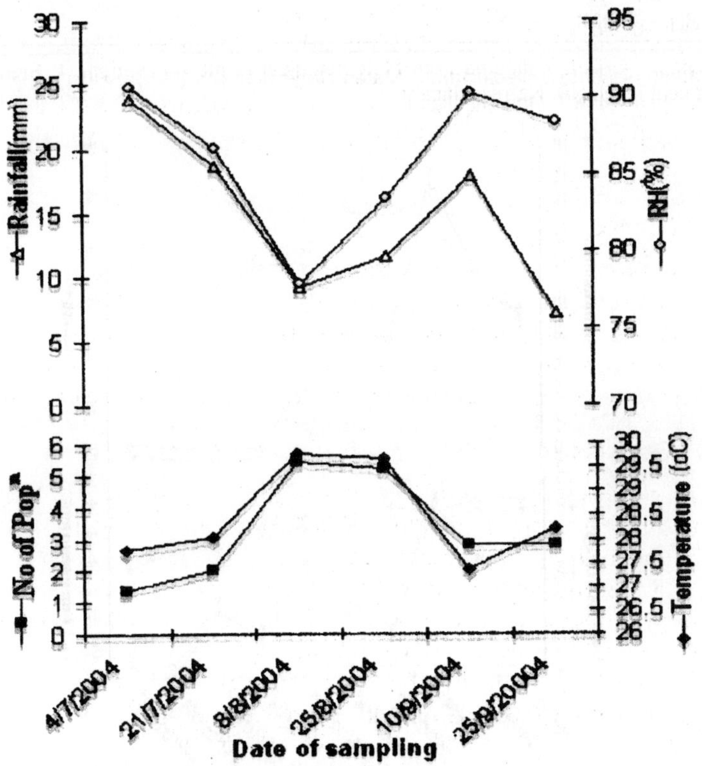

Figure 54.1: Graph Showing the Effect of Abiotic Factors on *R. foveicollis* in Katigorah During July, 04– September, 04

Table 54.2: Seasonal Incidence or *R. fovelcollis* in Alenpur on *Lagenaria vulgaris* (Bottle gourd) During August, 04–December, 04

Date of Sampling	*No of Pop^n*	*Temperature (°C)*	*Rainfall (mm)*	*RH (%)*
13/8/2004	1.2+	29.8++	9.25++	77.93++
28/8/2004	1.8	29.69	11.59	82.44
11/9/2004	2.6	27.38	17.93	90.23
26/9/2004	0.6	28.24	7.12	88.37
7/10/2004	1.0	26.65	7.53	88.73
24/10/2004	1.6	26.62	3.94	83.94
12/11/2004	0.6	24.78	0	83.6
26/11/2004	1.0	23.08	0	80.73
15/12/2004	0	22.73	0	76.4
30/12/2004	0.2	19.44	0.39	82.69

'F' test: 4.50 (NS)

't'

Temp: –27.00**

Rainfall: –2.74*

RH: –61.20**

+: Based on 5 quadrates; ++: Data collected from Meteorological Deptt. (Guwahati); *: Significant at 5 per cent level; **: Significant at 1 per cent level; NS: Non-significant.

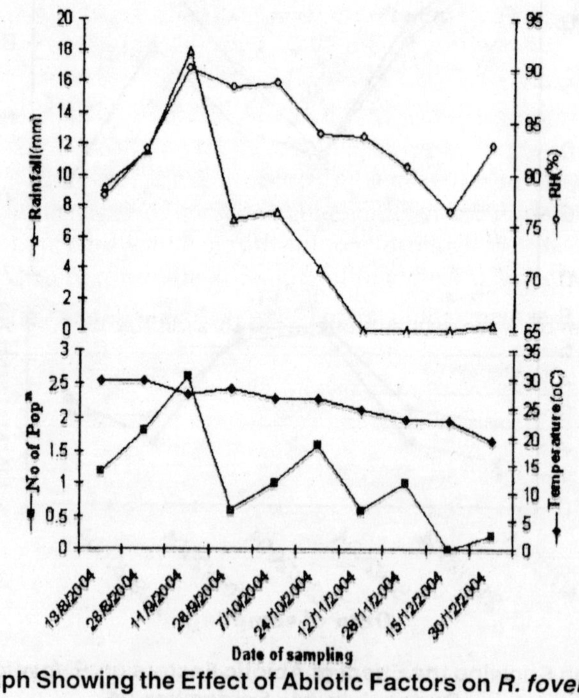

Figure 54.2: Graph Showing the Effect of Abiotic Factors on *R. foveicollis* in Alenpur During August, 04–December, 04

During winter maximum population (1.8/m²) recorded on last week of February, 05 and minimum (0.2/m²) recorded in the beginning of December, 04 I Katigorah. Regarding Alenpur maximum population (5.2/m²) on last part of February, 05 and minimum (1.0/m²) on last part of March, 05 were recorded. Multiple correlation was found to be significant ($P < 0.01$) with all the abiotic factors in Katigorah whereas insignificant ($P < 0.05$) in Alenpur. Partial correlation (t-test) showed significant ($P < 0.01$) with temperature and R.H. but rainfall showed insignificant ($P < 0.05$) for both the sites (Tables 54.3 and 54.4; Figures 54.3 and 54.4).

Table 54.3: Seasonal Incidence of *R. foveicollis* in Katigorah on *Lagenaria vulgaris* (Bottle gourd) During December, 04–February, 05

Date of Sampling	*No of Pop^n*	*Temperature (°C)*	*Rainfall (mm)*	*RH (%)*
5/12/2004	0.2+	22.73	0++	76.4
20/12/2004	0.6	19.44	0.39	82.69
4/1/2005	0.8	18.67	0	83.1
21/1/2005	1.2	18.94	0.07	77.5
6/2/2005	1.4	21.54	0	66.9
24/2/2005	1.8	23.38	8.94	80.08

'F'-test: 188.29**

't'-

Temp: –24.54**

Rainfall: –0.42 (NS)

RH: –30.61**

+: Based on 5 quadrates; ++: Data collected from Meteorological Deptt. (Guwahati); *: Significant at 5 per cent level; **: Significant at 1 per cent level; NS: Non-significant.

Table 54.4: Seasonal Incidence of *R. foveicollis* in Alenpur on *Lagenaria vulgaris* (Bottle gourd) During January, 05–April, 05

Date of Sampling	*No of Pop^n.*	*Temperature (°C)*	*Rainfall (mm)*	*RH (%)*
20/1/2005	1.4+	18.94++	0.07++	77.5++
6/2/2005	2.0	21.54	0	66.9
21/2/2005	5.2	23.38	8.93	80.08
8/3/2005	1.4	25.10	14.59	77.37
23/312005	1.0	23.88	17.52	80.56
9/4/2005	3.4	26.54	5.57	71.67

'F' –test: 0.77 (NS)

't'-

Temp: –8.68**

Rainfall: –1.70 (NS)

RH: –32.50**

+: Based on 5 quadrates; ++: Data collected from Meteorological Deptt. (Guwahati); *: Significant at 5 per cent level; **: Significant at 1 per cent level; NS: Non-significant.

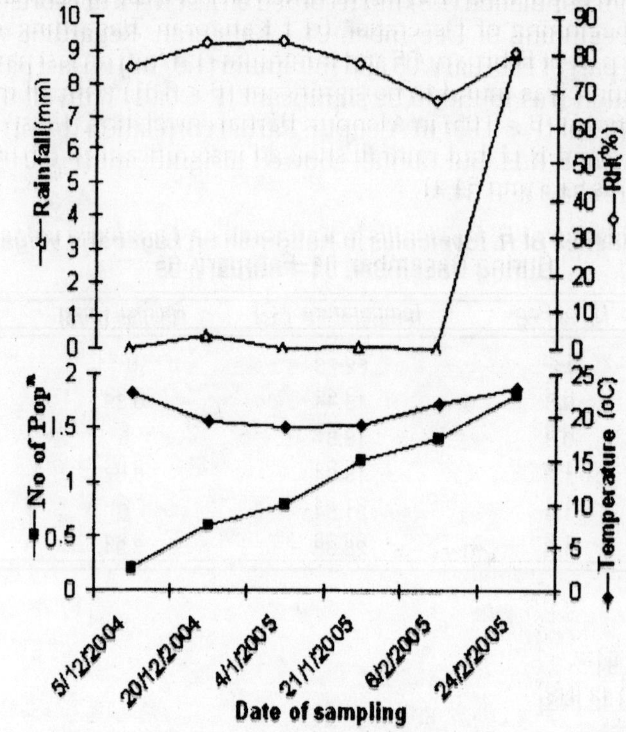

Figure 54.3: Graph Showing the Effect of Abiotic Factors on *R. foveicollis* in Katigorah During December, 04–February, 05

Bio-efficacy was tested with two biopesticides and three synthetic pesticides. The data on effectiveness of a single spray of two biopesticides against the insect-pest in the adult stage are presented in the Table 54.5. Out of two biopesticides Calpaste (0.4 per cent) afforded cent per cent mortality after 1 day of treatment whereas Larvocel (0.5 per cent) gave cent per cent mortality after 3 days of treatment. ANOVA was employed which indicated significant performance ($P < 0.05$) after 1 day of treatment thereafter showed insignificant upto 7 day of application by using both the pesticides (Table 54.5).

Table 54.5: Bioefficacy of Biopesticides against *R. foveicollis*

Biopesticides	*Conc. (%)*	*Pre-treat Pop*	*% Mortality After Days*			
			1	*3*	*5*	*7*
Call Paste	0.40	9	100+ (90)++	88.88+ (70) ++	66.66+ (54.16) ++	66.66+ (54.16) ++
Larvocel	0.50	9	19.44 (21.110)	100 (90)	100 (90)	72.22 (52.24)
	CD at 5%		8.53*	1.53 (NS)	1.53 (NS)	0.11 (NS)

+: Based on three replications: each consisted of one sq. mt. area; ++: Figures in parentheses are average of transformed value = Arcsin $\sqrt{\text{percentage}}$; *: Significant at 5 per cent; NS: Non-significant.

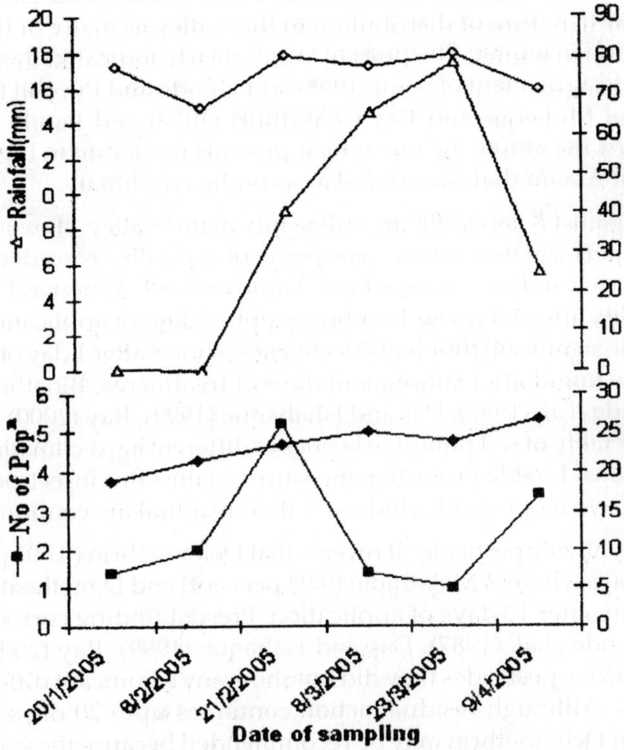

Figure 54.4: Graph Showing the Effect of Abiotic factor on *R. foveicollis* in Alenpur During January, 05–April, 05

In case of synthetic pesticides cent per cent mortality was recorded by Deltamethrin (0.001 per cent) after 5 days of treatment and Dimethoate (0.03 per cent) and Malathion (0.03 per cent) afforded cent per cent mortality after 10 days of treatment. However ANOVA test indicated insignificant ($P < 0.05$) difference among all the pesticides during the sampling periods (Table 54.6).

Table 54.6: Bio-efficacy of Synthetic Pesticides against *R. foveicollis*

Chemical Insecticides	*Conc. (%)*	*Pre-treat Pop.*	*% Mortality After Days*				
			1	*5*	*10*	*15*	*20*
Deltamethrin	0.001	20	91.66+ (71.93)++	100+ (90)++	95.83+ (76.14)++	94.44+ (75.97)++	86.11+ (67.04)++
Dimethoate	0.03	6	66.66 (54.16)	83.33 (68.59)	100 (90)	50 (44.48)	66.66 (54.16)
Malathion	0.03	10	47.22 (42.90)	80.55 (62.87)	100 (90)	80.55 (62.97)	72.22 (57.24)
	CD at 5%		1.24 (NS)	1.32 (NS)	1.27 (NS)	0.86 (NS)	0.38 (NS)

+: Based on three replications: each consisted of one sq. mt. area; ++: Figures in parentheses are average of transformed value = Arcsin $\sqrt{\text{percentage}}$; NS: Non-significant.

This species is peculiar in nature of distribution in this valley as many of the authors indicated that it undergoes hibernation in winter. The present study clearly indicated their abundance during winter season which is in disagreement of Saini (1958) and Shinde and Purohit (1978). But our study corroborates the finding of Mukerjee and Ray Chaudhuri (1959) and Pande *et al.* (1987). During autumn and winter seasons the abiotic factors which prevails moderate to high may favours their abundance in this valley of Assam that considered as a conducive climate.

Use of biopesticides against *R. foveicollis* are still scanty in this valley. However, Calpaste (0.4 per cent) gives very effective performance where cent per cent mortality recorded only after 1 day of treatment, thereafter its efficacy reduces and continued upto an week. Whereas Larvocel (0.5 per cent) shows cent per cent mortality after 3 days and continues upto 5 days of application. The effectiveness continues upto an week. The significant different effectiveness shows after 1 day of application whereas no significant effectiveness found after subsequent days of treatments. Bioefficacy of biopesticides was earlier studied by Pande *et al.* (1987), Das and Ishahaque (1999), Ray (2000) which indicates 21.0 per cent to 88.0 per cent mortality of red pumpkin beetles in different agro-climatic conditions of India. Present finding indicates considerable protection measures against this insect-pest by using both the biopesticides. Use of these two biopesticides indicates their residual life continues upto an week.

As regards the use of synthetic pesticides it reveals that Deltamethrin (0.001 per cent) affords cent per cent mortality after 5 days whereas Malathioin (0.03 per cent) and Dimethoate (0.03 per cent) also gives cent per cent mortality after 10 days of application. Present finding corroborates the works of Krishnaiah *et al.* (1979), Pande *et al.* (1987), Das and Isahaque (1999), Ray (2000), Rajak and Singh (2002). As regards the efficacy of pesticides they did not show any significant different effectiveness in all the sampling occasions. Although residual action continues upto 20 days but as far as health hazard is concern the use of Deltamethrin may be recommended because the synthetic pyrethroid is easily photodegradable and less mammalian toxicity followed by Malathion.

References

Al-Ali, A.S., Al Neamy, I.K. and Alwan, M.S., 1982. On the biology and host preference of *Aulacophora foveiciollis*, Lucas (Coleoptera : Galerucidae). *Z. Ang. Ent.*, 84: 82–86.

Bogawat, J.K. and Pandey, S.N., 1967. Food preference in *Aulacophora* spp. *Indian J. Ent.*, 29(4): 349–352.

Butani, D.K. and Jotwani, M.G., 1983. Insects as limiting factors in vegetable production. *Pesticides*, 17: 6–13.

Das, S.K. and Ishahaque, N.M.D.M., 1999. Control of red pumpkin beetle, *Aulacophora foveicollis* (Lucas). *J. Agric. Sci. Soc.*, NE India, 123(2): 112–117.

Johri, R. and Johri, P.K., 2003a. Food preference of red pumpkin beetle, *Aulacophora foveicollis* (Lucas) at Kanpur in Uttar Pradesh. *J. Appl. Zool. Res.*, 14(1): 80–81.

Kadam, M.V. and Patel, G.A., 1957. Pests of crucifers, chillies, onions, cucurbits and bhindi crops and how to fight them. Pub. Govt. of Maharashtra, Bombay, pp. 100.

Krishnaiah, K., Jagon, M.N. and Prasad, V.G., 1979. Evaluation of insecticides for the control of major pest of musk-melon. *Ind. J. Ent.*, 41: 311–315.

Mukherjee, M.K. and Ray Chaudhuri, D.N., 1959. Biology of *Aulacophora foveicollis* (Lucas) (Coleoptera : Chrysomelidae). *Proc. Zool. Soc.*, 12(1): 15–18.

Khan, S.M. and Wasim, M., 2001. Assessment of different plaint extracts for their repellency against red pumpkin beetle (*Aulacophora foveicollis* Lucas) attacking muskmelon (*Cucumis melo* L.) crop. *J. Biol. Sci.*, 1(4): 198–200.

Melamed-Madjar, V., 1960. Studies on red pumpkin beetle in Israel. *Ktavim*, 10: 139–145.

Mehta, P.K. and Sandhu, G.S., 1992. Influence of cucurbitacins on the feeding activity of red pumpkin beetle, *Aulacophora foveicollis* (Lucas). *J. Insect. Sci.*, 5(2): 187–189.

Pande, Y.D., Ray, D.C. and Ghosh, D., 1987. Some ecological observations on the red pumpkin beetle *Raphidopalpa foveicollis* (Lucas) (Chrysomelidae : Coleoptera) and toxicity *Hyptis saveolens* leaf extract to the adult beetles in Tripura. *Indian Biologist*, 14(1): 22–27.

Ray, D.C., 2000. Field studies on *Raphidopalpa foveicollis* (Lucas) (Chrysomelidae : Coleoptera) extent of damage caused and evaluation of certain insecticides and plant extracts. *Ind. J. Env. and Ecoplan.*, 3(3): 579–586.

Rajak, D.C. and Singh, H.M., 2002. Comparative efficacy of pesticides against red pumpkin beetle, *Aulacophora foveicollis* on musk-melon. *Ann. Pl. Protec. Sci.*, 10(1): 147–148.

Saini, R.S., 1958. All the bionomics and life-histories of three species of *Aldacophora* (Chrysomelidae : Coleoptera) from India. *Proc. Nat. Acad. Sci.*, Section B. 28: 365–371.

Saini, R.S., 1959. Studies on the food preference of *Aulacophora. Madhya Bharati*, 8: 55–57.

Shinde, C.B. and Purohit, M.L., 1978. Population study of red pumpkin beetle (*Aulacophora foveicollis* Lucas)-a serious insect-pest of cucurbits. *Sci. and Cult.*, 44(7): 335.

Singh, S.V., Mishra, A., Bisen, R.S. and Malik, Y.P., 2000. Host preference of red pumpkin beetle *Aulacophora foveicollis* and melon fruit fly *Dacus Cucurbitae. Indian J. Ent.*, 62(3): 242–246.

Thomas, C. and Jacob, S., 1994. Biological efficacy of curbofuran against the red pumpkin beetle *Raphidopalpa foveicollis* Lucas infesting bitter gourd. *Indian J. Ent.*, 56(2): 164–168.

Chapter 55

Crop Density, Growth and Yield Attributes of Lowland Rice as Influenced by Different Level of Fertilizer Nitrogen Substitution through Poultry and Livestock Wastes

S. Ramesh[1], S. Ravi[1] and B. Chandrasekaran[2]

[1]**Department of Agronomy, Tamil Nadu Agricultural University, Coimbatore – 641 003, India**

[2]**Director of Research, Tamil Nadu Agricultural University, Coimbatore – 641 003, India**

ABSTRACT

A field experiment was laid out in sandy clay soil at Agriculture College and Research Institute, Killikulam, Tamil Nadu during the *Kar* season (June–September) to study the growth and yield attributes of lowland rice as influenced by substitution of inorganic fertilizer N through poultry and livestock wastes. 100 per cent N substitution through poultry manure caused significant reduction in plant density (60 m^{-2}) as against optimum plant population of 80 m^{-2}. At all stages *viz.*, tillering, flowering and harvest, the application of N as 50 per cent dried poultry manure (DPM) and 50 per cent N as fertilizer N recorded highest plant height. The LAI, number of tillers m^{-2} and DMP was highest with application of 25 per cent N as pig manure plus 75 per cent N as fertilizer nitrogen. The yield attributes such as productive tiller m^{-2} were significantly higher with 25 per cent N substitution through pig manure. The panicle length, number of grains $panicle^{-1}$ and 1000 grain weight was maximum with 50 per cent N as dried poultry manure plus 50 per cent N as fertilizer N. This study may help to optimise N level substitution with different organic manures.

Keywords: *Rice, Fertilizer nitrogen, Poultry, Livestock wastes.*

Introduction

In the mid sixties during the green revolution, there was a sudden spurt in the use of chemical fertilizers and lesser use of organic resources. In spite of this increase in fertilizer use, the overall consumption of fertilizer level is just 74 kg ha^{-1}, which is below the nutrient requirement of soil to sustain productivity and fertility. There is a wide gap between crop removal and addition of plant nutrients through fertilizers and it is expected to be about 6 metric tonnes during 2000 A.D. This gap could be made good by the application of organic manures *viz.*, poultry, piggery, sheep or goat manure (Swaminathan, 1987). In general, there are good relationship between total soil N and crop yields. An integrated approach involving organic manures and chemical fertilizers will go a long way in building up of soil fertility on a permanent basis and the system will supply most of nutrients in a judicious way and efficiency of nutrient uptake by the crop will be enhanced. Under Thambirabarani command area, rice is a major crop grown in about 1.32 lakh ha. Information on the efficiency of different organic and inorganic sources are scanty and hence present investigation was undertaken to study the plant population, growth and yield attributes of rice as influenced by the organic manures and fertilizer application.

Materials and Methods

A field experiment was conducted at Agricultural College and Research Institute, Killikulam, Tamil Nadu Agricultural University, India, during the *Kar* season (June–September) with the objective to find out the feasibility of substitution of inorganic fertilizer N through poultry manure and livestock wastes and their effect on plant population, growth and yield attributes of low land rice. The soil at the experimental site was moderately drained, deep and sandy clay (44.9 per cent clay, 8.4 per cent silt, 31.3 per cent coarse sand and 14.2 per cent fine sand) with pH of 6.9, electrical conductivity of 0.42 dSm^{-1}, available N of 250 kg ha^{-1}, available P_2O_5 of 16 kg ha^{-1}, available K_2O of 139 kg ha^{-1} and organic carbon of 0.69 g kg^{-1}.

The experiment was conducted in randomised block design with 18 treatments replicated thrice. The treatments consisted of fertilizer nitrogen substituted through poultry manure, pig manure, farm yard manure and sheep manure at different levels of 0 per cent, 25 per cent, 50 per cent and 100 per cent as per the treatment Table 55.1. Fertilizers in the form of urea, super phosphate and muriate of potash were used in the study. The nutrient content of organic manures were analysed and given below in Table 55.2.

Recommended level of fertilizer 120 : 60 : 60 kg NPK was followed and applied as per the treatments (0, 50, 75 and 100 per cent inorganic fertilizer). Based on the nitrogen content of the different manures, the quantity required for the different level of N substitution was calculated on dry weight basis and applied to the respective plots, one week before transplanting was applied in three splits and applied at basal, tillering and panicle initiation stages. The phosphatic fertilizer was applied fully as basal and potassium fertilizers was applied in two split dose as at basal and at panicle initiation stage. The growth attributes *viz.*, plant population, plant height, LAI, number of tillers m^{-2}, DMP (kg ha) and yield attributes *viz.*, number of panicles m^{-2}, panicle length, number of grains panicle-l and thousand grain weight were recorded as per standard procedure to study the effect of N substitution with different organic manures.

Table 55.1: The Structure of Treatments Adopted in the Study

Sl.No.	Treatments	Notations
1.	100% N through inorganic source	T_1
2.	100% N through FYM	T_2
3.	75% N through FYM + 25% N through inorganic	T_3
4.	50% N through FYM + 50% N through inorganic	T_4
5.	25% N through FYM + 75% N through inorganic	T_5
6.	100% N through dried poultry manure	T_6
7.	75% N through dried poultry manure + 25% N through inorganic	T_7
8.	50% N through dried poultry manure + 50% N through inorganic	T_8
9.	25% N through dried poultry manure + 75% N through inorganic	T_9
10.	100% N through pig manure	T_{10}
11.	75% N through pig manure + 25% N through inorganic	T_{11}
12.	50% N through pig manure + 50% N through inorganic	T_{12}
13.	25% N through pig manure + 75% N through inorganic	T_{13}
14.	100% N through deep litter sheep manure	T_{14}
15.	75% N through deep litter sheep manure + 25% N through inorganic	T_{15}
16.	50% N through deep litter sheep manure + 50% N through inorganic	T_{16}
17.	25% N through deep litter sheep manure + 75% N through inorganic	T_{17}
18.	Control (No manure and fertilizer)	T_{18}

Table 55.2: Nutrient Content of the Organic Manures

Sl.No.	Source	N%	P%	K%
1.	Farm yard manure	0.50	0.30	0.42
2.	Poultry manure	0.74	0.60	0.50
3.	Pig manure	0.56	0.50	0.40
4.	Sheep manure	0.78	0.40	0.45

Results and Discussion

Growth Attributes

The results revealed that application of organic manures like pig manure, sheep manure and FYM under 100 per cent substitution level did not cause any reduction in plant population. Hundred per cent N substitution through poultry manure caused adverse significant effect that reduced the plant population to a tune of 60 hills m^{-2} instead of normal plant population of 80 hills m^{-2}. The reason attributed to the reduction in plant population in poultry manure treatment was due to high soluble salts, NH_4-N and nitrate that caused suffocation and phytotoxicity and ultimately the plant dries. The reduction in population due to excess poultry manure application was reported earlier by Weil *et al.* (1979). The ammonium content of the pig manures is not so high as in poultry manure and did not inhibit germination or establishment as found by Dahama (1996). FYM application also resulted in better seedling establishment (Singh and Rajat De, 1987). Substrate application of organic and inorganic forms of nitrogen in combination have a profound influence on the growth and yield attributes of rice. At all the stages of crop growth *viz.*, tillering, flowering and harvest, substitution of 50 per cent of chemical fertilizer N with poultry manure registered significantly highest plant height (54.0, 84.0, 96.17) (Table 55.3). The reason attributed to this is probably the organic form of nutrients, available slowly and steadily throughout the crop period as and when the crop required. Further the nutrient release pattern of the poultry manure coincides with the critical stages of crop growth. Similar results of increased plant height with application of poultry manure plus inorganic fertilizers was reported by Budhar *et al.* (1991). Tiller production was significantly highest with treatment combination of 25 per cent N through pig manure 75 per cent N as inorganic fertilizer at tillering, flowering and harvest stage (422, 644, 733). The increased tiller production might be due to the complementary nature of both the sources which are more advantageous to the rice crop. Similar response was also reported by Pandey and Tripathi (1992). LAI at flowering stage, the highest LAI (6.70) was recorded with 60 per cent N through poultry manure plus 50 per cent N through chemical fertilizer which was on par with 75 per cent N supplied through poultry manure and 25 per cent N through inorganic fertilizer (6.60). These findings was in accordance with Budhar *et al.* (1991). Similar results of increased plant growth due to poultry manure in combination with inorganic fertilizers have been reported by Abusaleha (1981) and Dhandapani (1982). The maximum DMP was recorded at all the stages of crop growth with combination of 25 per cent N as pig manure plus 75 per cent N through inorganic fertilizer (1052, 8620, 13235 kg ha^{-1}) and it was on par with substitution of 50 per cent N through pig manure and 25 per cent through poultry manure (Table 55.3). Even though the substitution of 50 per cent N as poultry manure registered higher plant height, LAI and more number of grains as individual plants, because of the lesser plant population, it produced lower level of DMP only. The increased DMP with the 25 per cent N through pig manure may be due to the increased nutrient availability and higher NPK uptake by the plants at all the stages. This findings fall in line with Juang and Chang (1992).

Yield Attributes

Regarding the combination of organic N and chemical fertilizer, the highest productive tiller production of 506 m^{-2} was recorded with the substitution of 25 per cent N through pig manure plus 75 per cent N as chemical fertilizer (T_{13}), 50 per cent N through pig manure with tiller production of 502 m^{-2} (T_{12}) was next in order and it was comparable with T_{13} (Table 55.4). Favourable influence of this combination on crop growth nutrients availability of the soil and supply and consequent increase in the photosynthates might have influenced more number of panicle m^{-2} formation. Highest panicle length (24.50 cm), number of grains panicle^{-1} (120) and test weight (19.87 g) was recorded with the substitution of 50 per cent N through poultry manure plus 50 per cent N through chemical fertilizer. Poultry manure is a rich source of micronutrients especially Zn and B which play a significant role in manipulation of plant growth by entering into the physiological and biochemical process and increased the photoassimilate production. The greater quantity of photosynthates (source) produced with the substitution of 50 per cent N as chemical fertilizer and 50 per cent N as poultry manure was evidenced by observing increased plant height, LAI which might have increased the size of the sink like panicle length, number of grains panicle^{-1} and 1000 grain weight. Similar result of increased grain panicle^{-1} due to application of poultry manure along with the fertilizers was reported by Budhar *et al.* (1991).

Table 55.3: Effect of Different Organic Manures and Fertilizer N Levels on Plant Density and Growth Attributes of Rice

Treatments	Plant Density	Plant Height (cm)			Tillers m^{-2}			LAI	DMP $kg\,ha^{-1}$)		
		T	F	H	T	F	H		T	F	H
T_1	80.0	46.90	74.85	87.90	361	542	616	5.90	906	7399	11385
T_2	79.0	32.99	57.00	74.50	277	422	480	4.32	670	5238	8676
T_3	80.0	37.60	63.09	75.99	297	451	503	4.74	745	5867	9268
T_4	80.0	40.0	67.90	80.49	326	501	569	5.10	812	6745	10358
T_5	80.0	40.23	68.80	80.60	347	528	600	5.30	829	6886	10560
T_6	60.0	49.82	78.00	89.00	342	528	600	6.19	842	6990	10719
T_7	64.5	53.45	82.30	95.50	358	549	620	6.60	905	7581	11547
T_8	70.0	54.0	84.0	96.17	378	575	654	6.70	977	8011	12320
T_9	79.0	49.24	78.10	89.73	414	629	715	6.26	1023	8438	13049
T_{10}	80.0	45.80	73.00	82.58	352	541	614	5.69	887	7326	11296
T_{11}	80.0	47.30	74.89	88.29	384	583	663	5.83	970	7924	12286
T_{12}	80.0	50.23	78.33	90.10	417	635	722	6.32	1039	8576	13235
T_{13}	80.0	50.79	81.60	94.60	422	644	733	6.57	1052	8620	13446
T_{14}	79.0	35.40	62.00	75.00	323	492	554	4.62	757	6292	9618
T_{15}	80.0	37.99	64.19	76.47	325	495	560	4.80	771	6409	9840
T_{16}	80.0	41.59	69.50	80.99	350	534	606	5.40	840	6942	10664
T_{17}	80.0	45.99	73.90	83.87	357	545	545	619	5.77	896	7574
T_{18}	80.0	30.11	53.00	71.12	256	387	440	4.02	590	4653	7626
SEd	1.47	0.89	1.48	1.57	7.10	10.8	12.2	0.11	17.5	144.4	223.2
CD (P = 0.05)	2.99	1.82	3.01	3.19	14.4	21.9	24.9	0.23	35.6	293.4	453.6

T: Tillering; F: Flowering; H: Harvest.

Table 55.4: Yield Attributes of Rice as Influenced by Different Organic Manures and Fertilizer N Level Substitution

Treatments	Productive Tillers m^{-2}	Panicle Length (cm)	Grains $Panicle^{-1}$	1000 Grain Weight
T_1	430	20.60	103.00	19.41
T_2	321	18.70	82.00	18.20
T_3	355	18.76	86.97	18.49
T_4	385	19.00	93.99	18.90
T_5	388	19.20	95.00	19.03
T_6	401	22.90	113.00	19.80
T_7	439	24.20	118.00	19.82
T_8	465	24.50	120.00	19.87
T_9	498	22.40	110.10	19.60

Contd...

Table 55.4–Contd...

Treatments	Productive Tillers m^{-2}	Panicle Length (cm)	Grains Panicle^{-1}	1000 Grain Weight
T_{10}	424	20.40	101.00	19.27
T_{11}	470	22.30	110.00	19.55
T_{12}	502	22.50	111.00	19.61
T_{13}	506	22.60	112.00	19.60
T_{14}	361	18.80	88.00	18.53
T_{15}	364	18.90	90.00	18.56
T_{16}	399	19.30	96.00	19.06
T_{17}	437	20.90	105.00	19.51
T_{18}	292	17.60	77.00	18.17
SEd	8.39	0.42	2.04	0.35
CD (P = 0.05)	17.05	0.85	4.16	0.72

References

Abusaleha, 1981. Studies on the effect of organic NS inorganic form of nitrogen on bhendi (*Abelmoschus esculentus* (L.) Moench). *M.Sc.(Ag.) Thesis*, TNAU, Coimbatore.

Budhar, M.N., Palaniappan, S.P. and Rangasamy, A., 1991. Effect of farm wastes and green manures on lowland rice. *Indian J. Agron.*, 36(2): 251–252.

Dahama, A.K., 1996. *Organic Farming for Sustainable Agriculture.* Agro-Botanical Publishers, India, Bikaner.

Dhandapani, S., 1982. Studies on the effect of organic vs. inorganic form of nitrogen on cauliflower. *M.Sc. (Ag.) Thesis*, TNAU, Coimbatore.

Juang, T.C. and Chang, Y.S., 1992. Effect of application of compost and manure on crop growth. Nitrogen uptake under rice-com rotation. *Soil Fertil.*, pp. 18–39.

Pandey, N. and Tripathi, R.S., 1992. Grain yield of lowland rice (*Oryza sativa*) as influenced by integrated use of inorganic and organic nitrogen fertilizer. *Indian J. Agron.*, 37(3): 561–562.

Singh, R.K. and Rajat De, 1987. Organic manures and fertilizer management practices for dryland wheat. *Fertil. News*, 32(7): 33–36.

Swaminathan, M.S., 1987. Inaugural address. *Proc. Symp. on Sustainable Agriculture.* The role of the green manure crops in rice farming systems, 25–29 May, IRRI, Los Banos, Philippines.

Weil, R.R., Krontje, W. and Jones, G.D., 1979. Physical condition of a Davidson Clay Loam after five years of heavy poultry manure applications. *J. Environ. Qual.*, 8: 387–392.

Chapter 56

Growth, Yield, Nutrient Uptake and Soil Fertility Status of the Succeeding Rice Crop as Influenced by the Residual Effect of Nitrogen Substitution through Livestock Wastes in the Preceding Rice Crop

S. Ramesh[1], S. Ravi[1] and B. Chandrasekaran[2]

[1]Department of Agronomy, Tamil Nadu Agricultural University, Coimbatore - 641 003, India

[2]Director of Research, Tamil Nadu Agricultural University, Coimbatore - 641 003, India

ABSTRACT

A study was undertaken at Agricultural College and Research Institute, Killikulam, Tamil Nadu to find out the technical feasibility and economic viability of inorganic N substitution through poultry manure and other livestock wastes and their effect on growth and yield of lowland rice (*Oryza sativa*) during *Kar* season (June–September) and their residual effect on the succeeding rice crop of *Pishanam* (October–January) under Thambirabarani command area. Growth and yield attributes, yield, nutrient uptake and fertility status of the succeeding *Pishanam* rice were significantly influenced by the residual effect of organic manures and fertilizers applied to the preceding rice crop. 100 per cent N substitution through pig manure in the preceding crop (*Kar* season) recorded the highest plant height of 89.95 cm, number of tillers m^{-2} (685 m^{-1}, leaf area index (5.20), dry matter production (10854 kg ha^{-1}), productive tillers m^{-2} (480 m^{-1}, panicle length (22.50 cm), grains per panicle (115.20) and grain yield (4481 kg ha^{-1}) in the succeeding crop; it was comparable with 75 per cent N application through pig manure and 25 per cent N through inorganic form. Application of full dose of N as pig manure to the (*Kar* rice) first crop registered the highest N uptake of 95.60 kg ha^{-1} in the succeeding *Pishanam* season crop and was comparable with 75 per cent N substitution with pig manure. Similarly, the organic carbon content, available N, available P and K were highest with 100 per cent N substitution through pig manure in the preceding crop and it was comparable with 75 per cent N substitution through pig manure.

Keywords: *Rice, Yield, Nutrient uptake, Livestock wastes, Residual effect.*

Introduction

Rice (*Oryza sativa* L.) is cultivated under diverse agroclimatic conditions in developing countries with the modem high yielding rice varieties contributing significantly to total food production. The response of this HYV to fertilizer was high but on the long term the sole application of inorganic fertility leads to deterioration of soil fertility and productivity. There is a wide gap between crop removal and addition of plant nutrients through fertilizers and it is expected to be about 6 metric tonnes during 2000 A.D. This gap could be made good by the application of organic manures *viz.*, poultry, piggery, sheep or goat manure (Swaminathan, 1987). India is having about 20 per cent of livestock population of the world, with a waste excretion of 4.2 metric tonnes of N, 1.2 metric tonnes of P_2O_5 and 1.95 metric tonnes of K_2O. Farm yard manure is considered as a repository of plant nutrients apart from improving the physico-chemical and biological processes of soil (Dahiya and Singh, 1980). Poultry industry in India has great importance on high monetary returns. Poultry manure is rich in plant nutrient and serves as a soil conserving material (Eno, 1966). In urban areas, recycling of piggeries waste is the only means of efficient and useful way of disposal. Pig manure is a good source of essential nutrients. The effectiveness of the pig faeces increased, when it is used in conjunction with NPK fertilizers (Udayasoorian *et al.*, 1983). Sheep manure is another organic domestically available and its application increased the yield of rice (Ramasamy, 1990). An integrated approach involving organic manures and chemical fertilizers will go a long way in building up of soil fertility on a permanent basis. Under Thambirabarani command area, rice is the major crop grown in about 1.32 lakh ha. Information on the efficacy of residual effect of different organic and inorganic sources on the succeeding rice crops is scanty and hence the present study was undertaken.

Materials and Methods

Field experiments were conducted at Agricultural College and Research Institute, Killikulam during the *Pishanam* season (October–January) to study the residual effect of substitution of inorganic fertilizer N through poultry manure and other livestock wastes in the preceding *kar* season crop (June-September) under the Thambirabarani command area. The soil of the experimental field is moderately drained, deep, sandy clay (44.9 per cent clay, 8.4 per cent silt, 31.3 per cent coarse sand and 14.2 per cent fine sand) with 6.9 pH, electrical conductivity of 0.42 dsm^{-1}. The fertility status of the soil was classified as low in available N of 250 kg ha^{-1}, medium in available P_2O_5 of 16 kg ha^{-1}, medium in available K_2O of 129 kg ha^{-1} and organic carbon of 0.69 9 kg^{-1}.

The field experiment was laid out in a randomised block design replicated thrice with various level of substitution of the inorganic N with the organic manure as per the treatment given below for the *Kar* season crop (Table 56.1).

Table 56.1: The Structure of Treatments Adopted in the Study

Sl.No.	*Treatments*	*Notations*
1.	100% N through inorganic source	T_1
2.	100% N through FYM	T_2
3.	75% N through FYM + 25% N through inorganic	T_3
4.	50% N through FYM + 50% N through inorganic	T_4
5.	25% N through FYM + 75% N through inorganic	T_5
6.	100% N through dried poultry manure	T_6
7.	75% N through dried poultry manure + 25% N through inorganic	T_7
8.	50% N through dried poultry manure + 50% N through inorganic	T_8
9.	25% N through dried poultry manure + 75% N through inorganic	T_9
10.	100% N through pig manure	T_{10}
11.	75% N through pig manure + 25% N through inorganic	T_{11}
12.	50% N through pig manure + 50% N through inorganic	T_{12}
13.	25% N through pig manure + 75% N through inorganic	T_{13}
14.	100% N through deep litter sheep manure	T_{14}
15.	75% N through deep litter sheep manure + 25% N through inorganic	T_{15}
16.	50% N through deep litter sheep manure + 50% N through inorganic	T_{16}
17.	25% N through deep litter sheep manure + 75% N through inorganic	T_{17}
18.	Control (No manure and fertilizer)	T_{18}

Recommended level of fertilizer 120 : 60 : 60 kg NPK ha^{-1} was followed for *kar* season crop. Based on the nitrogen content of the different manures, the quantity required for the different level of N substitution was calculated on dry weight basis and applied to the respective plots, one week before transplanting and incorporated well into the field. The nitrogenous fertilizer was applied in three splits at basal, tillering and panicle initiation stages. The phosphatic fertilizer was applied fully as basal and potassium fertilizer was applied in two split dose one at basal and other at panicle initiation stage. The residual crop rice was raised in the same field during *Pishanam* season one week was allowed for the decomposition of rice stubbles after incorporation. The plots were prepared by manual digging. Seedlings of ADT 39 rice were transplanted with a spacing 15 × 10 cm. Fertilizers were not applied to any of the plots. The growth and yield attributes, grain and straw yield were recorded by adopting the standard procedures. The nutrient uptake at different crop stages was calculated by multiplying percentage of nutrient content by DMP and expressed as kg ha^{-1}. Organic carbon content, available N, P and K content in post harvest soil samples were determined by standard procedures and expressed as kg ha^{-1}.

Results and Discussion

Growth and Yield Attributes

The growth and yield attributes of succeeding rice (*Pishanam*) was significantly influenced by the residual effect of organic manures and fertilizer applied to the previous crop (*Kar* season). Substitution of 100 per cent N through pig manure in *Kar* season recorded the highest plant height of 89.95 cm in the *Pishanam* season and it was followed by 75 per cent N as pig manure plus 25 per cent N as chemical fertilizer (88.20 cm) and was comparable with each other. In the residual crop highest tiller production (685 m^{-2}), LAI (5.2), DMP (10854 kg ha^{-1}) was recorded with the application of 100 per cent N as pig manure during first crop (Kar season) and it was on par with 75 per cent N application as pig manure and remaining 25 per cent N as chemical fertilizer (Table 56.2). This might be due to the increased soil fertility and residual effect of available nutrients after the first crop. The cumulative effect of increase in plant height, LAI, higher nutrient uptake leads to increase in DMP with 100 per cent N substitution as pig manure. Beneficial effect of humus contributed by the organic manures, might have favoured the optimum environment for the increased uptake of nutrient by plants as reported by Mani (1991). The increase in the source like plant height, LAI, DMP due to increased soil nutrient and higher uptake which hastened the translocation of photoassimilates to sink and ultimately increased the yield components and yield.

Table 56.2: Residual Effect of Different Organic Manures and Fertilizer N Levels on Growth and Yield Attributes of Rice

Treatments	*Harvest Stage*					
	Plant Height (cm)	*No. of Tillers m^{-2}*	*LAI*	*DMP kg ha^{-1}*	*Productive Tillers m^{-2}*	*Grains $Panicle^{-1}$*
T_1	88.20	441	4.58	7205	300	83.10
T_2	82.00	573	4.94	8600	384	99.20
T_3	82.30	542	4.97	8594	380	98.30
T_4	82.10	50	4.95	8024	352	94.00
T_5	78.30	487	4.84	7924	341	92.60
T_6	86.70	629	5.10	10077	443	108.00
T_7	85.80	611	5.07	9784	428	105.00
T_8	78.40	500	4.85	8000	345	93.00
T_9	74.30	442	4.65	7295	307	84.30
T_{10}	89.95	685	5.20	10854	480	115.20
T_{11}	88.20	664	5.15	10655	466	113.00
T_{12}	86.31	618	5.09	9903	436	106.00
T_{13}	85.73	561	4.96	8834	392	101.00
T_{14}	81.70	501	4.93	7984	348	93.20
T_{15}	78.10	494	4.83	7821	340	92.00
T_{16}	78.00	481	4.82	7739	339	91.00
T_{17}	74.60	446	4.71	7405	311	85.00
T_{18}	70.10	402	3.98	6198	267	74.00
SEd	2.04	10.79	0.09	173.16	7.55	1.95
CD (P = 0.05)	4.14	21.92	0.20	351.85	15.34	3.96

Grain Yield

Application of different organic manures and fertilizer levels to the preceding rice crop exhibited a significant residual effect on the succeeding crop (*Pishanam*) grain yield. 100 per cent N substitution through pig manure in *Kar* season crop recorded highest grain yield of 4481 kg ha^{-1} in the *Pishanam* crop and it was comparable with 75 per cent N as pig manure plus 25 per cent N as chemical fertilizer with grain yield of 4400 kg ha^{-1} (Table 56.3). The increased yield obtained in pig manure application might have resulted due to the cumulative effect of higher DMP, nutrient uptake and yield components. Similar results of increased yield due to residual effect of pig manure was reported by Maskina *et al.* (1988), Andrasi and Koposcsi (1989) and Gutser *et al.* (1987). 100 per cent N application through inorganic fertilizer in *Kar* season recorded grain yield of 2892 kg h^{-1} in the *Pishanam* season due to the poor residual effect on the inorganic fertilizer application. The reduction in yield was due to the inadequate residual nutrients available in the field. Sharma and Mittra (1989) reported that reduction in yield in the succeeding crop due to lesser residual effect of inorganic fertilizer. There was not much variation in the yield of the first crop and residual crop due to Farm Yard Manure (FYM) application. This was in confirmity with Soni and Sikarwar (1983).

Table 56.3: Grain Yield (kg ha^{-1}) and Nutrient Uptake (kg ha^{-1}) of Rice as Influenced by the Residual Effect of Organic Manures and Fertilizer N Levels

Treatments	*Grain Yield (kg ha^{-1})*	*Nutrient Uptake (kg ha^{-1})*		
T_1	2892	72.39	8.63	73.12
T_2	3500	84.04	13.26	84.58
T_3	3485	83.09	13.11	83.59
T_4	3235	79.20	12.80	80.01
T_5	3187	78.39	11.67	79.12
T_6	4150	89.20	14.31	92.14
T_7	4025	87.94	13.87	89.50
T_8	3207	78.93	12.74	79.81
T_9	2973	72.77	9.81	73.97
T_{10}	4481	95.60	15.08	98.76
T_{11}	4400	92.84	14.64	95.91
T_{12}	4075	88.40	14.19	91.43
T_{13}	3600	84.30	13.35	85.21
T_{14}	3229	79.00	12.77	77.61
T_{15}	3169	77.90	10.80	78.67
T_{16}	3133	76.97	1.23	79.74
T_{17}	2917	73.21	9.84	73.82
T_{18}	2125	67.74	7.61	69.01
SEd	71.36	1.64	0.25	1.67
CD (P = 0.05)	142.73	3.34	0.51	3.40

Nutrient Uptake

Application of different organic manures and fertilizers level to the preceding crop showed significant variation in nutrient uptake in the succeeding residual crop. The difference in nutrient uptake due to different treatment combinations ranged from 66.74 to 95.60 kg ha^{-1}. Application of full dose of N as pig manure to the *Kar* rice crop recorded the highest N (95.60 kg ha^{-1}), P (15.08 kg ha^{-1}) and K (98.76 kg ha^{-1}) uptake in the succeeding *Pishanam* season crop and it was comparable to 75 per cent N as pig manure plus 25 per cent as chemical fertilizer (Table 56.3). The increased N uptake with pig manure might have been due to the increased quantity of DMP and also higher nitrate, concentration of soil. Increased N uptake might have also influenced higher P uptake due to the positive correlation between N and P nutrients. Since pig manure contains 0.5 per cent phosphorus which further added to the soil P by 25 kg ha^{-1}. It falls in the same line of Colburn and Varco (1994). K uptake also followed the similar trend.

Soil Fertility Status

Different organic manures and fertilizers applied to the *Kar* season rice crop exhibited a significant variation in the organic carbon content of the *Pishanam* residual crop. Application of 100 per cent N application through pig manure have registered the highest organic carbon content of 0.845 per cent and it was comparable to 75 per cent N as pig manure plus 25 per cent N as chemical fertilizer with organic carbon content of 0.833 per cent (Table 56.4). 100 per cent N as pig manure application to the preceding rice crop (*Kar* season) recorded highest soil available N of 282.90 kg ha^{-1}, available P_2O_5 of 20.72 kg ha^{-1} and available K of 158.00 kg ha^{-1} and it was comparable with 75 per cent N substitution with pig manure. The organic carbon content at all the levels of substitution of inorganic N with organic manures was higher than initial organic carbon status of the soil due to the positive influence of organic matter on building up of soil fertility. This was in accordance with the report of Maskina *et al.* (1988). Even though fertilizers (or) organic manures were not applied to the *Pishanam* crop, the root biomass, stubbles and solubilization of native soil nutrients led to increase in soil N compared to initial N status of the soil. Similar trend was also noticed on the P and K content of soil. Overall residual fertility status of the residual crop sequence was considerably improved by the combination of organic manure and inorganic fertilizer.

Table 56.4: Residual Effect of Organic Manures and Fertilizer N Levels on Organic Carbon Content (%) and Postharvest Available Soil Nutrient (kg ha^{-1}) of Rice

Treatments	*Organic Carbon (%)*	*Available N kg ha^{-1}*	*Available P kg ha^{-1}*	*Available K kg ha^{-1}*
T_1	0.670	235.42	13.70	138.66
T_2	0.788	263.68	17.35	148.14
T_3	0.779	262.18	17.04	147.30
T_4	0.769	258.65	16.76	145.58
T_5	0.753	253.45	16.36	144.85
T_6	0.823	268.40	18.79	153.32
T_7	0.809	263.20	18.19	151.54
T_8	0.761	259.60	16.58	145.34
T_9	0.732	254.0	14.83	141.79
T_{10}	0.845	282.90	20.72	158.00
T_{11}	0.833	277.78	20.12	155.70
T_{12}	0.815	268.50	18.64	153.91
T_{13}	0.790	263.18	17.48	148.68
T_{14}	0.764	256.50	15.98	143.39
T_{15}	0.750	254.30	16.30	144.41
T_{16}	0.738	251.41	16.66	145.40
T_{17}	0.709	250.72	14.65	140.58
T_{18}	0.504	179.60	11.10	126.77
SEd	0.015	6.53	0.339	3.02
CD (P = 0.05)	0.03	13.28	0.69	6.14

References

Andrasi, I. and Kaposcsi, I., 1989. Field utilization of pig manure. Sertes hightragya Zantofoldi haszonositasa. *Noventermela*, 38(2): 159–168.

Coburn, S. and Varco, J.J., 1994. Effects of anaerobic swine lagoon effluent on soil extractable plant nutrients. In: *Soil Sci. Soc. Am. 58th Annual Meeting, Seattle.* 13–18th November, Washington, p. 325.

Dahiya, S.S. and Singh, R., 1980. Effect of farmyard manure and $CaCo_3$ on the dry matter, yield and nutrients uptake by oats (*Avenua sativa*). *Pl. Soil*, 56(3): 391.

Eno, C.P., 1966. Chicken manure: Its production, value preservation and disposition. *Florida Agric. Exp. Stan. Circ.*, S–140.

Gutser, R., Amberger A. and Vilsmeier, K., 1987. Effects of differently treated slurries on oats and rye grass in pot trial. In: *Abfallstoffeals Dunger. Proc. 99th VDLUFA, Congress*, September.

Mani, A.K., 1991. Effect of organic and inorganic fertilizer N on yield of rainfed ragi. *Madras Agric. J.*, 78(5–8): 210–212.

Maskina, M.S., Singh, Y. and Singh, B., 1988. Response of wetland rice to fertilizer N in a soil amended with cattle, poultry and pig manures. *Biol. Wastes*, 26: 1–8.

Ramasamy, A., 1990. Yield maximization in lowland transplanted rice through nitrogen integrated use of organic manures and fertilizer N under varying plant density. *Unpub. M.Sc. (Ag.) Thesis*, Tamil Nadu Agric. Univ., Coimbatore, India.

Sharma, A.R. and Mittra, B.N., 1989. Effect of N and P on rice and their residual effect on succeeding wheat/gram crop. *Indian J. Agron.*, 34(1): 40–44.

Soni, P.N. and Sikarwar, H.S., 1983. Nitrogen substitution with farmyard manure in rice-wheat sequence. *Indian J. Agron.*, 28(4): 392–396.

Swaminathan, M.S., 1987. Inaugural address. In: *Proc. Symp. Sustainable Agriculture: The Role of the Green Manure Crops in Rice Farming Systems*, 25–29th, May, IRRI, Los Banos, Philippines.

Udayasoorian, C., Krishnamoorthy, K.K. and Sree Ramulu, U.S., 1983. Utilization of livestock wastes in agriculture. In: *Proc. Nat. Sem. Utilization of Organic Wastes*, 24–25th, March, Tamil Nadu Agricultural University, Madurai, India, pp. 211–218.

Chapter 57

Agrometeorological Assessment and Amelioration of Rural Food Security

S. Venkataraman*

Retired Director, India Met. Department and Former WMO/FAO Agromet Expert
59/19, Nav Sahyadri Society, Pune - 411 052

ABSTRACT

Food security is defined various forms and facets of food security are outlined. Importance of micro-level food security for the farm labourer is stressed. Apparent nature of food security base on available current data is brought out. A method for agrometeorologically assessing contribution of dryland production to food security is proposed. Agroclimatic analyses for assessing potential food security and steps for enhancing current levels of rural food security are indicated.

Keywords: *Urban, Rural, National, Regional and Micro level, Apparent and Potential food securities, Enhancement, Optimal use local resources.*

Introduction

Following Swaminathan and Medrano (2004), "Food Security " may be defined as availability of adequate amounts of staple food grains and protein-rich protective foods, like oilseeds and pulses, at prices that are economically worthwhile for the farmer and also affordable by the empowered earnings

* E-mail: svr@sridhar-v.com.

of the unorganized, weaker sections of the populace, like the landless farm labourer. There are national, regional and local food securities. Urban food security will involve collection of food grain surpluses from farmers at prices not lower than Minimal Support Price, MSP and storage and movement of food stocks at low costs and with minimal losses. Food security for rural populace would ideally require maximal local availability of required amount of staple food grains and protective foods. For food grains, oilseeds and pulses there are strongly ingrained local preferences for specific crops. From the climatic point of view the required staple food grains can be grown ubiquitously, with some subsidisation if necessary, to ensure local availability. However, in the case of pulses and oilseeds, raising locally preferred crop may either not be possible or worthwhile. The above have to be kept in view in planning sustainable food security.

Facets of Food Security

In national food security shortfalls in Kharif crop production can be made good from irrigated areas in the rabi season. Shortfalls, if still persisting, can be made up from limited use of irrigated areas in the summer season. There is a difference in making good the shortfalls of a particular crop through increased production of (*i*) the same crop and (*ii*) of other substitute crops across seasons and areas. Besides local unpreparedness, as mentioned above, substitution of locally preferred pulses and oilseeds by others pose problems of storage and movement of substitute produce to the consuming populace. In regional food security losses in crop production from dryland areas and irrigated areas due to rainfall and temperature vagaries respectively can be made good from other areas in which the crop has realized good rains and ideal temperature regimes. National and regional food securities, even if achieved, do not alleviate the hardships of the farmers and the farm labourers in the affected regions. Crop insurance can take care of the hardships of affected farmers. Relief works to provide non-farm employment to enhance the purchasing power of the landless labourer have to be organized on a micro-level basis.

Thus food security has many distinct features that need to be addressed. In this one has to differentiate apparent food security from potential food security and look into optimal use of local resources for ensuring enhancement and sustainability of micro-level food security. The above aspects are dealt with below.

Apparent Food Security

Unit area crop yields can be related to the duration of occupancy of the field by them (Swaminathan, 1968; Venkataraman and Muchinda, 1988). Water is the major factor in duration of field occupancy by crops. The quantum of water locally available as irrigation, rainfall and groundwater for raising crops in relation to that required to ensure adequate availability of staple food and protective crops is an important factor in assessment of local food security. The amount of gross irrigated acreage under surface and groundwater irrigation is a measure of prevalent food security. In any region considerable areas are rain-dependant for crop culture. A measure of contribution from dryland areas towards overall local food security is necessary. Rainfall over short periods of time shows extremely high inter-yearly variations at a place. Therefore, to assess contributions from dryland areas towards local food security it is first of all necessary to delineate homogenous rainfall zones in the dry farming tract (Venkataraman, 2001). Then in each zone at representative stations, from analyses of actually realized rainfall over a long series of years, the percentage frequencies of occurrence of various durations of crop-life durations, in terms of weeks have to be determined (Venkataraman, 2003). Once this is done, the ratio of (*i*) sums of products of the frequency percentage and crop-life duration in weeks associated with it to (*ii*) 52 times the sum of the frequency percentages can give a measure of the fraction of the year that can be considered as productive for dryland cropping. Multiplying the dryland acreage by the above fraction will give the productive dryland acreage, which can then be added to the gross irrigated acreage. The ratio of gross productive acreage to the total arable area will give a measure of apparent food security.

Potential Food Security

The term Apparent Food Security has been used in the preceding paragraph since it is assumed that (*a*) the gross irrigated acreage is the result of optimal use of both surface irrigation and groundwater and (*b*) gross dryland production is the maximum possible under the rainfall vagaries. However, (*i*) crops are generally over-irrigated (*ii*) groundwater is mostly used for raising non food security crops in the high water duty periods and (*iii*) differences in yields on farmers' fields with those at nearby research stations has been reported to be widening with increase in rainfall (Sivakumar *et al.*, 1983). The problems related to the above need to be addressed to assess and/or realise potential food security.

Efficient Use of Water Resources

For any given location it is agroclimatically possible to (*i*) select food security crops and their sequencing suited to local climate and (*ii*) to determine the possible gross irrigated acreage for a given quantity of irrigation water. The two will maximize local gross production of food security crops under surface irrigation. Strategic use of groundwater for critical irrigations for (*i*) saving rainfed food security crops during droughts and (*ii*) extending the maturity periods of irrigated food security crops will maximize food security and limiting such strategic use to average annual recharge of groundwater reserves by rainfall will help conserve groundwater and help sustain food security. In the case of rainfed crops (*a*) collection of surface runoff from rains, prevention of evaporative depletion from such water storages and re-use of the rainfall water to combat drought situations (*b*) dissemination of technology available at a research station for (*i*) coping with inadequate rains and (*ii*) maximizing benefits from good rains to dryland farmers in neighboring areas and (*c*) provision of medium range crop-weather based agronomic advisories will help to considerably lessen the prevalent uncertainties in dryland crop production and help augment local food security.

Suggestions for Enhancement of Micro-level Food Security

The state departments of agricultural statistics should undertake collection of basic data required for assessment of micro-level, rural, apparent food security. The state departments of agricultural extension should ensure transfer of weather oriented agronomic technology for irrigated and rainfed crops available at a research stations to farmers in neighbouring areas for real time use. The Agrimet divisoins of State Agricultural Universities must carry out agroclimatic analyses for upgrading apparent food security to potential food security, principally through optimal and conjunctive use of locally available water resources. Last but not the least state and central governments should legislate to facilitate management of land and water resources on a watershed basis though a confederation of agricultural land cooperative societies.

References

Sivakumar, M.V.K., Singh, P. and Williams, J.H., 1983. In: *Alfisols in the Semi Arid Tropics*. A Consultants' Workshop, ICRISAT, Hyderabad, pp. 15–30.

Swaminathan, M.S., 1968. Genetic Manipulation of Productivity Per Day. Special Lecture, *ICAR Symposium on Cropping Patterns in India*.

Swaminathan, M.S. and Medarano, P., 2004. *Towards a Food Secure India: A Call for Policy Initiatives and Public Action*. Publication M.S. Swaminathan Research Foundation and World Food Programme of FAO, pp. ii to iv.

Venkataraman, S., 2001. A simple and rational agroclimatic method for rainfall zonation in dryland areas. *Ind. J. Environ. and Ecoplan.*, 5: 135–144.

Venkataraman, S., 2003. Agrometeorological aspects and assessment of proneness to crop droughts. *J. Curr. Sci.*, 3: 301–304.

Venkataraman, S. and Muchinda, M.R., 1988. Influence of temperature and moisture on maturation periods of rainfed maize. *Productive Farming*, September issue, p. 20–25.

Chapter 58

Natural Enemies of *Helicoverpa armigera* (Hubn.) on Pigeon Pea from Western Maharashtra

T.V. Sathe and T.M. Chougale

Department of Zoology, Shivaji University, Kolhapur – 416 004, India

ABSTRACT

Helicoverpa armigera (Hubn.) is polyphagous pest of agricultural crops. It causes severe damage to pigeon pea *Cajanus cajan* (Millusp). Hence, natural enemies of this pest have been studied with respect to their biodiversity, occurrence and mortalities in pest.

Keywords: Grampod borer, Natural enemies, Pigeon pea, Western Maharashtra.

Introduction

Helicoverpa armigera (Hubn.) is polyphagous pest of agricultural crops, causing considerable damage to more than 180 host plants. It is very difficult to control with pesticides since it has developed resistance to several traditional pesticides like endosulphan, pyrethroids etc. (Jayaraj, 1988). Hence, natural control/biological control would worth for pesticidal use. Secondly, the pesticides cause many serious problems like air and water pollution, health hazards, killing of beneficial organisms, pest resurgence, secondary pest-out-break, etc. From Western Maharashtra, very little attention is paid on natural enemies of *Helicoverpa armigera*. Sathe (1986, 1992), Sathe *et al.* (1986,87), Sathe *et al.* (2003) etc. have reported some natural enemies of pests from Kolhapur district of Maharashtra.

Materials and Methods

A weekly survey and collection of natural enemies of *H. armigera* were made from the fields of pigeon pea from Western Maharashtra, specially Kolhapur, Sangli, Satara and Pune districts during the years 2003–2006. During the course of studies, extensive collection of *H. armigera* eggs, larvae, pupae and adults have been made to screen the insect parasitoids.

The collected material was reared on pigeon pea pods in laboratory for parasitoid emergence. Similarly, record of predators was also made by observing predators feeding on *H. armigera*. Such predators were collected from the field and later identified. Observations were also made on occurrence of natural enemies of *H. armigera* on pigeon pea crop in Western Maharashtra.

Results and Discussion

The survey study revealed that a very large number of insect parasitoids and predators were found attacking various stages of *H. armigera* (Table 58.1).

Table 58.1: List of Natural Enemies of *H. armigera* from Western Maharashtra

Sl.No.	*Name*	*Stage Attacked*	*Occurrence*
(A)	**Parasitoids**		
1.	*Campoletis chlorideae* Uchida	Larva	November–February
2.	*Charops adita*	Larva	November–December
3.	*Apanteles* sp.	Larva	November–January
4.	*A. ruficrus*	Larva	November–January
5.	*Trichogramma minutum*	Egg	October–February
6.	*Ecthromorpha* sp.	Pupal	November–January
7.	*Enicospilus* sp.	Larva	November–January
8.	*Bracon* sp.	Larva	November–January
9.	*Diagdegma fenestralis*	Larva	September–February
10.	*Eriborus trochanteratus*	Larva	September–January
11.	*Tachinid* fly	Larva	October–December
(B)	**Predators**		
1.	*Monochilus sexmaculatus*	Egg + Larva	September–February
2.	*Scymnus* sp.	Egg + Larva	December–January
3.	*Chrysopa carnea*	Egg. + Larva	December–January
4.	*Praying mantid*	Egg + Larva	August–February
5.	*Coccinella* sp.	Egg	December–January
6.	Pentatomid bug	Larva	August–January
(C)	**Vertebrate**		
1.	Crows		
	Corvus splendens	Larva	October–January
	C. macrorhynchos	Larva	September–February
2.	Squirrels		
	Funambulus palmarum	Larva	September–February

H. armigera is commonly known as grampod borer and recorded from several states of India, namely Andhra Pradesh, Bihar, Assam, Punjab, Haryana, Uttar Pradesh, Himachal Pradesh, Madhya

Pradesh, Rajasthan, Orissa, Karnataka, Tamil Nadu, West Bengal and Maharashtra etc. It causes severe damage to pigeon pea and other pulse crops in Western Maharashtra. The parasitoid *Compoletis chlorideae* and *Trichogramma* spp. have great potential in causing mortalities in larvae and eggs of pest respectively. The dipterous Tachinid fly attack older instars and is potential natural enemy of *H. armigera*. *C. chlorideae* attack second instars while Tachinids attacked 4th instar onwards. *C. chlorideae* parasitised, maximum, 52 per cent, *Apanteles ruficrus* attacked about 7–10 per cent pest larvae, *Enicosopilus* sp. 5 per cent larvae. While *Trichogramma sp.* parasitised 20–40 per cent of eggs of *H. armigera*. *D. fenestralis* caused about 13 per cent parasitism in the fields. While *Eriborus trochanteratus* caused 7–10 per cent mortality in 3rd and 4th instars of *H. armigera* by parasitism. In general, the above natural enemies have good impact on suppression of population of *H. armigera* in Western Maharashtra.

The predators namely *Menochilus* sp., *Chrysopa* were found potential, on egg and 1st instar stage. Likely, crows, *C. splendens* were found quite potential in causing moralalities in 3rd and 4th instar larvae of *H. armigera* and caused higher mortalities. Other predatory species were less effective on pigeon pea agroecosystems.

Acknowledgement

Authors are thankful to DST, New Delhi, for financial assistance and sanction of research project SP/SO/C–07–99, Dt. 19.12.2002.

References

Jayaraj, S., Uthamasamy, S., M. Gopalan, R.J. Rabindra, 1990. *Heliothis Management*, pp. 1–328.

Townes, H., Townes, M. and Gupta, V.K., 1961. *Mem. Amar. Ent. Inst.*, 1: 1–572.

Sathe, T.V., 1986. New records of natural enemies of *Exelastis atomosa* Walsingham, a pigeon pea pest in Kolhapur, India. *Oikoassay*, 3(1): 17.

Sathe, T.V., 1992. Natural enemies of some insect pests of economic importance. *Oikoassay*, 9: 15–17.

Sathe, T.V., Gosavi, N.B. and Devgire, Q.V., 1986. Parasitic complex associated with *Chapra mathais* Fab. (Lep.: Hesperiidae), a paddy pest in Kolhapur. *Geobios New Report*, 5: 59–60.

Sathe, T.V., Santhakumar M.V., Salve, U. and Ingawale, D.M., 1987. New record of natural enemies of *Spodoptera exigua* (Hubn.) in Kolhapur, India. *Oikoassay*, 4(1): 21–22.

Sathe, T.V., S.A. Inamdar and R.K. Dawale, 2003. *Indian Pest Parasitoids*. DPH, New Delhi, pp. 1–145.

Chatper 59

Effect of BGA and Sea Weed Extract (Plant Growth Stimulant) and Fertilizer on Yield of Mungbean (*Vigna radiata*) Variety Vaibhav

D.D. Dudhade and B.M. Jamadagni

Pulses Improvement Project, Mahatma Phule Krishi Vidyapeeth, Rahuri - 413 722 (India)

ABSTRACT

In absence of any fertilizer treatments the foliar sprays of Bio force increased the yield significantly. The efficacy of foliar sprays was increased in presence of the fertilizer application at sowing. Three sprays (15, 30 and 45 DAS) of Bio-Force were most effective giving the average 1563 kg /ha of seed yield irrespective of the fertilizer levels. Ttte fertilizers also had their own effect in absence of Bio-Force.

Keywords: *Mungbean, Foliar sprays.*

Introduction

Low and variable seed yield is a major problem limiting the production and rapid expansion of grain legumes including mungbean in tropics. The serious problems of flower drop and poor pod setting which limited crop yield in mungbean has not yet solved. Some growth substances are being increasingly employed as an aid to enhance yield. (Brenner, 1987 and Setia *et al.*, 1991). Use of certain plant growth regulators was found to be successful in some crops to over come such constraints by increasing photosynthetic efficiency, prevent senescence (McLaren, 1982). Hence, an experiment was conducted to study the effect of Bio-Force (Plant growth stimulant) on yield of Mungbean [*Vigna radiata* (L.) Wilczek] variety vaibhav.

Materials and Methods

The field experiment was conducted in Strip Plot Design with three replications. The horizontal treatments were three levels of fertilizer *viz.*, (*i*) Control, (*ii*) RD (20 kg N + 40 kg P_2O_5/ha), (*iii*) RD + 60 kg K_2O/ha. In vertical strips four treatments of foliar application of BGA (Blue Green Algae and Sea Weed) extract were allotted. They were *viz.*, (*i*) Control, (*ii*) 2 spray Preflowering (20 DAS) and poding (45 DAS), (*iii*) 3 sprays (15, 30 and 45 DAS) and (*iv*) 4 sprays (15, 30, 45 and 60 DAS). The gross and net plot size were 4.0 × 3.0 m and 3.80 × 2.40 m. The fertilizers were given as per the treatments below the seed rows which was 30 cm apart at sowing. Each treatment was replicated thrice. The sowing was done on 6 July 2002 and harvested on 17 September 2002. For foliar sprays of Bio-Force, received from Nirmal Seed Pvt., Ltd. Pachora – 424 201, was used for testing. The rate of application was 1 ml flit of water at each spray.

Result and Discussion

The data on seed yield (kg /ha) of Vaibhav Mung under the treatments of foliar sprays of Bio-Force in presence of different fertilizer treatments are given in Table 59.1.

Table 59.1: Effect of Bio-Force on Seed Yield (kg/ha) of Mungbean Variety Vaibhav Under Different Fertilizer Treatments

Bio-Force Spray	*Fertilizer Yield (kg /ha)*			*Mean Yield (kg/ha)*
	Absolute Control	*RD N : P 20 : 40*	*RD + K_2O N : P : K 20 : 40 : 60*	
Control	884	1127	1161	1057
2 Sprays (20 and 40 DAS)	1258	1393	1523	1391
3 Sprays (15, 30 and 45 DAS)	1427	1404	1859	1563
4 Sprays (15, 30, 45 and 60 DAS)	1360	1486	1597	1481
Mean	**1232**	**1353**	**1535**	

	Bio-Force	*Fertilizer*	*Interactions*	
			Bio-Force at the Same Level of Fertilizer	*Fertilizer at the Level of Bio-Force*
SE ±	72	42	127	125
C.D. at 5%	249	165	NS	NS

It is revealed that in absence of any fertilizer treatments the foliar sprays of Bio-Force increased the seed yield significantly. Under absolute control, the grain yield was 884 kg /ha. With 2 sprays of Bio-Force *i.e.* at 20 and 45 DAS, the yield increased to 1258 kg /ha and it reached the maximum of 1427 kg /ha with 3 sprays *i.e.* at 15,30 and 45 DAS. Patel *et al.* (1997) have reported the enhancement in yield mungbean by foliar sprays of Kinetin (KIN) 10^{-6} M. Foliar spray of PGR stimulated and efficiency of developing sink (seed) to utilize more photo assimilates and this mobilization towards sink resulting in increased final yield (Brenner, 1987). The treatments of 4 sprays did not show increase in yield over that of 3 sprays. The efficacy of foliar sprays was increased in presence of the fertilizer application at sowing. Two foliar sprays of Bio-Force (20 and 45 DAS respectively) given to the crop nourished with RD gave the yield levels of 1393 kg /ha. The combination of 3 sprays of Bio-Force and a fertilizer dose of (20 kg N + 40 kg P_2O_5 + K_2O/ha) exhibited the highest level of grain yield (1859 kg /ha). Thus, the effect of Bio-Force was amplified by in presence of the NPI fertilizer. In general, 3 sprays of Bio-Force were most effective giving the average 1563 kg /ha of seed yield irrespective of the fertilizer levels. The fertilizers also had their own effect in absence of Bio-Force.

The above study indicated that, it is essential to apply a fertilizer dose of NPK @ 20 : 40 : 60 kg /ha for obtaining satisfactory levels of yield. Further, the efficacy of fertilizers is increased by application of Bio-Force at 15, 30 and 45 DAS.

References

Brenner, M.L., 1987. *Martinus Nijhofj; Dordrecht*, pp. 475–493.

McLaren, J.S., 1982. *Chemical Manipulation of Crop Growth and Development*. Butterworths, London, p. 4–1.

Patel, *et al.*, 1997. *Indian J. Pulses Res.*, 10 (1): 78–80.

Setia, R.C. *et al.*, 1991. *Recent Advances in Plant Biology*, (Eds.) Malik, C.P. and Abrol, Y.P. Narendra Publishers, New Delhi, pp. 17–75.

Chapter 60

Effect of Phosphorus and Seed Rate on the Yield of Bold Seeded Kabuli Chickpea

D.D. Dudhade and B.M. Jamadgni

Pulses Improvement Project, Mahatma Phule Krishi Vidyapeeth, Rahuri – 413 722, India

ABSTRACT

A field experiment was conducted to find out suitable seed rate and optimum dose of phosphorus for kabuli chickpea. There was significant linear increase in grain yield with seed rate in kabuli seed KAK-2. The seed rate 125 kg/ha exhibited 1907 kg/ha which was 39.5 per cent more than that under 75 kg seed rate /ha. The crop responded significantly to phosphorus levels with higher grain yield 1875 kg/ha under 60 kg P_2O_5/ha.

Keywords: Seed rate, Phosphorus, Kabuli seed, B : C ratio.

Introduction

Chickpea (*Cicer arietinum* L.) is traditionally grown under rainfed condition; however response to fertilizer application is also reported under rainfed condition (Raghu and Choudhary, 1983.) One of the ways of increasing the yield is by means of balanced fertilizer application of chickpea. Legumes are normally heavy feeders on phosphorus. Phosphorus application in chickpea promotes root growth, nodulation, nitrogen fixation, photosynthesis, improves grain quality and enhance yield. (Chaudhary *et al.*, 1974). The root growth as well as plant development may differ in new plant types of gram cultivars. Efficiency of phosphorus utilization may differ under different seed rates and phosphorus levels. No information is available on the behaviour of recently developed kabuli chickpea to phosphorus and seed rate in Maharashtra. The present experiment was therefore undertaken to study the effect of phosphorus and seed rate on the growth and yield of bold seeded kabuli chickpea.

Materials and Methods

A field experiment was conducted at Pulses Improvement Project, of Mahatma Phule Krishi Vidyapeeth Rahuri Dist. Ahmednagar in *rabi* seasons of 2000–01 to 2002–03, to find out a suitable seed rate and phosphorus level for kabuli chickpea. The nine treatment combinations comprised of three seed rates *viz.*, 75, 100 and 125 kg/ha and three levels of phosphorus *i.e.*, 0, 30 and 60 kg ha^{-1} in a Factorial Randomized Block Design with four replications. The experimental plot had medium black soil (available nitrogen 257 kg /ha, available phosphorus 14.7 kg/ha and available potash 750 kg/ha). A basal dose of 25 kg N kg/ha and phosphorus as per treatment in the form of urea and single super phosphate was applied at the time of sowing. The gross and net plot size were 4.0 × 3.0 m and 3.80 × 2.40 m. Crop was sown in rows 30 cm apart on 6, 12 November and 7 October in 2000, 2001 and 2002 respectively. The crop was harvested on 15 February, 1 March and 3 February in 2001, 2002 and 2003.

Results and Discussion

From the pooled data in Table 60.1, it is revealed that there was significant linear increase in grain yield with seed rate in kabuli seed KAK-2. The seed rate 125 kg/ha exhibited 1907 kg /ha which was 39.5 per cent more than that under 75 kg seed rate/ha. Higher yield due to higher seed rate was mainly because of higher plant population. Similar results have been reported by Singh and Yadav (1985) who recorded higher grain yield at higher seed rate of 100 kg/ha.

Table 60.1: Seed Yield of Kabuli Chickpea KAK-2 of Different Seed Rates, Phosphorus Levels and its Cost of Cultivation (Data pooled over three years)

Treatments	Yield kg/ha			Pooled Mean (kg/ha)	% Yield increase Over Control	Cost of Cultivation (Rs/ha)	Gross Returns (Rs/ha)	Net Return (Rs/ha)	B : C Ratio
	2000–2001	2001–2002	2002–2003						
(A) **Seed rate**									
75 kg/ha	1721	1202	1181	1368	–	11534	34200	22666	2.96
100 kg/ha	2039	1415	1412	1622	18.6	13823	40550	26727	2.93
125 kg/ha	2218	1696	1808	1907	39.5	14879	45200	30321	3.03
SE ±	42	58	56	33					
CD at 5%	120	170	163	93					
(B) **Phosphorus levels**									
0 kg P_2O_5/ha	1809	1257	1090	1385		12855	34625	21770	2.69
30 kg P_2O_5/ha	1992	1369	1550	1637	18.1	13501	40925	27424	3.03
60 kg P_2O_5/ha	2178	1687	1759	1875	35.3	14146	46875	32729	3.31
SE ±	42	58	56	33					
CD at 5%	120	170	163	93					
Interaction A × B									
SE ±	71	101	97	57					
CD at 5%	NS	NS	NS	NS					
CV%	7.17	14.06	13.22	12.15					

Market rate of grain: Rs. 2500/q.

The crop responded significantly to phosphorus levels with higher grain yield 1875 kg/ha under 60 kg P_2O_5/ha. The increase in grain yield of kabuli chickpea with P was due to better and efficient nodulation, which might have resulted in increased assimilation of nitrogen by kabuli chickpea and thus recorded higher number of pods/plant with bolder seeds. This ultimately resulted in higher grain yield, as also reported by Singh and Yadav (1985).

The interaction was not significant (Table 60.2.), however economic analysis revealed that the kabuli chickpea KAK-2 when sown with 125. kg seed rate by giving 60 kg P_2O_5 along with 25 kg N/ha is most remunerative as it gave 93.60 per cent higher yield over 75 kg seed rate and 0 kg P_2O_5 /ha. This combination exhibited highest net returns (Rs. 40712 /ha) and with B : C ratio 3.80.

Table 60.2: (Interaction Table) Seed Yield of Kabuli Chickpea KAK-2 of Different Seed Rates, Phosphorus Levels and its Cost of Cultivation (Data pooled over three years)

Sl.No.	*Treatments* *Seed rate +* *P_2O_5 kg/ha*	*Pooled Mean (kg/ha)*	*% Yield Increase Over Control*	*Cost of Cultivation (Rs/ha)*	*Gross Returns (Rs/ha)*	*Net Return (Rs/ha)*	*B : C Ratio*
1.	75 + 0 kg/ha	1141	–	12195	28525	16330	2.33
2.	75 + 30 kg/ha	1371	20.15	12518	34275	21757	2.73
3.	75 + 60 kg/ha	1592	39.52	12840	39800	26960	3.09
4.	100 + 0 kg/ha	1411	23.66	13339	35275	21936	2.64
5.	100 + 30 kg/ha	1632	43.03	13662	41550	21636	3.04
6.	100 + 60 kg/ha	1823	59.77	13995	45575	31580	3.25
7.	125 + 0 kg/ha	1605	40.66	13867	40125	26258	2.89
8.	125 + 30 kg/ha	1909	67.30	14190	47725	33535	3.36
9.	125 + 60 kg/ha	2209	93.60	14513	55225	40712	3.80
	SE ±	57					
	CD at 5%	NS					
	CV%	12.15					

Market rate of grain: Rs. 2500/q.

On the basis of above results, it is concluded that the cultivation of chickpea by using 125 kg seed rate and 60 kg P_2O_5/ha with basal dose is remunerative.

References

Chaudhary, S.L., S. Ram and G. Giri, 1974. *Indian J. of Agron.*, 19(4): 274–276.

Raghu, J.S. and S.D. Choubey, 1983. *Indian J. of Agron.*, 28: 239–242.

Singh, S.C. and D.S. Yadav, 1985. *Indian J. of Agron.*, 30(4): 414–416.

Chapter 61

Plankton Diversity in Riverine Ecosystem of South Assam and Tripura

Dilip Nath and D.C. Ray*

Department of Ecology and Environmental Science, Assam University, Silchar – 788 011

ABSTRACT

Plankton diversity in four river bodies of South Assam and Tripura was undertaken during September, 2004 to August, 2005. Out of four riverine ecosystems 25 plankton species were recorded *Spirogyra* sp. showed highest per cent occurrence followed by *Oscillatoria* sp. in river Deo. Simpson's diversity index (λ) was found to be moderate in river Deo and lowest in river Jatinga. Sorensen coefficient indicated highest similarity between Baleshwar and Jatinga rivers (0.64) followed by river Dhaleshwari and river Jatinga.

***Keywords**: Plankton, Diversity, Similarity and Dissimilarity.*

Introduction

Plankton are economically and ecologically important group of aquatic organisms. They play a key role in the primary and secondary productivity. Phytoplankton a chlorophyll-bearing organism responsible for the primary production in the fresh water zones and for biogenic oxygen of the water during day time. Otherwise a number of non-insect animal species have plankotonic life stages (Davis *et al.*, 1996). Diversity indicates the degree of complexity of community structure. It is a function of number of species (richness) and the abundance. Diversity has often been related to environmental characteristics of water masses and the energy within the community.

* Corresponding Author: E-mail: raydulal@yahoo.co.in.

Ecological statistics includes numerous quantitative methodologies for analyzing the in the biotic communities. Several workers have used diversity indices (Madupratap *et al.*, 1981; Goswdlni and Goswami, 1990; Gajbhiye *et al.*, 1991; Terdalker and Pai, 2001; Lande, 2004), similarities (Sharma, 2000) and relationship between phyto and zooplankton (Hosrnani, 2002).

Keeping the above statement in view the present study has been carried out for the assessment of plankton population diversity collected from four river stations of South Assam and Tripura.

Materials and Methods

Plankton samples were collected by using Haron tentor plankton net (200μ mesh size) from 0–6 metres water column. Specimens were preserved immediately in 5 per cent Formalin solution and identified followed by standard methods (Edmondson, 1959; Koste, 1978; Hosmani and Bharari, 1980; Michael and Sharma, 1988). Species diversity (Simpson's index) and similarity and dissimilarity (Sorensen coefficient) was conducted.

Table 61.1: The Occurrence of Plankton in Four Riverine System

Plankton	*Rivers*			
Genus/Species	*Deo*	*Dhaleshwari*	*Baleshwar*	*Jatinga*
Anaboena	−	+	+	+
Nostoc sp.	−	−	+	+
Oscillatoria sp.	+	−	−	−
Microcystis sp.	−	+	+	+
Chlorella sp.	−	+	−	+
Ankistrodesmus sp.	+	+	+	+
Spirogyra sp.	+	−	+	−
Cosmerium sp.	−	−	+	−
Pinnularia sp.	+	−	+	+
Diatoma sp.	+	−	+	−
Phytodeptmus annae	+	−	−	−
Diaptomus sp.	−	+	−	−
Camptocercus sp.	−	+	−	−
Arcella sp.	−	−	+	+
Difflugia sp.	−	−	−	+
Paramoecium sp.	+	−	−	−
Volvox sp.	−	+	+	+
Brachionus sp	−	−	+	+
Fillinia sp.	−	−	+	+
Daphnia sp.	−	−	−	+
Simocephalus sp.	−	−	+	−
Bosminia sp.	−	−	+	+
Alona sp.	−	−	+	+
Cyclops sp.	−	−	+	−
Moina sp.	−	−	−	+

Results and Discussion

Collected data were presented in Table 61.1. Regarding the occurrence of plankton the maximum was recorded as *Spirogyra* sp. (35.17 per cent) only from river Baleshwar and minimum (0.38 per cent) from river Deo. The second dominating group (7.72 per cent) was recorded as *Oscillatoria* sp. which was found only in river Deo (Tripura). *Ankistrodesmus* sp. only the plankton which was commonly found in all study sites which attains a third dominating group (5.01 per cent) in river Baleshwar. As regards the Simpson's diversity index of plankton it was highest (0.42) in river Deo followed by river Baleshwar (0.37). The least index showed in river Jatinga (0.10) (Table 61.2). Although species richness was higher in river Jatinga but it showed less diversity index.

Table 61.2: Simpson's Diversity Index (λ)

River	Diversity
Deo	0.42
Dhaleshwari	0.27
Baleshwar	0.37
Jatinga	0.10

Sorensen cofficient indicated highest similarity (0.64) between Baleshwar and Jatinga rivers followed by Dhaleshwari and Jatinga rivers (0.50 per cent). Least similarity (0.15) was noticed between river Deo and river Dhaleshwari (Table 61.3).

It is observed that river Deo constitutes mainly phytoplankton. This may be due to the absence of zooplankton, but this observation disagrees with Lefevre (1942) who found difference among 20 different species of algae in their ability to support contaminated growth of *Daphnia* cultures and part of the differences seemed to be the digestibility.

Table 61.3: Sorensen Similarity Index (Cs)

River	Similarity	Dissimilarity
Deo vs. Dhaleshwari	0.15	0.85
Deo vs. Baleshwar	0.33	0.67
Deo vs. Jatinga	0.19	0.81
Dhaleshwari vs. Baleshwar	0.34	0.66
Dhaleshwari vs. Jatinga	0.50	0.50
Baleshwar vs. Jatinga	0.64	0.36

In case of river Baleshwar and river Jatinga Copepodes are present and phytoplankton are abundant which disagrees the finding of Hosmani (2002). Occurrence of *Ankistrodesmus* sp. recorded from all the river system which is a single species corroborates the findings of George (1961) and Pennak (1963) who observed the occurrence of different species of same genus at a time but disagrees the finding of Hosmani (2002).

Plankton diversity highest recorded from Deo river which belongs to Tripura a separate state. It may be due to less anthropogenic activity which it shows less diversity compared to other three rivers which belongs to southern part of Assam. Similarity of plankton communities is highest between Baleshwar and Jatinga rivers may be the close proximity of point of source.

References

Davis, C.S., Ashijan, C.J. and Alantalo, P., 1996. Zooplankton diversity. Ocenus. Reports on Research from Woods Hole Ocenographic Institution, 39: 7–8.

Edmondson, W.T., 1959. *Freshwater Biology*, 2nd Ed. Wiley and Sons, New York, pp. 1248.

Gajbhiye, S.N., Stephen, R., Nair, V.R. and Desai, B.N., 1991. Copepodes of the near shore waters of Bombay. *Indian J. Marine Science*, 20: 187–194.

George, M.G., 1961. Diurnal variations in two aballow ponds in Delhi, India. *Hydrobiologia*, 18: 265–273.

Goswami, S.C. and Goswami, U., 1990. Diel variation in Minicoy Lagoon and Kavaratti Atoll (Lakshadweep Islands). *Indian J. Marine Science*, 19: 120–125.

Hosmani, S.P., 2002. Phytoplankton-zooplankton relationship in four freshwater bodies of Dharwar. *Ind. J. Env. and Ecoplan.*, 6(1): 23–28.

Hosmani, S.P. and Bharati, S.G., 1980. Limnological studies in ponds and lakes in Dharwar. Comparative phytoplankton ecology of four water bodies. *Phykos*, 19: 27–43

Koste, W., 1978. *Rotaria*. Gebruder Borntaeger, Berlin, Stuttgart, pp. 234.

Lande, V.W., 2004. Zooplankton assessment in the coastal waters of Kakinada and Mumbai. *Indian J. Env. and Ecoplan.*, 8(1): 75–80.

Lefevre, M., 1942. L'utilization des algues dicandouce par les cledoceros. *Bull. Biol. Fr. Blog.*, 76: 250–276.

Madhupratap, M., Sreekumaran, S.R., Nair, C.T.A. and Nair, V.R., 1981. Major crustacean groups and zooplankton diversity around Andaman-Nicobar Islands. *Indian J. Marine Science*, 10: 266–269.

Michael, R.G. and Sharma, B.K., 1988. *Fauna of India: Indian Cledocera (Crustacea : Brachipoda : Cladocera)*. Zool. Surv. India, Govt. of India, pp. 262.

Pennak, R.W., 1963. Ecological affinities and origin of free living. Acelomate freshwater invertebrates in the lower metazoa. In: *Comparative Biology and Phytogeny*, (Ed.) E.C. Dougherty. Univ. California Press, pp. 435–451.

Sharma, B.K., 2000. Rotifers from some tropical flood-plain lakes of Assam (N.E. India). *Tropical Ecology*, 41(2): 175–181.

Terdalkar, S. and Pai, I.K., 2001. Statistical approaches for computing diversity of zooplankton in the Andaman sea. *Tropical Ecology*, 42(2): 243–250.

Chapter 62

The Occurrences of the Heavy Metals from Three Reservoirs of Satara District (Maharashtra), India

Sandhya M. Pawar and Sanjay S. Sathe

Department of Biological Sciences, Padmabhushan Dr. Vasantraodada Patil Mahavidyalaya, Tasgaon, DistrictSangli – 416 312, India

ABSTRACT

The present work aims to study the level of heavy metals in different water reservoirs from Satara district and also to analyse other water quality parameters like pH, total hardness, electrical conductivity, free CO_2, dissolved oxygen, sodium, potassium, nitrates and phosphates. The analysis shows a low level of these metals below the permissible limits as the standards given by different health organizations.

Introduction

Heavy metals are one of the most hazards environmental pollution. Industrial effluents are discharged into sewage canals of cities causing serious pollution and health hazards (Baddesha and Rao 1986). The heavy metals like Pb, Cd, Cu and Zn are mostly absorbed and get accumulated in various parts of plants as free metals, which may adversely affect the plant growth and metabolism. (Barman and Lal, 1194) Some of the heavy metals are get contaminated into aquatic systems as result of natural activities (Weathering of soils and rocks from volcanic eruption) and from a variety of human activities involving the tanneries, mining, electroplating industries and various other industries producing pesticides and plants.

The heavy metals accumulate in the sediments due to adsorption process more over the ability to adsorb heavy metals is enhanced due to presence of organic particles. (Jackson, 1978) The deposition of heavy metals occurs in association with fine particles of silt and clay. They decrease root respiration and nutrient uptake by the plants, which inhibit cell mitosis in root meristmatic regions (Jameel, 2001).

The sub-metals such as Manganese, Iron, Copper and Zinc are essential micronutrients while others such as Mercury; Cadmium and lead are not required even *in* small amount by any organism. Virtually all metals including the essential metal micronutrients are toxic if exposure levels are sufficiently high. The Cadmium, Chromium, Copper, Lead, Mercury, Nickel and Zinc are particular relevance in fresh water. The increased circulation of toxic metals in recent times resulted in invariable build up of such toxic substances in the human food chain. Heavy metals are rapidly absorb to particulate materials as like Detritus, Plankton, suspended sediments and they are assimilated by living organisms. On a similar survey many workers, (Sharma and Konsal, 1986; Patel *et al.*, 2002) have been reported that industrial waste water contains high amount of elements, like Fe, Cu, Zn, Cd, Pb, Ni, Cr, Co, As and Hg which affect the soil, water and plant system. The concentration of metals dissolved in the water may give a highly misleading picture of the degree of metal pollution. Therefore the survey was undertaken to judge the suitability of different effluents in water for the drinking and irrigation.

Study Area

Kas Reservoir

It is situated 30 km away in the northern west part of Satara city. It is constructed at the origin of Urmodi River.

In 1882 the tank was constructed, at the time it's expenditure was Rs. 261000. The length of tank is 720 feet and depth of tank is 60 feet. The total area 7.03 sq km. From the tank 11 to 12 Lac gallon water is supplied to the Satara city. It is supplied by gravity force to city.

Kanher Reservoir

It is a artificial (man made) reservoir built on Venna River near Kanher. It is situated in the northern west part of Medha Tahsil of Satara Distrct. It is about 15 km away from city.

It's construction is began in 1976 and completed in 1988. It is about 1955 mts in length, 50.30 mts in height and has capacity of storage 286 million gallon of water.

Mahadare Reservoir

It is one of natural reservoir constructed at the foot of Yawateshwar by honorable Chh. Pratapsinh Maharaj to supply the water to the city.

It is situated in Mahadare village, 6 km away from city. The length of this tank is 260 feet, width is 257 feet and depth is 30 feet. It is constructed totally by stone. From this tank daily 5000 gallon water is supplied to the city.

Materials and Methods

The water samples were collected from all these three reservoirs in pre-sterilized plastic bottles according to standard method of APHA (1995) and by Manivasakam (1984). The samples were analyzed for different physico- chemical parameters as per method, described by Trivedy and Goel (1984). The traces of the heavy metals as Fe, Mn, Zn, Cu, Pb, Cd, Cr, Co and Ni were analyzed by Atomic Absorption Spectrophotometers.

Results and Discussion

The results of analysis of physico-chemical parameters are represented in Table 62.1 and characteristic of heavy metals of these reservoirs presented in Table 62.2. In last 25 years metals have received great attention because they provide a coded history of lake's environmental. (Pennington, 1981; Kiggey *et al.;* Jain and Salman, 1995 and Someshwara Rao *et al.*, 1997). Heavy metal is continuously realized into aquatic environment from natural process that is volcanic activity and weathering of rocks. Heavy metals as well as pesticides have a unique property and accumulation over a period of time along a food chain and very high levels can be accumulated in organisms from very low concentration in water and sediments.

Table 62.1: Annual Range of Some Physico-chemical Parameters in Kas, Kanher and Mahadare Reservoirs from March 2004 to April 2005

Sl.No.	*Parameters*	*Sites*		
		Water Reservoirs		
		Kas	*Kanher*	*Mahadare*
1.	pH	6.2–7.1	6.30–7.50	7.10–8.5
2.	Electrical conductivity	0.027–0.044	0.113–0.190	0.208–0.407
3.	Dissolved oxygen	3.15–8.51	3.00–7.49	4.05–8.10
4.	Free CO_2	2.64–12.0	4.4–10.2	5.5–16.4
5.	Total hardness	28–60	46–98	60–195
6.	Sodium	4.0–9.0	7.2–19.0	13.0–26.5
7.	Potassium	< 0.05–0.16	0.5–1.2	0.80–1.83
8.	Nitrates	2.4–8.0	10.0–19.0	15.0–24.0
9.	Phosphates	0.002–0.180	0.0002–0.280	0.013–0.220

All values are expressed in mg/Liter except pH and E.C.

Table 62.2: Annual Range of Heavy Metals in Kas, Kanher and Mahadare Reservoirs March 2004 to April 2005

Sl.No.	*Heavy Metals*		*Sites*		
			Water Reservoirs		
			Kas	*Kanher*	*Mahadare*
1.	Lead	ppm	0.004	BLD	0.003
2.	Chromium	ppm	0.002	0.004	0.008
3.	Cadmium	ppm	0.0128	0.0003	0.0200
4.	Arsenic	ppm	BLD	BLD	BLD
5.	Nickel	ppm	BLD	BLD	BLD
6.	Cyanide	ppm	BLD	BLD	BLD
7.	Iron	ppm	2.12	2.40	2.40
8.	Manganese	ppm	12	1.6	BLD
9.	Zinc	ppm	1.16	0.56	1.16
10.	Copper	ppm	0.028	0.011	0.016

BLD: Below Detectable Level.

The permissible limit presented by FAO (1992) for heavy metal is for Zn-2mg/L, Cu-0.2mg/L, Pb-0.04 to 0.5 mg/L, Cd-0.01 mg/L, Co-0.05mg/L, Cr-0.10 mg/L and for Fe-0.1 0 mg/L.

In the present investigation the heavy metals like Arsenic, Nickel and Cynide are not detected in these reservoirs. In drinking water Cadmium more, than 0.1 mg/L causes Bronchitis, Anemia, Renal stone formation, copper and zinc are found to be essential for proper metabolic functions where as other like Cd and Pb are highly toxic to aquatic organism and consequently to the consumers (Grepe *et al.*, 2000). Hypertension and Arteriosclerosis in animal human beings (Manivasakam, 1987; W.H.O., 1988). While water having 5 mg/L of chromium are toxic to animals (W.H.O., 1988). The Chromium values detected are 0.002 mg/L, 0.004 mg/L and 0.008 mg/L for Kas, Kanher and Mahadare reservoirs, respectively while Cadmium values recorded 0.0128 mg/L, 0.003 mg/L and 0.020 mg/L for these three reservoirs respectively. These values are with in the permissible limit of BIS (1991). Similar observations were recorded by Kaushik *et al.* (1997) for different reservoirs in Gwalior regions. The lead was found to be 0.003 to 0.004 mg/L. All the reported values were under the permissible limits (WHO Standard, 1983). The manganese ranged between 1.60 to 12 mg/L. The values of the Zinc reported between 0.56 to 1.16 mg/L. These values are under the permissible limits (USPH Standard, 1980) The Copper ranged between 0.011 to 0. 028 mg/L. All the values of it were beyond the permissible limits (WHO Standard, 1983). All these observations indicates that the water from all these reservoirs is highly potable and without any organic, pollution of heavy metals.

Acknowledgement

Authors are thankful to U.G.C. New Delhi and W.R.O. Pune for financial assistance to their minor research projects. Similarly thanks due to Principal Dr. R.V. Shejwal for encouragement and providing necessary facilities.

References

APHA, 1995. *American Health Association Standard Methods for Examination Water and Wastewater*, 19th Edition, New York.

BIS, 1991. *Bureau of Indian Standard Drinking Water Specification* (First revision), I.S. 10500.

Bruno, K., 1995. *Wastewater Treatment and Use in Agriculture,* (Ed.) Percal, M.B. Irrigation and Drainage Paper (4), FAO Rome, p. 13–19.

Grepe, M.S., Moreno, V.J. and Patat, M.L., 2000. Cadmium, zinc and copper accumulation in the squid III argentinus from southwest Atlantic ocean. *Mar. Biol.*, 136: 1039–1044.

Kaushik, S., Sabu, B.K., Lawania, R.K. and Tiwari, R.K., 1997. Occurrence of heavy metals in Lentic water of Gwalior Region. *Poll. Res.*, 16(4): 237–239.

Lloyd, R., 1961. *The Toxicity of Mixture of Zinc and Copper Sulphates Rainbow Trout.*

Manivasakam, N., 1984. *Physico-chemical Examination of Water Sewage and Industrial Effluent.* Pragati Prakashan, Meerut, U.P. p. 3–12.

Manivasakam, N., 1987. *Industrial Effluents*, Shakti publication, Coimbotore.

Narayan, T.N. N.S. and Madhyastha, M.N., 1985. *Heavy Metal Pollution in India: A Review Current Pollution Research in India.* Environment Pollution, Karad.

Patel, K.P., Pondya, R.R., Maliwal, G.L., Patel, K.C. and Ramani, V.P., 2002. Suitability of industrial effluences for irrigation around Bharuch and Ankleshwar industrial zone in Gujarat. *Pollution Res.*, Each (Accepted).

Sharma, V.K. and Kansal, B.D., 1986. Heavy metal contamination of soils and plants with sewage irrigation, *Pollution Res.* Each, 4: 86–91.

Trivedi, R.K. and Goel, P.K., 1984. *Chemical and Biological Method for Water Pollution Studies.* Environmental Publish, Karad, India.

WHO, 1988. *Guidelines for Drinking Water Quality,* Volume 2, WHO, Geneva.

Chapter 63

Growth and Yield Response of Rice to Solid Waste of a Paper Mill of Orissa

B. Padhy[1], P.K. Gantaye[2], K.C. Lenka[1] and Sabita K. Padhy[1]

[1]Division of Physiology and Biochemistry, Department of Botany, Berhampur University, Berhampur - 7, Orissa

[2]Department of Botany, Rayagada College, Rayagada - 1, Orissa

ABSTRACT

The present piece of work is concerned with impact of solid waste of a paper mill (J.K. Paper mill, Rayagada, Orissa) on vegetative growth and yield response of three cultivars of *indica* rice (Jagannath, Annapurna and Sarathi) carried out by pot-culture method. Different concentrations (1.0, 2.5, 5.0 and 10 per cent) of solid waste of paper mill (PMW) applied into the culture-pot considerably reduced vegetative growth (production of tillers and leaves per plant and plant height), yield per plant and components of yield (production of number of panicle per plant and its length, grain setting and weight of 1000 grains). The poor vegetative growth of the test cultivars, resulted due to application of solid waste, is the clear prove of sodicity toxicity of the PMW. The decreased trend of yield per plant was due to higher per cent of pollen and spikelet sterility. Among three test cultivars. Annapurna was found to be highly affected than Jagannath and Sarathi. The alkalinity and sodicity nature of waste were mostly responsible for decrease of vegetative growth and grain yield of the test crop.

Keywords: Paper mill, Solid waste, Rice, Vegetative growth, Yield and Components of yield.

Introduction

Rice, among the cereals is the most stable food crop, occupies about 39.6 million hectares or 37 per cent of the total area under cereal cultivation in India. In order to cope us with population explosion of the globe several strategies have, however, been involved to increase rice production. The rice production depends on water supply and soil characteristics such as salinity, acidity, alkalinity, nutrient contents etc. Generally, application of different exogenous agents like pesticides, fungicides, chemical fertilizers and industrial effluents and wastes contaminate the soils. These chemicals directly or indirectly alter the soil character and play important role on growth and yield of concerned crop plants.

The industrial wastes discharged in to nature include various gases, liquid or solid-wastes whose chemical nature and composition vary with type of industry and the mode of waste treatment. Solid wastes, the discharged and unused products in solid form of the concerned industry, are being dumped at several places or disposed off around the nearby industries in shape of land filling which, in due course, are being washed away by various means and enter into crop fields and natural water resources. Many such instances on leaching of metals and salts from solid waste are being well documented (Wong and Tom, 1977; Tyler, 1981) and this create salt stress condition to the crop plants in the field. A salt stress condition can bring about damage and stunted growth with reduced yield (Russel, 1950).

The problem of solid waste in paper and pulp industry start right from the raw material procurement stage. This off plant pollutant includes solid wastes as cutting wastes from wood, bamboo, leaves, branches, twigs etc. The major solid wastes include lime sludge, fly ash, limekiln rejects and waste papers. The most troublesome ecological problem faced by pulp and paper industries is the disposal of sludge. The sludge are thin aqueous suspensions of waste materials discharged by the factories at various points such as clarifier sludge, broke washings, clay dyestuffs, bleaching reagents etc. These are hard to dewater because of hydrous nature of the fine pulp fibers. The disposed solid waste in due course washed away by rainwater and enter into the near by crop fields either directly or indirectly.

In paper industry lime is normally used for converting sodium carbonate present in green liquor to sodium hydroxide. The calcium carbonate generated in the above process is normally called "lime sludge." The quantity of lime sludge generated per day varies from 200 to 300 tonnes depending upon the type of plant and consumption of raw materials.

It is observed that J.K. Paper Mill lime sludge are being disposed near by road sides, cultivated land and river banks which directly or indirectly pollute the environment. Though a lot of work has been done on effect of solid waste of other paper and pulp industries on some plants (Gomati and Oblisami, 1992; Khanna *et al.*, 1990; Rao and Vidyavati, 1988; Rajananna and Oblisami, 1979) systems, little work has been carried out on the effect of solid waste of J.K. Paper Mill on crop plants. Hence, it is felt quite reasonable to find out the effect of solid-waste of J.K. Paper Mill on growth and yield performance of 3 improved cultivars of rice.

Materials and Methods

Three improved cultivars of rice (*Ortza sativa* L. cvs. Jagannath, Annapurna and Sarathi) were chosen as plant material in the present investigation for their good agronomical characters.

Pure line seeds of *O. sativa* L. cvs. Jagannath, Annapurna and Sarathi were procured from the Regional Agricultural Research Station of Orissa, University of Agriculture and Technology (OUAT) located at Berhampur. Healthy seeds of uniform, shape, colour and size were surface sterilized with 0.03 per cent formalin solution for 3 hours, then washed thoroughly with water followed by distilled water and then allowed to germinate in petridish lined with moist blotting paper in a seed germinating chamber maintained at 30±2°C. The sprouting seeds were allowed to grow under light in the seedling growth chamber provided with 2.5±0.5 K.lux light intensity from 2 fluorescent tube lights and allowed to grow under oven field. After a week of transplantation the seedlings were thinned to have 5 plants per pot.

The disposed off and sun-dried solid wastes (Lime sludge) obtained from the J.K. paper mill situated at Rayagada were powdered and mixed with cow dung manure and garden soil mixture in a proportion of 1 : 8 (v/v) of the pots to have 1.0, 2.5, 5.0 and 10 per cent (v/v) of solid waste in different sets with 5 pots in each set. The pots containing equal volume of soil and cow-dung manure mixture only were served as control (c). After 10 days of soaking the seedlings grown in growth chamber were transplanted into earthen ware pots (25 cm × 25 cm size) containing well mixture of cow-dung manure and garden soil and different concentrations of PMW at the rate of 8 seedlings per-pot and allowed to grow under open field. After a week of transplantation, the seedlings were thinned to have 5 seedlings per pot. Care was taken for periodical watering in all the pots.

Production of tillers per plant, number of green leaves per plant, plant height were recorded at the time of flowering in both treated and control sets, following the methods adopted by Padhy (1980). The total grain, yield per plant was calculated by collecting 1000 fertile grains from different panicles of each plant following the methods adopted by Bhattacharjee, *et al.* (1913).

All the data collected from both treated and control sets of plants were subjected to statistical analysis to calculate Standard Errors (S.E.).

Results and Discussion

Vegetative Growth Parameters

It includes the following parameters:

Production of Tillers per Plant

The solid waste of paper mill showed a reduced trend in the production of tillers per plant compared to control. All the test cultivars of rice exhibited positive correlation between reduction in tiller production and increase of solid waste concentration. However Jagannath variety was found to be most adversely affected by solid waste of paper mill. The degree of reduction in production of tiller among the cultivars was as follows: Jagannath > Sarathi > Annapurna.

Production of Leaves on Main Shoot

Production of leaves on main shoot is considered as an important parameter of vegetative growth of cereals. The treatment with solid waste considerably checked the development of leaves per plant in all the cultivars tried compared to control. Thus, higher the concentration of solid waste, lesser was the production of leaves per plant. The degree of effectiveness of reduction in production of leaves on main shoot was as follows: Jagannath > Annapurna > Sarathi.

Height of the Plants

Heights of any cereal plant play a vital role on productivity of the concerned crop. The solid waste of paper mill partially inhibited the plant growth resulting reduction in plant height. Positive correlations were marked between increase in solid waste concentration and rate of decrease in plant height in all the test cultivars of rice. Although all the test cultivars exhibited similar trend compared with their respective control plants. Annapurna cultivar was found to be more sensitive than Jagannath and Sarathi.

Table 63.1: Vegetative Growth Response of Three Cultivars of Rice to Different Concentrations of Solid of the Paper Mill (Mean of 20 plants ± S.E) Date of sowing 1st June, 2004 (Parameters recorded at the time of flowering)

Treatments	*Name of the Cultivar*	*Number of Tiller per Plant*	*Number of Green Leaves on Main Shoot*	*Number of Total Green Leaves per Plant*	*Height of the Plant (cm)*
Control	Jagannath	15.81±0.28	3.62±0.02	38.81±1.02	56.38±0.11
1.00%	–do–	14.66±0.91	3.45±0.01	30.71±0.91	54.07±0.42
2.50%	–do–	10.11±0.88	3.20±0.03	25.33±1.01	58.81±0.01
5.00%	–do–	8.37±0.09	3.04±0.01	18.11±0.93	48.01±0.92
10.00%	–do–	5.08±0.08	2.63±0.03	12.01±0.08	40.73±0.88
Control	Annapuma	12.15±0.81	3.25±0.01	31.21±0.62	31.75±0.88
1.00%	–do–	10.78±0.91	3.11±0.03	28.01±0.92	28.71±0.71
2.50%	–do–	9.44±082	2.87±0.01	25.31±0.97	25.03±0.71
5.00%	–do–	8.11±0.09	2.75±0.03	20.02±0.93	24.77±0.03
10.00%	–do–	6.07±0.01	2.51±0.02	15.19±0.97	22.37±0.01
Control	Sarathi	9.41±0.02	3.32±0.02	22.51±0.68	52.11±0.03
1.00%	–do–	8.91±0.01	3.00±0.08	18.21±0.81	50.08±0.07
2.50%	–do–	6.71±0.03	2.74±0.01	15.43±0.88	48.11±0.11
5.00%	–do–	5.03±0.07	2.60±0.02	12.11±0.81	40.22±0.88
10.00%	–do–	4.08±0.01	2.44±0.01	9.03±0.77	38.07±0.83

Table 63.2: Pollen Sterility in Three Cultivars of Rice Influenced by Different Concentrations of Solids Waste of the Paper Mill (Mean of 20 observation ± SE) Date of sowing 1st June 2004

Treatments	*Name of the Cultivar*	*Total Number of Pollen Grains per Focus*	*Total Number of Fertile Pollen Grains per Focus*	*% of Pollen Sterility*
Control	Jagannath	67.15±0.21	52.11±0.17	22.39
1.00%	–do–	60.24±0.15	45.10±0.21	25.13
2.50%	–do–	58.55±0.18	43.47±0.15	25.75
5.00%	–do–	61.33±0.21	43.91±0.15	28.4
10.00%	–do–	55.45±0.14	38.60±0.22	30.38
Control	Annapurna	65.25±0.11	48.48±0.16	25.7
1.00%	–do–	59.75±0.61	43.18±0.15	27.73
2.50%	–do–	60.24±0.13	41.04±0.18	31.87
5.00%	–do–	58.35±0.15	37.32±0.15	36.04
10.00%	–do–	59.44±0.25	36.25±0.21	39.01
Control	Sarathi	62.34±0.15	46.65±0.16	25.16
1.00%	–do–	57.25±0.18	42.55±0.22	25.67
2.50%	–do–	60.54±0.21	44.38±0.15	26.69
5.00%	–do–	59.53±0.17	42.26±0.12	28.77
10.00%	–do–	58.80±0.11	40.21±0.14	31.61

Table 63.3: Yield Response (Components of Yield) of Three Cultivars of Rice Influenced by Different Concentrations of Solid Waste of the Paper Mill (Mean of 20 plants ± S.E) Date of sowing 1st June 2004

Treatments	*Name of the Cultivar*	*Number of Panicles per Plant*	*Length of the Panicle (cm)*	*Total Number of Spikelets per Panicle*	*Total Number of Fertile Grains per Panicle*	*% of Spikelet Sterility*	*Weight of 100 Grains (gm)*
Control	Jagannath	7.12±0.14	18.11±0.89	135.41±1.11	105.41±1.22	22.15	20.18±0.02
1.00%	–do–	6.32±0.02	17.06±0.83	125.71±1.08	102.70±0.91	18.3	19.33±0.01
2.50%	–do–	5.03±0.01	15.81±0.91	102.53±1.01	83.4±0.83	25.49	18.11±0.02
5.00%	–do–	4.01±0.03	15.08±0.73	98.08±0.87	70.51±0.91	28.1	17.45±0.01
10.00%	–do–	3.57±0.05	14.61±0.88	90.31±0.83	63.16±0.81	30.06	17.22±0.22
Control	Annapurna	5.61±0.03	16.73±1.81	125.11±1.08	93.80±1.22	25.03	18.41±0.01
1.00%	–do–	5.01±0.01	15.82±0.08	121.00±1.03	88.33±0.09	27	17.32±0.04
2.50%	–do–	4.23±0.02	14.52±0.09	114.13±1.07	78.70±0.07	31.04	15.41±001
5.00%	–do–	3.61±0.01	14.00±0.11	97.05±1.10	62.98±0.08	35.1	14.03±0.06
10.00%	–do–	3.05±0.02	13.51±0.05	90.71±1.09	56.24±0.10	38	13.51±0.02
Control	Sarathi	5.31±0.01	17.51±0.83	115.03±0.91	86.83±0.87	24.51	18.73±0.01
1.00%	–do–	4.72±0.03	16.33±0.07	108.01±0.91	81.01±0.08	25	17.81±0.04
2.50%	–do–	4.51±0.04	15.05±0.05	101.22±0.95	74.80±0.60	26.1	16.53±0.01
5.00%	–do–	3.77±0.01	14.41±0.07	90.05±0.99	64.81±0.08	28.03	15.82±0.01
10.00%	–do–	3.01±0.03	13.50±0.05	84.10±0.15	58.20±0.03	30.8	15.05±0.02

Table 63.4: Grain Yield Per Plant (in gms) of Three Cultivars of Rice Influenced by Different Concentrations of Solid Waste of the Paper Mill (Mean of 20 plants ± S.E.)

Treatment	*Name of the Cultivars*		
	Jagannath	*Annapurna*	*Sarathi*
Control	15.145±0.085	9.687±0.72	8.635±0.078
1.00%	12.546±0074	7.664±0676	6809±0.095
2.50%	7.637±0.062	5.130±0.044	5.576±0.078
5.00%	4.933±0.093	3.189±0.099	3.865±0.091
10.00%	3.882±0.086	2.317±0.097	2.636±0.089

Components of Yield

It includes the following parameters:

Production of Number of Panicles per Plant

All concentrations of paper mill solid waste considerably checked the production of number of panicles per plant in all the cultivars tried positive correlations were noticed between increase of solid waste concentration with decrease in the production of panicles per plant. Among three cultivars the degree of reduction in production of panicles per plant was as follows: Jagannath > Annapurna > Sarathi.

Panicle Length

In all the test cultivars of rice, the length of the panicles significantly reduced compared with their respective control values. Higher the concentration of solid waste less was the panicle length. Sarathi cultivar was found to be more sensitive followed by Jagannath and Annapurna.

Total Number of Fertile Grains per Panicle (Grain Setting)

The application of solid waste of paper mill considerably reduced the development of grains per panicle in all the cultivars of rice tested compared to respective control plants. Higher the concentration of solid waste applied in soil lower was the grain development. The degree of sensitivity on grain production by the application of solid waste among three cultivars of rice was as follows: Annapurna > Sarathi > Jagannath.

Weight of 1000 Grains

Grain weight, in general, is the reflection of proper grain filling during its course of development after fertilization. Application of solid waste of paper mill considerably caused poor grain filling resulting lower grain weight in all the 3 test cultivars of rice and exhibited positive correlations with that of increase in the application of solid waste in the soil. The least grain weight recorded in Annapurna followed by Jagannath and Sarathi.

Grain Yield per Plant

Changes in any parameters of vegetative growth and components of yield reflect on grain yield of the concerned crop. It was marked in all the three test cultivars of rice that higher the concentration of solid waste application lower was the yield efficiency. The treatments indicate positive correlations between increase of solid waste concentration in the soil and decrease in grain yield per plant. This parameter correlated with weight of 1000 grains. The degree of decrease in yield/plant in test cultivars was as follows: Annapurna > Jagannath > Sarathi.

Generally the solid wastes and effluents of paper and pulp industries contain higher amount of Calcium, Sodium, Potassium, Sulphate, and Chloride besides other chemicals. These substances cause alkalinity in the soil. Qadar (1990) reported that higher sodicity condition in the soil cause higher mortality of the rice seedlings. Subramanyam *et al.* (1984) and Rajannan and Oblisami (1979) reported that the excess amount of Calcium and Magnesium in water cause injuries to crop plants. Similar reports are also available on toxic effects of paper mill effluent on the growth, morphology and chloroplast structure by Rao and Vidhyavati (1988) on 2 species of *cosmarium*. Hence, the solid waste containing higher quantity of various cations and anions might have influenced on production of tillers leaf per plant and plant height.

The alkalinity of the soil caused by the toxic substance present in the solid waste might have checked the formation of panicle in tillers. The reports of Qadar (1988 a) and Dragon and Gaul (1974) on growth and yield parameters of rice in relation to alkali soil and sodicity toxicity agree with the present findings.

The weight of grains depends on the availability of assimilate and their accumulation in spikelet during grain filling in cereals. It is thus suspected that the assimilates might have not properly translocated from leaves and accumulated in spikelets. Onkware (1990, 1993) reported that salt stress cause poor grain filling and low grain weight in finger millet. The sodicity or alkaline condition of soil due to application of solid waste of paper mill might have checked the proper grain filling resulting low main weight. The present findings corroborate with findings of Misra (1998).

Grain yield per plant in all the test cultivars of rice was remarkably reduced in the plants treated with all concentrations of solid waste of paper which might be due to reduction in vegetative growth, lower assimilation rate, reduction in the development of fertile tillers per plant and size of the panicle. Further the reduction of yield/plant might be influenced by the reduction of parameters of yield components and lower grain setting due to higher pollen and spikelet sterility.

Hence, it is concluded that the decrease of yield per plant in treated sets was due to presence of toxic substances in solid waste which considerably reduced the parameters of yield that reflected on yield efficiency of the test rice crops in this investigation. Therefore, it is suggested that solid waste of J.K. paper mill should not be dump near and around the crop fields, which may directly or indirectly hamper the growth, development and yield aspects of any crop.

Acknowledgements

The authors are grateful to Head of the department of Botany, Berhampur University, Berhampur for providing laboratory and library facilities; Deputy Secretary, U.G.C. (Regional office), Kolkata for awarding Teacher Fellowship to Mr. Gantayat and Officer-in-charge, Regional Agricultural Research Station of Q.U.A.T for supplying pure-line seeds to carry out this investigation.

References

Bhattacharjee, D.P., Ramakrishnayaa, G. and Ghosh, A.K., 1973. Analysis of yields components and productive efficiency of rice varieties under soil moisture deficient. *Oryza*, 10(2): 17–28.

Dargan, K.S. and Gaul, B.L., 1974. For paddy in alkali soil, seedling age and planting date vital. *Indian Farm.*, 24: 11–12.

Gomathi, V. and Oblisami, G., 1992. Effect of pulp and paper mill effluent on germination of three crops. *Ind. J. Environ. Health*, 34(4): 326, 328.

Khanna, P.K., Mitter, D., Marwaha, S.S. and Kennedya, J.K., 1990. Characterization and biobleaching of paper mill effluents. *Biopaper J.*, 10: 16–18.

Misra, J., 1998. Impact of water stress and certain industrial wastes on yield and parameters of yield in rice. *Ph.D. Thesis in Science (Botany)*, Berhampur University, Berhampur, Orissa, India.

Onkware, A.O., 1990. The effect of salt stress on water relations and photosynthesis in finger millet. *Indian J. Plant Physiol.*, 33: 177–180.

Onkware, A.O., 1993. The germination, growth and grain production of salt stressed finger millet (*Eleusine coracana* L. Gaertn). *Indian J. Plant Physiol.*, 36(2): 77–81.

Padhy, B., 1980. Impact of photoperiod and seasonal sowing in rice with some studies on biochemical and histological aspects. *Ph.D. Thesis in Science (Botany)*, Berhampur University, Berhampur, Orissa, India.

Qadar, A., 1988. Differential sodicity tolerance of growth and yield parameters in genotypes of rice (*Oryza sativa* L.). *Ind. J. Agric. Sci.*, 58: 607–611.

Qadar, A., 1990. Effects of seedling age of two rice varieties on their sodicity tolerance. *Ind. J. Plant Physiol.*, 38(2): 162–163.

Rajannan, G. and Oblisami, G., 1979. Effects of paper factory effluents on soil and crop plants. *Ind. J. Environ. Hlth.*, 21: 120–130.

Rao, B.D. and Vidyavati, 1988. Toxicity of paper mill effluents on two species of *Cosmarium*. *Vegetos.*, 1(2): 87–90.

Russel, E.J., 1950. *Soil Conditions and Plant Growth*. Longmans Green Co., London.

Subrahamanyam, P.V.R., Juwarker, A.S. and Sundaresan, B.B., 1984. Utilization of pulp and paper mill waste for crop irrigation. In: *Proc. Asian. Chem. Conf. on Priorities in Chemistry in Development of Asia*, Kuala Lumpur, Malaysia, pp. 26–31.

Tyler, G., 1981. Leaching of metals from the A-horizon of a source forest soil. *Water, Air and Soil Poll.*, 15: 353.

Wong, M.H. and Tom, F.Y., 1977. Soil and vegetation contamination by iron ore tailings. *Environ. Pollut.*, 17: 195.

Chapter 64

Fluctuation of AM Fungi Infection and its Importance on Certain Forest Tree Species

M.G. Nadagouda, R.H. Ratageri, N.M. Rolli and H.C. Lakshman

P.G. Department Post graduate and Research in Botany, Karnataka University, Dharwad - 580 003, India

ABSTRACT

Fluctuation of AM fungal colonization was determined on 57 tree species out of which fifteen tree rhizospheric soil sample revealed *Glomus* species were predominated over *Gigaspore* or *sclerocystis.* The hyphae were profusely branched moderately in eleven plants and four trees had higher branched hyphae. Nineteen trees showed more effective colonization, twenty two tree exhibited moderate root colonization and lower colonization was recorded in sixteen trees. Laboratory growth experiments on *Albizzia lebbeck* showed significant plant growth, nodulation and Nitrogen fixation. Plants received the inoculum of *Rhizobium, Azotobecter* and mycorrhizal fungi. Similar results were observed in *Pongamia pinnata* at Ninety days harvest. However, *Anogeissus latifolia* showed the tripartite inoculation of *Glomus fasciculatum, Glomus marcrocarpum plus, Acaulospora calospora* brought a significant plant height, dry matter, per cent of root colonization and P uptake. The experiments revealed that there were lot of variation in the colonization but there is need of specific fungi which influence the plants biomass production.

Keywords: Fluctuation, Varied mycorrhizal colonization, Forest tree species.

Introduction

The need for increased food production in most developing countries associated in many cases with a reduction of the areas of arable land, leaves no options for farmers but to intensive the yields per unit area through the use of improved crops varieties irrigation and fertilization.

The utilization of biofertilizer is considered today by many scientists as a promising alternative, particularly for a country like India where scientific capability is available to develop and promote such technologies. Phosphorus is the second most important of the key elements for plant metabolism and growth. Research on soil microorganisms, which increase phosphorus uptake by plants has received a lot of attention over the last 30 years. In Karnataka *Albizzia lebbeck, Pongamia pinnata* and *Angeossus latifolia* three tree species widely used for plantations especially in agro forestry systems. In Karnataka, these are important species of choice by farmers to increase the productivity of their land. By virtue of their fast growth and well-known for yielding good timber, fuel and fodder. A huge quantity of seedlings is required by farmers, panchayat and the forest department for undertaking the plantation of these valuable species.

It is said that Dharwad is a Chota Mahabaleshwar attached to Western Ghats of Karnataka. The geographical location is lying in between 14°48′ and 15°50′ North Longitude 74°48′ and 76°20′ East latitude northwestern part of Karnataka. It is the prime source of perennial rivers and trees of southwestern part of India. Trees occurring in these forests regain are classified into tree types; soil builders, soil improvers and soil depleters. In the afforestation programmes while the first two categories of trees are to be encouraged, the last one need to be avoided. The role of microorganisms, particularly mycorrhizae in the building and improving soil characters is well recoginsed (Sutton, 1978).

The production of quality seedlings in nursery is important for revegetation of the ever-increasing degrading forests of the tropics. The soil used to raise seedlings may not contain the optimum population of microbes needed for a healthy raising of seedlings. Bios augmentation with native arbuscular mycorrhizal fungi improves to quality of seedlings in nurseries (Bagyraj *et al.*, 1989 and Muttu Kumar *et al.*, 2001).

However, research work on the association of mycorrhizal in forest plant, species of Dharwad region is scanty. The present work reports the extent of AM fungal association in Dharwad district forest plant species and greenhouse pot by inoculating studies native fungi and *azotobacter* to raise good seedlings at nursery stage.

Materials and Methods

An intensive, survey was conducted to assess the association of AM fungi in Dharwad district forest tree species soil and root samples were collected from polythen bags with proper labeling. Roots were properly washed in running tap water and cleared in a near boiling 10 per cent aqueous solution of KOH for 48 hr. Roots were stained in Trypan blue following several washings in distilled waters to drain out the KOH (Phillips and Hayman, 1970). The stained roots were cut into 1 cm segments, 80–100 such segments were picked up and examined under the microscope. V AM colonization was determined by Nicoloson' s formula (1955) as follow:

$$\text{Per cent Colonization} = \frac{\text{Number of Root Segments Colonized}}{\text{Total No. of Segments Examined}} \times 100$$

The spore density of VAM fungi was quantities in 1 kg of soil following the wet sieving and decanting technique of Geredemann and Nicolson (1963) and the frequency of occurrence was calculated by Norton's formula (1978) as follow. The identification of VAM fungi was based on taxonomic keys prepared, by Hall (1984). The physiochemical characteristics of soil Dharwad is shown in Table 64.1.

$$\text{Absolute Frequency} = \frac{\text{Number of Samples Containing a Species}}{\text{Total No. of Segments Examined}} \times 100$$

$$\text{Relative Frequency} = \frac{\text{Frequency of Species}}{\text{Sum of Frequencies of All the Species}} \times 100$$

Results and Discussion

The present study an intensive survey for the prevalence of AM fling forest tree species of Dharwad district, revealed that these symbionts were found to have association with, varied types of tree species. The results of the physico-chemical analysis of rhizosphere soil shown in Table 64.1. Most of the tree species had prominent AM fungal colonization in the form of pesides and orbusvcules or bout. The frequency of AMF colonization and spore number varied with different most genera. A selected fifteen tree species has clearly noted down in (Table 64.2). The genus glomus was most abundant, next followed by Acaulospora, Gigaspora, Scutellospora and Sclerosisis AM fungal propagates. Also differed qualitatively. For instance, the rhizosphere of fifteen plants recorded the dominance of one species to each. However percentage of AM fungal colonization was cartage rised in three type *i.e.*, higher per cent, moderate per cent and lower incidence of AM fungal colonization was observed in 57 tree species, belonging to 18 anagiosper families (Tables 64.3–64.5). The degree of AMF colonization was varied with three species. Highly colonized roots were seen in 17 tree species, with colonization range from 61 to 100 per cent (Table 64.3). Moderate AM fungal colonization was recorded in twenty-two tree species, with colonization range from 46 to 55 per cent (Table 64.4). Lower incidence of colonization was observed in sixteen tree species, with colonization range from 37 to 45 per cent (Table 64.5).

Table 64.1: Physio-chemical Characteristics of Dharwad District

Sl.No.	*Parameters*	*Value*
1.	pH	69.72
2.	EC	20.1–10.4 mmhos/cm
3.	Texture (Sand : Silt : Clay)	52 : 24 : 14 per cent
4.	Exchangeable Sodium	90–88 per cent
5.	SAR	730–950 per cent
6.	$CaCO_3$	1–3 per cent
7.	Total porosity	34.9–40.6 per cent
8.	Non capillary porosity	2.4–5.9 per cent
9.	Intrinsic Permeability	0.01–0.08 per cent

Growth parameters *viz.*, plant height, nodules number, Dry weights nitrogen and phosphorus content in shoots, of *Albizzia lebbeck* was recorded (Table 64.6) for 90 days. VAM fungal inoculation resulted in a significant difference in to growth of *Albizzia lebbeck* plants. The extent of increase or decrease varied with *Rhizobium* and *Azotobacter* inoculum used (Table 64.6). Plants heights were significantly increased 5–8 fold over the control. Similarly, the increase in dry weight, number of nodules, phosphorus and nitrogen content of shoots recorded maximum, when the plants received

Table 64.2: Occurrence of AM Fungal Spores in Rhizosphoric Soils of Dharwad District

Sl.No.	Plant Sciences	Heliphae	Vesicles	Arbuscles	Tree Species Predominated AMF Spores
1.	*Acacia catechu* Willd.	++	+	–	*Glomus mossae, Gl. Fasciculatum*
2.	*Acacia nilotica* Lam.	++	+	+	*Gl. Macrocarpum, Gl. Mossae*
3.	*Albizza procera* Benth.	+++	+	–	*Gl. Fasciculatum., Gl. Geosporum*
4.	*Azadirachta indica* Juss.	++	–	–	*Gigaspora calospora, Gl. mossae*
5.	*Aegle marmelous* Corr.	+++	+	+	*Gl. Caladonius, Gl. Macrocarpum*
6.	*Casuarina equsilifolia* Roxb.	++	+	–	*Gl. Albidium, Sclerocystis coremodies*
7.	*Dalbergia sissoo* Roxb.	++	+	+	*Gl. Monosporum, Gl. mossae*
8.	*Diptrocarpus tubinatus* Gart.	++	–	–	*Sclerocystis sinusa*
9.	*Hardwickia binata* Roxb.	++	+	–	*Gl. multicaulis*
10.	*Eugenia bractiata* Roxb.	+++	+	+	*Gl. mossae, Gl. macrocarpum*
11.	*Tectona grandis* Linn.	++	+	+	*Sclerocystis coremoides, Gl. Geosporum*
12.	*Terminalia tementosa* WSA,	+++	+	+	*Gl. Reticulates*
13.	*Tamarindus indica* Linn.	++	+	–	*Gl. Mossae, Gl. Fasciculatum*
14.	*Syzgium cumini* DC.	+++	+	–	*Gl. Margarita*
15.	*Zizyphus mauritiana* Lam.	++	+	–	*Gl. Mossae, Gl. Macrocarpum*

++: Moderate hyphae within cortex; +++: High profarely branched hyphae within the cortex.

Table 64.3: Effective AM Fungal Colonization in Forestry Tree Species of Dharwad District

Sl.No.	Tree Species	Per Cent Root Colonization	AMF Spores/100g Soil
1.	*Acacia catechu* Willd.	61.4	112
2.	*Acacia arabica* Willd.	73.1	173
3.	*Albizzia lebbeck* Benth.	63.6	102
4.	*Albizzia procera* Benth.	56.1	181
5.	*Azadirachta indica* Juss.	68.3	144
6.	*Aegle marmelos* Corr.	100.0	103
7.	*Anacardium occidentale* Linn.	66.4	170
8.	*Artocarpus integrifolia* Linn.	98.3	192
9.	*Artocarpus hetrophylla* Lam.	91.6	107
10.	*Borassis blafellifer* Linn.	83.1	189
12.	*Tectoha grandis* Linn.	76.3	201
13.	*Hardmickia binata* Roxb.	65.7	165
14.	*Terminalia bellarica* Roxb.	84.1	289
15.	*Terminalia tementosa* W and A.	88.4	109
16.	*Terminalia chebula* Retz.	92.3	116
17.	*Tamarindus indica* Linn.	74.6	201
18.	*Phyllnthus emblica* Linn.	62.7	179
19.	*Bombasa stricta* Roxb.	82.4	194
20.	*Syzgium cumini* DC.	97.3	252

Rhizobium, mycorrhiza (*Glomas fasciculatum*) and *Azotobactor* inoculation. The plant height and root was drastically increased in dual inoculated plants of *Pongomia pinnata* (Table 64.7). *Azotobactor* or *Rhizobium* had not showed significantly, in comparison to mycorryizal (*Glomus macro carpum*) inoculation. In *Pongamia pinnata* plant height, dry weight and nodule number and nitrogen content was significantly higher, when the plants received mycorrhiza, *Rhizobium* and *Azotobactor* inoculation compare to uninoculated plants under agroforestry ecosystems, the use of *Rhizobium* and *Azotobactor* and P-mobilising microses (*Glomus mascrocarpum*) as tree seedlings might have an influence biogrowth through the better uptake of P and N providing resistance to drought and to increase the tolerance or resistance to invading root pathogens. In case of *Anogeossus latifolia*, the seeds inoculated with co-inoculation of *Glomus macrocarpum* or *Glomus fasciculation* single inoculation registered better plant growth and establishment over untreated controls. Dual inoculation exerted better effect of plant height over the control. However, very significantly increased plant height (102 cm), plant dry matter per cent of root colonization and phosphorus content in shoots was recorded due to combined inoculation (Table 64.8).

Table 64.4: Moderate AM Fungal Colonization in Tree Species of Dharwad District

Sl.No.	*Tree Species*	*Per Cent Root Colonization*	*AMF Spores/100g Soil*
1.	*Acacia nilotica* Lam.	55.2	104
2.	*Acacia mangium* L.	57.5	198
3.	*Acacia pennata* (L.) Willd.	63.2	103
4.	*Dalbergia sisso* Roxb.	52.1	215
5.	*Bauhinia racemosa* Lam.	49.3	106
6.	*Bauhinia varigata* Linn.	48.4	211
7.	*Indigofera tinctoria* Linn.	51.4	501
8.	*Calliandra brevipus* Roxb.	53.7	251
9.	*Diptro carpus tubinatus* Gart.	46.3	114
10.	*Cassia auriculata* Linn.	53.9	352
11.	*Cassia fistula* Linn.	48.7	181
12.	*Sesaabnia grandiflora* Pers.	47.8	256
13.	*Leucaena leucocephala* Bentho	51.4	132
14.	*Thespecia populanea* Soland.	52.3	124
15.	*Engenia montana* Lam.	51.5	210
16.	*Pterocarpus marsupium* Roxb.	45.4	158
17.	*Eugenia bracteata* Roxb.	54.2	102
18.	*Acacia leucocephala* Link.	53.3	153
19.	*Lassianthus coffeodes*	48.7	212
20.	*Rhamnus wighti* WSA.	49.5	128
21.	*Rubus moluccanus* Linn.	46.4	103
22.	*Ternstrodemia japonia* DC.	47.5	192

Table 64.5: Lower Incidence AM Fungal Colonization in Forestry Tree Species of Dharwad District

Sl.No.	*Tree Species*	*Per Cent Root Colonization*	*AMF Spores/100g Soil*
1.	*Acacia ferruginea* DC.	41.3	196
2.	*Angofeissus latifolia* L.	44.7	102
3.	*Ficus religiosa* Linn.	46.5	244
4.	*Acacia auriculiformis* Roxb.	43.6	545
5.	*Acacia dealbata* Benth.	39.2	321
6.	*Casuarina equisetifolia* Roxb.	39.4	142
7.	*Albizzia odoratissima*	44.3	601
8.	*Dalbergia paniculata*	43.1	341
9.	*Erythrina indica* Lamk.	44.9	210
10.	*Enterolobium saman* (Jacq.) Prain.	45.4	412
11.	*Pongamia pinnata* DC.	43.9	251
12.	*Phoenix sylvestis* (L.) Roxb.	44.6	199
13.	*Prospis cineraria* Linn.	43.4	105
14.	*Prosopis juliflora* Linn.	45.8	118
15.	*Zizyphus mauritiona* Lam.	45.3	214
16.	*Santsalum album* Linn.	37.8	236

Table 64.6: Effect of AM Fungi and Plant Height Rhizobium and Azotobacter with Regard to Dry Matter of Shoot Per Cent VAM Colonization P and N Uptake in *Albizzia lebbeck* Shoots at 90 Days

Treatment	*Plant Height (cm)*	*Nodules (No./Plant)*	*Total Dry Matter (g/Plant)*	*% VAMP Colonization*	*Nitrogen (mg/Plant)*	*Phosophorus Uptake (mg/Plant)*
Control	14.9	1.3	2.1	–	51.3	48.4
AMF *fasciculatum*	21.1	2.2	5.8	57.3	86.2	91.3
Rhizobium	17.9	6.7	4.3	42.3	93.8	97.8
Azotobacter	17.3	3.5	4.1	41.1	91.6	104.2
AMF + *Rhizobium*	42.9	14.6	14.3	46.8	103.3	121.4
AMF + *Azotobacter*	37.2	16.3	9.8	47.1	114.4	133.1
Rhizobium + Azatobacter	36.1	15.6	9.5	46.8	128.5	136.4
AMF + *Rh + Az*	72.6	19.2	27.3	62.1	129.4	138.5
LSD = 0.05	8.10	0.02	0.05	5.16	0.72	0.96

AMF: Arbuscular Mycorrhizal Fungi (*Glomus faciculatum*) Soils Mixed inoculum 20 gm

Rh: *Rhizobium* (1.0×10^{-5} cells/ml)

Az: *Azotobacter* (1.5×10^{-5} cells/ml)

Species of *Glomus fasciculatum*, *Glomus macro carpium* and *Gigaspora callospora* were dominant in this region. This might be due to the high sporulation capacity and high viability of *Glomus* Spp., while others were scanty due to the adverse edaphic conditions, longer reproductive times and shorter viability. Similar observations were made by (Sieverding, 1991; Jamaluddin *et al.*, 2002).

Table 64.7: Effect of VAM, *G. macrocarpum*, *Rhizobium* and *Azotobacter* on *Pongamia pinnata* Plant with Regard to Plant Height, Root Length Fresh and Dry Weight of Shoot and Roots Number of Root Nodules and N Content in Nodules per Plant at 90 Days

Treatment	Plant Height (cm)	Root Length (cm)	Fresh Weight		Dry Weight		Number of Root Nodules/ Plant	Nitrogen (mg/Nodule) Dry Wt.
			Shoot Plant (g)	Root Plant (g)	Shoot Plant (g)	Root Plant (g)		
Control	15.7	9.2	5.5	1.7	2.1	7.1	1.11	21.6
AMF (*G. macrocarpum*)	21.4	17.5	18.3	2.1	7.1	1.12	1.78	32.4
Rhizobium	19.5	21.3	13.5	1.8	4.5	1.01	4.3	52.8
Azotobacter	18.6	21.1	12.8	1.5	4.3	1.22	2.2	52.8
AMF + *Rhizobium*	47.6	24.1	23.4	5.2	10.7	2.53	7.1	79.3
AMF + *Azotobacter*	34.3	22.5	19.7	5.0	7.3	1.72	5.4	67.1
Rhizobium + *Azotobacter*	32.3	23.1	17.1	4.8	7.0	1.64	11.2	62.3
AMF + *Rh* + *Azo*	64.9	33.4	27.6	6.1	14.7	2.66	14.5	98.5
LSD = 0.05%	5.11	2.05	1.12	1.05	0.05	0.03	0.07	0.32

Table 64.8: Effect of VAM (*G. fasciculatum*, *G. macrocarpum* and *Acaulospora calospora*) with Dual Inoculation in Respect to Plant Height, Dry Matter Shoot, VAM Colonization and P Content of *Angeossus latifolia* at 90 Days

Treatment	Plant Height (cm)	Total Dry Matter (g/Plant)	% VAM Colonization	Phosphorus Content in Shoot (mg/Plant)
Control	17.3	4.0	–	0.05
G. fasciculatum	29.7	9.2	48.2	0.17
G. macrocarpum	29.1	9.0	46.8	0.14
Acaulospora calospora	21.3	5.1	44.5	0.12
G. fa + *G. mac*	55.1	16.7	49.7	0.21
G. fa + *A. cal*	49.5	11.6	45.5	0.19
G. fa + *G. mac*	78.2	32.1	61.4	0.34
G. mac + *A. cal*	58.7	17.6	48.2	0.23
G. fa + *G. mac* + *A. cal*	114.2	58.2	64	0.42
LSD = 0.05%	16.02	0.10	7.05	0.11

A. Cal: *Acaulospora callospora; G. fa: Glomus fasciculatum; B. G. mac: Glomus macrocalpum.*

The present study reveals the importance of native arbuscular mycorrhizal fungal importance on the growth and development of three tree species *Albizzia labbeck, Pongamia pinnata* and *Anogessus latifolia* at 90 days. Seedling though there were difference in response of the plants to different inoculum potentials of the indigenous arbuscular mycorrhizal fungi there was always a positive response. An improvement in the quality of seedlings was observed in terms of growth, biomass production, nutrient uptake as compared to control. Arbuscular mycorrhizal fungi improve the plant growth and development of seedling (Ikram *et al.*, 1992; Ravikumar *et al.*, 1997), of the different treatment. In conclusion, the results confirmed that appropriate quality of AM fungi, *Azotobacter, Rhizobium* and *Gigospora* would help in production of quality seedlings for nursery practices.

References

Abbott, L.K. and Robson, A.D., 1977. Growth stimulation of sub-terranean colover with AM fungi. *Australian Journal of Agricultural Research*, 28: 639–645.

Abril, A.B. and Bucher, E.H., 2004. Nutritional sources of the fungus cultured by leaf-cutting ants. *Applied Soil Ecology*, 26(3): 243–247.

Bagyaraj, D.J., Brya Reddy, M.S. and Nalini, P.A., 1989. Selection of efficient inoculant VA mycorrhizal fungus for *Leucaena*. *Forest Ecology and Management*, 27: 81– 85.

Caporn, S.J.M., Song, W. and Read, D.J., 1995. The effect of repeated nitrogen fertilization on mycorrhizal infection in heather [*Caluna vulgaris* (L) Hull]. *New Phytologist*, 129(4): 605–609.

Fay, P., Mitchell, D.T. and Osborne, B.A., 1996. Photosynthesis and nutrient-use efficiency of barley in response to low arbuscular mycorrhizal colonization and addition of phosphorus. *New Phytologist*, 132(3): 425–433.

Gamble, J.S., 1922. *A Manual of Indian Timbers*. Sampson Low, Marston and Company Ltd., London, pp. 331

Gerdemann, J.W. and Nicolson, T.H., 1963. Spores of mycorhizal endogone species extracted from soil by we sieving and decanting. *Translation of British Mycological Society*, 46: 235– 244

Gomez, K.A. and Gomez, A.A., 1984. *Statistical Procedures for Agricultural Research*, 2nd edn. (An International Rice Research Institute Book). John Wiley and Sons, New York, pp. 680.

Gordon, J.C., Wheeler, C.T. and Perry, D.A., 1979. Symbiolic N fixation in the. management of temperate forests *Oregon State University Bulletin*, pp. 501.

Ikram, A., Mahmmed, A.W., Ghani, M.N., Ibrahim, M.T. and Zainal, A.B., 1992. Field nursery inoculation of *Hevea brasilensis* Muell. Arg. Seedlings root stock with vesicular arbuscular mycorrhizal fungi (VAM) fungi. *Plant and Soil*, 145: 231–236.

Jamaludin, Chandran, K.K. and Malakar, G.H., 2002. Studies on VAM fungi associated with tree species planted in sludge garden at the Ballarpur Paper mills, Maharashtra. *Mycorrhiza News*, 13(4): 10–12.

Muthukumar, T., Udaiyan, K. and Rajeshkannan, V., 2001. Response of neem (*Azadurachta indica* A. Juss) to indigenous arbuscular mycorrhizal fungi, phosphate-solubilising and asymbiotic nitrogen fixing bacteria under tropical nursery conditions. *Biology and Fertility of Soils*, 34: 417–426.

Philips, J.H. and Hayman, D.S., 1970. Improved procedures for clearing roots and staining parasitic and VAM fungi for rapid assessment of infection. *Transactions of the British Mycological Society*, 55: 158–161.

Ravikumar, R., Ananthakrishnan, G., Appasamy, T. and Ganapathi, A., 1997. Effect of endomycorrhizae (VAM) on bamboo seeding growth and biomass productivity. *Forest Ecology and Management*, 98: 205–208.

Sieverding, E., 1991. Vesicular arbuscular mycorrhiza management in tropical agroecosystem. Deutsche Gesellschaft far Technische Zusammenarbeit (GTZ), Germany, pp. 371.

Chapter 65

Arbuscular Mycorrhizae (AM) Fungal Association in Some Rare, Medicinal Plants

R.H. Ratageri, M.G. Nadagouda, N.M. Rolli and H.C. Lakshman

P.G. Department Post graduate and Research in Botany (Microbiology Lab), Karnataka University, Dharwad - 580 003, India

ABSTRACT

Medicinal plants belongs to eighteen family, of which twenty six plants were screened for their AM fungal association. There was no correlation between spore population and spore number. Except *Araceae, commelinaceae, santalaceae* and *zygophyllaceae piperaceae* and *moringaceae* per cent root colonization and spore number correlated to each other. Thirty six AM fungal spores were isolated from *Madhuca indica, Glorious superba* and *Santalum indica* showed diverged spore population with *Glomus* occupies top slat, then *Acaulospora* and *Scuttelospora* respectively. Inoculation of *Glomus fasciculatum* to *Madhuca indica* showed a significant plant height and biomass production. *Glomus mosseae* five fold increased plant growth was recorded in *Glorious superba* influenced macro and micro nutrient uptake was significant in mycorrhiza inoculated plants over the non-mycorrhizal plants. On contrary, magnesium concentration was higher in non mycorrhizal plants than that of mycorrhizal plants.

Keywords: *Rare medicinal plants, Mycorrhizal plants, Biomass production, Spore population.*

Introduction

World is endowed with a rich wealth of medical plants. Herbs have always been the principal from of medicine in India and presently they are becoming popular throughout the developed world. It is estimated that around 70,000 plant species from lichens to flowering trees, have been used at one time or another for medicinal purposes. Therefore, conservation and maintenance of traditional medical plants is most essential to ensure access to traditional forms of health care. (Purohit and Prajapati, 2003).

Arbuscular mycorrhizal (AM) fungi are the most important groups of symbiotic organisms. They normally colonize 85 per cent of terrestrial plants. These fungi enter the root tissue and form special. structures called vesicles and arbuscular. AM fungi play an important role in improving the nutrient uptake and growth of the plant species in adverse conditions (Smith and Read, 1997). It is well documented that arbuscular mycorrhizal fungi aid in the absorption of phosphorus and other elements from the soil (Jeffries, 1987). They help in the, establishment of seedlings in bare and degraded soil (Bethlenfalvery *et al.*, 1984; Kidd and Proctor, 2001). It has been reported that AM fungi increase the plant tolerance to water stress and salinity stress (Feng *et al.*, 2002). Due to the presence of alkaloid substances, Arbuscular Mycorrhiza (AM) fungal association in medicinal plants has been ruled out by Mohan Kumar and Mahadevan (1984). However, in recent years, reports of AM fungal association in medicinal plants (Lakshman, 1992; Malani *et al.*, 2002; Hemlatha and Selvaraj, 2003). But the information on rare, endangered, endemic and threatened medicinal plants with AM fungal association is very scanty. Therefore, the importance of such association in growth, biomass production and nutrient uptake on *Madhuca indica, Glorica superba* and *Santalum album* have been investigated.

Materials and Methods

A survey of AM fungi in twenty four medicinal plants, which are rare, endangered, endemic and threatened. This study has been carried out in May 2004. Collection of rhizosphere soil along with root was undertaken in Dharwad district geographically it lying in between. The rhizospheric soil samples and root samples were collected from different localities and brought to the laboratory. Roots were carefully washed and cleaned in 10 per cent KOH and stained with 0.05 per cent trepan blue in lacto phenol (Phillips and Hayman, 1970). The percentage of root colonization was done based on the number of root colonization by AM fungi. AM fungi propagules were isolated from rhizospheric soil using the wet sieving and decanting technique (Gerdemann and Nicolson, 1963). The number of AM propagules present in soil was calculated per 50 g. dry weight of the soil. The species level identification of different AM fungi was done following the keys provided by Trappe (1982) and Schenck and Perez (1990). Physico-chemical characteristics of soil samples such as pH and electric conductivity was carried out according to (Subbaiah and Asija, 1956). Soil organic carbon was estimated by the method of Walkey and Black (1934) and soil Phosphorus and determined by the method of Olsen *et al.* (1963). Nitrogen in soil samples was estimated by the Micro Kjeldhal method (Bremner, 1960).

Pot cultures were raised in separate pots containing sterilized soil and pure sand in 1 : 1 ratio mixed inoculum of *Glomus fasciculatum* was given to seedlings to *Madhuca indica* and *Santalum album* after having cultured in the hosts *Eleusine coracana. Allium cepa* was used as hosts for *Glomus mosseae* which was inoculated to *Glorious superba* and *Santalum album* in green house experiments. Pot experiments were conducted in 20 × 25 cm pots filled with sterilized sandy loam soil. The potting mix had pH 6.8 and 2.6 ppm available phosphorus per kg soil. 10.7 ppm available potassium and 13.1 ppm Nitrogen per kg soil. 50 g mixed inoculum was uniformly spread 1 cm below in each pot before sowing the seeds of *Madhuca indica, Santalum album* and *Glorious superba*. Inoculum consists of hyphae, Chlamydo spore 214/50 g soil and chopped roots bits of host plants. No chemical fertilizer was applied throughout the growth period and plants were watered on alternate days. All the pots were arranged following a randomized block design. Plants were harvested once in 40 days for two intervals. Parameters like, plants growth, biomass production, per cent AM colonization, spore number per 50 g soil, Macro nutrients and micro nutrients mycorrhizae inoculated and control were determined.

Chemical analysis of plants and soil used for pot experiments was done according to procedures as already mentioned.

Results and Discussion

In the field survey, the number of rare and endangered endemic and threatened medicinal plants is shown (Table 65.1). Most of the medicinal plants growing in a nutritionally moderate or poor sandy loam soil, were found to grown with other forest plants. Microscopic examination of their roots revealed extensive colonization by AM fungi with 48–92 per cent level of infection (Table 65.2). A large number of inter and intra-metrical vesicles were between 120 µm and 149 µm in size. The vesicles were globose to subglobose and the subtending hyphae were simple. Based on the morphological character, the AM fungi were isolated and identified. Altogether thirty six AM fungi were isolated from root zone soils of. medicinal plants (Table 65.3). Among them *Glomus* species were predominant. However, *Acaulospora* were higher than sclrocysts species. Soil born auxiliary cells of *Gigaspora* and *Scutellospora* were also isolated.

Table 65.1: List of Twenty Six Rare Endangered Endemic and Threatened Medicinal Plants

Sl.No.	*Botanical Name*	*Family*	*Habitat*	*Status*
1.	*Acorus calamus* L.	*Araceae*	Herb	R
2.	*Aegle marmelos Corr.* Ex Roxb	*Rutaceae*	Tree	T
3.	*Artocarpus lakoocha* Roxb.	*Moraceae*	Tree	T
4.	*Barringotnia acutangala* Gaertn	*Myrtaceae*	Shrub	R
5.	*Butea manosperma* Lam.	*Papilionacea*	Tree	T
6.	*Canariurn strictum* Roxb.	*Campahulaceae*	Herb	E
7.	*Ceropegia ordorata* Hook	*Asclepiadaceae*	Herb	En
8.	*Commelina tricolour* Bomes	*Commelinaceae* L.	Herb	E
9.	*Crotalariz lutescene* Dalz.	*Papilionaceae*	Shrub	En
10.	*Garicinia indica* Choiss.	*Fumaricaceae*	Tree	T
11.	*Gernlia arborea* Roxb.	*Verbenaceae*	Tree	R
12.	*Glorica superba* L.	*Liliaceae*	Herb	T
13.	*Gymnema sylvestre* R.Br.	*Asclepiodaceae*	Twiner	R
14.	*Hemidismus indica* R.Br.	*Asclepiadaceae*	Twiner	En
15.	*Madhuca longifolia* Gmel.	*Sapotaceae*	Tree	R
16.	*Michelia champaca* L.	*Magnoliaceae*	Tree	T
17.	*Ophiorriza banesi* wight.	*Rubiaceae*	Herb	E
18.	*Myristica malabarica* Lam.	*Moringaceae*	Tree	R
19.	*Piper nigrum* L.	*Piperaceae*	Twiner	E
20.	*Ptericarpus marsupium* Lam.	*Papilionaceae*	Tree	R
21.	*Rauvolfia serpentina* benth Ex. Kurz	*Apocynaceae*	Herb	E
22.	*Rubia cardifolia* Benth.	*Rubiaceae*	Herb	E
23.	*Santalurn album* L.	*Santalaceae* L.	Tree	En
24.	*Todalia aristica* Juss.	*Rutaaceae*	Shrub	R
25.	*Tribulus terristris* L.	*Zygophyllaceae* L.	Herb	T
26.	*Vitex trifolia* L.	*Verbenaceae*	Shrub	R

R: Rare; E: Endangered; En: Endemic; T: Threatened.

Table 65.2: Twenty Six Rare Endangered Endemic and Threatened Medicinal Plants Showing Per Cent AMF Colonization and Spore Number

Sl.No.	Plant Species	% AMF Colonization	Spores/50 g Soil
1.	*Acorus calamus* L.	24.1	102
2.	*Aegle marmelos Corr.* Ex Roxb	91.2	199
3.	*Artocarpus lakoocha* Roxb.	72.1	151
4.	*Barringotnia acutangala* Gaertn	61.2	162
5.	*Butea manosperma* Lam.	54.3	143
6.	*Canarium strictum* Roxb.	68.5	202
7.	*Ceropegia ordorata* Hook	72.4	117
8.	*Commelina tricolour* Bomes	19.5	182
9.	*Crotalariz lutescene* Dalz.	48.2	178
10.	*Garicinia indica* Choiss.	66.1	171
11.	*Gemlia arborea* Roxb.	72.4	166
12.	*Glorica superba* L.	83.3	181
13.	*Gymnema sylvestre* R.Br.	59.6	164
14.	*Hemidismus indica* R.Br.	65.1	152
15.	*Madhuca longifolia* Gmel.	56.3	132
16.	*Michelia champaca* L.	67.2	129
17.	*Ophiorriza banesi* Wight.	74.8	104
18.	*Myristica malabarica* Lam.	83.9	211
19.	*Piper nigrum* L.	76.3	214
20.	*Ptericarpus marsupium* Lam.	53.7	102
21.	*Rauvolfia serpentina* Benth Ex. Kurz	77.3	113
22.	*Rubia cardifolia* Benth	74.4	119
23.	*Santalum album* L.	21.2	156
24.	*Todalia aristica* Juss.	86.2	142
25.	*Tribulus terristris* L.	14.6	126
26.	*Vitex trifolia* L.	68.1	136

R: Rare; E: Endangered; En: Endemic; T: Threatened.

Growth response and mycorrhizal development of plants raised in sandy loam soils were assessed for the impact of inoculation with two different AM fungi. The response of *Madhuca indica* and *Santalum album* inoculated with *Glomus fasciculatum* and *Glorious superba* received the inoculum of *G. mosseae* was varied. However the inoculated plants generally had greater plant height, biomass production and nutrient uptake (Tables 65.4, 65.5 and 65.6), compared to the uninoculated controls. However, no significant increase of magnesium concentration was observed in all experimental plants, which were inoculated by *G. fasciculatum* or *G. mosseae.* Much significant increased plant height was not observed on *Santalum album* inoculated with *G. fasciculatum,* although plants inoculated with *G. fasciculatum* to *Madhuca longifolia* showed marked growth response and *Glorious superba* showed an increase in plant growth and nutritional uptake in all the studied plants (Tables 65.4 and 65.5).

Table 65.3: The Association of Arbuscular Mycorrhizal Fungal at on Three Tree Species of Rare, Threatened and Endemic Medicinal Plants

Sl.No.	*Mycorrhizal Species*	*Host Species*		
		Madhuca indica (R)	*G. superba (T)*	*S. album (En)*
1.	*Acaulospora appendicula* (Spain) Siev and Sch.	–	+	–
2.	*A. delicata* (Walker) Pte. and Bloss	+	+	–
3.	*A. dentriculata* Sieverding and Toro	–	–	+
4.	*A. elegans* Trappe and Gerdemann	–	+	+
5.	*A. lacuuosa* Mortan	–	–	+
6.	*A. longula* Spain and Schenck	+	–	–
7.	*A. rugosa* Mortan	–	–	+
8.	*A. spinosa* Walker Trappe	+	–	–
9.	*A. sporocarpia* Berch	+	+	–
10.	*A. tuberculata* Janos and Trappe	–	–	+
11.	*Gigaspora candida* Bhattacharjee and Mukerji	–	–	–
12.	*G. ramispora spora* Spain	–	+	–
13.	*G. rosea* Nicolson and Schenck	–	+	–
14.	*Glomus aggregatum* Schenck, Smith and Koske	–	–	+
15.	*G. albidum* Walker and Rhodes	+	+	+
16.	*G. boreale* (Tnaxter) Trappe and Gerdemann	+	+	–
17.	*G. citricolum* Tang and Zang	–	–	+
18.	*G. clarum* Nicolson and Schenck	+	+	–
19.	*G. etunicatum* Becker and Gerdemann	+	+	–
20.	*G. fasciculatum* (Thereter) Gerd. and Trappe	+	+	+
21.	*G. fragile* (Berk and Brvous) Trappe and Gerdeman	+	+	–
22.	*G. geosporum* (Nicol and Gerd.) Walker	+	–	+
23.	*G. hoi* Berch and Trappe	–	–	+
24.	*G. macro carpum* Tal and Tal	+	–	+
26.	*G. microcarpum* Tul and Tul	+	–	+
27.	*G. mosseae* (Nicol and Gerd.) Gerd and Tappe	+	+	+
28.	*G. multicaule* Gerd and Trappe	+	–	–
29.	*G. tenerum* Tandy	–	–	+
30.	*Scleraykis chavispora* Trappe	–	+	+
31.	*S. indica* (Pat) Hohn.	–	+	–
32.	*S. rubiformis* Gerd and Trappe	+	–	–
33.	*Scutellospora aurigloba* (Hall) Wal and Sanders	–	–	+
34.	*S. calespora* (Nicol and Gerd) Walker and Sanders	+	+	–
35.	*S. gilmorei* (Trappe and Gerd) Walker and Sanders	–	+	–
36.	*S. tricalypta* (Herr and Ferr.) Walker and Sanders	–	–	+
37.	*S. verruscosa* (Koske and Walker) Walker and Sanders	+	–	–

Madhuca indica (R): Rare; *Gloriousa superba* (T): Threatened; *Santulum album* (En): Endamic; +: Present; –: Endangered.

Table 65.4: Effect of Arbuscular Mycorrhizal Fungi on the Growth Biomass Product, Per Cent AM Colonization, Spore Number, Macro and Micro Nutrient Status in *Madhuca indica* of 60 Days

Treatment	Plant Height	Total Plant Dry Weight	% AMF Coloni- zation	Spore No./50 g Soil	Macro (%)			Micro (ppm)		
					N	P	K	Zn	Cu	Mg
Control	19.71	2.92	–	–	1.51	0.11	1.07	1.8	2.2	2.3
G. fasciculatum	46.53	8.42	53.2	114	3.73	0.27	2.12	3.3	4.1	2.2
CD at 0.05%	7.15	3.45	11.3	10.2	0.08	0.005	0.05	0.002	0.001	0.001

Table 65.5: Effect of Arbuscular Mycorrhizal Fungi on the Growth Biomass Product, Per Cent AM Colonization, Spore Number, Macro and Micro Nutrient Status in *Glorica Superba* of 60 Days

Treatment	Plant Height	Total Plant Dry Weight	% AMF Coloni- zation	Spore No./50 g Soil	Macro (%)			Micro (ppm)		
					N	P	K	Zn	Cu	Mg
Control	17.64	3.81	–	–	1.73	0.12	1.12	2.1	1.7	2.1
G. fasciculatum	83.41	14.55	86.62	263	3.82	0.32	2.62	3.1.	3.8	1.6
CD at 0.05%	9.16	4.41	15.30	13.2	0.07	0.005	0.05	0.001	0.005	0.001

Inoculation on three medicinal plants with two AM fungi resulted in increased plant height, dry matter and nutrient content. However, there was no positive correlation between plant growth parameters and mycorrhizal colonization (Table 65.3). Mycorrhizal inoculation results in an increase in the number of spores in the rhizosphere soil and this was maximum in *G. fasciculatum* inoculation to *Madhuca longifolia* and *Santalum album.* The phosphorus, potassium, nitrogen, zinc and copper content in the shoots significantly higher compared to the uninoculated control (Tables 65.4–65.6). The P content was more pronounced in plants inoculated with *G. fasciculatum* or *G. mosseae.* This was more evident from the decrease in the P content of the soil. A similar result was achieved by (Ponder, 1984; Gupta and Janardhanan, 1991) on different tree species. Arbuscular mycorrhizal fungi are known to improve plant growth mainly through increased P uptake and other nutrients (Koide, 1991). Schubert and Hayman (1986) reported that different strains of AM fungi differ to the extent by which they increased nutrient uptake and plant growth. Hence, some workers suggested the need for selecting efficient AM fungi that can be used for inoculating different plants (Lakshman, 2001).

Table 65.6: Effect of Arbuscular Mycorrhizal Fungi on the Growth Biomass Product, Per Cent AM Colonization, Spore Number, Macro and Micro Nutrient Status in *Santalum album* of 60 Days

Treatment	Plant Height	Total Plant Dry Weight	% AMF Coloni- zation	Spore No./50 g Soil	Macro (%)			Micro (ppm)		
					N	P	K	Zn	Cu	Mg
Control	17.92	2.61	–	–	1.55	0.05	1.07	1.2	1.4	2.2
G. mosseae	39.53	7.47	48.32	103	2.92	0.19	2.16	2.6	3.1	1.8
CD at 0.05%	6.3	3.51	13.10	8.00	0.06	0.005	0.005	0.002	0.003	0.002

In the present study, AM status is higher in all the mycorrhizae inoculated plants compared to the control plants. Higher root colonization allows more host-fungus contact and the exchange of nutrients helps in better growth (Smith and Read, 1997). AM fungi differ greatly in their symbiotic effectiveness, which depends on their preference for particular soils or host plant specificity (Dickie *et al.*, 2002), direct ability to stimulate plant growth and competitive ability. These results indicate that the natural population of medicinal plants grown in different localities is associated with AM fungi, predominated by species of *Glomus*. In this study, *Glomus fasciculatum*.

G. mosseae caused higher plant growth, biomass production root colonization, number of spore and uptake of macro and micro elements. I could conduct the field and laboratory experimental data is a major contribution of AMF role benefactor and this data can pave the way for further expansion and production of medicinal plant under semi-arid tropical conditions.

References

Bethlen Falvey, G.J., Dakessian, S. and Pacovsky, R.S., 1984 Mycorrhizae in a southern California desert: ecological implication. *Can. J. Bot.*, 62: 519–524.

Bremner, J.M., 1960. Determination of nitrogen in soil by Micro Kjeldhal method. *J. Agricultural Science*, 55: 11–33.

Feng, G., Zhang, F.S., Li, X.L., Tian, C.Y., Tang, C. and Rengel, Z., 2002. Improved tolerance of Maize plants to salt stress by arbuscular mycorrhiza (AM) related to higher accumulation of soluble sugars in roots. *Mycorrhiza*, 12(4): 185–190.

Gerdemann, J.W. and Nicolson, T.Hs., 1963. Spores of mycorrhizal Endogone species extracted from soil by wet-sieving and decanting. *Trans. Brit. Mycol. Soc.*, 46: 235–244.

Gupta, M.L. and Janardhanan, K.K., 1991. Mycorrhizal association of *Glomus aggregatum* with palmarosa enhance growth and biomass. *Plant and Soil*, 131: 261–263.

Hemalatha, M. and Selvaraj, T., 2003. Association of AM fungi with Indian borage [*Plectranthus ambionicus* (Lour.) *Spreng*] and its influence on growth and biomass production. *Mycorrhiza News*, 15(1): 18–21.

Jeffries, P., 1987. Use of mycorrhiza in agriculture. *Critical Review in Biotechnology*, 5: 319–357.

Kidd, P.S. and Proctor J., 2001. Why plants grow poorly as very acid soils: are ecologists missing the obvious? *J. Exp. Botany*, 52: 791–799.

Koide, R.T., 1991. Nutrient supply nutrient demand and plant response to mycorrhizal infection. *New Phytol.*, 117: 365–386.

Lakshman, H.C., 1992. Does medicinal plants require mycorrizal inoculations. *J. Conservation*, 119: 29–35.

Lakshman, H.C., 2001. VA: Mycorrhizae for sustainable Agriculture. *Mycorrhizae and Biopesticides*, 19: 23–29.

Mahankumar, V. and Mahadevan, A., 1984. Do secondary substances inhibit mycorrhizal association ? *Curr. Sci.*, 55: 936–937.

Malani, R.M., Prabhu, R.R. and Divkaran, M., 2002. Occurrence of VAM in the roots of *Phyllanthus fraernus*. *Webster Mycorrhiza News*, 14(2): 11–14.

Olsen, S.R., Watanabe, P.S. and Danielson, R.E., 1963. Phosphorus absorption by corn nots as affected by moisture and phosphorus concentration. *Soil Science Society of America Journal*, 25: 289–294.

Phillips, J.M. and Hayman, D.S., 1970. Improved procedure for cleaning roots and staining parasitic and vesicular-arbuscular mycorrhizal fungi for rapid assessment of infection. *Trans. Brit. Mycol. Soc.*, 54: 53–63.

Ponder, F. Jr., 1984. Growth and mycorrhizal development of potted white ash and black walnut fertilized by two methods. *Cant. J. Bot.*, 6: 501–512.

Purohit, S.S. and Prajapati, N.D., 2003. Medicinal plants: Local heritage with global importance. *Agrobios*, 1(8): 7–8.

Schenck, N.C. and Perez, Y., 1990. *Manual of Identification of VA Mycorrhizal Fungi Gaineville.* University of Florida, Florida, 241 pp.

Schubert, A. and Hayman, D.S., 1986. Plant growth responses to vesicular-arbuscular mycorrhiza XVI. Effectiveness of different Endophytes and different levels of soil phosphate. *New phytol.*, 103: 70–90.

Smith, S.E. and Read, D.J., 1997. *Mycorrhizal Symbiosis*, 2nd Edition. Academic press Inc., USA.

Subbaiah, B.V. and Asija, G.L., 1956 A rapid procedure for determination of available nitrogen in soils. *Current Science*, 25: 259–260.

Trappe, J.M., 1982. Synoptic key to the genera and species of zygomycetous mycorrhizal fungi. *Phyto Pathol.*, 72: 1102–1108.

Walkey, A. and Black, T.A., 1934. An examination of the Degtiare of method for determination of soil organic matter and proposed modification of the chromic acid titration. *Soil Science*, 37: 29–38.

Chapter 66

Foundry Industry and Latest Pollution Control Technologies

Y.C. Sharma

Environmental Laboratories, Department of Applied Chemistry, Institute of Technology, Banaras Hindu University, Varanasi - 221 005

ABSTRACT

Foundry industry is the backbone of every developing nation. This is one of the most polluted industries and after enaction and implementation of Air (prevention and control of pollution) Act, 1981, each industry has to adopt pollution control measures. The present article presents pollution aspects foundries and the existing pollution control technology. Emission in India in relevant cupolas and standards are discussed. An overview of various instruments which are normally employed for control of pollution, especially SPM, has been discussed.

Pollution

Out of the total amount of pollutants emitted into the atmosphere, approximately 90 per cent are gaseous substances and about 10 per cent are articulates consisting of solids and liquid substances. According to an estimate the total weight of the gaseous, liquid and solid pollutants entering the earth's atmosphere each year is 3×10^{12} kg (Gaur, 1990 and Majumdar, 1990). After arrival of industrial revolution concurrent with 19th century, pollution of the environment and especially air pollution is a topic of concern (Sarkar and Gadgil, 1989).

Volcanoes, storms etc. are the natural sources of air pollution but industries account for major share among man-made sources. Iron and steel production releases different types of pollutants (Table 66.1).

Table 66.1: Pollutants Emitted During Iron and Steel Manufacture

Shop	Flue Gases	Dust	CO (M_3/t)	SO_2	No_x	C_mH_n
Coke production	275–300	2–4	1–2	1–9	0.2–0.4	2.0–2.5
Sinter production	3500–5000	30–70	30–50	2.5–5.0	0.7–1.0	0.15–0.25
B.F. production	2000–2200	60–120	40–100	0.5–0.7	0.15–2.0	–
Steel making	2000–4000	13–17	1.5–2.5	0.4–1.4	1–2	–
Convert	–	25–40	80–90	0.05–0.20	0.1–0.5	–

Flue gas, dust, CO, SO_2, NO and hydrocarbons are the major pollutants released in major amounts.

Foundry Industries

Foundry Industry, unequivocally, constitutes the backbone of the diverse engineering infrastructure, but when it comes to the discussion of pollution, it is one of the most polluted industries. Other industries which account for rather greater air pollution are, thermal power plants, cement plants, oil refineries etc. Foundry emissions would be classified into: (*i*) Emissions from melting operations and (*ii*) Emissions from non-melting operations.

Iron melting is carried out in the furnaces like cupola, electric arc furnace, induction furnace, oil fired rotary and crucible furnaces. Out of these, oil fired rotary and crucible furnaces have limited applications, the major pollutants emitted from the main furnaces have been given in Table 66.2. The cupola furnace is economically most viable, simple and easily adaptable and thus finds the widest application. Main pollutants from cupola furnace are, SO_2, oxides of nitrogen, unburned coke, fly ash and particulates. The particulates are mainly metallic oxides, unburned coke and fly ash. The emission levels of grit, dust and smoke in Indian foundries are in the range of 5–10 kg/T of iron melted. Other pollutants are also quite significant.

Table 66.2: Pollutants Emitted from Different Furnaces

Furnaces	Pollutants
Cupola	Particulates, metallic oxides, unburnt hydrocarbons, CO and SO_2
Electric arc furnace	Particulates, CO, SO_2, NOx, CN and fluorides
Electric induction furnace	Particulates and metallic oxides

The non-melting operations in foundry industry include moulding and core-making, drying and ladle heating, sand preparation, metal pouring mould cooling, shake out, fettling and heat treatment. The details of these emissions are given in Table 66.3. Pollutants in form of saw dust and wood chips come out of pattern shop. It is clear from Table 66.3 that in all the melting operations dust, CO and SO_2 are the major pollutants.

Sources of Emission

Main sources of emission from cupola furnaces are the quality of scrap and processes involved in melting. Quality of fuel and raw materials, effects the emissions. If the charge contains oil and grease, it will give out thick volumes smoke with 500 T (Sengupta *et al.*, 1990; Jain and Khanna, 1982). If combustion of fuel is not uniform and incomplete, it results in excessive evolution of CO_2. Further, the release of pollutants throughout the melting operations is non-uniform because of non-uniform charge and air-charge, air-fuel, etc. ratio. Low quality coal allows results in greater degree of emission of fly ash and ash.

Table 66.3: Emissions from Different Foundry Operations

Operations	*Pollutants*
Moulding and core making	Dust and CO
Drying oven and ladle heating	Dust, CO and SO_2
Sand preparation	Dust
Metal pouring and mould cooling	Dust and CO
Shake out	Dust
Fettling	Dust
Heat treatment	CO and SO_2
Pattern shop	Saw dust and wood chips

Emission in Indian Cupolas

Amount of emissions in cupola depends on its melting capacity also. For a small size cupola of 1.0 t/hr capacity, 5080 M^3/h discharge rate, SPM is 2820 mg/NM^3 NOx recorded is 120 and amount of SO_2 emitted has been found to be 373 mg/NM^3. Emission for cupola of other capacities range given in Table 66.4.

Table 66.4: Standards of Cupola Dust of Different Countries

Country	*Dust Level Mg/NM³*	*Dust Level Kg/t*	*Melting Rate T/hr*	*Remarks*
Australia	250	–	–	Results be corrected to 12 per cent CO_2
France	–	2.0	< 2.0	–
UK	115	–	–	For hot blast cupola CO should be removed
Italy	250	–	< 4.0	Existing cold blast cupola
Japan	200–400	–	All sizes	–
Germany	1000	–	All sizes	Residential low population
USSR	80–100	0.25	> 14.0	At least 90 per cent CO level
USA	–	1.02–21.3	0.455	CO should not exceed 0.1 per cent
Yugoslavia	800–600	–	–	–

Emission standards for Indian cupola are based on melting rate and allowable dust levels. These are presented in Table 66.5 (Singh, 1987).

It is surprising and a point of discussion that for a cupola of melting rate of < 3 t/hr, for example 2.90 t/hr, allowable dust level is 450 mg/Nm^3 and for cupola (*e.g.* > 3.1 t/hr) melting rate the allowable dust level drastically becomes very stringent. There must be other points of consideration.

Table 66.5: Emission Standards for Indian Cupola

Melting Rate, t/hr	Allowable Dust Level, mg/Nm³
< 3	450
> 3	150

Pollution Control in Foundry Industries

Pollution control in foundries can essentially be achieved by adopting certain logical and useful decisions. It can be controlled by charging processes, replacing inferior quality raw materials, using adequate amount of coke and using pollution control equipments and maintenance of pollution control devices which is an expensive affair and is limited to large scale foundries. Whereas for small scale foundry units, use of superior quality raw materials including iron scrap, low ash coke and use of simple and economically viable instruments *e.g.*, wet scrubbers would be the best solutions (Phillip and Ketel, 1987), medium and large scale foundry.

Pollution Control by Instruments

In addition to the pollution control practices by using superior quality raw materials, clean scrap, etc. the abatement can be achieved by using instruments. The instruments are frequently used for reduction of articulate matter and for different operations namely sand moulding, sand reparation, shake out and drying plants. Modem foundries also use various energy efficient fume extraction systems also. The variation in gas flow and temperature during operation, melting etc., do not affect the efficiency of venturi scrubbers (Phillip and Ketel, 1987; Speight, 1978).

Main Problems of Foundry Emission

Basically six types of equipments used for collection particulates are available:

1. Settling Chambers
2. Inertial separators
3. Cyclones and multiclones
4. Filters
5. Scrubbers, and
6. Electrostatic precipitators

The systems for control of air pollution in foundry industry most of the times incorporate two or more equipments in series. This has many advantages. The first collector of the series removes coarser articles from the polluted air stream and fine articles are left for the secondary collectors. This enhances the efficiency of the secondary collector. In some cases if one of the collectors goes out of order the system remains functional. Series collectors may be used to separate materials in mixtures; core collector may separate waste materials, whereas the other may separate waste materials. Primary collector may act as a fine preventive device by inhibiting the combustible substances to enter into the second collector.

All the instruments can be used in foundries, but scrubbers, cyclones, filters and electrostatic precipitates yield better advantages (Phillip and Ketel, 1987; Speight, 1978). Particle size of the particulate material is important parameter which controls efficiency of these devices (Table 66.6).

Efficiency of cyclone will also increase due to increment in density, gas inlet velocity, inlet dust loading, length of cyclone and ratio of body diameter to gas outlet diameter.

Filtration is also very commonly used for cleaning the dust laden gas. For filtration, fabric or cloth filters and fibrous or deep filters are used. Each filter is of 120–420 mm diameter and its length is 2.10 m. Dust is collected at bottom of the hopper. Other filters which are used in reverse jet filters, envelope type fabric filters, multicompartment type bag house etc. Electrostatic precipitators are the best devices to control and minimize the dust or particulate matter from dust laden gas. They can be used for all kinds of waste gases. The ESP's work with very high efficiency even for the particles as small as 1/10 of a micron. Their efficiency is as high as 100 per cent.

Table 66.6: Comparison of the Relation Between Efficiency of the Relation Between Efficiency of Cyclones and Particle Size

Particle Size (μ)	*Efficiency*	
	Conventional (%)	*High Efficiency (%)*
< 5	< 50	50–80
5–20	50–80	80–95
15–40	80–95	95–99
> 40	95–99	95–99

Economical Aspects

Installation of any of the above pollution control devices will put additional financial burden on the foundry and before finalizing particular equipments, some factors *viz.*, installation cost, power consumption and maintenance cost must be considered. There are no fixed rates which could help in selection of a equipment, and final choice depends on many considerations.

References

Gaur, A.K., 1990. Effect of air pollution on humanity, vegetation and monuments. In: *Proc. Int. Conf Management of Pollution in Foundries*, India, pp. 7–28.

Jain, P.L. and Khanna, S., 1982. *Foundry Emissions and Control*, 1st Ed.

Mahajan, S.P., 1991. *Pollution Control in Process Industries*, 3rd Ed.

Majumdar, B., 1990. Air pollution control systems for modern foundries. In: *Proc. Int. Conf. Management of Pollution in Foundries*, India, pp. 65–72.

Phillipp and Ketel, S.J., 1987. Waste Materials Management in Integrated Iron and Steel Mills. *Steel Timese*, 215: 11.

Sarkar, M.K. and Gadgill, K., 1989. Air-pollution control and fuel conservation in coal fired reheating furnaces. *Indian J. Env. Prot.*, 9: 77–85.

Sengupta, B., Prasad, B.M. and Kumar, S.V.N.S.S., 1990. *Indian Foundry J.*

Singh, P., 1987. *Workshop on Risk Assessment Techniques and Management*, IIT Delhi.

Speight, G.E., 1978. Iron and steel works. In: *Industrial Air Pollution Handbook*, McGraw Hill, London.

Lund, H.F. and [illegible], 1982. [illegible].

Sengupta, B., Pandey, B.M. and Kumar, S.K., 1990. Indian Standard.

Index

A

Aceria lycopersicci wolff, 93
Acetate dialysite, 79
Actinomycete
  biodegration, 206
  fungal interaction, 181
  importance, 182
  isolation, 182
  population density, 181
Adiabatic compressibility, 36
Aedes aegypti sp., 275
Aerobic
  microbes, 204
  treatment, 204
Aeromonas hydrophilla, 205
  densities of, 13
  diseases by, 2
  habitat, 2
  hemolytic activity, 9
  identification of, 10–11
  infection outbreak, 12
  methods of control, 14
  occurrence of 13
  pathology, 3–6
  range of 13
  serology of, 11–13
  taxonomy, 3
  vaccination of 11–13
  virulence factor, 8–10
Aeromonas liquefaciens sp., 3
Ageratum conizoides sp., 271
Agglutination procedures, 11
Air pollution, 67, 333
Air quality
  index, 65, 67
  assessment of parameters, 65
  monitoring stations, 65
  seasonal variation, 68–69
Air quality parameters
  NO_x 65
  RSPM, 65
  SO_2, 65
  SPM, 65
Albino rats, 96
Albizzia lebbeck sp., 409
Alcohol effect on brain atpase, 108
Alcoholics drugs, 108
Algae flora in rice field study, 176
Algae inoculation to rice crop, 176
Algal
  biodegration, 206
  population, in river benthos, 235
Algal spirogyra sp., 206
Allium cepa sp., 271
Amaranthus spinosus sp., 271
Amylase, 85–86
Amylase activity, 85

Amylase activity of green gram germination seeds, 86

Amylase activity, statistical analysis, 86

Anaerobic / aerobic sequential step treatment, 207–208

Anaerobic
- reduction of azo dyes, 204
- treatment, 206–207

Anova test, 361

Antagonistic activity spectrum, 181

Antheroselerosis, 79

Anthraquinone dye degradation, 206

Anti fungal activity, 120

Antibody differential kinetics, 12

Antifungal sensitivity test, 120

Antimicrobial activity, 181

Antinomyces israelli sp., 180

Antioxidands, 79–82

Apis dorsata sp., 269

Apparent moral
- compressibility, 36
- volume, 36

Aquatic ecosystem, 281

Aquatic macrophytes, 338

Argemone hydrophica synthesis, 9

Argemone mexicana leaf extract, 155

Argemone mexicana leaf extract effect on
- dual culture of *Rhizoctonia solani* sp., 154–155
- dual culture of *Trichoderma viride* sp., 154–155
- fungi growth, 153

Argemone mexicana linn. (papavaraceae), 152

Argemone sobria extracellular protease, 13

Army worm, 135

Aromatic amines, 202

Arteriosclerosis, 79

Arbuscular mycorrhizae fungal, 416
- association, 415
- colorization, 409

Arbuscular mycorrhizae fungal spores occurrence in rhizosphoric soil of Dharwad district, 410

Arbuscular mycorrhizae fungi effect on
- growth biomass product, 420
- macro nutrients, 420
- micro nutrients, 420
- percentage am colonization, 420
- spore number, 420

Asparaginase, 185

Asparaginase, synthesis by vibrio succinogens, 187

Asparagines levels in blood, 187

Aspergillus gryzae sp., 86

Aspergillus terrus sp., 206

Aspidopterys indica sp., 271

Atpase activities in ethanol treated animals, 108

Atpase, 108–109

Auxochromes, 200

Azathioprine, 79

Azobactor inoculation, 411

Azo dye degradation by fungi, 205–206

Azodisalicylate (ADs), 207

Azodye biodegration, factor affecting, 208—210

Azodyes, 199
- as carcinogenic agent, 202
- compounds, 202
- synthesis, 200—201
- toxicity, 202

Azodyes, biological treatment, 199—210

Azodyes, in textile industries, 199
- intermediates of, 200
- structure of, 200

B

Bacillius cereus sp., 209

Bacterial tester strain, 95

Barbus stigma, 349

Basal dose, 74

Batch adsorption experiments, 23

Batch scale operation, 206

Bavistin doses, 58
- adverse effects, 58
- deletrions effects, 58

Bavistin effect on, morphological effect of
- bringal, 59
- chilli, 59
- tomato, 59

BCR *see* Benefit cost ratio

Bee flora, 269

Bee forage plants of *Apis dorsata* sp., 271

Benefit cost ratio, 125–127

Benthic algae as indicators, river water quality, 239–240

Bhia, 10

Bioagulation, 206

Biocontrol agent, 155

Bioefficacy, 360
Bioassay, 277
Black gram seeds, 345
Black tea, 95
Blood brain barrier, 108
Blood sampling, 79
Brain, 108–109
Branchitis, 5
Bresipalpus phoenicis sp., 92
Brinjal, 59–60
Brinjal seed, 58
Brinjal varietites analysis of economic loss, 126
Broth dilution method, 138–139
Bug of rice 135
Bulb geophytes , 161
Bull's eye, 171
Bull's eye, raw material characteristics, 173
Butylated hydoxytoluene, 80

C

C : N ratio, 313
Ca^{++} atpase activities, 108
Cabbage, 263
Cabbage butterfly, 264
Cadmium adsorption
  exothermic nature of, 26
  process of, 26
  removal percentage, 27
Cadmium amount determination, 23
Cadmium as contaminant, 30
Cadmium chloride concentration, 349
Cadmium effect on
biochemical changes, 30–31
  germination percentage, 30
Cadmium exposure effect, 348–353
Cadmium influence on
  germination of soybean 29–32
  photosynthetic pigments of soybean, 29–32
  seedling growth of soybean, 29–32
Cadmium pollution source, 23
Cadmium removal by economic method
  dynamic modeling, 25–26
Cadmium removal
  effect of pH, 25
  rate of, 25
  study of dynamics, 25
  from water, 22–26
  from waste water 22–26
Cadmium, adsorption on china clay
  concentration, 24
  contact time, 24
Cadmium, particle size, 23
Cajanus cajan, 271, 247
Calcium chloride, 85,86
Caliform detecting MPN test, 114
Camellia sinensis sp., 95
Capsicum fruitescens sp., 92, 247
Carbohydrate metabolism of *Vigna mungo*, 344
Cardiovascular disease, 79
Caribbean tunicate sp., 185
Carotenoid content of seedlings, 30
Carynespora cassiicola sp., 119
Cereals, 84
Chaterrvedi formula, 49
Chemical fertilizer effects, 365
Chickpea (*Cicer arietinum* L.), 387
Chikuwa preparation, 172
Chilli, 59–60
Chilli seeds, 58
Chlorophyll content of seedlings, 30.32
Chlorophyll stability index, 74
Chromium effect on biochemical changes, 30–31
Chromium influence on
  germination of soybean 29–32
  photosynthetic pigments of soybean 29–32
  seedling growth of soybean 29–32
Chromogen, 200
Chromophores, 200
Chronic rejection, 79
Chronic toxicity study, 349
Citric acid, 138–139
Citric acid effective range for *Proteus* sp., 139
Citrobacter strain, 190
Cluster bean (*Cyamposis tetragonalola*), 302
Cluster bean varieties, performance 302–304
Cobalt concentration in soil, 345
Coefficient of intraparticle diffusion, 26
Colchicines discovery, 247
Colletotrichum lindemuthianum sp., 119
Combination therapy, 188
Common carp, 12
Common vegetables
  mite pest scenario, 88–93
Compost, 309
Compost maturity test, 312

Composting experiment, heap method, 310
Composting methodology, 311
Conjugated diencs, 80
Copper pthalocyanine dye, degradation pathway, 206
Coriander
drought tolerance, 73
growth, 74
praline content, 74, 77
soil type, 74
Coriforms, 112–116
Correlation matrix, parameters, 225–226
Cowdung, characteristics, 312
Creatinine level in blood, 79
Critical difference (CD), 265–267
Crude extract effect, 277
Crude lipopolysactaride (LPS), 12
CTAB technique, 244
Cucumis pubscens willd, effect of colchicines, 247
Cyclosporine A, 79, 82
Cyst culture, 294

D

Debye Hukel theory, 36
Defoliators, 134
Didemnin B, 185
Dinitro salicylic acid method, 85
Disco fish, 171
Discorea alta species
genetic differentiation within, 224
samples of, 244
Disease related laser use survey at Indore, 157–159
Dissolved oxygen (DO) concentration, 290
Disulphide moiety, 86
Diurnal variation in Ayyanakere, 288—291
Diurnal variation in physiochemical characteristics of
Ayyanakere lake, 289
Diurnal variation of freshwater, 289
Diurnal variation of plankton in Ayyonaker lake, 290
DNA method, 244
Drinking water quality, 325
Dropper formation 161
Drosophila species study, 102
Drought tolerance in
crops plants, 74
options to minimize yield lasers, 74
strategies to breed, 74
Dry weight of
brinjal, 60
chilli, 60
leaves, 60
roots, 60
stem, 60
tomato, 60
Dye reduction rate, 209

E

Ear cutting insect pest, 135
EC-TDS analyzer, 338
Emission factor, 66
Emission in Indian cupolas, 425
Emission intensity air pollutants, 67
Emission of foundary, 424–425
Endoparasites of insects, 293
Energy,
affectivity, 45
conservation of, 45
Environmental audit
aims of, 43
approach of, 44
definition of 41–42
evolution of, 42
guidelines, 44
in Indian context, 41
material audit, 45
protocols, 44
Environmental conservation, 46
Enzyme activities of brain after alcoholization, 108
Emission intensity of line source, 70
Epicatechin (EC), 95
Epicatechin gallate (ECG), 95, 98
Epigallocatechin (EGC), 95, 98
Epigallocatechin gallete (EGCG), 95, 98
Epilogue, 46
Epithelial hyperplasia, 5
Eriophyid mite, 93
Eriphyids (erineum mite), 89
Eschirichia coli sp., 139
Escherichia coli k-12, 187
ESRD patients study, 79
blood sampling of, 79
ESRD, 79, 81–82
ESRS lipoprotein oxidation measurement, 79
Esterbauer sulphate method, 180
Ethanol, 108–109
Ethanol administration on rats, 285

Ethanol consumption, 107

Ethnoveterinary practices by Santhal tribe 163–166

Eutetranychus orientalis klein, 92

Evolulus alsionides sp., 271

Exophthalmia, 5

Extra cellulose enzymes, 182–183

F

Faridabad distinct, 47–48

groundwater balance, 48

in mansoon, 51

in non mansoon 51

seepage calculation of canals, 51

surface water irrigation, 51

total recharge, 51

Faridabad district annual ground water

rechange calcutions, 53

Fecal contamination

californ test 112

detection of, 112

Eijkman test, 114–115

H_2S test, 112–114

MPN test, 112–113

Fiber reactive azodyes, 201

Fishes pesticides and haematological picture, 258–259

Fishes, pesticides and histopathological changes, 259

effect on gills, 259

effect on kidney, 259

effect on liver, 259

Fishes, pesticides and reproduction, 259

Fishes, toxicity of chemical testing, 257

Flavonoids, 95

Flecorescent antibody test, 11

Fluidized bed anaerobic reactor, (fbr), 208

Foliar spray, 127

Folin phenol reajent, 80

Food security

apparent, 378

definition of, 377

facets of, 378

local, 378

microlevel, 379

national, 378

potential, 379

regional, 378

Forest tree species

fluctuation of AM fungi infection, 407–413

importance of, 407–413

Foundary emission, problems, 426

Foundary industry, 424

Foundary industry pollution control, 426

Fresh fish bull's eye, 172

Fresh irrigated pearl millet straw, characteristics, 311

Freshwater ecosystem, 288–289

Freshwater fish *Sarotheraden mossumbicus*, 349

Freshwater lake of Chickmagalore

diurnal variation, 289

phytoplankton, 289

water analysis, 289

Fruit borer, 125, 127

Fruit borer effect on brinjal, 125

Fruit damage, 126–127

Furnace pollutants, 424

Fusarium oxysporum, 119

Fym application, 366–567

G

Gam etocyst, 297

Gamont, 295

Generic sequential analysis of rivers, 237

Genetic variability in *Dioscorea alata*, 243–246

Genotypes, 146, 148–149

Geotricum candidum sp., 206

Geotropism, 161

Germinated green gram seeds (GGGS), 85–86

Germination seeds, 58

dry weight, 58–60

germination percentage 58–60

root length, 58–60

tomato, 58–60

Ginger (*Gingiber officinalerose*), 299

morphology of, 300

yield of, 300

Ginger cultivation, 299

Ginger varieties, evaluation, 294–301

Glomas fasciculation, 411–412

Glomus macro carpum sp., 411

Glorica superba sp., 416

Gluconeogenesis, inhibitory effect of ethanol, 285

Glucose fermentation, 11

Glue protein, 104

Glutamic oxaloacetic transaminase (GOT), 334

Glutamic pyruvic transaminase (GPT), 334

Glycogenesis, 285

Gram seeds, 85

Green gram amylase activation by calcium chloride, 84–86

Green gram germination time fixation, 85

Green gram seed, activity of amylase, 85

Green green, 85–86

Green tea, 95

Green tea, autimulagenicity, 95

Greenhouse experiment, 153, 155

Gross mansoon draft (MD), 52

Ground water rechange annual, 51

Ground water resource evaluation, 47–55

Ground water sampling
- location of Bhadrawati, 219

Groundwater
- balance, 54
- development level, 55
- draft, 53
- losses, 53
- quality, 217
- quality of Badravati town, 216
- sampling map in Bhadrawati, 217–218
- worthy areas, 49

Groundwater estimation committee (NABARD), 55

H

H_2S method, 112–116

Halophilic microorganism, 185

Haltius, 294

Hapanototype, 297

Harbor motile aeromonadas, 13

Heavy metal pollution, 29–30

Heavy metal stress, 345

Helianthus annus sp., 271

Helicoverpa armigera, natural enemies, 381

Heteropneustis fossilis sp., 349

Hieroglyphus bonian fab, 135

Hirmocystidae sp., 295

Holotrichia sp. 134

Honey bee
- collection of comb pollen, 269
- forage availability of, 269
- identification of pollen types, 269
- methods of collection, 269
- percentage composition, 272
- rearing of, 269
- study area, 269

Human carcinogen, 202

Hydrellia griseola fall, 135

Hydrophyte screening, 168

Hydrophytic plants, in Dharwad , 167–170

Hydrophytic plants, 167

I

Immunoenzyme procedure, 11

Immunosuppressive therapy of renal transplants, 82

Indian bean (sem), 145

Indian bean, seed invigoration, 145

Indian emission standards, 64

Indian industries, 41

Indian urbanization process, 63

Industrial activities
- environmental damage of, 42

Inhibition zone, 120

Inoculum preparation, 138

Insect pest scenario, 130–134

Insect pest species, 130

Insecticides

Intestine
- cadmium chloride exposure 350–352
- control of chronic test, 350–352

Invigoration treatment
- interaction, 148
- dry weight, 149
- fresh weight, 149

Invigoration treatment, 146–149

Ion exchange mechanism, 25

Ionic solutes, functions, 36

Irrigation water return flow recharge, 50

J

Jalgoan district, vehicle pollution data, 63

K

Kabuli chickpea
- effect of phosphours, 387–389
- seed rate, 387–389

Kanher reservoir, 395–396

Kar seabon crop, 371

Kas reservoir, 395–396

Klesiella sp. 137

L

Lagergren's model, 25

L asparagine therapy, 190

L asparagines enzyme, antitumour activity, 190

L asparoginase enzyme from marine
- aqctinomycetes, 189
- streptomyces cyllirus, 189

L. Orbonalis, fruit damage, 127

L. Varicornis, 135

Lablab bean of seedling, 146

Lag phase 81–82

Larval salivary gland, 104

Larval size, 104

Laser application in medical science, 157

Laser treatment, percentage of patient suffering, 158

L.asparaginase
- activity in marine sediments, 187
- antiturnour activity, 188
- enzyme from microorganism, 185
- isoforms, 185
- stimulation, 187
- treatment for lympoblastic leukemia, 188

Latechins, 95

Latic habitats, 234

LDL lipid proxidation, 79–80, 82

LDL+VLDL, copper ion induced oxidation, 82

LDL+VLDL fraction, 80

LDL+VLDL fraction, assay of lipid peroxidation, 80

LDL+VLDL isolation from serum, 80

L dopa, 108

Leaf extracts application, 155

Leaf extracts preparation method, 152–153

Leaf laters, 134

Leaf miners, 135

Leguminous seeds, 86

Leptocorisa acuta sp., 135

Leptomeningeal congestion in brain, 5

Leucinodes orbonalis sp., 124

L.glutaminase, 187

Line source, emission intensity, (EP), 66

Lipid proxidation, 82

Lipid peroxidation in

LDL, 80

Lipoprotein oxidation, 79–82

Liver
- cadmium chloride exposure, 350–352
- control of chronic test, 350–352
- glycogen level, 282–283
- histology of, 284
- metabolic site, 281
- serum glucose level, 282–283
- structure of, 282
- Low land rice plant population
- poultry manure treatment, 366–367

Low land rice productivity
- basal stage, 365
- level of fertilizers, 365
- organic manures, 365, 365, 367
- panicle initiation stage, 365
- phosphatic fertilizers application, 365
- plant population reduction of, 366
- potassium fertilizers, 365, 367
- structure of treatment, 366
- tillering stage 365, 367
- Low land rice
- crop density of, 364–369
- growth of, 364–369
- panicle formation, 367
- sufluenced of fwertilizer, 364–369
- yield attributes of, 364–369

Low land rice, treatment
- nitrogen fertilizer, 365
- pig manure, 365
- poultry manure, 365
- sheep manure, 365

Luffa acutangula sp., 247

Luffa cylindrical sp., 276

Lycopersicon esculentum mill, 142

M

M. Unipunctata sp., 135

Macrophytes, 338

Madhava indica sp., 416

Magnesium sulphate in river water mixture density, 37

Magnesium sulphate in urea water mixture, 37

Mahadare reservoir, 395—396

Mani reservoir, diversity of phytoplankton, 251–254

Mansoon rainfall recharge, 49

Mansoonal rainfall, 49

Marine actinomycetes, 180–181

Marine therapeutic enzymes, 185

Maturated pearl millet straw compost
- chemical characteristics, 313
- nutrients, contents of, 314

Medicinal plants used by Santhals, 164

Medicinal plants
- endangered andemic, 417
- theratened, 417

Mercury porosimeter, 23

Methionine, 302

Methods of
- Burstien, 80
- Scholnick, 80

Methods of ester Bauer sulphate, 80
Methods of
drought tolerance, 74
water use efficiency, 74
Mg^{++} atpase activities, 108
Microcystis, 291
Micronutrients, source, poultry manure, 367
Mineral salts, ultrasonic investigation, 35–38
Minimum inhibitory concentration, 138–139
Mite pest fauna, scenario, 90
Mode of injury, 133–134
Momordica charantia sp., 271
Monolepta higropilineata from Ramaghat, 294
Monsoon rechange (MR), 52
Mosquito rearing, 276
Motality renal diseased patient, 82
Motile aeromanadas virulence mechanism, 8
Motile aeromonad infection, 6
Motile aeromonadas
antigenic diversity, 11
densities of, 13
occurance of, 13
range of, 13
somatic antigen 12
MPN coliforms, 115
Mucuna seeds
active principles of, 108
treatment of, 108
Mucuria pruriens sp., 108–109
Mugil cephalus sp., 13
Mung bean variety vaibhav, effect of bioforce, 385
Mungbean (*vigna radiata*)
effect of, BGA, 384–386
effect of, fertilizers, 384–386
effect of, sea weed extracts, 384–386
Mycelium, 155
Mypiophyllum spiaatum sp., 13

N

Na^+ K^+ atpase activities, 108
National ambient air quality standards, 65
Necrosis, 5
Neem extracts statistical analysis, 264
Negative H_2S count, 114–115
Negative mpn count, 114–115
Nicolson formula, 408
Non mansoon rainfall recharge 49
Normalization factor(NA), 52
Normalized monsoon rechange, 52
Norton formula, 408

O

Ocimum basilicum sp., 271
Onion, spontaneous positive geotrophic
shoot development, 101–102
Oo cyst, 297
Organic manure nutrient content, 366
Organochlorides, 255
Organochlorodies, toxic effects, 257
Organophosphate, 257
Organophosphate toxic effect, 258
Oroton sparsiflous sp., 276
Ovary
cadmium chloride exposure, 350–352
control of chronic test, 350–352
Oxidation fermentation (OF), 11
Oxya chinensis, 135
Oxytetracycline drug, 14

P

P. argyrophyla, effect, 121
P. bettle
effect, 121
leaf extracts, 122
methanol extracts, 122
Padobutrazol, 142–144
Paclobutrazol effect in salt stressed tomato, 143
P. aminoarobenzene (PAAB), 205
biological oxidation of, 205
Pangomia pinnata sp., 411
Paper industry lime, 400
Paper mill of Orissa, 399
Paper mill solid waste concentration, 403
Passive haemagglutination, 12
Pearl millet, 310
Pearl millet straw, 311
Percent of inhibition analysis, 120
Percentage of lithophytic algal in
rivers of Andhra pradesh in polluted stations, 236
rivers of Andhra pradesh in unpolluted stations, 236
Percentage yield
of treated crop, 124
of untreated crop, 124

Peroxidase, 142–143

Pesticides, biological magnification, 257

Phagoeytized bacteria, 6

Phanerochacte chryosporium sp., 206

Phaseolus radiatus sp., 247

Phtipnkton diversity at Gopnath, 315–323

Phyla modiflora, 271

Physiochemical characteristics of Dharwad district, 410

Phytopathogenic fungi, 121

Phytopathogenic fungi in intro sensitivity study, 118

Phytophagous mite, 89

Phytophathogenic fungi, effect of

P. Argyrophyla, 121

Phytoplankton, 281, 338

  population dynamics, 317–319

  similarity indices of, 320

  qualitative estimation, 252

Phytotoxicity, 366

Pigeon pea from Western Maharashtra, 381

Piper species, 119, 122

Plankotonic life stages, 390

Plankton, 390

Plankton analysis, 291

Plant bioregulator mediated biochemical changes, 142

Plant derived frengicides, 119

Plant extracts, 119–120

Plant multiprotectants, 142

Pollen foraging behaviour of

  Apis dorsata, 268

  Rock bee, 268

Pollutant

  concentration, 65–66

  emission intensity, 66

  emission rates, 66

  in iron manufacture, 424

  in steel manufacture, 424

Pollution control by instruments, 426

Pollution control technologies, 423–427

Pollution, 423

Polymerase chain reaction (PCR) technique, 11

Polypeptide chain, 86

Polyphagotarsonemus latus banks, 92

Polysulphane membrane, 79

Potato dextrose agar (PDA); 120

Potential dye metabolites, 203

Pro audit questionnaire, 44

  process of 43–44

  programme of, 43

  resource conservation, 43

  workbook, 44

Proline, 74, 77

Proteus sp. 137

Protocol for broth dilution method, 138

Pseudomanas nitro reducens sp., 205

Pseudomonas sp. 137

PST studies, 102

Pupation height, 102

Pupation site preference (PSP), 101

Pyricularia orism sp., 206

R

Rhizoctonia solani sp., 152

Rhizoctonia solani, integrated control, 155

Rhizoctonia solani growth in petridish 154

Raphidodalpa aulacophorae sp., 294

Raphidopalpa foreicallis, 294

  distribution of, 362

  effect of abiotic factors, 357–361

  seasonal incidence of, 357–359

  synthetic pesticides, 361

  use of biopesticides, 362

Raphidopalpa spatulatus sp., 294

Rat river

  effect of ethanol, 281–285

  effect of *Mucuna pruriens*, 281–285

Rate constant of adsorption, 25

Rattus norvegicus sp., 108

Rattus norvegicus, 281

Reacting substances

Reactive oxygen species (ROS), 95

Red pumpkin bettle, 356, 362

Red sore disease, 6

  clinical isolates of, 8

  diagnosis of 10–11

  etiological agent of 6

  etiology of 6

Renal transplant

  lipoprotein oxidation measurement, 79

Reneal transplant patients, 79–82

Renel transplantation, 79

Reserviors of Satara distrcit, 394

Reservoir morphometric features, 252

Respinable suspended particulate matter (RSPM), 65–67

Retractocephalus monoleptae sp., 295
life cycle, 296
Rhizoctonia solani integrated control, 151
Rhizoctonia solani sp., 119
Rhizomatous herbaceous perennial, 299
Rice agroecosystem, insect pests' scenario, 129–135
Rice ecosystem of Ranchi region, 130
account of insect pest scenario, 131
nature of pest complex of rice,132
status of pest complex of rice 132
succession of pest complex of rice, 132
Rice gall fly, 135
Rice growth and yield, effect of fertilizers, 373–374
organic manure, 373–374
Rice hispa, 134–135
Rice in rainfed agroecosystem, 130
Rice skipper, 134
Rice soil fertility, 375
River ecosystem
study of, 234
Riverine ecosystem of South Asia, 390–392
Riverine ecosystem of Tripura, 390–392
Riverine system, occurrence of plankton, 391
Rivers of Andhra pradesh
physiological aspect, 234–241
water quality, 234
Root weevil, 134
Root zones insect pests. 134
Rphidopalpa foreicollis
insect pest, 356, 360
pollution dynamics, 356
population dynamics of, 355–362
Rural food security, 375
agrometeorological assessment, 377–379
amelioration, 377–379
Related water content, 74, 77

S

S. karnatakensis, 187
S. venezulae, 187
S9 fraction, 96
Salinity, 142
Salmonella typhimurium
reverse mutation assay, 96
tester strain, 98
Santalum album sp., 416
Santhal tribals, 163
Sap suckers, 134
Sausage stored change in
biochemical characteristics, 174
microbiological characteristics, 174
physical characteristic, 174
Scieszko scheme, 3
Seed invigoration
dry weight, effect, 149
fresh weight, effect, 149
germination, effect, 147
root length, effect, 147–148
vigour index, effect, 148
Seed invigoration, effect on,
germination, 147
shoot length 148
vigour index 148
root length 147
Seeds, 58
of brinjal, 58
of chilli, 58
of tomato, 58
Seepage from canal during mansoon period, 52
Septate gregarines, 293
Septicemia, 5
Serial dilution plate technique, 310
Serratia marcescens sp., 190
Serum glucose, 285
Serum glutamate oxalate transaminase(SGOT), 285
Serum glutamate pyruvate transominase (SGPT), 285
Silica gel fractions effect, 278
Simpson's diversity index, 392
Simpson's index, 391
Sludge treatment of wastes, 204
Sodium chloride stress, 142
Sodium sulphate, in urea water minture
density, 37
velocity, 37
Sodium sulphate, in urea water mixture
adiabatic compressibility, 38
apparent moral compressibility, 38
apparent moral volume, 38
Soil
biological processes, 371
physio chemical processes, 371
Solanum elaegnfolium sp., 276
Solanum torvum sp., 271

Solute solvent interaction, 38
Sonicated polyvalent bacteria, 12
Sorensen similarity index (CS), 392
Soxhlet extraction, 95
Soybean morphological parameters, 30
Soybean, germination studies, 29–32
Species sequential analysis of rivers, 237
Spinosus, 294
Staphylococci sp. 137, 139
Stem borers, 135
Stink bug, 135
Streak plate method, 310
Streptomyces chromofuscus sp., 206
Streptomyces collinase sp., 187
Streptomyces vinidosporns sp., 206
Streptomyces, sp. 181
Streptomycetes life cycle, 183
Streptomycetes marinesis sp., 181
Streptomycetes, antibiotics, 184
Succession, 134
Surface water sources, recharge, 50
Suspended parteulate methods, (SPM), 63
Sustenance of life, 260
Synadenium grandi sp., 276

T

Ta 100 strain, 96
TBARs levels, 81
Tenuipalids (false spider mite), 89
Tenuipalpid mite, 92
Termite, 134
Testis
  cadmium chloride exposure, 353
  control of chronic test, 353
Tetraanychus macfarlanei sp., 92
Tetrahymena phriformis sp., 13
Tetramethony propane sp., 80
Tetranychid mite, 89
Tetranychus mescaledonicus sp., 91–92
Textile effluents, 202
Textile effluents treatment, 202
  azodye reduction by anaerobic bacterium, 203
Theaflavins (TF), 95
Therapeutic enzymes, microbinal source, 186
Theraun tolerant coliform (TTC), 114–115
Thiobarbituric acid reacting substances (TABARs), 80
Thiophene 2 carboxylic (T2C), 182
Three point, 23
Tiller production, 367
Tomato, 58,60
Tomato seeds, 58
Tomato, enhanced salinity tolerance, 141–143
Tomato, total amino acid content, 142
Total coliform (TC), 112
Toxicity consideration, 201
Toxinomic diagnosis, 295
Toxoid, 12
Traffic densities at air monitoring stations, 70
Triadimefon, 142
Triazole compounds, 142
Trichloderma viride pure culture s, 152
Trophozoite development, 295
Trophozoite, 295
TC coliforms, 115
Turmeric species, 305
  morphology of, 306
  rhizome yield of, 307
  yield of, 306
Turmeric varieties in Andhra Pradesh, 305
Two spotted spider mite (TSM), 89

U

Ultrasonic velocity, 35
Unit area crop field, 379
Upflow anaerobic sludge blanket (UASB), 207
Urapathogens, 139
Urban areas, air pollution
Urban areas, pollution, 63
Urinary tract infection (UTI), 137

V

Value added products, preparation, 171–174
Vam effect, 413
Varietal resistance
Vegetative specialization in monocotyledons , 162
Vehicle emission estimation, 66
Vigour index, 146–148
Vigour index of seedling, 146
Vigour length, 146

W

Water
  bicarbonate, 229
  calcium hardness, 330

caleivm, 228
carbonate, 330
chloride, 229
chemical oxygen demand, 228
colour, 217
dissolved oxygen, 330
E. coli, 230
electrical conductivity (EC), 220—221
fluoride, 230, 329
magenesium, 228
magnenium hardness, 331
nitrate, 230, 329
non carbonate hardness, 330
odour, 328
pH, 220, 329
phosphate, 230
physiochemical characteristics, 252, 327–328
potassium, 229
sodium, 229
source, 326
sulfate, 229
temperature, 328
total alkalinity, 329
total hardness, 330
turbidity, 220
Water pollutants
pathological effects of, 260
toxic effects of, 260
Water pollution, 255–260
Water pollution, pesticides, 255
Water pollution, sources, 256
Water quality data of Bhadrawati, 221–224
Water resources, efficient use, 379
Water samples of Dharwad, 338
Water table factuation (WTF), 49
White grub, 134
Whole cell antigen, 13
Whorl maggol, 135
Wild yams, 243
Winged yam, 243
Wistar strain, 96, 281
World's oceans
agriculture pollutants, 256
industrial pollutants, 256

Y

Yellow fever mosquito, 275
Yield response of rice, 399–405

Z

Zea mays, 271
Zooplanktons, 316
density, 321
population dynamics, 320–321
similarity indices, 323